# CHRIS CUTRONE

# MARXISM AND

# POLITICS

## ESSAYS ON CRITICAL THEORY AND THE PARTY 2006-2024

sublation
press

MARXISM AND POLITICS:
ESSAYS ON CRITICAL THEORY AND THE PARTY, 2006–2024

First Published by Sublation Media 2024
Copyright © 2024 Chris Cutrone
Cover image: Stephanie A. Karamitsos, "A Different Bubble" (2018)

Commissioned and Edited by Douglas Lain

A Sublation Press Book
Published by Sublation Media LLC

Distributed by Itasca Books

su**blation**
**press**

www.sublationmedia.com

Print ISBN: 979-8-9901591-1-2
eBook ISBN: 979-8-9901591-2-9

Printed in the United States of America

# Contents

## Socialism and capitalism

## Epilegomena

## Postscripta

## Appendix

# Foreword

The aim of the experiments was to send an emissary into time
to summon the past and future to the aid of the present.
— Chris Marker, *La Jetée* (1962)

At the outset, I must refer the reader to my prior volume of writings published by Sublation, *The Death of the Millennial Left: Interventions 2006–2022* (2023). The essays collected in the present book were the result of my role as a teacher in my extra-curricular capacities as Chief Pedagogue for the Platypus Affiliated Society, of which I was a founding member.

As I conceived and announced it when I started writing these essays, it was a matter of "turning the internal pedagogy outward," namely, making it public, and engaging the "Left" on this basis. There were broadly two phases to this effort, each in the aftermath of a downturn on the Millennial Left: a turn to reconsiderations of "Marxism" after the collapse of the anti-war movement and eruption of the financial crisis with Obama's election in 2008; and to questions of the meaning of "socialism" after the failure of anti-austerity protests, Occupy Wall Street and the Arab Spring — but before the advent of new "socialist" parties with Podemos in Spain and SYRIZA in Greece, or Jeremy Corbyn's ascension to leadership of the Labour Party in the U.K. and the Bernie Sanders campaign for nomination by the Democratic Party after Obama's Presidency, the latter of which led to the refound positive currency of the word "socialism" in mainstream American political discourse and the joining of massive numbers of politicized Millennials in the Democratic Socialists of America.

As a college professor, my responsibilities are to the subject matter of my intellectual knowledge and scholarly expertise. In Platypus, my obligations have been somewhat different, since they involve "politics" — or at least the semblance thereof — and are in the public sphere that is fundamentally different from the private space that defines the academic classroom. It is appropriate therefore that my essays from this time be published for more widespread reading, and are taken together as a coherent whole. My prior book, *The Death of the Millennial Left*, provides the political-historical context for the more theoretically-oriented and deeply historical register of the essays collected in this volume.

That said, as I wrote in the Preface to my previous book, it is not a matter of my political commitments and beliefs guiding my theory, but rather the opposite: my theoretical perspective informing my view of present capitalist politics and of "Left" responses to it. — It must necessarily seem to come from "Left field," so to speak, if not another planet.

I wrote far more words and a much greater number of essays on Marxist theory and history than I did remarking on contemporary political events — as it turns out, nearly three times as much.

The issue is the motivation for these writings assembled here, namely, Platypus's engagements with the self-educational process of the Millennial Left over its many years and paths of peregrination. The various moments of the Millennial Left were the different occasions for my attempts at clarifying the history and theory of Marxism, to participate in the earnest investigation into and learning from Marxist history that was attempted in the past two decades. I wrote out of my experience of this history as recalled in the present: less from my own "activist" past and concerns, which were three or four decades old, and more in accompanying its new students, trying to see things through their eyes, or at least thereby to challenge my own assumptions and preoccupations — something I do routinely when teaching historical material in my academic role. I could not assume *a priori* any singular purpose or direction, as the Millennials' investigations — as that of any genuine students — were exploratory and open-ended.

Still, there are certain abiding themes linking and threaded through all of the essays collected here — not provided by me so much as their historical moment. And in hindsight, as indicated by the sub-title of this book, there has come into focus an inexorable task around which everything has orbited as if about a dark star or at least an eclipsed sun: the need for a socialist party and a Marxist self-consciousness of its true mission and purpose.

One key concern that comes forth in these essays has been the need to address and show how the longstanding conflicts and oppositions on the Left, between supposed "authoritarian" vs. "libertarian" traditions of socialism or communism — the source of a compulsory meme for the Millennials, intersecting this antinomical axis with another, that of the purported binary of capitalism vs. socialism — either had been overcome by or had not applied to original historical Marxism. This allowed me to put aside entirely the sundry fruitless dead-end pseudo-"debates" within ostensible "Marxism" and the greater "Left" that have blocked developments for so long. The reader will note how I actively avoid, because I do not accept, the terms of these longstanding "debates." Alongside the Millennial Left, I have sought a new direction from history.

This was something I thought was possible for the Millennial Left to do — or to have done, since unfortunately they ultimately have not done so and now no longer will.

My two students who first summoned me to my role as teacher of the Millennial Left were themselves a bit older (graduate students), and came from an anarchist background. They commended my ability to transcend the "authoritarian" vs. "libertarian" divide — but quit Platypus when we came around to reading Lenin. The younger students stayed on, excited to violate the taboos forbidding this history. As I quipped at the time, using a title from my own adolescent education, I was going to allow them to explore uninhibited "everything you always wanted to know about Marxism but were afraid to ask."

In the aftermath of the Millennial retreat from such encouraging openness, the question is not the potential and hence imperative for the reconstruction of a true Marxist perspective out of the historical wreckage palpable when I was writing these essays during the Millennial Left moment, but rather any possible future for doing so that could and should come with new generations of interest in and curiosity about Marxism: the questions and problems presented by the abandoned and overgrown monument of Marxism — an artifact of a lost world that is nevertheless inevitably rediscovered from time to time by the intrepid and unwary lost children making their ways through the jungle of capitalism.

The Millennials did not themselves add anything lasting to this archaeological dig, as their own efforts were so ephemeral and — seemingly eagerly — cut short, not even leaving evidence of iconoclastic vandalism, nor any other remaining traces of their all-too-brief temporary encampment. What followed them has not been another generation of explorers resuming this work of investigation, but the grim reenactment ceremonies of a Zoomer cargo-cult at the vacated site in the shadow of the Monolith, where the bones of past sacrificial victims are wielded as weapons.

This book is less a set of "messages in a bottle" washed ashore by waves of the past crashing against our time, and more my own inscribed Golden Disc to be carried by the *Voyager* deep space probe after its fissile power core has gone cold, adrift on the cosmic tides and gravitational attractions of interstellar history, among its constantly shifting constellations.

\* \* \*

I must address the purpose and spirit of these essays.

The unfortunate generational narcissism of the Millennials is striking in comparison to my own experience that informed my approach to history. As a member of "Gen X," I knew that a great deal had happened in the past and weighed heavily on the mind of the present. The Millennials by contrast have seemed to think that history began with them. In this they have been very much like the 1960s Baby Boomer New Left cohort, who thought that they were going to proceed to right the world in ways their forebears could not possibly have done due to their supposed ignorance and backwardness. They thought that only they and their time were socially and historically conscious, aware of the horrors of oppression and exploitation to which previous generations had been blind. I myself could never have had such an illusion, coming of age as I did in a time — the so-called "End of History" — anxious to put to rest the utopianism of the past, of which Marxism was seemingly the greatest and most dangerous form.

My essays have been less theses of their own than readers' guides to or even annotated bibliographies of what I consider priority material in the existing corpus of writings by and about Marxism, leading attention and drawing focus, in order to not lose sight of their unifying red thread. But it is important to note that my writings cannot substitute for reading the original historical Marxist works I reference. My own experience reading and learning Marxism instructed and directed me: I am aware of how much in Marxism remains opaque, causing the eyes to glaze over, and it tends to be the most important parts. It is the most difficult to understand and even impossible to comprehend aspects of Marxism that are its most urgent matters. The strangeness of Marxism is what makes it most worthwhile to consider.

I addressed the issues and problems raised in these essays through engagements with the preceding generations of the "Left," specifically that of the 1960s New Left — perhaps the last genuine attempt to regain knowledge of Marxism — often through their writings, but sometimes in person through public forum panel discussions as well as in private conversations: Andrew Feenberg, Douglas Kellner, Paul Leblanc, Lars Lih, Mike Macnair, Leo Panitch, Robert Pippin, Moishe Postone, Adolph Reed, Gillian Rose, and others. I also addressed prominent figures whom I have not met such as Alain Badiou and Slavoj Žižek. In these writings I sought to prompt discussion through articulating explicitly what is almost never said — indeed, actively silenced.

There were two particular engagements that motivated many of my essays in this volume: what has been called the "great Lenin debate" that culminated in 2011–12, before, during and after the anti-austerity and Occupy movement and Arab Spring; and the subsequent debate on Lukács's early Marxist writings. Both of these were centered on discussion fostered by the Communist Party of Great Britain (CPGB), whose prominent member Mike Macnair was an important interlocutor in each debate. They were connected by and through another conversation motivated by the Millennial Left, what was once called the "party question" in the history of Marxism.

At the dawn of the Millennial Left, in 2005, Lars Lih had published a new translation of and book on Lenin's *What is to be Done?* (1902), and the founding editor and publisher of *Jacobin* magazine, Democratic Socialists of America member Bhaskar Sunkara had taken up Mike Macnair's book *Revolutionary Strategy* (2009) in the task of forging "Left unity" and finding a path to a political party for socialism that had eluded prior generations, going back to the 1930s. Macnair and Lih had emphasized the "Kautskyist" background for Lenin — something my former comrades in the Spartacist League had also foregrounded. I spoke on a panel with Lih on Lenin's Marxism, and I wrote a critical review of Macnair's book that was published in the CPGB's newspaper, the *Weekly Worker*: I have debated Macnair on the topic of the party, both in person and in print on several occasions. Many members of the Democratic Socialists of America (DSA) have been influenced by Lih and Macnair's writings on Lenin and Second International Marxism more generally, and I sought to contribute to their learning from Lenin.

My participation in the debate around Georg Lukács's book *History and Class Consciousness* (1923) and related contemporaneous writings was prepared by my long study of and scholarly work on Theodor W. Adorno's Marxism, during which I helped disinter and spur translation and publication of the 1956 conversation between Frankfurt Institute for Social Research director Max Horkheimer and Adorno on the project, ultimately abandoned, of writing a new *Communist Manifesto* for the 20th century — after the experience of the failure of Marxism to achieve socialism, which they intended to be nonetheless "Leninist." — It seemed a shocking revelation to everyone but me that Adorno and other Frankfurt School Critical Theorists had been admirers and followers of Lenin. Other previously unknown writings by Horkheimer and Adorno were the occasions for several of the essays collected here.

The relevance of this historical material is not self-evident, and indeed the obscurity of the Marxism of the Frankfurt School is a good indicator of what is usually neglected as the esoteric content of Marxism, whether that of Lenin, Rosa Luxemburg, Leon Trotsky, Karl Kautsky, Walter Benjamin, Adorno, Horkheimer, Marcuse, among many others — or that of Marx and Engels themselves.

I refer the reader to the recent books by my close friend and collaborator Spencer Leonard, who has introduced and published two volumes of political writings by Marx and Engels on Bonapartism and imperialism, the selection of which was motivated by the needs of our common teaching in Platypus.[1]

As part of Platypus's project of educating the Millennial Left on this historically forgotten thought of Marxism, I made a deliberate and even systematic effort to focus on what is usually glossed over or even suppressed — and for younger people, what is often completely invisible — in Marxism. This means reading Marxism against the grain of its own history — especially considering that the last 100 years, the 20th century, as I discuss in several of my essays here, was the time of the self-liquidation and active forgetting of Marxism, repressed less by its opponents than by its purported "proponents" themselves — this is not least the meaning of the vexed and even controversial term "Stalinism," a word that still elicits immediate hatred of anyone who utters it on the "Left," as a despised "Trot." Yes, I have been touched by Trotsky and the Frankfurt School, so widely vilified by past generations of the "Left," but in ways that were evidently unique, as I had to maintain Marxism against both "Trotskyism" and the late but to my mind confused currency during my own lifetime of Frankfurt School Critical Theory, as it was rediscovered after the failure of the 1960s New Left.

One Marxist concept that elicits scorn or mere bemusement that I discuss in several of these essays is the "dictatorship of the proletariat" — as I describe it, the centrally defining but also most controversial idea in Marxism, denounced by its avowed opponents and renounced by its ostensible adherents. As with all else in the history of Marxism on which I have written, this has been taken as a negative rather than positive object: the dictatorship of the proletariat as the missing goal or task that defines the present absence of Marxism.

I have been aware since a young age that my interest in Marxism has made me strangely unwelcome on the "Left." This has also meant that what I found so impressive and never forgot about Marxism, and which used to be taken for granted by and about it, has become peculiar — a blind-spot towards which it is very difficult to draw attention without being suspected

---

1    Spencer A. Leonard, *Marx and Engels on Bonapartism: Selected Journalism, 1851–59* and *Marx and Engels on Imperialism: Selected Journalism, 1856–62* (Lanham, MD: Lexington Books, 2023).

of trying to trick or mislead through optical illusion or sleight-of-hand. "Why is Cutrone going on about *that*? He must be up to no good." Marxism was an unwelcome inconvenience, which was often identified with me as a personal idiosyncrasy. — This was, ultimately, the opinion even of my own personal mentors on the Left and in Marxism. (For discussion of the influence of my own teachers, see the Prologue to *The Death of the Millennial Left*, on my "Paths to Marxism.") This despite my own doubts and misgivings about Marxism and my eager willingness to hear any and all arguments against it. My interest in Marxism has been driven by honest curiosity. My commitment to it has been not primarily to the answers or solutions it might provide but the questions and problems it poses. They have not gone away in my lifetime, and I suspect they will not any time soon.

It is not for me to claim that Marxism is in any way "good." Rather, so long as anyone is still interested in or curious about Marxism, I have felt it my duty to stand for its authentic memory against its myriad falsifications or just plain oblivion. — A thankless task, but one of which I remain convinced will eventually prove crucial and essential to get beyond capitalism: not least because, whatever we might call its essential character, clearly the modern world faces new and unprecedented problems in history.

But I have been aware that preserving the memory of Marxism will not necessarily be through fidelity or "orthodoxy." Indeed some of the greatest insights into Marxism have been by non- and even anti-Marxists. I am open to potential post-Marxist and even non-Marxist paths to freedom — if earned and not falsely assumed by mere ignorance, which results merely in sub-Marxism, avoiding the profound problems Marxism presents. Marxism might want to be forgotten, but it must be actually overcome — in practical reality and not merely in "theory" — in order to do so. The history of the Millennial Left refracted indirectly in its many facets and aspects in these essays was one of trying to actively remember Marxism and thus hopefully truly — and not falsely — forget it.

This task has so far failed, and so my writings collected in this book have proved necessary to publish. They thus close a definite chapter of history, both in the world and of my own life and thinking. While I always suspected that I was writing less for my own formative moment, and really for the time — now past — of the Millennial Left, specifically, and more for posterity, it is nonetheless sobering to confront that fact marked by this publication. I used to joke that my writings were destined immediately for "the archive" — this is what both these books form now. It is my wish that, as I intended when originally writing them, these essays will spark and help illuminate further investigation into the history of Marxism, according to the light of the stars guiding my own learning and teaching: Marx, Lenin and Adorno.

\* \* \*

This book was originally conceived in 2018 to be published alongside another collection of essays by Platypus, *Marxism in the Age of Trump* (2018), to which I contributed and edited. This was meant to mark what I called the "death" of the Millennial Left in 2017. The Millennial reconsideration of original historical Marxism came to an end at that time, along with interest in refounding an independent socialist party, in favor of the DSA and participation in capitalist politics via the Bernie Sanders campaign and election of the Squad "Democratic socialists" etc.

Publishing this book now, in 2024, has the unintended effect of marking the centenary of Lenin's death in 1924. Unlike Philip Cunliffe, whose counterfactual history novel, *Lenin Lives!* (2017) was in part inspired by my writings on Lenin, and who has marked the 100th anniversary of Lenin's death this year with a call to bury Lenin along with the rest of the 20th century Left's heritage,[2] I think we not only should but must remember Lenin. — Not in order to try repeating his history — and certainly not to repeat his distorted after-effects in "Marxist-Leninist" Stalinism (and "Trotskyism") — but to recall the task Lenin set himself as a follower of Marx.

---

2   "Lenin's lesson for Western liberals: Authoritarianism is a symptom of a corrupted Left," *Unherd,* January 19, 2024.

# Preamble

Prologue

# A short history of the Left

## Marx and 1848

Marx was not the author but the brilliant critical participant of the Left in the 19th Century. Socialism and communism were not invented by Marx, Engels and their collaborators (and opponents) on the Left, but issued from the contradictions of modern society itself, as expressed in the French Revolution of 1789 and in the modern labor movement that emerged with the Industrial Revolution in the early 19th Century. Marx's great insight was to regard the Left itself as symptomatic of capitalism that does not oppose it from without but from within, *immanently*. Nevertheless Marx endorsed the Left, the modern socialist workers movement, and sought to push it further and provoke recognition of how it pointed beyond itself.

Marx's thought originated in the immanent critique of emancipatory politics after 1789, in French socialism, German Idealist philosophy, and British political economy. By 1848, the time of Marx and Engels's *Communist Manifesto* and the revolutionary uprisings in France, Germany, and other parts of Europe (triggered by the global economic depression of the 1840s), the politics of social equality and democracy had become more complicated and profound than a Rousseauian civilizational critique of modern society (Proudhon's slogan "property is theft") could comprehend — or hope to overcome. By 1848, radical democracy, in forms of revolt by the "bourgeois" (urban) "third estate" (including workers), had come to grief: capital was threatened by social democracy, for it pushed beyond its forms of social reproduction. The aftermath of failed revolution in 1848 saw the advent of emphatic forms of "mass" politics and the modern national parliamentary-Bonapartist state with which we still live today.

After the post-1848 crisis on the Left, Marx engaged the critical-dialectical conception of capitalism, recognizing it as a form of emancipation that (re)constitutes a specific form of domination over society: the imperative to produce "surplus value" and thus capitalize on labor in forms mediated and measured in labor-time. Capital became a form of wealth measurable as an investment of social labor, a form of preservation and stake of value on the future, but one in which "dead" labor dominates the living.

After 1917, Lukács recovered Marx's grasp of the contradictory but constitutive identity and non-identity of social exploitation and domination under capitalism, giving rise to forms of discontent and agency — *ideologies*, including on the "Left" — that reproduce and perpetuate a society dominated by capital, a contradiction of social being and consciousness for subjects of the commodity form.

For Marx, capitalism itself sets the stage for and provokes emancipatory social potential that it also constrains. As social form, capital points beyond itself.

## Lenin, Luxemburg and 1917

At the turn of the 20th Century, the younger generation of radicals in Second International Social Democracy took for granted the revolutionary character of their Marxist forebears (Kautsky, Plekhanov), but uneasily came up against problems in the movement they so enthusiastically championed. The standard bearers of the revolutionary Marxist mandate found themselves shockingly isolated on the Left with the outbreak of World War in 1914. Russia proved to be the "weakest link" in the world system of capitalism, becoming the epicenter of revolutionary political struggle, but with the paradoxical outcome of what Lenin called a "deformed workers' state" administering "state capitalism" on the frontier-backwater of global capital, which too soon "recovered" from the crisis of the war. Luxemburg and her comrades in Germany supported the Bolsheviks, but as Marxists remained critical, knowing that October 1917 advanced the necessity of global revolution, posing a "problem" in Russia that could not be "solved" there. Struggling to remain true to the principles of Marxism, actually Lenin, Luxemburg and their cohort transformed the Marxist movement, but in very uneven ways that, with the ultimate failure and betrayal of the anti-capitalist revolution opened in 1917–19, set the stage for the later degeneration of the Left — not least in its self-understanding.

## Trotsky

When Stalin announced the policy of "socialism in one country" he was not thereby explicitly overthrowing a revolutionary Marxist perspective but rather accommodating circumstances of the Russian Revolution by 1924. Even those revolutionaries less cynical than Stalin and the Bolsheviks he manipulated and murdered did not countenance that only the risky politics of worldwide Communism had any hope of preserving, let alone furthering, the very modest gains of 1917. In the absence of this, the exigencies of "preserving the revolution" demanded ever higher sacrifices, an unfolding catastrophe for humanity.

## Adorno

The disintegration of revolutionary Marxism by the 1930s presented an acute problem for critical consciousness on the Left. The radical crisis of war and social revolution 1914–19 produced its reactionary complement, the virulent movement of fascism and a resumption of world war that by 1945 had devastated the Left. In the wake of counterrevolution and reaction after 1919 emerged the "authoritarian character" structure of social and political subjectivity that was expressed pervasively, not only in black- and brown-shirt rallies, but also in the Popular Front and, later, "nationalism" in the "Third World." The "authoritarian personality," with its characteristic wounded narcissism and sado-masochism, evinced a regressive "fear of freedom."

"Marxism" became part of the ideology of the reactionary social reality of "advanced" capitalism, but one which yet, smoldering with history, pointed beyond the terms of the "bourgeois" ideology whose vacancy it had come to occupy. In the period of triumphant counter-revolution that characterized the high 20th Century, the question and problem of critical social consciousness re-emerged. Recovering the critical intent of Marxian theory and practice proved an obscure issue by the 1960s, but one that haunted the Left in the social-political disorientation and occultation of the tasks and project of emancipation that is the most profound legacy of defeated and failed revolution.

### From '68 — and '89 — to today

By the 1960s, the "Left" increasingly denied the rights and responsibilities of strategically placed populations at the heart of global capital to change the course of history. — As Susan Sontag succinctly expressed it in 1967, "the white race is the cancer of human history."[1] — Embraced was a passive expectation of the crowding onto the historical stage by "subalterns," with no critical regard for the actual political forms this takes. — As Adorno put it at the advent of decolonization: "Savages are not more noble" (1944).[2] — Such abdication took diverse forms of self-abnegation — including racist enthusiasms for "cultural difference" — evacuating politics.

The revolutionary Left, already in a state of deep decomposition after 1945, received the last nail in its coffin with the abdication of the role of critical social consciousness in the wake of the "New" Left — but prepared long before. The post-'60s disenchantment of the Left cast a long shadow across the 1970s–80s, and culminated in 1989–92 with the destruction of the Soviet Union and the "end of history" — an end to any ("grand") projects of emancipatory social transformation. The "New Left" got the world it deserved; attempts to sustain its pseudo-radical anti-Marxism are efforts to resuscitate a ghost.

Adorno's observation that "wrong life cannot be lived rightly" (1944)[3] has been mistaken to be an existential and not a political problem. But the problem of practice is not ethical but concerns opening actual social-political possibilities for emancipation.

An emancipated world in which the freedom of each would be a precondition for the freedom of all, achieved through social solidarity that

---

1    Susan Sontag, "What's Happening in America?" *Partisan Review* 34, no. 1 (Winter 1967), 57–8.
2    *Minima Moralia*, trans. E.F.N. Jephcott (London: Verso, 2005), 52.
3    Ibid., 39.

provides "from each according to his ability, to each according to his need" (Marx), whose vision motivated the historical Left, seems scarcely conceivable today.

But, just as it is quite possible, manifestly, to be oppressed without realizing the reasons for it — the meaning of "alienation" — unfulfilled potential can yet persist despite lack of awareness of it: a non-identity of subject and object. The possibility of critical consciousness of emancipation survives its apparent demise, however unconsciously it tasks us today. The role of consciousness is vital for any possible social emancipation.

(July 2006)

# Prologue

# Do we need Adorno?

## Marxism became a "message in a bottle"
## — can we yet receive it?

Horkheimer and Adorno's 1956 conversation took place in the aftermath of the Khrushchev speech denouncing Stalin. This event signaled a possible political opening, not in the Soviet Union so much as for the international Left. Horkheimer and Adorno recognized the potential of the Communist Parties in France and Italy, paralleling Marcuse's estimation in his 1947 "33 Theses":

> The development [of history since Marx] has confirmed the correctness of the Leninist conception of the vanguard party as the subject of the revolution. It is true that the communist parties of today are not this subject, but it is just as true that only they can become it. . . . The political task then would consist in reconstructing revolutionary theory within the communist parties and working for the praxis appropriate to it. The task seems impossible today. But perhaps the relative independence from Soviet dictates, which this task demands, is present as a possibility in Western Europe's . . . communist parties.[1]

Horkheimer and Adorno's conversation in *Towards a New Manifesto*[2] was part of a greater crisis of Communism (uprising in Hungary, emergence of the post-colonial Non-Aligned Movement, split between the USSR and Communist China) that gave rise to the New Left. Verso's title was

---

1   In *Collected Papers of Herbert Marcuse: Technology, War and Fascism*, ed. Douglas Kellner (London: Routledge, 1998), 227.

2   Reprinted first in *New Left Review* 65 (September – October 2010). Citations from *Towards a New Manifesto*, trans. Rodney Livingstone (New York: Verso, 2011).

not misleading: this was the time of the founding of *New Left Review*, to which C. Wright Mills wrote his famous "Letter to the New Left" (1960),[3] calling for greater attention to the role of intellectuals in social-political transformation.

As Adorno put the matter, "I have always wanted to . . . develop a theory that remains faithful to Marx, Engels and Lenin." Horkheimer responded laconically, "Who would not subscribe to that?"[4] It is necessary to understand what such statements took for granted.

The emphasis on Marxism as an account of "exploitation," rather than of social-historical *domination*, is mistaken. Marx called "capital" the domination of society by an alienated historical dynamic of value-production (M–C–M' [Money-Commodity-Money']). At stake here is the proletarianization of bourgeois society after the Industrial Revolution, or, as Lukács put it in *History and Class Consciousness* (1923), how the fate of the workers becomes that of society as a whole. This went back to Marx and Engels in the 1840s: Engels had written a precursor to the *Communist Manifesto*, a "Credo" (1847), in which he pointed out that the proletariat, the working class after the Industrial Revolution, was unlike any other exploited group in history, in both its social being and consciousness. The danger was that the working class would mistake their post-Industrial Revolution condition for that of pre-industrial bourgeois society, with its ethos of work. As the Abbé Sieyès had put it, in his 1789 revolutionary pamphlet "What is the Third Estate?," while the Church's First Estate with its property of communion with Divinity "prays," and the aristocratic Second Estate with its property of honor in noble chivalry "fights," the commoner Third Estate "works," with no property other than that of labor. Bourgeois society was the result of the revolt of the Third Estate. But the separate classes of increasing numbers of workers and ever fewer capitalists were the products of the division of bourgeois society in the Industrial Revolution, over the value of the property of labor, between wages and capital. This was, according to Marx, the "crisis" of bourgeois society in capital, recurrent since the 1840s.

---

3   *New Left Review* I/5 (September – October 1960).

4   op. cit. 103.

At issue is the "bourgeois ideology" of the "fetish character of the commodity," or, how the working class misrecognized the reasons for its condition, blaming this on exploitation by the capitalists rather than the historical undermining of the social value of labor. As Marx explained in *Capital*, the workers exchanged, not the products of their work as with the labor of artisans, but rather their *time*, the accumulated value of which is *capital*, the means of production that was the private property of the capitalists. But for Marx the capitalists were the "character-masks of capital," agents of the greater social imperative to produce and accumulate value, where the source of that value in the exchange of labor-time was being undermined and destroyed. As Horkheimer stated it in "The Authoritarian State" (1940), the Industrial Revolution made "not work but the workers superfluous."[5] The question was, how had history changed since the earlier moment of bourgeois society (Adam Smith's time of "manufacture") with respect to labor and value?

Adorno's affirmation of Lenin on subjectivity was driven by his account of the deepening problems of capitalism in the 20th century, in which the historical development of the workers' movement was bound up. Adorno did not think that the workers were no longer exploited. See Adorno's 1942 essay "Reflections on Class Theory" and his 1968 speech "Late Capitalism or Industrial Society?," which he published in the U.S. under the title "Is Marx Obsolete?"[6] In "Reflections on Class Theory," Adorno pointed out that Marx and Engels's assertion that the entire history of civilization was one of "class struggles" was actually a *critique* of history as a whole; that the dialectic of history in capital was one of *unfreedom*; and that only the complete dehumanization of labor was potentially its opposite, the liberation from work. "Late Capitalism or Industrial Society?" pointed out that the workers were not paid a share of the economic value of their labor, which Marx had recognized in post-Industrial Revolution capitalism was infinitesimal, but rather their wages were a cut of the profits of *capital*, granted to them for political reasons, to prevent revolution. The

---

5   In *The Essential Frankfurt School Reader*, ed. Andrew Arato and Eike Gebhardt (New York: Continuum, 1985), 95.

6   Both in *Can One Live After Auschwitz?: A Philosophical Reader*, ed. Rolf Tiedemann, trans. Rodney Livingstone, (Stanford: Stanford University Press, 2009).

ramifications of this process were those addressed by the split in the social-ist workers' movement — in Marxism itself — that Lenin represented.

The crisis of Marxism was grasped by the Frankfurt School in its for-mative moment of the 1920s. In "The Little Man and the Philosophy of Freedom" (in *Dämmerung*, 1926–31) Horkheimer explained how the "present lack of freedom does not apply equally to all."[7] An element of freedom exists when the product is consonant with the interest of the pro-ducer. All those who work, and even those who don't, have a share in the creation of contemporary reality." This followed Lukács's *History and Class Consciousness*, which prominently quoted Marx and Engels from *The Holy Family* (1845):

> The property-owning class and the class of the proletariat rep-resent the same human self-alienation. But the former feels at home in this self-alienation and feels itself confirmed by it; it recognizes alienation as its own instrument and in it possesses the semblance of a human existence. The latter feels itself destroyed by this alienation and sees in it its own impotence and the reality of an inhuman existence.[8]

And the necessary corrective was not the feeling of this oppression, but the theoretical and practical consciousness of the historical potential for the transformation of "bourgeois social relations," at a global scale: "Workers of the world, unite!" This could only take place through the growth and greater accumulated historical self-awareness of the workers' movement for socialism. But the growth of the workers' movement had resulted in the crisis of socialism, its division into revolutionary Communism and reformist Social Democracy in WWI and the revolutions that followed (in Russia, Germany, Hungary and Italy). Reformist Social Democracy had succumbed to the "reification" of bourgeois ideology in seeking to preserve the workers' interests, and had become the counterrevolutionary bulwark

---

7   *Dawn and Decline: Notes 1926-31 and 1950-1969*, trans. Michael Shaw (New York: Continuum, 1978), 50–52.

8   *History and Class Consciousness: Studies in Marxist Dialectics*, trans. Rodney Livingstone (Cambridge, MA: MIT Press, 1971), 149.

of continued capitalism in the post-WWI world. There was a civil war in Marxism. The question was the revolutionary necessity and possibility of Communism that Lenin expressed in the October 1917 Revolution that was meant to be the beginning of global revolution. Similarly, for the Frankfurt School, the Stalinism that developed in the wake of failed world revolution, was, contrary to Lenin, the reification of "Marxism" itself, now become barbarized bourgeois ideology, the affirmation of work, rather than its dialectical *Aufhebung* (negation and transcendence through fulfillment and completion).

To put it in Lenin's terms, from *What is to be Done?* (1902), there are two "dialectically" interrelated — potentially contradictory — levels of consciousness, the workers' "trade union" consciousness, which remains within the horizon of capitalism, and their "class consciousness," which reveals the world-historical potential beyond capitalism. The latter, the "Hegelian" critical self-recognition of the workers' class struggle, was the substance of Marxism: the critique of communism as the "real movement of history." As Marx put it in his celebrated 1843 letter to Ruge, "Communism is a dogmatic abstraction . . . infected by its opposite, private property." And, in his 1844 *Economic and Philosophical Manuscripts*, Marx stated unequivocally that,

> Communism is the position as the negation of the negation, and is hence the actual phase necessary for the next stage of historical development in the process of human emancipation and rehabilitation. *Communism* is the necessary form and the dynamic principle of the immediate future, but communism as such is not the goal of human development, the form of human society.

For Marx, communism demanded an "immanent critique" according to its "dialectical" contradictions, heightened to adequate historical self-awareness. The issue is the potential abolition of wage-labor by the wage-laborers, the overcoming of the social principle of work by the workers. Marx's "Hegelian" question was, how had history made this possible, in theory and practice?

While Horkheimer and Adorno's historical moment was not the same as Marx's or Lenin's, this does not mean that they abandoned Marxism, but rather that Marxism, in its degeneration, had abandoned them. The experience of Communism in the 1930s was the purge of intellectuals. So the question was the potential continued critical role of theory: how to follow Lenin? In "Imaginative Excesses" (orphaned from *Minima Moralia* 1944–47 — the same time as the writing of Horkheimer and Adorno's *Dialectic of Enlightenment*), Adorno argued that the workers "no longer mistrust intellectuals because they betray the revolution, but because they might want it, and thereby reveal how great is their own need of intellectuals."[9]

Adorno and Horkheimer are thus potentially helpful for recovering the true spirit of Marxism. Their work expresses what has become obscure or esoteric about Marxism. This invites a blaming of their work as culpable, instead of recognizing the unfolding of history they described that had made Marxism potentially irrelevant, a "message in a bottle" they hoped could still yet be received. It is unfortunate if their conversation isn't.

Contribution to symposium "Do we need Adorno?"
by *nonsite.org* (September 17, 2012)

---

9   Published as "Messages in a Bottle," trans. Edmund Jephcott, *New Left Review* I/200, (July – August 1993), 12–14.

# Lenin

# 1917

## The decline of the Left in the 20th century
## Toward a theory of historical regression

In place of the old bourgeois society, with its classes and class antagonisms, we shall have an association, in which *the free development of each is the condition for the free development of all*.

— Friedrich Engels and Karl Marx[1]

Hegel links the freedom of each to the freedom of all as something of equal value. But in doing so he regards the freedom of the individual only in terms of the freedom of the whole, through which it is realized. Marx, by contrast, makes the free development of each the precondition for the correlative freedom of all.

— Karl Korsch[2]

The year 1917 is the most enigmatic and hence controversial date in the history of the Left. It is therefore necessarily the focal point for the Platypus philosophy of history of the Left, which seeks to grasp problems in the present as those that had already manifested in the past, but have not yet been overcome. Until we make historical sense of the problems associated with the events and self-conscious actors of 1917, we will be haunted by their legacy. Therefore, whether we are aware of this or not, we are tasked with grappling with 1917, a year marked by the most profound attempt to change the world that has ever taken place.

The two most important names associated with the revolution that broke out in 1917 in Russia and in 1918 in Germany are the Second International

---

1   *Manifesto of the Communist Party* (1848).
2   Introduction to Marx's *Critique of the Gotha Programme* (1922).

Marxist radicals Vladimir Lenin and Rosa Luxemburg, each of whom played fateful roles in this revolutionary moment. Two Marxian critical theorists who sought to follow Luxemburg and Lenin to advance the historical consciousness and philosophical awareness of the problems of revolutionary politics, in the wake of 1917, are Georg Lukács and Karl Korsch.

While neither Lenin nor Luxemburg survived the revolutionary period that began in 1917, both Lukács and Korsch ended up disavowing and distancing themselves from their works, both published in 1923, that sought to elaborate a Marxian critical theory of the revolutionary proletarian socialist politics of Lenin and Luxemburg. Lukács adapted his perspective to the prevailing conditions of Stalinism in the international Communist movement and Korsch became a critic of "Marxist-Leninist" Bolshevism, and an important theorist of "Left" or "council communist" politics. Meanwhile, Luxemburg was pitted against Lenin in a similar degeneration and disintegration of the revolutionary consciousness that had informed the revolution of 1917.

The forms that this disintegration took involved the arraying of the principles of liberalism against those of socialism, or libertarianism against authoritarianism. Lenin and Lukács became emblems of authoritarian socialism, while Luxemburg and Korsch became associated with more libertarian, if not liberal, concerns.

But what remains buried under such a misapprehension of the disputed legacy of 1917 is the substance of agreement and collaboration, in the revolutionary Marxist politics of that moment, among all these figures. Behind the fact of Luxemburg's close collaboration and practical political unity with Lenin lies the intrinsic relationship of liberalism with socialism, and emancipation with necessity. Rather than associating Lenin with revolutionary necessity and Luxemburg with desirable emancipation in such a one-sided manner, we need to grasp how necessity, possibility, and desirability were related, for both Luxemburg and Lenin, in ways that not only allowed for, but actually motivated their shared thought and action in the revolution that opened in 1917.

Both Lenin and Luxemburg sought to articulate and fulfill the concerns of liberalism with socialism — for instance in Lenin's (qualified) endorsement of self-determination against national oppression.

Lukács and Korsch were among the first, and remain the best, to have rigorously explored the theoretical implications of the shared politics of Luxemburg and Lenin, in their works *History and Class Consciousness* and "Marxism and Philosophy," respectively. Both Lukács and Korsch approached what they considered the practical and theoretical breakthrough of the Third International Marxist communism of Luxemburg and Lenin by returning to the "Hegelian" roots of Marxism, a reconsideration of its "idealist" dimension, as opposed to a "materialist" objectivistic metaphysics that lied behind "economism," for example.

This involved, for Lukács and Korsch, an exploration of Lenin and Luxemburg's break from the objectivistic "vulgar Marxism" of the politics and theory of the Second International, exemplified by Karl Kautsky. Lukács's term for such objectivism was "reification"; Korsch addressed it by way of Marx's approach to the philosophical problem of "theory and practice," which, he argued, had become "separated out" in the Second International period, their "umbilical cord broken," while Lenin and Luxemburg had tried to bring them back into productive tension and advance their relation through their revolutionary Marxism.

Ironically, while the title of Lukács's work is *History and Class Consciousness*, it was concerned with a more "philosophical" exposition and categorial investigation of the problem of "reification" and the commodity form as socially mediating, following Marx in *Capital*. Meanwhile, Korsch's "Marxism and Philosophy" actually addressed the historical vicissitudes of the theory-practice problem in Marx and Engels's lifetime and in the subsequent history of the Marxism of the Second International. In both cases, there was an attempt to grasp the issue of subjectivity, or the "subjective" dimension of Marxism.

But it was this focus on subjectivity from which both Lukács and Korsch broke in their subsequent development: Lukács disavowed what he pejoratively called the attempt to "out-Hegel Hegel," making his peace with Stalinist "dialectical materialism," while (later) attempting to found a "Marxist ontology." Korsch, on the other hand, distanced himself from what he came to call, pejoratively, the "metaphysical" presuppositions of Marxism — even and, perhaps, especially as practiced by Lenin, though also, if to a lesser extent, by Luxemburg and even by Marx himself — pushing him ultimately to call for "going beyond Marxism."

In this complementary if divergent trajectory, Lukács and Korsch reflected, in their own ways, the return of the "vulgar Marxism" that they had sought to supersede in their theoretical digestion of 1917 — a return marked by the Stalinization of the international Communist movement beginning in the 1920s. For example, Theodor W. Adorno was excited to meet Lukács in Vienna in 1925, only to be repulsed at Lukács's disavowal of the work that had so strongly inspired Adorno and his colleagues in the Frankfurt School, such as Walter Benjamin and Max Horkheimer. Korsch, who had also, like Lukács, been associated with the Frankfurt School from its inception, had come by the end of the 1930s to scorn the Frankfurt critical theorists as "Marxist metaphysicians," while in the 1960s Lukács wrote contemptuously of them as having taken up residence at the "Grand Hotel Abyss," explicitly deriding them for following his early work. In such disavowals can be found evidence for the repression of the problems Lukács and Korsch had sought to address in elaborating Marxian theory from Lenin and Luxemburg's revolutionary thought and action in 1917–19.

Likewise, in subsequent history, the relation between "means" and "ends" for the Marxist radicals Lenin and Luxemburg in the moment of 1917 became obscured, Lenin being caricatured as believing, in some Machiavellian fashion, that the "ends justified the means," or exemplifying "revolutionary will." Luxemburg was equally caricatured as an upholder of principled emancipatory means in extolling the virtues of practical defeat, seemingly happy to remain a Cassandra of the revolution. Biographically, this is crudely reconciled in the image of Luxemburg's quixotic martyrdom during the Spartacist uprising of 1919, and Lenin's illness and subsequent removal from political power at the end of his life, condemned to watch, helpless, the dawn of the Stalinist authoritarianism to which his political ruthlessness and pursuit of revolutionary ends had supposedly led.

In either case, rather than serving as an impetus for a determined investigation of these revolutionary Marxists' thought and action at the level of the basis for their self-understanding and political judgment — models from which we might be able to learn, elaborate, and build upon further — they have been regarded only as emblems of competing principles, in the abstract (e.g., on the question of the Constituent Assembly, over which they had differed only tactically, not principally). So Lenin's writings and actions are scoured for any hint of authoritarian inhumanity, and Luxemburg's for anything that can be framed for its supposedly more humane compassion. At the same time, the futility of both their politics has been naturalized: It is tacitly understood that neither what Lenin nor Luxemburg aspired to achieve was actually possible to accomplish — either in their time or in ours.

In the words of Adorno's writing on the legacy of Lenin, Luxemburg, Korsch, and Lukács, in his last completed book, *Negative Dialectics*, this way of approaching 1917 and its significance evinced "dogmatization and thought-taboos."[3] The thought and action of Lenin and Luxemburg are now approached dogmatically, and they and their critical-theoretical inheritors, Lukács, Korsch, Benjamin, and Adorno, are approached only with a powerful thought-taboo firmly in place: that the revolutionary moment of 1917 was doomed to failure, and that its fate was tragically played out in the character of the revolutionary Marxism of its time. Their Marxism is thus buried in an attempt to ward off the haunting accusation that it did not fail us, but rather that we have failed it — failed to learn what we might from it. But, like Lukács and Korsch in their subsequent development, after they convinced themselves of the "errors of their ways," we have not recognized and understood, but only rationalized, the problematic legacy of 1917.

1917 remains a question — and it is the very same question that Lenin and Luxemburg went about trying to address in theory and practice — whether we ask it explicitly of ourselves now or not. It is the great tabooed subject, even if that taboo has been enforced, either by a mountain of calumny heaped upon it, or the "praise" it earns in Stalinist — or "Trotskyist" — "adherence."

For example, it remains unclear whether the "soviets" or "workers' councils" that sprung up in the revolutions of 1917–19 could have ever been proven in practice to be an adequate social-political means (for beginning) to overcome capitalism. The Lukács of the revolutionary period

3   Trans. E. B. Ashton (New York: Continuum, 2007), 143.

recognized, in "The Standpoint of the Proletariat," the third part of his essay on "Reification and the Consciousness of the Proletariat," the danger that

> [As Hegel said,] directly before the emergence of something qualitatively new, the old state of affairs gathers itself up into its original, purely general, essence, into its simple totality, transcending and absorbing back into itself all those marked differences and peculiarities which it evinced when it was still viable. . . . [I]n the age of the dissolution of capitalism, the fetishistic categories collapse and it becomes necessary to have recourse to the "natural form" underlying them.[4]

Lukács recognized that the "producers' democracy" of the "workers' councils" in the revolutionary "dictatorship of the proletariat" was intrinsically related to, and indeed the political expression of, an intensification of the "reification" of the commodity form. Nevertheless, it seems that the attempt, by Lenin and Trotsky's Bolsheviks, to bring "all power to the soviets" in the October Revolution of 1917, and by Luxemburg's Spartacists in the German Revolution that followed, is something we can learn from, despite its failure. For this revolutionary moment raises all the questions, and at the most profound levels, of the problematic relationship between capitalism and democracy that still haunt us today.

Similarly, Korsch recognized that the revolutions of 1917–19 were the outcome of a "crisis of Marxism" that had previously manifested in the Second International, in the reformist "revisionist" dispute, in which the younger generation of radicals, Luxemburg, Lenin, and Trotsky, first cut their teeth at the turn of the century. But, according to Korsch in 1923, this "crisis of Marxism" remained unresolved. The unfolding of 1917 can thus be said to be the highest expression of the "crisis of Marxism" that Luxemburg, Lenin, and Trotsky — and Korsch and Lukács after them — recognized as manifesting the highest expression of the *crisis of capitalism*, in the period of war, revolution, counterrevolution, civil war, and reaction that set the

---

4  *History and Class Consciousness: Studies in Marxist Dialectics*, trans. Rodney Livingstone (Cambridge, MA: MIT Press, 1971), 208.

stage for subsequent 20th century history. Arguably, the world never really overcame or even recovered from this crisis of the early 20th century, but has only continued to struggle with its still unresolved aftermath.

In this sense 1917 was not, in the self-understanding of its thinkers and actors, an attempt to leap from the realm of necessity, but rather the attempt to advance a necessity — the necessity of social revolution and transformation — to a higher stage, and thus open a new realm of possibility. The enigmatic silence surrounding the question of 1917 is masked by a deafening din of opprobrium meant to prevent our hearing it. It remains, as Benjamin put it, an "alarm clock that in each minute rings for sixty seconds," whether we (choose to) hear it or not.[5] But the degree to which those who have come later have done so, the repression of 1917 has been achieved only at the cost of a regression that, as Benjamin put it, ceaselessly consumes the past and our ability to learn from it, ceding the meaning of history and its sacrifices to our enemies, and rendering those sacrifices in past struggles vain.

Recognizing the nature of the difficulty of 1917, that the problems we find in this moment comprise the essence of its potential pertinence for us, may be the first step in our recognizing the character of the regression the Left has undergone since then. Like a troubling memory in an individual's life that impinges upon consciousness, the memory of 1917 that troubles our conceptions of social-political possibilities in the present might help us reveal the problems we seek to overcome, the same problems against which Lenin and Luxemburg struggled. Even if a failure, theirs was a brilliant failure from which we cannot afford to be disinherited.

Presented at the Left Forum 2009 on a panel organized by Platypus around four significant moments in the progressive diremption of theory and practice over the course of the 20th century: 2001 (Spencer A. Leonard), 1968 (Atiya Khan), 1933 (Richard Rubin) and 1917.

Originally published in *Platypus Review* 17 (November 2009)

---

5   "Surrealism," in *Walter Benjamin: Selected Writings*, vol. 2 *1927–1930*, ed. Michael W. Jennings (Cambridge, MA: Harvard University Press), 218.

# Lenin's liberalism

## Introduction

Lenin's Marxist politics has been profoundly misconstrued and distorted, both positively and negatively, as supposedly having wanted to strip capitalist society of its deceptive veneer and assert the unadorned proletariat as the be-all and end-all of "socialist" society. Certainly not merely the later Stalinist history of the Soviet Union, but also practices of the Soviet state under Lenin's leadership in the Civil War, so-called "War Communism," and the Red Terror, lent themselves to a belief in Lenin as a ruthless destroyer of "bourgeois" conditions of life. But, then, what are we to make, for instance, of Lenin's pamphlets on *The State and Revolution* and *"Left-Wing" Communism: An Infantile Disorder*? For they emphasized both the necessary persistence of "bourgeois right" among the workers in the long transition from socialism to communism, requiring the continuation of state mediation, and the fact that Marxists had understood their effort as trying to overcome capital "on the basis of capitalism" itself. A prime example of Lenin's insistence on the mediation of politics in society was his opposition to Trotsky's recommendation that labor unions be militarized and subsumed under the state. Lenin wanted to preserve, rather, the important non-identity of class, party, and state in the Soviet "workers' state," which he recognized as necessarily carrying on, for the foreseeable future, "state capitalism" (characterized by "bureaucratic deformations" due to Russian conditions). Lenin thus wanted to preserve the possibility of politics *within* the working class, a theme that reached back to his first major pamphlet, *What is to be Done?* Lenin's "last struggle"[1] was to prevent the strangling of politics in the Soviet state, a danger he regarded not merely in terms of Stalin's leadership, but the condition of the Bolsheviks more generally. For instance, Lenin critically noted Trotsky's predilection for "administrative" solutions.

Georg Lukács, Karl Korsch, and Theodor Adorno, teasing out a "Hegelian" dimension to Lenin's Marxism, derived from Lenin's theoretical writings and political practice an elaboration of the Marxist theory of social mediation in capital, through the politics of proletarian socialism, that sought to recover Lenin from a bad utopian perspective of the desire to do away with politics altogether. Rather, such Marxist critical theory following Lenin understood overcoming the "alienation" and "reification" of capital as providing the possibility for the *true practice of politics*, a neglected but vital contribution Lenin made to the development of Marxism. Lenin did not attempt to destroy modern forms of political mediation, but rather to achieve the true mediation of theory and practice, in politics freed from society dominated by capital. This was the content of Lenin's liberalism, his "dialectical" Marxist attempt, not to negate, but rather to fulfill the *desiderata* of bourgeois society, which capital had come to block, and which could only be worked through "immanently."

## The controversy about Lenin

Lenin is the most controversial figure in the history of Marxism, and perhaps one of the most controversial figures in all of history. As such, he is an impossible figure for sober consideration, without polemic. Nevertheless, it has become impossible, also, after Lenin, to consider Marxism without reference to him. Broadly, Marxism is divided into avowedly "Leninist" and "anti-Leninist" tendencies. In what ways was Lenin either an advance or a calamity for Marxism? But there is another way of approaching Lenin, which is as an expression of the historical crisis of Marxism. In other words, Lenin as a historical figure is unavoidably significant as manifesting a crisis of Marxism. The question is how Lenin provided the basis

---

1   Moshe Lewin, *Lenin's Last Struggle* (Ann Arbor: University of Michigan Press, 2005).

for advancing that crisis, how the polarization around Lenin could provide the basis for advancing the potential transformation of Marxism, in terms of resolving certain problems. What is clear from the various ways that Lenin is usually approached is that the necessity for such transformation and advance of Marxism has been expressed only in distorted ways. For instance, the question of Marxist "orthodoxy" hinders the proper evaluation of Lenin. There was a fundamental ambiguity in the way Marxism addressed its own historical crisis, in the question of fidelity to and revision of Marx, for instance in the so-called "Revisionist Dispute" of the late 19th century. Lenin was a leading anti-revisionist or "orthodox" Marxist. This was also true of other Second International radical Marxists, such as Rosa Luxemburg and Leon Trotsky. In what ways did these figures, and above all Lenin, think that being true to Marx was required for the advancement and transformation of Marxism?

The Frankfurt School Critical Theorist Theodor Adorno, in his 1966 book *Negative Dialectics*, wrote of the degeneration of Marxism due to "dogmatization and thought-taboos." There is no other figure in the history of Marxism who has been subject to such "dogmatization and thought-taboos" as much as Lenin. For Adorno, figures in the history of Marxism such as Lenin or Luxemburg or Kautsky should not be approached in terms merely of their theoretical perspectives or practical actions they took or advocated, but rather in their *relation* of theory and practice, or, *why* they thought they *did* what they did *when* they did so. As Adorno put it, theory and practice have a changing relation that "fluctuates" historically.[2]

Lenin, among other Marxists, thought that the political party served an important function with regard to *consciousness*, and wrote in *What is to be Done?* of the key "importance of the *theoretical struggle*" in forming such a party. Lenin thought that theory was not simply a matter of generalization from experience in terms of trial and error, as in traditional (pre-Kantian) epistemology, but, importantly, in the Hegelian "dialectical" sense of *history*: this is how Lenin understood "theory." As Lenin put it, history did not advance in a line but rather in "spirals," through repetitions and regressions, and not simple linear "progress." In this respect, the past could be an

---

2   *Negative Dialectics*, trans. E. B. Ashton (New York: Continuum, 1973), 143.

*advance* on the present, or, the present could seek to *attain* moments of the past, but under changed conditions. And such changed conditions were themselves not to be regarded simply as "progressive." Rather, there was an important ambivalence to history, in that it exhibited both progress and *regress*. In his 1915 Granat Encyclopedia entry on Karl Marx, describing "dialectics" from a Marxian perspective, Lenin wrote,

> In our times, the idea of development, of evolution, has almost completely penetrated social consciousness, only in other ways, and not through Hegelian philosophy. Still, this idea, as formulated by Marx and Engels on the basis of Hegel's philosophy, is far more comprehensive and far richer in content than the current idea of evolution is. A development that repeats, as it were, stages that have already been passed, but repeats them in a different way, on a higher basis ("the negation of the negation"), a development, so to speak, that proceeds in spirals, not in a straight line; a development by leaps, catastrophes, and revolutions; "breaks in continuity"; the transformation of quantity into quality; inner impulses towards development, imparted by the contradiction and conflict of the various forces and tendencies acting on a given body, or within a given phenomenon, or within a given society; the interdependence and the closest and indissoluble connection between *all* aspects of any phenomenon (history constantly revealing ever new aspects), a connection that provides a uniform, and universal process of motion, one that follows definite laws — these are some of the features of dialectics as a doctrine of development that is richer than the conventional one.[3]

With Marxism, the "crisis" of bourgeois society was recognized. The crisis of bourgeois society circa 1848 was what Marx called "capital," a provocative characterization. The spiral development through which

---

3   *Karl Marx: A Brief Biographical Sketch with an Exposition of Marxism*, II. "The Marxist Doctrine," in Lenin, *Collected Works* vol. 21 (Moscow: Progress Publishers, 1974). Originally published in 1915.

Lenin, among other Second International radicals such as Luxemburg and Trotsky, thought that history in the modern era had regressed through the "progress" since Marx and Engels's time in 1848, the moment of the *Communist Manifesto*, showed how and why the subsequent development of Marxism sought to re-attain 1848. Was history since 1848 progress or regress? In a certain sense, it was both. In this history, bourgeois society appeared to both fulfill and negate itself. In other words, bourgeois society had become more itself than ever; in other respects, however, it grew distant from its earlier achievements and even undermined them. (For instance, the recrudescence of slave labor in the decades leading up to the U.S. Civil War.) The Second International radicals thus sought to return to the original potential of bourgeois society in its first moment of crisis, circa 1848. As Karl Kraus put it, in a way that registered deeply with Walter Benjamin and Adorno, "Origin is the goal."[4] Even though the crisis of capital or bourgeois society grew, the question was whether the crisis *advanced*. The Second International radicals recognized that while the crisis of capital, in Marx's sense, grows, the crisis must be made to advance, as history does not progress automatically. It was in this sense that there was, potentially, a return of the 1848 moment in the development of Marxism itself, which was the attempt to make the growing crisis — what Luxemburg and Lenin called "imperialism," and what Lenin termed capitalism's "highest stage" — a historical advance.

The paradox of such development and transformation of Marxism itself through the return to the past moment of potential and resultant "crisis" was expressed well by Karl Korsch, who wrote, in his 1923 essay on "Marxism and Philosophy,"

> [The] transformation and development of Marxist theory has been effected under the peculiar ideological guise of a return to the pure teaching of original or true Marxism. Yet it is easy to understand both the reasons for this guise and the real character of the process which is concealed by it. What theoreticians

---

4   Cited by Walter Benjamin in "On the Concept of History," *Selected Writings*, vol. 4 *1938–40* (Cambridge, MA: Harvard, 2003), 395.

like Rosa Luxemburg in Germany and Lenin in Russia have done, and are doing, in the field of Marxist theory is to liberate it from the inhibiting traditions of [Social Democracy]. They thereby answer the practical needs of the new revolutionary stage of proletarian class struggle, for these traditions weighed "like a nightmare" on the brain of the working masses whose objectively revolutionary socioeconomic position no longer corresponded to these [earlier] evolutionary doctrines. The apparent revival of original Marxist theory in the Third International is simply a result of the fact that in a new revolutionary period not only the workers' movement itself, but the theoretical conceptions of communists which express it, must assume an explicitly revolutionary form. This is why large sections of the Marxist system, which seemed virtually forgotten in the final decades of the nineteenth century, have now come to life again.[5]

So, what were these "revolutionary" aspects of Marxism that were recovered in the course of the "crisis of Marxism" (Korsch's phrase), and how did Lenin help recover them?

### Lenin and the political party

Lenin made a portentous but indicative remark in the first footnote to his book *What is to be Done?*, in which he stated that,

> Incidentally, in the history of modern socialism [there] is a phenomenon . . . in its way very consoling, namely . . . the strife of the various trends within the socialist movement. . . . [In] the[se] disputes between Lassalleans and Eisenachers, between Guesdists and Possibilists, between Fabians and Social-Democrats, and between Narodnaya Volya adherents and Social-Democrats . . . really [an] international battle

---

5  Karl Korsch, "Marxism and Philosophy," in *Marxism and Philosophy*, ed. and trans. Fred Halliday (New York: Monthly Review Press, 2008), 67–68.

with socialist opportunism, [will] international revolutionary Social-Democracy . . . perhaps become sufficiently strengthened to put an end to the political reaction that has long reigned in Europe?[6]

In other words, could working through the issue of opportunist-reformist "revisionism" within Marxism be the means for overcoming capital? This would appear to be the self-centrality of Marxism taken to its fullest flower. But there was a rationale to this. Not only did Lenin (subsequent to *What is to be Done?*) want the Mensheviks thrown out of Russian Social Democracy (Lenin agreed with the Mensheviks on excluding the so-called "economistic" tendencies of Marxism and the Jewish Bund workers' organizations), but a seldom remarked fact was that Luxemburg, too, wanted the reformist Revisionists thrown out of the German Social Democratic Party (Kautsky waffled on the issue). Lenin and Luxemburg wanted to split the Second International from its reformists (or, "opportunists").

Lenin not only thought that splits, that is, political divisions, in the Left or the workers' movement were *possible* and *desirable*, but also *necessary*. The only differences Lenin had with figures such as Luxemburg or Kautsky were over particular concrete instances in which such splits did or could or should have occurred. For instance, Luxemburg thought that the split in Russian Social Democracy in 1903 was premature and so did not concur with Lenin and the Bolsheviks on its benefits. And, importantly, the question was not merely over *whether* a political split could or should take place, but *how*, and, also, *when*. Politics was a *historical* phenomenon.

There is the specific question of the "party" as a form of politics. Marx and Engels had written in the *Communist Manifesto* that, "The Communists do not form a separate party opposed to the other working-class parties." So, this would appear to present a problem in the case of Lenin, who is notorious for the "party question." But it poses a problem for the question of Marxism in general, for Marxism confronted other, opposed, political tendencies in the working class, for instance anarchism in the First International. What had changed between Marx and Engels's time and Lenin's?

---

6   Lenin, *What Is to Be Done? Burning Questions of Our Movement* (1902).

As Marxists, Lenin and Luxemburg considered themselves to be vying for leadership of the social democratic workers' movement and its political party; they didn't simply identify with either the party or the movement, both of which originated independently of them. Both the workers' movement and the social-democratic party would have existed without Marxism. For them, the party was an instrument, as was the workers' movement itself. In responding to Eduard Bernstein's remark that the "movement is everything, the goal nothing," Luxemburg went so far as to say that without the goal of socialism the workers' movement was nothing, or perhaps even worse than nothing, in that it exacerbated the problem of capitalism, for instance giving rise to the "imperialist" form of capitalism in the late 19th century. How were the social-democratic movement and its political parties understood by Marxists? For considering this, it is necessary to note well Marx's critique of the Gotha Programme that had founded the German SPD and Engels's subsequent critique of the Erfurt Programme that had made Marxism the official perspective of the Social Democratic Party. They critiqued these programmes because that's what Marxists do: critique. No matter what had been written in these programmes, it was certain to elicit critiques from Marx and Engels.

The Marxists, that is, Marx and Engels, seem to have reluctantly gone along with the formation of a permanent party of social democracy, but not without serious reservations and caveats. The endorsement of party politics was provisional and conditional. For instance, in 1917, Lenin himself threatened to quit the Bolshevik party. Lenin thought that he could quit the party and continue to lead the revolution, that he would quit the party in order to lead the revolution.

Luxemburg's biographer, British political scientist J.P. Nettl, traced the question of the social-democratic party to a set of problematic conceptions, all of which were challenged in practice and theory by the radical Left in the Second International, in figures such as Luxemburg and Lenin. The party could be conceived as an interest-aggregator and pressure-group on the state, advancing the interests of the working class. Or it could be conceived, as it was most overtly by its leadership, under its organizational leader August Bebel and its leading theorist Karl Kautsky, as a "state within the state," or what Nettl termed an "inheritor party," aiming to take power.[7] Involved in the latter was a theory not only of revolution but also of socialism, both of which were problematical. Specifically troublesome was the idea of building up the working class's own organization within capitalism so that when its final crisis came, political power would fall into the hands of the social democrats, who had organized the working class in anticipation of such an eventuality. But these were conceptions that were challenged and critiqued, not only by later radicals such as Luxemburg and Lenin, but also by Marx and Engels themselves. Marxists such as Marx and Engels and Lenin and Luxemburg were, rightly, deeply suspicious of the social-democratic party as a permanent political institution of the working class.

## The problem of party-politics

To situate this discussion properly, it is important to return to the classical liberal scorn for political parties. There was no term of political contempt greater than "party man," or "partisan" politics, which violated not only the value of individuals thinking for themselves but also, perhaps more importantly, the very notion of politics in the liberal-democratic conception, especially with regard to the distinction between the state and civil society. Whereas the state was compulsory, civil society institutions were voluntary. While political parties, as forms of association, could be considered civil society organizations, the articulation of such formations with political power in the state struck classical liberal thinkers as particularly dangerous. Hegel, for one, explicitly preferred hereditary monarchy over democracy as a form of executive authority, precisely because it was free of such a problem. For Hegel, civil society would remain more free under a monarchy than under democracy, in which he thought political authority could be distorted by private interests. The danger lay in the potential for a civil society group to capture state power in its narrow, private interests. Moreover, in the classical liberal tradition, the idea of the professional "politician" was severely objectionable; rather, state-political figures rose

---

7    J. P. Nettl, "The German Social Democratic Party 1890-1914 as Political Model," *Past and Present* 30 (April 1965).

through other civil society institutions, as entrepreneurs, professors, priests, etc., and only reluctantly took on the duty of public office: "It's a dirty job, but somebody has to do it."

This problem of modern politics and its forms recurred in the late 19th and early 20th centuries to thinkers such as Robert Michels, a student and associate of Max Weber, similarly concerned with the problem of modern "bureaucracy," who, in a landmark study, compared the German SPD to the Democratic Party in the U.S., specifically with regard to the issue of the "party machine," with its "ward bosses," or machine-party politics, and the resulting tendency towards what Michels called "oligarchy."[8] Michels had been a member of the SPD, in its radical wing, until 1907. (Michels, who also studied the Socialist Party in Italy, went on to join Italian fascism under the former Socialist Benito Mussolini, because he thought fascism was a solution to the problem of "bureaucracy," but that's another story.) So the problem of party-politics was a well-known issue in Lenin's time. For Second International radical Marxists such as Luxemburg and Lenin, the workers' social-democratic party was not to be an interest-aggregator and permanent political institution of social power like the Democratic Party in the U.S. (which ultimately became the party of the labor unions). What, then, was the function of the social-democratic party, for figures such as Lenin and Luxemburg?

Obviously, Lenin's concerns with politics were not the same as those of liberals, who sought to prevent the ossification of political authority from stymieing the dynamism of civil society in capitalism. For Lenin's concern was above all with revolution, that is, fundamental social transformation. But was the issue of politics thus so different in Lenin's case? This raises the important issue of how social revolution and transformation were related to "politics," in the modern sense. That is, whether Lenin was interested in the "end" of politics as conceived in liberalism and practiced under capitalism, or instead concerned with overcoming the obstacle to the practice of politics that capitalism had become. How was overcoming the *social* problem capitalism had become a new beginning for the true practice of

---

8   *Political Parties: A Sociological Study of the Oligarchical Tendencies of Modern Democracy* (1911).

*politics?* In this sense, it is important to address how political mediation was brought into being but ultimately shaped and distorted by the modern society of capital, especially after the Industrial Revolution.

"Politics" is a modern phenomenon. Modern politics is conditioned by the crisis of capital in modern history. Traditional civilization, prior to the bourgeois, capitalist epoch, was subject to crises that could only be considered natural or divine in origin. Modern society is subject, for Marxists (as well as for liberals), rather, to human-made crisis thus potentially subject to politics. Bourgeois politics indeed responds to the permanent crisis of capitalism — in a sense, that's all it does — but in inadequate terms, naturalizing aspects of capitalism that should be regarded as changeable, but can only be so regarded, for Marxists, as radically and consistently changeable, from a proletarian or working-class socialist perspective. Thus, modern politics has been haunted by the "specter of communism," or socialism. As Marx put it, in *The Eighteenth Brumaire of Louis Bonaparte,* "Every demand of the simplest bourgeois financial reform, of the most ordinary liberalism, of the most formal republicanism, of the most insipid democracy, is . . . stigmatized as 'socialism.'"[9]

Furthermore, the concrete meaning of socialism or communism is subject to change. For Marxists, the demand for socialism in the 19th century was itself an *engine* of capitalist development, *historically.* The story of socialism, then, is bound up with the development of capital, and the question of whether and how its crisis was growing and advancing.

Moreover, the question of party-politics *per se* is a post-1848 phenomenon, in which modern socialism was bound up. In other words, the crisis of bourgeois society in capital after the Industrial Revolution and the failure of the "social republic" in 1848, was the crisis of bourgeois society *as liberal.* The rise of party-politics was thus a feature of the growing authoritarianism of bourgeois society, or, the failure of liberalism. As such, socialism needed to take up the problems of bourgeois society in capital that liberalism had failed to anticipate or adequately meet, or, to take up the cause of liberalism that bourgeois politics had dropped in the post-1848 world. For Marx, the problem was found most saliently in Louis Bonaparte's popular

---

9   *Marx-Engels Reader,* 2nd edition, ed. Robert C. Tucker (New York: Norton, 1978), 602.

authoritarianism against the liberals in Second Republic France, culminating in the *coup d'état* and establishment of the Second Empire. As Marx put it, the capitalists were no longer and the workers not yet able, politically, to master the bourgeois society of capital. Party-politics was thus bound up with the historical phenomenon of Bonapartism.

## Lenin and the crisis of Marxism

The period of close collaboration between Luxemburg and Lenin around the 1905 Russian Revolution saw Luxemburg leveling a critique of the relation that had developed between the social-democratic party and the labor unions in her pamphlet on *The Mass Strike, the Political Party, and the Trade Unions*. (Also, during this time Luxemburg wrote a defense of Lenin against the Menshevik charge of "Blanquism," which she called "pedantic," and thought said more of the reformist opportunism of those leveling the charge against Lenin than about its target.[10]) In her *Mass Strike* pamphlet, Luxemburg delineated specific and non-identical roles for the various elements she mentioned in her title, that is to say, general strike committees, political parties, and labor unions (not mentioned specifically were the "soviets," or workers' councils). In this sense, the "mass strike" was for Luxemburg a *symptom* of the historical development and crisis of social democracy itself. This made it a *political* and not merely tactical issue. That is, for Luxemburg, the mass strike was a phenomenon of how social democracy had developed its political parties and labor unions, and what new historical necessities had thus been brought into being. Luxemburg's pamphlet was, above all, a critique of the social-democratic party, which she regarded as a historical symptom. This was prefigured in Luxemburg's earlier pamphlet on *Reform or Revolution?*, where she addressed the question of the *raison d'être* of the social-democratic movement (the combination of political party and labor unions).

From this perspective of regarding the history of the workers' movement and Marxism itself as *intrinsic* to the history of capitalism, then, it becomes possible to make sense of Lenin's further articulations of politics

---

10   Rosa Luxemburg, "Blanquism and Social Democracy" (1906).

in his later works, *The State and Revolution* and *"Left-Wing" Communism: An Infantile Disorder*, as well as in the political disputes that attended the young Soviet state that had issued from the Russian Revolution and had endured the Civil War and stabilization of international capitalism in the aftermath of WWI. Lenin maintained a strictly minimal conception of the state, restricting it to the monopoly of authority for the exercise of force, precisely in order to avoid an all-encompassing conception of the state as the be-all and end-all of politics. Similarly, Lenin deemed "infantile" the impatience of supposed radicals with existing forms of political mediation, such as parliaments, stating unequivocally that while Marxism may have "theoretically" surpassed a liberal conception of the state, this had not yet been achieved "politically," that is, in practice. In response to Trotsky's recommendation that labor unions be militarized in the Soviet state, Lenin maintained that unions needed to remain independent not only of the state, but also of the Communist Party itself. The workers needed the ability, according to Lenin, of asserting their rights against the party and the state. Lenin recognized the necessity of an articulated non-identity of state, political parties, and other voluntary civil society institutions such as labor unions. This was grounded in Lenin's perspective that capitalist social relations could not be abolished in one stroke through political revolution, that, even though the state had been "smashed," it was reconstituted, not on the basis of a new social principle, but on the continuation of what Lenin called "bourgeois right," long after the political overthrow and even social elimination of a separate capitalist class. "Bourgeois right" persisted precisely among the workers (and other previously subordinate members of society) and so necessarily governed their social relations, necessitating a state that could thus only "wither away." Politics could be only slowly transformed.

Finally, there is the question of Adorno's continued adherence to Lenin, despite what at first glance may appear to be some jarring contradictions with respect to Lenin's own perspective and political practice. For instance, in a late essay from 1969, "Critique," Adorno praised the U.S. Constitutional system of "divisions of powers" and "checks and balances" as essential to preserving the critical function of reason in the exercise of political authority.[11] But this was an *example* for Adorno, and not necessarily to be hypostatized as such. The making common of executive and legislative authority in the "soviet" system of "workers' councils" was understood by Lenin, as Adorno well knew, to coexist with separate civil society organizations such as political parties, labor unions and other voluntary groups, and so did not necessarily and certainly did not intentionally violate the critical role of political mediation at various levels of society.

It has been a fundamental mistake to conflate and confuse Lenin's model of *party* politics for a form of *state* in pursuing socialism. Lenin presupposed their important non-identity. The party was meant to be one element among many mediating factors in society and politics. Moreover, Lenin's party was meant to be one among many parties, including multiple parties of the working class, vying for its adherence, and even multiple "Marxist" parties, differing in their relation of theory and practice, or means and ends.

By contrast, there was nothing so repressive and authoritarian as the Kautskyan (or Bebelian) social-democratic "party of the whole class" (or, the "one class, one party" model of social democracy, that is, that since the capitalists are of one interest in confronting the workers, the workers need to be unified against the capitalists). The social-democratic party, after all, waged the counterrevolution against Lenin and Luxemburg.

Lenin preserved politics by splitting Marxism. For this, Lenin has never been forgiven. But, precisely for this, Lenin needs to be remembered.

Presented at the Left Forum 2011 on the panel "Lenin's Marxism" with Paul LeBlanc of the International Socialist Organization and Lars T. Lih, author of *Lenin Reconsidered: "What is to be Done" in Context*, organized by Platypus at Pace University in NYC.

Originally published in *Platypus Review* 36 (June 2011)

---

11  In *Critical Models: Interventions and Catchwords*, trans. Henry W. Pickford (New York: Columbia University Press, 1998).

# Lenin's politics[1]

The principal mistake made by those who contemplate Lenin's political thought and action is due to assumptions that are made about the relation of socialism to democracy. Lenin was not an "undemocratic socialist" or one who prioritized socialism as an "end" over the "means" of democracy. Lenin did not think that once a majority of workers was won to socialist revolution democracy was finished. Lenin was not an authoritarian socialist.[2]

Socialism is meant to transcend liberalism by fulfilling it.[3] The problem with liberalism is not its direction, supposedly different from socialism, but rather that it does not go far enough. Socialism is not anti-liberal. The 20th century antinomy of socialism versus liberalism, as expressed in Isaiah Berlin's counterposing of "positive and negative freedoms" or "freedom to [social benefits] versus freedom from [the state],"[4] or the idea that social justice conflicts with liberty, travesties (and naturalizes) and thus degrades the actual problem, which is not a clash of timeless principles — liberalism versus democracy — but a historically specific contradiction of capitalism. To clarify this, it is necessary to return to a Marxist approach, such as Lenin's.

The error consists of addressing a dialectical approach to politics such as Lenin's in an undialectical and eclectic manner, as if there were a number of criteria to be checked off (anticapitalism, democracy, etc.), rather

---

1    A rejoinder to David Adam, "Lenin the liberal: A reply to Chris Cutrone," *Platypus Review* 40 (October 2011).

2    See my "The Decline of the Left in the 20th century: Toward a Theory of Historical Regression: 1917," *Platypus Review* 17 (November 2000), in this volume.

3    See my "Lenin's Liberalism," *Platypus Review* 36 (June 2011), in this volume.

4    See Isaiah Berlin, "Two Concepts of Liberty" (1958), in *Four Essays on Liberty* (Oxford University Press, 1969).

than a set of intrinsically interrelated historical problems to be worked through together. The actual dialectic of the historically interrelated developments of capitalism, democracy, and the struggle for socialism demands a dialectical approach in both practice and theory. The reason that various moments of Lenin's thought and action can appear contradictory is due to an undialectical interpretation of Lenin, not to Lenin himself. Lenin is subject to the same interpretive problem as Marx: the question of Lenin cuts to the heart of Marxism.[5]

This is recognizable by way of considering Lenin's various discussions of the state, political parties, and society.[6] Lenin assumed that these were not the same thing and did not assume that "socialism" meant making them into the same thing. Most of Lenin's readers (both followers and detractors) either praise or denounce Lenin, mistakenly, for his supposed attempts to make society into an undifferentiated totality. Not only what Lenin said, but what he did shows otherwise. Furthermore, one must take into account how Lenin avowedly sought to be true to Marx, whether one judges Lenin to have been successful in this or not. Therefore, at least in part, one must reckon with the problem of evaluating Lenin as a Marxist.

It is a fundamental error to regard Lenin as a largely unconscious political actor who was reduced to theoretically "justifying" his actions. Readers often commit the fallacy of projecting their own inclinations or fears onto Lenin and misinterpret him accordingly. On the contrary, one must address what Lenin said and did in terms of the coherence of his own self-understanding. For this, it is necessary to regard the historical, that is, social and political, circumstances within which Lenin not only acted but spoke. From the various available records, Lenin did not write treatises but political pamphlets, moreover with propagandistic purpose, including his most "theoretical" works such as *The State and Revolution* (1917).

What is clear is that Lenin did not advocate the partyification of the state (or statification of the party) or the statification of society — in this crucial respect, Lenin remained a "liberal." Both of these phenomena of Stalinization post-date Lenin and need to be addressed in terms of a process

---

5    See Tamas Krausz, "Lenin's Legacy Today," *Platypus Review* 39 (September 2011).
6    See Spartacist League, *Lenin and the Vanguard Party* in *Workers Vanguard* (1978).

beginning after Lenin's medical retirement, the dangers of which Lenin was well aware and against which he struggled, in vain, in his final years.[7]

The ban on factions that seems to impugn Lenin's motives and show a supposed continuity between him and Stalin can be addressed rather straightforwardly. Lenin came in 1921 to advocate banning organized factions — not dissent! — within the Russian Communist Party, precisely because of the differentiated realities of the party, the state, and society in the Soviet workers' state of the former Russian Empire. Many careerist state functionaries had joined the party (though, according to Lenin, they deserved only to be "shot"), and the party-controlled state faced a deeply divided society, in which he thought that the party could become a plaything in the hands of other state and greater societal forces. The ban on factions was meant not only to be merely a temporary measure, but it should be noted that Lenin did not call for such ban on factions in the Communist International, which was considered a single world party divided into national sections. The ban on factions was meant to address a danger specific to the Bolsheviks being a ruling governmental party under certain conditions, and it was inextricably tied to the contemporaneous implementation of the New Economic Policy. One might interpret the ban as directed against the Left, whereas in fact it was directed against the Right, that is, directed against the power of the status quo in the former Russian Empire swamping the politics of social revolution. So, the ban on factions was a self-consciously limited and specifically local compromise to Lenin's mind, and not at all the expression of any kind of principle. It is a serious mistake to regard it otherwise. The fact that the ban on factions helped lead to Stalinism does not make it into an "original sin" by Lenin. Revolution beyond the Soviet Union was the only way to ameliorate the problems of Bolshevik rule, as Rosa Luxemburg, for one, recognized.[8]

The other mistake, indicative of a fundamental misunderstanding of the relation of the struggle for proletarian socialism to democracy and the politics of the state, is to regard problems of economics and politics as similar in kind. There is no contradiction between democracy in politics and

---

7    See Moshe Lewin, Lenin's Last Struggle (New York: Pantheon, 1968).

8    See Rosa Luxemburg, "The Russian Tragedy" (1918).

hierarchy of authority in various concrete activities, whether economic or military. The question is one of social and political leadership and responsibility. Is a factory responsible only to its own employees, or to society as a whole? Lenin was certainly not a syndicalist or "council communist," that is, Lenin did not think that socialist politics can be adequately pursued by labor unions or workers' councils (or more indeterminate "democratic assemblies") alone, but this does not mean Lenin was undemocratic. The issue of democracy in economic life cannot be considered in an unmediated way without doing violence to the societal issues involved. The point of "democratizing the economy" is not to be understood properly as simply workplace democracy. This is because socialism is not merely a problem of the organization of production, let alone merely an economic issue. Socialism is not merely democratic. Rather, democracy poses the question of society and, from a Marxist perspective, the "social question" is capitalism. Marxism recognizes the need for democracy in capitalism. Lenin addressed the possibility of overcoming the necessity of the state or, more precisely, the need for democracy. Marxism agrees with anarchism on the goal of superseding democracy, but disagrees on how to get there from here. Marxism recognizes the need for a democratic state posed by capitalism that cannot be wished away.

The society and state in question were addressed by Lenin with respect to the "dictatorship of the proletariat," which is, importantly, not a national state. His vision was for a workers' state at a global scale. Because the bourgeois state is a global and not a national phenomenon, neither is the Marxist vision of the "workers' state." Lenin did not pursue a national road to socialism. As a Marxist, he recognized that, under capitalism, "the state" — of which various national states were merely local components — was essentially the "dictatorship of the bourgeoisie." This did not mean that there were no political struggles among the capitalists to which various nation states could and did become subject. Rather, the need for socialism was tied to a need for a global state as well as a truly free global civil society already expressed under capitalism.[9] Only by understanding what Marx

---

9    See Immanuel Kant, "Idea for a Universal History from a Cosmopolitan Point of View," trans. Lewis White Beck, in *Kant on History* (Indianapolis: Bobbs-Merrill, 1963).

meant by the "dictatorship of the bourgeoisie" in liberal democracy can we understand what Lenin meant by the "dictatorship of the proletariat" in a revolutionary "workers' state."[10]

Lenin was a liberal because he understood the necessity of politics within the working class, which does not and cannot take place outside the domains of bourgeois rights and politics, but which is rather inevitably and necessarily part and parcel of them. Lenin did not advocate the unmediated politicization of society, which he knew would be regressive, whether understood in authoritarian or "libertarian" terms. The Soviet workers' state in Lenin's time was indeed like the Paris Commune of 1871, if it had been led by Marx and Engels, had fought off Versailles, and had held on to power.

The Russian Revolution presented new problems, not with regard to *socialism*, which was never achieved, but rather with regard to the *revolution*, which failed. Like the Commune, the revolution that opened in 1917 was abortive. Isolation in Russia was defeating: the failure of the German Revolution 1918–19 was the defeat of the revolution in Russia. Stalinism was the result of this defeat, and adapted itself to it. Lenin already contended with this defeat, and distinguished his Marxism from both Right opportunism and ultra-Leftism.[11] The question is, what can we learn about this failure, from Lenin's perspective?

Because democratic discontents, the workers' movement, and anti-capitalist and socialist political parties, operate in a differentiated totality of bourgeois society that must be transformed, they are subject to politicization and the problems of democratic self-determination that liberal bourgeois society has historically placed on the agenda. Proletarian socialism, in Lenin's view no less than Marx's, does not nullify these problems but seeks to allow them a fuller scope of activity. Lenin advocated not only a workers' "state," but also workers' political parties and other workers' civil society institutions such as labor unions and workers' publications, which the struggle for socialism necessitated. This is true after the revolution even

---

10  The reason why the global state under capital tends toward liberal democracy at the core but tolerates tyranny in its subordinate domains or peripheral extremities is the expediency or convenience of opportunism; despotism in the center, by contrast, is highly politically contentious and untenable. Indeed, it has led to world wars.

11  See Lenin, *"Left-Wing" Communism: An Infantile Disorder* (1920).

more than before because the workers' social revolution is meant to build upon the existing society. Lenin was an avowed Marxist "communist." As Marx put it, communism seeks a society in which the "free development of each is the condition for the free development of all."[12]

Both "libertarian" and authoritarian tendencies in socialism tend to avoid the importance of Lenin's Marxism on this score, because both tendencies tend to conflate society and politics. This is not only anti-liberal but illiberal — and un-Marxist — whether understood hierarchically or "democratically." Capitalism is already a "grassroots" and thus a democratic phenomenon, and not merely a baleful hierarchy of authority: its problem goes beyond democracy.

The proletarian socialist revolution, in Lenin's view as well as Marx's, was not meant to bring about the Millennium, but rather to clear certain obstacles to the struggle for the working class's social and political self-determination (not exclusively as a matter of the state), which Marx and Lenin thought could lead society beyond capitalism. Moreover, this was conceived largely "negatively," in terms of problems to be overcome. The revolution, in Marxist terms, does not produce an emancipated society ready-made, but only, perhaps, political forms through which emancipatory social transformation, otherwise blocked by capitalism, might be pursued and developed further. Lenin, like Marx, thought that overthrowing both the rule of capitalist private property in the means of production and the subjection of society to the vicissitudes of the market, the classic demands of proletarian socialism as it had developed after the Industrial Revolution, might allow this.

Neither Marx nor Lenin came with blueprints for an emancipated society in hand. Rather, Lenin, following Marx, advocated pursuing the forms of the struggle for socialism that had emerged historically in and through the development of the workers' movement itself. Historical Marxism did not formulate independent schemes for emancipation, but sought the potential social-emancipatory content of emergent political phenomena in light of history. Lenin as well as Marx advocated the workers' right to rule, but followed other socialists in doing so. It is necessary to address Lenin as

---

12 Marx and Engels, *Manifesto of the Communist Party* (1848).

a consistent advocate of workers' power, and consider how he understood the meaning of this in the struggle for socialism.

Socialism in the original Marxist sense that Lenin followed does not seek to undo but rather tries to press further the gains of historically "bourgeois" liberal democracy. Liberalism is not meant to be negated but fulfilled by democracy, just as bourgeois society is not meant to be torn down but transcended in overcoming capitalism. Liberal and democratic concerns need to answer to the historical tasks of emancipatory social transformation, not timeless political "principles."

Lenin himself was very clear on this, even if neither most of his supposed followers nor his detractors have been. The problem is anti-Marxist interpretive bias that is blinding.

Originally published in *Platypus Review* 40 (October 2011)

# The relevance of Lenin today

If the Bolshevik Revolution is — as some people have called it — the most significant political event of the 20th century, then Lenin must for good or ill be considered the century's most significant political leader. Not only in the scholarly circles of the former Soviet Union, but even among many non-Communist scholars, he has been regarded as both the greatest revolutionary leader and revolutionary statesman in history, as well as the greatest revolutionary thinker since Marx.

*– Encyclopedia Britannica*

## 2011 – year of revolution?

*Time* magazine nominated "the protester," from the Arab Spring to the #Occupy movement, as "Person of the Year" for 2011.[1] In addressing the culture of the #Occupy movement, *Time* listed some key books to be read, in a sidebar article, "How to stock a protest library."[2] Included were *A People's History of the United States* by Howard Zinn, *The Prison Notebooks* by Antonio Gramsci, *Multitude* by Michael Hardt and Antonio Negri, and *Welcome to the Desert of the Real* by Slavoj Žižek.

*Time's* lead article by Kurt Andersen compared the Arab Spring and #Occupy movement to the beginnings of the Great French Revolution in 1789, invoking the poem "The French Revolution as It Appeared to Enthusiasts at Its Commencement" by William Wordsworth. Under the title "The Beginning of History," Andersen wrote that,

---

1   Kurt Andersen, "The Protester," *Time* 175 no. 28 (December 26, 2011 – January 2, 2012).
2   *Time* 175 no. 28 (print edition), 74.

Aftermaths are never as splendid as uprisings. Solidarity has a short half-life. Democracy is messy and hard, and votes may not go your way. Freedom doesn't appear all at once. . . . No one knows how the revolutions will play out: A bumpy road to stable democracy, as in America two centuries ago? Radicals' taking over, as in France just after the bliss and very heaven? Or quick counterrevolution, as in France 60 years later [in 1848]?[3]

The imagination of revolution in 2011 was, it appears, 1789 without consequences: According to Wordsworth, it was "bliss . . . in that dawn to be alive" and "to be young was very heaven." In this respect, there was an attempt to exorcize the memory of revolution in the 20th century — specifically, the haunting memory of Lenin.

## 1789 and 1917

There were once two revolutions considered definitive of the modern period, the French Revolution of 1789 and the Russian Revolution of 1917. Why did Diego Rivera paint Lenin in his mural "Man at the Crossroads" (1933) in Rockefeller Center, as depicted in the film *Cradle Will Rock* (1999), about the Popular Front against War and Fascism of the 1930s? "Why not Thomas Jefferson?," asked John Cusack, playing Nelson Rockefeller, ingenuously. "Ridiculous!," Ruben Blades, playing Rivera, responded with defiance, "Lenin stays!"

Still, Jefferson, in his letter of January 3, 1793 to U.S. Ambassador to France William Short, wrote,

The tone of your letters had for some time given me pain, on account of the extreme warmth with which they censured the proceedings of the Jacobins of France. . . . In the struggle which was necessary, many guilty persons fell without the forms of trial, and with them some innocent. These I deplore as much as any body, and shall deplore some of them to the day of

---

3   Ibid., 75.

my death. But I deplore them as I should have done had they fallen in battle. It was necessary to use the arm of the people, a machine not quite so blind as balls and bombs, but blind to a certain degree. A few of their cordial friends met at their hands, the fate of enemies. But time and truth will rescue and embalm their memories, while their posterity will be enjoying that very liberty for which they would never have hesitated to offer up their lives. The liberty of the whole earth was depending on the issue of the contest, and was ever such a prize won with so little innocent blood? My own affections have been deeply wounded by some of the martyrs to this cause, but rather than it should have failed, I would have seen half the earth desolated. Were there but an Adam and an Eve left in every country, and left free, it would be better than as it now is.[4]

The image of 18th century Jacobins and 20th century Bolsheviks haunts any revolutionary politics, up to today. Lenin characterized himself as a "revolutionary social democrat," a "Jacobin who wholly identifies himself with the organization of the proletariat . . . conscious of its class interests."[5] What did it mean to identify as a "Jacobin" in Lenin's turn-of-the-20th century socialist workers' movement? Was it to be merely the most intransigent, ruthless revolutionary, for whom "the ends justify the means," like Robespierre?

But the question of "Jacobinism" in subsequent history, after the 18th century, involves the transformation of the tasks of the bourgeois revolution in the 19th century. To stand in the tradition of Jacobinism in the 19th century meant, for Lenin, to identify with the workers' movement for socialism. Furthermore, for Lenin, it meant to be a *Marxist*.

### 1848?

There is another date besides 1789 and 1917 that needs to be considered: 1848. This was the time of the "Spring of the Nations" in Europe. But these

---

4    Thomas Jefferson, *The Declaration of Independence and Other Writings* (Verso Revolutions Series), ed. Michael Hardt (London: Verso, 2007), 46–47.

5    Lenin, *One Step Forward, Two Steps Back* (1904).

revolutions failed. This was the moment of Marx and Engels's *Communist Manifesto*, published in anticipation of the revolution, just days before its outbreak. So, the question is not so much, How was Lenin a "Jacobin"?, but, rather, How was Lenin a "Marxist"? This is because 1848, the defining moment of Marxism, tends to drop out of the historical imagination of revolution today,[6] whereas for Marxism in Lenin's time 1848 was the lodestar.

Rosa Luxemburg, in her speech to the founding congress of the German Communist Party (Spartacus League), "On the Spartacus programme" (1918), offered a remarkable argument about the complex, recursive historical dialectic of progression and regression issuing from 1848. Here, Luxemburg stated that,

> Great historical movements have been the determining causes of today's deliberations. The time has arrived when the entire socialist programme of the proletariat has to be established upon a new foundation. We are faced with a position similar to that which was faced by Marx and Engels when they wrote the *Communist Manifesto* seventy years ago. . . . With a few trifling variations, [the formulations of the *Manifesto*] . . . are the tasks that confront us today. It is by such measures that we shall have to realize socialism. Between the day when the above programme [of the *Manifesto*] was formulated, and the present hour, there have intervened seventy years of capitalist development, and the historical evolutionary process has brought us back to the standpoint [of Marx and Engels in the *Manifesto*]. . . . The further evolution of capital has . . . resulted in this, that . . . it is our immediate objective to fulfill what Marx and Engels thought they would have to fulfill in the year 1848. But between that point of development, that beginning in the year 1848, and our own views and our immediate task, there

---

6   See my "Egypt, or history's invidious comparisons: 1979, 1789, and 1848," *Platypus Review* 33 (March 2011), in *Death of the Millennial Left: Interventions 2006–2022*. Also see my "The Marxist hypothesis: A response to Alain Badiou's 'communist hypothesis,'" *Platypus Review* 29 (November 2010), in this volume.

lies the whole evolution, not only of capitalism, but in addition
that of the socialist labor movement.

This is because, as Luxemburg had put it in her 1900 pamphlet *Reform or
Revolution*, the original contradiction of capital, the chaos of production
versus its progressive socialization, had become compounded by a new
"contradiction," the growth in organization and consciousness of the workers' movement itself, which in Luxemburg's view did not ameliorate but
exacerbated the social and political crisis and need for revolution in capital.

By contrast, however, see Luxemburg's former mentor Karl Kautsky's
criticism of Lenin and Luxemburg, for their predilection for what Kautsky
called "primitive Marxism." Kautsky wrote that, "All theoreticians of communism delight in drawing on primitive Marxism, on the early works,
which Marx and Engels wrote before they turned thirty, up until the revolution of 1848 and its aftermath of 1849 and 1850."[7]

### Marxism and "Leninism"

In 2011, it seems, *Time* magazine, among others, could only regard revolution in terms of 1789. This is quite unlike the period of most of the
20th century prior to 1989 — the centenary of the French Revolution also
marked the beginning of the collapse of the Soviet Union — in which 1789
could be recalled only in terms of 1917. A historical link was drawn between
Bolshevism and the Jacobins. In the collapse of 20th century Communism,
not only the demon of 1917 but also 1789 seemed exorcized.

Did 1917 and 1789 share only disappointing results, the terror and
totalitarianism, and an ultimately conservative, oppressive outcome, in
Napoleon Bonaparte's Empire and Stalin's Soviet Union? 1917 seems to
have complicated and deepened the problems of 1789, underscoring
Hegel's caveats about the terror of revolution. It would appear that Napoleon stands in the same relation to Robespierre as Stalin stands to Lenin.
But the problems of 1917 need to be further specified, by reference to 1848

---

7   This is in Kautsky's critique of Karl Korsch's rumination on Luxemburg and Lenin in
    "Marxism and philosophy" (1923), "A destroyer of vulgar Marxism" (1924), trans. Ben
    Lewis, *Platypus Review* 43 (February 2012).

and, hence, to Marxism, as a post-1848 historical phenomenon.[8] The question concerning Lenin is the question of Marxism.[9]

This is because there would be no discussing Marxism today without the role of the Bolsheviks in the October Revolution. The relevance of Marxism is inevitably tied to Lenin. Marxism continues to be relevant either because of or despite Lenin.[10] But what is the significance of Lenin as a historical figure from the point of view of Marxism?

For Marx, history presented new tasks in 1848, different from those confronting earlier forms of revolutionary politics, such as Jacobinism. Marx thus distinguished "the revolution of the 19th century" from that of the 18th.[11] But where the 18th century seemed to have succeeded, the 19th century appeared to have failed: history repeated itself, according to Marx, "the first time as tragedy, the second time as farce."[12] Trying to escape this debacle, Marxism expressed and sought to specify the tasks of revolution in the 19th century. The question of Lenin's relevance is how well (or poorly) Lenin, as a 20th century revolutionary, expressed the tasks inherited from 19th century Marxism. How was Lenin, as a Marxist, adequately (or inadequately) conscious of the tasks of history?

The recent (December 2011) passing of Christopher Hitchens (1949–2011) provides an occasion for considering the fate of Marxism in the late 20th century.[13] Hitchens's formative experience as a Marxist was in a tendency of Trotskyism, the International Socialists, who, in the 1960s and early 1970s period of the New Left, characterized themselves, as Hitchens once put it, as "Luxemburgist." This was intended to contrast with "Leninism," which had been, during the Cold War, at least associated, if not simply equated, with Stalinism. The New Left, as anti-Stalinist, in large measure considered itself to be either anti-Leninist, or, more generously,

---

8 See my "1873–1973: The century of Marxism: The death of Marxism and the emergence of neo-liberalism and neo-anarchism," *Platypus Review* 47 (June 2012), in this volume.

9 See Tamas Krausz, "Lenin's legacy today," *Platypus Review* 39 (September 2011).

10 See my "Lenin's liberalism," *Platypus Review* 36 (June 2011), in this volume. Also see my "Lenin's politics," *Platypus Review* 40 (October 2011), in this volume.

11 See Karl Marx, *The Eighteenth Brumaire of Louis Bonaparte* (1852).

12 Ibid.

13 See Spencer Leonard, "Going it alone: Christopher Hitchens and the death of the Left," *Platypus Review* 11 (March 2009).

post-Leninist, going beyond Lenin. The New Left sought to leave Lenin behind — at least at first. Within a few short years of the crisis of 1968, however, the International Socialists, along with many others on the Left, embraced "Leninism."[14] What did this mean?

## The New Left and the 20th century

Prior to the crisis of the New Left in 1968, "Leninism" meant something very specific. Leninism was "anti-imperialist," and hence anti-colonialist, or, even, supportive of Third World nationalism, in its outlook for revolutionary politics. The relevance of Leninism, especially for the metropolitan countries — as opposed to the peripheral, post-colonial regions of the world — seemed severely limited, at best.

In the mid-20th century, it appeared that Marxism was only relevant as "Leninism," a revolutionary ideology of the "underdeveloped" world. In this respect, the metropolitan New Left of the core capitalist countries considered itself to be not merely post-Leninist but post-Marxist — or, more accurately, post-Marxist because it was post-Leninist.

After the crisis of 1968, however, the New Left transitioned from being largely anti-Leninist to becoming "Leninist." This was when the significance of Maoism, through the Great Proletarian Cultural Revolution in China, transformed from seeming to be relevant only to peasant guerilla-based revolutionism and "new democracy" in the post-colonial periphery, to becoming a modern form of Marxism with potential radical purchase in the core capitalist countries. The turn from the 1960s to the 1970s involved a neo-Marxism and neo-Leninism. The ostensibly Marxist organizations that exist today are mostly characterized by their formation and development during this renaissance of "Leninism" in the 1970s. Even the anti-Leninists of the period bear the marks of this phenomenon, for instance, anarchism.

The New Left leading up to 1968 was an important moment of not merely confrontation but also cross-fertilization between anarchism and

---

14 See Tony Cliff, *Lenin*, 4 vols. (London: Pluto Press, 1975, 1976, 1978 and 1979). See also the critique of Cliff by the Spartacist League, *Lenin and the Vanguard Party* in *Workers Vanguard* (1978).

Marxism. This was the content of supposed "post-Marxism": see, for example, the ex-Marxist, anarchist Murray Bookchin, who protested against the potential return of Leninism in his famous 1969 pamphlet, *Listen, Marxist!* In this, there was recalled an earlier moment of anarchist and Marxist rapprochement — in the Russian Revolution, beginning as early as 1905, but developing more deeply in 1917 and the founding of the Communist International in its wake. There were splits and regroupments in this period not only among Social Democrats and Communists but also among Marxists and anarchists. It also meant the new adherence to Marxism by many who, prior to World War I and the Russian Revolution, considered themselves "post-Marxist," such as Georg Lukács.

The reconsideration of and return to "Marxism/Leninism" in the latter phase of the New Left in the 1970s, circa and after the crisis of 1968, thus recapitulated an earlier moment of reconfiguration of the Left. The newfound "Leninism" meant the New Left "getting serious" about politics. The figure of Lenin is thus involved in not only the division between "reformist" Social Democrats and "revolutionary" Communists in the crisis of World War I and the Russian and other revolutions (such as in Germany, Hungary, and Italy) that followed, or the division between liberalism and socialism in the mid-20th century context of the Cold War, but also between anarchists and Marxists, both in the era of the Russian Revolution and, later, in the New Left. It is in this sense that Lenin is a world-historical figure in the history of the Left.[15] "Leninism" meant a turn to "revolutionary" politics and the contest for power — or so, at least, it seemed.

But did Lenin and "Leninism" represent a progressive development for Marxism, either in 1917 or after 1968? For anarchists, social democrats and liberals, the answer is "No." For them, Lenin represented a degeneration of Marxism into Jacobinism, terror, and totalitarian dictatorship, or, short of that, into an authoritarian political impulse, a lowering of horizons — Napoleon, after all, was a Jacobin! If anything, Lenin revealed the truth of Marxism as, at least potentially, an authoritarian and totalitarian ideology, as the anarchists and others had warned already in the 19th century.

---

15 See my "The decline of the Left in the 20th century: Toward a theory of historical regression: 1917," *Platypus Review* 17 (November 2000), in this volume.

For avowed "Leninists," however, the answer to the question of Lenin as progress is "Yes": Lenin went beyond Marx. Either in terms of anti-imperialist and/or anti-colonialist politics of the Left, or simply by virtue of successfully implementing Marxism as revolutionary politics "in practice," Lenin is regarded as having successfully brought Marxism into the 20th century.

But perhaps what ought to be considered is what Lenin himself thought of his contribution, in terms of either the progression or regression of Marxism, and how to understand this in light of the prior history leading into the 20th century.

### Lenin as a Marxist

Lenin's 1917 pamphlet, *The State and Revolution*, did not aspire to original-ity, but was, rather, an attempted synthesis of Engels and Marx's various writings that they themselves never made: specifically, of the *Communist Manifesto*, *The Civil War in France* (on the Paris Commune), and *Critique of the Gotha Programme*. Moreover, Lenin was writing against subsequent Marxists' treatments of the issue of the state, especially Kautsky's. Why did Lenin take the time during the crisis, not only of the collapse of the Tsarist Russian Empire but of the First World War, to write on this topic? The fact of the Russian Revolution is not the only explanation. World War I was a far more dramatic crisis than the Revolutions of 1848 had been, and a far greater crisis than the Franco-Prussian War that had ushered in the Paris Commune. Socialism clearly seemed more necessary in Lenin's time. But was it more *possible*? Prior to World War I, Kautsky would have regarded socialism as more possible, but after World War I, Kautsky regarded it as less so, and with less necessity of priority. Rather, "demo-cracy" seemed to Kautsky more necessary than, and a precondition for the possibility of socialism.

For Lenin, the crisis of bourgeois society had matured. It had grown, but had it *advanced*? For Lenin, the preconditions of socialism had also been eroded and not merely further developed since Marx's time. Indeed Kautsky, Lenin's great Marxist adversary in 1917, regarded WWI as a set-back and not as an opportunity to struggle for socialism. Lenin's opponents considered him fanatical. The attempt to turn the World War into a civil war — socialist revolution — seemed dogmatic zealotry. For Kautsky, Lenin's revolutionism seemed part of the barbarism of the War rather than an answer to it.

Marx made a wry remark, in his writing on the Paris Commune, that the only possibility of preserving the gains of bourgeois society was through the "dictatorship of the proletariat." Marx savaged the liberal politician who put down the Commune, Adolphe Thiers. However, in his *Critique of the Gotha Programme*, Marx regarded his followers as having regressed behind and fallen below the threshold of the bourgeois liberals of the time. Marx castigated his ostensible followers for being less "practically internationalist" than the cosmopolitan, free-trade liberals were, and for being more positive about the state than the liberals.

Lenin marshaled Marx's rancor, bringing it home in the present, against Kautsky. World War I may have made socialism apparently less possible, but it also made it more necessary. This is the dialectical conception of "socialism or barbarism" that Lenin shared with Rosa Luxemburg, and what made them common opponents of Kautsky. Luxemburg and Lenin regarded themselves as "orthodox," faithful to the revolutionary spirit of Marx and Engels, whereas Kautsky was a traitor — "renegade." Kautsky opposed democracy to socialism but betrayed them both.

### The relevance of Lenin today: political and social revolution

All of this seems very far removed from the concerns of the present. Today, we struggle not with the problem of achieving socialism, but rather have returned to the apparently more basic issue of democracy. This is seen in recent events, from the financial crisis to the question of "sovereign debt"; from the Arab Spring to Occupy Wall Street; from the struggle for a unified European-wide policy, to the elections in Greece and Egypt that seem to have threatened so much and promised so little. The need to go beyond mere "protest" has asserted itself. Political revolution seems necessary — again.

Lenin was a figure of the struggle for socialism — a man of a very different era.[16] But his self-conception as a "Jacobin" raises the issue of regarding Lenin as a radical *democrat*.[17] Lenin's identification for this was "revolutionary social democrat" — someone who would uphold the need for revolution to achieve democracy with adequate social content. In this respect, what Lenin aspired to might remain our goal as well. The question that remains for us is the relation between democracy and capitalism. Capitalism is a source of severe discontents — an undoubted problem of our world — but seems intractable. It is no longer the case, as it was in the Cold War period, that capitalism is accepted as a necessary evil, to preserve the autonomy of civil society against the potentially "totalitarian" state. Rather, in our time, we accept capitalism in the much more degraded sense of Margaret Thatcher's infamous expression, "There is no alternative!" But the recent crisis of neoliberalism means that even this ideology, predominant for a generation, has seemingly worn thin. Social revolution seems necessary — again.

But there is an unmistakable shying away from such tasks on the Left today. Political party, never mind revolution, seems undesirable in the present. For political parties are defined by their ability and willingness to take power.[18] Today, the people — the *demos* — seem resigned to their political powerlessness. Indeed, forming a political party aiming at radical democracy, let alone socialism — a "Jacobin" party — would itself be a revolutionary act. Perhaps this is precisely the reason why it is avoided. The image of Lenin haunting us reminds that we could do otherwise.

It is Lenin who offers the memory, however distant, of the relation between political and social revolution, the relation between the need for democracy — the "rule of the people" – and the task of socialism. This is the reason that Lenin is either forgotten entirely — in an unconscious

---

16  See my "1873–1973: The century of Marxism," *Platypus Review* 47 (June 2012), in this volume.

17  See Ben Lewis and Tom Riley, "Lenin and the Marxist Left after #Occupy," *Platypus Review* 47 (June 2012).

18  See Peter Nettl, "The German Social Democratic Party 1890–1914 as a political model," *Past & Present* 30 (April 1965), 65–95.

psychological blind-spot[19] — or is ritualistically invoked only to be demonized. Nevertheless, the questions raised by Lenin remain.

The irrelevance of Lenin is his relevance.

Presented at the School of the Art Institute of Chicago on December 17, 2011.

Originally published in *Weekly Worker* 922 (July 12, 2012) and *Platypus Review* 48 (July – August 2012)

---

19 But Lenin is more than the symptom that, for instance, Slavoj Žižek takes him to be. See "The Occupy movement, a renascent Left, and Marxism today," *Platypus Review* 42 (December 2011 – January 2012).

# Lenin at 150

On the occasion of the 150th anniversary of Lenin's birth, I would like to approach Lenin's meaning today by critically examining an essay written by the liberal political philosopher Ralph Miliband on the occasion of Lenin's 100th birthday in 1970[1] — which was the year of my own birth. The reason for using Miliband's essay to frame my discussion of Lenin's legacy is that the DSA Democratic Socialists of America magazine *Jacobin* republished Miliband, who is perhaps their most important theoretical inspiration, in 2018 as a belated treatment of the 100th anniversary of the Russian Revolution of 1917 — or perhaps as a way of marking the centenary of the ill-fated German Revolution of 1918, which failed as a socialist revolution but is usually regarded as a successful democratic revolution, issuing in the Weimar Republic under the leadership of the Social-Democratic Party of Germany (SPD). There is a wound in the apparent conflict between the desiderata of socialism and democracy, in which the Russian tradition associated with Lenin is opposed to and by the German tradition associated with social democracy, or, alternatively, "democratic socialism," by contrast with the supposedly undemocratic socialism of Lenin, however justified or not by "Russian conditions." The German model seems to stand for conditions more appropriate to advanced capitalist and liberal democratic countries.

Ralph Miliband is most famously noted for his perspective of "parliamentary socialism." But this was not simply positive for Miliband but critical, namely, critical of the Labour Party in the UK. — It must be noted that Miliband's sons are important leaders in the Labour Party today,

---

1   "Lenin's *The State and Revolution*," *Jacobin* (August 2018).

among its most prominent neoliberal figures. Preceding his book on parliamentary socialism, Miliband wrote a critical essay in 1960, "The sickness of Labourism," written for the very first issue of the newly minted *New Left Review* in 1960, in the aftermath of Labour's dismal election failure in 1959, Miliband's criticism of which, of course, the DSA/*Jacobin* cannot digest let alone assimilate. The DSA/*Jacobin* fall well below even a liberal such as Miliband — and not only because the U.S. Democratic Party is something less than the UK Labour Party, either in composition or organization. Miliband's perspective thus figures for the DSA/*Jacobin* in a specifically symptomatic way, as an indication of limits and, we must admit, ultimate failure, for instance demonstrated by the recent fate of the Bernie Sanders Campaign as an attempted "electoral road" to "socialism," this year as well as back in 2016 — the latter's failure leading to the explosion in growth of the DSA itself. Neither Labour's aspiration to socialism, whether back in the 1960s or more recently under Jeremy Corbyn's leadership, nor the DSA's has come to any kind of even minimal fruition. Thus the specter — the haunting memory — of Lenin presents itself for our consideration today: How does Lenin hold out the promise of socialism?

Previously, I have written on several occasions on Lenin.[2] So I am tasked to say something today that I haven't already said before. First of all, I want to address the elephant in the room (or is it the 800lb gorilla?), which is Stalinism, the apparent fate of supposed "Leninism" — which is also a demonstrated failure, however it is recalled today in its own peculiar way by the penchant for neo-Stalinism that seems to be an act of defiance, épater la bourgeoisie [shock the bourgeoisie], on the part of young (or not so young) Bohemian "Leftists," in their deeply disappointed bitterness and antipathy towards the political status quo. "Leninism" means a certain antinomian nihilism — against which Lenin himself was deeply opposed.

An irony of history is that Lenin's legacy has succumbed to the very thing against which he defined himself and from which his Marxism sharply departed, namely Narodnism, the Romantic rage of the supposedly "revolutionary" intelligentsia, who claimed — understood themselves — to

---

2   See my: "The Decline of the Left in the 20th Century: Toward a Theory of Historical Regression: 1917"; "Lenin's liberalism"; "Lenin's politics"; "The relevance of Lenin today"; and "1917-2017," all in this volume.

identify with the oppressed and exploited masses, but really for whom the latter were just a sentimental image rather than a reality. Lenin would be extremely unhappy at what he — and indeed what revolution itself, let alone "socialism" — has come to symbolize today. Lenin was the very opposite of a Mao or a Che or Fidel. And he was also the opposite of Stalin. How so?

The three figures, Lenin, Stalin, and Trotsky, form the heart of the issue of the Russian Revolution and its momentous effect on the 20th century, still reverberating today. Trotsky disputed Stalin and the Soviet Union's claim to the memory of Lenin, writing, in "Stalinism and Bolshevism" on the 20th anniversary of the Russian Revolution in 1937, that Stalinism was the "antithesis" of Bolshevism[3] — a loaded word, demanding specifically a dialectical approach to the problem. What did Lenin and Trotsky have in common as Marxists from which Stalin differed? Stalin's policy of "socialism in one country" was the fatal compromise of not only the Russian Revolution, but of Marxism, and indeed of the very movement of proletarian socialism itself. Trotsky considered Stalinism to be the opportunist adaptation of Marxism to the failure of the world socialist revolution — the limiting of the revolution to Russia.

This verdict by Trotsky was not affected by the spread of "Communism" after WWII to Eastern Europe, China, Korea, Vietnam, and, later, Cuba. Each was an independent ostensibly "socialist" state — and by this very fact alone represented the betrayal of socialism. Their conflicts, antagonism and competition, including wars both "hot" and "cold," for instance the alliance of Mao's China with the United States against Soviet Russia and the Warsaw Pact, demonstrated the lie of their supposed "socialism." Of course each side justified this by reference to the supposed capitulation to global imperialism by the other side. But the point is that all these states were part of the world capitalist status quo. It was that unshaken status quo that fatally compromised the ostensibly "socialist" aspirations of these national revolutions. Suffice it to say that Lenin would not have considered the outcome of the Russian Revolution or any subsequently that have sought to follow in its footsteps to be socialism — at all. Lenin would not

---

3   *Socialist Appeal* 1, no. 7 (September 25, 1937), 4–5, and vol. 1, no. 8 (October 2, 1937), 4–5.

have considered any of them to represent the true Marxist "dictatorship of the proletariat," either. For Lenin, as for Marxism more generally, the dictatorship of the proletariat (never mind socialism) required the preponderant power over global capitalism world-wide, that is, victory in the core capitalist countries. This of course has never yet happened. So its correctness is an open question.

In his 1970 Lenin centenary essay, Miliband chose to address Lenin's pamphlet on *State and Revolution*, an obvious choice to get at the heart of the issue of Lenin's Stalinist legacy. But Miliband shares a great deal of assumptions with Stalinism. For one, the national-state framing of the question of socialism. But more importantly, Miliband like Stalinism elides the non-identity of the state and society, of political and social power, and hence of political and social revolution. Miliband calls this the problem of "authority." In this is evoked not only the liberal-democratic but also the anarchist critique of not merely Leninism but Marxism itself. Miliband acknowledges that indeed the problem touched on by Lenin on revolution and the state goes to the heart of Marxism, namely, to the issue of the Marxist perspective on the necessity of the dictatorship of the proletariat, which Marx considered his only real and essential original contribution to socialism.

In 1917, Lenin was accused of "assuming the vacant throne of Bakunin" in calling for "all power to the soviets [workers and soldiers councils]." — Indeed, Miliband's choice of Lenin's writings, *The State and Revolution*, written in the year of the 1917 Russian Revolution, is considered Lenin's most anarchist or at least libertarian text. Lenin's critics accused him of regressing to pre-Marxian socialism and neglecting the developed Marxist political perspective on socialist revolution as the majority action by the working class, reverting instead to putschism or falling back on minority political action. This is not merely due to the minority numbers of the industrial working class in majority peasant Russia but also and especially the minority status of Lenin's Bolshevik Communist Party, as opposed to the majority socialists of Socialist Revolutionaries and Menshevik Social Democrats, as well as of non-party socialists such as anarchist currents of various tendencies, some of whom were indeed critical of the anarchist legacy of Bakunin himself. Bakunin is infamous for his idea of the "invisible dictatorship" of conscious revolutionaries coordinating the otherwise spontaneous action of the masses to success — apparently repeating the early history of the "revolutionary conspiracy" of Blanqui in the era of the Revolution of 1848. But what was and why did Bakunin hold his perspective on the supposed "invisible dictatorship"? Marxism considered it the corollary — the complementary "opposite" — of the Bonapartist capitalist state, with its paranoiac Orwellian character of subordinating society through society's own complicity in the inevitable authoritarianism — the blind social compulsion — of capitalism, to which everyone was subject, and in which both and neither everyone's and no one's interests are truly represented. Bakunin's "invisible dictatorship" was not meant to dominate but facilitate the self-emancipation of the people themselves. — So was Lenin's — Marxism's — political party for socialist revolution.

Lenin has of course been accused of the opposite tendency from anarchism, namely of being a Lassallean or "state" socialist. Lenin's *The State and Revolution* drew most heavily on Marx's *Critique of the Gotha Programme*, attacking the Lassalleanism of the programme of the new Social-Democratic Party of Germany at its founding in 1875. So this raises the question of the specific role of the political party for Marxism: Does it lead inevitably to statism? The history of ostensible "Leninism" in Stalinism seems to demonstrate so. The antinomical contrary interpretations of Lenin — libertarian vs. authoritarian, statist vs. anarchist, liberal vs. democratic — are not due to some inconsistency or aporia in Lenin or in Marxism itself — as Miliband for one thought — but are rather due to the contradictory nature of capitalism itself, which affects the way its political tasks appear, calling for opposed solutions. The question is Marxism's self-consciousness of this phenomenon — Lenin's awareness and consciously deliberate political pursuit of socialism under such contradictory conditions.

The history of Marxism regarding rival currents in socialism represented by Lassalle and Bakunin must be addressed in terms of how Marxism thought it overcame the dispute between social and political action — between anarchism and statism — as a phenomenon of antinomies of capitalism, namely, the need for both political and social action to overcome the contradiction of capitalist production in society. This was the necessary role of the mass political party for socialism, to link the required social and political action. Such mediation was not meant to temper or alleviate the contradiction between political and social action — between statism and anarchism — but rather to embody and in certain respects exacerbate the contradiction.

Marxism was not some reconciled synthesis of anarchism and statism, a happy medium between the two, but rather actively took up — "sublated," so to speak — the contradiction between them as a practical task, regarding the conflict in the socialist movement as an expression of the contradiction of capitalism, from which socialism was of course not free. There is not a question of abstract principles — supposed libertarian vs. authoritarian socialism — but rather the real movement of history in capitalism in which socialism is inextricably bound up. Positively: Lenin called for overcoming capitalism on the basis of capitalism itself, which also means from within the self-contradiction of socialism.

Lenin stands accused of Blanquism. The 19th century socialist Louis Auguste Blanqui gets a bad rap for his perspective of "revolutionary conspiracy" to overthrow the state. For Blanqui, such revolutionary political action was not itself meant to achieve socialism, but rather to clear the way for the people themselves to achieve socialism through their social action freed from domination by the capitalist state.

Miliband is at best what Marx/ism would have considered a "petit bourgeois socialist." But really he was a liberal, albeit under 20th century conditions of advanced late capitalism. What does this mean? It is about the attitude towards the capitalist state. The predecessor to Bakunin, Proudhon, the inventor of "anarchism" per se, was coldly neutral towards the Revolution of 1848, but afterwards oriented positively towards the post-1848 President of the 2nd Republic, Louis Bonaparte, especially after his coup d'état establishing the 2nd Empire. This is because Proudhon, while hostile to the state as such, still considered the Bonapartist state a potential temporary ally against the capitalist bourgeoisie. Proudhon's apparent opposite, the "statist socialist" Ferdinand Lassalle had a similar positive orientation towards the eventual first Chancellor of the Prussian Empire Kaiserreich, Bismarck, as an ally against the capitalist bourgeoisie — Bismarck who infamously said that the results of the 1848 Revolution demonstrated that not popular assemblies but rather "blood and iron" would solve the pressing political issues of the day. In this was recapitulated the old post-Renaissance alliance of the emergent bourgeoisie — the new free city-states — with the Absolutist Monarchy against the feudal aristocracy.

The 20th century social-democratic welfare state is the inheritor of such Bonapartism in the capitalist state — Bismarckism, etc. For instance, Efraim Carlebach has written of the late 19th century Fabian socialist enthusiasm for Bismarck from which the UK Labour Party historically originated[4] — the Labour Party replaced and inherited the role of the Liberal Party in the UK, which had represented the working class, especially its organization in labor unions. The Labour Party arose in the period of Progressivism — progressive liberalism — and progressive liberals around the world, such as for instance Theodore Roosevelt in the U.S., were inspired by Wilhelmine Germany that was founded by Bismarck, specifically Bismarck as the founder of the welfare state. Bismarck's welfare state provisions were made long before the socialists were any kind of real political threat. The welfare state has always been a police measure and not a compromise with the working class. Indeed socialists historically rejected the welfare state — this hostility only changed in the 1930s, with the Stalinist adoption of the People's Front against fascism and its positive orientation towards progressive liberal democracy.

Pre-WWI Wilhelmine Germany was considered at the time progressive and indeed liberal, part of the greater era's progressive liberal development of capitalism — which was opposed by contemporary socialists under Marxist leadership. But by conflating state and society in the category of "authority," further obscured by the question of "democracy," Miliband expresses the liquidation of Marxism into statism — Miliband assumes the Bonapartism of the capitalist state, regarding the difference of socialism as one of mere policy, for instance the policies pursued by the state that supposedly serve one group — say, capitalists or workers — over others. This expresses a tension — indeed contradiction — between liberalism and democracy. This contradiction is often mistaken for that of liberalism versus socialism, as for instance by the post-20th century "Left" going back to the 1930s Stalinist era of the Communist Party's alliance with progressive liberals in support of FDR's New Deal, whose history is expressed today by DSA/*Jacobin*.

For Lenin, by contrast, the issue of politics — and hence of proletarian socialism — is not of what is being done, but rather of who is doing it. The criterion of socialism for Marxism such as Lenin's is the activity of the working class — or lack thereof. The socialist revolution and the political regime of the dictatorship of the proletariat was not for Lenin the achievement of socialism but rather its mere precondition, opening the door to the self-transformation of society beyond capitalism led by the — "dictatorship," or social preponderance, preponderance of social power — of the working class. Without this, it is inevitable that the state serves rather not the interests of the capitalists as a social group but rather the imperatives of capital, which is different. For Lenin, the necessary dictatorship of the proletariat was the highest form of capitalism — meaning capitalism brought to the highest level of politics and hence of potentially working through its social self-contradictions — and not yet socialism — meaning not yet even the overcoming of capitalism.

By equating the capitalist welfare state with socialism, with the only remaining criterion the democratic self-governance of the working class, Miliband by contrast elided the crucial Marxist distinction between the dictatorship of the proletariat and socialism. For Miliband, what made the state socialist or not was the degree of supposed "workers' democracy." — In this way, Miliband serves very well to articulate the current DSA/*Jacobin* identification of its political goals with "democratic socialism." But, like Miliband, DSA/*Jacobin* falls prey to the issue of the policies pursued by the state as the criterion of socialism, however without Miliband's recognition of the difference between (social-democratic welfare state) policies pursued by capitalist politicians vs. by the working class itself.

Lenin pursued the political and social power — the social and political revolution — of the working class as not the ultimate goal but rather the "next necessary step" in the history of capitalism leading — hopefully — to its self-overcoming in socialism. As a Marxist, Lenin was very sober and clear-eyed — unsentimental — about the actual political and social tasks of the struggle for socialism — what they were and what they were not.

In harking back to the manifest impasse of the mid-20th century capitalist welfare state registered by Miliband, however through identifying this with the alleged limits of Lenin's and greater Marxism's consciousness of the problem, but without proper recognition of its true nature in capitalism, those such as DSA/*Jacobin* actively obfuscate, bury and forget, not Marxism such as Lenin's, or the goal of socialism, but rather the actual problem of capitalism they are trying to confront, obscuring it still further.

The "Left" today such as DSA/*Jacobin* wants the restoration of pre-neoliberal progressive capitalism, for instance the pre-neoliberal politics of the UK Labour Party — or indeed simply the pre-neoliberal Democrats. Their misuse of the label "socialism" and abuse of "Marxism," including even the memory of Lenin and their bandying about of the word "revolution," is overwrought and in the service of progressive capitalism. This is an utter travesty of socialism, Marxism, and the memory of Lenin.

On the 150th anniversary of Lenin's birth, we owe him at least the thought that what he consciously recognized and actually pursued as a Marxist be remembered properly and not falsified — and certainly not in the interest of seeking, by sharp contrast to Lenin, the "democratic" legitimation of capitalism, which even liberals such as Ralph Miliband acknowledged to be a deep problem afflicting contemporary society and its supposed "welfare" state. By reckoning with what Marxists such as Lenin understood as the real problem and actual political tasks of capitalism, there is yet hope that we will resume the true socialist pursuit of actually overcoming it.

## Postscript: On *Jacobin*'s defense of Miliband contra Lenin

Longtime DSA member and Publisher and Editor of *Jacobin* magazine Bhaskar Sunkara responded to my critique of Ralph Miliband by interviewing Leo Panitch of the *Socialist Register* on Jacobin's YouTube broadcast *Stay at Home*.[5] Sunkara has previously stated that rather than a follower of Lenin or Kautsky, he is a follower of Miliband. Sunkara and Panitch were eager to defend Miliband's socialist *bona fides* against my calling him a liberal, but

---

5    Episode 29 (April 27, 2020).

what they argued confirmed my understanding of Miliband as a liberal and not a socialist let alone a Marxist. The issue is indeed one of the state and revolution. It is not, as Panitch asserted in the interview, a matter of political "pluralism" in socialism.

Panitch, who claims Miliband as an important mentor figure, spoke at a Platypus public forum panel discussion in Halifax in January 2015 on the meaning of political party for the Left, and observed in his prepared opening remarks that in the 50 years between 1870 and 1920 — Lenin's time — there took place the first and as yet only time in history when the subaltern have organized themselves as a political force.[6] In his interview with Sunkara on Miliband, Panitch now claims that Lenin's strategy — which was that of 2nd International Marxism as a whole, for instance by Karl Kautsky, Rosa Luxemburg, Eugene Debs, et al. — of replacing the capitalist state with the organizations of the working class that had been built up by the socialist political party before the revolution, was invalidated by the historical experience of the 20th century. Instead, according to Panitch, the existing liberal democratic capitalist state was to provide the means to achieve socialism. This is because it is supposedly no longer a state of capitalists but rather one committed to capitalism: committed to capital accumulation. But Marxism always considered it to be so: Bonapartist management of capitalism in political liberal democracy.

Panitch claims that Miliband's critique of the UK Labour Party was in its Fabian dogma of "educating the ruling class in socialism through the state," whereas socialists would instead "educate the working class in socialism through the state." But Lenin and other Marxists considered the essential education of the working class in the necessity of socialism to take place through its "class struggle" under capitalism — its struggle as a class to constitute itself as a revolutionary force — in which it built its civil social organizations and political parties aiming to take political and social — state — power. Panitch condemns Lenin for his allegedly violent vision of the overthrow of the capitalist state and replacing it with a revolutionary workers state — the infamous "dictatorship of the proletariat" always envisioned by Marxism.

---

6    Transcript published in *Platypus Review* 74 (March 2015).

Thus Panitch condemns the Marxist perspective on proletarian social-ist revolution per se. But the question for Lenin and other Marxists was not revolution as a strategy — they were not dogmatic "revolutionists" as opposed to reformists — but rather the inevitability of capitalist crisis and hence the inevitability of political and social revolution. The only question was whether and how the working class would have the political means to turn the revolution of inevitable capitalist crisis into potential political and social revolution leading to socialism. By abandoning this Marxist per-spective on revolution — which Miliband himself importantly did not rule out — Panitch and Sunkara along with DSA/*Jacobin* do indeed articulate a liberal democratic and not proletarian socialist let alone Marxist politics.

Presented at a Platypus teach-in on the 150th anniversary of Lenin's birth, April 22, 2020.

Originally published in *Platypus Review* 126 (May 2020)

# Critical theory

# History

# "Let the dead bury the dead!"

The new *Mayday* magazine (UK) and Platypus have been in dialogue on the issues of anarchism and Marxism and the state of the "Left" today in light of history.[1]

*Principia Dialectica,* another new British journal, also has taken note[2] of Platypus, specifically with our interview of Moishe Postone on "Marx after Marxism."[3]

In their note of us, *Principia Dialectica* cites our interview with Postone to say that "Postone's reflections on Lukács are certainly bracing, and enough to challenge any cryogenically frozen leftoid stuck in 1917." Platypus raises the Bolshevik Revolution of 1917, which Lukács regarded as follows:

> Only the Russian Revolution really opened a window to the future; the fall of Czarism brought a glimpse of it, and with the collapse of capitalism it appeared in full view. At the time our knowledge of the facts and the principles underlying them was of the slightest and very unreliable. Despite this we saw — at last! at last! — a way for mankind to escape from war and capitalism.[4]

---

1  See my "Organization, political action, history, and consciousness: on anarchism and Marxism," *Platypus Review* 2 (February 2008), in *Death of the Millennial Left: Interventions 2006–2022*; and Trevor Bark, "Half-time team talk: Mayday (UK) response on anarchism and Marxism," *Platypus Review* 4 (April – May 2008).

2  "Weird gonzo leftoid journal," *Principia Dialectica* (April 15, 2008).

3  "Marx after Marxism: An interview with Moishe Postone," *Platypus Review* 3 (March 2008).

4  *History and Class Consciousness,* trans. Rodney Livingstone (Cambridge, MA: MIT Press, 1972), xi.

But Platypus raises Bolshevism and its historical moment less as a rallying cry than as a question and problem. 1917 should be followed not by an exclamation point but a question mark, but one that has not lost its saliency but only become a more profound enigma in subsequent history. What was to Lukács and others of the time a brief glimpse of emancipatory potential has only become more obscure, but without becoming any less penetrating.

— But today the danger is not being frozen in 1917 but rather 1968.

*Principia Dialectica* distributed the leaflet "Let the dead bury the dead!" at the May '68 Jamboree at Conway Hall in London on May 10, 2008. This leaflet uses a great deal of Platypus rhetoric, on the "fossilized" and undead character of today's "Left," on anarchism being an enduring "bad conscience" of the failures of Marxism, etc., and involves not only this plagiarism but an unacknowledged response to our statements on the necessary return to the history of the revolutionary Marxist tradition. At the same time, this leaflet rehearses precisely those aspects of a non-/ anti-Marxian and/or "anarchist" approach we have addressed previously in our articles in dialogue with Mayday.[5]

The problem with this *Principia Dialectica* statement is that it has no cognizance of the issue of historical *regression*. Necessarily, this involves a non-dialectical and non-immanent understanding of capitalism as a "system," resulting in an insistence on an (historically impossible) "outside" of capitalism. — Regarding the announcement appended below their leaflet, for a meeting on "What is value, and how to destroy it?," the point, following Marx, is not to "destroy" (the social) "value" (of capital and proletarian labor), but rather to realize and overcome it on its own basis, and so would mean *redeeming* the very great sacrifices humanity has already made — and continues to make — in the history of capitalism.

Corollary to the one-sided view of and opposition to "value" (and what it means socially) is an unjustified yet assumed progressive view of history. This is unwarranted especially in light of the state of the "Left" today, 40 years after 1968, which has not shown any progress. — Otherwise, why call the "Leftist" commemoration of 1968 that *Principia Dialectica* picketed with its

---

5   See my "Organization, political action, history, and consciousness: on anarchism and Marxism," *Platypus Review* 2 (February 2008), in *Death of the Millennial Left: Interventions 2006–2022*.

leaflet, a "wake" conducted by "embalmed" "mummies?" But, like all anarchism, *Principia Dialectica* has no (need for a) theory of history (of capital). An incoherent view of capitalism and its recent history both underlies and results from the leaflet's ambivalent salute and adieu to 1968. As Moishe Postone has pointed out, the combined and equally inappropriate triumphalism and melancholy of post-1968 politics results from the undigested character of the Marxist tradition from which the 1960s "New" Left sought to depart:

> [T]he emancipatory potential of general social coordination [i.e., Marxist "planning"] . . . should [not] be dismissed. But that potential can only be realized when it is associated with the historical overcoming of capital, the core of our form of social life. . . . Without such an analysis of capital, however, one that is not restricted to the mode of distribution, but that can, nevertheless, address the emancipatory impulses expressed by traditional Marxism . . . our conceptions of emancipation will continue to oscillate between a homogenizing general (whether effected via the market or the state) and particularism, an oscillation that replicates the dualistic forms of commodity and capital themselves.[6]

As such, the *Principia Dialectica* leaflet commemorating 1968 is a symptom of what Postone calls the post-1960s postmodernist politics of "premature post-capitalism," which imagines that the necessity for proletarian labor in mediating the conditions of modern social life and its potential emancipatory transformation has already been overcome in practice, however ripe its overcoming has been historically in *theory*.

As Lars Lih has pointed out,[7] the reconsideration of history for an anti-capitalist politics adequate to our time would mean indeed redeeming

---

6    "Theorizing the Contemporary World: Brenner, Arrighi, Harvey," (2006) in *Political Economy of the Present and Possible Global Future(s)*, eds. Rob Albritton, Bob Jessop, Richard Westra (London: Anthem Press, 2010), 22-23.

7    "Lenin and the Great Awakening," in *Lenin Reloaded*, eds. Sebastian Budgen, Stathis Kouvelakis, Slavoj Žižek (Durham: Duke University Press, 2007), 283–296.

and realizing what *Principia Dialectica* disdainfully calls "proletarian Messianism." — Precisely Walter Benjamin's understanding of the historical significance of such "Messianism," and its negative philosophy of history in the period of defeat and regression on the Left after 1917–19, provides the necessary guiding insight for such redemption. As Theodor W. Adorno interpreted Benjamin, "The only philosophy which can be responsibly practiced in face of despair is the attempt to contemplate all [historical] things as they would present themselves from the standpoint of [their potential] redemption."[8]

Rather than attempts at redeeming the modern (and still on-going) history of the industrial proletariat, and realizing and fulfilling — and going beyond — this necessity of what Marx called proletarian self-transcendence/self-abolition (Aufhebung), however, the "Left" has (ever since 1917–19, but especially after 1968) regressed behind this task. This is why the revolutionary Marxism of 2nd International radicalism of Lenin, Luxemburg, Trotsky, et al. — as well as the thought and politics of Marx himself — can still "flash up" as a historical image that haunts us and won't go away, despite all efforts at exorcism by varieties of "post-Marxism."

The very problematic history of the Marxist revolutionary "tradition" — as well as of the modern workers movement — requires *redemption*. And this is not simply desirable or possible, but actually unavoidably necessary.

Historical "anarchism" and its various offspring (e.g., Situationism) remain the deserved forms of the "bad conscience" of the failures of historical ("traditional") Marxism, but anarchism is nevertheless a symptomatic regression to pre-Marxian socialism (of Proudhon et al.).

Marxism was not a mistaken detour because it failed historically. Rather, the continued recrudescence of anarchism proves in a certain sense that a reconstitution of the Marxian point of departure remains necessary. A revisiting — and "repetition" — of the Marxian critique of (pre-Marxian as well as post-Marx-ist) socialism is in order. — As Adorno put it, the return of anarchism "is that of a ghost," which however "does not invalidate the [Marxian] critique" of it.[9]

---

8   "Finale," in *Minima Moralia*, trans. E.F.N. Jephcott (London: Verso, 2005), 247.

9   "Resignation," in *Critical Models: Interventions and Catchwords*, trans. Henry W. Pickford (New York: Columbia University Press, 2005), 292.

For Adorno, anarchism manifested "the impatience with theory."[10] Ironically, such impatience with theory is corollary to the dismissal of the industrial proletariat as "Subject" of human emancipation (through its self-transformation and overcoming). This dismissal is seen in the *Principia Dialectica* celebration of the "happy unemployed" and the calls to "never work ever" and thus (try to) remain "outside" the "system." But as the historical Marxian critique of "actually existing socialism" — and the history of capitalism to date — has shown, there is no secure let alone emancipated state outside of capitalism that has been possible. Capitalism will be overcome from within (its own historical logic), or not at all.

As Adorno put it, "Only if the extremes [of the theoretically armed revolutionary intellectuals, and the industrial working class] come together will humanity survive."[11] — Platypus is noted — and attacked — for being on the one hand too intellectual and on the other hand too committed to a proletarian path to social emancipation beyond capital. Thus our indication of this dual necessity of theory and practice finds its critical affirmation — even when our project remains unacknowledged rather than singled out by our interlocutors.

The history of the failed Marxian attempted departures from symptomatic socialism (from Marx's departure from Proudhon, to Lenin, Luxemburg, Trotsky and Lukács's departure from the politics of 2nd International Social Democracy and its "vulgar Marxism," to Trotsky and the Frankfurt School's departures from Stalinized 3rd International Communism) still tasks us, but not as ritual invocation devoid of the actual content of historical self-understanding, but only as this history allows for its critical apprehension — in the critique of the present and how we got here.

Originally published in *Platypus Review* 5 (May – July 2008)

---

10  "Resignation," in *Critical Models*, trans. Henry W. Pickford (New York: Columbia University Press, 1998), 292.

11  "Imaginative Excesses" (orphaned from *Minima Moralia*), published as "Messages in a Bottle," trans. Edmund Jephcott, *New Left Review* I/200 (July – August 1993), 12–14.

## Postscript: Against Debord's Nihilism

*Principia Dialectica* has responded to our critique of their *détournement* of our "death of the Left" rhetoric with a noisy disclaimer.

But to hold up Guy Debord's "Situationism" circa 1968 against two centuries of the critical theory and politics of Marx, Engels, Lenin, Luxemburg, Trotsky, Lukács, Korsch, Benjamin, Adorno, et al. — to say nothing of the contributions to enlightenment of Kant, Hegel, Nietzsche, Weber, Durkheim, Freud, et al. — requires either a great deal of gall, or is meant only in jest.

We suspect the latter, and so seek, at the very least, to prevent the misappropriation — really, abuse — of Moishe Postone's work by such bad faith efforts as *Principia Dialectica*. — Otherwise:

The title of the *Principia Dialectica* rejoinder to Platypus cites Amy Winehouse's 2006 song "Rehab," which sounds like a 1960s-era pop song, another piquant, if immediately dated and musty British appropriation and slick commodification of American culture. But, although Winehouse sang that she wouldn't "go to rehab, no, no, no," as it turned out, later she did!

This story does in fact speak to the principal intention of Platypus, to learn from the past and prevent its pathological repetition: The understandable desire to escape the past in a manic fit of ecstatic optimism is tragic to the extent that it is unrealistic and lands one precisely where one has sworn never to return; it is farcical to the degree that this is repeated — over and over again.

Note to advocates of today's already obsolete early 1990s-era rehabilitation of Situationism and other post-1960s politics of anarchism, *autonomia*, "post-work," etc.: If you find yourself disagreeing with all or several of the most outstanding historical Marxist critical theorists and political actors listed above and/or the enlightened thought about modern humanity from the 17th–19th centuries from which the best Marxists drew and developed their insights, you can be sure that you are in denial and not on any road to recovery.

Whether you like it or not, and one way or another, you will find yourself "back to rehab" — in some form of political social democracy, liberalism, conservatism, or worse, or by being simply depoliticized and folded back into the rhythm of mainstream existence — or, in a dead-end of self-destruction, whether intoxicated or not. Debord's suicide — motivated very differently from Benjamin's, Debord being more pathetic than tragic — should stand as a warning to any and all of his wannabe followers. For, going down this highway, you will sooner or later either render yourself entirely useless politically, or you'll end up dropping the attempt at emancipatory politics altogether — as indeed Debord's Situationism had done already from the very beginning.

Platypus, by contrast, seeks to foster recognition by a new generation of thinkers and actors that there might be a point to developing and instrumentalizing ourselves for the possibility of human enlightenment and emancipation, and not complacently wasting ourselves away in a narcissistic narcosis of self-dosing on the gaiety of futility.

Note to young contrarian "rebels": The "system" is going to consume you one way or another, no matter what you do, so it might as well be in ways that push the envelope of possibility and move oneself and others as far in the directions of human betterment and development of further potential as possible.

What *Principia Dialectica* says about class struggle, "proletarian" empowerment and capital is of course true: this is all immanent to and perpetuating of the "system." Where *Principia Dialectica*, as all anarchism, goes wrong (but perhaps instructively) is in their Romantic nihilism. But the system is our reality — in and through it is the only direction in which our hope might lie.

The world doesn't need any more Hölderlins; as Hegel said, the "unhappy consciousness" is regressive, falls below the threshold with which it is tasked, and so cannot fulfill itself, but must overcome itself.

Debord's notes on cocktail napkins can't help us do that.

## Coda

Anselm Jappe of the Krisis-Gruppe, in his 1993 book *Guy Debord* cites Debord's affinity with Lukács with the following quotation, "The only possible basis for understanding this world is to oppose it; and such opposition will be neither genuine nor realistic unless it contests the totality."[12] *Principia Dialectica* also turns to Jappe for the concept of capital as the "automaton" or "automatic subject."[13]

The question, however, is not one of affirming vs. opposing the social "totality" and the proletariat as being already the "subject-object of history," but rather *transforming* the alienated totality of domination in an emancipatory manner, and the possibility of the working class *becoming* an actual subject of social emancipation in the process of overcoming capital: Lukács was not *positing* something but politically *advocating* it, and we need to understand *why*.

According to Hegel, one becomes a subject only in the process of self-overcoming and transformation. This side of such an emancipatory process, the proletariat remains an "object" of the "automatic subject" of capital, which is an expression of the industrial working class's alienated social agency in value production. What is missing from *Principia Dialectica* is precisely the sense of history — for instance, why Lukács's book was titled *History and Class Consciousness*. The question is not what kind of subject the proletariat *is*, but what it *could be* — in the activity of its *self-abolition*, in, through and beyond capital, on the basis of labor as a *socially mediating* activity that becomes a form of *self-domination* under capital, its alienated product.

But Lukács recognized such revolutionary socialist politics as the "completion" of "reification," and so that this is not the end goal of emancipation but rather a *necessary stage* for the possible overcoming of capital. That, in the USSR, etc. and in Stalinist and social democratic and other nationalist-reformist working class politics in the 20th century, the proletariat participated in the reconstitution of capital and not in its revolutionary overcoming, was the *result* of the failure of the 1917–19 anti-capitalist revolution, not its *cause* — or the original animus of the Marxism of Lenin, Luxemburg and Trotsky.

---

12  Trans. Donald Nicholson-Smith (Berkeley: University of California Press, 1993), 27. Also in Jappe's pamphlet "An Imbecile's Guide to Guy Debord's *Concept of the Spectacle*" (Treason Press, 2004).

13  In Jappe's *Adventures of the Commodity: For a New Critique of Value* (Munich: 2003/05).

Debord's Situationism is just as much an adaptation to this failure as any other form of the "politics" of post-Marxism in the 20th century. Debord and his followers went along with the lie that Lenin led to Stalin, with all the confusion this entailed. The goal is indeed the overcoming of proletarian labor — the society of work — as mediating and thus dominating modern human history. The question is, *how*?

Postscript and coda published June 14, 2008

# Capital in history

## The need for a Marxian philosophy of history of the Left

I want to speak about the meaning of *history* for any purportedly Marxian Left.

We in Platypus focus on the history of the Left because we think that the narrative one tells about this history is in fact one's theory of the present. Implicitly or explicitly, in one's conception of the history of the Left, is an account of how the present came to be. By focusing on the history of the Left, or, by adopting a Left-centric view of history, we hypothesize that the most important determinations of the present are the result of what the Left has done or failed to do historically.

For the purposes of this talk, I will focus on the broadest possible framing for such questions and problems of capital in history, the broadest possible context within which I think one needs to understand the problems faced by the Left, specifically by a purportedly Marxian Left.

I will not, for example, be focusing so much on issues for Platypus in the history of the various phases and stages of capital itself, for instance our contention that the 1960s represented not any kind of advance, but a profound retrogression on the Left. I will not elucidate our account of how the present suffers from at least 3 generations of degeneration and regression on the Left: the first, in the 1930s, being tragic; the second in the 1960s being farcical; and the most recent, in the 1990s, being sterilizing.

But, suffice it to say, I will point out that, for Platypus, the recognition of regression and the attempt to understand its significance and causes is perhaps our most important point of departure. The topic of this talk is the most fundamental assumption informing our understanding of regression.

For purposes of brevity, I will not be citing explicitly, but I wish to indicate my indebtedness for the following treatment of a potential Marxian philosophy of history, beyond Marx and Engels themselves, and Rosa Luxemburg, Lenin and Trotsky, to Georg Lukács, Karl Korsch, Walter Benjamin, Theodor Adorno, and, last but not least, the Marx scholar Moishe Postone. And, moreover, I will be in dialogue, through these writers, with Hegel, who distinguished philosophical history as the story of the development of freedom. — For Hegel, history is only meaningful the degree to which it is the story of freedom.

Capital is completely unprecedented in the history of humanity, hence, any struggle for emancipation beyond capital is also completely unprecedented. While there is a connection between the unprecedented nature of the emergence of capital in history and the struggle to get beyond it, this connection can also be highly misleading, leading to a false symmetry between the transition *into* and *within* different periods of the transformations of modern capital, and a potential transition *beyond* capital. The revolt of the Third Estate, which initiated a still on-going and never-to-be-exhausted modern history of bourgeois-democratic revolutions, is both the ground for, and, from a Marxian perspective, the now potentially historically obsolescent social form of politics from which proletarian socialist politics seeks to depart, to get beyond.

Hegel, as a philosopher of the time of the last of the great bourgeois-democratic revolutions marking the emergence of modern capital, the Great French Revolution of 1789, was for this reason a theorist of the revolt of the Third Estate. Marx, who came later, after the beginning of the Industrial Revolution of the 19th century, faced problems Hegel did not.

It has often been stated, but not fully comprehended by Marxists that Marx recognized the *historical* mission of the class-conscious proletariat, to overcome capitalism and to thus do away with class society. Traditionally, this meant, however paradoxically, either the end of the pre-history or the beginning of the true history of humanity. — In a sense, this duality of the possibility of an end and a true beginning, was a response to a Right Hegelian notion of an end to history, what is assumed by apologists for capital as a best of all possible worlds.

Famously, in the *Communist Manifesto*, Marx and Engels stated that all history hitherto has been the history of class struggles; Engels added a clever footnote later that specified "all *written* history." We might extrapolate from this that what Engels meant was the history of civilization; history as class struggle did not pertain, for instance, to human history or social life prior to the formation of classes, the time of the supposed "primitive communism." Later, in 1942, Adorno, following Benjamin, wrote that such a conception by Marx and Engels of all of history as the history of class struggles was in fact a *critique* of all of history, a critique of *history* itself.[1]

So in what way does the critique of *history* matter in the critique of *capital*? The problem with the commonplace view of capitalism as primarily a problem of exploitation is that it is in this dimension that capital fails to distinguish itself from other forms of civilization. What is new in capital is social *domination*, which must be distinguished both logically and historically, structurally and empirically, from exploitation, to which it is not reducible. Social domination means the domination of society by capital. This is what is *new* about capital in the history of civilization; prior forms of civilization knew overt domination of some social groups over others, but did not know as Marx recognized in capital a social dynamic to which all social groups — all aspects of society as a whole — are subject.

So we must first draw a demarcation approximately 10,000 years ago, with the origins of civilization and class society, when the great agricultural revolution of the Neolithic Age took place, and human beings went from being nomadic hunter-gatherers to becoming settled agriculturalists. The predominant mode of life for humanity went from the hunter-gatherer to the peasant, and was this for most of subsequent history.

Several hundred years ago, however, a similarly profound transformation began, in which the predominant mode of life has gone from agricultural peasant to urban worker: wage-earner, manufacturer, and industrial producer.

More proximally, with the Industrial Revolution in the late-18th to early-19th centuries, certain aspects of this "bourgeois" epoch of civilization and society manifested themselves and threw this history of the emergence of modernity into a new light. Rather than an "end of history" as bourgeois

---

1 Theodor W. Adorno, "Reflections on Class Theory," in *Can One Live After Auschwitz?: A Philosophical Reader*, ed. Rolf Tiedemann, trans. Rodney Livingstone and others (Stanford: Stanford University Press, 2009), 93. Adorno is following Benjamin's "Theses on the Philosophy of History" (1940).

thinkers up to that time had thought, modern social life entered into a severe crisis that fundamentally problematized the transition from peasant- to worker-based society.

With Marx in the 19th century came the realization that bourgeois society, along with all its categories of subjectivity including its valorization of labor, might itself be transitional, that the end-goal of humanity might not be found in the productive individual of bourgeois theory and practice, but that this society might point beyond itself, towards a potential qualitative transformation at least as profound as that which separated the peasant way of life from the urban "proletarian" one, indeed a transition more on the order of profundity of the Neolithic Revolution in agriculture that ended hunter-gatherer society 10,000 years ago, more profound than that which separated modern from traditional society.

At the same time that this modern, bourgeois society ratcheted into high gear by the late-18th century, it entered into crisis, and a new, unprecedented historical phenomenon was manifested in political life, the "Left." — While earlier forms of politics certainly disputed values, this was not in terms of historical "progress," which became the hallmark of the Left.

The Industrial Revolution of the early 19th century, the introduction of machine production, was accompanied by the optimistic and exhilarating socialist utopias suggested by these new developments, pointing to fantastical possibilities expressed in the imaginations of Fourier and Saint-Simon, among others.

Marx regarded the society of "bourgeois right" and "private property" as indeed already resting on the social constitution and mediation of labor, from which private property was derived, and asked the question of whether the trajectory of this society, from the revolt of the Third Estate and the manufacturing era in the 18th century to the Industrial Revolution of the 19th century, indicated the possibility of a further development.

In the midst of the dramatic social transformations of the 19th century in which, as Marx put it in the *Manifesto*, "all that was solid melted into air," as early as 1843, Marx prognosed and faced the future virtual proletarianization of society, and asked whether and how humanity in proletarian form might liberate itself from this condition, whether and how, and with what necessity the proletariat would "transcend" and "abolish itself." As early as the 1844 *Manuscripts*, Marx recognized that socialism (of Proudhon et al.) was itself symptomatic of capital: proletarian labor was *constitutive* of capital, and thus its politics was *symptomatic* of how the society conditioned by capital might reveal itself as transitional, as pointing beyond itself. — This was Marx's most fundamental point of departure, that proletarianization was a substantial social problem and not merely relative to the bourgeoisie, and that the proletarianization of society was not the overcoming of capital but its fullest realization, and that this — the proletarianized society of *capital* — pointed beyond itself.

Thus, with Marx, a philosophy of the history of the Left was born. For Marx was not a socialist or communist so much as a thinker who tasked himself with understanding the *meaning* of the emergence of proletarian socialism in *history*. Marx was not simply the best or most consistent or radical socialist, but rather the most *historically*, and hence critically, *self-aware*. By "scientific" socialism, Marx understood himself to be elaborating a form of knowledge aware of its own conditions of possibility.

For a Hegelian and Marxian clarification of the specificity of the modern problem of social freedom, however, it becomes clear that the Left must define itself not sociologically, whether in terms of socioeconomic class or a principle of collectivism over individualism, etc., but rather as a matter of consciousness, specifically historical consciousness.

For, starting with Marx, it is consciousness of history and historical *potential* and *possibilities*, however apparently utopian or obscure, that distinguishes the Left from the Right, not the struggle against oppression — which the modern Right also claims. The Right does not represent the past but rather the foreclosing of possibilities in the present.

For this reason, it is important for us to recognize the potential and fact of regression that the possibilities for the Left in theory and practice have suffered as a result of the abandonment of *historical* consciousness in favor of the *immediacies* of struggles against *oppression*.

Marx's critique of symptomatic socialism, from Proudhon, Lassalle, Bakunin, et al., to his own followers in the new German Social-Democratic Party and their program at Gotha (as well as in Engels's subsequent critique of the Erfurt Programme), was aimed at maintaining the Marxian vision corresponding to the horizon of possibility of post-capitalist and post-proletarian society.

Unfortunately, beginning in Marx's own lifetime, the form of politics he sought to inspire began to fall well below the threshold of this critically important consciousness of history. And the vast majority of this regression has taken place precisely in the name of "Marxism." Throughout the history of Marxism, from the disputes with the anarchists in the 1st International Workingmen's Association, and disputes in the 2nd Socialist International, to the subsequent splits in the Marxist workers' movement with the Bolshevik-led Third, Communist International and Trotskyist Fourth International, a sometimes heroic but, in retrospect, overwhelmingly tragic struggle to preserve or recover something of the initial Marxian point of departure for modern proletarian socialism took place.

In the latter half of the 20th century, developments regressed so far behind the original Marxian self-consciousness that Marxism itself became an affirmative ideology of industrial society, and the threshold of post-capitalist society became obscured, finding expression only obtusely, in various recrudescent utopian ideologies, and, finally, in the most recent period, with the hegemony of "anarchist" ideologies and Romantic rejections of modernity.

But, beyond this crisis and passage into oblivion of a specifically Marxian approach, the "Left" itself, which emerged prior to Hegel and Marx's attempts to philosophize its historical significance, has virtually disappeared. The present inability to distinguish conservative-reactionary from progressive-emancipatory responses to the problems of society conditioned by capital, is inseparable from the decline and disappearance of the social movement of proletarian socialism for which Marx had sought to provide a more adequate and provocative self-consciousness at the time of its emergence in the 19th century.

Paradoxically, as Lukács, following Luxemburg and Lenin, already pointed out, almost a century ago, while the apparent possibility of overcoming capital approaches in certain respects, in another sense it seems to retreat infinitely beyond the horizon of possibility. Can we follow Luxemburg's early recognition of the opportunism that always threatens us, not as some kind of selling-out or falling from grace, but rather the manifestation of the very real fear that attends the dawning awareness of what grave risks are entailed in trying to fundamentally move the world beyond capital?

What's worse — and, in the present, prior to any danger of "opportunism" — with the extreme coarsening if not utter disintegration of the ability to apprehend and transform capital through working-class politics, has come the coarsening of our ability to even recognize and apprehend, let alone adequately understand our social reality. We do not suffer simply from opportunism but from a rather more basic disorientation. Today we are faced with the problem not of changing the world but more fundamentally of understanding it.

On the other hand, approaching Marxian socialism, are we dealing with a "utopia?" — And, if so, what of this? What is the significance of our "utopian" sense of human potential beyond capital and proletarian labor? Is it a mere dream?

Marx began with utopian socialism and ended with the most influential if spectacularly failing modern political ideology, "scientific socialism." At the same time, Marx gave us an acute and incisive critical framework for grasping the reasons why the last 200 years have been, by far, the most tumultuously transformative but also destructive epoch of human civilization, why this period has promised so much and yet disappointed so bitterly. The last 200 years have seen more, and more profound changes, than prior millennia have. Marx attempted to grasp the reasons for this. Others have failed to see the difference and have tried to re-assimilate modern history back into its antecedents (for instance, in postmodernist illusions of an endless medievalism: see Bruno Latour's 1993 book *We Have Never Been Modern*).

What would it mean to treat the entire Marxian project as, first and foremost, a recognition of the history of modernity *tout court* as one of the *pathology of transition*, from the class society that emerged with the agricultural revolution 10,000 years ago and the civilizations based on an essentially peasant way of life, through the emergence of the commodity form of social mediation, to the present global civilization dominated by capital, towards a form of humanity that might lie beyond this?

With Marx we are faced with a self-consciousness of an obscure and mysterious historical task, which can only be further clarified theoretically through transformative practice – the practice of proletarian socialism. But this task has been abandoned in favor of what are essentially capital-*reconstituting* struggles, attempting to cope with the vicissitudes of the dynamics of modern history. But this re-assimilation of Marxism back into ideology characteristic of the revolt of the Third Estate means the loss of the true horizon of possibility that motivated Marx and gave his project meaning and urgency.

Can we follow Marx and the best historically revolutionary Marxists who followed him in recognizing the forms of discontent in the pathological society we inhabit as being themselves symptomatic of and bound up with the very problem against which they rage? Can we avoid the premature post-capitalism and bad, reactionary utopianism that attends the present death of the Left in theory in practice, and preserve and fulfill the tasks given to us by history? Can we recognize the breadth and depth of the problem we seek to overcome without retreating into wishful thinking and ideological gracing of the accomplished fact, and apologizing for impulses that only seem directed against it, at the expense of what might lie beyond the traps of the suffering of the present?

We urgently need an acute awareness of our historical *epoch* as well as of our fleeting moment *now*, within it. — We must ask what it is about the present moment that might make the possibility of recovering a Marxian social and political consciousness viable, and how we can *advance* it by way of *recovering* it.

For the *pathology* of our modern society mediated by capital, of the proletarian form of social life and its self-objectifications, the new forms of humanity it makes possible, which are completely unprecedented in history, grows only worse the longer delayed is taking the possible and necessary steps to the next levels of the struggle for freedom.

The pathology grows worse, not merely in terms of the various forms of the destruction of humanity, which are daunting, but also, perhaps more importantly – and disturbingly – in the manifest worsening social conditions and capacities for practical politics on the Left, and our worsening theoretical awareness of them. If there has been a crisis and evacuation of Marxian thought, it has been because its most fundamental context and point of departure, its awareness of its greater *historical* moment, the possibility of an *epochal* transition, has been forgotten, while we have not ceased to share this moment, but only lost sight of its necessities and possibilities. Any future emancipatory politics must regain such awareness of the *transitional* nature of capitalist modernity and of the reasons why we pay such a steep price for failing to recognize this.

Presented at the Marxist-Humanist Committee public forum on "The Crisis in Marxist Thought," hosted by Platypus in Chicago on July 25, 2008.

Originally published in *Platypus Review* 7 (October 2008)

# Remember the future![1]

Historical consciousness articulates the problem of what "ought" to be with what "is." The question is how the necessities of emancipatory struggles in the present relate to those of the past. The tasks revealed by historical Marxism have not been superseded but only obscured and forgotten, at the expense of emancipatory social politics in the present.

## Dunayevskaya and post-Trotskyism

The problem with Raya Dunayevskaya lies in the belief that there has been any real theoretical or practical political progress since the failure of the revolutions of 1917–19. This imagined progress is explicitly or implicitly assumed in all "Trotskyism" and post-Trotskyism.

Contrary to the prevailing views of post-Marxism, the high-water mark of progress in the movement for human freedom was in the practical politics and theoretical self-understanding of Lenin and Trotsky's Bolsheviks in Russia and Rosa Luxemburg's Spartacists in Germany. We have not progressed beyond the horizon of such political practice and its theory, but only regressed and fallen below this threshold. We urgently need to attain its spirit anew.

For the past half century, revolutionary "Left" politics, Marxist or otherwise, have remained stuck in the antinomies of "spontaneity" and "organization," "participatory democracy" and "vanguardist" politics, etc. Meanwhile, the historical moment of 1917–19 and its protagonists in thought and action remain enigmas to us.

---

1  A rejoinder to Peter Hudis's "Re-thinking the Crisis of Capital in Light of the Crisis of the Left" *Platypus Review* 8 (November 2008).

A repressed historical fact: neither Lenin nor Luxemburg was a "vanguardist" or a "spontaneist." These and other phantasies — indeed, any apparent resolution to, and progress beyond, the genuine political problems of social emancipation beyond capital revealed in 1917–19 — are pernicious illusions.

Dunayevskaya never properly registers the problem of regression. The most problematic assumption is that coming later means knowing better. But newly emergent forms of "resistance to capital" might be symptomatic of regression, and thereby not point beyond capitalist social relations any more — and perhaps far less — than proletarian socialism did in the early 20th century. It is not a matter of such new forms of politics expressing advances in social-political consciousness, but rather the effects of the horizon of a Marxian anti-capitalist politics slipping away.

Hudis's conception of capital as the domination of living labor by abstract labor leads to his equating all forms of resistance to capital as forms of "living labor's" protest against and purportedly immanent attempt to overcome capital.

Such an analysis finds "new" forms of anticapitalism in the social movements of the 1960s "New Left" (e.g. women's and gay liberation, black power, anti-colonization). The "New Left," however, actually represented a turning away from the problem of capital.

Why? Because only through proletarian socialism does the problem of the "contradiction" of capital — the self-contradictory character of proletarian labor in both its "abstract" and "concrete" dimensions — come to light. For capital is not merely the abstract dimension dominating the concrete, "living" dimension. It is rather the ways the abstract and concrete dimensions are related through market or state forms. Capital is the mode of self-relation of the proletariat and its consequences as a social-historical totality. All forms of "resistance to capital" constitute its reproduction in an on-going way.

Proletarian socialism, on the other hand, is the movement that reveals the self-contradiction of capital most explicitly and intensely in its reproduction. Other symptomatic forms of coping with the capital dynamic do so only more obscurely. Only proletarian socialism, the most acute manifestation of the self-contradiction of capital, concretely points beyond it.

We need a proletarian socialist politics to manifest the problem of capital for us, so that we can begin to formulate a politics for getting beyond it.

The degree to which an approach such as Hudis's attempts to be more open-minded about social struggles and their relation to the problem of capital, it actually conceals more than it reveals. Capital is a form of life, however "alienated," and not just a form of domination "over" life. Hence, one cannot take the position of "life" against capital, of "living labor" against "abstract labor," without naturalizing capital at another, deeper level.

## Marx's political vision: the "dictatorship of the proletariat"

Recognizing capital as a form of life also means recognizing the truly radical difference between a post-capitalist society and the society of capital. It is, in fact, too radical for us to really foresee, despite humanity's struggle to realize it over the course of more than a century. To clarify the relationship between the historical present and a possible future, it is helpful to consider Marx's political thinking on socialism.

Marx's understanding of socialist politics is expressed most clearly in his notion of the "dictatorship of the proletariat." For Marx, the "dictatorship of the proletariat" is not merely the overcoming of abstract labor by living labor, but rather the highest expression of their contradiction in the subjectivity of the commodity form.

Further, it expresses the contradiction of the democratic will of the producers in both their particular-"concrete" and "abstract"-general social dimensions. For example, the "participatory"-democratic ordering of the site of production will conflict with the more abstract "representative" democracy of political forms at a more general social level. In fact, the political circumstances of socialism would likely produce social conflicts, and hence politics. In a sense it would be, by comparison with the present, the first time in which authentic social-politics can be practiced.

In this sense, the "dictatorship of the proletariat" marks the end of politics as we know it, and the beginning of politics in a new and more advanced sense, with the working class and its activity helping to point beyond the social dynamic of capital. I disagree with Hudis that historical revolutionary Marxist protagonists such as Luxemburg, Lenin and Trotsky adopted a fundamentally different conception of the future of politics than Marx. Each of them, to the contrary, recognized the necessary leading, "vanguard" role of the working class in the attempt to democratize, or bring under conscious human control, the social process set in motion by capital.

The dynamic of capital does not evaporate through the activity of the working class. Quite the contrary, it is through this activity that capital, as Marx understood it, comes into being. Through the "dictatorship of the proletariat," however, the working class plays the necessarily leading role globally in addressing the problem of capital and its effects. In other words, it is the political means by which the social problem of capital is revealed so that it can begin to be overcome.

The proletariat then becomes for the first time, in Lukács's Hegelian-Marxist terms, the subject-object of (its own) history. At the same time, the proletariat as a class begins to cease being the self-contradictory "subject-object" it is today under capital. The proletariat, when these conditions are met, becomes itself for the first time while ceasing to be what it has been — constituted by and reconstitutive of capital — and thus begins to overcome and abolish itself.

The most potentially "participatory" concrete form of democracy, that of "the producers," must be recognized as the highest expression of the subjectivity of the commodity form, the subject-object relation of the proletariat with its own social activity of labor — and not as its "negation."

Hence, evading or otherwise abandoning Marx's conception of the "dictatorship of the proletariat" means abandoning the struggle to overcome capital. We need to remember what this actually meant by way of studying the most developed expressions to date of such a politics. We must remember the tasks of the past still informing our present by recalling what it was that revolutionary Marxism sought to accomplish, despite its historical failure.

### Remember the future!

The political thought and action bound up in the revolutionary moment of 1917–19 comprise a complex, rich heritage we neglect at our peril. This heritage, that of Luxemburg, Lenin and Trotsky and theorists in their wake, such as Lukács, Korsch, Benjamin and Adorno, is in the form of a set of problems to be worked through and not ready-made solutions. In order to recognize these outstanding problems of capital we must remember the future whose horizons of possibility informed the politics of the best traditions of revolutionary Marxism. Despite the limitations of Marxism as a historical movement, we nevertheless remain within the horizon of the history of capital and its social effects, whether politics today recognizes it or not. Hence, apparently paradoxically, it is by recognizing the horizons of possibility of capital as revealed in the past that we may recognize the limits humanity needs to overcome to realize its potential, emancipated future.

For example, in the earlier Marxist movement of the 2nd International (1889–1914), the women's liberation movement took place as an integral part of the struggle for socialism, to which it was neither subordinated nor from which it was separated. Such Marxist socialists as August Bebel and Clara Zetkin, among countless other, now-forgotten, participants in this movement, achieved profound insights into the relation of traditional gender roles and sexuality to the radically changed circumstances of modern capitalism. They recognized how capitalism both drew upon and radically reconstituted, on a new and different basis, such "traditional" oppressive aspects of society. Furthermore, they recognized the obstacle to women's emancipation capital had become and thus the fundamental connection between women's and sexual oppression and other problems in modern society. It was only because of the subsequent degeneration and conservatization of this movement, due to a series of failures and defeats, that a separate "feminist" movement had to come into being in the course of the regression of the 20th Century. Embracing the history of feminism thus amounts to naturalizing and adapting to such defeat and lowering the horizons of social politics.

Over-attentiveness to newly emergent — though concrete — forms of "resistance" to capitalism amounts to chasing our tails in the present and tailing after the effects of capital. Such over-attentiveness does not broaden but narrows our horizons; it does not, as Luxemburg demanded, engage, seize hold of and attempt to guide, in however limited ways, the changes in and of capital, so that we might get beyond them. "Resistance" in the present represents attempts to cope with and thus catch up with the social dynamics of capital. And the terms of such resistance have only worsened over time with the waning and disappearance of proletarian socialist politics.

Far from pointing to a post-capitalist society, such forms of social struggle under capital actually represent the limits of the present and its future, but only in obscure form, and thus not the actual breadth of the horizon of a potential future of and beyond capital. They express not the potentially new future beyond capital, but only the trailing edge, the wake of the newly emerging past in the present.

The post-'60s "new social movements" such as feminism and other forms of politics of social identity have expressed reconstituted forms of participation in capital. Not "getting beyond" the working class as might have been thought, such movements have opened the way to new and reconstituted forms of proletarianization. Moreover, they have done so in ways that have obscured the problem of the social totality in which they have taken place — the central role of the working class in the reconstitution of capital. The illusion is that such new forms of politics mean getting beyond the necessity of proletarian socialism, when in fact they have meant the avoidance of this task.

Such purportedly post-proletarian forms of politics have represented new forms of capital in an already-captured future of the present. They do not help us recognize the actual necessary tasks of a politics in, through and beyond capital. Only a proletarian socialist politics could do this. We need to remember the horizon of this politics, or remain forever trapped, knowingly or not, by its unfulfilled potential and betrayed possibilities.

Originally published in *Platypus Review* 8 (November 2008)

# Against dogmatic abstraction

## A critique of Cindy Milstein on anarchism and Marxism

At the Left Forum 2010, held at Pace University in New York City in March, Cindy Milstein, director of the Institute for Anarchist Studies, spoke at a panel discussion on anarchism and Marxism, chaired by Andrej Grubacic, with fellow panelists Roxanne Dunbar-Ortiz and Andrew Curley. The topic of Milstein's talk was the prospect for the "synthesis of anarchism and Marxism" today.[1] The relation between anarchism and Marxism is a long-standing and vexing problem, for their developments have been inextricably intertwined.

Milstein began her talk by remarking on the sea-change that had occurred over the course of the last "10–20 years," in which the "default pole on the Left" had gone from "authoritarian to libertarian," so that now what she called "authoritarian perspectives" had to take seriously and respond to libertarian ones, rather than the reverse, which had been the case previously. Authoritarian Marxists now were on the defensive and had to answer to libertarian anarchists.[2] Milstein commented on her chagrin when she realized that a speaker she found favorable at a recent forum was in fact from the ISO (International Socialist Organization), because the speaker had "sounded like an anarchist." For Milstein, this was important

---

1   Video documentation of Milstein's talk at the Left Forum 2010 can be found on You-Tube under "Cindy Milstein at the Left Forum (1)" from March 22, 2010.

2   It is unclear by her "10–20 year" periodization whether Milstein meant this negatively, with the collapse of Stalinism or "authoritarian/state socialism" beginning in 1989, or positively, with the supposedly resurgent Left of the "anti/alter-globalization" movement exemplified by the 1999 protests against the World Trade Organization in Seattle and the World Social Forum starting in 2001 at Porto Alegre, Brazil. Milstein was probably referencing both.

because it meant that, unlike in the past, the Left could now potentially proceed along essentially "libertarian" lines.

Milstein offered two opposed ways in which the potential synthesis of anarchism and Marxism has proceeded to date, both of which she critiqued and wanted to surpass. One was what she called the prevalent "anarchistic activism" today that found expression, for example, in the Invisible Committee's 2005 pamphlet *The Coming Insurrection* and in the rash of campus occupations at the height of the recent financial crisis. While Milstein praised aspects of this contemporary expression of a certain anarchistic impulse, she expressed concern that it also replicated "the worst aspects of Marxism, its clandestine organizing and vanguardism." Milstein found a complementary problem with the Marxist Left's attempts (e.g., by the ISO, et al.) to "sound anarchist" in the present circumstances, for she thought that they did so dishonestly, in order to recruit new members to Marxism. The way Milstein posed these problems already says a great deal about her sympathies and actual purpose in posing the question of a potential synthesis of anarchism and Marxism. For, in her view, whereas the anarchistic Left of the Invisible Committee and campus activists makes an honest mistake, the Marxists have more nefarious motives.[3] Milstein's critique of the contemporary anarchistic politics expressed by the Invisible Committee's manifesto and associated ethic of "occupy everything" was that, in its extreme emphasis on "autonomy," it is subject to what she called "individualist nihilism," and so lost sight of the "collective."

Milstein sought to reclaim the moniker of the "Left" exclusively for a revolutionary politics that does not include social democratic or liberal "reformist" political tendencies. (She made a special point, however, of saying that this did not mean excluding the history of "classical liberalism," of Thomas Paine, Jean-Jacques Rousseau, and others, which she still found relevant.) Her point was to raise the question of how it might be possible to achieve a non-authoritarian or "libertarian" version of "socialism," or anti-capitalism informed by Marxism. Milstein identified the problem, common to both Marxism and present-day forms of anarchism, as the

---

3    Ever since the Marx-Bakunin split in the International Workingmen's Association or First International, anarchists have characterized Marxists as authoritarians hijacking the revolutionary movement.

failure to properly prefigure an emancipated society of "libertarian social-ism" in revolutionary politics. Marxism, on this view, retains a crucial role to play. Milstein asserted that anti-capitalism was the *sine qua non* of any purported revolutionary politics. According to Milstein, what was missing from contemporary anarchism, but which Marxism potentially provided, was the "socialist," or revolutionary anti-capitalist dimension that could be found in Marx's critical theoretical analysis of capitalism in *Capital*. To Mil-stein, this was the key basis for any possible rapprochement of anarchism and Marxism.

It is therefore necessary to address the different conceptions of cap-italism, and thus anti-capitalism, that might lie behind anarchism and Marxism, in order to see if and how they could participate in a common "libertarian socialist" anti-capitalist politics, moving forward.

Historically, anarchists have complained of the split in the First Inter-national Workingmen's Association, in which the Marxists predominated and expelled the anarchists. The history of the subsequent Second or Socialist International, which excluded the anarchists, was peppered with anarchist protest against their marginalization in this period of tremendous growth in the revolutionary socialist workers' movement.[4] The crisis in the Second International that took place in the context of the First World War (1914–18) saw many former anarchists joining the radicals Lenin, Luxemburg and Trotsky in forming the Third International at the time of the Russian, German, Hungarian and Italian working class revolutions of 1917–19. (For instance, the preeminent American Trotskyist James P. Cannon had, prior to the Bolshevik Revolution, been an anarchist militant in the Industrial Workers of the World.)[5] To be sure, there were many anar-chists who remained inimical to, sought to compete politically with, and even fought militarily against Marxism throughout this later period (as in the case of the Russian Civil War), but the splits and realignments among anarchists and Marxists at that time have been a bone of contention in the history of revolutionary socialism ever since then. These two moments, of

---

4   See James Joll, *The Second International 1889–1914* (New York: Praeger, 1956).

5   See Bryan D. Palmer, *James P. Cannon and the Origins of the American Revolutionary Left 1890–1928* (Champaign: University of Illinois Press, 2007).

the First and Third Internationals, are joined by the further trauma of the Spanish Civil War of the 1930s, in which Marxists again fought anarchists.

So how does this "ancient history" appear in the present? Milstein is content to continue a long tradition among anarchists and "left" or libertarian communists and socialists, in which anarchism is opposed to Marxism along the lines of libertarian versus authoritarian politics. But is this indeed the essential, crucial difference between anarchism and Marxism?

Although Milstein approached the question of a present-day synthesis of anarchism and Marxism in an apparently open way, her perspective was still that of a rather dogmatic anarchism, adhering to principles rather than historical perspectives. What Milstein offered was the possibility, not of a true synthesis, but rather of re-assimilating Marxism back into its pre- and non-Marxian or "socialist" historical background.

Two figures of historical anarchism not mentioned by Milstein in her talk, but who can be regarded in terms of the emergence and further development of Marx's own perspectives on capitalism and socialism, are, respectively, Pierre-Joseph Proudhon (1809–65) and Mikhail Bakunin (1814–76). Marx's thought responded in its initial stages to the formulation of socialism by Proudhon, who was perhaps the most influential socialist at the time of Marx's youth. Bakunin, on the other hand, started out as an admirer of Marx's work, completing the first Russian translation the *Communist Manifesto* while also attempting to undertake a translation of *Capital* (the latter project was abandoned unfinished).

One figure Milstein did mention, Murray Bookchin (1921–2006), who taught her anarchism, was a famous critical interlocutor with Marxism, writing the New Left pamphlet *Listen, Marxist!*.[6] Bookchin was himself a former Marxist, first as a mainstream Third International Communist, later a Trotskyist, before ultimately turning to anarchism out of disenchantment with Marxism. More precisely, it was disenchantment with the practice of Marxist politics that motivated Bookchin's turn to anarchism. Like her mentor, Milstein's approach appears to be motivated by a Marxist anti-capitalism in theory and a libertarian anarchist politics in practice. But

---

6  In *Post-Scarcity Anarchism* (Montreal-Buffalo: Black Rose Books, 1986), 195–244. Originally published 1969.

how does this relate to the actual historical differences between anarchism and Marxism, in both theory and practice?

Marx's critique of capital was formulated and emerged strongly out of his critical engagement with Proudhon's "anarchist" socialism. Proudhon could be considered the first "libertarian socialist." Proudhon in fact invented the term "anarchism." He also famously coined the phrase "property is theft." Proudhon, like Marx, engaged and was influenced by not only British political economy and French socialism, but also Hegelian philosophy. Proudhon admitted to having only "three masters: the Bible, Adam Smith, and Hegel."[7] Marx's personal relationship with Proudhon was broken by Marx's critique of Proudhon's 1847 book, *System of Economical Contradictions: or, The Philosophy of Poverty*. Marx's book-length critique was titled, in his typically incisive style of dialectical reversal, *The Poverty of Philosophy*. It is significant that Marx worked towards a critique of Proudhonian socialism at the same time as he was beginning to elaborate a critique of the categories of political economy, through the case of Proudhon's 1840 book *What is Property?*, in the unpublished 1844 *Economic and Philosophic Manuscripts*.

By addressing Proudhon's opposition to capital as symptomatic, and trying to get at the shared presuppositions of both capitalist society and its discontents, as expressed by Proudhon, Marx attempted to grasp the historical essence of capital more fundamentally, and the possibility of capital being reproduced in and through the forms of discontent it generated. This meant taking a very historically specific view of capital that could regard how the prevailing forms of modern society and its characteristic forms of self-understanding in practice, and their discontents, in political ideology, shared a common historical moment in capital. Proudhon's thought, Marx argued, was not simply mistaken, but, as an acute symptom of capital, necessitated a critical understanding of what Proudhon was trying to grasp and struggle through. Marx's "critique of political economy," and attempt to "get at the root" of capital in "humanity itself," as a historical phenomenon, can thus be said to have begun with his critique of Proudhon.

---

7  Cited by J.A. Langlois in his preface to *P.J. Proudhon: His Life and Works* (1875).

For Marx, Proudhon offered not the overcoming, but rather the purest expression of the commodity form in capital, in the call to "abolish private property." The unintended effect of the abolition of property would, according to Marx, actually render society itself into one great "universal capitalist" over its members. For Marx understood "capital" as the contradiction of modern society with itself.[8] Just as each member of capitalist society regarded himself as his own property, a commodity to be bought and sold, so society regarded itself as capital. As Marx put it, in the 1844 *Manuscripts*,

> Communism is the position as the negation of the negation [of humanity in capital], and is hence the actual phase necessary for the next stage of historical development in the process of human emancipation and rehabilitation. Communism is the necessary form and the dynamic principle of the immediate future, but communism as such is not the goal of human development, the form of human society.[9]

This is what Proudhon, according to Marx, did not recognize about "socialism."

It is precisely such historical specification of the problems of capital and its discontents, and of any purported attempts to get beyond capital, that distinguishes Marx's approach from that of anarchism and non-Marxian socialism. In his critique of capital and its discontents, Marx did not pose any principles against others, abstractly, but rather tried to understand the actual basis for the principles of (anti)capitalism from within.

This relates to Marx's later dispute with his erstwhile admirer Bakunin. Bakunin was most opposed to what he believed to be Marx's and Marx's followers' embrace of the "state" in their concept of political revolution leading to socialism. Where Bakunin, in characteristic anarchist manner,

---

8   For example, Proudhon advocated replacing money with labor time credits and so did not recognize, as Marx noted early on and elaborated in detail later in *Capital*, how, after the Industrial Revolution and the introduction of machine production, labor-time undermined itself as a measure of social value.

9   *Economic and Philosophic Manuscripts of 1844*, in *Marx-Engels Reader*, 2nd edition, ed. Robert C. Tucker (New York: Norton, 1978), 93.

claimed to be opposed to the state *per se*, Marx and his best followers — such as that great demon for anarchists, Lenin,[10] in *The State and Revolution* (1917) — sought to grasp the necessity of the state as a function of capital, seeking to attack the conditions of possibility of the need for something like state authority in capital itself. Departing from regarding the state as an invidious *cause* of (political) unfreedom, Marx and the best Marxists sought to find out how the state, in its modern, capitalist, pathological, and self-contradictory form, was actually an *effect* of capital. The difference between Marxism and anarchism is in the understanding of the modern capitalist state as a historically specific phenomenon, a symptom, as opposed to a transhistorical evil.

Milstein's mentor Bookchin provides a good example of this kind of problem in anarchism with respect to historical specificity in opposition to capitalism. Opposed to the individualistic "egoism" of Proudhonian anarchism and of others such as Max Stirner,[11] Bookchin sought to find an adequate form of social life that in principle could do away with any pernicious authority. Bookchin found this in the idea, taken from Bakunin and Peter Kropotkin (1842–1921), of local communitarian "mutualism," as opposed to the tyranny of the capitalist state. For Bookchin, the anarchist opposition to capital comes down to a matter of the most anthropologically appropriate principle of society. (It is notable that Noam Chomsky offers a similar anarchist perspective on human nature as inherently socialist.)

Milstein's diagnosis and prescription for what ails today's Left is concerned with its supposed lack of, or otherwise bad principles for, proper

---

10  Lenin wrote in *"Left-Wing" Communism: An Infantile Disorder* (1920) that,

> [D]riven to frenzy by the horrors of capitalism . . . anarchism is characteristic of all capitalist countries. The instability of such revolutionism, its barrenness, and its tendency to turn rapidly into submission, apathy, phantasms, and even a frenzied infatuation with one bourgeois fad or another — all this is common knowledge. . . .

> Anarchism was not infrequently a kind of penalty for the opportunist sins of the working-class movement. The two monstrosities complemented each other. (*The Lenin Anthology*, ed. Robert C. Tucker (New York: Norton, 1975), 559–560.)

11  See Max Stirner, *The Ego and its Own* (London: Rebel Press, 1993). Originally published 1845. Sometimes translated as *The Individual and his Property*.

political organizing, in terms of both an adequate practice of anti-capitalist revolutionary politics and the emancipated society of "libertarian social-ism" towards which it strives.

The eminently practical political issue of "how to get there from here" involves an understanding and judgment of not only the "how" and the "there," but also the "here" from which one imagines one is proceeding. The question is whether we live in a society that suffers from bad principles of organization, extreme hierarchy, and distantly centralized authority, or from a deeper and more obscure problem of social life in modern capi-talism that makes hierarchy and centralization both possible and indeed necessary. Where Marx and a Marxian approach begin is with an examina-tion of what anarchism only presupposes and treats *a priori* as the highest principle of proper human social life. Marxists seek to understand where the impulse towards "libertarian socialism" originates historically. Marxists consider "socialism" to be the historical product and not simply the antith-esis of capitalism. Marxists ask, what necessity must be overcome in order to get beyond capital? For socialism would be not simply the negation, but also the completion of capitalism. Marx nonetheless endorsed it as such. This was the heart of Marx's "dialectical" approach to capital.

By contrast, for Milstein, following Bookchin, socialism differs fun-damentally in principle from capitalism. The problem with Marx and historical materialism was that it remained too subject to the exigencies of capitalism in the 19th to early 20th century era of industrialization. Similarly, the problem with the historical anarchism of Proudhon, Bakunin, and Kropotkin was that it had not yet adequately formulated the proper political principles for the relations of the individual in society. Bookchin thought that the possibility for this had been achieved in the late 20th cen-tury, in what he called "post-scarcity anarchism," which would allow for a return to the social principles of the traditional human communities that had been destroyed by capitalism and the hierarchical civilizational forms that preceded it.[12] Even though Bookchin thought that Marx's funda-mental political perspective of proletarian socialism had been historically

---

12 See Bookchin, *Post-Scarcity Anarchism* (1970); "Beyond Neo-Marxism," *Telos* 36 (1979); and *Toward an Ecological Society* (1980).

superseded, he nevertheless found support for his approach in Marx's late ethnographic notebooks.[13]

On the contrary, an approach properly following Marx would try to understand and push further the aspiration towards a socialist society that comes historically as a result of and from within capital itself. Rather than taking one's own supposed "anti-capitalism" simply as given, a Marxian approach seeks—as Marx put it in a famous 1843 letter to Arnold Ruge calling for the "ruthless criticism of everything existing," including first and foremost the Left[14]—to "show the world why it is struggling, and [that] consciousness of this is a thing it must acquire whether it wishes or not."[15]

For Milstein, the problems afflicting today's "anti-capitalist movement" can be established and overcome in principle *a priori*. According to Milstein, the Left must only give up its "individualistic nihilism" and "conspiratorial vanguardism" in organized politics in order to achieve socialism. This means Marxists must give up their bad ideas and forms of organization and become anarchists, or "libertarian socialists," if they are to serve rather than hinder the revolution against capital.

But, as the young, searching 25 year-old political radical Marx wrote (in his 1843 letter to Ruge),

> In fact, the internal obstacles seem almost greater than external difficulties. For . . . the question "where to?" is a rich source of confusion . . . among the reformers, but also every individual must admit to himself that he has no precise idea about what ought to happen. . . . [However] we do not anticipate the world with our dogmas but instead attempt to discover the new world through the critique of the old. I am therefore not in favor of our hoisting a dogmatic banner. Quite the reverse. We must

---

13  These writings by Marx are also the subject of a recent book by the Marxist-Humanist Kevin B. Anderson, *Marx at the Margins* (Chicago: University of Chicago Press, 2010).

14  Elsewhere, Marx wrote, "Our task is that of ruthless criticism, and much more against ostensible friends than against open enemies; and in maintaining this our position we gladly forego cheap democratic popularity." ("Gottfried Kinkel," in *Neue Rheinische Zeitung: Politisch-Ökonomische Revue* no. 4, 1850.)

15  Marx, letter to Arnold Ruge (September 1843), in *Marx-Engels Reader*, 12–15.

try to help the dogmatists to clarify their ideas. In particular, communism is a dogmatic abstraction and . . . only a particular manifestation of the humanistic principle and is infected by its opposite, private property. The abolition of private property is therefore by no means identical with communism and communism has seen other socialist theories, such as those of . . . Proudhon, rising up in opposition to it, not fortuitously but necessarily, because it is only a particular, one-sided realization of the principle of socialism. And by the same token, the whole principle of socialism is concerned only with one side, namely the *reality* of the true existence of man. . . . This does not mean that we shall confront the world with new doctrinaire principles and proclaim: Here is the truth, on your knees before it! It means that we shall develop for the world new principles from the existing principles of the world. . . . Our programme must be: the reform of consciousness not through dogmas but by analyzing . . . consciousness obscure to itself. . . . It will then become plain that the world has long since dreamed of something of which it needs only to become conscious for it to possess it in reality.[16]

Marx counterposed his own unique perspective sharply against that of other "socialists," whom he found to be unwittingly bound up in the categories of capital against which they raged. This has remained the case for virtually all "anti-capitalists" up to the present. Marx grasped this problem of anti-capitalism at the dawn of the epoch of industrial capital that arose with the disintegration of traditional society, but to whose unprecedented and historically specific social and political problems we continue to be subject today.

Marx departed from anarchism and other forms of symptomatic "socialism" with reason, and this reason must not be forgotten. Marx's task remains unfinished. Only this "clarification" of "consciousness obscure to

---

16  Ibid.

itself" that Marx called for can fulfill the long "dream" of anarchism, which otherwise will remain denied in reality.

Originally published in *Platypus Review* 25 (July 2010)

# Chinoiserie

## A critique of the Revolutionary Communist Party, USA's "new synthesis"[1]

## Prologue

David Bholatat adopted, as epigraph for his essay "Beyond Equality," the following passage from Joseph Schumpeter's classic 1942 book *Capitalism, Socialism and Democracy*:

> First and foremost, socialism means a new cultural world.... But second—what cultural world? . . . Some socialists are ready enough with folded hands and the smile of the blessed on their lips, to chant the canticle of justice, equality, freedom in general and freedom from "the exploitation of man by man" in particular, of peace and love, of fetters broken and cultural energies unchained, of new horizons opened, of new dignities revealed. But that is Rousseau adulterated with some Bentham.[2]

Bholat's essay follows Schumpeter in seeking to demonstrate the inadequacy and problematic character of the call for social "equality," for which he finds warrant in Marx's critique of capital. This is most notable in Marx's statement, echoing the French socialist Louis Blanc, that an emancipated

---

1   Review of *Communism: The Beginning of a New Stage, a Manifesto from the RCP, USA* (2008); and Raymond Lotta, Nayi Duniya, and K. J. A., "Alain Badiou's 'Politics of Emancipation': A Communism Locked Within the Confines of the Bourgeois World," *Demarcations* 1 (Summer – Fall 2009).

2   David Bholat, "Beyond Equality," *Rethinking Marxism* vol. 22 no. 2 (April 2010), 272–284.

society beyond capital would be governed by the principle of providing "from each according to his ability, to each according to his need."[3]

Jean-Jacques Rousseau (1712–78) argued, in his 1754 *Discourse on the Origin of Inequality*, that society alone produced "inequality," since in nature there are only "differences." Marx sought to fulfill Rousseau's demand for a society freed from the necessity of commensurability, of making alike what is unlike, in the commodity form of labor — a society freed from the exigencies of the exchange of labor.

Jeremy Bentham (1748–1832), the founder of Utilitarian philosophy at the end of the 18th century, famously called for society to provide "the greatest good for the greatest number." Marx considered his project to fulfill this aspiration as well.

The modern society of capital has indeed sought to achieve these various *desiderata*, of the individual diversity of incommensurable difference, as well as increased wellbeing of all its members, but has consistently failed to do so. A Marxian approach can be regarded as the *immanent* critique of capital, the critique of capital on its own ground, as expressed by the classical "bourgeois" liberal thinkers such as Rousseau and Bentham at the dawn of modern capitalist society, in that capital fails to fulfill its promise, but it would be desirable to accomplish this.

Schumpeter, writing in the mid-20th century, thought that modern society was moving inexorably toward "socialism," and that this was due to the unique and potentially crucial role that modern society allowed "intellectuals" to play. The far greater access to education that modern capitalist society made possible entailed the emergence of a stratum of people who could articulate problems for which they were not directly responsible on behalf of social groups to which they did not belong. This meant the possibility of a more radical critique and the fostering and mobilizing of broader social discontents than had been possible in pre-capitalist society. This role for intellectuals, combined with the inherent structural social problems of capital and the rise of "democratic" politics, created a potentially

---

3    Marx, *Critique of the Gotha Program* (1875), in *The Marx-Engels Reader*, 2nd edition, ed. Robert C. Tucker (New York: Norton, 1978), 531.

revolutionary situation in which "socialism," or the curtailment of capitalist entrepreneurship, was the likely outcome.

Bholat concluded his essay "Beyond Equality" by citing favorably Slavoj Žižek and Jacques Derrida's critiques, respectively, of "Marx's tolerance for the defects of first-phase communism," and of the principle of "equality before the law."[4]

The possibility of a "dialectical" transformation, the simultaneous negation and fulfillment of capital, its *Aufhebung* through a "proletarian socialist" politics, as capital's simultaneous historical realization and overcoming — as Marx conceived it, following Hegel — has proven elusive, but continues to task theoretical accounts inspired by Marxism.

### Entre nous

The Maoist Revolutionary Communist Party (RCP), USA published in 2008 the manifesto, *Communism: The Beginning of a New Stage*. This was followed, in short order, by the launching of a new theoretical journal, *Demarcations*, whose inaugural issue included a lengthy critique of Alain Badiou by RCP members* Raymond Lotta, Nayi Duniya, and K. J. A., titled "Alain Badiou's 'Politics of Emancipation': A Communism Locked Within the Confines of the Bourgeois World." Taken together, these and other recent writings of the RCP amount to a significant departure and change in orientation for their tendency of American Maoism. This is noteworthy as they are one of the most prominent Marxist Left organizations in the U.S., helping to organize, for instance, the major anti-war group The World Can't Wait. The RCP's spokesperson Sunsara Taylor is regularly invited to represent the radical Left on Fox News and elsewhere. Recently, the RCP has conducted a campaign of interventions featuring Lotta and Taylor as speakers at college and university campuses, including the top elite schools throughout the U.S., on the topic of communism today, in light of the history of the 20th century revolutions in Russia and China and their defeats. In this, the RCP demonstrates a reorientation towards intellectuals as potential cadres for revolutionary politics.[5]

---

4   Bholat, "Beyond Equality," 282.
5   See "An Open Letter from Raymond Lotta to Tony Judt and the NYU Community on the Responsibility of Intellectuals to the Truth, Including and Especially the Truth

The RCP's critique of the latter-day and post-Maoist "communist" Alain Badiou's conception of "radical, anarchic equality" is a part of their program of demonstrating "How Communism Goes Beyond Equality and Why it Must." It strongly resembles David Bholat's critique of the traditional Marxist Left in "Beyond Equality." For, as Bholat wrote, "in light of the world-historical failure of Marxism," the "one-sided emphasis of historical left movements on equity . . . might be reevaluated today," for such discontents remained "vulnerable to fascist elements motivated by *ressentiment* and revenge" that "represented a reactionary desire . . . to return to a romanticized, precapitalist moment."[6]

So, some clarification — and radicalization — of discontents has appeared necessary. For what is offered by such apparently disparate perspectives as Bholat and the RCP is what might be called a "post-postmodernist" politics, in which the radical reconsideration of the experience of 20th century Marxism seems in order. This links to Badiou and Žižek's attempts to advance what they call the "communist hypothesis." Žižek has spoken of "the Badiou event" as opening new horizons for both communism and philosophy. Badiou and Žižek share a background in Lacanian and Althusserian "post-structuralist" French thought, in common with other prominent post-New Left thinkers — and former students of Louis Althusser — such as Etienne Balibar and Jacques Rancière. Althusser found, in the Russian and Chinese Revolutions, a salutary challenge to the notion of the Hegelian "logic of history," that revolutionary change could and indeed did happen as a matter of contingency.[7] Althusser took great inspiration from Mao in China and Lenin in Russia for advancing the possibility of emancipation against a passive expectancy of automatic evolution in the historical process of capital.

---

about Communism," *Revolution* 180 (October 25, 2009), in which Lotta states that,

> Yes, revolutionary power must be held on to: a new state power and the overall leadership of a vanguard party are indispensable. But leadership must be exercised in ways that are, in certain important and crucial respects, different from how this was understood and practiced in the past. This [RCP's] new synthesis recognizes the indispensable role of intellectual ferment and dissent in socialist society.

6   Bholat, "Beyond Equality," 282.
7   See Louis Althusser, "Contradiction and Overdetermination" (1962), *New Left Review* I/41 (January – February 1967), 15–35. Also in *For Marx* (1965), trans. Ben Brewster (London: New Left Books, 1977), 87–116.

Michel Foucault took Althusser as license to go for an entire historiography of contingency.[8] For Badiou, this means that emancipation must be conceived of as an "event," which involves a fundamental reconsideration of ontology.[9] There is a common background for such postmodernist politics, also, in Sartre's "existentialist" Marxism, the anti-Cartesian phenomenology of Henri Bergson and Maurice Merleau-Ponty, and the "Spinozist" materialism of Georges Bataille.[10] The coincidence of vintage 1960s Maoist New Left Marxism with contemporaneous French thought — Foucault, Deleuze, Derrida — has resulted in a veritable *chinoiserie* prominent in reconsiderations of Marxism today.[11] But what does the — distinctively French — image of China say about the potential for a reformulated Leftist politics?[12]

## Rousseau

The mid-18th century Enlightenment *philosophe* Rousseau stands as the central figure at the critical crossroads for any consideration of the historical emergence of the Left.[13] Rousseau has haunted the self-understanding

---

8    See, for instance, Michel Foucault, "Nietzsche, Genealogy, History" (1971), in *Language, Counter-Memory, Practice: Selected Essays and Interviews*, ed. D. F. Bouchard (Ithaca: Cornell University Press, 1977), 139–164, in which Foucault ignored that Nietzsche's famous *On the Genealogy of Morals* (1887) was "a polemic" against any such "genealogy," and so turned Nietzsche, in keeping with Foucault's own intent, from a philosopher of freedom into freedom's "deconstructionist":

> In this sense, genealogy returns to the . . . history that Nietzsche recognized in [his 1874 essay "On the Use and Abuse of History for Life"]. . . . [But] the critique of the injustices of the past by a truth held by men in the present becomes the destruction of the man who maintains knowledge by the injustice proper to the will to knowledge. (164)

9    See Alain Badiou, *Being and Event*, trans. Oliver Feltham (New York: Continuum, 2007).

10   See the interview with Badiou by Filippo del Luchesse and Jason Smith, conducted in Los Angeles February 7, 2007, " 'We Need a Popular Discipline': Contemporary Politics and the Crisis of the Negative," *Critical Inquiry* 34, no. 4 (Summer 2008), 645–659.

11   See Richard Wolin, *The Wind from the East: French Intellectuals, the Cultural Revolution, and the Legacy of the 1960s* (Princeton: Princeton University Press, 2010).

12   See Peter Hallward's essay on Badiou's *Logiques des Mondes (Logics of Worlds)*, "Order and Event," *New Left Review* 53 (September – October 2008).

13   As James Miller, author of *The Passion of Michel Foucault* (2000), put it in his 1992 introduction to Rousseau's *Discourse on the Origin of Inequality* (Indianapolis: Hackett, 1992),

of Marxism, and indeed of revolutionary politics more generally, if only for the problematic influence he exercised on the pre-Marxian Left, most infamously in the ideas of the radical Jacobins such as Robespierre in the Great French Revolution. Lenin famously described himself as a "Jacobin indissolubly joined to the organization of the proletariat, which has become conscious of its class interests."[14] Modern conservatism was in an important sense founded by Edmund Burke's (1729–97) anti-Jacobin critique of Rousseau.

In his critique of Bruno Bauer's *The Jewish Question* (1843), the young Marx cited the following from Rousseau's *Social Contract* (1762):

> Whoever dares undertake to establish a people's institutions must feel himself capable of changing, as it were, human nature, of transforming each individual, who by himself is a complete and solitary whole, into a part of a larger whole, from which, in a sense, the individual receives his life and his being, of substituting a limited and mental existence for the physical and independent existence. He has to take from man his own powers, and give him in exchange alien powers which he cannot employ without the help of other men.

Marx wrote that this was "well formulated," but only as "the abstract notion of political man," concluding that,

The principle of freedom and its corollary, "perfectibility" ... suggest that the possibilities for being human are both multiple and, literally, endless. ... Contemporaries like Kant well understood the novelty and radical implications of Rousseau's new principle of freedom [and] appreciated his unusual stress on history as the site where the true nature of our species is simultaneously realized and perverted, revealed and distorted. A new way of thinking about the human condition had appeared. ... As Hegel put it, "The principle of freedom dawned on the world in Rousseau, and gave infinite strength to man, who thus apprehended himself as infinite." (xv)

14  Quoted by Rosa Luxemburg in *Organizational Questions of Russian Social Democracy* (1904), available in English translation as *Leninism or Marxism?* in *The Russian Revolution and Leninism or Marxism?* (Ann Arbor: University of Michigan Press, 1961). Luxemburg's pamphlet was a critique of Lenin, *One Step Forward, Two Steps Back: The Crisis in our Party* (1904).

Human emancipation will only be complete when the real, individual man has absorbed into himself the abstract citizen; when as an individual man, in his everyday life, in his work, and in his relationships, he has become a *species-being*; and when he has recognized and organized his own powers as *social* powers so that he no longer separates this social power from himself as *political* power.[15]

The RCP's Lotta, Duniya and K.J.A., under the chapter heading "Why Alain Badiou is a Rousseauist, and Why We should *not* be," point out that Rousseau's perspective is that of "bourgeois society":

The forms and content of equality in bourgeois society correspond to a certain mode of production: capitalism, based on commodity production and the interactions it engenders: private ownership, production for profit not need, and exploitation of wage-labor. Commodity production is governed by the exchange of equivalents, the measure of the labor time socially necessary to produce these commodities; that is, by an equal standard.[16]

Like Bholat following Derrida in "Beyond Equality," Lotta, Duniya, and K.J.A. attack "the standard of 'equality before the law' of bourgeois jurisprudence [as] a standard that serves the equal treatment of the capitalist property holders in a society governed by capitalist market relations," adding that, "for the dispossessed, formal equality masks the condition of fundamental powerlessness." What Lotta et al. dismiss as "formal equality" is not the liberal conception formulated by Rousseau that Marx cited favorably, precisely in its recognition of the "alienation" of the "changing" of "human nature" in society. Rather, the RCP writers let slip back in the

---

15  Marx, "On *The Jewish Question*," in *Marx-Engels Reader*, 2nd edition, ed. Robert C. Tucker, 46. This essay was written by Marx in 1843 as a response to Bruno Bauer's *The Jewish Question*, of the same year.

16  Raymond Lotta et al., "Alain Badiou's 'Politics of Emancipation:' A Communism Locked Within the Confines of the Bourgeois World."

one-sided conception of "politics" that Marx criticized and sought to over-come. For them, the opposition between the social and political that Marx diagnosed as symptomatic of modern capitalist society becomes instead the rigged game between exploiters and exploited. Note the need that Marx identified for the "individual" to "[recognize] and [organize] his own pow-ers as *social* powers so that he no longer separates this social power from himself as *political* power," something quite different from simply removing the "mask" of false "equality" from the condition of the "dispossessed" in "bourgeois democracy." Where does the RCP's perspective of revolution-ary politics originate? This is made apparent in the central section of their critique of Badiou over the interpretation of the Shanghai Commune, an event in the Great Proletarian Cultural Revolution (GPCR) in China.

### *La Commune*

The GPCR is dear to both Badiou and the RCP. This was the greatest event in the history of Marxism to take place in the era of the 1960s–70s New Left, and it exerted a profound attraction and influence over many at the time. The RCP is a direct product of its broad international impact. It seemed to justify Mao's claim to be the leading international (and not merely Chinese) opponent of "revisionism," i.e. of the abdication of proletarian socialist rev-olution in favor of reformism. Apart from factual questions about what really happened during the Cultural Revolution and the substance of Mao's own politics, both in China and internationally (thoughtful Maoists do not deny the distortion of Mao's politics by nationalism, but they tend to gloss over the intra-bureaucratic aspects of the GPCR), the issue of what the Cultural Revolution and Maoism more generally might *mean* to people, both then and now, is of more pressing concern. After all, the two most forthright arguments in favor of "communism" today are made by Maoists, Badiou and the RCP. It is also significant that both favor the appellation of "communist" over "Marxist," which both do on the grounds of their under-standing of the Cultural Revolution.

The Cultural Revolution is the basis for regarding Mao as making a unique and indispensable contribution to communism. What the Cul-tural Revolution means to Maoists is fundamentally informed by their conception of capitalism. So, rather than taking sides in or analyzing the social and political phenomenon of the Cultural Revolution *per se*, it is necessary to examine what has been taken to be its significance. The Chinese Cultural Revolution is perhaps the most significant recent "Jacobin" moment in the history of Marxism, raising again, in the latter part of the 20th century, long-standing questions about the relation between socialism and democracy — the issue of "communism," in the strict sense.

The significance of the Shanghai Commune of 1967 is contested by Badiou and the RCP. For Badiou it was a model akin to the 1792–94 radical Jacobin period of the French Revolution. In the Shanghai Commune radicalized students ("Red Guards") overthrew the local Communist Party apparatus, spreading into a workers' revolt. While initially enthusiastic about this spontaneous "anti-revisionist" upsurge against conservative elements in the CP, Mao and his followers ultimately rejected the Shanghai Commune as a model. They advocated instead the "revolutionary committee" in which the Maoist Communist Party cadres' paramount leading political character could be preserved. Badiou criticizes this straitjacketing of communism in the "party-state," whereas the RCP defends Mao's politics of rejuvenating the Party and purging it of "capitalist roaders" as the necessary and sole revolutionary path.

Badiou, by contrast, sees Mao's eventual rejection of the Shanghai Commune as a betrayal of "egalitarianism." For him, the "party-state" is a brake on the radical "democratic" egalitarianism that characterizes "communism" as a historically recurrent political phenomenon. The RCP critiques this conception of "equality" and "direct democracy" as "concealing class interests" and thus being unable to "rise above particular interests." For instance, according to the RCP, as long as there remains a distinction between "intellectual and manual labor," intellectuals can come to dominate the social process, even under socialism, thus reproducing a dynamic constantly giving rise to the possible return to capitalism, which is understood primarily as a matter of social and political hierarchy. To the RCP, Badiou is thus prematurely egalitarian.

Badiou conceives of the relation between freedom and equality as an ontological one, in the mathematical terms of set theory, transhistoricizing it. The RCP, while recognizing the historically specific nature of

capitalist class struggle, conceives of the role of the revolutionary proletarian party as the political means for *suppressing* tendencies towards
social inequality. In either case, neither Badiou nor the RCP conceives
of the transformation of the capitalist mode of production that would
allow for overcoming the socially pernicious aspects of specifically capitalist forms of inequality, the dangers of which are understood by Badiou
and the RCP rather atavistically. Marx, by contrast, looked forward to the
potential for overcoming the conditions of possibility for the reproduction of capitalist class dynamics in the mode of production itself: capital's
overcoming of the need to accumulate the value of surplus labor-time.
Marx saw the historical potential to overcome this socially mediating
aspect of labor in automated machine production. However, Marx also
foresaw that, short of socialism, the drive to accumulate surplus-value
results in producing a surplus population, an "industrial reserve army" of
potential "workers" who thus remain vulnerable to exploitation. A politics based only in their "democratic" discontents can result, not in the
overcoming of the social need for labor, but in the (capitalist) demand
for more labor. Or, as Max Horkheimer, director of the Marxist Frankfurt
Institute for Social Research, put it, machines "have made not work but
the workers superfluous."[17]

For the RCP, Mao in the Cultural Revolution addressed in new and
effective ways problems of the "transition to socialism" never attempted
under Stalin. The RCP criticizes Stalin for his failed "methods" in advancing the transition to socialism, a failure Mao overcame in the Cultural
Revolution in China 1966–76. The RCP celebrates the egalitarian-eman-
cipatory impulse of the Cultural Revolution while also praising Mao's
guidance and political leadership of the process by which the "capitalist"
road to China's development was politically overcome and avoided. This
struggle ended, according to the RCP, with Mao's death and the subsequent purging of his followers, known as the "Gang of Four," in 1976,
embarking China upon its capitalist development up to the present.

---

17 "The Authoritarian State," in *The Essential Frankfurt School Reader*, ed. Andrew Arato
and Eike Gebhardt (New York: Continuum, 2005), 95.

Badiou explicitly attacks the limitations of Marxism in general, and not merely the "party-state" form of political rule (for which he holds Marxism responsible), for failing to recognize how the emancipatory striving of "equality" goes "beyond class." This is why he favors the designation "communism" to "Marxism." The RCP (rightly) smells a rat in this attempt by Badiou to take communism "beyond" anti-capitalist class-struggle politics. But in so doing they do not pause to reflect on the subordinate position of class struggle in Marx's own conception of the possibility of overcoming capital.

For Marx, the political-economic struggle of the specifically modern classes of capitalists and workers is a projection of the contradiction of capital. The RCP, by contrast, regards the class struggle as constituting the social contradiction in capital. This flows from their understanding of the contradiction of capital as existing between the socialized forces of production and the privatized and hence capitalist relations of production. Privileged empowerment, whether in the form of capitalist private property or in more developed intellectual capacities, is the source rather than the result of the contradiction of capital in the RCP's traditional "Marxist" view. For the RCP, Badiou's perspective of radical democratic "equality" does not address such inherent social advantage that intellectuals would enjoy even under socialism, presenting the constant threat of defeating the struggle for socialism.[18]

But the RCP does not stop at upholding Mao in the Cultural Revolution as a model for revolutionary politics. Rather, they attempt a "new synthesis" in which the relation of Marx, Lenin and Mao as historical figures is reformulated to provide for a 21st century socialist politics that could still learn from but overcome the limitations of the 20th century experience of the Russian and Chinese Revolutions.

---

18 There is an important affinity here with the anarchism of Noam Chomsky and Michael Albert, who consider Marxism to be an ideology of the aspirations to social domination by the "coordinator class" of intellectuals, which is how they understand the results of, e.g., the Russian and Chinese Revolutions. In this view, Marxism is the means by which the intellectuals harness the class struggle of the workers for other, non-emancipatory ends. Their understanding of the "party-state" is the regime of the coordinator class.

## The "new synthesis"

According to a traditional Maoist view, the RCP considers the historical trajectory from Marx through Lenin to Mao as a progress in the theory and practice of the struggle for socialism. But they also detect distinct limitations among all three historical figures and so regard them as importantly complementary rather than successive. For the RCP's "new synthesis," Marx and Lenin can still address the shortcomings of Mao, rather than the latter simply building upon the former. How so?

It is important first to consider the significance of this change in the RCP's thinking from traditional Maoism. The RCP's "new synthesis" was the cause of a split in the RCP, with some, including Mike Ely, going on to form the Kasama Project. The RCP replies to criticism of their current articulations of the limitations of the Russian and Chinese Revolutions with reference to earlier criticism of the RCP, over the course of the past three decades, for reducing Communism to a "tattered flag" in their reconsideration of this history. But the RCP should be commended for taking this risk.

The RCP struggles in explaining and relating the limitations of the three principal thinkers in the tradition they look towards for "communism." With Marx, there is the limitation of relatively lacking historical experience of socialist revolution. Only the Paris Commune figures for this history. With Lenin, the limitations of the Bolshevik Revolution are displaced in the RCP's evaluation of, not Lenin, but Stalin's attempt to build "socialism" in the 1920s–30s. Like the disastrous Great Leap Forward in China (1958–61), the first Five-Year Plan in the Soviet Union (1928–33), a period of "revolutionary" militancy in the history of Stalin's rule, is glossed over by the RCP in evaluating the Russian and Chinese 20th century experiences of attempts to "build socialism."[19]

---

19  The first Five-Year Plan in the USSR saw the accelerated collectivization of agriculture, in which the Communists unleashed "class struggle" in the countryside, with great popular participation. This coincided with the Communist International's policy of refusing any political alliances with reformists, whom they dubbed "social fascists" during this period, which they considered the advent of revolution, following the Great Crash. Such extremism caused, not only mass starvation and brutalization of life in the USSR — whose failures to "build socialism" were blamed on "Trotskyite wreckers," leading to the Purge

For the RCP, Mao represents a breakthrough. Through his leadership of the Chinese Communist Party, the limitations of the experience of Stalinism in the Soviet Union were overcome, in the Cultural Revolution in China of the 1960s–70s. But none of these are examples of success — socialism, let alone communism, has not yet been achieved — and they do not exactly add up, but rather require a "synthesis."

Mao provides a salutary contribution only the degree to which the Cultural Revolution overcame the problem of Stalinist "methods," which are considered bureaucratic and authoritarian in the sense of stifling revolutionary initiative: Stalin did the right things but in the wrong ways. Not secretly manipulated purge "trials," but people's justice would have been the better way to stave off the threat of the "capitalist road" in the USSR of the 1930s. Most telling about the RCP's "new synthesis" is how they conceive its first two figures. For the RCP, a combination of Marx and Lenin taken without Mao becomes a perspective of "Eurocentric world revolution." This is because, in the RCP's estimation, there is a significant difference between Lenin and "Leninism," the degree to which the former, according to the RCP, "did not always live up" to the latter, and the latter is assimilated to what are really phenomena of Stalinism and Maoism, building "socialism in one country," in which Mao's own practice, especially in the Cultural Revolution, takes priority. But this begs the question of the Marxist perspective on "world revolution" — and the need for revolution in the U.S., which Marx and Lenin themselves thought was key. Instead, the problem of socialism in China dominates the RCP's historical imagination of revolution.

## World revolution

Kant, in his theses in "Idea for a Universal History from a Cosmopolitan Point of View" (1784), addressed Rousseau as follows. Kant warned of the danger that,

---

Trials in the mid- to late 1930s — but also the eventual victory of the Nazis in Germany. Just as the Purge Trials in the USSR were in response to failures of the Five-Year Plans, the Cultural Revolution in China was a response to the failure of the Great Leap Forward.

[T]he vitality of mankind may fall asleep. . . . Until this last step to a union of states is taken, which is the halfway mark in the development of mankind, human nature must suffer the cruelest hardships under the guise of external well-being; and Rousseau was not far wrong in preferring the state of savages, so long, that is, as the last stage to which the human race must climb is not attained. . . . [Mere civilization,] however, is nothing but pretense and glittering misery. In such a condition the human species will no doubt remain until . . . it works its way out of the chaotic conditions of its international relations.[20]

Marx considered his political project to be a continuation of Kant's, no less than Rousseau's or Bentham's, albeit under the changed historical conditions of post-Industrial Revolution capitalism, in which "international relations" expressed not merely an unenlightened state, but the social contradictions of the civilization of global capital.[21] Writing on the Paris Commune of 1870–71, Marx addressed the antithetical forms of cosmopolitanism in capital:

---

20  Immanuel Kant, "The Idea for a Universal History from a Cosmopolitan Point of View," in *Kant on History*, trans. Lewis White Beck (Indianapolis: Bobbs-Merrill, 1963), 11–25.

21  See, for instance, the British Trotskyist Cliff Slaughter's argument, in "What is Revolutionary Leadership?" (1960), in which he pointed out about Stalinism that,

> As a part of [the process of Stalinization], certain theoretical distortions of Marxism play an important part. Above all, Marxism is twisted into an economic determinism. The dialectic is abstracted from history and reimposed on social development as a series of fixed stages. Instead of the rich variety and conflict of human history we have the natural series of slavery, feudalism, capitalism and socialism through which all societies pass. . . . An apparent touch of flexibility is given to this schematic picture by the doctrine that different countries will find their "own" roads to Socialism, learning from the USSR but adapting to their particular national characteristics. This is of course a mechanical caricature of historical materialism. The connection between the struggles of the working class for Socialism in, say, Britain, Russia and Vietnam, is not at all in the greater or lesser degree of similarity of social structure of those countries, but in the organic interdependence of their struggles. Capitalism is an international phenomenon, and the working class is an international force.

From *Labour Review* 5 no. 3 (October – November 1960), 93–96 & 105–111.

If the Commune was thus the true representative of all the healthy elements of French society, and therefore the truly national government, it was, at the same time, as a working men's government, as the bold champion of the emancipation of labor, emphatically international. Within sight of that Prussian army, that had annexed to Germany two French provinces, the Commune annexed to France the working people all over the world. . . . The [preceding] Second Empire [by contrast] had been the jubilee of cosmopolitan blackleggism, the rakes of all countries rushing in at its call for a share in its orgies and in the plunder of the French people.[22]

The RCP remains hampered by the Stalinist perspective of building "socialism in one country," at the expense of a direct politics of world revolution that characterized the Marxism of Marx's own time, in the First International. And so the RCP fails to recognize the degree to which Marx's own politics was "emphatically international" in nature. As Marx scholar Moishe Postone put it,

Now, the revolution, as imagined by Trotsky — because it's Trotsky who really influences Lenin in 1918 — entailed the idea of permanent revolution, in that, revolution in the East would spark revolution in the West. But I think Trotsky had no illusions about the Soviet Union being socialist. This was the point of his debate with Stalin. The problem is that both were right. That is, Trotsky was right: there is no such thing as "socialism in one country." Stalin was right, on the other hand, in claiming that this was the only road that they had open to them once revolution failed in the West, between 1918–1923. Now, did it have to be done with the terror of Stalin? That's a very complicated question, but there was terror and it was enormous, and we don't do ourselves a service by neglecting

---

22  *The Civil War in France,* in *Marx-Engels Reader,* 638.

that. In a sense it becomes an active will against history, as wild as claiming that "history is on our side."[23]

Bob Avakian, the leader of the RCP, writing about "Leninism as the bridge," put the matter of the relation between Marx, Lenin and Mao this way: "Marxism without Leninism is Eurocentric social-chauvinism and social democracy. Maoism without Leninism is nationalism (and also, in certain contexts, social-chauvinism) and bourgeois democracy."[24] But Avakian and the RCP have a fundamental ambivalence about Lenin. In the same article, Avakian wrote that, "as stressed before there is Leninism and there is Lenin, and if Lenin didn't always live up to Leninism, that doesn't make Leninism any less than what it is." This is because, for the RCP, "Leninism" is in fact Stalinism, to which they recognize Lenin's actual politics cannot be assimilated. It is therefore a standing question of what remains of Marx and Lenin when they are unhitched from the Stalinist-Maoist train of 20th century "communism," the eventual course of the Russian and Chinese Revolutions to which the RCP points for inspiration and guidance. But the RCP's imagination has always been fired more by the Chinese than the Russian experience. If "Leninism" was a historical "bridge," it led to Mao's China.

### The image of China

China has provided a Rococo mirror reflecting global realities, whether in the 18th or the 20th and 21st centuries. The Middle Kingdom has stood, spectacular and confounding, for attempts to comprehend in social imagination both civilization and barbarism, now as then. The *ancien régime* at Versailles awaiting its historical fate would have liked to close itself up in a Forbidden City; the fervid imaginations of the 18th century *philosophes* such as Rousseau would have liked to breach the walls of its decadent customs. Both projected their world through the prism of China, which

---

23 "Marx after Marxism," interview by Benjamin Blumberg and Pam C. Nogales C., *Platypus Review* 3 (March 2008).
24 *Conquer the World? The International Proletariat Can and Must*, part III, *Revolution* 50 (1981), p. 38.

seemed to condense and refract at once all the splendors and horrors — Kant's "glittering misery" — of society. This has also been true of the Left from the latter part of the 20th century to the present. The very existence of China has seemed to suggest some obscure potential for the future of humanity, both thrilling and terrifying. What if China were indeed the center of the world, as many on the Left have wished, ever since the 1960s?

If today China strikes the imagination as a peculiar authoritarian "communist" capitalist powerhouse that may end up leading the world in the 21st century, in the 1960s the Cultural Revolution symbolized China. Immediately prior to the student and worker upheaval in France of May 1968, Jean-Luc Godard directed his film *La Chinoise* (1967) about young revolutionaries in Paris. At around the same time, Horkheimer worried about the appearance of "Chinese on the Rhine," as students began reading and quoting from Mao's Little Red Book. If in the 18th century the Jacobin revolutionaries wanted France not to be China, in the 1960s would-be French revolutionaries wanted China to be the revolutionary France of the late 20th century.

In his critique of Jacobinism, Burke wrote that,

[T]he age of chivalry is gone: that of sophisters, economists, and calculators, has succeeded. . . . The unbought grace of life . . . is gone! . . . All the pleasing illusions . . . which harmonized the different shades of life, and which, by a bland assimilation, incorporated into politics the sentiments which beautify and soften private society, are to be dissolved by this new conquering empire of light and reason.

On this scheme of things, a king is but a man; a queen is but a woman; a woman is but an animal; and an animal not of the highest order. . . . On the scheme of this barbarous philosophy, which is the offspring of cold hearts and muddy understandings . . . laws are to be supported only by their terrors, and by the concern, which each individual may find in them, from his

> own private speculations, or can spare to them from his own
> private interests.[25]

Still, the Jacobin terror continues. Today in Communist China, a bribery case in producing chemically adulterated pharmaceuticals, baby milk formula, and pet food results in a death sentence, to prevent any decrease in demand from the United States. Chinese authorities dismiss the criticism made on human rights grounds, pointing to the need to be vigilant against a constant threat of "corruption." No doubt American consumers wonder what such swift "justice" could do to improve corporate behavior in the U.S.

The connection between revolutionary France and China in the bourgeois epoch, from the 18th century through the 20th century to the present, is summed up well in an apocryphal quip supposedly made by the Chinese Communist Premier Zhou Enlai, in response to a question about the historical significance of the French Revolution: Zhou said it was still "too soon to tell." Because of its Revolution in the 20th century, China came to have cast upon it the long shadow of Jacobinism and Rousseau's 18th century critique of social inequality. But, as Marx discovered long ago, inequality is not the *cause* but the *effect* of capital. Such confusion has contributed to the perspective of "Third World" revolution that had its heyday in the post-WWII Left — after the 1949 Chinese Revolution — and that still stalks the imagination of emancipatory politics today. Not only post-postmodernist neo-communists such as Badiou, but also Maoists in the more rigorous 1960s–70s tradition such as the RCP, remain beholden to the specter of inequality in the modern world.

China, as a result of its 20th century revolutionary transformation, has gone from being like the India of the 18th century, its traditional ways of life breaking down and swamped in pre-capitalist obscurity, confronted with the dynamics of global capitalism, to becoming something like a potential Britain of the 18th century — the manufacturing "workshop of the world" — albeit in the profoundly changed circumstances of the 21st century. As Marx, in a 1858 letter to Engels, pointed out about his own time,

---

25 *Reflections on the Revolution in France* (1790), J. C. D. Clark, ed. (Stanford: Stanford University Press, 2001), 239–240.

There is no denying that bourgeois society has for the second time experienced its 16th century, a 16th century which, I hope, will sound its death knell just as the first ushered it into the world. The proper task of bourgeois society is the creation of the world market, at least in outline, and of the production based on that market. . . . For us, the difficult *question* is this: [in Europe] revolution is imminent and will, moreover, instantly assume a socialist character. Will it not necessarily be *crushed* in this little corner of the earth, since the *movement* of bourgeois society is still in the *ascendant* over a far greater area?[26]

What the 16th century meant to Marx was the "primitive accumulation of capital," the process by which society was transformed, through the liquidation of the peasantry, in the emergence of the modern working class and the bourgeois social relations of its existence. If this process continued in the 19th century, beyond Britain, through the rest of Europe and the United States and Japan, in the 20th century it proceeded in Asia — through the Russian and Chinese Revolutions. The reconstitution of capital in the 19th century, unleashing a brutal process of late colonial expansion, was, to Marx's mind, not only unnecessary and hence tragic, but also *regressive* and potentially *counterrevolutionary*. Marx's warning should have resounded loudly through the "revolutionary" history of Marxism in the 20th century, but was instead repressed and forgotten.

For Marx and Engels, it was not a matter of China and other countries, newly swept into the maelstrom of capitalist development by the mid-19th century, "catching up" with Britain and other more "advanced" areas, but rather the possibility of the social and political turbulence in such "colonial" zones having any progressive-emancipatory impact on global capital at its core. As Marx wrote, in *The Class Struggles in France, 1848–50*, about the relation of England to other countries,

---

26 See "Europocentric World Revolution," *Marx-Engels Reader*, 676. This selection, which omits the first sentence, is from a letter from Marx to Engels dated October 8, 1858.

Just as the period of crisis began later [elsewhere] than in England, so also did prosperity. The process originated in England, which is the demiurge of the bourgeois cosmos. [Elsewhere] the various phases of the cycle repeatedly experienced by bourgeois society assume a secondary and tertiary form. . . . Violent outbreaks naturally erupt sooner at the extremities of the bourgeois body than in its heart, because in the latter the possibilities of accommodation are greater than in the former. On the other hand, the degree to which revolutions [elsewhere] affect England is at the same time the [barometer] that indicates to what extent these revolutions really put into question bourgeois life conditions, and to what extent they touch only their political formations.

On this all the reactionary attempts to hold back bourgeois development will rebound just as much as will all the ethical indignation and all the enraptured proclamations of the democrats.[27]

This means that the "democratic" politics that engenders "ethical indignation" at the rank inequality in global capital remains woefully inadequate to the task of overcoming the "bourgeois world" within which the RCP accuses Badiou et al. of remaining "locked." For subsequent history has clearly shown that the Chinese Revolution under Mao remained trapped in global capital, despite the "socialist" ferment of the Great Proletarian Cultural Revolution that gripped the imagination of the international Left of the time, "Maoist" and otherwise.[28] Without revolutionary socialist

---

27  In *Marx-Engels Reader*, 593.

28  For instance, even many avowed "Trotskyists" were fascinated and inspired by the GPCR. See, for example, Gerry Healy and David North's International Committee of the Fourth International's British journal *Newsline* of January 21, 1967, where an article by Michael Banda stated that "the best elements led by Mao and Lin Piao have been forced to go outside the framework of the Party and call on the youth and the working class to intervene [in this] anti-bureaucratic [fight]." See David North, *The Heritage We Defend: A Contribution to the History of the Fourth International* (Detroit: Labor Publications, 1988), 424. North, who became critical of Banda's positive perspective on Mao in the Cultural Revolution, is currently the leader of the international tendency of which the Socialist Equality Party is the U.S. section.

consequences in the "heart" of the bourgeois world, revolutions in countries such as China cannot, according to Marx, "really put into question bourgeois life conditions" but "touch only their political formations." As Engels put it, in a 1882 letter to the leading German Social Democratic Party Marxist theorist Karl Kautsky,

> [T]he countries inhabited by a native population, which are simply subjugated . . . must be taken over for the time being by the [world] proletariat and led as rapidly as possible towards independence. How this process will develop is difficult to say. . . . [Such places] will perhaps, indeed very probably, produce a revolution . . . and [this] would certainly be the best thing for us. We shall have enough to do at home. Once Europe is reorganized [in socialism], and North America, that will furnish such colossal power and such an example that the semi-civilized countries will follow in their wake of their own accord. Economic needs alone will be responsible for this. But as to what social and political phases these countries will then have to pass through before they likewise arrive at socialist organization, we to-day can only advance rather idle hypotheses.[29]

### "Locked within the confines of the bourgeois world"

Despite the RCP's critique of the post-1960s New Left neo-communism of Badiou, and its partial recognition that Marx and the best of Marxism sought to go beyond "bourgeois" discontents and demands for equality in capital, the RCP perspective on Marxism remains compromised by its focus on capitalist inequality. This leads to an ambivalent and confused conception of the potential role of "intellectuals" in revolutionary politics — a role highlighted in the mid-20th century by even such unreservedly "bourgeois" perspectives such as that of Joseph Schumpeter, and also by

---

29  See "Europocentric World Revolution," *Marx-Engels Reader*, 677. The complete letter from Engels to Kautsky of September 12, 1882 is available on the *Marxist Internet Archive*.

figures influential for the 1960s New Left such as C. Wright Mills.[30] The RCP, along with other tendencies of post-New Left politics preoccupied by problems of inequality and hierarchy, such as neo-anarchism, suspects intellectuals of containing the germ for reproducing capitalism through inequality. Likewise, the RCP remains confused about the supposed problem of a "Euro-" or "Western"-centric perspective on "world revolution." In this sense, the RCP remains trapped by the preoccupations of 1960s-era New Left Maoism in which they originated, despite their attempts to recover the critical purchase of the earlier revolutionary politics of Marx and Lenin. Despite their intended critical approach to this history, they fail to consider how Maoism may have represented a *retreat* rather than an *advance* from such revolutionary Marxism. For, as Lenin recognized, the best of Marxist revolutionary politics was not opposed to but rather necessarily stood within the tradition of Rousseau and the radical bourgeois intellectual "Jacobin" legacy of the 18th century, while attempting to transcend it.[31] Like it or not, and either for ill or for good, we remain "locked in the bourgeois world," within whose conditions we must try to make any possible revolution.

Originally published in *Platypus Review* 26 (August 2010)

* Note: It should not be assumed that writers for *Demarcations* are members of the RCP.

---

30 See C. Wright Mills, "Letter to the New Left," *New Left Review* I/5 (September – October 1960), 18–23.

31 Georg Lukács addressed such transcendence in his eulogy, "Lenin—Theoretician of Practice" (1924). It is included as part of the "Postscript 1967," in Lukács, *Lenin: A Study on the Unity of His Thought*, trans. Nicholas Jacobs (Cambridge, MA: MIT Press, 1970), in which Lukács described Lenin as follows:

> In the chain of democratic revolutions in modern times two types of leaders, poles apart, made their appearance, embodied by men such as Danton and Robespierre, in both reality and literature. ... Lenin is the first representative of an entirely new type, a *tertium datur*, as opposed to the two extremes. (93)

But Marx was also a representative of this new type of revolutionary intellectual.

# The Marxist hypothesis

## A response to Alain Badiou's "communist hypothesis"

### Against Badiou

Alain Badiou's recent book (2010) is titled with the phrase promoted by his and Slavoj Žižek's work for the last few years, "the communist hypothesis."[1] This is also the title of Badiou's 2008 essay in *New Left Review*[2] on the historical significance of the 2007 election of Nicolas Sarkozy to the French Presidency.[3] There, Badiou explains his approach to communism as follows:

> What is the communist hypothesis? In its generic sense, given in its canonic *Manifesto*, "communist" means, first, that the logic of class — the fundamental subordination of labour to a dominant class, the arrangement that has persisted since Antiquity — is not inevitable; it can be overcome. The communist hypothesis is that a different collective organization is practicable, one that will eliminate the inequality of wealth and even the division of labour. The private appropriation of massive fortunes and their transmission by inheritance will disappear. The existence of a coercive state, separate from civil society, will no longer appear a necessity: a long process of reorganization based on a free association of producers will see it withering away.[4]

---

1  *The Communist Hypothesis* (London: Verso, 2010). The book is printed in a pocket-sized red hardcover on which is emblazoned a gold star — a *Little Red Book* (viz., *Quotations from Chairman Mao Tse-Tung*) for our time?

2  "The Communist Hypothesis," *New Left Review* 49 (January – February 2008), 29–42.

3  The other book to originate from Badiou's 2008 essay in *New Left Review* is *The Meaning of Sarkozy* (London: Verso, 2008).

4  "The Communist Hypothesis," 34–35.

Badiou goes on to state that,

> As a pure Idea of equality, the communist hypothesis has
> no doubt existed since the beginnings of the state. As soon
> as mass action opposes state coercion in the name of egali-
> tarian justice, rudiments or fragments of the hypothesis start
> to appear. Popular revolts — the slaves led by Spartacus, the
> peasants led by Müntzer — might be identified as practical
> examples of this "communist invariant." With the French
> Revolution, the communist hypothesis then inaugurates the
> epoch of political modernity.[5]

Badiou thus establishes "communism" as the perennial counter-current to
civilization throughout its history.

Badiou divides what he calls the modern history of the "communist
hypothesis" into two broad periods, or "sequences," from 1792–1871
and from 1917–76. The first, from Year One of the revolutionary French
Republic through the defeat of the Paris Commune, Badiou describes as
the "setting in place of the communist hypothesis." The second, from the
October 1917 Revolution in Russia to Mao's death and the end of the Great
Proletarian Cultural Revolution in China, Badiou calls the sequence of "pre-
liminary attempts at . . . [the] realization [of the communist hypothesis]."[6]

The two periods remaining in this historical trajectory sketched by
Badiou, 1871–1917 and 1976 to the present, Badiou describes as "intervals" in which "the communist hypothesis was declared to be untenable,"
"with the adversary in the ascendant."[7]

But the period from 1871–1917 saw the massive growth and development of Marxism (alongside and indeed bound up with the last great
flowering of bourgeois society and culture in the *Belle Époque*[8]), and

---

5   Ibid., 35.
6   Ibid., 35–36.
7   Ibid., 36–37.
8   See Theodor W. Adorno, "Those Twenties," in *Critical Models: Interventions and Catch-
    words*, trans. Henry Pickford (New York: Columbia University Press, 1998), 41–48,
    originally published in 1961, in which Adorno stated that, "Already in the twenties,

culminated in the crisis of war and revolution, which Badiou's account avoids — or, more precisely, evades. That is, this period raises the question of Marxism as such, and its significance in history.

## The Marxist hypothesis

A very different set of historical periodizations, and hence a different history, focused on other developments, might be opposed to Badiou's. Counter to Badiou's "communist hypothesis," which reaches back to the origins of the state in the birth of civilization millennia ago, a "Marxist hypothesis" would seek to grasp the history of the specifically modern society of capital, the different historical phases of capital as characterized by Marx's and other Marxists' accounts, beginning in the mid-19th century. But, as Nietzsche scholar Peter Preuss put it, "the 19th century had discovered history and all subsequent inquiry and education bore the stamp of this discovery. This was not simply the discovery of a set of facts about the past but the discovery of the historicity of man."[9]

Marx is the central figure in developing the critical recognition of history as an invention of the 19th century.[10] (The other names associated

---

as a consequence of the events of [the failure of the German Revolution in] 1919, the decision had fallen against that political potential that, had things gone otherwise, with great probability would have influenced developments in Russia and prevented Stalinism." So, "that the twenties were a world where 'everything may be permitted,' that is, a utopia . . . only seemed so" (43). Indeed, according to Adorno, "The heroic age . . . was actually around 1910" (41). See note 13, below.

9  Introduction to Friedrich Nietzsche, *On the Advantage and Disadvantage of History for Life* (Indianapolis: Hackett, 1980), 1.

10  See Louis Menand's 2003 Introduction to the republication of Edmund Wilson's *To the Finland Station: A Study in the Writing and Acting of History* (New York: New York Review of Books, 2003), originally published in 1940, in which Menand cites Wilson's statement that "Marx and Engels were the *philosophes* of a second Enlightenment" (xvi). Furthermore, Menand points out that,

> Marxism gave a meaning to modernity. . . . Marxism was founded on an appeal for social justice, but there were many forms that such an appeal might have taken. Its deeper attraction was the discovery of meaning, a meaning in which human beings might participate, in history itself. (xiii)

with this consciousness of history are Hegel and Nietzsche; relating these three thinkers is a deep problem, long pondered by Marxists.[11])

The Marxist hypothesis is based on Marx's theoretical and political engagement with the problem he articulated throughout his life, from the *Communist Manifesto* to *Capital*, and includes the political thought and action inspired by and seeking to follow and develop upon Marx. This problem is the historical specificity of capital — and hence of history itself. For the Marxist hypothesis is that capital is the source of what Kant called "universal history."[12]

By contrast with Badiou's history of the "communist hypothesis," a history of the "Marxist hypothesis" will be complicated, layered, not quite linear, and non-eventful. It is divided into the different periods in the history of Marxism: from 1848–95, the publication of Marx and Engels's *Communist Manifesto* to Engels's death, to 1914–19, the crisis of Marxism in war and revolution; and from 1923–40, post-Bolshevik Marxism, to 1968–89, the "New Left" and the collapse of "Communism." These are periods in the history of Marxism, which are conceived as the history of what Marx called "capital." This is the history of capital and its potential overcoming, as expressed in the history of Marxism.[13]

Such history is motivated by the need for what Karl Korsch called, in his 1923 essay "Marxism and Philosophy," the historical-materialist analysis and critique of Marxism itself, or a Marxist history and theory of Marxism.[14] This would be a history of the emergence, crisis, and decline of Marxism as expressing the possibility of getting beyond capital, as Marx

---

11  See, for example, Theodor W. Adorno, *History and Freedom: Lectures 1964–65*, ed. Rolf Tiedemann, trans. Rodney Livingstone (Cambridge: Polity, 2006).

12  Immanuel Kant, "Idea for a Universal History from a Cosmopolitan Point of View," in *Kant on History*, trans. Lewis White Beck (Indianapolis: Bobbs-Merrill, 1963), 11–25.

13  For instance, the title of Lenin's pamphlet *Imperialism: The Highest Stage of Capitalism* (1916) indicates what the historical era of "imperialism" meant to Lenin and other contemporary Marxists: the eve of revolution. The self-understanding of the Marxists of the late 19th and early 20th centuries grounded the history of Marxism itself in the history of capital, even if their propagandistic rhetoric had the unfortunate character of calling the crisis of capital expressed by Marxism "inevitable." See note 18, below.

14  See Karl Korsch, "Marxism and Philosophy," *Marxism and Philosophy*, trans. Fred Halliday (New York: Monthly Review Press, 2008). Originally published in 1923.

and the best Marxists understood this. Today, as opposed to Korsch's time in 1923, this would include consideration of the possibility that the potential Marxism expressed missed its chance, and has carried on only in a degenerate, spectral way, until passing effectively into history. That such an account is possible at all is what motivates the fundamental "hypothesis" of Marxism, or the Marxist hypothesis — the hypothesis that Marxism, as a perspective and politics, could be the vital nerve center of modern history. For Marxism is the grandest of all Grand Narratives of history, with reason. Today, the question is what *was* Marxism?

For most Marxists in the 20th century (and hence also for Badiou), the period of Marxism from 1871–1917, which saw the foundation and growth of the parties of the Second International, was the era of "revisionism," in which Marxist revolutionary politics was swamped by reformism. But this was also the period of the *struggle against* the reformist revision of Marxism by Marx and Engels's epigones, such as Bebel, Bernstein, Kautsky, and Plekhanov. This struggle against reformism was conducted by the students of these very same disciples of Marx, and involved a complex change, itself an important historical transition, in which the students were disappointed by and came to surpass their teachers.[15]

The greatest achievement of the struggle against reformism in the Second International was the Bolshevik leadership of the October Revolution, followed by the (however abortive) revolutions in Germany, Hungary and Italy, and the establishment of the Third "Communist" International.[16] The world crisis of war and revolution 1914–19 should be regarded properly as the *Götterdämmerung* of Marxism, which raised the crisis of capital to

---

15  See Lars T. Lih's extensive work on Lenin's "Kautskyism," for instance in *Lenin Rediscovered: What is to be Done? in Context* (Chicago: Haymarket Books, 2008).

16  In a portentous first footnote to his book *What is to be Done?* (1902), Lenin put it this way:

> Incidentally, in the history of modern socialism [there] is a phenomenon ... in its way very consoling, namely ... the strife of the various trends within the socialist movement. ... [In] the disputes between Lassalleans and Eisenachers, between Guesdists and Possibilists, between Fabians and Social-Democrats, and between Narodnaya Volya adherents and Social-Democrats ... really [an] international battle with socialist opportunism, [will] international revolutionary Social-Democracy ... perhaps become sufficiently strengthened to put an end to the political reaction that has long reigned in Europe?

the realm of politics, in a way not seen before or since. The crisis of Marxism 1914–19 was a civil war among Marxists. On one side, the younger generation of radicals that had risen in and ultimately split the Second International and established the Third, most prominently Lenin, Luxemburg, and Trotsky, led the greatest attempt to change the world in history. They regarded their division in Marxism as expressing the necessity of human emancipation.[17] That their attempt must be judged today a failure does not alter its profound — and profoundly enigmatic — character.[18]

---

17 See Leon Trotsky, "Art and Politics in Our Epoch," a June 18, 1938 letter to the editors of *Partisan Review*.

> Not a single progressive idea has begun with a "mass base," otherwise it would not have been a progressive idea. It is only in its last stage that the idea finds its masses – if, of course, it answers the needs of progress. All great movements have begun as "splinters" of older movements. . . . The group of Marx and Engels came into existence as a "splinter" of the Hegelian Left. The Communist [Third] International germinated during [WWI] from the "splinters" of the Social Democratic [Second] International. If these pioneers found themselves able to create a mass base, it was precisely because they did not fear isolation. They knew beforehand that the quality of their ideas would be transformed into quantity. These "splinters" . . . carried within themselves the germs of the great historical movements of tomorrow.

18 See Korsch, *Marxism and Philosophy*:

> [A] transformation and development of Marxist theory has been effected under the peculiar ideological guise of a return to the pure teaching of original or true Marxism. Yet it is easy to understand both the reasons for this guise and the real character of the process which is concealed by it. What theoreticians like Rosa Luxemburg in Germany and Lenin in Russia have done, and are doing, in the field of Marxist theory is to liberate it from the inhibiting traditions of [Social Democracy]. They thereby answer the practical needs of the new revolutionary stage of proletarian class struggle, for these traditions weighed "like a nightmare" on the brain of the working masses whose objectively revolutionary socioeconomic position no longer corresponded to these [earlier] evolutionary doctrines. The apparent revival of original Marxist theory in the Third International is simply a result of the fact that in a new revolutionary period not only the workers' movement itself, but the theoretical conceptions of communists which express it, must assume an explicitly revolutionary form. This is why large sections of the Marxist system, which seemed virtually forgotten in the final decades of the nineteenth century, have now come to life again. (67–68)

I have elaborated further on the significance of Korsch's important essay in my review of Korsch, "Marxism and Philosophy," in this volume.

The stakes of the Revolution attempted by the Second International radicals, inspired by Marx, cannot be overestimated. For Marx and his followers, the epoch of capital was both the culmination of history and marked the potential end of pre-history and the true beginning of human history, in communism.[19] As Walter Benjamin put it, "humanity is preparing to outlive culture, if need be"[20] — that is, to survive civilization, as it has been lived for an eon.[21]

## The specter of Marx

While Marx and Engels had written of the "specter" of communism, today it is the memory of Marx that haunts the world. This difference is important to register: Marx and Engels could count on a political movement — communism — that they sought to clarify and raise to self-consciousness of its

---

19  Adorno, in "Reflections on Class Theory" (originally written in 1942), provides the following unequivocally powerful interpretation of the perspective of Marx and Engels's *Communist Manifesto*:

> According to theory, history is the history of class struggles. But the concept of class is bound up with the emergence of the proletariat. . . . By extending the concept of class to prehistory, theory . . . turns against prehistory itself. . . . By exposing the historical necessity that had brought capitalism into being, political economy became the critique of history as a whole. . . . All history is the history of class struggles because it was always the same thing, namely, prehistory. (*Can One Live After Auschwitz? A Philosophical Reader*, ed. Rolf Tiedemann (Stanford: Stanford University Press, 2003), 93–94.)

20  Walter Benjamin, "Experience and Poverty," in *Selected Writings*, vol. 2 *1927–34* (Cambridge, MA: Harvard University Press, 1999), 735. Originally published in 1933.

21  The term used to describe this effect is the "Anthropocene." Jeffrey Sachs, in the second of his 2007 Reith Lectures, "Survival in the Anthropocene" (Peking University, Beijing, April 18, 2007), characterized it this way:

> "The Anthropocene" – a term that is spectacularly vivid, a term invented by one of the great scientists of our age, Paul Crutzen, to signify the fact that human beings for the first time have taken hold not only of the economy and of population dynamics, but of the planet's physical systems, Anthropocene meaning human-created era of Earth's history. The geologists call our time the Holocene – the period of the last thirteen thousand years or so since the last Ice Age – but Crutzen wisely and perhaps shockingly noted that the last two hundred years are really a unique era, not only in human history but in the Earth's physical history as well.

historical significance. Today, by contrast, we need to remember not the historical political movement so much as the form of critical consciousness given expression in Marxism. This must be traced back to the thought and political action of Marx himself.

If Marx is mistaken for an affirmer and promulgator of "communism" as opposed to what he actually was, its most incisive critic (from within), we risk forgetting the most important if fragile achievement of history: the consciousness of potential in capital. As Marx wrote early on, in an 1843 letter to Arnold Ruge that called for the "ruthless criticism of everything existing," "Communism is a dogmatic abstraction and ... only a particular manifestation of the humanistic principle and is infected by its opposite, private property."[22]

The potential for emancipated humanity expressed in communism that Marx recognized in the modern history of capital is not assimilable without remainder to pre- or non-Marxian socialism. Marx's thought and politics are not continuous with the Spartacus slave revolt against Rome or the teachings of the Apostles — or with the radical egalitarianism of the Protestants or the Jacobins. As Marx put it, "*Communism* is the necessary form and the dynamic principle of the immediate future, but communism as such is not the goal of human development, the form of human society."[23] Communism, as a form of discontent in capital, thus demanded critical clarification of its own meaning, and not one-sided endorsement. For Marx thought that communism was a means and not an end in itself.

So what does it mean that, today, we continue, politically, to have "communism" — in Badiou's sense of demands for "radical democratic equality" — but not "Marxism?" Badiou's periodization of the history of modern communism in the history of civilization dissolves Marxism into one of its constituent parts – or at least submerges it in this history. But Marx sought, in his own thought and politics, to comprehend and

---

22 "For the ruthless criticism of everything existing," letter to Arnold Ruge (September, 1843), in *Marx-Engels Reader*, 2nd edition, ed. Robert C. Tucker (New York: Norton, 1978), 12–15.
23 *Economic and Philosophic Manuscripts of 1844*, in *Marx-Engels Reader* (New York: Norton, 1978), 93.

transcend the specifically modern phenomenon of communism, that is, the modern social-democratic workers' movement emerging in the 19th century, as a constituent of *capital*, as a historically specific form of humanity. So, what would it mean, today, to view the history of the modern society of capital through the figure of Marx? The possibility of such a project is the Marxist hypothesis.

## "Marx-ism"

It goes a long way in making sense of the most important historical figures of communism after Marx, such as Engels, Kautsky, Plekhanov, Lenin, Luxemburg, Trotsky, Bukharin, Lukács, Stalin, and Mao, among others, to evaluate them as followers of Marx. It is significant that they themselves sought to justify their own political thought and action in such terms — and were regarded for this by their political opponents as sectarian dogmatists, disciples of Marxism as a religion. But how did they think that they were following Marx? What are we to make of the most significant and profound political movement of the last two centuries, calling itself "Marxist," and led by people who, in debate, never ceased to quote Marx at each other? What has been puzzled over in such disputes, and what were — and are still, potentially — the political consequences of such disagreement over the meaning of Marx?

Certainly, Marxism has been disparaged as a religion, and Marx as a prophet. (For instance, Leszek Kolakowski dismissed Marxism as the "farcical aspect of human bondage."[24]) But what of Marx as a philosopher? If Marx has been widely discredited as a political thinker, nevertheless, in 2005, for instance, a survey of BBC listeners[25] polled Marx as the "greatest philosopher of all time," well ahead of Socrates, Kant, Nietzsche, and others. On the face of it, this does not seem like a particularly plausible judgment of Marx, either in terms of his own thinking and practice or of "philosophy" as a discipline, unless Marx's philosophy is understood as indicating how we have not yet overcome the problems he identified

---

24 *Main Currents in Marxism* (New York: Norton, 2005), 1212.
25 "Marx wins In Our Time's Greatest Philosopher vote" (July 13, 2005).

in modern society.[26] As far as the reputation of Marx as a thinker is concerned, we seem to have been left with "Marxism" but without Marx's own "communist" politics: "Marxism" has survived as an "analysis," but without clear practical importance; "communism" has survived as an ethic without effective politics. How might we make sense of this?

The Marxist hypothesis is that the relation between Marx and "communism" needs to be posed again, but in decidedly non-traditional ways, casting the history of Marxism in a critical light. For it is not that communism found a respected comrade in Marx — perhaps more (or less) estimable than others — but that Marx's thought and political action form an irreducibly singular model that can yet task us, and to which we must still aspire. Hence, the continued potential purchase of "Marx-ism." The question is not, as Badiou would have it, what is the future of communism, but of Marx.

To address any potential future of Marxism, it is necessary to revisit Marx's own Marxism and its implications.

### Marx in 1848

Marx pointed out about the revolution in Germany, in which he immediately involved himself after writing the *Manifesto*, that the capitalists were more afraid of the workers asserting their bourgeois rights than they were of the Prussian state taking away theirs. This was not because of a conflicting class interest between the capitalists and Junkers (Prussian landed aristocracy), but rather because of the emerging authoritarianism in post-Industrial Revolution capital, at a global scale. For such authoritarianism was also characteristic of the revolution of 1848 in France, in which Napoleon's nephew Louis Bonaparte's rule, as the first elected President of the Second Republic (1848–52), and then, after his *coup d'etat*, as Emperor

---

26 See Robert Pippin, "*Critical Inquiry* and Critical Theory: A Short History of Nonbeing," *Critical Inquiry* 30, no. 2 (Winter 2004), 424–428. Pippin wrote that,

> [T]he dim understanding we have of the post-Kantian situation with respect to, let's say, "the necessary conditions for the possibility of what isn't" . . . is what I wanted to suggest. I'm not sure it will get us anywhere. Philosophy rarely does. Perhaps it exists to remind us that we haven't gotten anywhere. (428)

of the Second Empire (1852–70), could not be characterized as expressing the interest of some *non*-bourgeois class (the "peasants," whom Marx
insisted on calling, pointedly, "petit bourgeois"), but rather of *all* the classes
of bourgeois society, including the "lumpenproletariat," in crisis by the
mid-19th century.[27] As Marx put it mordantly, in *The Eighteenth Brumaire
of Louis Bonaparte* (1852), bourgeois fanatics for order were shot down on
their balconies in the name of defense of the social order.[28] The late 19th
century rule of Napoleon III and Bismarck — and Disraeli — mirrored
each other. Marx analyzed the authoritarianism of post-1848 society, in
which the state seems to rise over civil life, as a situation in which the bourgeoisie were no longer and the proletariat not yet able to master capital.[29]
This was the crisis of bourgeois society Marx recognized. Badiou's account,
on the other hand, is rather a history of ruling class power opposed by the
resistance of the oppressed. As early as 1848 Marx was not a theorist of
*classes* but *capital*, of which modern socio-political classes were "phantas-
magorical" projections.[30] Marx sought to situate, not capital in the history
of class struggle, but history in capital,[31] to which social struggles and their
history were subordinate.[32]

---

27  See *The Class Struggles in France 1848–50* (originally published in 1850) and *The Eighteenth Brumaire of Louis Bonaparte* (originally published in 1852).
28  *Eighteenth Brumaire*, in *Marx-Engels Reader*:

Every demand of the simplest bourgeois financial reform, of the most ordinary
liberalism, of the most formal republicanism, of the most insipid democracy, is
simultaneously castigated as an "attempt on society" and stigmatized as "socialism." … Bourgeois fanatics for order are shot down on their balconies by mobs of
drunken soldiers, their domestic sanctuaries profaned … in the name of property,
of family … and of order. … Finally, the scum of bourgeois society forms … the
"saviour of society." (602–603)
29  Engels summed this up well in his 1891 Introduction to Marx, *The Civil War in France*
(1871), in *Marx-Engels Reader*, 620.
30  See Marx, *Capital: A Critique of Political Economy*, trans. Ben Fowkes (London: Penguin, 1990), 165.
31  See my "Capital in History: The need for a Marxian philosophy of history of the Left,"
*Platypus Review* 7 (October 2008), in this volume.
32  See Platypus Historians Group, "Introduction to the history of the Left: Changes in the
meaning of class struggles," *Platypus Review* 3 (March 2008).

## Capitalism, communism, and the "state of nature"

Jean-Jacques Rousseau had raised a hypothetical "state of nature" in order to throw contemporary society into critical relief. In so doing, Rousseau sought to bring society closer to a "state of nature." Liberal, bourgeois society was a model and an aspiration for Rousseau. For Rousseau, it was human "nature" to be free.[33] Humans achieved a higher "civil liberty" of "moral freedom" in society than they could enjoy as animals, with mere "physical" freedom in nature. Indeed, as animals, humans are not free, but rather slaves to their natural needs and instincts. Only in society could freedom be achieved, and humans free themselves from their natural, animal condition.[34] When Rousseau was writing, in the mid-18th century, the promise of freedom in bourgeois society was still on the horizon. Bourgeois society aspired to proximity to the "state of nature" in the sense of bringing humanity, both individually and collectively, closer to its potential, to better realize its freedom. With Marx, communism, too, aimed for the realization of this potential. The imagination of a "primitive communism," closer to a "state of nature" of unspoiled human potential, recapitulated the Rousseauian vision of bourgeois society as emancipation. But, in capitalism, bourgeois society had come to violate its own promised potential. It had become a "state of nature," not in Rousseau's sense, but rather according to Hobbes, a "war of all against all" — a conception that Rousseau had critiqued. Society was not to be the suspension of hostilities, but the realization of freedom. Moreover, humanity in society exhibited a "general will," not reducible to

---

33  As James Miller, author of *The Passion of Michel Foucault* (2000), put it in his 1992 introduction to Rousseau's *Discourse on the Origin of Inequality* (Indianapolis: Hackett, 1992),

>  The principle of freedom and its corollary, "perfectibility" . . . suggest that the possibilities for being human are both multiple and, literally, endless. . . . Contemporaries like Kant well understood the novelty and radical implications of Rousseau's new principle of freedom [and] appreciated his unusual stress on history as the site where the true nature of our species is simultaneously realized and perverted, revealed and distorted. A new way of thinking about the human condition had appeared. . . . As Hegel put it, "The principle of freedom dawned on the world in Rousseau, and gave infinite strength to man, who thus apprehended himself as infinite." (xv)

34  See Rousseau, *The Social Contract*, Ch. 8 "Civil Society," translated by Maurice Cranston (London: Penguin, 1968), 64–65. Originally published in 1762.

its individual members: more than the sum of its parts. Not a Leviathan, but a "second nature," a rebirth of potential, both collectively and individually. Human nature found the realization of its freedom in society, but humans were free to develop and transform themselves, for good or ill. To bring society closer to the "state of nature," then, was to allow humanity's potential to be better realized. Communism, according to Marx, was to follow Rousseau, not Hobbes, in realizing bourgeois society's aspirations and potential. But, first, communism had to be clear about its aims.

## Communism: not opposed to, but in, through, and beyond the bourgeois society of capital

The Marxist hypothesis is that Marx's thought and politics correspond to a moment of profound transformation in the history of modern society, indeed, in the history of humanity: the rise of "industrial capital" and of the concomitant "social-democratic" workers' movement that attended this change. This was expressed in the workers' demand for *social* democracy, which Marx thought needed to be raised to greater self-consciousness to achieve its aims.[35] Marx characterized the moment of industrial capital as marking the crisis in modern society — or even, an event and crisis in "natural history"[36] — in which humanity faced the choice, as Luxemburg put it (echoing Engels) of "socialism or barbarism."[37] This was because classical bourgeois forms of politics that had emerged in the preceding era of the rise of manufacturing capital in the 17th and 18th centuries, liberalism and democracy, proved to be inadequate to the problems and tasks of modern society since the 19th century — Marx's moment. With Marx, humanity

---

35  See Marx, "For the ruthless criticism of everything existing."

36  See note 21, above. See also Adorno, "The Idea of Natural History" (originally written in 1932), trans. Robert Hullot-Kentor, *Telos* 57 (1985): "[I]t is not a question of completing one theory by another, but of the immanent interpretation of a theory. I submit myself, so to speak, to the authority of the materialist dialectic" (124).

37  See Luxemburg, *The Crisis in German Social Democracy* (AKA *The Junius Pamphlet*, originally published in 1915).

faces a new, unforeseen task. However, unfulfilled, this task has fallen into neglect today.[38]

In the transformed circumstance of capital, liberalism and democracy became *necessary* precisely in their *impossibility*, and thus pointed to their "dialectical" *Aufhebung* — completion and transcendence through negation, or self-overcoming.[39] Liberalism and democracy became not only mutually contradictory but each became self-contradictory in capital. It is thus not a matter of communism *versus* liberal democracy — as Badiou and Žižek take it to be. Communism was, for Marx, the political movement that pointed to the possibility of overcoming the necessity of liberalism and democracy, or the transcending of the need for "bourgeois" politics per se. But this was to be achieved through the politics of the demands for the *bourgeois* rights of the working class. Marx regarded the socialism and communism that had emerged in his time as expressing a late, and hence self-contradictory and potentially incoherent form of bourgeois radicalism — expressing the *radicalization* of bourgeois society — but that demanded redemption. Marx sought the potential in capital of going beyond demands for greater liberalism and democracy. Subsequent "communism" lost sight of Marx on this, and disintegrated into the 20th century antinomy of socialism and liberalism.[40] The Marxist hypothesis is that Marx recognized

---

38  See Korsch, *Marxism and Philosophy*:

> [Marx wrote, in the Preface to *A Contribution to the Critique of Political Economy* (1859), that] "[Humanity] always sets itself only such problems as it can solve; since, looking at the matter more closely it will always be found that the problem itself arises only when the material conditions for its solution are already present or are at least understood to be in the process of emergence." This dictum is not affected by the fact that a problem which supersedes present relations may have been formulated in an anterior epoch. (58)

39  On this point, see some of Marx's earliest writings, which provided the points of departure for his more mature work, such as "Contribution to the Critique of Hegel's *Philosophy of Right*" (1843), "On [Bruno Bauer's] *The Jewish Question*" (1843), and *The Poverty of Philosophy* (1847).

40  But, for Marx and Engels, there was no necessary contradiction between the freedom of the individual and that of the collective, or, in this sense, between liberalism and socialism: "In place of the old bourgeois society, with its classes and class antagonisms, we shall have an association, in which *the free development of each is the condition for the free development of all*" (*Manifesto of the Communist Party*, in *Marx-Engels Reader*, 491).

the possibility, not of opposition, but of a qualitative transformation, in, through, and beyond bourgeois society.

Originally published in *Platypus Review* 29 (November 2010)

---

For further discussion of this antinomic degeneration and disintegration of the original Marxian perspective, see my "1917" in this volume. See also my "Friedrich Hayek and the legacy of Milton Friedman: Neo-liberalism and the question of freedom (in part, a response to Naomi Klein)," and also my "Obama and Clinton: 'Third Way' politics and the 'Left,'" both in *Death of the Millennial Left: Interventions 2006–2022*.

# Badiou's "communism"
# — a gerontic disorder

Perhaps the most condemnatory thing that could be said of Badiou's "communism" was something Badiou himself wrote, when he defined "communism" as a "Kantian regulatory idea," a norm to be aspired to, rather than a concrete reality to be achieved. This not only besmirched the historical Marxist idea of "communism," but also Kant! For Kant addressed freedom as something that could and should be, not as a utopia. And Marx remained deeply engaged in practical politics. Leon Trotsky wrote, more than a hundred years ago, after the 1905 Russian Revolution, that "Marxism converted socialism into a science, but this does not prevent some 'Marxists' from converting Marxism into a Utopia." Trotsky also wrote that, "[I]n academies . . . it might be possible artificially to detain the proletariat for fifty, a hundred or five hundred years, but in the course of all-round life in capitalist society, on the basis of unceasing class struggle[,] . . . [t]he growth of the consciousness of the proletariat transforms this class struggle, gives it a deeper and more purposeful character."[1] Trotsky was not a utopian any more than Kant or Marx were.

However, as we know, such "unceasing class struggle" that Trotsky had in mind, which could "transform" the "consciousness of the proletariat" and potentially "give it a deeper and more purposeful character," is precisely what the world has been missing, for at least a generation. The Marxist vision for proletarian socialism has passed, almost completely into oblivion. Badiou's late redefinition of "communism" is a response — an adaptation — to this historical reality. Indeed, Trotsky was writing at the crest of 2nd International Marxism, which developed in the period from

---

1 *Results and Prospects* (1906).

1871 to 1917, whose history Badiou deliberately seeks to bury. Badiou characterizes this period, like our own, as an "interval," in which "the communist hypothesis was declared to be untenable," "with the adversary in the ascendant."[2] What is the basis of Badiou's judgment of this period, 1871 to 1917, in which, not only did bourgeois society go through its last great flowering, in the *Belle Époque*, but Marxism flourished as an international workers' movement, commanding a dedication to socialist revolution by millions in the core capitalist countries? The period between the Paris Commune and the October Revolution was *not* in any way like ours; it was not cynical, but optimistic in the sense of historical mission and the real potential of human progress. Badiou shares the skepticism that has developed regarding such historical potential. Indeed, we can say that Badiou is typical of the 1960s-era New Left in this regard. Badiou cannot recognize 2nd Intl. Marxism as an advance. Moreover, Badiou is, in Trotsky's sense, "academic," despite his avowed intentions. The last thing Badiou imagines is that he has conceded. Badiou's entire philosophy was developed out of concern for "fidelity," resisting the apostasies of the 1968 generation in the decades that followed. — The question is, to what does Badiou claim fidelity? Certainly not Marxism.

What has sanctioned Badiou to bury the admittedly obscure history of the first wave of Marxism in the 2nd Intl., today? And why does Badiou find an affinity in our moment with that of the pre-WWI world, which otherwise seems so unlikely? In certain respects, Badiou is rather optimistic in finding such an affinity, hoping that today we are in a period of preparation for the realization of more radical social transformation — "revolution" — down the road. Badiou thus tries to keep fidelity to "the revolution" in his estimation of the present. But which "revolution?" Badiou is clear that his model for revolution is May 1968 in France and the contemporaneous Great Proletarian Cultural Revolution in China. Presumably, in the latter case, this means a commitment to Mao and "Marxism-Leninism." But, beneath this, there is a certain unmistakable pessimism to the characterization of the formative era of Lenin's Marxism in the 2nd Intl., as being, like ours, one of conservative reaction. — Was the growth of Marxism in

---

2    *The Communist Hypothesis* (London: Verso, 2010), 36–7.

the late 19th and early 20th centuries really a retreat, after the defeat of the Paris Commune? Or, has Badiou mistaken one revolution for another? Badiou has maintained fidelity, not to "communism," in Marx's sense, but rather to "democracy," that is, the eternal *bourgeois* revolution. It is thus significant that Badiou dates modern communism, not to Marx in 1848, but to the Jacobins in 1792. This obscures the history that came between.

The truth is that Badiou's "communism" is deeply anti-Marxist. Not merely non-Marxist, in the sense of what it tends to leave out, but actually hostile to historical Marxism. Perhaps this is unremarkable. Perhaps it is not a problem in itself. But it may bear some inquiry into the potential consequences that might flow from this. Perhaps Badiou is quietly acknowledging that Marxism may have become an obstacle to the kind of social change that, in his estimation, is possible and desirable — and necessary. That is a real question. Does Marxism speak to the needs of the present? But to consider this — to consider what Badiou may have to offer as an alternative to Marxism — we must address what Badiou means by "communism."

Badiou defines communism as "radical democratic equality." The "hypothesis" that motivates communism, according to Badiou, is that,

> the logic of class — the fundamental subordination of labour to a dominant class, the arrangement that has persisted since Antiquity — is not inevitable; it can be overcome.... [A] different collective organization is practicable, one that will eliminate the inequality of wealth and even the division of labour.... The existence of a coercive state, separate from civil society, will no longer appear a necessity: a long process of reorganization based on a free association of producers will see it withering away.[3]

Furthermore,

> As a pure Idea of equality, the communist hypothesis has no doubt existed since the beginnings of the state. As soon as mass action opposes state coercion in the name of egalitarian

---

3   Ibid., 34–5

justice, rudiments or fragments of the hypothesis start to appear. Popular revolts — the slaves led by Spartacus, the peasants led by Müntzer — might be identified as practical examples of this "communist invariant." With the French Revolution, the communist hypothesis then inaugurates the epoch of political modernity.[4]

However, the potential for emancipated humanity expressed in communism that Marx recognized in the modern history of capital is not assimilable without remainder to pre- or non-Marxian socialism. Marx's thought and politics are not continuous with the Spartacus slave revolt against Rome or the teachings of the Apostles — or with the radical egalitarianism of the Protestants or the Jacobins. So what was Marx's distinct contribution? As Marx put it, "*Communism* is the necessary form and the dynamic principle of the immediate future, but communism as such is not the goal of human development, the form of human society."[5] This was because, according to Marx, "Communism is a dogmatic abstraction and . . . only a particular manifestation of the humanistic principle and is infected by its opposite, private property."[6] Marx was not the preeminent communist of his time but rather its critic, seeking to push it further. The best Marxists who followed, such as Lenin, Luxemburg and Trotsky, similarly sought to push their respective political movement of "revolutionary social democracy" in the 2nd Intl. further. In so doing, they revealed and grappled with the form of capital of their moment in history, what they called "imperialism," seeking to make it into capital's "highest" and last stage, the eve of revolution. Badiou, by contrast, addresses inequality as a timeless, perennial problem. He thus departs fundamentally from Marx and Marxism, and liquidates the revolution of capital.

Badiou conceives of the relation between freedom and equality as an ontological one, in the mathematical terms of set theory, transhistoricizing

---

4    Ibid., 35.

5    *Economic and Philosophic Manuscripts of 1844*, in *Marx-Engels Reader*, 2nd edition, ed. Robert C. Tucker (New York: Norton, 1978), 93.

6    "For the ruthless criticism of everything existing," letter to Arnold Ruge (September, 1843), in *Marx-Engels Reader* (New York: Norton, 1978), 12–15.

it. Badiou's background is in Lacanian and Althusserian "post-structuralist" French thought, in common with other prominent New Left-era thinkers — and former students of Louis Althusser — such as Étienne Balibar and Jacques Rancière. Althusser found, in the Russian and Chinese Revolutions, a salutary challenge to the notion of the Hegelian "logic of history," that revolutionary change could and indeed did happen as a matter of contingency. Althusser took great inspiration from Mao in China and Lenin in Russia for advancing the possibility of emancipation against a passive expectancy of automatic evolution in the historical process of capital. For Badiou, this means that emancipation must be conceived of as an "event," which involves a fundamental reconsideration of ontology. Badiou does not conceive of the transformation of the capitalist mode of production that would allow for overcoming the socially pernicious aspects of specifically capitalist forms of inequality. By contrast, Marx looked forward to the potential for overcoming the conditions of possibility for the reproduction of capitalist class dynamics in the mode of production itself: capital's overcoming of the need to accumulate the value of surplus labor-time. Marx saw the historical potential to overcome this socially mediating aspect of labor, expressed, for instance, in automated machine production. However, Marx also foresaw that, short of socialism, the drive to accumulate surplus-value results in producing a surplus population, an "industrial reserve army" of potential "workers" who thus remain vulnerable to exploitation. A politics based only in their "democratic" discontents can result, not in the overcoming of the social need for labor, but in the (capitalist) demand for more labor, the demand to be put to work. Or, as Max Horkheimer, director of the Marxist Frankfurt Institute for Social Research, put it, machines "have made not work but the workers superfluous."[7] Marx anticipated this when he warned that realization of the socialist demand to abolish "private property" would (merely) make society as a whole into one giant capitalist dominating its members. Marx even went so far as to analogize this with socialist calls to abolish marriage as a "bourgeois" institution, which he

---

7    "The authoritarian state," in *The Essential Frankfurt School Reader*, ed. Andrew Arato and Eike Gebhardt (New York: Continuum, 1985), 95.

said would result only in universal prostitution — indeed, that capitalism was already bringing this about.[8]

For Marx, elimination of a separate capitalist class would not in itself be emancipatory unless a transformation in the "mode of production" and its social relations came about. Marx did not think that the capitalists were the cause, but the effect of capital, calling them its "character masks." Nonetheless, Marx endorsed, however critically, the traditional socialist demand to abolish private property and "expropriate the expropriators," regarding this as a necessary *first step*: necessary, but not sufficient, to realize a society beyond the mode of production and social relations of capital. As Lenin underscored this, in *The State and Revolution*, on the eve of the October 1917 Revolution in Russia, such social relations of bourgeois society, namely, the mutual exchange of labor as the form of social solidarity in capital, could only be transformed gradually and thus "wither away," and not be abolished and replaced at a stroke. The proletarian socialist revolution was supposed to open the door to this transformation. But, since then, the history of the Russian and Chinese Revolutions showed another potential, that is, the reconstitution of capital, under the guise of "socialism." Marx had already foreseen such a possibility in the limited consciousness of his socialist and communist contemporaries of the 19th century, and he criticized them "ruthlessly" for this. Marx and Lenin recognized a problem in "socialism" itself that their supposed followers have neglected or avoided.

All this remains hidden to Badiou. But it was precisely this Marxist approach to capital as a "mode of production," or form of society, that distinguishes Marx from other socialists or communists, and motivated revolutionaries who followed Marx, such as Lenin, maintaining that Marxism pursued the possibility of overcoming capital "on the basis of capitalism" itself. Badiou situates emancipatory possibilities rather atavistically, in a pre-historical ontology, to which the philosophy of mathematics — for instance, the question of "number and numbers" (the title of one of his books)[9] — can be an adequate guide. For Badiou, in a procedure that recalls a self-criticism session or assembly at a "reeducation" camp, matter

---

8   *Economic and Philosophic Manuscripts of 1844*, op. cit., 83.
9   Trans. Robin MacKay (Cambridge: Polity Press, 2008). Originally published 1990.

itself, in its open-ended recombinations, poses the solution to what Marx called "communism," the "riddle of history." Each element must be broken down to its radical potentiality for permutation — for instance, in the Maoist "revolutionary people," for emancipatory change to take place. It is not for nothing that Badiou conceives of revolution not as a process but an event, or, that his conception of "process" is founded on a conception of the "event." On the other hand, Badiou finds Marxists such as Lenin (and Marx himself) conceding to the existing social hierarchies and thus betraying the "idea of communism," for instance in the party-state, which Badiou regards in retrospect as a "failed experiment." Thus, Badiou.

What of Marx and Marxism? Marx distinguished capitalist inequality from that of the traditional caste system that had characterized civilization for millennia before the emergence of bourgeois society in the post-Renaissance world. As Adorno pointed out, to call all of history the "history of class struggles" was to indict all of ("recorded") history, and to thus consign it to the mere "pre-history" of authentic humanity. But this humanity was itself historically specific, and emergent — to the era of capital. Just as traditional inequality was not the *cause* of the form of community that the ancients regarded as being divine in origin, capitalist inequality was not the cause but the *effect*, the product of the cosmos of capital. Marx's magnum opus, *Capital*, explored how the post-Industrial Revolution society of capital produced a new form of inequality, between capitalist and worker, but one liable to be cast and responded to in the form of the original Revolt of the Third Estate that had ushered in modern bourgeois society in the 17th and 18th centuries. Marx found an important disparity — a self-contradiction — to have developed between the political aspirations of the subjects of capital, for "social democracy," and the potential of capital to go beyond bourgeois society and its forms of politics — liberalism and democracy. This did not make Marx and those who followed him illiberal or anti-democratic, but they did regard liberalism and democracy — the combined libertarian and social-egalitarian impulses in modern politics — as *means* and not *ends* in and of themselves. This is because they regarded capitalism itself as a process and not merely a state of being. Marx and his best followers, such as Lenin, looked forward not merely to more liberalism and more democracy, but to the potential transcendence of the *need* for both liberalism and democracy, an "end" to politics as presently practiced. But not all at once, and not by denying them in the present. Capital is not an eternal event of inequality that needs to be met with the event of revolution. Badiou does not deny liberalism and democracy, but rather unconsciously reaffirms their present, bourgeois forms, at a deeper and more obscure level. Badiou's ontology of "radical egalitarian democracy," provides not a critical recognition, but a philosophical affirmation of the way bourgeois society already proceeds, however contradictorily. Badiou mystifies.

The challenge is to recognize the symptomatic character of liberalism and democracy in the crisis of capital, as it had developed in the 19th century, setting the stage for the history that came later. But such symptomology was not to be "cured" in the sense of elimination, but rather undergone and worked through — as Nietzsche put it, modernity is an "illness, but the way pregnancy is an illness," bringing forth new life.[10] The problem, as Marx recognized it, was that, by the mid-19th century, when bourgeois society entered into crisis, after the Industrial Revolution, and became "proletarianized," humanity faced a situation in which, as Engels later described it, the capitalists were no longer and the workers not yet able to master the society of capital. Marx regarded this as the source of the authoritarianism of the modern, capitalist (nation-)state, despite the promises of classical bourgeois liberalism for a minimal state and a free, cosmopolitan civil society that would, for instance, reduce legislatures to, at most, sites of public debate and political recognition of social facts already accomplished on the ground — what Kant, for one, expected. But the bourgeoisie could no longer and the proletariat not yet rule modern society. The genie of capital had been let loose. The historical task of emancipating humanity had thus fallen from the bourgeois to the proletarian members of society. Marxists have recognized that this is the situation in which the world has remained stuck ever since then — ever since the failed "social democratic" Revolutions of 1848, on the eve of which Marx and Engels had published their inaugural *Manifesto*. For Marx, the demand for "social democracy" was part of the history of capital, to be worked through "immanently" and transcended. But none of this registers for Badiou. Marx

---

10  See *On the Genealogy of Morals: A Polemic* (1887), part II, sections 16–19.

marked a potential turning point for humanity; he was not merely one in a chain of prophets reaching back for thousands of years. He was thinker and political actor for our, modern time.

The cost of liquidating the specific history of capital — its peculiar constraint on society and its potential beyond itself — is Badiou's reduction of "communism" to the perennial complaint of the subaltern, the millennial dream of social equality, as a specter haunting the world that has more in common with eschatological "justice," posed by religion at the end of time, than with the pathology of the modern, bourgeois world of capital, in which humanity actually suffers today. We must awaken from this nightmare — the vain wish that things be otherwise — of the oppressed. For we are not only oppressed, but *tasked* by capital.

Nevertheless, the failure of historical Marxism has made Badiou an evidently adequate symptomatic expression of our time — its confusion and diminished expectations, well shy of the epochal transformation that had motivated Marx and the best Marxists, historically. We must remember Marxism, so we can forget Badiou: forget the time that made such ideology — such naturalization, indeed ontologization — of defeat so appealing, and finally consign it, where it belongs, to pre-history.

Presented on a panel with Nayi Duniya (*Demarcations* journal), co-author of "Alain Badiou's 'Politics of Emancipation': A Communism Locked Within the Confines of the Bourgeois World," and Bruno Bosteels (Cornell University) at the Left Forum 2011, Pace University, New York, March 19, 2011; and on the panel "Badiou and post-Maoism: Marxism and communism today," with Mike Ely, Joseph Ramsey and John Steele at the third annual Platypus Affiliated Society International Convention, the School of the Art Institute of Chicago, April 30, 2011.

# Adorno's Leninism

## Adorno's political relevance

Theodor W. Adorno, who was born in 1903 and lived until 1969, has a continuing purchase on problems of politics on the Left by virtue of his critical engagement with two crucial periods in the history of the Left: the 1930s "Old" Left and the 1960s "New Left." Adorno's critical theory, spanning this historical interval of the mid-20th century, can help make sense of the problems of the combined and ramified legacy of both periods.

Adorno is the key thinker for understanding 20th century Marxism and its discontents. As T. J. Clark has put it, Adorno "[spent a lifetime] building ever more elaborate conceptual trenches to outflank the Third International."[1] The period of Adorno's life, coming of age in the 1920s, in the wake of the failed international anti-capitalist revolution that had opened in Russia in 1917 and continued but was defeated in Germany, Hungary and Italy in 1919, and living through the darkest periods of fascism and war in the mid-20th century to the end of the 1960s, profoundly informed his critical theory. As he put it in the introduction to the last collection of his essays he edited for publication before he died, he sought to bring together "philosophical speculation and drastic experience."[2] Adorno reflected on his "drastic" historical experience through the immanent critique, the critique from within, of Marxism. Adorno thought Marxism had failed as an emancipatory politics but still demanded redemption, and that this could be achieved only on the basis of Marxism itself. Adorno's critical theory was a Marxist critique of Marxism, and as such reveals key aspects of Marxism that had otherwise

---

1    In "Should Benjamin Have Read Marx?" *Boundary* 30, no. 1 (Spring 2003).
2    Introduction to *Catchwords* [June 1969] in *Critical Models: Interventions and Catchwords*, trans. Henry W. Pickford (New York: Columbia University Press, 1998), 126.

become buried, as a function of the degenerations Marxism suffered from the 1930s through the 1960s. Several of Adorno's writings, from the 1930s–40s and the 1960s, illustrate the abiding concerns of his critical theory throughout this period.

In the late 1920s, the director of the Frankfurt Institute for Social Research Max Horkheimer wrote an aphorism titled "The Little Man and the Philosophy of Freedom" that is an excellent conspectus on the politics of Marxism.[3]

The "Marxist clarification of the concept of freedom" that Horkheimer calls for is the usually neglected aspect of Marxism. Marxism is usually regarded as an ideology of material redistribution or "social justice," championing the working class and other oppressed groups, where it should be seen as a philosophy of freedom.

There is a fundamentally different problem at stake in either regarding capitalism as a materially oppressive force, as a problem of exploitation, or as a problem of human freedom. The question of freedom raises the issue of possibilities for radical social-historical transformation, which was central to Adorno's thought. Whereas by the 1930s, with the triumph of Stalinist and social-democratic reformist politics in the workers' movement, on the defensive against fascism, Marxism had degenerated into an ideology merely affirming the interests of the working class, Marx himself had started out with a perspective on what he called the necessity of the working class's own self-abolition.[4]

Marx inquired into the potential overcoming of historical conditions of possibility for labor as the justification for social existence, which is how he understood capitalist society. Marx's point was to elucidate the possibilities for overcoming labor as a social form. But Marx thought that this could only happen in and through the working class's own political activity. How was it possible that the working class would abolish itself?

---

3   In *Dawn and Decline: Notes 1926-31 and 1950-1969*, trans. Michael Shaw (New York: Continuum, 1978), 50–52.

4   *Critique of Hegel's Philosophy of Right*, 1843.

## Politics not pre-figurative

Mahatma Gandhi said, "Be the change you want to see in the world." This ethic of "pre-figuration," the attempt to personally embody the principles of an emancipated world, was the classic expression of the moral problem of politics in service of radical social change in the 20th century. During the mid-20th century Cold War between the "liberal-democratic" West led by the United States and the Soviet Union, otherwise known as the Union of Workers' Councils Socialist Republics, the contrasting examples of Gandhi, leader of non-violent resistance to British colonialism in India, and Lenin, leader of the October 1917 Bolshevik Revolution in Russia and of the international Communist movement inspired by it, were widely used to pose two very different models for understanding the politics of emancipation. One was seen as ethical, remaining true to its intentions, while the other was not. Why would Adorno, like any Marxist, have chosen Lenin over Gandhi? Adorno's understanding of capitalism, what constituted it and what allowed it to reproduce itself as a social form, informed what he thought would be necessary, in theory and practice, to actually overcome it, in freedom.

Adorno, as a Marxist critical theorist, followed the discussion by Leon Trotsky, who had been the 26 year-old leader of the Petersburg Soviet or Workers' Council during the 1905 Revolution in Russia, of the "pre-requisites of socialism" in his 1906 pamphlet *Results and Prospects*, where he wrote about the problem of achieving what he called "socialist psychology," as follows:

> Marxism converted socialism into a science, but this does not prevent some "Marxists" from converting Marxism into a Utopia. . . .
>
> [M]any socialist ideologues (ideologues in the bad sense of the word — those who stand everything on its head) speak of preparing the proletariat for socialism in the sense of its being morally regenerated. The proletariat, and even "humanity" in general, must first of all cast out its old egoistical nature, and altruism must become predominant in social life, etc. As

we are as yet far from such a state of affairs, and "human nature" changes very slowly, socialism is put off for several centuries. Such a point of view probably seems very realistic and evolutionary, and so forth, but as a matter of fact it is really nothing but shallow moralizing.

It is assumed that a socialist psychology must be developed before the coming of socialism, in other words that it is possible for the masses to acquire a socialist psychology under capitalism. One must not confuse here the conscious striving towards socialism with socialist psychology. The latter presupposes the absence of egotistical motives in economic life; whereas the striving towards socialism and the struggle for it arise from the class psychology of the proletariat. However many points of contact there may be between the class psychology of the proletariat and classless socialist psychology, nevertheless a deep chasm divides them.

The joint struggle against exploitation engenders splendid shoots of idealism, comradely solidarity and self-sacrifice, but at the same time the individual struggle for existence, the ever-yawning abyss of poverty, the differentiation in the ranks of the workers themselves, the pressure of the ignorant masses from below, and the corrupting influence of the bourgeois parties do not permit these splendid shoots to develop fully. For all that, in spite of his remaining philistinely egoistic, and without his exceeding in "human" worth the average representative of the bourgeois classes, the average worker knows from experience that *his simplest requirements and natural desires can be satisfied only on the ruins of the capitalist system.*

The idealists picture the distant future generation which shall have become worthy of socialism exactly as Christians picture the members of the first Christian communes.

Whatever the psychology of the first proselytes of Christianity may have been — we know from the Acts of the Apostles of cases of embezzlement of communal property — in any case, as it became more widespread, Christianity not only failed to regenerate the souls of all the people, but itself degenerated, became materialistic and bureaucratic; from the practice of fraternal teaching one of another it changed into papalism, from wandering beggary into monastic parasitism; in short, not only did Christianity fail to subject to itself the social conditions of the milieu in which it spread, but it was itself subjected by them. This did not result from the lack of ability or the greed of the fathers and teachers of Christianity, but as a consequence of the inexorable laws of the dependence of human psychology upon the conditions of social life and labour, and the fathers and teachers of Christianity showed this dependence in their own persons.

If socialism aimed at creating a new human nature within the limits of the old society it would be nothing more than a new edition of the moralistic utopias. Socialism does not aim at creating a socialist psychology as a pre-requisite to socialism but at creating socialist conditions of life as a pre-requisite to socialist psychology.[5]

In this passage, Trotsky expressed a view common to the Marxism of that era, which Adorno summed up in a 1936 letter to Walter Benjamin as follows:

[The] proletariat . . . is itself a product of bourgeois society. . . . [T]he actual consciousness of actual workers . . . [has] absolutely no advantage over the bourgeois except . . . interest in the revolution, but otherwise bear[s] all the marks of mutilation of the typical bourgeois character. . . . [W]e maintain our solidarity with the proletariat instead of making of our own necessity a virtue of the proletariat, as we are always tempted to do — the proletariat which itself experiences the same necessity and needs us for knowledge as much as we need the

---

5    In *The Permanent Revolution & Results and Prospects* 3rd edition (New York: Pathfinder Press, 1969), 82 and 97–99.

proletariat to make the revolution . . . a true accounting of the relationship of the intellectuals to the working class.[6]

Adorno's philosophical idea of the "non-identity" of social being and consciousness, of practice and theory, of means and ends, is related to this, what he called the priority or "preponderance" of the "object." Society needs to be changed before consciousness.

Adorno's thought was preceded by Georg Lukács's treatment of the problem of "reification," or "reified consciousness." Citing Lenin, Lukács wrote, on "The Standpoint of the Proletariat," the third section of his 1923 essay "Reification and the Consciousness of the Proletariat," that,

> Reification is . . . the necessary, immediate reality of every person living in capitalist society. It can be overcome only by *constant and constantly renewed efforts to disrupt the reified structure of existence by concretely relating to the concretely manifested contradictions of the total development, by becoming conscious of the immanent meanings of these contradictions for the total development.* But it must be emphasized that . . . the structure can be disrupted only if the immanent contradictions of the process are made conscious. Only when the consciousness of the proletariat is able to point out the road along which the dialectics of history is objectively impelled, but which it cannot travel unaided, will the consciousness of the proletariat awaken to a consciousness of the process, and only then will the proletariat become the identical subject-object of history whose praxis will change reality. If the proletariat fails to take this step the contradiction will remain unresolved and will be reproduced by the dialectical mechanics of history at a higher level, in an altered form and with increased intensity. It is in this that the objective necessity of history consists. The deed of the proletariat can never be more than to take the next step in the process.

---

6   Letter of March 18, 1936, in Adorno et al., *Aesthetics and Politics* (London: Verso, 1980), 123–125.

Whether it is "decisive" or "episodic" depends on the concrete circumstances [of this on-going struggle.]⁷

Lukács thought that,

Lenin's achievement is that he rediscovered this side of Marxism that points the way to an understanding of its practical core. His constantly reiterated warning to seize the "next link" in the chain with all one's might, that link on which the fate of the totality depends in that one moment, his dismissal of all utopian demands, i.e. his "relativism" and his "Realpolitik": all these things are nothing less than the practical realization of the young Marx's [1845] *Theses on Feuerbach*.⁸

In his third "Thesis" on Feuerbach, Marx wrote that,

The materialist doctrine that men are products of circumstances and upbringing, and that, therefore, changed men are products of other circumstances and changed upbringing, forgets that it is men who change circumstances and that it is essential to educate the educator himself. Hence, this doctrine necessarily arrives at dividing society into two parts, one of which is superior to society.

The coincidence of the changing of circumstances and of human activity can be conceived and rationally understood only as revolutionizing practice.⁹

So, what, for Adorno, counted as "revolutionary practice," and what is the role of "critical theory," and, hence, the role of Marxist "intellectuals," in relation to this?

---

7   *History and Class Consciousness*, trans. Rodney Livingstone (Cambridge, MA: MIT Press, 1971), 197–198.

8   Ibid., 221n60.

9   In *The Marx-Engels Reader*, 2nd edition, ed. Robert C. Tucker (New York: Norton, 1978), 144.

## The politics of Critical Theory

In his 1936 letter to Benjamin, Adorno pointed out that,

> [I]f [one] legitimately interpret[s] technical progress and alien-
> ation in a dialectical fashion, without doing the same in equal
> measure for the world of objectified subjectivity . . . then the
> political effect of this is to credit the proletariat directly with an
> achievement which, according to Lenin, it can only accomplish
> through the theory introduced by intellectuals as dialectical
> subjects. . . . "Les extrèmes me touchent" ["The extremes touch
> me" (André Gide)] . . . but only if the dialectic of the lowest
> has the same value as the dialectic of the highest. . . . Both
> bear the stigmata of capitalism, both contain elements of
> change. . . . Both are torn halves of an integral freedom, to
> which, however, they do not add up. It would be romantic to
> sacrifice one to the other . . . [as] with that romantic anarchism
> which places blind trust in the spontaneous powers of the pro-
> letariat within the historical process — a proletariat which is
> itself a product of bourgeois society.[10]

This conception of the dialectic of the "extremes" was developed by Adorno in two writings of the 1940s, "Reflections on Class Theory," and "Imagina-tive Excesses."[11] In these writings, Adorno drew upon not only Marx and the best in the history of Marxist politics, but also the critical-theoretical digestion of this politics by Lukács.

In his 1920 essay on "Class Consciousness," Lukács wrote that,

> *Only the consciousness of the proletariat can point to the way that*
> *leads out of the impasse of capitalism.* As long as this conscious-
> ness is lacking, the crisis remains permanent, it goes back to

---

10  *The Complete Correspondence 1928–40*, ed. Henri Lonitz, trans. Nicholas Walker (Cam-bridge, MA: Harvard University Press, 1999), 129–130.

11  Published as "Messages in a Bottle," trans. Edmund Jephcott, *New Left Review* I/200, (July – August 1993), 12–14.

its starting-point, repeats the cycle until after infinite sufferings
and terrible detours the school of history completes the education of the proletariat and confers upon it the leadership of
mankind. But the proletariat is not given any choice. As Marx
says, it must become a class not only "as against capital" but also
"for itself;" that is to say, the class struggle must be raised from
the level of economic necessity to the level of conscious aim
and effective class consciousness. The pacifists and humanitar-
ians of the class struggle whose efforts tend whether they will
or no to retard this lengthy, painful and crisis-ridden process
would be horrified if they could but see what sufferings they
inflict on the proletariat by extending this course of education. But the proletariat cannot abdicate its mission. The only
question at issue is how much it has to suffer before it achieves
ideological maturity, before it acquires a true understanding of
its class situation and a true class consciousness.

Of course this uncertainty and lack of clarity are themselves the symptoms of the crisis in bourgeois society. As
the product of capitalism the proletariat must necessarily be
subject to the modes of existence of its creator. This mode
of existence is inhumanity and reification. No doubt the very
existence of the proletariat implies criticism and the negation
of this form of life. But until the objective crisis of capitalism
has matured and until the proletariat has achieved true class
consciousness, and the ability to understand the crisis fully, it
cannot go beyond the criticism of reification and so it is only
negatively superior to its antagonist. . . . Indeed, if it can do
no more than negate some aspects of capitalism, if it cannot
at least aspire to a critique of the whole, then it will not even
achieve a negative superiority. . . .

The reified consciousness must also remain hopelessly
trapped in the two extremes of crude empiricism and abstract
utopianism. In the one case, consciousness becomes either
a completely passive observer moving in obedience to laws
which it can never control. In the other it regards itself as a

power which is able of its own — subjective — volition to master the essentially meaningless motion of objects.[12]

In "The Standpoint of the Proletariat," Lukács elaborated further that,

[T]here arises what at first sight seems to be the paradoxical situation that this projected, mythological world [of capital] seems closer to consciousness than does the immediate reality. But the paradox dissolves as soon as we remind ourselves that we must abandon the standpoint of immediacy and solve the problem if immediate reality is to be mastered in truth. Whereas[,] mythology is simply *the reproduction in imagination of the problem in its insolubility.* Thus immediacy is merely reinstated on a higher level. . . .

Of course, [the alternative of] "indeterminism" does not lead to a way out of the difficulty for the individual. . . . [It is] nothing but the acquisition of that margin of "freedom" that the conflicting claims and irrationality of the reified laws can offer the individual in capitalist society. It ultimately turns into a mystique of intuition which leaves the fatalism of the external reified world even more intact than before[,] [despite having] rebelled in the name of "humanism" against the tyranny of the "law." . . . Even worse, having failed to perceive that man in his negative immediacy was a moment in a dialectical process, such a philosophy, when consciously directed toward the restructuring of society, is forced to distort the social reality in order to discover the positive side, man as he exists, in one of its manifestations. . . . In support of this we may cite as a typical illustration the well-known passage [from Marx's great adversary, the German socialist Ferdinand Lassalle]: "There is no *social way* that leads out of this social situation. The vain efforts of *things* to behave *like human beings* can be seen in the English [labor] strikes whose melancholy outcome is familiar enough.

---

12 *History and Class Consciousness*, 76–77.

The *only* way out for the workers is to be found in *that sphere within which* they can still be *human beings. . . ."*

[I]t is important to establish that the abstract and absolute separation[,] . . . the rigid division between *man as thing,* on the one hand, and *man as man,* on the other, is not without consequences . . . [T]his means that every path leading to a change in this reality is systematically blocked.

This disintegration of a dialectical, practical unity into an inorganic aggregate of the empirical and the utopian, a clinging to the "facts" (in their untranscended immediacy) and a faith in illusions[,] as alien to the past as to the present[,] is characteristic. . . .

The danger to which the proletariat has been exposed since its appearance on the historical stage was that it might remain imprisoned in its immediacy together with the bourgeoisie.[13]

In "Reflections on Class Theory," Adorno provided a striking reinterpretation of Marx and Engels's *Communist Manifesto* as a theory of emancipation from history:

According to [Marxian] theory, history is the history of class struggles. But the concept of class is bound up with the [historical] emergence of the proletariat. . . . By extending the concept of class to prehistory, theory denounces not just the bourgeois . . . [but] turns against prehistory itself. . . . By exposing the historical necessity that had brought capitalism into being, [the critique of] political economy became the critique of history as a whole. . . . All history is the history of class struggles because it was always the same thing, namely, prehistory. . . . This means, however, that the dehumanization is also its opposite. . . . Only when the victims completely assume the features of the ruling

---

13  Ibid., 194–196.

civilization will they be capable of wresting them from the dominant power.[14]

Adorno elaborated this further in the aphorism "Imaginative Excesses," which was orphaned from the published version of Adorno's book *Minima Moralia: Reflections from Damaged Life* (1944–47). Adorno wrote that,

> Those schooled in dialectical theory are reluctant to indulge in positive images of the proper society, of its members, even of those who would accomplish it. . . . The leap into the future, clean over the conditions of the present, lands in the past. In other words: ends and means cannot be formulated in isolation from each other. Dialectics will have no truck with the maxim that the former justify the latter, no matter how close it seems to come to the doctrine of the ruse of reason or, for that matter, the subordination of individual spontaneity to party discipline. The belief that the blind play of means could be summarily displaced by the sovereignty of rational ends was bourgeois utopianism. It is the antithesis of means and ends itself that should be criticized. Both are reified in bourgeois thinking. . . . [Their] petrified antithesis holds good for the world that produced it, but not for the effort to change it. Solidarity can call on us to subordinate not only individual interests but even our better insight. . . . Hence the precariousness of any statement about those on whom the transformation depends. . . . The dissident wholly governed by the end is today in any case so thoroughly despised by friend and foe as an "idealist" and daydreamer. . . . Certainly, however, no more faith can be placed in those equated with the means; the subjectless beings whom historical wrong has robbed of the strength to right it, adapted to technology and unemployment, conforming and squalid, hard to distinguish from the wind-jackets of

---

14 In *Can One Live After Auschwitz?: A Philosophical Reader*, ed. Rolf Tiedemann, trans. Rodney Livingstone, (Stanford: Stanford University Press, 2003), 93–110.

fascism: their actual state disclaims the idea that puts its trust in them. Both types are theatre masks of class society projected on to the night-sky of the future . . . on one hand the abstract rigorist, helplessly striving to realize chimeras, and on the other the subhuman creature who as dishonour's progeny shall never be allowed to avert it.

What the rescuers would be like cannot be prophesied without obscuring their image with falsehood. . . . What can be perceived, however, is what they will not be like: neither personalities nor bundles of reflexes, but least of all a synthesis of the two, hardboiled realists with a sense of higher things. When the constitution of human beings has grown adapted to social antagonisms heightened to the extreme, the humane constitution sufficient to hold antagonism in check will be mediated by the extremes, not an average mingling of the two. The bearers of technical progress, now still mechanized mechanics, will, in evolving their special abilities, reach the point already indicated by technology where specialization grows superfluous. Once their consciousness has been converted into pure means without any qualification, it may cease to be a means and breach, with its attachment to particular objects, the last heteronomous barrier; its last entrapment in the existing state, the last fetishism of the status quo, including that of its own self, which is dissolved in its radical implementation as an instrument. Drawing breath at last, it may grow aware of the incongruence between its rational development and the irrationality of its ends, and act accordingly.

At the same time, however, the producers are more than ever thrown back on theory, to which the idea of a just condition evolves in their own medium, self-consistent thought, by virtue of insistent self-criticism. The class division of society is also maintained by those who oppose class society: following the schematic division of physical and mental labour, they split themselves up into workers and intellectuals. This division cripples the practice which is called for. It cannot be arbitrarily set aside. But while those professionally concerned with things of the mind are themselves turned more and more into technicians, the growing opacity of capitalist mass society makes an association between intellectuals who still are such, with workers who still know themselves to be such, more timely than thirty years ago [at the time of the 1917 Bolshevik Revolution]. . . . Today, when the concept of the proletariat, unshaken in its economic essence, is so occluded by technology that in the greatest industrial country [the United States of America] there can be no question of proletarian class-consciousness, the role of intellectuals would no longer be to alert the torpid to their most obvious interests, but to strip the veil from the eyes of the wise-guys, the illusion that capitalism, which makes them its temporary beneficiaries, is based on anything other than their exploitation and oppression. The deluded workers are directly dependent on those who can still just see and tell of their delusion. Their hatred of intellectuals has changed accordingly. It has aligned itself to the prevailing commonsense views. The masses no longer mistrust intellectuals because they betray the revolution, but because they might want it, and thereby reveal how great is their own need of intellectuals. Only if the extremes come together will humanity survive.[15]

## The problem of means and ends

A principal trope of Stalinophobic Cold War liberalism in the 20th century was the idea that Bolshevism thought that the "ends justify the means," in some Machiavellian manner, that Leninists were willing to do anything to achieve socialism. This made a mockery not only of the realties of socialist politics up to that time, but also of the self-conscious relation within Marxism itself between theory and practice, what came to be known as "alienation." Instead, Marxism became an example for the liberal caveat, supposedly according to Kant, that something "may be true in theory but not in

---

15  Published as "Messages in a Bottle."

practice." Marxist politics had historically succumbed to the theory-practice problem, but that does not mean that Marxists had been unaware of this problem, nor that Marxist theory had not developed a self-understanding of what it means to inhabit and work through this problem.

As Adorno put it in his 1966 book *Negative Dialectics*,

> The liquidation of theory by dogmatization and thought taboos contributed to the bad practice. . . . The interrelation of both moments [of theory and practice] is not settled once and for all but fluctuates historically. . . . Those who chide theory [for being] anachronistic obey the *topos* of dismissing, as obsolete, what remains painful [because it was] thwarted. . . . The fact that history has rolled over certain positions will be respected as a verdict on their truth content only by those who agree with Schiller that "world history is the world tribunal." What has been cast aside but not absorbed theoretically will often yield its truth content only later. It festers as a sore on the prevailing health; this will lead back to it in changed situations.[16]

What this meant for Adorno is that past emancipatory politics could not be superseded or rendered irrelevant the degree to which they remained unfulfilled. A task could be forgotten but it would continue to task the present. This means an inevitable return to it. The most broad-gauged question raised by this approach is the degree to which we may still live under capital in the way Marx understood it. If Marx's work is still able to provoke critical recognition of our present realities, then we are tasked to grasp the ways it continues to do so. This is not merely a matter of theoretical "analysis," however, but also raises issues of practical politics. This means inquiring into the ways Marx understood the relation of theory and practice, most especially his own. Adorno thought that this was not a matter of simply emulating Marx's political practice or theoretical perspectives, but rather trying to grasp the relation of theory and practice under changed conditions.

---

16  Trans. E. B. Ashton (Continuum: New York, 1983), 143–144.

This articulated non-identity, antagonism and even contradiction of theory and practice, observable in the history of Marxism most of all, was not taken to be defeating for Adorno, but was in fact precisely where Marxism pointed acutely to the problem of freedom in capital, and how it might be possible to transform and transcend it. Adorno put it this way, in a late, posthumously published essay from 1969, "Marginalia to Theory and Praxis," inspired by his conflicts with both student activists and his old friend and colleague Herbert Marcuse, who he thought had regressed to a Romantic rejection of capital:

> If, to make an exception for once, one risks what is called a grand perspective, beyond the historical differences in which the concepts of theory and praxis have their life, one discovers the infinitely progressive aspect of the separation of theory and praxis, which was deplored by the Romantics and denounced by the Socialists in their wake — except for the mature Marx.[17]

As Adorno put it in a [May 5, 1969] letter to Marcuse,

> [T]here are moments in which theory is pushed on further by practice. But such a situation neither exists objectively today, nor does the barren and brutal practicism that confronts us here have the slightest thing to do with theory anyhow.[18]

In his final published essay, "Resignation" (1969), which became a kind of testament, Adorno pointed out that,

> Even political undertakings can sink into pseudo-activities, into theater. It is no coincidence that the ideals of immediate action, even the propaganda of the [deed], have been resurrected after the willing integration of formerly progressive

---

17  In *Critical Models*, trans. Henry W. Pickford (New York: Columbia University Press, 1998), 266.

18  "Correspondence on the German Student Movement," trans. Esther Leslie, *New Left Review* I/233 (January – February 1999), 127.

organizations that now in all countries of the earth are developing the characteristic traits of what they once opposed. Yet this does not invalidate the [Marxist] critique of anarchism. Its return is that of a ghost. The impatience with [Marxian] theory that manifests itself with its return does not advance thought beyond itself. By forgetting thought, the impatience falls back below it.[19]

This is almost a direct paraphrase of Lenin, who wrote in his 1920 pamphlet *"Left-Wing" Communism: An Infantile Disorder* that,

[D]riven to frenzy by the horrors of capitalism . . . anarchism is characteristic of all capitalist countries. The instability of such revolutionism, its barrenness, and its tendency to turn rapidly into submission, apathy, phantasms, and even a frenzied infatuation with one bourgeois fad or another — all this is common knowledge. . . .

Anarchism was not infrequently a kind of penalty for the opportunist sins of the working-class movement. The two monstrosities complemented each other.[20]

Adorno paralleled Lenin's discussion of the "phantasms" of non-Marxian socialism, and defense of a Marxist approach, stating that, "Thought, enlightenment conscious of itself, threatens to disenchant the pseudo-reality within which actionism moves."[21] Immediately prior to Adorno's comment on anarchism, he discussed the antinomy of spontaneity and organization, as follows,

Pseudo-activity is generally the attempt to rescue enclaves of immediacy in the midst of a thoroughly mediated and rigidified society. Such attempts are rationalized by saying that the small

---

19 In *Critical Models*, trans. Henry W. Pickford (New York: Columbia University Press, 1998), 292.

20 *The Lenin Anthology*, ed. Robert C. Tucker (New York: Norton, 1975), 559–560.

21 *Critical Models*, 291.

change is one step in the long path toward the transformation of the whole. The disastrous model of pseudo-activity is the "*do-it-yourself.*" . . . The do-it-yourself approach in politics is not completely of the same caliber [as the quasi-rational purpose of inspiring in the unfree individuals, paralyzed in their spontaneity, the assurance that everything depends on them]. The society that impenetrably confronts people is nonetheless these very people. The trust in the limited action of small groups recalls the spontaneity that withers beneath the encrusted totality and without which this totality cannot become something different. The administered world has the tendency to strangle all spontaneity, or at least to channel it into pseudo-activities. At least this does not function as smoothly as the agents of the administered world would hope. However, spontaneity should not be absolutized, just as little as it should be split off from the objective situation or idolized the way the administered world itself is.[22]

Adorno's poignant defense of Marxism was expressed most pithily in the final lines with which his "Marginalia to Theory and Praxis" concludes, that,

Marx by no means surrendered himself to praxis. Praxis is a source of power for theory but cannot be prescribed by it. It appears in theory merely, and indeed necessarily, as a blind spot, as an obsession with what it being criticized. . . . This admixture of delusion, however, warns of the excesses in which it incessantly grows.[23]

Marxism is both true and untrue; the question is how one recognizes its truth and untruth, and the necessity — the inevitability — of its being both.

Adorno acknowledged his indebtedness to the best of historical Marxism when he wrote that,

---

22  Ibid., 291–292.
23  Ibid., 278.

The theorist who intervenes in practical controversies nowadays discovers on a regular basis and to his shame that whatever
ideas he might contribute were expressed long ago — and usually better the first time around.[24]

Presented at the Platypus Affiliated Society second annual
International Convention, Chicago, May 29, 2010.

---

24 "Sexual Taboos and the Law Today" (1963), in *Critical Models*, trans. Henry W. Pickford (New York: Columbia University Press, 1998), 71.

# The politics of Critical Theory

The political origins of Frankfurt School Critical Theory have remained opaque, for several reasons, not least the taciturn character of the major writings of its figures. The motivation for such reticence on the part of these theorists is itself what requires explanation: why they engaged in self-censorship and the encryption of their ideas, and consigned themselves to writing "messages in a bottle" without immediate or definite addressee. As Horkheimer put it, the danger was in speaking like an "oracle;" he asked simply, "To whom shall we say these things?"[1] It was not simply due to American exile in the Nazi era or post-World War II Cold War exigency. Some of their ideas were expressed explicitly enough. Rather, the collapse of the Marxist Left in which the Critical Theorists' thought had been formed, in the wake of the October 1917 Revolution in Russia and the German Revolution and civil war of 1918–19, deeply affected their perspective on political possibilities in their historical moment. The question is, in what way was this Marxism?

A series of conversations between Horkheimer and Adorno from 1956, at the height of the Cold War, provide insight into their thinking and how they understood their situation in the trajectory of Marxism in the 20th century. Selections from the transcript were recently published in the *New Left Review* (2010), under the title "Towards a New Manifesto?" The German publication of the complete transcript, in Horkheimer's collected works, is under the title "Discussion about Theory and Praxis," and their discussion was indeed in consideration of rewriting the *Communist Manifesto* in light of intervening history. Within a few years of this, Adorno began

---

1   Theodor Adorno and Max Horkheimer, "Towards a New Manifesto," trans. Rodney Livingstone, *New Left Review* 65 (September – October 2010), 46.

but abandoned work on a critique of the German Social-Democratic Party's Godesberg Programme, which officially renounced Marxism in 1959, on the model of Marx's celebrated critique of the Gotha Programme that had founded the SPD in 1875. So, especially Adorno, but also Horkheimer, had been deeply concerned with the question of continuing the project of Marxism well after World War II. In the series of conversations between them, Adorno expressed his interest in rewriting the Communist Manifesto along what he called "strictly Leninist" lines, to which Horkheimer did not object, but only pointed out that such a document, calling for what he called the "re-establishment of a socialist party," "could not appear in Russia, while in the United States and Germany it would be worthless." Nonetheless, Horkheimer felt it was necessary to show "why one can be a communist and yet despise the Russians." As Horkheimer put it, simply, "Theory is, as it were, one of humanity's tools."[2] Thus, they tasked themselves to try to continue Marxism, if only as "theory."

Now, it is precisely the supposed turning away from political practice and retreat into theory that many commentators have characterized as the Frankfurters' abandonment of Marxism. For instance, Martin Jay, in *The Dialectical Imagination*,[3] or Phil Slater, in his book[4] offering a "Marxist interpretation" of the Frankfurt School, characterized matters in such terms: Marxism could not be supposed to exist as mere theory, but had to be tied to practice. But this was not a problem new to the Frankfurt Institute in exile, that is, after being forced to abandon their work in collaboration with the Soviet Marx-Engels Institute, for example, which was as much due to Stalinism as Nazism. Rather, it pointed back to what Karl Korsch, a foundational figure for the Institute, wrote in 1923: that the crisis of Marxism, that is, the problems that had already manifested in the era of the Second International in the late 19th century (the so-called "Revisionist Dispute"), and developed and culminated in its collapse and division in World War I and the revolutions that followed, meant that the "umbilical

---

2  Ibid., 57.

3  *The Dialectical Imagination: A History of the Frankfurt School and the Institute of Social Research, 1923-1950* (Berkeley: University of California Press, 1973).

4  *Origin and Significance of the Frankfurt School: A Marxist Perspective* (London: Routledge, 1977).

cord" between theory and practice had been already "broken."[5] Marxism stood in need of a transformation, in both theory and practice, but this transformation could only happen as a function of not only practice but also theory. They suffered the same fate. For Korsch in 1923, as well as for Georg Lukács in this same period, in writings seminal for the Frankfurt School Critical Theorists, Lenin and Rosa Luxemburg were exemplary of the attempt to rearticulate Marxist theory and practice. Lenin in particular, as Lukács characterized him, the "theoretician of practice," provided a key, indeed the crucial figure, in political action and theoretical self-understanding, of the problem Marxism faced at that historical moment. As Adorno remarks, "I have always wanted to . . . develop a theory that remains faithful to Marx, Engels and Lenin."[6] So, the question becomes, "faithful" in what way?

Several statements in two writings by Horkheimer and Adorno's colleague, Herbert Marcuse, his "33 Theses" from 1947, and his book *Soviet Marxism* from 1958, can help shed light on the orientation of the members of the Frankfurt School towards the prior politics of "communism," specifically of Lenin. Additionally, several letters from Adorno to Horkheimer and Benjamin in the late 1930s explicate Adorno's positive attitude towards Lenin. Finally, writings from Adorno's last year, 1969, the "Marginalia to Theory and Praxis" and "Resignation," restated and further specified the content of his "Leninism" in light of his critique of the 1960s New Left. The challenge is to recognize the content of such "Leninism" that might otherwise appear obscure or idiosyncratic, but actually points back to the politics of the early 20th century that was formative of Adorno and his cohort. Then, the question becomes, what was the significance of such a perspective in the later period of Adorno's life? How did such "Leninism" retain purchase under changed conditions, such that Adorno could bring it to bear, critically, up to the end of his life? Furthermore, what could Adorno's perspective on "Leninism" reveal about Lenin himself? Why and how did Adorno remain a Marxist, and how did Lenin figure in this?

---

5    "Marxism and Philosophy" (1923), in *Marxism and Philosophy*, trans. Fred Halliday (New York: Monthly Review Press, 1970), 53.
6    "Towards a New Manifesto," 59.

One clear explanation for Adorno's "Leninism" was the importance of consciousness in Adorno's estimation of potential for emancipatory social transformation. For instance, in a letter to Horkheimer critical of Erich Fromm's more humane approach to Freudian psychoanalysis, Adorno wrote that Fromm demonstrated "a mixture of social democracy and anarchism . . . [and] a severe lack of . . . dialectics . . . [in] the concept of authority, without which, after all, neither Lenin's [vanguard] nor dictatorship can be conceived of. I would strongly advise him to read Lenin." Adorno thought that Fromm thus threatened to deploy something of what he called the "trick used by bourgeois individualists against Marx," and wrote to Horkheimer that he considered this to be a "real threat to the line . . . which [our] journal takes."[7]

But the political role of an intellectual, theoretically informed "vanguard" is liable to the common criticism of Leninism's tendency towards an oppressive domination over rather than critical facilitation of social emancipation. A more complicated apprehension of the role of consciousness in the historical transformation of society can be found in Adorno's correspondence on Benjamin's essay "The Work of Art in the Age of Mechanical Reproduction" in 1936. There, Adorno commended Benjamin's work for providing an account of the relationship of intellectuals to workers along the lines of Lenin. As Adorno put it in his letter to Benjamin,

> The proletariat . . . is itself a product of bourgeois society. . . . [T]he actual consciousness of actual workers . . . [has] absolutely no advantage over the bourgeois except . . . interest in the revolution, but otherwise bear[s] all the marks of mutilation of the typical bourgeois character. . . . We maintain our

---

7  Adorno to Horkheimer, March 21, 1936, quoted in Rolf Wiggershaus, *The Frankfurt School: Its History, Theories, and Political Significance*, trans. Michael Robertson (Cambridge, MA: The MIT Press, 1986/94), 266. Moreover, Adorno wrote that,

   "If one is concerned to achieve what might be possible with human beings, it is extremely difficult to remain friendly towards real people . . . a pretext for approving of precisely that element in people by which they prove themselves to be not merely their own victims but virtually their own hangmen." See Adorno to Horkheimer, June 2, 1941, quoted in Wiggershaus, *The Frankfurt School*, 268.

solidarity with the proletariat instead of making of our own necessity a virtue of the proletariat, as we are always tempted to do — the proletariat which itself experiences the same necessity and needs us for knowledge as much as we need the proletariat to make the revolution. I am convinced that the further development of the . . . debate you have so magnificently inaugurated . . . depends essentially on a true accounting of the relationship of the intellectuals to the working class. . . . [Your essay is] among the profoundest and most powerful statements of political theory that I have encountered since I read [Lenin's] *The State and Revolution.*[8]

Adorno likely had in mind as well Lenin's *What is to be Done?* or *"Left-Wing" Communism: An Infantile Disorder.* In the former, Lenin (in)famously distinguished between "trade union" and "socialist consciousness." But in the latter work, Lenin described the persistent "bourgeois" social conditions of intellectual work per se that would long survive the proletarian socialist revolution, indeed (reiterating from *What is to be Done?*) that workers became thoroughly "bourgeois" by virtue of the very activity of intellectual work (such as in journalism or art production), including and perhaps especially in their activity as Communist Party political cadre. For Lenin, workers' political revolution meant governing what would remain an essentially bourgeois society. The revolution would make the workers for the first time, so to speak, entirely bourgeois, which was the precondition of their leading society beyond bourgeois conditions.[9] It was a moment, the next necessary step, in the workers' self-overcoming, in the emancipatory transformation of society in, through and beyond capital. Marxism was not

---

8    "Correspondence with Benjamin," *New Left Review* I/81 (September – October 1973), 66–68.

9    As Lenin wrote in *"Left-Wing" Communism: An Infantile Disorder*:

The most shameless careerism . . . and vulgar petty-bourgeois conservatism are all unquestionably common and prevalent features engendered everywhere by capitalism, not only outside but also within the working-class movement. . . . [T]he overthrow of the bourgeoisie and the conquest of political power by the proletariat — [creates] these very same difficulties on a still larger, an infinitely larger scale.

extrinsic but intrinsic to this process, as the workers' movement itself was. As Adorno put it to Horkheimer, "It could be said that Marx and Hegel taught that there are no ideals in the abstract, but that the ideal always lies in the next step, that the entire thing cannot be grasped directly but only indirectly by means of the next step."[10] Lukács had mentioned this about Lenin, in a footnote to his 1923 essay in *History and Class Consciousness*, "Reification and the Consciousness of the Proletariat," that,

> Lenin's achievement is that he rediscovered this side of Marxism that points the way to an understanding of its practical core. His constantly reiterated warning to seize the "next link" in the chain with all one's might, that link on which the fate of the totality depends in that one moment, his dismissal of all utopian demands, i.e. his "relativism" and his "Realpolitik": all these things are nothing less than the practical realisation of the young Marx's *Theses on Feuerbach*.[11]

This was not fully achieved in the revolution that began to unfold from 1917 to 1919 in Russia, Germany, Hungary, and Italy, but was cut short of attaining the politics of the socialist transformation of society. Thirty years later, in the context of the dawning Cold War following the defeat of the Nazis in World War II, Marcuse's "33 Theses" tried to take stock of the legacy of the crisis of Marxism and the failure of the revolution:

> [Thesis 3:] [T]o uphold without compromise orthodox Marxist theory . . . [i]n the face of political reality . . . would be powerless, abstract and unpolitical, but when the political reality as a whole is false, the unpolitical position may be the only political truth . . .
>
> [Thesis 32:] [T]he political workers' party remains the necessary subject of revolution. In the original Marxist conception, the party does not play a decisive role. Marx assumed

---

10 "Towards a New Manifesto," 54.

11 In *History and Class Consciousness: Studies in Marxist Dialectics* (1923), trans. Rodney Livingstone (Cambridge, MA: The MIT Press, 1971), 221 n60.

that the proletariat is driven to revolutionary action on its own, based on the knowledge of its own interests, as soon as revolutionary conditions are present. . . . [But subsequent] development has confirmed the correctness of the Leninist conception of the vanguard party as the subject of the revolution. It is true that the communist parties today are not this subject, but it is just as true that only they can become it. Only in the theories of the communist parties is the memory of the revolutionary tradition alive, which can become the memory of the revolutionary goal again . . .

[Thesis 33:] The political task then would consist in reconstructing revolutionary theory.[12]

As Marcuse put it in 1958, in *Soviet Marxism,*

During the Revolution, it became clear to what degree Lenin had succeeded in basing his strategy on the actual class interests and aspirations of the workers and peasants. . . . Then, from 1923 on, the decisions of the leadership increasingly dissociated from the class interests of the proletariat. The former no longer presuppose the proletariat as a revolutionary agent but rather are imposed upon the proletariat and the rest of the underlying population.[13]

Adorno's commentary in conversation with Horkheimer in 1956, in a passage not included in the *New Left Review* translation, titled "Individualism," addressed what he called the problem of subjectivity as socially constituted, which he thought Lenin had addressed more rigorously than Marx. Adorno said that,

Marx was too harmless; he probably imagined quite naïvely that human beings are basically the same in all essentials and

---

12  In *Technology, War, and Fascism*, ed. Douglas Kellner (New York: Routledge, 1998), 217 and 226–227.

13  (New York: Columbia University Press, 1958), 149.

will remain so. It would be a good idea, therefore, to deprive them of their second nature. He was not concerned with their subjectivity; he probably didn't look into that too closely. The idea that human beings are the products of society down to their innermost core is an idea that he would have rejected as milieu theory. Lenin was the first person to assert this.[14]

What this meant for Adorno was that the struggle to overcome the domination of society by capital was something more and other than the class struggle of the workers against the capitalists. It was not merely a matter of their exploitation. For it was not the case that social subjects were products of their class position so much as bourgeois society under capital determined all of its subjects in a historical nexus of unfreedom. Rather, class position was an expression of the structure of this universal unfreedom. As Horkheimer wrote, in "The Little Man and the Philosophy of Freedom,"

> In socialism, freedom is to become a reality. But because the present system is called "free" and considered liberal, it is not terribly clear what this may mean . . .
>
> The businessman is subject to laws that neither he nor anyone else nor any power with such a mandate created with purpose and deliberation. They are laws which the big capitalists and perhaps he himself skillfully make use of but whose existence must be accepted as a fact. Boom, bust, inflation, wars and even the qualities of things and human beings the present society demands are a function of such laws, of the anonymous social reality . . .
>
> Bourgeois thought views this reality as superhuman. It fetishizes the social process . . .
>
> [T]he error is not that people do not recognize the subject but that the subject does not exist. Everything therefore depends

---

14 "Diskussion über Theorie und Praxis" (1956), in Max Horkheimer, *Gesammelte Schriften*, vol. 19, Nachträge, Verzeichnisse und Register (Frankfurt: S. Fischer, 1996), 71, quoted in Detlev Claussen, *Theodor W. Adorno: One Last Genius* (Cambridge, MA: Harvard University Press, 2008), 233.

on creating the free subject that consciously shapes social life. And this subject is nothing other than the rationally organized socialist society which regulates its own existence.... But for the little man who is turned down when he asks for a job because objective conditions make it impossible, it is most important that their origin be brought to the light of day so that they do not continue being unfavorable to him. Not only his own lack of freedom but that of others as well spells his doom. His interest lies in the Marxist clarification of the concept of freedom.[15]

Such a clarification of what would constitute a progressive-emancipatory approach to the problem of capital was cut short by the course of Marxism in the 20th century. It thus also became increasingly difficult to "bring to the light of day" the "origins" of persistent social conditions of unfreedom. In many respects, the crisis of Marxism had been exacerbated but not overcome as a function of the post-World War I revolutionary aftermath. This involved a deepening of the crisis of humanity: the Frankfurt Institute Critical Theorists were well aware that fascism as a historical phenomenon was due to the failure of Marxism. Fascism was the ill-begotten offspring of the history of Marxism itself.

A decade after 1917, Horkheimer wrote, in a passage titled "Indications," that,

The moral character of a person can be infallibly inferred from his response to certain questions. . . . In 1930 the attitude toward Russia casts light on people's thinking. It is extremely difficult to say what conditions are like there. I do not claim to know where the country is going; there is undoubtedly much misery. . . . The senseless injustice of the imperialist world can certainly not be explained by technological inadequacy. Anyone who has the eyes to see will view events in Russia as the continuing painful attempt to overcome this terrible social

---

15 *Dawn and Decline: Notes 1926-31 and 1950-69*, trans. Michael Shaw (New York: Seabury, 1978), 50–52.

injustice. At the very least, he will ask with a throbbing heart whether it is still under way. If appearances were to be against it, he will cling to this hope like the cancer patient to the questionable report that a cure for his illness may have been found.

When Kant received the first news of the French Revolution, he is said to have changed the direction of his customary stroll from then on.[16]

Despite what occurred in the unfolding of developments in 20th century history, Horkheimer and Adorno never reversed course. Are we yet ready to receive their messages in a bottle?

Presented at the third annual Platypus Affiliated Society International Convention, held April 29 – May 1, 2011 at the School of the Art Institute of Chicago, on a panel discussion with Nicholas Brown of the University of Illinois at Chicago, Andrew Feenberg of Simon Fraser University in Vancouver and Richard Westerman of the University of Chicago.

Originally published in *Platypus Review* 37 (July 2011)

---

16  Ibid., 72–73.

# Class consciousness (from
# a Marxist perspective) today

For Marxists, the division of modern socioeconomic classes is not the cause of the problem of capitalism but rather its effect.

Modern classes are different from ancient separations between castes, such as between the clergy or priestly caste, and the noble aristocracy or warrior caste, and the vast majority of people, "commoners," or those who were ignorant of divinity and without honor, who, for most of history, were peasants living through subsistence agriculture, a mute background of the pageantry of the ancient world.

Modern, "bourgeois" society, or the society of the modern city, is the product of the revolt of the Third Estate, or commoners, who had no property other than that of their labor: "self-made" men. During the French Revolution, the Third Estate separated itself from the other Estates of the clergy and aristocracy, and declared itself the National Assembly, with the famous Tennis Court Oath. This fulfilled the call of the Abbé Sieyès, who had declared in his revolutionary pamphlet *What is the Third Estate?*, that while under the *ancien régime* the Third Estate had been "nothing," now it would be "everything."

As the 20th century Marxist Critical Theorist Theodor Adorno put it, "society is a concept of the Third Estate."[1] What he meant by this was that unlike the previous, ancient civilization in which people were divinely ordered in a Great Chain of Being, the Third Estate put forward the idea that people would *relate* to one another. They would do so on the basis of their "work," or their activity in society, which would find purchase not in

---

1    "Society" in *Salmagundi*, no. 10/11 (Fall 1969 – Winter 1970).

a strict hierarchy of traditional values, but rather through a "free market" of goods. People would be free to find their own values in society.

Modern society is thus the society of the Third Estate, after the overthrow of the traditional authority of the Church and the feudal aristocrats. Modern, bourgeois society is based on the values of the Third Estate, which center on the values of work. The highest values of modern society are not religion or the honor of a warrior code, but rather material productivity and efficiency, being a "productive member of society." From this perspective, the perspective of modern bourgeois society, all of history appears to be the history of different, progressively developing "modes of production," of which capitalism is the latest and highest. The past becomes a time of people toiling in ignorance and superstition, held back by conservative customs and arrogant elites from realizing their potential productivity and ingenuity. The paradigmatic image of this state of affairs is Galileo being forced to recant his scientific insight under threat by the Church.

With the successful revolt of the Third Estate it appeared that humanity attained its "natural" condition of Enlightenment, in relation both to the natural world and in humans' relations with each other. Seemingly unlimited possibilities opened up, and the Dark Ages were finally brought to an end.

With the Industrial Revolution of the late 18th to early 19th centuries, however, a new "contradiction" developed in bourgeois society, that of the value of *capital* versus the value of the wages of *labor*. With this contradiction came a new social and political conflict, the "class struggle" of the workers for the value of their wages against the capitalists' imperative to preserve and expand the value of capital. This came to a certain head in the 1840s, known at the time as the "hungry '40s," the first world-wide economic crisis after the Industrial Revolution, which seemed to go beyond a mere adjustment of the market, but pointed to new and deeper problems.

This new conflict between the workers and capitalists that raged in the mid-19th century was expressed in the desire for "socialism," or of society becoming true to itself, and the value of the contributions of all society's members being recognized and their being allowed to participate fully in the development and political direction of humanity. This was expressed in the Revolutions of 1848, the "Spring of the Nations" in Europe that resulted from the crisis of the 1840s, which called for the "social republic" or "social democracy," that is, democracy adequate to the needs of society as a whole.

For the socialists of the time, the crisis of the 1840s and revolutions of 1848 demonstrated the need and possibility for getting beyond capitalism.

In late 1847, two young bohemian intellectuals, Karl Marx and Friedrich Engels, were commissioned by the Communist League to write a manifesto ahead of the potential revolutions that appeared on the horizon. Issued mere days ahead of the revolutions of 1848, the *Communist Manifesto* was a survey of the contradictory and paradoxical situation of modern society, its simultaneous radical possibilities and self-destructive tendencies in capitalism.

For Marx and Engels, as good followers of Hegel's dialectic of history, the phenomenon of contradiction was the appearance of the possibility and necessity for change.

Marx and Engels could be confident of the apparent, manifest crisis of modern society and the need for radical change emerging in their time. They were not the originators of socialism or communism but rather tried to sum up the historical experience of the struggle for socialism in their time. They did not seek to tell the workers their interest in overcoming capitalism, but rather tried to help clarify the workers' own consciousness of their historical situation, the crisis of bourgeois society in capital.

What Marx and Engels recognized that perhaps distinguished them from other socialists, however, was the utterly unique character of the modern, post-Industrial Revolution working class. What made the modern working class, or "industrial proletariat" different was its subjection to mass unemployment. Marx and Engels understood this unemployment to be not a temporary, contingent phenomenon due to market fluctuations or technical innovations putting people out of work, but rather a permanent feature of modern society after the Industrial Revolution, in which preserving the value of capital was in conflict with the value of workers' wages. Unlike Adam Smith in the pre-industrial era, who observed that higher wages and lower profits increased productivity in society as a whole, after the Industrial Revolution, increased productivity was not due to workers' greater efficiency but rather that of machines. This meant, as the director of the Marxist Frankfurt Institute for Social Research Max Horkheimer put it, that "machines made not work but the workers superfluous."[2]

On a global scale, greater productivity increased not employment and wealth but rather *unemployment* and *impoverishment*, as capitalism destroyed traditional ways of life (for instance of the peasants) but failed to be able to provide meaningful productive employment and thus participation in society for all, as originally envisioned in the revolt of the Third Estate and promised in the bourgeois revolution against the hierarchy of the *ancien régime*. The promise of the modern city is mocked by the mushrooming of slum cities around the world. The old world has been destroyed but the new one is hardly better. The promise of freedom is cruelly exploited, but its hope dashed.

Marxists were the first, and have remained the most consistent in recognizing the nature and character of this contradiction of modern society.

The difference between Marx's time and ours is not in the essential problem of society, its self-contradictory form of value between wages and capital, but rather in the social and political conflicts, which no longer take the form primarily, as in Marx's time, of the "class struggle" between workers and capitalists. "Class" has become a passive, objective category, rather than an active, subjective one, as it had been in Marx's day and in the time of historical Marxism. What Marxists once meant by "class consciousness" is no more.

This lends a certain melancholy to the experience of "class" today. Privilege and disadvantage alike seem arbitrary and accidental, not an expression of the supposed worth of people's roles in society but only of their luck, good or bad fortune. It becomes impossible to derive a politics from class position, and so other politics take its place. Conflicts of culture, ethnicity and religion replace the struggle over capitalism. Impoverished workers attack not orders whose privileges are dubious in the extreme, but rather each other in communal hatred. Consciousness of common class situation seems completely obscured and erased.

Not as Marx foresaw, workers with nothing to lose but their chains, but the unemployed masses wield their chains as weapons against each other.

---

2   "The Authoritarian State," in *The Essential Frankfurt School Reader*, ed. Andrew Arato and Eike Gebhardt (New York: Continuum, 1985), 95.

Meanwhile, in the background, underlying and overarching everything, capitalism continues. But it is no longer recognized. This is not surprising, however, since proper recognition of the problem could only come from practically engaging it as such. The issue is why it seems so undesirable to do so, today. Why have people stopped struggling for socialism?

We hear that we are in the midst of a deepening economic and social crisis, the greatest since the Great Depression of the early 20th century. But we do not see a political crisis of the same order of magnitude. It is not, as in the 1930s, when communism and fascism challenged capitalism from the Left and the Right, forcing massive social reform and political change.

This is because the idea of socialism — the idea of society being true to itself — has been disenchanted. With it has gone the class struggle of the workers against the capitalists that sought to realize the promise of freedom in modern society. It has been replaced with competing notions of social justice that borrow from ancient values. But since the sources of such ancient values, for instance religions, are in conflict, this struggle for justice points not to the transformation of society as a whole, but rather its devolution into competing values of different "cultures." Today in the U.S., it seems to matter more whether one lives in a "red or blue state," or what one's "race, gender, and sexuality" are, than if one is a worker or a capitalist — whatever that might mean. Cultural affinities seem to matter more than socioeconomic interests, as the latter burn. People cling to their chains, as the only things that they know.

Originally published in *Platypus Review* 51 (November 2012)

# Revolution without Marx?
# Rousseau, Kant and Hegel

## Introduction

Bourgeois society came into full recognition with Rousseau, who in the *Discourse on the Origin of Inequality* and *On the Social Contract*, opened its radical critique. Hegel wrote: "The principle of freedom dawned on the world in Rousseau." Marx quoted Rousseau favorably that "Whoever dares undertake to establish a people's institutions must feel himself capable of changing, as it were, human nature . . . to take from man his own powers, and give him in exchange alien powers which he cannot employ without the help of other men." Rousseau posed the question of society, which Adorno wrote is a "concept of the Third Estate."[1] Marx recognized the crisis of bourgeois society in the Industrial Revolution and workers' call for socialism. But proletarian socialism is no longer the rising force it was in Marx's time. So what remains of thinking the unrealized radicalism of bourgeois society without Marx? Kant stated that if the potential of bourgeois society was not fully achieved as the "mid-point" of freedom then Rousseau may have been right to prefer savagery against civilization's "glittering misery." Nietzsche warned that we might continue to be "living at the expense of the future": "Perhaps more comfortably, less dangerously, but at the same time in a meaner style, more basely."[2] How have thinkers of the revolutionary epoch after Rousseau, Adam Smith, Kant, Hegel, Benjamin Constant, and Nietzsche himself, contributed to the possibility of emancipation in a world after Marxism?

---

1    "Society" in *Salmagundi*, no. 10/11 (Fall 1969 – Winter 1970).
2    *On the Genealogy of Morals*, in *On the Genealogy of Morals and Ecco Homo*, trans. and ed. Walter Kaufmann (New York: Random House, 2010), 20.

## Marx and Rousseau

Marx's favorite quotation of Rousseau, from *On the Social Contract*, goes as follows:

> Whoever dares undertake to establish a people's institutions must feel himself capable of changing, as it were, human nature, of transforming each individual, who by himself is a complete and solitary whole, into a part of a larger whole, from which, in a sense, the individual receives his life and his being, of substituting a limited and mental existence for the physical and independent existence. He has to take from man his own powers, and give him in exchange alien powers which he cannot employ without the help of other men.[3]

Marx wrote that this was "well formulated," but only as "the abstract notion of political man," concluding that,

> Human emancipation will only be complete when the real, individual man has absorbed into himself the abstract citizen; when as an individual man, in his everyday life, in his work, and in his relationships, he has become a species-being; and when he has recognized and organized his own powers as social powers so that he no longer separates this social power from himself as political power.[4]

What did Marx mean by "social powers" as opposed to the "political power" from which it has been "separated?" A key passage from Marx's *Grundrisse* articulates well the new modern concept of freedom found in Rousseau:

> The ancient conception, in which man always appears (in however narrowly national, religious, or political a definition)

---

3   *On The Jewish Question* (1843).
4   Ibid.

as the aim of production, seems very much more exalted than the modern world, in which production is the aim of man and wealth the aim of production. In fact, however, when the narrow bourgeois form has been peeled away, what is wealth, if not the universality of needs, capacities, enjoyments, productive powers etc., of individuals, produced in universal exchange? What, if not the full development of human control over the forces of nature – those of his own nature as well as those of so-called "nature"? What, if not the absolute elaboration of his creative dispositions, without any preconditions other than antecedent historical evolution which make the totality of this evolution – i.e., the evolution of all human powers as such, unmeasured by any previously established yardstick – an end in itself? What is this, if not a situation where man does not reproduce in any determined form, but produces his totality? Where he does not seek to remain something formed by the past, but is in the absolute movement of becoming? In bourgeois political economy – and in the epoch of production to which it corresponds – this complete elaboration of what lies within man, appears as the total alienation, and the destruction of all fixed, one-sided purposes as the sacrifice of the end in itself to a wholly external compulsion. Hence in one way the childlike world of the ancients appears to be superior; and this is so, insofar as we seek for closed shape, form and established limitation. The ancients provide a narrow satisfaction, whereas the modern world leaves us unsatisfied, or, where it appears to be satisfied, with itself, is vulgar and mean.[5]

As the intellectual historian and critic of Michel Foucault's historicism, James Miller, put it in introduction to Rousseau,

The principle of freedom and its corollary, "perfectibility," ... suggest that the possibilities for being human are both multiple and,

5   Karl Marx, *Grundrisse*, trans. Martin Nicolaus.

literally, endless. . . . Contemporaries like Kant well understood the novelty and radical implications of Rousseau's new principle of freedom [and] appreciated his unusual stress on history as the site where the true nature of our species is simultaneously realized and perverted, revealed and distorted. A new way of thinking about the human condition had appeared.[6]

Another contemporary intellectual historian, Louis Menand, writing in introduction to the republication of Edmund Wilson's history of socialism, *To the Finland Station*, described this new way of thinking in Marx and Engels as follows:

In premodern societies, the ends of life are given at the beginning of life: people do things in their generation so that the same things will continue to be done in the next generation. Meaning is immanent in all the ordinary customs and practices of existence, since these are inherited from the past, and are therefore worth reproducing. The idea is to make the world go not forward, only around. In modern societies, the ends of life are not given at the beginning of life; they are thought to be created or discovered. The reproduction of the customs and practices of the group is no longer the chief purpose of existence; the idea is not to repeat, but to change, to move the world forward. Meaning is no longer immanent in the practices of ordinary life, since those practices are understood by everyone to be contingent and time-bound. This is why death, in modern societies, is the great taboo, an absurdity, the worst thing one can imagine. For at the close of life people cannot look back and know that they have accomplished the task set for them at birth. This knowledge always lies up ahead, somewhere over history's horizon. Modern societies don't know what will count as valuable in the conduct of life in the long run, because they have no way of

---

6    Introduction to Rousseau, *Discourse on the Origin of Inequality* (Indianapolis: Hackett, 1992), xv.

knowing what conduct the long run will find itself in a position to respect. The only certain knowledge death comes with is the knowledge that the values of one's own time, the values one has tried to live by, are expunge-able. . . . Marxism gave a meaning to modernity. It said that, wittingly or not, the individual performs a role in a drama that has a shape and a goal, a trajectory, and that modernity will turn out to be just one act in that drama. Historical change is not arbitrary. It is generated by class conflict; it is faithful to an inner logic; it points toward an end, which is the establishment of the classless society. Marxism was founded on an appeal for social justice, but there were many forms that such an appeal might have taken. Its deeper attraction was the discovery of meaning, a meaning in which human beings might participate, in history itself. When [Edmund] Wilson explained, in his introduction to the 1972 edition of *To the Finland Station*, that his book had been written under the assumption that "an important step in progress has been made, that a fundamental 'breakthrough' had occurred," this is the faith he was referring to. . . . Marx and Engels were the *philosophes* of a second Enlightenment.[7]

Peter Preuss, writing in introduction to Nietzsche's *On the Advantage and Disadvantage of History for Life*, pointed out that,

Man, unlike animal, is self-conscious. He is aware that he is alive and that he must die. And because he is self-conscious he is not only aware of living, but of living well or badly. Life is not wholly something that happens to man; it is also something he engages in according to values he follows. Human existence is a task. . . . The 19th century had discovered history and all subsequent inquiry and education bore the stamp of this discovery. This was not simply the discovery of a set of facts about the past

---

7   Foreword to Edmund Wilson, *To the Finland Station* (New York: New York Review of Books, 2003), xv–xviii.

but the discovery of the historicity of man: man, unlike animal, is a historical being. Man is not wholly the product of an alien act, either natural or divine, but in part produces his own being. The task of existing is a task precisely because it is not a case of acting according to a permanent nature or essence but rather of producing that nature within the limitations of a situation. History is the record of this self-production; it is the activity of a historical being recovering the past into the present which anticipates the future.[8]

Lifting the task of human freedom in modern society out of its current historical obscurity today is difficult precisely because we have reverted to regarding ourselves as products of an "alien act," and so proceed according to a model of "social justice" owing to the Ancients' "closed . . . form and established limitation" that loses Marxism's specific consciousness of society in history. But such consciousness of history was not at all original to Marxism but rather had roots in the antecedent development of the self-conscious thought of emergent bourgeois society in the 18th century, beginning with Rousseau and elaborated by his followers Kant and Hegel. The radicalism of bourgeois thought conscious of itself was an essential assumption of Marxism, which sought to carry forward the historical project of freedom.

If, as Menand put it, Marx and Engels were *"philosophes* of a Second Enlightenment" in the 19th century, then what of the 18th century Enlightenment of which Rousseau was perhaps the most notorious *philosophe*? What remains of this 18th century legacy for the struggle to emancipate society today?

## Rousseau in the 18th century

The Classicism of the 18th century Enlightenment had its distinctive melancholy, already, reaching back in historical fragments, broken remnants of

---

8 Introduction to Nietzsche, *The Advantage and Disadvantage of History for Life* (Indianapolis: Hackett, 1980), 1–2.

Ancient forms, for inspiration to the modern task of freedom. Rilke, at the turn of the 20th century, expressed this wistful sense of modern freedom in his poem "Archaic Torso of Apollo":

> We cannot know his legendary head
> with eyes like ripening fruit. And yet his torso
> is still suffused with brilliance from inside,
> like a lamp, in which his gaze, now turned to low,
> gleams in all its power. Otherwise
> the curved breast could not dazzle you so, nor could
> a smile run through the placid hips and thighs
> to that dark center where procreation flared.
> Otherwise this stone would seem defaced
> beneath the translucent cascade of the shoulders
> and would not glisten like a wild beast's fur:
> would not, from all the borders of itself,
> burst like a star: for here there is no place
> that does not see you. You must change your life.[9]

The scholar of German Idealist philosophy, Robert Pippin, wrote that after Kant's critical turn,

> some new way of conceiving of philosophy adequate to the realization of the radically historical nature of the human condition was now necessary. . . . The problem of understanding properly (especially critically) conceptual, artistic, and social change was henceforth at the forefront[.][10]

This new conception was found in Rousseau. Rousseau wrote that while animals were machines wound up for functioning in a specific natural environment, humans could regard and reflect upon their own machinery

---

9    From *Ahead of All Parting: Selected Poetry and Prose of Rainer Maria Rilke*, translated by Stephen Mitchell (New York: Modern Library, 2015).

10   "*Critical Inquiry* and Critical Theory: A Short History of Non-Being," *Critical Inquiry* 30, no. 2 (Winter 2004), 425.

and thus change it. This was Rousseau's radical notion of "perfectibility" which was not in pursuit of an ideal of perfection but rather open-ended in infinite adaptability. Unlike animal species, humans could adapt themselves to live in any environment and thus transform "outer nature" to suit them, thus transforming as well their own "inner nature," giving rise to ever-new possibilities. This was the new conception of freedom, not freedom to be according to a fixed natural or Divine form, but rather freedom to transform and realize new potential possibilities, to become new and different, other than what we were before.

### Rousseau and Kant

Rousseau understood the most radical possibilities of freedom-in-transformation to take place in society, the site of new and "alien powers which he cannot employ without the help of other men." Rousseau described this as the sacrifice of "natural liberty" for "moral freedom," the freedom to act in unnatural ways. For Rousseau, such freedom was radically ambivalent: it could be for good or for ill. However, the problem of society in which humanity had fallen could only be "solved" socially, not individually. This is why Rousseau was liable to be read later antinomically, as either anarchist or authoritarian: Rousseau gave expression to the radical ambiguity of freedom as it was revealed in modern society, the crossroads of civilization that bourgeois society represented. As Kant put it, in his "Idea for a Universal History from a Cosmopolitan Point of View" written in 1784, the same year as his famous essay answering the question, "What is Enlightenment?,"

> The vitality of mankind may fall asleep. . . . Until this last step to a union of states is taken, which is the halfway mark in the development of mankind, human nature must suffer the cruelest hardships under the guise of external well-being; and Rousseau was not far wrong in preferring the state of savages, so long, that is, as the last stage to which the human race must climb is not attained. . . . [Mere civilization,] however, is nothing but pretense and glittering misery. In such a condition the

human species will no doubt remain until . . . it works its way out of the chaotic conditions of its international relations.[11]

Rousseau was profoundly inspirational for Kant with respect to the fundamental "philosophical" issue of the relation of theory and practice. Specifically, Rousseau originated the modern dialectic of theory and practice, what Rousseau called their "reflective" and Kant called their "speculative" relation. In Kant's First Critique, the *Critique of Pure Reason*, and his summary of his argument there and reply to critics of it, the *Prolegomena to Any Future Metaphysics*, Kant articulated the "conditions of possibility" for concepts or categories of understanding as being those of practice.

What this meant in Kant was that, while "things-in-themselves" were inaccessible to us, things do become objects of our theoretical understanding, by virtue of being objects of our practical engagement: Objects were "concrete" in the sense of being concretions of the various practical and thus conceptual relations we have with them. Furthermore, as Hegel put it, in the *Science of Logic*, objects were not "identical" with themselves — there was a non-identity of an object and its own concept — because they were subject to transformed, that is, changed, practices. So, objects were not approximations of always inaccurate theoretical models of conceptual understanding, but our concepts change as a function of changes in practice that were nonetheless informed by theoretical concepts. Concepts were "inductive" rather than "deductive" because they were not abstractions from empirical observation as generalizations from experience, but rather objects were "concretions of abstractions" in the sense of being determined in a web of practical relations. Rationalist metaphysics had a real basis in issues of practice. Furthermore, such practical relations were social in nature, as well as subject to historical change — change that is brought about subjectively by agents of practice who transform themselves in the process of transforming objects. What objects are for subjects changes as a function of changing practical relations.

In his essay "What is Enlightenment?," Kant had articulated a distinction between "public" and "private" reason in order to demonstrate that,

---

11  In *Kant on History*, trans. Lewis White Beck (Indianapolis: Bobbs-Merrill, 1963), 21.

enmeshed in the web of practical relations in society, we are condemned to exercise merely "private reason" in pursuit of our self-interest as individual "cogs in the machine" of society. It was only in the exercise of "public reason" that we were potentially free of such self-interest determined by our positions in society, to exercise reason as "anyone" — as any rational subject or any political citizen — from a position transcendent of such compromised interested practice. For Kant, such exercise of "public reason" expressed, however indirectly, the possibility of changes in social practice: the way things "ought" to be as opposed to how they "are" at present.

## Hegel and the philosophy of history

Hegel built upon Kant and Rousseau in his pursuit of the "philosophy of history" of accounting for such change in freedom, or "reason in history." The issue of Hegelianism is a notoriously but ultimately needlessly difficult one: how to include the "subjective factor in history." Hegel's sense of the actuality of the rational in the real turns on the relation of essence and appearance, or, with what necessity things appear as they do. What is essential is what is practical, and what is practical is subjective as well as objective. In this view, theoretical reflection on the subjective dimension of experience must use metaphysical categories that are not merely handy but actually constitutive of social practices in which one is a subject.

Rousseau, in his *Discourse on the Origin of Inequality*, had raised a hypothetical "state of nature" in order to throw his contemporary society into critical relief. In so doing, Rousseau sought to bring society closer to a "state of nature." Liberal, bourgeois society was a model and an aspiration for Rousseau. For Rousseau, it was human "nature" to be free. Humans achieved a higher "civil liberty" of "moral freedom" in society than they could enjoy as animals, with mere "physical" freedom in nature. Indeed, as animals, humans are not free, but rather slaves to their natural needs and instincts. Only in society could freedom be achieved, and humans free themselves from their natural, animal condition. When Rousseau was writing, in the mid-18th century, the promise of freedom in bourgeois society was still on the horizon. Bourgeois society aspired to proximity to the "state of nature" in the sense of bringing humanity, both individually and collectively, closer to its potential, to better realize its freedom.

For Rousseau, in his reflections *On the Social Contract*, society exhibited a "general will" not reducible to its individual members: more than the sum of its parts. Not Hobbes's "Leviathan," but rather a "second nature," a rebirth of potential, both collectively and individually. Human nature found the realization of its freedom in society, but humans were free to develop and transform themselves, for good or for ill. For Rousseau and the 18th century revolutionaries he inspired, to bring society closer to the "state of nature," then, was to allow humanity's potential to be better realized. But, first, society had to be clear about its aims, in practice as well as in theory. Rousseau was the first to articulate this new, modern task of social freedom.

The question Rousseau poses, then, is the speculative or dialectical relation of theory and practice, today. How might we raise the originally Rousseauian question of critical-theoretical reflection on our practices, from within the conditions of "second nature" that express our condition of freedom — including our self-imposed conditions of unfreedom? That is the issue of "public reason" today, as much as it was in Rousseau's time.

As Hegel put it, in his *Introduction to the Philosophy of History*,

> When we look at this drama of human passions, and observe the consequences of their violence and of the unreason that is linked not only to them but also (and especially) to good intentions and rightful aims; when we see arising from them all the evil, the wickedness, the decline of the most flourishing nations mankind has produced, we can only be filled with grief for all that has come to nothing. And since this decline and fall is not merely the work of nature but of the will of men, we might well end with moral outrage over such a drama, and with a revolt of our good spirit (if there is a spirit of goodness in us). Without rhetorical exaggeration, we could paint the most fearful picture of the misfortunes suffered by the noblest of nations and states as well as by private virtues — and with that picture we could arouse feelings of the deepest and most helpless sadness, not to be outweighed by any consoling outcome. We can

strengthen ourselves against this, or escape it, only by thinking that, well, so it was at one time; it is fate; there is nothing to be done about it now. And finally — in order to cast off the tediousness that this reflection of sadness could produce in us and to return to involvement in our own life, to the present of our own aims and interests — we return to the selfishness of standing on a quiet shore where we can be secure in enjoying the distant sight of confusion and wreckage. . . . But as we contemplate history as this slaughter-bench, upon which the happiness of nations, the wisdom of states, and the virtues of individuals were sacrificed, the question necessarily comes to mind: What was the ultimate goal for which these monstrous sacrifices were made? . . . World history is the progress in the consciousness of freedom — a progress that we must come to know in its necessity. . . . The Orientals knew only that one person is free; the Greeks and Romans that some are free; while we [moderns] know that all humans are implicitly free, qua human. . . . The final goal of the world, we said, is Spirit's consciousness of its freedom, and hence also the actualization of that very freedom. . . . It is this final goal — freedom — toward which all the world's history has been working. It is this goal to which all the sacrifices have been brought upon the broad altar of the earth in the long flow of time.[12]

Hopefully, still.

Presented on a panel at the Left Forum 2013, followed by Spencer Leonard's "Adam Smith, revolutionary" and Sunit Singh's "Nietzsche's untimeliness," at Pace University, NYC, on June 9, 2013.

Originally published in *Platypus Review* 61 (November 2013)

---

12  Hegel, *Reason In History: A General Introduction to the Philosophy of History* (Indianapolis: Bobbs-Merrill, 1953).

# Adorno and Freud

## The relation of Freudian psychoanalysis
## to Marxist critical social theory

Adorno's *Habilitationsschrift* was on Kant and Freud. It ended with Marx. Why did Adorno think that Marx addressed the problems of both Kantian and Freudian accounts of consciousness?

The distinction between Kant and Freud turns on the psychoanalytic concept of the "unconscious," the by-definition unknowable portion of mental processes, the unthought thoughts and unfelt feelings that are foreign to Kant's rational idealism. Kant's "critical" philosophy was concerned with how we can know what we know, and what this revealed about our subjectivity. Kant's philosophical "critiques" were investigations into conditions of possibility: Specifically, Kant was concerned with the possibility of change in consciousness. By contrast, Freud was concerned with how conscious intention was constituted in struggle with countervailing, "unconscious" tendencies: how the motivation for consciousness becomes opaque to itself. But like Kant, Freud was not interested in disenchanting but rather strengthening consciousness.

For both Kant and Freud, the greater possibilities for human freedom are to be found in the conquests of consciousness: To become more self-aware is to achieve greater freedom, and this freedom is grounded in possibilities for change. The potential for the qualitative transformation of consciousness, which for both Kant and Freud includes affective relations and hence is not merely about "conceptual" knowledge, underwrites both Kantian philosophy and Freudian psychotherapy.

But both Kantian and Freudian accounts of consciousness became utopian for Adorno. Adorno's Marxist "materialist" critique of the inadequacies of Kant and Freud was concerned with redeeming the *desiderata* of their approaches to consciousness, and not simply "demystifying" them. For Adorno, what Kant and Freud both lacked was a critical theory of capital; a capacity for the self-reflection, as such, of the subjectivity of the commodity form. Marx provided this. For Adorno, both Kant and Freud were liable to be abused if the problem of capital was obscured and not taken as the fundamental historical frame for the problem of freedom that both sought to address. What was *critical* about Kantian and Freudian consciousness could become unwittingly and unintentionally *affirmative* of the status quo, as if we were already rational subjects with well-developed egos, as if we were already free, as if these were not our *tasks*. This potential self-undermining or self-contradiction of the task of consciousness that Adorno found in Kant and Freud could be explicated adequately only from a Marxian perspective. When Adorno deployed Freudian and Kantian categories for grasping consciousness, he deliberately rendered them aporetic. Adorno considered Kant and Freud as providing descriptive theories that in turn must be subject to critical reflection and specification — within a Marxian socio-historical frame.

For Adorno, the self-opacity of the subject or, in Freud's terms, the phenomenon of the "unconscious mental process," is the expression of the self-contradiction or non-identity of the "subject" in Hegelian-Marxian terms. Because Kantian consciousness is not a static proposition, because Kant was concerned with an account of the possibility of a self-grounded, "self-legislated" and thus *self-conscious* freedom, Adorno was not arraying Freud against Kant. Adorno was not treating Kant as naïve consciousness, but rather attending to the historical separation of Freud from Kant. Marx came between them. The Freudian theory of the unconscious is, for Adorno, a description of the self-alienated character of the subjectivity of modern capital. Freud can be taken as an alternative to Marx — or Kant — only the degree to which a Marxian approach fails to give adequate expression to historical developments in the self-contradiction of the subjectivity of the commodity form.

One thinker usually neglected in accounts of the development of Frankfurt School Critical Theory is Wilhelm Reich. For Adorno, perhaps the key phrase from Reich is "fear of freedom."[1] This phrase has a deeper connotation than might at first be apparent, in that it refers to a dynamic process and not a static fact of repression. "Repression," in Freud's terms, is *self*-repression: It constitutes the self, and hence is not to be understood as an "introjection" from without. The potential for freedom itself produces the reflex of fear in an intrinsic motion. The fear of freedom is thus an index of freedom's possibility. Repression implies its opposite, which is the potential transformation of consciousness. The "fear of freedom" is thus grounded in freedom itself.

Reich derived the "fear of freedom" directly from Freud. Importantly, for Freud, psychopathology exists on a spectrum in which the pathological and the healthy differ not in kind but degree. Freud does not identify the healthy with the normal, but treats both as species of the pathological. The normal is simply the typical, commonplace pathology. For Freud, "neurosis" was the unrealistic way of coping with the new and the different, a failure of the ego's "reality principle." The characteristic thought-figure here is "neurotic repetition." Neurosis is, for Freud, fundamentally about repetition. To free oneself from neurosis is to free oneself from unhealthy repetition. Nonetheless, however, psychical character is, for Freud, itself a function of repetition. The point of psychoanalytic therapy is not to eliminate the individual experience that gives rise to one's character, but rather to allow the past experience to recur in the present in a less pathological way. This is why, for Freud, to "cure" a neurosis is not to "eliminate" it but to *transform* it. The point is not to unravel a person's psychical character, but for it to play out better under changed conditions. For it is simply inappropriate and impractical for a grown person to engage adult situations "regressively," that is, according to a pattern deeply fixed in childhood. While that childhood pattern cannot be extirpated, it can be transformed, so as to be better able to deal with the new situations that are not the repetition of childhood traumas and hence prove intractable to past forms of mastery. At the same time, such forms of mastery from childhood need to be satisfied and not denied. There is no more authoritarian character than the child. What are

---

1 "Ideology as a Material Force," in *The Mass Psychology of Fascism*, trans. Vincent Carfagno (New York: Farrar, Straus and Giroux, 1970), 31.

otherwise "authoritarian" characteristics of the psyche allow precisely these needs to be satisfied. "Guilt," that most characteristic Freudian category, is a form of libidinal satisfaction. Hence its power.

Perhaps the most paradoxical thought Reich offered, writing in the aftermath of the 1933 Nazi seizure of power, was the need for a Marxian approach to attend to the "*progressive* character of fascism." "Progressive" in what sense? Reich thought that Marxism had failed to properly "heed the unconscious impulses" that were otherwise expressed by fascism. Fascism had expressed the emergence of the qualitatively new, however paradoxically, in the form of an apparently retrograde politics. Reich was keen to point out that fascism was not really a throwback to some earlier epoch but rather the appearance of the new, if in a pathological and obscured form. Walter Benjamin's notion of "progressive barbarism" similarly addressed this paradox, for "barbarism" is not savagery but decadence.[2]

Reich thought that learning from Freud was necessary in the face of the phenomenon of fascism, which he regarded as expressing the failure of Marxism. It was necessary due to Freud's attention to expanding and strengthening the capacity of the conscious ego to experience the new and not to "regress" in the neurotic attempt to master the present by repeating the past. Freud attended to the problem of achieving true, present mastery, rather than relapsing into false, past forms. This, Freud thought, could be accomplished through the faculty of "reality-testing," the self-modification of behavior that characterized a healthy ego, able to cope with new situations. Because, for Freud, this always took place in the context of, and as a function of, a predominantly "unconscious" mental process of which the ego was merely the outmost part and in which were lodged the affects and thoughts of the past, this involved a theory of the transformation of consciousness. Because the unconscious did not "know time," transformation was the realm of the ego-psychology of consciousness.

For Reich, as well as for Benjamin and Adorno, from the perspective of Marxism the Freudian account of past and present provided a rich description of the problem of the political task of social emancipation in its

---

2   "Experience and Poverty" in *Arcades Project*, trans. Howard Eiland and Kevin McLaughlin (Cambridge: Belknap Press, 1999), 732.

*subjective* dimension. Fascism had resulted from Marxism's failure to meet the demands of individuals outpaced by history. Reich's great critique of "Marxist" rationalism was that it could not account for why, for the most part, starving people do not steal to survive and the oppressed do not revolt. By contrast, in the Freudian account of emancipation from neurosis, there was both a continuity with and change from prior experience in the capacity to experience the new and different. This was the ego's freedom. One suffered from neurosis to the degree to which one shielded oneself stubbornly against the new. This is why Freud characterized melancholia, or the inability to grieve, as a narcissistic disorder: it represented the false mastery of a pre-ego psychology in which consciousness had not adequately distinguished itself from its environment. The self was not adequately bounded, but instead engaged in a pathological projective identification with the object of loss. The melancholic suffered not from loss of the object, but rather from a sense of loss of self, or a lack of sense of self. The pathological loss was due to a pathological affective investment in the object to begin with, which was not a proper or realistic object of libidinal investment at all. The melancholic suffered from an unrealistic sense of both self and other.

In the context of social change, such narcissism was wounded in recoil from the experience of the new. It thus undermined itself, for it regressed below the capacities for consciousness. The challenge of the new that could be met in freedom becomes instead the pathologically repressed, the insistence on what Adorno called the "ever-same." There is an illusion involved, both of the emergently new in the present, and in the image of the past.[3]

---

3    See Robert Hullot-Kentor, *Things Beyond Resemblance: Collected Essays on Theodor W. Adorno* (New York: Columbia University Press, 2006), 83:

> [Siegfried] Kracauer . . . pointed out [in his review of Adorno's *Kierkegaard: Construction of the Aesthetic*] that . . . [Adorno's] methodology derived from the concept of truth developed by Benjamin in his studies of Goethe and the Baroque drama: "In the view of [Benjamin's] studies, the truth-content of a work reveals itself only in its collapse. . . . The work's claim to totality, its systematic structure, as well as its superficial intentions share the fate of everything transient, but as they pass away with time the work brings characteristics and configurations to the fore that are actually images of truth." This process could be exemplified by a recurrent dream: throughout its recurrences its images age, if imperceptibly; its

214 · Critical theory: History

But such "illusion" is not only pathological, but constitutive: it comprises the "necessary form of appearance," the thought and felt reality of past and present in consciousness. This is the double-movement of both the traumatically new and of an old, past pathology. It is this double-movement, within which the ego struggles for its very existence in the process of undergoing change within and without that Adorno took to be a powerful description of the modern subject of capital. The "liquidation of the individual" was in its dwindling present, dissolved between past and future. The modern subject was thus inevitably "non-identical" with itself. Reich had provided a straightforward account of how accelerating social transformations in capital ensured that characteristic patterns of childhood life would prove inappropriate to adult realities, and that parental authority would be thus undermined. Culture could no longer serve its ancient function.

Freud's account of the "unconscious mental process" was one salient way of grasping this constitutive non-identity of the subject. Freud's ego and id, the "I" and "it" dimensions of consciousness, described how the psychical self was importantly not at one with itself. For Adorno, this was a description not only of the subject's constraint but its potential, the dynamic character of subjectivity, reproductive of both a problem and a task.

In his 1955 essay "Sociology and Psychology," Adorno addressed the necessary and indeed constitutive antinomy of the "individual" and "society" under capital.[4] According to Adorno, there was a productive tension and not a flat contradiction between approaches that elaborated society from the individual psyche and those that derived the individual from the social process: both were at once true and untrue in their partiality. Adorno's point was that it was inevitable that social problems be approached in such one-sided ways. Adorno thus derived two complementary approaches: critical psychology and critical sociology. Or, at a

---

historical truth takes shape as its thematic content dissolves. It is the truth-content that gives the dream, the philosophical work, or the novel its resilience. This idea of historical truth is one of the most provocative rebuttals to historicism ever conceived: works are not studied in the interest of returning them to their own time and period, documents of "how it really was," but rather according to the truth they release in their own process of disintegration.

4   Trans. Irving N. Wohlfarth, *New Left Review* I/46–47 (November – December 1967 & January – February 1968).

different level, critical individualism and critical authoritarianism. Under capital, both the psychical and social guises of the individual were at once functionally effective and spurious delusional realities. It was not a matter of properly merging two aspects of the individual but of recognizing what Adorno elsewhere called the "two torn halves of an integral freedom to which however they do not add up."[5] It was true that there were both social potentials not reducible to individuals and individual potentials not straightforwardly explicable from accounts of society.

The antagonism of the particular and the general had a social basis, but for Adorno this social basis was itself contradictory. Hence there was indeed a social basis for the contradiction of individual and society, rather than a psychical basis, but this social basis found a ground for its reproduction in the self-contradiction of the psychical individual. A self-contradictory form of society gave rise to, and was itself reproduced through, self-contradictory individuals.

The key for Adorno was to avoid collapsing what should be critical-theoretical categories into apologetic or affirmative-descriptive ones for grasping the individual and society. Neither a social dialectic nor a split psyche was to be ontologized or naturalized, but both required historical specification as dual aspects of a problem to be overcome. That problem was what Marx called "capital." For Adorno, it was important that both dialectical and psychoanalytic accounts of consciousness had only emerged in modernity. From this historical reality one could speculate that an emancipated society would be neither dialectical nor consist of psychological individuals, for both were symptomatic of capital. Nevertheless, any potential for freedom needed to be found there, in the socially general and individual symptoms of capital, described by both disciplines of sociology and psychology.

Hence, the problem for Adorno was not a question of methodology but of critical reflexivity: how did social history present itself through individual psychology (not methodological individualism but critical reflection on the individuation of a social problem). The "primacy" of the

5   Letter from Adorno to Benjamin (August 2, 1935), in "Letters to Walter Benjamin," *New Left Review* I/81 (September – October 1973).

social, or of the "object," was, for Adorno, not a methodological move or preferred mode of analysis, let alone a philosophical ontology, but was meant to provoke critical recognition of the problem he sought to address.

In his speech to the 1968 conference of the German Society for Sociology, titled "Late Capitalism or Industrial Society?," Adorno described how the contradiction of capital was expressed in "free-floating anxiety."[6] Such "free-floating anxiety" was expressive of the undermining of what Freud considered the ego-psychology of the subject of therapy. Paranoia spoke to pre-Oedipal, pre-individuated problems, to what Adorno called the "liquidation of the individual." This was caused by and fed into the further perpetuation of authoritarian social conditions.

For Adorno, especially as regards the neo-Freudian revisionists of psychoanalysis as well as post- and non-Freudian approaches, therapy had, since Freud's time, itself become repressive in ways scarcely anticipated by Freud. Such "therapy" sought to repress the social-historical symptom of the impossibility of therapy. Freud had commented on the intractability of narcissistic disorders such as melancholia, but these had come to replace the typical Freudian neuroses of the 19th century such as hysteria. The paranoiac-delusional reality of the authoritarian personality had its ground of truth, a basis, in society. The "fear of freedom" was expressed in the individual's retreat from ego-psychology, a narcissistic recoil from an intractable social reality. Perhaps this could be recognized as such. This, for Adorno, was the emancipatory potential of narcissism.

In his essay "Freudian Theory and the Pattern of Fascist Propaganda" (1951),[7] Adorno characterized the appeal of fascist demagogy precisely in its being recognized by its consumers as the lie that one chooses to believe, the authority one spites while participating in it by submitting to it in bad faith. This was its invidious power, the pleasure of doing wrong, but also its potential overcoming. An antisocial psychology, not reducible to the sociopathic, had been developed which posed the question of society, if at a different level than in Freud's time. It was no longer situated in

---

6   In *Can One Live After Auschwitz?: A Philosophical Reader*, ed. Rolf Tiedemann, trans. Rodney Livingstone and others (Stanford: Stanford University Press, 2009), 125.

7   In *The Essential Frankfurt School Reader*, ed. Andrew Arato and Eike Gebhardt (New York: Continuum, 1985).

the "family romance" of the Oedipal drama but in society writ large. But this demanded recognition beyond what was available in the psychotherapeutic relationship, because it spoke not to the interaction of egos but to projective identification among what Freud could only consider wounded narcissists. For Adorno, we are a paranoid society with reason.

There had always been a fine line between therapy, providing for an individual's betterment through strengthening the ego's "reality principle," and adaptation to a bad social reality. For Adorno, the practice of therapy had come to tip the balance to adaptation — repression. The critical edge of Freudian psychoanalysis was lost in its unproblematic adoption by society — in its very "success." Freudian psychoanalysis was admitted and domesticated, but only the degree to which it had become outmoded. Like so much of modernism, it became part of kitsch culture. This gave it a repressive function. But it retained, however obscurely, a "utopian" dimension: the idea of being an ego at all. Not the self constituted in interpellation by authority, but in being for-itself.

After Freud, therapy produced, not problematic individuals of potential freedom, but authoritarian pseudo-individuals of mere survival. For Freud it was the preservation of the individual's potential for self-overcoming and not mere self-reiteration that characterized the ego. For Adorno, however, the obsolescence of Freudian ego-psychology posed the question and problem of what Adorno called "self-preservation." For Adorno, this was seen in individuals' "unworthiness of love."

If psychoanalytic therapy had always been above all pragmatic, had always concerned itself with the transformation of neurotic symptoms in the direction of better abilities to cope with reality, then there was always a danger of replacing neuroses with those that merely better suited society. But if, as Freud put it early on, as a result of psychotherapy the individual finds herself pressing demands that society has difficulty meeting, then that remained society's problem.[8] It was a problem *for* the individual, but not simply *of* or "with" the individual. Freud understood his task as helping a neurotic to better equip herself for dealing with reality, including, first and foremost, *social* realities — that is, other individuals. Freud recognized

---

8   In "The Psychotherapy of Hysteria," in *Studies on Hysteria.*

the *challenge* of psychoanalysis. It was not for Freud to deny the benefits of therapy even if these presented new problems. Freud conceived psychical development as an open-ended process of consciousness in freedom.

The problem for Adorno was how to present the problem of society as such. Capital was the endemic form of psychology and not only sociology. What was the *psychological* basis for emancipatory transformation? For the problem was not how the individual was to survive society, but rather how society would survive the unmet demands presented by its individuals — and how society could transfigure and redeem the suffering, including psychically, of individual human beings. These human beings instantiated the very substance of that society, and they were the individuals who provided the ground for social transformation.

An emancipated society would no longer be "sociological" as it is under capital, but would be truly social for the first time. Its emancipated individuals would no longer be "psychological," but would be truly "individual" for the first time. They would no longer be merely derivative from their experience, stunted and recoiled in their narcissism. In this sense, the true, diverse individuation, what Adorno called "multiplicity," towards which Freudian psychoanalytic therapy pointed, could be realized, freed from the compulsions of neurotic repetition, including those of prevailing patterns of culture. At the same time, the pathological necessity of individual emancipation from society would be overcome. Repetition could be non-pathological, non-repressive, and elaborated in freedom. The self-contradiction of consciousness found in the Freudian problematic of ego-psychology, with its "unconscious mental process" from which it remained alienated, would be overcome, allowing for the first time the Kantian rationalism of the adequately self-aware and self-legislating subject of freedom in an open-ended development and transformation of human reason, not as a cunning social dialectic, but in and through individual human beings, who could be themselves for the very first time.

Originally published in *Platypus Review* 24 (June 2010)

# Sexuality and gender in capitalism[1]

In my presentation, I will be drawing from but not citing a variety of readings we do in Platypus, including Georg Lukács's book *History and Class Consciousness* (1923), Theodor W. Adorno's essay "Sexual Taboos and the Law Today" (1963) and John D'Emilio's essay "Capitalism and Gay Identity" (1983), as well as University of Chicago Professor Moishe Postone's interpretation of Marx's critique of capital.[2]

I want to start with a quotation from Juliet Mitchell's groundbreaking essay "Women: The Longest Revolution," published in the *New Left Review* in 1966, that will establish some categories I wish to explore in considering a Marxist approach to problems of sexuality and gender in capital:

> Socialism will be a process of change, of becoming. A fixed image of the future is in the worst sense ahistorical. . . . As Marx wrote (in *Precapitalist Economic Formations*): "What is progress if not the absolute elaboration of humanity's creative dispositions . . . unmeasured by any previously established yardstick[,] an end in itself . . . the absolute movement of becoming?" . . . The liberation of women under socialism will

---

1   On Juliet Mitchell, "Women: The Longest Revolution," *New Left Review* I/40 (November – December 1966), 11–37.

2   *History and Class Consciousness*, trans. Rodney Livingstone (Cambridge, MA: MIT Press, 1972); "Sexual Taboos and the Law Today," in *Critical Models: Interventions and Catchwords*, trans. Henry Pickford (New York: Columbia University Press, 2005); "Capitalism and Gay Identity," in *Powers of Desire: The Politics of Sexuality*, edited by Ann Snitow, Christine Stansell, and Sharan Thompson. New Feminist Library Series (New York: Monthly Review Press, 1983); *Time, Labor, and Social Domination: A Reinterpretation of Marx's Critical Theory* (Cambridge: Cambridge University Press, 1993).

> [be] ... a human achievement, in the long passage from Nature
> to Culture which is the definition of history and society.[3]

Here, Mitchell concludes her essay with an emphasis on the issue of "becoming," or the open-ended transformation of gender and sexuality that capital makes possible but constrains.

To illustrate the problem regarding the history of the Left, including Marxism, on issues of gender and sexuality, it should suffice to address a poorly registered shift that occurred in the 20th century in the social imagination and ideology of discontents with capital between two crucial periods, the early 20th century "Old Left" of the 1930s and '40s, and the "New Left" of the 1960s and '70s. In the earlier period, of the "Old" Left, the predominant form of discontent and grievance regarding capitalism, which had some continuity with similar forms of the 19th century workers' movement, was how capitalism undermined the working class family and sexual life, breaking up the "hearth and home," and denying the benefits of the bourgeois family to the workers, in exploiting not only men but also women and children. In the late 20th century "New Left," by contrast, there was a reversal of the discontent and grievance with capitalism, in that it made women and children (and men) prisoners of the "bourgeois" family. Where once capitalism was seen as barring the family life of the workers, now capitalism was seen as depending upon and thus keeping workers constrained in the conventional family. Where once the demand was to have the freedom to have a family, there arose the demand to abolish the family along with capitalism. Where once, in supposed "Marxism-Leninism," that is, Stalinist, Maoist, and Guevarist, etc., Communism, the family was regarded as the "fighting unit of socialism," for "New Left" Marxists, the family was seen as a bulwark of capitalism. Similarly, where once, in such supposed "Marxism," homosexuality and other "deviance" was seen as the result of "bourgeois decadence," for the "New Left," sexual liberation found pride of place. What accounts for this shift?

As shown by the fact that today, paradoxically, a central concern of politics around homosexuality is the demand for equal rights to marital

---

3   "Women: The Longest Revolution," 37.

and "family" status, it is not a simple matter of "progress," in which at one time Marxists had been unaware of the depth of issues of gender and sexual oppression, and then came to be aware, trying to incorporate issues of gender and sexuality into their critiques of capital. For, as Mitchell points out, not only Marx and Engels themselves, but also later Marxists, such as the German Social-Democratic Party leader August Bebel, as well as younger Marxist political activists, such as Lenin, Rosa Luxemburg, and Trotsky, were very much aware of how gender and sexual liberation were central concerns for overcoming capital. For instance, in the late 19th century, August Bebel was the first modern parliamentarian to call for the decriminalization of homosexuality. When Bebel's party later inherited power in the Weimar Republic after the German Revolution of 1918 at the end of the First World War, it became the first modern democratic state to decriminalize homosexuality, but only after the Bolsheviks had already done so in the Russian Revolution of 1917. It was the demise of the Weimar Republic with the 1933 Nazi seizure of power that recriminalized homosexuality (and, incidentally, this was one of very few laws implemented by the Nazis that was not repealed with their defeat at the end of World War II). In the Soviet Union, it was only in the process of conservatization that occurred through Stalinism, the degeneration of the Russian Revolution, that homosexuality was recriminalized, and the conventional heterosexual family was reinforced (for instance through the recriminalization of abortion and the restoration of legal obstacles to divorce) around the same time, in the 1930s. As a result, subsequent "Marxists" took as axiomatic the celebration of heterosexuality and the family, and the pathologization of homosexuality, neither of which had been the case for earlier Marxist radicals.

Thus, conventional but false "Marxist" accounts that came later have posed the issue of "gender vs. class," or, in "socialist feminist" versions, have tried to demonstrate the "interconnectedness" of "gender, sexuality and class," where what needed to be addressed was how gender or sexuality could, equally as well as socioeconomic "class" accounts could do, describe the problem of capital, in terms of the problem of emancipatory transformation. To do so it would be necessary to show how gender and sexuality are in themselves issues of class, or, perhaps more importantly, how class is an issue of sexuality and gender. For gender and sexuality are capital.

That is, they comprise its conditions of reproduction, as much as socio-economic classes do. And, like modern classes, gender and sexuality have themselves been formed by the history of capital.

One way to disentangle the problems that have usually beset and confounded purported "Marxist" anti-capitalist approaches to gender and sexual liberation is to recognize that a Marxian account of capital is concerned with conditions of possibility and not causal-deterministic explanations for oppression. So, the question would not be how capitalism *causes* sexual and gender oppression, which could indeed be shown, but, rather, how capital could be grasped as the historically specific social *condition of possibility* for forms of sexual and gender constraint and oppression. This is especially important with regard to how, in the modern era, sexuality and gender roles have taken a variety of forms, but all nonetheless remained problematical and ultimately constraining of social possibilities for developing greater human potential.

The modern era of capital, beginning in the late 18th and early 19th centuries, has demonstrated a great deal of potential, in a variety of different forms, for sexual life and gender relations. Such potential has been inherent in the overcoming of traditional ways of life in capital. Conservatives have responded to such changes as the dangerous break-down of traditional values, but, from the beginning, Marxists, among other bohemian socialists of the 19th and early 20th centuries, had been interested in how to push such potential further, in an open-ended way. They regarded capital as a constraint, an obstacle to this. At the same time, however, they regarded capital as the inevitable condition of possibility for emancipatory transformation. As regards changes already underway, Marxists found them expressing potential capital already embodied. Marxists thus distinguished themselves sharply from conservative responses to capital's dynamic of change. Capital undermined traditional ways of life, but not nearly enough, according to Marxism, because modern capitalist society allowed for the reproduction of (new forms of) gender and sexual oppression. Capital not only undermined, but allowed the recrudescence of the worst forms of supposed "traditional" ways of life.

An example I'd like to raise is the phenomenon of the return of the traditional sexual prostitution of boys in Afghanistan after the U.S.-led NATO coalition ousted the Taliban. This has been chronicled in a recent PBS *Frontline* documentary.[4] Whereas the former Soviet client regime and the Taliban radical Islamic fundamentalists, each in their own ways and for their own reasons, had suppressed the practice of the "dancing boys" in Afghanistan, the post-U.S. invasion and occupation regime, while formally outlawing it, has largely tolerated its return. This is because the Mujahideen fighters (for instance of the Russian- and Indian- and then U.S.-backed Northern Alliance) that had fought the Soviet-backed regime and then had been ousted in turn by the Taliban, but now form pillars of the new, post-NATO intervention regime, had cultivated the practice of "dancing boy" prostitution among themselves over the course of the past 30 years. Indeed, their opposition to Afghanistan's pro-Soviet regime in the 1970s and '80s could be attributed almost as much to their adherence to this "traditional" sexual practice as to their opposition to the unveiling, education, public life and rights of women. As one adherent put it in the Frontline documentary, "Women are for children, but boys are for pleasure." In Afghanistan, as elsewhere, the nexus of pressure of a money economy with conditions of wretched, abject poverty, massive social dislocation, including conditions of far-ranging migrant labor markets, and some dubious "traditional" cultural values, results in the worst of both modern and traditional forms of social life. How would a Marxist approach address a phenomenon like the Afghan "dancing boys?"

While there is no simple, straightforward answer, it is clear that "dancing boy" prostitution in Afghanistan today bears only superficial resemblance to anything that was practiced traditionally in a prior historical era, itself nothing to celebrate. So the practice can and should be condemned, as in the liberal sensibility of the Frontline documentary, directed at scandalizing a Western audience towards opposing present U.S. and NATO/European policy in Afghanistan that tolerates such abuses by the regime they have fostered there. But opposing the prostitution of the "dancing boys" on the basis of some "hetero-normative" (and hence homophobic) assumption of conventional sexual and gender life elsewhere, such as found in America and Europe, is problematic, to say the least, however much it may appear to

---

4   *The Dancing Boys of Afghanistan*, directed by Najibullah Quraishi (2010)

be a possible improvement, as advocates in Afghanistan seeking to put an end to the "dancing boys" may imagine.

Such supposed "traditional" practices of male intergenerational, pederastic homosexuality that finds grotesque expression today in Afghanistan can obviously in no way be found to express the full potential of male homosexuality — or of child sexuality, for that matter. So, the solution is not to try to get Afghan men to adopt a more "normal" sexual orientation towards relations with (adult) women and the modern (Western) marriage based on love and (heterosexual) intimacy, which is highly unlikely under present social conditions in a place like Afghanistan, anyway. And, as anyone concerned with sexual and gender emancipation in places like America and Europe would point out, not only the conventional forms of intimate life and family practices that take place hegemonically "here," but also those found in the gay/lesbian/bisexual/transgender subcultures, are hardly the final word in terms of sexual and gender emancipation. And, just as importantly, as can be observed in the society of "law and order" such as practiced in places like the U.S., criminalization of sexual practices of any kind offers no solution.

Another example I'd raise is female genital mutilation, as "traditionally" practiced in parts of Africa and the Middle East and also among immigrant communities from such places in North America and Europe. While socio-biologists have desperately tried to find a biological-evolutionary "reason" for female orgasm, it turns out to be entirely extraneous from survival imperatives of natural selection. As one writer put it, female orgasm, unlike the male orgasm, seems to exist naturally just "for fun." Biology is a *condition*, and not a "destiny." There is nothing simply "natural" about human biological conditions. But these can indeed play out in a variety of different ways, depending on *society*. It can also, for instance, allow whole cultures to practice the sexual mutilation of — the excising of sexual pleasure from — female children, as occurs routinely for millions of girls around the world each year. It is a "voluntary" practice, by and among women. But this is only an extreme example of how "culture" shapes "nature," or, how society forms "sexuality," through gender roles, among other practices, all of which, to one degree or another, could be understood as forms of "mutilation," including psychologically, when seen from the standpoint of *potential emancipation*. How would Marxists respond? — Especially, as regards female genital mutilation, when what is at stake concerns marital eligibility, and, hence, a whole host of life-chances for women, if the "traditional" practice is abrogated. We could broaden this concern in addressing the phenomenon of "honor killings" of women for sexual infractions, including involuntary ones such as being raped, in the Arab world and elsewhere. Even more broadly, sex work, especially as a global phenomenon, for instance among millions of migrant workers, points to problems of life chances, for the men who are clients no less than for the women who are prostituted. It is not merely a matter of gender oppression, although gender oppression as a condition certainly plays a key role. Clearly, as in the case of the Afghan "dancing boys," what is required is some kind of increased scope for both individual and collective possibilities. The task is to grasp *capital*, the social-historical moment of the present in a process of *becoming*, as a matter of economics, politics and culture, including gender and sexuality, as embodying both potential and constraint for such possibilities. How could a less destructive way for humanity be opened?

Addressing capital as the fundamental and global context for such phenomena is a challenging but necessary requirement for even beginning to approach the question and problem of what it would take to open possibilities for gender and sexual practices for the vast majority, if not simply the totality of humanity in our modern epoch. In the forms of purportedly "inhuman" practices as can be found in the phenomena of gender and sexuality with which the present world is rife, can be seen, in however distorted form, potential possibilities for *becoming human*, in ways that can only be barely imagined today. As Mitchell warned in her essay more than 40 years ago, we need to attend to the problem of our present discontents taking static, hypostatized forms, and beware of the normative principles we may be tempted to offer against manifest destructive practices we face and want to overcome. For what is necessary is to grasp the "movement of becoming" in capital that must be transformed, from the break-down of tradition, as well as the specious re-positing of "tradition" in the face of the onslaught of modernity, into a truly "human achievement" of emancipation.

Presented at the University of Chicago, May 18, 2010.

# The mass psychology
# of capitalist democracy

The Frankfurt School in the 1920s–30s incorporated the categories of Freudian psychoanalysis as descriptive of the mediation of the contradiction of the commodity form in individual consciousness. This critical appropriation of psychoanalytic categories was in response to the collapse of preceding forms of political mediation in which the contradictions of capitalism manifested, for instance between socialism and liberalism.

Freudian categories were not meant to supplement let alone replace Marxian critical-theoretical categories for the Frankfurt School, but rather psychoanalytic approaches to psychology were themselves regarded as symptoms of social-historical development — and crisis. In other words, the question was why had not Marx, Hegel or Kant, among others, developed a theory of unconscious mental processes, prior to Freud? And why had Freud's theory of the unconscious emerged when it did, in the late 19th and early 20th century. (The closest to a registration of the psychological unconscious was by William James, also in the late 19th century, roughly contemporaneously with but in ignorance of Freud. — One must place to one side the earlier Romantic conception by Schelling, which had a different concern, not psychological but rather philosophical and moreover theological.) Furthermore, why had Freudian psychoanalysis achieved widespread currency and plausibility when it did, in the early-mid 20th century? And, what changes had occurred in the meaning and purchase of Freudian psychoanalysis, especially with respect to the so-called "neo-Freudian revisionism" after Freud, but also regarding Freud's later, "metapsychological" speculations?

What such concerns raised by the Frankfurt School — what Marcuse called the "obsolescence of the Freudian concept of man"[1] — was the transformation of society that took place in the late 19th and early-mid 20th century, and how this related to the failure of Marxism, politically — the failure of the revolution 1917–19. This was the lodestar for the Frankfurt School's perspective on history, the key period 1848–1917, through which they considered the problems of modern society. This is found especially in Walter Benjamin's *Arcades Project*, which was focused on the mid-19th century moment, circa 1848, as anticipating the 20th century. It was as part of this project that Benjamin wrote his famous "Theses on the philosophy of history," actually titled "On the concept of history," the aphorisms which were to serve as prolegomena to the *Arcades Project* as a whole. It was there that Benjamin engaged Freudian psychoanalytic categories most extensively, building upon and deepening his investigation into the melancholy of modernity that he had previously charted in his work on Proust and Kafka.

As a symptom of what Freud called a "narcissistic disorder" — that is, an inability and problematic form of self-love — melancholia challenged Freud's clinical concept of the ego: Freud thought that melancholia was perhaps beyond psychoanalytic therapy's effectiveness. This was because for Freud the therapeutic process of transference was short-circuited by the patient's identification that was problematically projective and prevented the relation to another — the therapist — as an other. The other was both too closely and too distantly related; the difference was too great and too little.

Such projective identification was found by Benjamin in Baudelaire's work, about which Benjamin wrote that, "Here it is the commodity itself that speaks." This has been mistakenly read as meaning merely that Baudelaire was granting subjectivity to commodities as articles of consumption, whereas for Benjamin the critical point was rather that the speaker was a commodity. As Adorno put it in a letter to Benjamin about his work on Baudelaire, "The fetish character of the commodity is not a fact of consciousness; rather it is dialectical, in the eminent sense that it produces

---

1   In *Five Lectures: Psychoanalysis, Politics, and Utopia* (Boston: Beacon Press, 1970).

consciousness."[2] That is, for Adorno, the commodity form of subjectivity is the very source of consciousness — of self-consciousness in the Hegelian sense. Benjamin wrote that the commodity is the most empathic thing imaginable, in that it only realizes its being-in-itself through being-for-another, however ambivalently. Adorno wrote to Benjamin that this is a function of both "desire and fear."

Such ambivalence was fundamental to Freud's conception of the primordial origins of the psyche: the primary narcissism's originary wounding encounter with parental authority, with the first other, the mother. It is the introduction of the third figure of the father that for Freud allows for others to be others, in an essential triad that interrupts the original dyad of mother-and-child. The further relation with which the child must reckon, between the mother and father, or of the other with another, was key for Freud to the development of a balanced sense of self that transcended the reversible and ambivalent projective identification with the primary caregiver in infancy. Overcoming the threat to the relation to the mother that the father represents in the Oedipus complex also overcomes the narcissistic identification that threatens to obliterate the nascent sense of self in the infantile merging with the other. Until the introduction of this essential third, the danger is the radical ambivalence regarding difference, which is perceived as a deadly threat: the fear of as well as the desire to obliterate the psyche represented by the mother as object of both love and hate.

For Freud such primordial originary narcissism subsists in later psychical development: it is enlisted and transformed in the process of being transcended. However, there is occasion for regressing to this primary narcissistic state: there are traumas that overwhelm the fragile development of the ego, beyond its original — and originally problematic — narcissism, returning it to that condition. It was not coincidental that Freud turned his attention to the question of melancholia and narcissism in the context of WWI and the traumas experienced there, in which Freud found a model for penetrating the developmental sources for narcissistic disorders such as melancholia.

---

2    August 2, 1935 in "Letters to Walter Benjamin" *New Left Review* I/81 (September – October 1973).

The Marxist appropriation of Freud's clinical theory of primary narcissism by Benjamin and Adorno was in the social context of the contradictions of capitalism that overwhelmed the sense of self in the ego. The Freudian therapeutic question of "Why did I do that?" was overwhelmed in the contradictory social dynamics of capitalism, in which the responsible individual was both demanded and rendered intolerable. WWI only expressed in drastic form the fundamental character of the situation of the human being in modern capitalism. For the Frankfurt School, modern society already by the mid-19th century was contradictory respecting individual human beings, and this found expression and registration in the very phenomenon of "psychology" itself — the self-contradictory character of the logic of the psyche. Freud's apprehension of the contradiction between consciousness and "unconscious mental processes" expressed this in acute form, and was itself regarded by Benjamin and Adorno as a phenomenon of society. But Freud's desirable intention to strengthen the resources for the individual psyche was rendered utopian — impossible — in modern society. As Freud himself observed in one of his earliest published reflections on analytic therapy, however, this was society's problem — therapy may produce individuals with demands that society cannot meet. But these demands were socially legitimate even if they remained denied. A contradiction of capitalism was found in the contradiction between the individual and society in a very precise sense.

Now, what were the political ramifications and implications of this? The Frankfurt School Critical Theorists were keen to recognize those political forms that appealed to the abdication of the responsibility of the individual through problematic narcissistic identification, short-circuiting the ego, and seemingly justifying the condition of paranoid ambivalence — both desire and fear for objects of simultaneous hate and love — what Anna Freud termed "identification with the aggressor" in society. This was a dynamic that the Frankfurt School thinkers found as well in "revolutionary politics" — perhaps especially so, in that fascism offered a form of social revolution in mobilizing the masses for political action, however reactionary.

But the problem ran deeper than the dramatic outward expression of fascism. As Wilhelm Reich pointed out, the "fear of freedom" was characteristic of the "average unpolitical person," who was nonetheless "authoritarian" in psychical comportment.[3] So, what was necessary, then, was recognizing the unconscious authoritarianism of the individual's condition in modern society.

For Adorno, this was to be found in the form of identification not only with overt fascist demagogy but also with what his friend and mentor Siegfried Kracauer called the "inconspicuous surface-level expressions" of everyday social life and its mass-cultural forms, what Adorno called the psychical "pattern" that was found in exaggerated, acute form in fascist "propaganda," but was not qualitatively or essentially different from commercial advertising.[4] Adorno found a constitutive ambivalence there, in which the subject found pleasure in the conformist "going along" with the lie while still recognizing it as false: the psychical satisfaction in the "will to believe" in what one knew to be false.

Adorno characterized this as simultaneously looking up and down at the object of authority, placing oneself above and below it. The pleasure of the audience for fascist propaganda was in the combined admiration and contempt for the demagogue, who was not only exalted but also degraded in the viewer's estimation. When confronted by his friend Karl Jaspers about the Nazi mistreatment of his Jewish wife, Heidegger replied that Hitler had "such wonderful hands." In this the demagogical "leader" was an object of projective identification for the subject: the subject rehearsed his own overestimation of himself and self-derogation, not merely in sharing the mentality of the propaganda, as both idealized and unworthy, but in recognizing one's own contemptible character in granting the demagogy a hearing, let alone authority. The pleasure in fascist buffoonery is precisely in its ridiculousness that is nonetheless performed in earnest — with deadly seriousness. This was the authentically democratic basis for fascism — in the psychology of the masses, who, acting precisely as a "mass," abdicated their actual democratic responsibility for political authority.

---

3   "Ideology as a Material Force," in *The Mass Psychology of Fascism*, trans. Vincent Carfagno (New York: Farrar, Straus and Giroux, 1970), 26.

4   Krakauer, "The Mass Ornament," in *The Mass Ornament* (Cambridge: Harvard University Press, 1995), 75; Adorno, "Freudian Theory and the Pattern of Fascist Propaganda," in *The Essential Frankfurt School Reader*, ed. Arato and Gebhardt (New York: Continuum, 1985).

As Tocqueville put it, in a democracy the people gets the government it deserves. This was rendered paradoxical in modern capitalism, in that the public disavows responsibility for the leaders that it nonetheless elects, in this way reinforcing the authoritarianism one would otherwise deplore: it is what one really wants in the abdication for responsibility that renders one actually contemptible. One's desire is unworthy. The authoritarian ritual is the rehearsal of this political abdication, what Reich called the "fear of freedom." In the Frankfurt School's time, the masses failed to make the revolution, which meant that they deserved the fascist reaction, but felt that they could both blame and punish the revolutionaries for the reaction that followed as well as disclaim responsibility for fascism, feeling "misled" by it. But the point is that they misled themselves, precisely through indulging the paranoiac mentality of fascism in which the narcissistic ego could lose itself, a bitter but nonetheless comforting pleasure of regressing through the dissolution of individual identity in the fascist mass. As Benjamin pointed out, fascism gave the masses an opportunity to "express themselves," but only by abdicating themselves.[5] This is true not only of fascism, but is endemic in modern politics.

An example from U.S. politics will suffice to demonstrate how this works today, despite the absence of revolutionary political crisis. When the President gives his State of the Union address to Congress and the wider public, he is flanked behind by his Vice President as leader of the Senate and by the Speaker of the House of Representatives. Moreover, the Justices of the Supreme Court as well as the members of Congress are present, with certain hand-picked representatives of the public also in the audience.

In each case, the television viewers have audience members in attendance as proxy observers, whose reactions serve as cues. This goes to the most absurd ritual practiced at these events, the applause that punctuates the President's speech. It is entirely predictable which "side of the aisle" — which representatives of the two parties, Republicans and Democrats — will applaud or give a standing ovation to particular statements in the speech. The rehearsed, mechanical quality of such audience responses

---

5 "The Work of Art in the Age of Mechanical Reproduction" (1935) in *Illuminations*, ed. Hannah Arendt, trans. Harry Zohn (New York: Schocken Books, 1968), 241.

demonstrate the political contentlessness of the President's speech: the reactions are not to the President's policies but rather to his power; one waits for what the President will say in suspense, but there will be no surprise, or, if something startling is said then this will be in expectation of a stumble rather than a prerogative. There is an embarrassed awkwardness attending such occasions of public power. For it is not the President's power that is being rehearsed so much as his powerlessness — at least in any substantial matter of change. One expects and responds only to the performance, not the policy. Did the President give a good speech? What were the benchmarks of the speech's success? Not the President as policy-maker but as speech-giver. The humiliating performance of the President provides for the public's abasement of the political power to which they are nonetheless subject. Indeed, whenever unexpected Presidential action is taken, it is almost always unpopular and regarded as a misstep: one thinks of the Iraq invasion and the TARP economic bailout and stimulus measures. The President is radically divided between person and role: the role is granted unrealistic authority; the person debased.

The rating on performance expresses and reinforces the conservatism of such phenomena. One witnesses the drama more or less indulgently towards all the participants; one indulges oneself in the rehearsal, but with a combination of radically opposed values: enthrallment and circumspect distance. One knows that it is merely a performance, but a performance that is granted a spurious substance, like a sports game, with all the passions of fandom. One watches not only the President and his audience, but also oneself, ambivalently. The enigma of power remains intact, its authority unpenetrated. The effects of policy and hence the consequential character of politics remain unclear, and this suits the viewers perfectly well, as it provides solace for their abdication of responsibility. Everyone does what is expected, but no one takes action. The people get the government that they not only actually but importantly feel themselves to deserve, one which simultaneously flatters and humiliates them, and in ways that allow them to hide and lose themselves in the process, disappearing into an anonymous public, which also preserves themselves, narcissistically — allows them to be "subjects" without risking themselves, either psychologically or politically.

In a classic moment for the concerns of Freudian psychoanalysis, the social subject and hence society remains opaque to itself: the therapeutic question, "Why did I do that?" is occluded by the unasked question of politics, "What have we done?"

Presented on a panel with Isaac Balbus and Marilyn Nissim-Sabat
at the conference "Which Way Forward for Psychoanalysis?"
held at the University of Chicago, May 18, 2013.

# Critical authoritarianism[1]

## Immanent critique

Whenever approaching any phenomenon, Adorno's procedure is one of *immanent dialectical critique*. The phenomenon is treated as not accidental or arbitrary but as a necessary form of appearance that points beyond itself, indicating conditions of possibility for change. It is a phenomenon of the necessity for change. The conditions of possibility for change indicated by the phenomenon in question are explored immanently, from within. The possibility for change is indicated by a phenomenon's self-contradictions, which unfold from within itself, from its own movement, and develop from within its historical moment.

Everything is taken not merely as it "is," as it happens to exist, but rather as it "ought" to be, as it could and should be, yielding as-yet unrealized potentials and possibilities. So it is with "authoritarianism," in Adorno's view. For Adorno, the key is how psychological authoritarianism is self-contradictory and points beyond itself. Adorno is interested in the "actuality" of authoritarianism: as Wilhelm Reich put it, the "progressive character of fascism;"[2] as Walter Benjamin put it, the "positive concept of barbarism."[3]

---

1   On Adorno's "Remarks on *The Authoritarian Personality*," published for the first time in *Platypus Review* 91 (November 2016).

2   "[T]he mass basis of fascism, the rebelling lower middle classes, contained not only reactionary but also powerful progressive social forces. This contradiction was overlooked [by contemporary Marxists]." Wilhelm Reich, "Ideology as Material Power," in *The Mass Psychology of Fascism* (1933/46), trans. Vincent Carfagno (New York: Farrar, Straus and Giroux, 1970), 3–4.

3   "Experience and Poverty" (1933), in *Selected Writings,* vol. 2 *1927–34,* ed. Howard Eiland and Michael W. Jennings, (Cambridge, Massachusetts: Belknap, Harvard, 1999), 732.

This demands a critical approach rather than a merely descriptive or analytically positive or affirmative approach. For something can be affirmed either in its justification and legitimation or in its denunciation. In either case, the phenomenon is left as it is; whereas, for Adorno, as a Marxist, "the point is to *change* it."[4]

So, what possibilities for change are indicated by authoritarianism, and how are such possibilities pointed to by the categories of Freudian psychoanalysis? For Adorno, it is unfortunate that social contradiction has passed from ideology and politics in society to individual psychology (indeed, this expresses a political failure), but there it is.[5] The "F-scale" is misleading, as Adorno notes, in that it might — despite its being posed as a "scale" — be mistaken for a matter of difference in kind rather than degree. Meaning that, for Adorno, everyone is more or less susceptible to fascism — everyone is more or less authoritarian.

The competing aspects of the individual psyche between liberal individuality and authoritarian tendencies is itself the self-contradiction of authoritarianism Adorno sought to explore. In capitalism, liberalism is the flip-side of the same coin as fascism. Individualism and collectivism are an antinomy that express capitalist contradiction. For individualism violates true individuality and collectivism violates the true potential of the social collectivity. Individuality and collectivity remain unfulfilled *desiderata*, the aspirations and goals of bourgeois society, its emancipatory promise. For Adorno (as for Marx), both are travestied in capitalism — mere "shams."

Authoritarianism is an expression of that travesty of society. Fascism is the sham collectivity in which the sham individuality hides itself; just as liberalism is the sham individuality that conceals the collective condition of

---

4   Marx, "Theses on Feuerbach" (1845).

5   See Max Horkheimer, "On the Sociology of Class Relations" (1943) and my discussion of it, "Without a Socialist Party, there is no Class Struggle, only Rackets," *nonsite.org* (January 11, 2016), in this volume. In "The Authoritarian State" (1940/42), Horkheimer wrote that,

> Sociological and psychological concepts are too superficial to express what has happened to revolutionaries in the last few decades: their will toward freedom has been damaged, without which neither understanding nor solidarity nor a correct relation between leader and group is conceivable. (*The Essential Frankfurt School Reader*, eds. Andrew Arato and Eike Gebhardt [New York: Continuum, 1985], 95–117.)

society. That collective condition is not a state of being but the task of the need for socialism beyond capitalism. Fascism as well as liberalism expresses that unfulfilled need and tasking demand for socialism in capitalism.

So what would it mean to critique authoritarianism in an immanently dialectical manner? What is the critical value of authoritarianism, in Adorno's view? How can the potential possibility pointing beyond capitalism be expressed by authoritarianism and revealed rather than concealed by individual psychology? How is society critically revealed in authoritarianism, pointing to socialism?

## Psychology

In "Sociology and psychology"[6] Adorno diagnoses the division of psychology from sociology as itself a symptom of contradiction in society — of the actual separation and contradiction of the individual and the collective in capitalism.

In *The Authoritarian Personality*,[7] Adorno et al. wrote that the fascist personality was characterized by identification with technology, the love for instruments as "equipment." Here, Adorno found the emancipatory potential beyond capitalism precisely in such identification and imitation: it becomes a matter of the form of individuation. In "Imaginative excesses," orphaned from *Minima Moralia*,[8] Adorno wrote that,

> [N]o . . . faith can be placed in those equated with the means; the subjectless beings whom historical wrong has robbed of the strength to right it, adapted to technology and unemployment, conforming and squalid, hard to distinguish from the

---

6 "Sociology and Psychology" (1955). Originally written by Adorno for a festschrift celebrating Max Horkheimer's sixtieth birthday, the piece was published in English translation in two parts in the *New Left Review*, I/46 (November – December 1967), 63–80, and I/47 (January – February 1968), 79–97.

7 Theodor W. Adorno, Else Frenkel-Brunswik, Daniel Levinson, and Nevitt Sanford, *The Authoritarian Personality* (New York: Harper & Brothers, 1950).

8 Adorno, "Imaginative Excesses," an unpublished piece intended for *Minima Moralia* (1944–47), published as section X of "Messages in a Bottle," trans. Edmund Jephcott, *New Left Review*, I/200 (July – August 1993), 12–14.

wind-jackets of fascism the subhuman creature who as dishonour's progeny shall never be allowed to avert it.

The bearers of technical progress, now still mechanized
mechanics, will, in evolving their special abilities, reach the
point already indicated by technology where specialization
grows superfluous. Once their consciousness has been converted into pure means without any qualification, it may cease
to be a means and breach, with its attachment to particular
objects, the last heteronomous barrier; its last entrapment in
the existing state, the last fetishism of the status quo, including
that of its own self, which is dissolved in its radical implementation as an instrument. Drawing breath at last, it may grow aware
of the incongruence between its rational development and the
irrationality of its ends, and act accordingly.

In "On the Fetish-Character in Music and the Regression of Listening,"
Adorno seeks to redeem authoritarianism in his conclusion when he offers
that, "Even discipline can take over the expression of free solidarity if freedom becomes its content." He goes on that, "As little as authoritarianism is
a symptom of progress in consciousness of freedom, it could suddenly turn
around if [individual psychology], in unity with the society, should ever leave
the road of the always-identical"[9] — that is, in going beyond capitalism. Here,
critical authoritarianism is met by a critical individualism in which "collective powers are liquidating an individuality past saving, but against them only
individuals are capable of consciously representing the aims of collectivity."[10]
What are the aims of the collectivity expressed by the identification with
technology? What Adorno following Benjamin called "mimesis"[11] Freud

---

9   In *Essays on Music*, ed. Richard Leppert, trans. Susan H. Gillespie (Berkeley;
    Los Angeles: University of California Press, 2002), 314. Originally published
    in 1938.

10  Ibid., 315.

11  See Walter Benjamin, "On the Mimetic Faculty," *Selected Writings*, vol. 2 *1927–
    34*, Michael W. Jennings, Howard Eiland and Gary Smith, eds. (Cambridge,
    MA: Harvard University Press, 1999), 720–722: "The child plays at being not
    only a shopkeeper or teacher, but a windmill and a train" (720).

analyzed psychologically as "identification." Adorno wrote that "the pressure to be permitted to obey . . . is today more general than ever." But what Marx called the "industrial forces of production" are constrained and distorted by the "bourgeois social relations of production" in capitalism. There is a homologous contradiction within the individual personality.

In "Reflections on Class Theory," Adorno wrote that,

> Dehumanization is no external power, no propaganda, however conceived, no exclusion from culture. It is precisely the intrinsic reality of the oppressed in the system, who used formerly to stand out because of their wretchedness, whereas today their wretchedness lies in the fact that they can never escape. That they suspect that the truth is propaganda, while swallowing the propaganda culture that is fetishized and distorted into the madness of an unending reflection of themselves.
>
> This means, however, that the dehumanization is also its opposite. In reified human beings reification finds its outer limits. They catch up with the technical forces of production in which the relations of production lie hidden: in this way these relations lose the shock of their alien nature because the alienation is so complete. But they may soon also lose their power. Only when the victims completely assume the features of the ruling civilization will they be capable to wresting them from the dominant power.[12]

## Society

Karl Marx regarded the "necessity of the dictatorship of the proletariat" as a phenomenon of "Bonapartism" — the rise to power of Louis Bonaparte as a result of the failure of the Revolution of 1848 in France. This was Marx's difference from the anarchists: the recognition of the necessity of the state in capitalism.[13] Hence one should regard Marx on the dictatorship of the

---

12  In *Can One Live After Auschwitz?: A Philosophical Reader*, ed. Rolf Tiedemann, trans. Rodney Livingstone and others (Stanford: Stanford University Press, 2009), 93–110.

13  See Karl Marx, *The Eighteenth Brumaire of Louis Bonaparte* (1852) Ch. VII, where he finds

proletariat as a "critical Bonapartist."[14] Bonapartism expressed an objective societal need rather than a subjective attitude. Bonapartist response to

---

that political atomization leads inexorably to the authoritarian state in Bonapartism:

> Insofar as millions of families live under conditions of existence that separate their mode of life, their interests, and their culture from those of the other classes, and put them in hostile opposition to the latter, they form a class. Insofar as there is merely a local interconnection ... and the identity of their interests forms no community, no national bond, and no political organization among them, they do not constitute a class. They are therefore incapable of asserting their class interest in their own name, whether through a parliament or a convention. They cannot represent themselves, they must be represented. Their representative must at the same time appear as their master, as an authority over them, an unlimited governmental power which protects them ... and sends them rain and sunshine from above. The[ir] political influence ... therefore, finds its final expression in the executive power which subordinates society to itself.

Marx's discussion of the French peasants of the mid-19th century also applied to what he called the "lumpenproletariat" as a constituent of Bonapartism, and so would apply to the working class in capitalism today without a political party organized for the struggle to achieve socialism. The "sack of potatoes" or of "homologous magnitudes" is what Adorno, among others, characterized as the "masses" in the 20th century. (For instance, Benjamin wrote in the Epilogue to "The Work of Art in the Age of Mechanical Reproduction" (1936) that fascism gave the masses the opportunity to express themselves while depriving them of their right to change society.)

Adorno paraphrases Marx here when he writes that,

> The masses are incessantly molded from above, they must be molded, if they are to be kept at bay. The overwhelming machinery of propaganda and cultural industry evidences the necessity of this apparatus for the perpetuation of a set-up the potentialities of which have outgrown the status quo. Since this potential is also the potential of effective resistance against the fascist trend, it is imperative to study the mentality of those who are at the receiver's end of today's social dynamics. We must study them not only because they reflect these dynamics, but above all because they are the latter's intrinsic anti-thesis. ("Remarks on 'The Authoritarian Personality'").

The manifestation — and potential resolution — of this contradiction of the masses in capitalism that otherwise resulted in Bonapartism was through the politics of socialism: Marx's "dictatorship of the proletariat" was to be achieved by the mass-political socialist party. Marx broke with the anarchists over the latter's refusal to take "political action" and to thus consign the working class to merely "social action." i.e. to avoid the necessary struggle for state power.

14 See my "Proletarian dictatorship and state capitalism," *Weekly Worker* 1064 (June 25, 2015), in this volume.

the objective social crisis and contradiction of capitalism pointed beyond itself and so required a dialectical critique, which Marx thought the anarchist Pierre-Joseph Proudhon failed to provide by treating Bonapartism as objectively determined, apologizing for it, as did the sentimental socialist Victor Hugo who treated Bonapartism as a monstrous historical accident like a "bolt from the blue."[15] Fatalism and contingency were two sides of the same contradiction that obscured a necessity that could be addressed properly only in a dialectical way. These are the terms in which Adorno addressed "authoritarianism."

Adorno's "critical authoritarianism" addresses what the "immanent dialectical critique" of authoritarianism would mean, both in terms of Freudian psychoanalytic categories of description, and in terms of (absent) politics for socialism. Adorno's *Dream Notes* records a dream of his participating in a gang-rape, as a primal scene of fascism.[16] The "delightful young mulatto . . . the kind of woman one sees in Harlem" who catches his eye admonishes him that "This is the style of the Institute." The homosexuality and sado-masochism of authoritarianism in pre-Oedipal psychology; the desire as well as fear to "liquidate the ego" in ambivalence about individuality; critical (as opposed to methodological or affirmative) individualism; the desire and fear of collectivity in authoritarian collectivism; projection, identification and counter-identification providing for social cohesion as well as for separation and atomization — these are the themes of Adorno's critical approach to psychology in late capitalism.

A similar thought was articulated contemporaneously by Frantz Fanon in *Black Skin, White Masks*, which characterizes negrophobic racism as "repressed homosexuality" and a "narcissistic disorder." Fanon describes the Freudian approach to rape fantasies as a masochistic fear and desire that is an internalized projection of parental authority, a self-sadism. One fears what one wishes to happen; a wish is a way of mastering a fear by internalizing it; a fear is a way of repressing a wish. The reason rape is so traumatic is that it activates and violates such infantile experiences. There is the experience of parental seduction harking back to the anal phase of libido development,

---

15   Karl Marx, Preface to the 1869 edition of *The Eighteenth Brumaire of Louis Bonaparte* (1852).

16   "New York, 8 February 1941," in *Dream Notes* (Cambridge: Polity Press, 2007), 5–6.

when the child experiences itself as unable to control its excretion, which is experienced as disturbingly involuntary, a blow to narcissism in the difficulty of toilet training, seeking to please the parents' expectations. The parents' cleaning of the infant is pleasurably stimulating, and the child internalizes the parent's simultaneous desire and disgust, attraction and repulsion, which becomes the complex of feelings, the combination of shame and guilt with pleasure, that the child takes in its own bodily functions. Humiliation at loss of self-control is a formative experience of transforming narcissism into identification. The infant's desire for the parents is an identification with the feared power.[17] The parents embody the ego-ideal of self-control. This is channeled later through gendered object-libido in the Oedipus complex as genital pleasure, but retains the sado-masochistic qualities of the anal phase, which precedes gender identification and so exhibits more basic, homosexual (ungendered) qualities that prevents the recognition of difference and individuality. In a narcissistic — authoritarian — society everyone becomes trapped in a static and self-reinforcing identity, where the need was actually to allow the opening to non-identity of freedom: the freedom to "overcome oneself" allowed by the healthy ego.

Fanon sought to provide an account of how "racial narcissism" — the failure of the individual ego — could yet point beyond itself, specifically in its treacherously dyadic character of Self and Other, to the need that was blocked: "the world of the You."[18]

Adorno brings into his discussion of *The Authoritarian Personality* a key background writing for Fanon's *BSWM*, Jean-Paul Sartre's *Anti-Semite and Jew*, which assumes, as Adorno does, contemporary anti-Semitism as a norm and not an aberration. He states simply that what needs to be explained is why anyone is "*not* anti-Semitic." But this pointed not to a problem of psychology but of *society*. As Adorno commended Sartre's treatment of anti-Semitism:

---

17  See Anna Freud, "Identification with the Aggressor," Ch. IX, *The Ego and the Mechanisms of Defence* (1936).

18  Frantz Fanon, *Black Skin, White Masks* (1952), trans. Charles Lam Markmann, (London: Pluto Press, 2002), 181.

We distinguish between anti-semitism as an objective social phenomenon, and the anti-semite as a peculiar type of individuality similar to Sartre's exposé which, for good reasons, is called "Portrait of the Antisemite" rather than "Psychology of Anti-semitism." This kind of personality is accessible to psychological analysis. . . . It would be quite impossible to reduce the objective phenomenon of present-day anti-semitism with its age-old background and all social and economic implications, to the mentality of those who, to speak with Sartre, have to make their decision in regard to this issue. Today, each and every man is faced with a tremendous bulk of objectively existing prejudices, discriminations and articulate anti-semitic attitudes. The accumulated power of this objective complex is so great and apparently so far beyond individual powers of resistance that one might indeed ask, why are people not antisemitic, [sic] instead of asking why certain kinds of people are anti-semitic. Thus, it would be naïve to base a prognosis of anti-semitism, this truly "social" disease, on the diagnosis of the individual patients.[19]

This means that the self-contradiction expressed by (non-)racism is one of society as well: the racist society points beyond itself objectively as well as subjectively, socially as well as individually. Racism as a problem contains the key to its own solution.[20] Anti-Semitic demagogues identified with Jews when imitating their stereotypical mannerisms;[21] white racists

---

19  "Remarks on *The Authoritarian Personality* by Adorno, Frenkel-Brunswik, Levinson, Sanford," published in *Platypus Review* 91 (November 2016).

20  This is because, according to Adorno, "Those who are incapable of believing their own cause . . . must constantly prove to themselves the truth of their gospel through the reality and irreversibility of their deeds." Violent action takes the place of thought and self-reflection; but this suggests the converse, that critical thinking could prevent such disastrous action. See Adorno, "Education after Auschwitz" (1966), in *Critical Models: Interventions and Catchwords*, ed. and trans. Henry W. Pickford (New York: Columbia University Press, 1998), 191–204.

21  See Theodor W. Adorno, "Freudian Theory and the Pattern of Fascist Propaganda" (1951), in *The Culture Industry*, ed. J. M. Bernstein (London and New York: Routledge, 2001), 132–157.

of the Jim Crow era performed minstrel shows in black-face. As Fanon put it, "Long ago the black man admitted the unarguable superiority of the white man, and all his efforts are aimed at achieving a white existence;" "For the black man there is only one destiny. And it is white."[22] Racism will end when black people become white. Or, as Adorno put it in "Reflections on Class Theory," "Only when the victims completely assume the features of the ruling civilization will they be capable to wresting them from the dominant power." Racism's abolition will be its *Aufhebung*: it will be its *Selbstaufhebung*, its self-completion as well as its self-negation. So will be the overcoming of authoritarianism in capitalism more generally.

The infamous "F-scale" of *The Authoritarian Personality* is a *scale*, which means that authoritarianism or predisposition to fascism is not a difference in kind but of degree: Everyone is more or less authoritarian. The most authoritarian thing would be to deny — to fail to recognize — one's own authoritarianism.

Originally published in *Platypus Review* 91 (November 2016)

---

22  Frantz Fanon, *Black Skin, White Masks*, 178.

# Philosophy

# History, theory

I want to begin, straightaway, with something Richard raised,[1] on which I would like to try to elaborate, by way of properly motivating the more "positive" aspect of Platypus's theory. Not how we are misrecognized, as either neoconservatives, crypto-Spartacists or academic Left-liberals, and what this says "negatively" about our project, as if in a photonegative, as Richard has discussed, but rather how we positively think about the intellectual content of our project.

Let me begin with a thought experiment: What if the Spartacist critique of the 1960s New Left and Moishe Postone's critique of the New Left, as disparate and antithetical as they might appear, were both correct? In other words, what if, paradoxically, the problem of the 1960s New Left was that it was simultaneously "too traditional" and "not traditional enough" in its Marxism?

What if the Spartacists were right that Stalinism and Trotskyism (and Bolshevism more generally) were not to be conflated, as they were in both Stalinophilic New Leftism, of Maoism and Che Guevarism, etc., and Stalinophobic neo-anarchism, Situationism, etc.? And what if Postone was correct, that Trotskyism, as part of "traditional Marxism," was unable to deal with the problem of mid-20th century capitalism's differences from earlier forms, and not able to address why revolutionary proletarian class consciousness, as it had previously manifested, did not continue, but seemed to become either irrelevant or, worse, affirmative of the status quo of the "administered society" of "organized" capitalism in the mid-20th century?

---

1   Richard Rubin, "The Platypus Synthesis: Four types of ambiguity," *Platypus1917* (June 15, 2009).

What both the Spartacists and Postone are unable to address, however, is why both of their perspectives, which purported to grasp the problem of capital more deeply and in broader historical context than others in the post-1960s New Left, found virtually no adherents. If we in Platypus say that both the Spartacists and Postone are correct, but both fail to adequately account for their own forms of consciousness, this raises an interesting paradox that points back to issues of historical interpretation for the Spartacists and Postone's points of departure, namely, Bolshevism as revolutionary Marxism, and Marx's own Marxism.

We could say that the problem of the Spartacists and Postone point to two different aspects of temporality in the history of the Left, that the Spartacists act as if no historical time intervenes between themselves and 1917, and Postone acts as if the progression of historical transformation leaves the Marxist tradition permanently superseded.

Both the Spartacists and Postone acknowledge, in however a limited fashion, the problem of regression; in the case of the Spartacists, the regression is post-1917, and for Postone it is post-1968, but both consider regression in only a linear and static manner, as if the emancipatory moments of 1917 and 1968 wait to be resumed at some time in a future that never comes. — And, behind both of these, lies 1848, which also continues to haunt our world, as taken up by the Situationists, "Left-" and "council" or "libertarian" communists and "anarchists." What if all three are correct, that we are indeed haunted by 1848, 1917 and 1968, that these moments actually circumscribe present possibilities? Then the question would be: How so?

The point would be, *contra* both the Spartacists and Postone, to grasp how and why the pertinence of history changes and fluctuates, over time, and as a function of the present. The point would be to be able to grasp a non-linear conception of historical progression — and regression. If, according to the Spartacists, the moment of the Bolshevik Revolution remains permanently relevant, and, for Postone, Marx remains permanently relevant, this side of overcoming capital, then we ought to be able to explain how this is so, and in ways the Spartacists and Postone themselves have been unable to do. This is precisely what Platypus sets out to do.

Please let me begin again, with four quotations, to be considered in constellation. The first is from Walter Benjamin's 1940 "Theses on the Philosophy of History":

> Karl Kraus said that "Origin is the goal." History is the subject of a structure whose site is not homogenous, empty time, but time filled by the presence of the now. Thus, to Robespierre ancient Rome was a past charged with the time of the now which he blasted out of the continuum of history. The French Revolution viewed itself as Rome incarnate. It evoked ancient Rome the way fashion evokes costumes of the past. Fashion has a flair for the topical, no matter where it stirs in the thickets of long ago; it is a tiger's leap into the past. This jump, however, takes place in an arena where the ruling class gives the commands. The same leap in the open air of history is the dialectical one, which is how Marx understood the revolution.[2]

In attempting to read the history of the accelerated demise and self-liquidation of the Left after the 1960s, reading it, as Benjamin put it, "against the grain," we in Platypus face a problem discussed by Nietzsche in his 1873 essay "On the Use and Abuse of History for Life":

> A person must have the power and from time to time use it to break a past and to dissolve it, in order to be able to live. . . . People or ages serving life in this way, by judging and destroying a past, are always dangerous and in danger. . . . It is an attempt to give oneself, as it were, a past after the fact, out of which we may be descended in opposition to the one from which we are descended.[3]

However, as Karl Korsch wrote, in his 1923 essay on "Marxism and Philosophy":

---

2  In *Illuminations*, ed. Hannah Arendt (New York: Schocken, 1969), 261.
3  Translation by Ian Johnstone, available online.

[Marx wrote (in his 1859 *Preface to A Contribution to the Critique of Political Economy*) that] "[Humanity] always sets itself only such problems as it can solve; since, looking at the matter more closely it will always be found that the problem itself arises only when the material conditions for its solution are already present or are at least understood to be in the process of emergence." [But] this dictum is not affected by the fact that a problem which supersedes present relations may have been formulated in an anterior epoch.[4]

As Adorno wrote, in his 1966 book *Negative Dialectics*:

The liquidation of theory by dogmatization and thought taboos contributed to the bad practice. . . . The interrelation of both moments [of theory and practice] is not settled once and for all but fluctuates historically. . . . Those who chide theory [for being] anachronistic obey the topos of dismissing, as obsolete, what remains painful [because it was] thwarted. . . . The fact that history has rolled over certain positions will be respected as a verdict on their truth content only by those who agree with Schiller that "world history is the world tribunal." What has been cast aside but not absorbed theoretically will often yield its truth content only later. It festers as a sore on the prevailing health; this will lead back to it in changed situations.[5]

We in Platypus consider ourselves, quite self-consciously, to be a function of such a return, under changed circumstances, to what was "cast aside but not absorbed theoretically." We think that such an approach as ours is only possible by virtue of the ways history, in failing to be transcended, continues to "fester," "yielding its truth content," but "only later." Our approach is informed by prior models for such an endeavor, namely, Trotsky and Adorno, and those who succeeded them, namely, the Spartacists and Moishe Postone.

---

4    In *Marxism and Philosophy*, trans. Fred Halliday (New York: New Left Books, 1970), 58.
5    trans. E. B. Ashton (New York: Continuum, 1983).

We think that figures of historical thought and action such as Marx, Lenin and Luxemburg, Trotsky, Lukács, Korsch, Benjamin and Adorno have an apparently fluctuating pertinence, but we consider them to remain in constellation with the present, however distantly, precisely because these historical figures "remain painful [because they were] thwarted," and because "history rolled over [their] positions" without their having been actually transcended and superseded, but only mistakenly "dismissed as obsolete." As Adorno put it, in one of his last essays, "Late Capitalism or Industrial Society?," or "Is Marx Obsolete?," if Marx has become obsolete, this obsolescence will only be capable of being overcome on the basis of Marx's own thought and model of historical action.[6] We in Platypus think the same goes for Luxemburg, Lenin and Trotsky, and Adorno himself.

If these historical figures are obsolete but still remain capable of holding our attention and imagination, then we are tasked with explaining any continued pertinence they have by reference to their own models of historical thought and action, and thus, in a sense, "transcending" them, but only through "remembering" them, and on the basis that they themselves provide for our understanding them. We want to transform the ways these figures haunt us in the present into a matter of actual gratitude as opposed to guilt (as Horkheimer and Adorno put it, in *The Dialectic of Enlightenment*, following Freudian psychoanalysis, about "The Theory of Ghosts"[7]).

We recognize that Marx and the best Marxists, such as Luxemburg, Lenin and Trotsky, will be transcended only by being fulfilled. We want to actually make them obsolete, whereas we find their (pseudo-) "obsolescence" declared by the "Left" today to be a function of trying to repress or ward them off instead. We begin with the discomfort of their memory, as an important symptom of history in the present.

But this involves a rather complicated historical approach, one that goes on in Platypus under the rubrics of "regression" and "critical" history, or history "against the grain" of events, which I would like to explicate now.

Nietzsche described what he called "critical history," or an approach to history that is critical of that history from the standpoint of the needs of

---

6    In *The Essential Frankfurt School Reader*, ed. Andrew Arato and Eike Gebhardt (New York: Continuum, 1985), 95.

7    Stanford: Stanford University Press, 2002, 178.

the present. Let me cite further from the passage of Nietzsche's "Use and Abuse of History for Life" I've already quoted to illustrate this point.
Nietzsche said that,

> Here it is not righteousness which sits in the judgment seat or, even less, mercy which announces judgment, but life alone, that dark, driving, insatiable self-desiring force.[8]

So the question becomes, how, if at all, does memory of historical Marxism serve the needs of the present? We in Platypus recognize both the obscurity of the heritage of revolutionary Marxism and the ways the alternative, non-revolutionary lineage of the "Left" in its decline has been naturalized and so is no longer recognized as such. Our point of departure is the hypothesis that the history of the Left, however obscure, is the actual history of the present, or, more accurately, in Hegelian terms, how the history of the Left is the history of the present in its "actuality," in its potential for change and transformation, and in its constraint of such potential. We are bound by the history of the Left, whether we recognize this or not.

For example, we follow Trotsky's caveat about the danger of being Stalinist in "method" if not in avowed "politics," and judge the "Left" today to be beholden to Stalinism in importantly unacknowledged ways. Ian Morrison wrote an article in the May issue of *The Platypus Review*,[9] on "Resurrecting the '30s," in which he cited C. Wright Mills on how the "nationalization" of the Left in the 1930s–40s was "catastrophic." We recognize this "nationalization," the narrowing of horizons for Leftist politics that has been taken for granted by the Left, especially after WWII, to be the very essence of Stalinism and its historical legacy in the present. More importantly, we recognize that such "nationalization" of Left politics was utterly foreign to the perspectives of Marx and the 2nd International radical Marxists, Lenin, Luxemburg and Trotsky. Hence, we find in their example a potential critical vantage-point regarding the subsequent historical trajectory of the Left.

Furthermore, Nietzsche described the danger of

---

8  op. cit.
9  *Platypus Review* 12 (May 2009).

[the] attempt to give oneself, as it were, a past after the fact, out of which we may be descended in opposition to the one from which we are descended. It is always a dangerous attempt, because it is so difficult to find a borderline to the denial of the past and because the second nature usually is weaker than the first.[10]

Richard Rubin, in his comments at our panel on "The Decline of the Left in the 20th Century" Friday night, spoke of how Trotsky and Benjamin provide the "hidden" or esoteric history of the 20th century, by contrast with its "real" history, exemplified by FDR and Hitler.[11] Our present world is more obviously descended from the history of Hitler and FDR, who in this sense made the world what it is today, as the effect of their actions. But how might we (come to) be descended also from Benjamin and Trotsky? Can we claim their history as ours, or are we condemned to being only the products of the history of Hitler, FDR and Stalin (and those who followed them)?

Does the historical possibility represented by Trotsky and Benjamin have any meaning to us today? Clearly their historical legacy of opposition is weaker than the other, dominant and victorious one. But was Trotsky and Benjamin's opposition to Stalin, FDR and Hitler so fruitless that we cannot make use of them in fighting against the continued effects of, and perhaps one day overcoming entirely, the legacy of the latter? It is in this sense that we can discuss the critique of the present available in history.

Benjamin contrasted such "critical history," of the "vanquished," which is related to but the converse of Nietzsche's, a critique of the present from the standpoint of history, as opposed to Nietzsche's critique of history from the standpoint of the present, to the affirmative history of the "victors," the affirmation of history as it happened. — But, first, we need to be very clear about what Benjamin meant by the "vanquished," who were not merely history's victims, but the defeated, those who actually struggled and lost: Benjamin's example was Rosa Luxemburg's Spartacus League in the German Revolution and Civil War of 1918–19. It was on behalf of such historically "vanquished" that Benjamin wrote that history needed to be read

---

10  op. cit.
11  "1933" *Platypus1917* (November 2009).

"against the grain" of the victories of the status quo that comprise the present. It is in memory of their sacrifices, the "anger and hatred" that emanates from the image of "enslaved ancestors," that Benjamin thought the struggle for emancipation in the present could be motivated by history, that history could serve the present, contrary to the way it otherwise oppresses it, in its affirmation of the status quo.

It is in this sense that we in Platypus do not claim so much that Marx, Luxemburg, Lenin and Trotsky, et al. were right, but rather we seek to make them right, retroactively. We do not claim their relevance, but seek to make them relevant. For they did not seek merely to find the crisis of capital, but to bring it about. Our critique of the present, initially, is what is available historically: how the present can be critiqued from the vantage-point of history.

The founder of the Spartacist League, James Robertson, once put it very well, in 1973 — in the aftermath of the '60s — that,

> The truth is historically conditioned; that is, the outlook of the Communist movement of the first four congresses of the Communist International rested upon a historic and successful upheaval of the revolutionary proletariat [in 1917]. A comparable theoretical breakthrough and generalization accompanied this massive revolutionary achievement. . . . It is as though the theoretical outlook of the proletarian vanguard in the period 1919–23 in the International stood atop a mountain. But since that time, from the period of the Trotskyist Left Opposition until his death and afterward, the proletariat has mainly witnessed defeats and the revolutionary vanguard has either been shrunken or its continuity in many countries broken. One cannot separate the ability to know the world from the ability to change it, and our capacity to change the world is on a very small scale compared to the heroic days of the Communist International.[12]

---

12 "In Defense of Democratic Centralism" (1973), substantially adapted into *Lenin and the Vanguard Party* in *Workers Vanguard* (1978).

Robertson pointed out how deeply mistaken, and indeed "arrogant," it was for us to assume that we know better than revolutionaries historically did. Our point is not to idolize the past but rather to instill an appropriate sense of humility towards it. Furthermore, the point is to be able to think in light of the past, how the past might help us think in the present. For, not only might we not know their past moments better than they did, but we might not know our present moment better than they might be able to prompt us to think about it. As Adorno wrote, in 1963,

> The theorist who intervenes in practical controversies nowadays discovers on a regular basis and to his shame that whatever ideas he might contribute were expressed long ago — and usually better the first time around.[13]

But repetition is regression. The second time around may not be better, but it might yet be productive in certain ways.

For it is not a matter of how these historical thinkers and actors we find important can be emulated in the present, practically, so much as it is a question of how far their perspective might see into the present. Not what would they do in the present, but what might they say to our present and its historical trajectory? So, initially, it is a matter of theory more than practice. Engaging the historical thought and action of our revolutionary Marxist forebears is not a matter of applying a ready-made theory, but rather tasks our own interpretative abilities. It demands that we think — not a simple matter. As Trotsky wrote to his followers in the 1930s, we must "learn to think," again. This is what distinguishes us from other supposedly "Marxist" organizations. And this is what informs our practice, what we actually make happen in the world, as Ian Morrison will discuss.

Approaching history this way allows us to pose certain questions. It does not provide answers. The positive content of historical ideas is in their ambiguity: this is what makes them live for us today, by contrast with the dead positivity of the pseudo-ideas — really, the suppression of

---

13  "Sexual Taboos and the Law Today" (1963), in *Critical Models: Interventions and Catchwords*, trans. Henry Pickford (New York: Columbia University Press, 2005), 71.

thinking — that we find on the fake "Left" today. For there is not merely the question of what we think about the past; but, also, and, perhaps most importantly, in our regressive moment today, the reciprocal one: what the past might think of us.

As Benjamin put it, history needs to be approached from the standpoint of its potential redemption. We think that the historical thought and action of Marxism demands to be redeemed, and that our world, dominated by capital, will continue to suffer so long as this task remains undone. We think that the constitutive horizon of our world was already charted, however preliminarily, by the revolutionary politics of historical Marxism, but that this horizon has become only blurred and forgotten since then. We in Platypus set ourselves the task of initiating thought about this problem, from deep within the fog of our present. We look back and see the revolutionary Marxists looking towards us from that faraway mountaintop. In their fleeting gaze we find an unfulfilled hope — and a haunting accusation.

Presented at the first annual Platypus Affiliated Society
International Convention, Chicago, June 12–14, 2009.

# On Karl Korsch's
# "Marxism and philosophy"

[Marx wrote,] "[Humanity] always sets itself only such problems as it can solve; since, looking at the matter more closely it will always be found that the problem itself arises only when the material conditions for its solution are already present or are at least understood to be in the process of emergence."[1] This dictum is not affected by the fact that a problem which supersedes present relations may have been formulated in an anterior epoch.

As scientific socialism, the Marxism of Marx and Engels remains the inclusive whole of a theory of social revolution . . . a materialism whose theory comprehended the totality of society and history, and whose practice overthrew it. . . . The difference [now] is that the various components of [what for Marx and Engels was] the unbreakable interconnection of theory and practice are further separated out. . . . The umbilical cord has been broken.[2]

## The problem of "Marxism and Philosophy" —
## Korsch and Adorno on theory and practice

Karl Korsch's seminal essay "Marxism and Philosophy" (1923) was first published in English, translated by Fred Halliday, in 1970 by Monthly

---

1  *Preface to A Contribution to the Critique of Political Economy* (1859).
2  Karl Korsch, "Marxism and Philosophy" (1923), in *Marxism and Philosophy*, trans. Fred Halliday (New York: Monthly Review Press, 2008).

Review Press. In 2008, they reprinted the volume, which also contains some important shorter essays, as part of their new "Classics" series.

The original publication of Korsch's essay coincided with Georg Lukács's 1923 landmark collection of essays, *History and Class Consciousness* (*HCC*). While Lukács's book has the word "history" in its title, it follows Marx's *Capital* in addressing the problem of social being and consciousness in a primarily "philosophical" and categorial manner, as the subjectivity of the commodity form. Korsch's essay on philosophy in Marxism, by contrast, is actually a historical treatment of the problem from Marx and Engels's time through the 2nd International to the crisis of Marxism and the revolutions of 1917–19. More specifically, it takes up the development and vicissitudes of the relation between theory and practice in the history of Marxism, which is considered *the* "philosophical" problem of Marxism.

Independently of one another, both Korsch's and Lukács's 1923 works shared an interest in recovering the Hegelian or "idealist" dimension of Marx's thought and politics. Both were motivated to establish the coherence of the Marxist revolutionaries Lenin and Luxemburg, and these 2nd International-era radicals' shared grounding in what Korsch called "Marx's Marxism." Their accomplishment of this is all the more impressive when it is recognized that it was made without benefit of either of the two most important texts in which Marx explicitly addressed the relation of his own thought to Hegel's, the 1844 *Economic and Philosophic Manuscripts* (first published in 1932) or the notes for *Capital* posthumously published as the *Grundrisse* (1939), and also without access to Lenin's 1914 notebooks on Hegel's *Science of Logic* (1929). Due to a perceived shortcoming in the expounding of revolutionary Marxism, the problem for Korsch and Lukács was interpreting Marxism as both theory and practice, or how the politics of Lenin and Luxemburg (rightly) considered itself "dialectical." Both Lukács and Korsch explicitly sought to provide this missing exposition and elaboration.

Lukács and Korsch were later denounced as "professors" in the Communist International, a controversy that erupted after the deaths of Luxemburg and Lenin. (Another important text of this moment was Lukács's 1924 monograph in eulogy, *Lenin: A Study on the Unity of his*

*Thought*.[3]) In the face of this party criticism, Lukács acquiesced and made his peace with Stalinized "orthodoxy." Eventually disavowing *History and Class Consciousness* as a misguided attempt to "out-Hegel Hegel," Lukács even attempted to destroy all the existing copies of the unpublished "Tailism and the Dialectic," his brilliant 1925 defense of *HCC*. (Apparently he failed, since a copy was eventually found in Soviet archives. This remarkable document was translated and published in 2000 as *A Defence of History and Class Consciousness*.[4])

Korsch responded differently to the party's criticism. Quitting the 3rd International Communist movement entirely, he became associated with the "Left" or "council" communism of Antonie Pannekoek, Paul Mattick, et al. Though making a choice very different from Lukács and distancing himself from official "Marxism-Leninism," Korsch also came to disavow his earlier argument in "Marxism and Philosophy." Specifically, he abandoned the attempt to establish the coherence of Lenin's theory and practice with that of Marx, going so far as to critique Marx's own Marxism. Thus, in "The Present State of the Problem of 'Marxism and Philosophy:' An Anti-Critique" (1930), included in *Marxism and Philosophy*, Korsch argues that, to the degree Marx shared a common basis with Lenin, this was an expression of limitations in Marx's own critical theory and political practice. Indeed, for Korsch it was a problem of "Marxism" in general, including that of Kautsky and Luxemburg. Ultimately, Korsch called for "going beyond" Marxism.

The complementary, if divergent, trajectories of Korsch and Lukács are indicative of the historical disintegration of the perspective both shared in their writings of 1923. Both had understood the "subjective" aspect of Marxism to have been clarified by Lenin's role in the October Revolution. The figure of Lenin was irreducible, and brought out dimensions of the Marxian project that otherwise lay unacknowledged. As Theodor W. Adorno put it in private discussion with Max Horkheimer in 1956,

> I always wanted to produce a theory that would be faithful to Marx, Engels and Lenin. . . . Marx was too harmless; he

---

3   Trans. Nicholas Jacobs (New York: Verso, 2009).
4   Trans. Esther Leslie (New York: Verso, 2000).

probably imagined quite naïvely that human beings are basically the same in all essentials and will remain so. It would be a good idea, therefore, to deprive them of their second nature. He was not concerned with their subjectivity; he probably didn't look into that too closely. The idea that human beings are the products of society down to their innermost core is an idea that he would have rejected as milieu theory. Lenin was the first person to assert this.[5]

In this discussion, Adorno also proposed to Horkheimer that they "should produce a reworked [version of Marx and Engels's] *Communist Manifesto* that would be 'strictly Leninist.'"[6]

No less than Lukács's *History and Class Consciousness*, Korsch's "Marxism and Philosophy" inspired the work of the Marxist critical theorists associated with the Frankfurt School — Horkheimer, Marcuse, Benjamin, and Adorno. But the reputation of Korsch's work has been eclipsed by that of Lukács. What the usual interpretive emphasis on Lukács occludes is that the Frankfurt School writers grappled not only with the problem of Stalinism but "anti-Stalinism" as well.[7] Both Korsch's and Lukács's post-1923

---

5 Max Horkheimer and Theodor Adorno, "Diskussion über Theorie und Praxis" (1956), in Horkheimer, *Gesammelte Schriften*, vol. 19 (Frankfurt: S. Fischer Verlag, 1996), 69–71; quoted in Detlev Claussen, *Theodor W. Adorno: One Last Genius* (Cambridge: Harvard University Press, 2008), 233.

6 Claussen, 233. Furthermore, while "Marx wrote his critique of the [SPD, German Social-Democratic Party's] Gotha Programme in 1875[,] Adorno had for some time planned to write a critique of the Godesberg Programme [in which the SPD formally renounced Marxism in 1959]" (Rolf Wiggershaus, *The Frankfurt School: Its History, Theories, and Political Significance*, trans. Michael Robertson [Cambridge, MA: MIT Press, 1995], 598).

7 From Phil Slater, *Origin and Significance of the Frankfurt School: A Marxist Perspective* (London: Routledge & Kegan Paul, 1977):

[Horkheimer wrote, in "The Authoritarian State" (1940),]

The concept of a transitional revolutionary dictatorship was in no way intended to mean the monopoly of the means of production by some new elite. Such dangers can be countered by the energy and alertness of the people themselves. . . . [The revolution that ends domination is as far-reaching as the will of the liberated. Any resignation is already a regression into prehistory. . . . The recurrence of political reaction and a new destruction of the beginnings of freedom cannot theoretically be ruled out, and certainly not as long as a hostile environment exists. No patented system worked out in advance can preclude regressions. The modalities of the new society are first found in the process of social transformation.] The theoretical conception which, following its first trail-blazers [such as Lenin and Luxemburg], will show the new society its way – the system of workers' councils – grows out of praxis. The roots of the council system go back to 1871, 1905, and other events. *Revolutionary transformation has a tradition that must continue.*

The Frankfurt School's respect for Lenin was due in large measure to his ability to retain the dynamic unity of party, theory and class, a unity subsequently lost. Marcuse's *Soviet Marxism* (1958) is here representative of the entire Frankfurt School:

> During the Revolution, it became clear to what degree Lenin had succeeded in basing his strategy on the actual class interests and aspirations of the workers and peasants. . . . Then, from 1923 on, the decisions of the leadership increasingly dissociated from the class interests of the proletariat. The former no longer presuppose the proletariat as a revolutionary agent but rather are imposed upon the proletariat and the rest of the underlying population.

Looking round for a possible *practical* exponent of [the] views of the Frankfurt School, one immediately encounters the figure of Trotsky. . . . [Trotsky maintained that the bureaucratism of the USSR] completely disregarded Lenin's conception of the dialectical interaction of party and class. . . . [Trotsky wrote that] the Marxist theoretician must still retain the concrete historical perspective of class struggle:

> [The causes for the downfall of the Social Democracy and of official Communism must be sought not in Marxist theory and not in the bad qualities of those people who applied it, but in the concrete conditions of the historical process.] It is not a question of counterposing abstract principles, but rather of the struggle of living social forces, with its inevitable ups and downs, with the degeneration of organizations, with the passing of entire generations into discard, and with the necessity which therefore arises of mobilizing fresh forces on a new historical stage. No one has bothered to pave in advance the road of revolutionary upsurge for the proletariat. [With inevitable halts and partial retreats it is necessary to move forward on a road crisscrossed by countless obstacles and covered with the debris of the past.] Those who are frightened by this had better step aside [Trotsky, "To Build Communist Parties and an International Anew," July 1933.]

The Frankfurt School, while upholding a number of principles (which became "abstract" in their passivity and isolation), did indeed, in this sense, step aside.

trajectories were critiqued by the Frankfurt School writers.[8] As Adorno put it in *Negative Dialectics* (1966),

> First Karl Korsch, later the functionaries of Diamat [Dialectical Materialism] have objected, that the turn to nonidentity would be, due to its immanent-critical and theoretical character, an insignificant nuance of neo-Hegelianism or of the historically obsolete Hegelian Left; as if the Marxist critique of philosophy had dispensed with this, while simultaneously the East cannot do without a statutory Marxist philosophy. The demand for the unity of theory and praxis has irresistibly debased the former to a mere underling; removing from it what it was supposed to have achieved in that unity. The practical visa-stamp demanded from all theory became the censor's stamp. In the famed unity of theory-praxis, the former was vanquished and the latter became non-conceptual, a piece of the politics which it was supposed to lead beyond; delivered over to power. The liquidation of theory by dogmatization and the ban on thinking contributed to bad praxis; that theory wins back its

---

One is not without some justification in asking whether Council Communism could perhaps be a concrete embodiment of many of the principles of the Frankfurt School. . . . [But] the Council Communists did not point out the soviets' [workers' councils'] own responsibility for the collapse of the revolutionary wave of 1918–19. (66–73)

8   The reverse was also true. Korsch, in distancing himself from his 1923 work that was so seminal for the Frankfurt School writers, also came to critique them:

> [Korsch] intended to try and interest Horkheimer and the [Frankfurt] Institute [for Social Research] in Pannekoek's book *Lenin as Philosopher* (1938) [which traced the bureaucratization of the USSR back to the supposedly crude materialism of Lenin's 1909 book *Materialism and Empirio-Criticism*]. . . . [Either] Korsch [or, the Director of the Institute, Horkheimer himself] would write a review for [the Institute's journal] the *Zeitschrift*. . . . Yet no such review appeared. . . . [Korsch suffered] total disillusionment with the Institute and their "impotent philosophy." Korsch [was] particularly bitter about the "metaphysician Horkheimer" (Slater, 73–74).

The record for Korsch's deteriorating relations with the Frankfurt Institute in exile is found in his private letters to Paul Mattick, editor of the journal *Living Marxism: International Council Correspondence*.

independence, is the interest of praxis itself. The relationship of both moments to each other is not settled for once and for all, but changes historically. Today, since the hegemonic bustle cripples and denigrates theory, theory testifies in all its powerlessness against the former by its mere existence.[9]

In this passage Adorno was addressing, not the Korsch of the 1923 "Marxism and Philosophy," but rather the later Korsch of the 1930 "Anti-Critique," distanced from the problem Adorno sought to address, of the constitutive non-identity of theory and practice. Adorno thought, like Korsch and Lukács in the early 1920s, that Lenin and Luxemburg's theoretical self-understanding, together with their revolutionary political practice, comprised the most advanced attempt yet to work through precisely this non-identity.[10]

In Adorno's terms, both the later Korsch and official "Diamat" (including Lukács) assumed "identity thinking," an identity of effective theory and practice, rather than their articulated non-identity, to which Korsch had drawn attention earlier in "Marxism and Philosophy." Such constitutive non-identity was, according to Korsch's earlier essay, expressed

---

9 Translated by Dennis Redmond, 2001. The first sentence of this passage, mentioning Korsch, is inexplicably missing from the 1973 Continuum edition of *Negative Dialectics* translated by E. B. Ashton (see "Relation to Left-wing Hegelianism," 143).

10 In a lecture of November 23, 1965, on "Theory and Practice," Adorno said,

> I should like to say that there is no intention here of advocating a relapse into contemplation, as was found in the great idealist philosophies and ultimately even in Hegel, despite the great importance of practice in the Hegelian system. . . . The late Karl Korsch . . . criticized Horkheimer and myself even more sharply, already in America and also later on, after the publication of *Dialectic of Enlightenment*. His objection was that we had regressed to the standpoint of Left Hegelianism. This does not seem right to me because the standpoint of pure contemplation can no longer be sustained. Though we should note, incidentally, that the polarity Marx constructs between pure contemplation on the one hand and his own political philosophy on the other does only partial justice to the intentions of Left Hegelianism. This is a difficult question . . . although we cannot deny the impressive political instincts which alerted Marx to the presence of the retrograde and, above all, nationalist potential in such thinkers as Bruno Bauer, Stirner and Ruge. (Adorno, *Lectures on Negative Dialectics*, trans. Rodney Livingstone [Cambridge: Polity Press, 2008], 52–53.)

symptomatically, in the subsistence of "philosophy" as a distinct activity in the historical epoch of Marxism. This was because it expressed a genuine historical need. The continued practice of philosophy was symptomatic expression of the need to transcend and supersede philosophy. Instead of this recognition of the actuality of the symptom of philosophical thinking, of the mutually constitutive separation of theory and practice, Korsch, by embracing council communism and shunning Marxian theory in the years after writing his famously condemned work, succumbed to what Adorno termed "identity thinking." By assuming the identity of theory and practice, or of social being and consciousness in the workers' movement, Korsch sought their "reconciliation," instead of discerning and critically grasping their persistent antagonism, as would necessarily be articulated in any purported politics of emancipation.

Just as Adorno tried to hold fast to the Lukács of *History and Class Consciousness* in the face of Lukács's own subsequent disavowals, the first sentence of Adorno's *Negative Dialectics* reiterated Korsch's statement in "Marxism and Philosophy" that "Philosophy cannot be abolished without being realized"[11]:

> Philosophy, which once seemed outmoded, remains alive because the moment of its realization was missed. The summary judgment that it had merely interpreted the world is itself crippled by resignation before reality, and becomes a defeatism of reason after the transformation of the world failed.[12]

Philosophy's end was its *self*-abolition. What Korsch prefaced to his statement helps to illuminate what Adorno meant. Korsch specified precisely what "the realization of philosophy" involves:

> Just as political action is not rendered unnecessary by the economic action of a revolutionary class, so intellectual action is not rendered unnecessary by either political or economic action.

---

11  *Marxism and Philosophy*, 97.
12  Translated by Redmond.

On the contrary it must be carried through to the end in theory and practice, as revolutionary scientific criticism and agitational work before the seizure of state power by the working class, and as scientific organisation and ideological dictatorship after the seizure of state power. If this is valid for intellectual action against the forms of consciousness which define bourgeois society in general, it is especially true of philosophical action. Bourgeois consciousness necessarily sees itself as apart from the world and independent of it, as pure critical philosophy and impartial science, just as the bourgeois State and bourgeois Law appear to be above society. This consciousness must be philosophically fought by the revolutionary materialistic dialectic, which is the philosophy of the working class. This struggle will only end when the whole of existing society and its economic basis have been totally overthrown in practice, and this consciousness has been totally surpassed and abolished in theory.[13]

This was the original Marxist "defense" of philosophy that Adorno reiterated in *Negative Dialectics*. Over four decades previously, in 1923, Korsch had explicitly tied it to Lenin's treatment of the problem of the state in *The State and Revolution* (1917). Just as, with the overcoming of capitalism, the necessity of the state would "wither," and not be done away with at one stroke, so too the necessity of "philosophical" thinking as it appeared in the epoch of capital would dissolve. This side of emancipation, "theoretical" self-reflection, thought's reflecting on its own conditions of possibility, remains necessary, precisely because it expresses an unresolved social-historical problem.

In "Marxism and Philosophy," Korsch analyzed Marxism as emergent from and historically continuous with the "revolt of the Third Estate," of the "bourgeois" liberal-democratic revolutionary epoch that preceded it. Korsch was concerned with Marx's continuity with Kant and Hegel. A problem that occurred to them, namely, of theory and practice, repeated itself, if in a more acute way, for Marx. It is a problem of the

---

13 *Marxism and Philosophy*, 97.

philosophy of revolution, or of the "theory of social revolution." This problem presents itself only insofar as it is conceived of as part and parcel of the social-historical process of transformation and not as contemplation from without. As it was for Hegel, Marx's fundamental "philosophical" issue is this: How is it possible, if however problematic, to be a self-conscious agent of change, if what is being transformed includes oneself, or, more precisely, an agency that transforms conditions both for one's practical grounding and for one's theoretical self-understanding in the process of acting?

Korsch addressed the question of revolution as a problem indicated by the liquidation and reconstitution of "philosophy" itself after the crisis and "decay of Hegelianism."[14] Why did philosophical development take a hiatus by 1848 and only appear to resume afterwards? What changed about "philosophy" in the interim? For Korsch recognized there was a curious blank spot or gap in the history of philosophy from the 1840s–60s, the period of Marxism's emergence. Korsch divided the relation of Marx's thought to philosophy roughly into three periods: pre-1848, circa 1848, and post-1848. These periods were distinguished by the different ways they related theory and practice: the first period was the critique of philosophy calling for its simultaneous realization and self-abolition; the second, the sublimation of philosophy in revolution; and the third, the recrudescence of the problem of relating theory and practice.

Korsch's third period in the history of Marxism extended into what he termed the "crisis of Marxism" beginning in the 1890s with the reformist "revisionist" dispute of Eduard Bernstein et al. against the "orthodox Marxism" of the 2nd International — when the "revolutionary Marxism" of Luxemburg and Lenin originated — and continuing into the acutely revolutionary period of 1917–19, from the Russian Revolution of 1917 through the German Revolution and civil war of 1918–19, to the Hungarian Soviet Republic (in which Lukács participated) and the workers' council movement in Italy (in which Antonio Gramsci participated) in 1919.

It was in this revolutionary period of the early 20th century that "Marx's Marxism" circa 1848 regained its saliency, but in ways that Korsch thought remained not entirely resolved as a matter of relating theory to

---

14  Ibid, 29.

practice. In "Marxism and Philosophy," Korsch found that while Lenin and Luxemburg had tried to better relate Marxian theory and practice than 2nd International Marxism had done, they had recognized this as an on-going task and aspiration and not already achieved in some finished sense. In the words of the epigraph from Lenin that introduces Korsch's 1923 essay, "We must organize a systematic study of the Hegelian dialectic from a materialist standpoint."[15] If Marxism continued to be subject to a "Hegelian dialectic," thus requiring the "historical materialist" analysis and explanation that Korsch sought to provide of it, this was because it was not itself the reconciled unity of theory and practice but remained, as theory, the critical reflection on the *problem* of relating theory and practice — which in turn prompted further theoretical development as well as practical political advances. As Adorno put it to Walter Benjamin in a letter of August 2, 1935,

> The fetish character of the commodity is not a fact of consciousness; rather it is dialectical, in the eminent sense that it produces consciousness. . . . [P]erfection of the commodity character in a Hegelian self-consciousness inaugurates the explosion of its phantasmagoria.[16]

Marxism was caught in the "phantasmagoria" of capital, while "exploding" it from within.

For the Korsch of "Marxism and Philosophy," Lenin and Luxemburg's "revolutionary Marxism" was bound up in the "crisis of Marxism," while advancing it to a new stage. As Korsch commented,

> This transformation and development of Marxist theory has been effected under the peculiar ideological guise of a return to the pure teaching of original or true Marxism. Yet it is easy to understand both the reasons for this guise and the real

---

15  "On the Significance of Militant Materialism" (1922).

16  Walter Benjamin, *Selected Writings*, vol. 3 *1935–38* (Cambridge: Harvard University Press, 2002), 54–56; Adorno et al., *Aesthetics and Politics* (London: Verso, 1980), 111–113.

character of the process which is concealed by it. What theoreticians like Rosa Luxemburg in Germany and Lenin in Russia have done, and are doing, in the field of Marxist theory is to liberate it from the inhibiting traditions of [Social Democracy]. They thereby answer the practical needs of the new revolutionary stage of proletarian class struggle, for these traditions weighed "like a nightmare" on the brain of the working masses whose objectively revolutionary socioeconomic position no longer corresponded to these [earlier] evolutionary doctrines. The apparent revival of original Marxist theory in the Third International is simply a result of the fact that in a new revolutionary period not only the workers' movement itself, but the theoretical conceptions of communists which express it, must assume an explicitly revolutionary form. This is why large sections of the Marxist system, which seemed virtually forgotten in the final decades of the nineteenth century, have now come to life again. It also explains why the leader of the Russian Revolution Lenin could write a book a few months before October [*The State and Revolution*, 1917] in which he stated that his aim was "in the first place to *restore* the correct Marxist theory of the State." . . . When Lenin placed the same question theoretically on the agenda at a decisive moment, this was an early indication that the internal connection of theory and practice within revolutionary Marxism had been consciously re-established.[17]

Korsch thus established the importance for what Adorno called the "historically changing" relation of theory and practice, making sense of their vicissitudes in the history of the politics of revolutionary Marxism. Furthermore, by establishing the character of the crisis of Marxism as a matter of theoretical reflection, Korsch re-established the role of consciousness in a Marxian conception of social revolution, why the abandonment or distancing of the practical perspective of revolution necessitates a degradation of theory.

---

17  *Marxism and Philosophy*, 67–68.

## Korsch and the 1960s "New Left" — the problem of "Leninism"

The 1970 publication of Korsch was an event for the Anglophone New Left. As Adolph Reed wrote,

> Leninism's elitism and denigration of consciousness had increasingly troubled me, but I feared I had no recourse without sacrificing a radical commitment. Korsch opened an entirely new vista, the "hidden dimension" of Western Marxism, and led to Lukács, a serious reading of Marcuse, and eventually the critical theoretical tradition.[18]

Reed's brief comment is cryptic and can be taken in (at least) two opposed ways, either that Korsch provided the redemption of Lenin or an alternative to Leninism.

Such 1960s-era "New Left" ambivalence about "Leninism" can be found in attenuated form in Fred Halliday's Translator's Introduction. In it, Halliday sticks closely to a biographical narrative of Korsch's work, seeking to bring out the coherence of Korsch's early and later periods, before and after "Marxism and Philosophy," while acknowledging the "erratic" character of Korsch's thought over the course of his life, and calling Korsch's tragic trajectory away from Lenin and Luxemburg's revolutionary Marxism a "fatal consequence" of the failure of the revolution.[19] By casting the issue of Korsch's work as "interesting" (if "erratic"), Halliday remained somewhat equivocal about the relevance of Korsch's key text, "Marxism and Philosophy," and thus about the continued pertinence of the revolutionary Marxism that Lenin shared with Luxemburg. What remained unresolved?

Halliday also suggests that Korsch's pre-1917 interests in the "syndicalist movement," the "positive content and actively democratic aspects of socialism, by contrast with the orthodox Marxism of the 2nd International

---

18   Adolph Reed, "Paths to Critical Theory," in Sohnya Sayres, *The 60s Without Apology*, ed. *Social Text* Staff (Minneapolis: University of Minnesota Press, 1985), 257–258; originally published in *Social Text* 9/10 (Spring – Summer 1984).

19   *Marxism and Philosophy*, 26.

which he thought defined itself merely negatively as the abolition of the capitalist mode of production,"[20] came to be expressed some years after the October Revolution, which witnessed "the decline in activity and the need for more critical reflection." At that time, Korsch returned to his earlier concerns, but with the tragic consequence of "lapsing into ultra-leftism and becoming cut off from the working class."[21]

Perhaps the motivation for Halliday's 1970 translation and publication of Korsch's "Marxism and Philosophy" was an affinity, after 1968, with Korsch's moment of "critical reflection" circa 1923. It may have expressed Halliday's hope that Korsch's further trajectory and fate might be avoided by the 1960s "New Left." In the wake of 1968, Halliday and others wanted to avoid the choice of either ultra-Leftism ("Luxemburgism") and "becoming cut off from the working class," or official "Leninism," and the 1923 Korsch seemed to provide a way out, through specific reflection on the problem of revolutionary political means and ends, in terms of articulating theory and practice.

### Forgetting the theory-practice problem — Korsch on spontaneity vs. organization and 1848 vs. 1917

In his 1930 "Anti-Critique" of the 1923 "Marxism and Philosophy," Korsch wrote,

> When the SPD became a "Marxist" party (a process completed with the Erfurt Programme written by Kautsky and Bernstein in 1891) a gap developed between its highly articulated revolutionary "Marxist" theory and a practice that was far behind this revolutionary theory; in some respects it directly contradicted it. This gap was in fact obvious, and it later came to be felt more and more acutely by all the vital forces in the Party (whether on the Left or Right) and its existence was denied only by the orthodox Marxists of the Centre. This gap can easily be

---

20  Ibid., 7–8.
21  Ibid., 26.

explained by the fact that in this historical phase "Marxism," while formally accepted by the workers' movement, was from the start not a true *theory*, in the sense of being "nothing other than a general expression of the real historical movement" (Marx). On the contrary it was always an *ideology* that had been adopted "from outside" in a pre-established form. In this situation such "orthodox Marxists" as Kautsky and Lenin made a permanent virtue out of a temporary necessity. They energetically defended the idea that socialism can only be brought to the workers "from outside," by bourgeois intellectuals who are allied to the workers' movement. This was also true of Left radicals like Rosa Luxemburg.[22]

According to Korsch, the Revolution of 1848 and the role of the workers' movement in it had provided "a rational solution for all the mysteries" of the contradiction between theory and practice that later 2nd International Marxists tried to sidestep by simply adopting Marxism as an ideology. Korsch commented that,

> [A]lthough [Second International Marxism's] effective practice was now on a *broader basis* than before, it had in no way reached the *heights* of general and theoretical achievement earlier attained by the revolutionary movement and proletarian class struggle on a *narrower basis*. This height was attained during the final phase of the first major capitalist cycle that came to an end towards 1850.[23]

Since the mid-19th century, Marxism, according to the Korsch of the "Anti-Critique," had grown ideological. Even Marx's *Capital* expressed a certain degeneration:

---

22  Ibid., 113–115.
23  Ibid., 116.

[T]he *theory* of Marx and Engels was progressing towards an ever higher level of theoretical perfection although it was no longer directly related to the *practice* of the worker's movement.[24]

In other words, the mature theory of Marx (and its development by Engels and their epigones) was itself "anachronistic" and thus unassimilable by the resurgent workers' movement of the last third of the 19th century.

Korsch abandoned his 1923 conception of Lenin and Luxemburg's rearticulation of 1848 in the theory and practice of 1917–19, the "transformation and development of Marxist theory . . . effected under the peculiar ideological guise of a return to the pure teaching of original or true Marxism." Marx's Marxism, especially in his mature writings, could only be the elaboration of 1848, in isolation from the workers' subsequent actual political practice, to which it became ideologically blind and blinding. No adequate "theory," that is, no "general expression of the real historical movement," had emerged since. This non-identity and divergence of theory and practice that began in the period of Marx's maturity and continued into the 20th century meant, for the Korsch of the 1930s, that Marxism, even in its most revolutionary forms, as with Lenin and Luxemburg, had developed, not to express, but rather to constrain the workers' movement. Marxism had become an ideology whose value could only be relative, not qualitatively superior to others.[25] When he died in 1961, Korsch was working on

---

24  Ibid., 117.

25  Such eclecticism on the Left has only deepened and become more compounded since Korsch's time, especially since the 1960s. However Marx may come up for periodic reconsideration, certain questions central to the Marxian problematic remain obscured.

As Fredric Jameson has written,

A Marx revival seems to be under way, predating the current [2007–09] disarray on Wall Street, even though no clear-cut political options yet seem to propose themselves. . . . The big ideological issues – anarchism, the party, economic planning, social classes – are still mainly avoided, on the grounds that they remind too many people of Communist propaganda. Such a reminder is unwanted, not so much because it is accompanied by the memory of deaths and violence . . . as simply and less dramatically because such topics now appear boring. ("Sandblasting Marx," *New Left Review* 55 January – February 2009).

For further discussion of the fluctuating currency and fortunes of Marxian approaches

a study of Marx's rival in the 1st International Workingmen's Association, the anarchist Mikhail Bakunin.[26]

Originally published in *Platypus Review* 15 (September 2009)

---

as a feature of modern history, see my "Symptomology: Historical transformations in social-political context," *Platypus Review* 12 (May 2009), in *Death of the Millennial Left*.

26  A. R. Giles-Peter, "Karl Korsch: A Marxist Friend of Anarchism," *Red & Black* (Australia) 5 (April 1973).

According to Giles-Peter, Korsch came to believe that the "basis of the revolutionary attitude in the modern bourgeois epoch would be an ethic Marx would have rejected as 'anarchist,'" and thus "explicitly rejected the elements of Marxism which separate it from anarchism."

As Korsch himself put it, in "Ten Theses on Marxism Today" (1950), trans. Giles-Peter in *Telos* 26 (Winter 1975–76),

> Marx is today only one among the numerous precursors, founders and developers of the socialist movement of the working class. No less important are the so-called Utopian Socialists from Thomas More to the present. No less important are the great rivals of Marx, such as Blanqui, and his sworn enemies, such as Proudhon and Bakunin. No less important, in the final result, are the more recent developments such as German revisionism, French syndicalism, and Russian Bolshevism.

Whereas Korsch in 1923 had grasped the essential and vital if transformed continuity between Marx and his precursors in the "revolutionary movement of the Third Estate" of the bourgeois liberal-democratic revolutions, by 1950 he wrote,

> The following points are particularly critical for Marxism: (a) its dependence on the underdeveloped economic and political conditions in Germany and all the other countries of central and eastern Europe where it was to have political relevance; (b) its unconditional adherence to the political forms of the bourgeois revolution; (c) the unconditional acceptance of the advanced economic conditions of England as a model for the future development of all countries and as objective preconditions for the transition to socialism; to which one should add; (d) the consequences of its repeated desperate and contradictory attempts to break out of these conditions.

## Rejoinder on Korsch

David Black's valuable comments and further historical exposition[27] of my review of Karl Korsch's *Marxism and Philosophy* have at their core an issue with Korsch's account of the different historical phases of the question of "philosophy" for Marx and Marxism. Black questions Korsch's differentiation of Marx's relationship to philosophy into three distinct periods: pre-1848, circa 1848, and post-1848. But attempting to defeat Korsch's historical account of such changes in Marx's approaches to relating theory and practice means avoiding Korsch's principal point. It also means defending Marx on mistaken ground. Black considers that Korsch's periodization — his recognition of changes — opens the door to criticizing Marx for inconsistency in his relation of theory to practice. But that is not so.

What makes Korsch's essay "Marxism and Philosophy" (1923) important, to Benjamin and Adorno's work for instance, and what relates it intrinsically to Lukács's contemporaneous treatment of the question of the "Hegelian" dimension of Marxism in *History and Class Consciousness*, is Korsch's discovery of the historically changing relation of theory and practice, and the self-consciousness of this problem, in the history of Marxism. This meant that the matter was, from a Marxian perspective, as Adorno put it in *Negative Dialectics*, "not settled once and for all, but fluctuates historically."[28] Indeed, as Adorno put it in a late essay,

> If, to make an exception for once, one risks what is called a grand perspective, beyond the historical differences in which the concepts of theory and praxis have their life, one discovers the infinitely progressive aspect of the separation of theory and praxis, which was deplored by the Romantics and denounced by the Socialists in their wake — except for the mature Marx.[29]

---

27  *Platypus Review* 18 (December 2009).

28  Theodor W. Adorno, *Negative Dialectics*, trans. E. B. Ashton (New York: Continuum Publishing, 1983), 143.

29  Theodor W. Adorno, "Marginalia to Theory and Praxis," in *Critical Models*, trans. Henry W. Pickford (New York: Columbia University Press, 1998), 266. This essay, a "dialectical epilegomenon" to his book *Negative Dialectics* that Adorno said intended to bring

However one may wish to question the nuances of Korsch's specific historiographic periodization of the problem of Marxism as that of the relation of theory and practice, both during Marx's lifetime and after, this should not be with an eye to either disputing or defending Marx or a Marxian approach's consistency on the matter. One may perhaps attempt a more fine-grained approach to the historical "fluctuations" of what Adorno called the "constitutive" and indeed "progressive" aspect of the "separation of theory and praxis." Korsch's point in the 1923 "Marxism and Philosophy," followed by Benjamin and Adorno, was that we must attend to this "separation," or, as Adorno put it, "non-identity," if we are to have a properly Marxian self-consciousness of the problem of "Marxism" in theory and practice. For this problem of the separation of theory and practice is not to be deplored, but calls for critical awareness. Marx was consistent in his own awareness of the relation of theory and practice. This meant that at different times Marx found them related in different ways.

By contrast, what has waylaid the sectarian "Marxist Left" has been the freezing of the theory-practice problem, which then continued to elude a progressive-emancipatory solution at any given moment. Particular historical moments in the theory-practice problem have become dogmatized by various sects, thus dooming them to irrelevance. So generations of ostensibly revolutionary "Marxists" have failed to heed the nature of Rosa Luxemburg's praise of Lenin and Trotsky's Bolsheviks in the October Revolution:

> All of us are subject to the laws of history. . . . The Bolsheviks
> have shown that they are capable of everything that a genuine
> revolutionary party can contribute within the limits of his
> torical possibilities. . . . What is in order is to distinguish the

---

together "philosophical speculation and drastic experience" (*Critical Models*, 126), was one of the last writings he finished for publication before he died in 1969. It reflected his dispute with fellow Frankfurt School critical theorist Hebert Marcuse over the student protests of the Vietnam War (see Adorno and Marcuse, "Correspondence on the German Student Movement," trans. Esther Leslie, *New Left Review* I/233, Jan.–Feb. 1999, 123–136). As Adorno put it in his May 5, 1969 letter to Marcuse, "[T]here are moments in which theory is pushed on further by practice. But such a situation neither exists objectively today, nor does the barren and brutal practicism that confronts us here have the slightest thing to do with theory anyhow" ("Correspondence," 127).

276 · Critical theory: Philosophy

essential from the non-essential, the kernel from the accidental excrescencies in the politics of the Bolsheviks. In the present period, when we face decisive final struggles in all the world, the most important problem of socialism was and is the burning question of our time. It is not a matter of this or that secondary question of tactics, but of the capacity for action of the proletariat, the strength to act, the will to power of socialism as such. In this, Lenin and Trotsky and their friends were the *first*, those who went ahead as an example to the proletariat of the world; they are still the *only ones* up to now who can cry with Hutten: "I have dared!" This is the essential and *enduring* in Bolshevik policy. In *this* sense theirs is the immortal historical service of having marched at the head of the international proletariat with the conquest of political power and the practical placing of the problem of the realization of socialism, and of having advanced mightily the settlement of the score between capital and labor in the entire world. . . . And in *this* sense, the future everywhere belongs to "Bolshevism."[30]

The Bolshevik Revolution was not itself the achievement of socialism and the overcoming of capitalism, but it did nevertheless squarely address itself to the problem of grasping history so as to make possible revolutionary practice. The Bolsheviks recognized, in other words, that we are tasked, by the very nature of capital, in Marx's sense, to struggle within and through the separation of theory and practice. The Bolshevik Revolution of October 1917 was the occasion and context for Korsch's rumination on the theory and practice of Marxism in his seminal 1923 essay on "Marxism and Philosophy."

In the extended aftermath of the failed revolution of 1917–19, the crisis of the Stalinization of Third International Communism and the looming political victory of fascism, Horkheimer, in an aphorism titled

---

30 "The Russian Revolution," in *The Russian Revolution and Leninism or Marxism* (Ann Arbor: University of Michigan Press, 1961), 80.

"A Discussion About Revolution," addressed himself to the same subject Luxemburg and Korsch had discussed, from the other side of historical experience:

> [A] proletarian party cannot be made the object of contemplative criticism. . . . Bourgeois criticism of the proletarian struggle is a logical impossibility. . . . At times such as the present, revolutionary belief may not really be compatible with great clear-sightedness about the realities.[31]

This is because, for Horkheimer, from a Marxian "proletarian" perspective, as opposed to a (historically) "bourgeois" one (including that of pre- or non-Marxian "socialism"), the problem is not a matter of formulating a correct theory and then implementing it in practice. It is rather a question of what Lukács called "historical consciousness." We should note well how Horkheimer posed the theory-practice problem here, as the contradiction between "revolutionary belief" and "clear-sightedness about the realities."

Horkheimer elaborated further that proletarian revolutionary politics cannot be conceived on the model of capitalist enterprise, and not only for socioeconomic class-hierarchical reasons, but rather because of the differing relation of theory and practice in the two instances; it is the absence of any "historical consciousness" of the theory and practice problem that makes "bourgeois criticism of the proletarian struggle" a *logical* "impossibility." As Lukács put it, in "Reification and the Consciousness of the Proletariat" (1923), "*a radical change in outlook is not feasible on the soil of bourgeois society*."[32] Rather, one must radically deepen — render "dialectical" — the outlook of the present historical moment. The point is that a Marxian perspective can find — and indeed has often found — itself far removed from the practical politics and (entirely "bourgeois") ideological consciousness of the working class. This has not invalidated Marxism, but rather called for a further Marxian critical reflection on its own condition.

---

31 Max Horkheimer, *Dawn and Decline: Notes 1926-31 and 1950-1969*, trans. Michael Shaw (New York: Seabury Press, 1978), 40-41.
32 Trans. Rodney Livingstone (Cambridge, MA: The MIT Press, 1972), 109-110.

In a letter of February 22, 1881 to the Dutch anarchist Ferdinand Domela Nieuwenhuis, Marx wrote,

> It is my conviction that the critical juncture for a new International Working Men's Association has not yet arrived and for that reason I regard all workers' congresses or socialist congresses, in so far as they are not directly related to the conditions existing in this or that particular nation, as not merely useless but actually harmful. They will always ineffectually end in endlessly repeated general banalities.[33]

How much more is this criticism applicable to the "Left" today! But, more directly, what it points to is that Marx recognized no fixed relation of theory and practice that he pursued throughout his life. Instead, he very self-consciously exercised judgment respecting the changing relation of theory and practice, and considered this consciousness the hallmark of his politics. Marx's *Eighteenth Brumaire of Louis Bonaparte* (1852) excoriated "bourgeois" democratic politics, including that of contemporary socialists, for its inability to simultaneously learn from *history* and face the challenge of the *new*.[34] How else could one judge that a moment has "not yet arrived" while calling for something other than "endlessly repeated banalities?"

---

33  Karl Marx to Domela Nieuwenhuis, 22 February 1881, in *Karl Marx and Friedrich Engels: Selected Correspondence, 1846-1895*, trans. Dona Torr (New York: International Publishers, 1942), 387.

34  As Luxemburg put it in 1915 in *The Crisis of German Social Democracy*, aka *The Junius Pamphlet*,

> Marx says [in *The Eighteenth Brumaire of Louis Bonaparte* (1852)]: "[T]he democrat (that is, the petty bourgeois revolutionary) [comes] out of the most shameful defeats as unmarked as he naïvely went into them; he comes away with the newly gained conviction that he must be victorious, not that he or his party ought to give up the old principles, but that conditions ought to accommodate him." The modern proletariat comes out of historical tests differently. Its tasks and its errors are both gigantic: no prescription, no schema valid for every case, no infallible leader to show it the path to follow. Historical experience is its only school mistress. Its thorny way to self-emancipation is paved not only with immeasurable suffering but also with countless errors. The aim of its journey — its emancipation depends on this — is whether the proletariat can learn from its own errors. Self-criticism,

Marx had a critical theory of the relation of theory and practice — recognizing it as a historically specific and not merely "philosophical" problem, or, a problem that called for the critical theory of the philosophy of history — and a political practice of the relation of theory and practice. There is not simply a theoretical or practical problem, but also and more profoundly a problem of relating theory and practice.

We are neither going to think our way out ahead of time, nor somehow work our way through, in the process of acting. We do not need to dissolve the theory-practice distinction that seems to paralyze us, but rather achieve both good theory and good practice in the struggle to relate them properly. It is not a matter of finding either a correct theory or correct practice, but of trying to judge and affect their *changing relation* and recognizing this as a problem of *history*.

Marx overcame the political pitfalls and historical blindness of his "revolutionary" contemporaries, such as the pre-Marxian socialism of Proudhon *et al.* leading to 1848, anarchism in the First International, and the Lassallean trend of the German Social-Democratic Party. It is significant that Marx's *Critique of the Gotha Programme* (1875) critiqued the residual Lassallean politics of the Social Democrats for being to the Right of the liberals on international free trade, etc., thus exposing the problem of this first "Marxist" party from the outset.[35]

Lenin, Luxemburg, and Trotsky, following Marx, recovered and struggled through the problem of theory and practice for their time, precipitating a crisis in Marxism, and thus advancing it. They overcame the

---

remorseless, cruel, and going to the core of things is the life's breath and light of the proletarian movement. The fall of the socialist proletariat in the present world war [WWI] is unprecedented. It is a misfortune for humanity. But socialism will be lost only if the international proletariat fails to measure the depth of this fall, if it refuses to learn from it.

35  Karl Marx, "Critique of the Gotha Program," in *Marx-Engels Reader*, 2nd edition, ed. Robert C. Tucker (New York: W. W. Norton, 1978), 533–534. Marx wrote,

In fact, the internationalism of the program stands *even infinitely below* that of the Free Trade party. The latter also asserts that the result of its efforts will be 'the international brotherhood of peoples.' But it also does something to make trade international. . . . The international activity of the working classes does not in any way depend on the existence of the International Working Men's Association.

"vulgar Marxist" ossification of theory and practice in the Second International, as Korsch and Lukács explained. It meant the Marxist critique of Marxism, or, an emancipatory critique of emancipatory politics — a Left critique of the Left. This is not a finished task. We need to attain this ability again, for our time.

Originally published in *Platypus Review* 20 (February 2010)

Parts included for presentation on the panel "Reconsiderations in Western Marxism: Lukács, Korsch, Adorno, Marcuse," with panelist Baolinh Dang, at the *Historical Materialism* conference, York University, Toronto, May 14, 2010; and on the panel "Hegel, Marx, and Modern Philosophy," with panelists Patrick Murray and Richard Westerman at the Weissbourd 2011 Annual Conference, the University of Chicago, May 6, 2011.

# Gillian Rose's "Hegelian" critique of Marxism[1]

Gillian Rose's magnum opus was her second book, *Hegel Contra Sociology* (1981). Preceding this was *The Melancholy Science: An Introduction to the Thought of Theodor W. Adorno* (1978), a work which charted Rose's approach to the relation of Marxism to Hegel in *Hegel Contra Sociology*.[2] Alongside her monograph on Adorno, Rose published two incisively critical reviews of the reception of Adorno's work.[3] Rose thus established herself early on as an important interrogator of Adorno's thought and Frankfurt School Critical Theory more generally, and of their problematic reception.

In her review of *Negative Dialectics*, Rose noted, "Anyone who is involved in the possibility of Marxism as a mode of cognition *sui generis* . . . must read Adorno's book."[4] As she wrote in her review of contemporaneous studies on the Frankfurt School,

> Both the books reviewed here indict the Frankfurt School for betraying a Marxist canon; yet they neither make any case for the importance of the School nor do they acknowledge the question central to that body of work: the possibility and

---

1   Book review: Gillian Rose, *Hegel Contra Sociology* (London: Verso, 2009). Originally published in 1981.

2   Rose, *The Melancholy Science* (London: Macmillan, 1978).

3   See Rose's review of the English translation of Adorno's *Negative Dialectics* (1973) in *The American Political Science Review* 70, no. 2 (June, 1976), 598–599; and of Susan Buck-Morss's *The Origin of Negative Dialectics: Theodor W. Adorno, Walter Benjamin and the Frankfurt Institute* (1977) and Zoltán Tar's *The Frankfurt School: The Critical Theories of Horkheimer and Adorno* (1977) in *History and Theory* 18, no. 1 (February 1979), 126–135.

4   Rose, Review of *Negative Dialectics*, 599.

desirability of defining such a canon. As a result both books overlook the relation of the Frankfurt School to Marx for which they are searching. . . . They have taken the writings [of Horkheimer, Benjamin and Adorno] literally but not seriously enough. The more general consequences of this approach are also considerable: it obscures instead of illuminating the large and significant differences within Marxism.[5]

Rose's critique can be said of virtually all the reception of Frankfurt School Critical Theory.

Rose followed her work on Adorno with *Hegel Contra Sociology*. The book's original dust jacket featured a blurb by Anthony Giddens, Rose's mentor and the *doyen* of sociology, who called it *"a very unusual piece of work . . . whose significance will take some time to sink in."* As Rose put it in *The Melancholy Science*, Adorno and other thinkers in Frankfurt School Critical Theory sought to answer for their generation the question Marx posed (in the 1844 *Economic and Philosophic Manuscripts*), "How do we now stand as regards the Hegelian dialectic?"[6] For Rose, this question remained a standing one. Hence, Rose's work on the problem of "Hegelian Marxism" comprised an important critique of the Left of her time that has only increased in resonance since then.

Rose sought to recover Hegel from readings informed by 20th century neo-Kantian influences, and from what she saw as the failure to fully grasp Hegel's critique of Kant. Where Kant could be seen as the bourgeois philosopher *par excellence*, Rose took Hegel to be his most important and unsurpassed critic. Hegel provided Rose with the standard for critical thinking on social modernity, whose threshold she found nearly all others to fall below, including thinkers she otherwise respected such as Adorno and Marx.

Rose read Marx as an important disciple of Hegel who, to her mind, nevertheless, misapprehended key aspects of Hegel's thought. According to Rose, this left Marxism at the mercy of prevailing Kantian preoccupations. As she put it, "When Marx is not self-conscious about his relation to

---

5   Rose, Review of *The Origin of Negative Dialectics* and *The Frankfurt School*, 126, 135.
6   Rose, *Melancholy Science*, 2.

Hegel's philosophy . . . [he] captures what Hegel means by actuality or spirit. But when Marx desires to dissociate himself from Hegel's actuality . . . he relies on and affirms abstract dichotomies between being and consciousness, theory and practice, etc."[7] In offering this Hegelian critique of Marx and Marxism, however, Rose actually fulfilled an important desideratum of Adorno's Marxist critical theory, which was to attend to what was "not yet subsumed," or, how a regression of Marxism could be met by a critique from the standpoint of what "remained" from Hegel.

In his deliberate recovery of what Rose characterized as Marx's "capturing" of Hegel's "actuality or spirit," Adorno was preceded by the "Hegelian Marxists" Georg Lukács and Karl Korsch. The "regressive" reading proposed by Adorno[8] that could answer Rose would involve reading Adorno as presupposing Lukács and Korsch, who presupposed the revolutionary Marxism of Lenin and Luxemburg, who presupposed Marx, who presupposed Hegel. Similarly, Adorno characterized Hegel as "Kant come into his own."[9] From Adorno's perspective, the Marxists did not need to rewrite Marx, nor did Marx need to rewrite Hegel. For Adorno the recovery of Marx by the Marxists — and of Hegel by Marx — was a matter of further specification and not simple "progress." This involved problematization, perhaps, but not overcoming in the sense of leaving behind.[10] Marx did not

---

7   *Hegel Contra Sociology*, 230–231.

8   See, for instance, Adorno, "Progress" (1962) and "Critique" (1969), in *Critical Models: Interventions and Catchwords*, trans. Henry W. Pickford (New York: Columbia University Press, 1998), 143–160 and 281–288.

9   Theodor W. Adorno, "Aspects of Hegel's Philosophy," in *Hegel: Three Studies*, trans. Shierry Weber Nicholsen (Cambridge, MA: MIT Press, 1994), 6.

10  See Georg Lukács, Preface (1922), *History and Class Consciousness: Studies in Marxist Dialectics* (1923), trans. Rodney Livingstone (Cambridge, MA: MIT Press, 1971):

The author of these pages . . . believes that today it is of practical importance to return in this respect to the traditions of Marx-interpretation founded by Engels (who regarded the "German workers' movement" as the "heir to classical German philosophy"), and by Plekhanov. He believes that all good Marxists should form, in Lenin's words "a kind of society of the materialist friends of the Hegelian dialectic." But Hegel's position today is the reverse of Marx's own. The problem with Marx is precisely to take his method and his system *as we find them* and to demonstrate that they *form a coherent unity that must be preserved*. The opposite is true of Hegel. The task he imposes is to separate out from the complex web of ideas with

seek to overcome Hegel, but rather was tasked to advance and fulfill his concerns. This comports well with Rose's approach to Hegel, which she in fact took over, however unconsciously, from her prior study of Adorno, failing to follow what Adorno assumed about Marxism in this regard.

Two parts of *Hegel Contra Sociology* frame its overall discussion of the challenge Hegel's thought presents to the critical theory of society: a section in the introductory chapter on what Rose calls the "Neo-Kantian Marxism" of Lukács and Adorno and the concluding section on "The Culture and Fate of Marxism." The arguments condensed in these two sections of Rose's book comprise one of the most interesting and challenging critiques of Marxism. However, Rose's misunderstanding of Marxism limits the direction and reach of the rousing call with which she concluded her book: "This critique of Marxism itself yields the project of a critical Marxism. . . . [P]resentation of the contradictory relations between Capital and culture is the only way to link the analysis of the economy to comprehension of the conditions for revolutionary practice."[11] Yet Rose's critique of Marxism, especially of Lukács and Adorno, and of Marx himself, misses its mark.

One problem regarding Rose's critique of Marxism is precisely her focus on Marxism as a specifically "philosophical" problem, as a problem more of thought than of action. As Lukács's contemporary Karl Korsch pointed out in "Marxism and Philosophy" (1923), by the late 19th century historians such as Dilthey had observed that "ideas contained in a philosophy can live on not only in philosophies, but equally well in positive sciences and social practice, and that this process precisely began on a large scale with Hegel's philosophy."[12] For Korsch, this meant that "philosophical" problems in the Hegelian sense were not matters of theory but practice. From a Marxian perspective, however, it is precisely the problem of capitalist society that is posed at the level of practice. Korsch went on to argue that "what appears as the purely 'ideal' development of philosophy in the 19th century can in fact only be fully and essentially grasped by relating

---

its sometimes glaring contradictions all the *seminal elements* of his thought and rescue them as a *vital intellectual force for the present*. (xlv)

11  *Hegel Contra Sociology*, 235.

12  Karl Korsch, "Marxism and Philosophy" (1923), in *Marxism and Philosophy*, trans. Fred Halliday (New York: Monthly Review Press, 1970 and 2008), 39.

it to the concrete historical development of bourgeois society as a whole."[13] Korsch's great insight, shared by Lukács, took this perspective from Luxemburg and Lenin, who grasped how the history of Marxism was a key part, indeed the crucial aspect, of this development, at the time of their writing in the first years of the 20th century.[14]

The most commented-upon essay of Lukács's collection *History and Class Consciousness* (1923) is "Reification and the Consciousness of the Proletariat," written specifically as the centerpiece of the book, but drawing upon arguments made in the book's other essays. Like many readers of Lukács, Rose focused her critique in particular on Lukács's argument in the second part of his "Reification" essay, "The Antinomies of Bourgeois Thought," neglecting that its "epistemological" investigation of philosophy is only one moment in a greater argument, which culminates in the most lengthy and difficult third part of Lukács's essay, "The Standpoint of the Proletariat." But it is in this part of the essay that Lukács addressed how the Marxist social-democratic workers' movement was an intrinsic part of what Korsch had called the "concrete historical development of bourgeois

---

13  Korsch, "Marxism and Philosophy," 40.

14  See, for instance: Rosa Luxemburg, *Reform or Revolution?* (1900), in which Luxemburg pointed out that all reforms aimed at ameliorating the crisis of capital actually exacerbated it; Vladimir Lenin, *What is to be Done?* (1902), in which Lenin supposed that overcoming reformist "revisionism" in international (Marxist) social democracy would amount to and be the express means for overcoming capitalism; and Leon Trotsky, *Results and Prospects* (1906), in which Trotsky pointed out that the various "prerequisites of socialism" not only developed historically independently but also, significantly, antagonistically. In *The State and Revolution* (1917), Lenin, following Marx, critiqued anarchism for calling for the "abolition" of the state and not recognizing that the necessity of the state could only "wither away" as a function of the gradual overcoming of "bourgeois right" whose prevalence would persist in the revolutionary socialist "workers' state" long after the overthrow of the bourgeoisie: the state would continue as a symptom of capitalist social relations without capitalists *per se.* In *Literature and Revolution* (1924), Trotsky pointed out that, as symptomatic products of present society, the cultural and even political expressions of the revolution could not themselves embody the principles of an emancipated society but could, at best, only open the way to them. For Lukács and Korsch (and Benjamin and Adorno following them — see Benjamin's 1934 essay on "The Author as Producer," in *Reflections*, trans. Edmund Jephcott [New York: Schocken, 1986], 220–238), such arguments demonstrated a dialectical approach to Marxism itself on the part of its most thoughtful actors.

society as a whole," in which its "philosophical" problem lived. The "philosophical" problem Korsch and Lukács sought to address was the "dialectic" of the political practice of the working class, how it actually produced and did not merely respond to the contradictions and potentially revolutionary crisis of capitalist society. It is because of Rose's failure to grasp this point that her criticism of Marx, Lukács, and Adorno amounts to nothing more than an unwitting recapitulation of Lukács's own critique of what he called "vulgar Marxism," and what Adorno called "positivism" or "identity thinking." Lukács and Adorno, following Lenin and Luxemburg, attempted to effect a return to what Korsch called "Marx's Marxism."

In examining Rose's critique of Lukács, Adorno, and Marx, and in responding to Rose's Hegelian interrogation of their supposed deficits, it becomes possible to recover what is important about and unifies their thought. Rose's questions about Marxism are those that any Marxian approach must answer to demonstrate its necessity — its "improved version," as Lukács put it, of the "Hegelian original" dialectic.[15]

---

15  Lukács, *History and Class Consciousness*, xlvi. Citing Lukács in her review of Buck-Morss and Tar on the Frankfurt School, Rose posed the problem of Marxism this way:

> The reception of the Frankfurt School in the English-speaking world to date displays a paradox. Frequently, the Frankfurt School inspires dogmatic historiography although it represents a tradition which is attractive and important precisely because of its rejection of dogmatic or "orthodox" Marxism. This tradition in German Marxism has its origin in Lukács's most un-Hegelian injunction to take Marxism as a "method" – a method which would remain valid even if "every one of Marx's individual theses" were proved wrong. One can indeed speculate whether philosophers like Bloch, Benjamin, Horkheimer, and Adorno would have become Marxists if Lukács had not pronounced thus. For other Marxists this position spells scientific "suicide." (Rose, Review of *The Origin of Negative Dialectics* and *The Frankfurt School*, 126.)

Nevertheless, Rose used a passage from Lukács's 1924 book in eulogy, *Lenin: A Study on the Unity of His Thought* as the epigraph for her essay: "[T]he dialectic is not a finished theory to be applied mechanically to all the phenomena of life *but only exists as theory in and through this application*" (126). Critically, Rose asked only that Lukács's own work – and that of other "Hegelian" Marxists – remain true to this observation.

## The problem of Marxism as Hegelian "science"

In the final section of *Hegel Contra Sociology,* in the conclusion of the chapter "With What Must the Science End?" titled "The Culture and Fate of Marxism," Rose addresses Marx directly. Here, Rose states that,

> Marx did not appreciate the politics of Hegel's presentation, the politics of a phenomenology [logic of appearance] which aims to re-form consciousness . . . [and] acknowledges the actuality which determines the formation of consciousness. . . . Marx's notion of political education was less systematic than [Hegel's].[16]

One issue of great import for Rose's critique of Marxism is the status of Hegel's philosophy as "speculative." As Rose wrote,

> Marx's reading of Hegel overlooks the discourse or logic of the speculative proposition. He refuses to see the lack of identity in Hegel's thought, and therefore tries to establish his own discourse of lack of identity using the ordinary proposition. But instead of producing a logic or discourse of lack of identity he produced an ambiguous dichotomy of activity/nature which relies on a natural beginning and an utopian end.[17]

Rose explicated this "lack of identity in Hegel's thought" as follows:

> Hegel knew that his thought would be misunderstood if it were read as [a] series of ordinary propositions which affirm an identity between a fixed subject and contingent accidents, but he also knew that, like any thinker, he had to present his thought in propositional form. He thus proposed . . . a "speculative proposition." . . . To read a proposition "speculatively" means that the identity which is affirmed between subject and predicate is seen

---

16  *Hegel Contra Sociology,* 232–233.
17  Ibid, 231.

equally to affirm a lack of identity between subject and predicate. ... From this perspective the "subject" is not fixed: ... Only when the lack of identity between subject and predicate has been experienced, can their identity be grasped. ... Thus it cannot be said, as Marx, for example, said [in his *Critique of Hegel's "Philosophy of Right"* (1843)], that the speculative proposition turns the predicate into the subject and therefore hypostatizes predicates, just like the ordinary proposition hypostatizes the subject. ... [Hegel's] speculative proposition is fundamentally opposed to [this] kind of formal identity.[18]

Rose may be correct about Marx's 1843 critique of Hegel. She severely critiqued Marx's 1845 "Theses on Feuerbach" on the same score.[19] What this overlooks is Marx's understanding of the historical difference between his time and Hegel's. Consequently, it neglects Marx's differing conception of "alienation" as a function of the Industrial Revolution, in which the meaning of the categories of bourgeois society, of the commodity form of labor, had become reversed.

Rose's failure to register the change in meaning of "alienation" for Marx compromised her reading of Lukács:

[M]aking a distinction between underlying process and resultant objectifications[,] Lukács was able to avoid the conventional Marxist treatment of capitalist social forms as mere "superstructure" or "epiphenomena;" legal, bureaucratic and cultural forms have the same status as the commodity form. Lukács made it clear that "reification" is the specific capitalist form of objectification. It determines the structure of all the capitalist social forms. ... [T]he process-like essence (the mode of production) attains a validity from the standpoint of the totality. ... [Lukács's approach] turned ... away from a logic of identity in the direction of a theory of historical mediation. The advantage of this

---

18 *Hegel Contra Sociology*, 51–53.
19 Ibid, 230.

approach was that Lukács opened new areas of social life to Marxist analysis and critique. . . . The disadvantage was that Lukács omitted many details of Marx's theory of value. . . . As a result "reification" and "mediation" become a kind of shorthand instead of a sustained theory. A further disadvantage is that the sociology of reification can only be completed by a speculative sociology of the proletariat as the subject-object of history.[20]

However, for Lukács the proletariat is not a Hegelian subject-object of history but a Marxian one.[21] Lukács did not affirm history as the given situation of the possibility of freedom in the way Hegel did. Rather, following Marx, Lukács treated historical structure as a problem to be overcome. History was not to be grasped as necessary, as Hegel affirmed against his contemporaries' Romantic despair at modernity. Rose mistakenly took Lukács's critique of capital to be Romantic, subject to the *aporiae* Hegel had characterized in the "unhappy consciousness." Rose therefore misinterpreted Lukács's revolutionism as a matter of "will":[22]

---

20  *Hegel Contra Sociology*, 30–31.

21  See Lukács, "Reification and the Consciousness of the Proletariat," 171–175:

> The *class meaning* of [the thoroughgoing capitalist rationalization of society] lies precisely in the fact that the bourgeoisie regularly transforms each new qualitative gain back onto the quantitative level of yet another rational calculation. Whereas for the proletariat, the "same" development has a different class meaning: it means the *abolition of the isolated individual*, it means that the workers can become conscious of the social character of labor, it means that the abstract, universal form of the societal principle as it is manifested can be increasingly concretized and overcome. . . . For the proletariat however, this ability to go beyond the immediate in search for the "remoter" factors means the *transformation of the objective nature of the objects of action.*

> The "objective nature of the objects of action" includes that of the working class itself.

22  Such misapprehension of revolutionary Marxism as voluntarism has been commonplace. Rosa Luxemburg's biographer, the political scientist J. P. Nettl, in the essay "The German Social Democratic Party 1890–1914 as Political Model" (in *Past and Present* 30 [April 1965], 65–95), addressed this issue as follows:

> Rosa Luxemburg was emphatically not an anarchist and went out of her way to distinguish between "revolutionary gymnastic," which was "conjured out of the air at will," and her own policy (see her 1906 pamphlet on *The Mass Strike, the Political Party and the Trade Unions*). . . . [Later Communist historians have burdened her]

Lukács's *History and Class Consciousness* is an attempt to give [Marx's] *Capital* a phenomenological form: to read Marx's

---

with the concept of spontaneity. . . . [But her's] was a dynamic, dialectic doctrine; organization and action revived each other and made each other grow. . . . It may well be that there were underlying similarities to anarchism, insofar as any doctrine of action resembles any other. A wind of action and movement was blowing strongly around the edges of European culture at the time, both in art and literature as well as in the more political context of Sorel and the Italian Futurists. . . . [But] most important of all, Rosa Luxemburg specifically drew on a Russian experience [of the 1905 Revolution] which differed sharply from the intellectual individualism of Bakunin, [Domela-]Nieuwenhuis and contemporary anarchism. She always emphasized self-discipline as an adjunct to action – the opposite of the doctrine of self-liberation which the Anarchists shared with other European action philosophies. (88–89)

The German Left evolved a special theory of action. . . . Where the German Left emphasized action against organization, Lenin preached organization as a means to action. But action was common to both – and it was this emphasis on action which finally brought the German Left and the Russian Bolsheviks into the same camp in spite of so many serious disagreements. In her review of the Bolshevik revolution, written in September 1918, Rosa Luxemburg singled out this commitment to action for particular praise. Here she saw a strong sympathetic echo to her own ideas, and analyzed it precisely in her own terms:

> With . . . the seizure of power and *the carrying forward* of the revolution the Bolsheviks have solved the famous question of a 'popular majority' which has so long oppressed the German Social Democrats . . . not through a majority to a revolutionary tactic, but through a revolutionary tactic to a majority ( *The Russian Revolution*)

With action as the cause and not the consequence of mass support, she saw the Bolsheviks applying her ideas in practice – and incidentally provides us with clear evidence as to what she meant when she spoke of majority and masses. In spite of other severe criticisms of Bolshevik policy, it was this solution of the problem by the Bolsheviks which definitely ensured them the support of the German Left. (91–92)

The possibilities adumbrated by modern sociology have not yet been adequately exploited in the study of political organizations, dynamics, relationships. Especially the dynamics; most pictures of change are "moving pictures," which means that they are no more than "a composition of immobilities . . . a position, then a new position, etc., *ad infinitum*" (Henri Bergson). The problem troubled Talcott Parsons among others, just as it long ago troubled Rosa Luxemburg. (95)

This was what Lukács, following Lenin and Luxemburg, meant by the problem of "reification."

analysis of capital as the potential consciousness of a universal class. But Lukács's emphasis on change in consciousness as *per se* revolutionary, separate from the analysis of change in capitalism, gives his appeal to the proletariat or the party the status of an appeal to a ... will.[23]

Nonetheless, Rose found aspects of Lukács's understanding of Marx compelling, in a "Hegelian" sense:

> The question of the relation between *Capital* and politics is thus not an abstract question about the relation between theory and practice, but a phenomenological question about the relationship between acknowledgement of actuality and the possibility of change. This is why the theory of commodity fetishism, the presentation of a contradiction between substance and subject, remains more impressive than any abstract statements about the relation between theory and practice or between capitalist crisis and the formation of revolutionary consciousness. It acknowledges actuality and its misrepresentation as consciousness.[24]

What is missing from Rose's critique of Lukács, however, is how he offered a dialectical argument, precisely through forms of misrecognition ("misrepresentation").[25]

---

23  *Hegel Contra Sociology*, 233.

24  Ibid.

25  As Lukács put it in the Preface (1922) to *History and Class Consciousness*,

> I should perhaps point out to the reader unfamiliar with dialectics one difficulty inherent in the nature of dialectical method relating to the definition of concepts and terminology. It is of the essence of dialectical method that concepts which are false in their abstract one-sidedness are later transcended (*zur Aufhebung gelangen*). The process of transcendence makes it inevitable that we should operate with these one-sided, abstract and false concepts. These concepts acquire their true meaning less by definition than by their function as aspects that are then transcended in the totality. Moreover, it is even more difficult to establish fixed meanings for concepts in Marx's improved version of the dialectic than in the Hegelian original. For if concepts are only the intellectual forms of historical realities then

This is why the theory of commodity fetishism has become central to the neo-Marxist theory of domination, aesthetics, and ideology. The theory of commodity fetishism is the most speculative moment in Marx's exposition of capital. It comes nearest to demonstrating in the historically specific case of commodity producing society how substance is ((mis-) represented as) subject, how necessary illusion arises out of productive activity.[26]

However, the contradiction of capital is not merely between "substance and subject," but rather a self-contradictory social substance, value, which gives rise to a self-contradictory subject.[27]

---

these forms, one-sided, abstract and false as they are, belong to the true unity as genuine aspects of it. Hegel's statements about this problem of terminology in the preface to the *Phenomenology* are thus even more true than Hegel himself realized when he said: "Just as the expressions 'unity of subject and object', of 'finite and infinite', of 'being and thought', etc., have the drawback that 'object' and 'subject' bear the same meaning as when *they exist outside that unity, so* that within the unity they mean something other than is implied by their expression: so, too, falsehood is not, *qua* false, any longer a moment of truth." In the pure historicization of the dialectic this statement receives yet another twist: in so far as the "false" is an aspect of the "true" it is both "false" and "non-false." When the professional demolishers of Marx criticize his "lack of conceptual rigor" and his use of "image" rather than "definitions," etc., they cut as sorry a figure as did Schopenhauer when he tried to expose Hegel's "logical howlers" in his Hegel critique. All that is proved is their total inability to grasp even the ABC of the dialectical method. The logical conclusion for the dialectician to draw from this failure is not that he is faced with a conflict between different scientific methods, but that he is in the presence of a *social phenomenon* and that by conceiving it as a socio-historical phenomenon he can at once refute it and transcend it dialectically. (xlvi–xlvii)

For Lukács, the self-contradictory nature of the workers' movement was itself a "socio-historical phenomenon" that had brought forth a revolutionary crisis at the time of Lukács's writing: from a Marxian perspective, the working class and its politics were the most important phenomena and objects of critique to be overcome in capitalist society.

26  Ibid, 232

27  See Moishe Postone, *Time, Labor and Social Domination: A Reinterpretation of Marx's Critical Theory* (Cambridge: Cambridge University Press, 2003).

## Rose's critique of the "sociological" Marxism of Lukács and Adorno

Rose's misconstrual of the status of proletarian social revolution in the self-understanding of Marxism led her to regard Lukács and Adorno's work as "theoretical" in the restricted sense of mere analysis. Rose denied the dialectical status of Lukács and Adorno's thought by neglecting the question of how a Marxian approach, from Lukács and Adorno's perspective, considered the workers' movement for emancipation as itself symptomatic of capital. Following Marx, Lukács and Adorno regarded Marxism as the organized historical self-consciousness of the social politics of the working class that potentially points beyond capital.[28] Rose

---

28  See Adorno, "Reflections on Class Theory" (1942), in *Can One Live After Auschwitz? A Philosophical Reader*, ed. Rolf Tiedemann (Stanford: Stanford University Press, 2003), 93–110:

> According to [Marxian] theory, history is the history of class struggles. But the concept of class is bound up with the emergence of the proletariat. . . . By extending the concept of class to prehistory, theory denounces not just the bourgeois . . . [but] turns against prehistory itself. . . . By exposing the historical necessity that had brought capitalism into being, [the critique of] political economy became the critique of history as a whole. . . . All history is the history of class struggles because it was always the same thing, namely, prehistory. (93–94)

> This means, however, that the dehumanization is also its opposite. . . . Only when the victims completely assume the features of the ruling civilization will they be capable of wresting them from the dominant power. (110)

This follows from Lukács's conception of proletarian socialism as the "completion" of reification ("Reification and the Consciousness of the Proletariat," in *History and Class Consciousness*):

> The danger to which the proletariat has been exposed since its appearance on the historical stage was that it might remain imprisoned in its immediacy together with the bourgeoisie. With the growth of social democracy this threat acquired a real political organisation which artificially cancels out the mediations so laboriously won and forces the proletariat back into its immediate existence where it is merely a component of capitalist society and not *at the same time* the motor that drives it to its doom and destruction. (196)

limited Lukács and Adorno's concerns regarding "misrecognition," characterizing their work as "sociological":

> The thought of Lukács and Adorno represent two of the most
> original and important attempts . . . [at] an Hegelian Marxism,
> but it constitutes a neo-Kantian Marxism. . . . They turned the
> neo-Kantian paradigm into a Marxist sociology of cultural
> forms . . . with a selective generalization of Marx's theory of
> commodity fetishism.[29]

But, according to Rose, this "sociological" analysis of the commodity form remained outside its object:

> In the essay "Reification and the Consciousness of the Prole-
> tariat" in *History and Class Consciousness*, Lukács generalizes
> Marx's theory of commodity fetishism by making a distinction
> between the total process of production, "real life-processes,"
> and the resultant objectifications of social forms. This notion
> of "objectification" has more in common with the neo-Kantian
> notion of the objectification of specific object-domains than
> with an "Hegelian" conflating of objectification, human praxis
> in general, with alienation, its form in capitalist society.[30]

Rose thought that Lukács thus undermined his own account of potential transformation: "Lukács's very success in demonstrating the prevalence of reification . . . meant that he could only appeal to the proletariat to

---

[E]ven the objects in the very centre of the dialectical process [i.e., the political
forms of the workers' movement itself] can only slough off their reified form after
a laborious process. A process in which the seizure of power by the proletariat
and even the organisation of the state and the economy on socialist lines are only
stages. They are, of course, extremely important stages, but they do not mean that
the ultimate objective has been achieved. And it even appears as if the decisive
crisis-period of capitalism may be characterized by the tendency to intensify reification, to bring it to a head. (208)

29  *Hegel Contra Sociology*, 29.
30  Ibid., 30.

overcome reification by apostrophes to the unity of theory and practice, or by introducing the party as *deus ex machina*."[31] In this respect, Rose failed to note how Lukács, and Adorno following him, had deeply internalized the Hegelian problematic of Marxism, how Marxism was not the (mis)application but the reconstruction of the Hegelian dialectic under the changed social-historical conditions of capital. For Rose, Lukács's concept of "reification" was too negative regarding the "totality" of capital, which she thought threatened to render capital non-dialectical, and its emancipatory transformation inconceivable. But Rose's perspective remains that of Hegel — pre-industrial capital.

## Hegel contra sociology – the "culture" and "fate" of Marxism

Just before she died in 1995, Rose wrote a new Preface for a reprint of *Hegel Contra Sociology*, which states that,

> The speculative exposition of Hegel in this book still provides the basis for a unique engagement with post-Hegelian thought, especially postmodernity, with its roots in Heideggerianism. . . .
> [T]he experience of negativity, the existential drama, is discovered at the heart of Hegelian rationalism. . . . Instead of working with the general question of the dominance of Western metaphysics, the dilemma of addressing modern ethics and politics without arrogating the authority under question is seen as the ineluctable difficulty in Hegel. . . . This book, therefore, remains the core of the project to demonstrate a nonfoundational and radical Hegel, which overcomes the opposition between nihilism and rationalism. It provides the possibility for renewal of critical thought in the intellectual difficulty of our time.[32]

Since the time of Rose's book, with the passage of Marxist politics into history, the "intellectual difficulty" in renewing critical thought has only

---

31  Ibid., 31.
32  Ibid., xviii.

gotten worse. "Postmodernity" has not meant the eclipse or end, but rather the unproblematic triumph, of "Western metaphysics" — in the exhaustion of "postmodernism."[33] Consideration of the problem Rose addressed in terms of the Hegelian roots of Marxism, the immanent critique of capitalist modernity, remains the "possibility" if not the "actuality" of our time. Only by facing it squarely can we avoid sharing in Marxism's "fate" as a "culture." For this "fate," the devolution into "culture," or what Rose called "pre-bourgeois society"[34], threatens not merely a form of politics on the Left, but humanity: it represents the failure to attain let alone transcend the threshold of Hegelian modernity, whose concern Rose recovered.

Originally published in *Platypus Review* 21 (March 2010)

---

33  Rose's term for the post-1960s "New Left" historical situation is "Heideggerian postmodernity." Robert Pippin, as a fellow "Hegelian," in his brief response to the *Critical Inquiry* journal's symposium on "The Future of Criticism," titled "*Critical Inquiry* and Critical Theory: A Short History of Nonbeing" (*Critical Inquiry* 30, no. 2 [Winter 2004], 424–428), has characterized this similarly, as follows:

> [T]he level of discussion and awareness of this issue, in its historical dimensions (with respect both to the history of critical theory and the history of modernization) has regressed.... [T]he problem with contemporary critical theory is that it has become insufficiently critical.... [T]here is also a historical cost for the neglect or underattention or lack of resolution of this core critical problem: repetition.... It may seem extreme to claim – well, to claim at all that such repetition exists (that postmodernism, say, is an instance of such repetition) – and also to claim that it is tied somehow to the dim understanding we have of the post-Kantian situation.... [T]hat is what I wanted to suggest. I'm not sure it will get us anywhere. Philosophy rarely does. Perhaps it exists to remind us that we haven't gotten anywhere. (427–428).

Heidegger himself anticipated this result in his "Overcoming Metaphysics" (1936–46), in *The End of Philosophy*, ed. and trans. Joan Stambaugh (Chicago: University of Chicago Press, 2003): "The still hidden truth of Being is withheld from metaphysical humanity. The laboring animal is left to the giddy whirl of its products so that it may tear itself to pieces and annihilate itself in empty nothingness" (87). Elsewhere, in "The End of Philosophy and the Task of Thinking" (1964), in *Basic Writings*, ed. David Farrell Krell (New York: HarperCollins, 1993), Heidegger acknowledged Marx's place in this process: "With the reversal of metaphysics which was already accomplished by Karl Marx, the most extreme possibility of philosophy is attained" (433).

34  *Hegel Contra Sociology*, 234.

# Defending Marxist Hegelianism against a Marxist critique

I am writing in response to Mike Macnair's 2003 critical review of books by John Rees and David Renton,[1] cited in Macnair's critique of Platypus.[2] I wish to refer also to my three letters and article in response.[3]

I find Macnair's analysis and critique of the political motivations and potential consequences of Rees's affirmative account of Marxist Hegelianism compelling and good. I agree with Macnair's conclusion that, despite Rees's former SWP/UK leader Alex Callinicos's anti-Hegelian Althusserianism, Rees considering "historical experience summed up in theory" was intrinsically connected to the SWP's concept of the party as one which "centralizes experience," with all the problems such a conception entails.

I wish to offer a rejoinder to Macnair's idea that such problematic conceptions of theory and political practice have roots in Lenin, Luxemburg and Lukács, Macnair's analysis of whom I find to be false. Also, I do not think that Macnair quite gets Hegel, although I agree with his characterization that "philosophy — as such — is inherently only a way of interpreting the world," and so limits Hegel's work for the political purposes under consideration.[4] Furthermore, I agree with Macnair's interpretation of Lenin with respect to the purposes of his polemical defense of Marxist approaches to philosophy in *Materialism and Empirio-Criticism* (1908). Moreover, I agree

---

1   "'Classical Marxism' and grasping the dialectic," *Weekly Worker* (September 11, 2003).
2   "No need for party?" *Weekly Worker* (May 12, 2011). See also Mike Macnair's "Theoretical dead end," (May 19, 2011); "The study of history and the left's decline," (June 2, 2011); and "Divided by a common language?" (June 30, 2011).
3   See Letters May 19, May 26 and July 7; and my article, "The philosophy of history" (June 9, 2011).
4   "Against philosopher kings," *Weekly Worker* (December 11, 2008).

with his central point that philosophical agreement cannot be the basis of agreement on political action.

However, as Nicholas Brown responded to comrade Macnair's question at the opening plenary on "The politics of Critical Theory" of the Platypus convention in Chicago on April 29 [2011], it is not possible to "Hegelianize" Marx, because Marx was more Hegelian than Hegel himself.[5] That is, Marx tried to achieve the "Hegelian" self-consciousness of his own historical moment. The question is, what relevance has Marx's Hegelianism today, and what is the relevance of taking such a Hegelian approach to the history of Marxism subsequent to Marx?

## Lukács, Lenin, Luxemburg

I disagree that Lukács's "subject" of history is the point of view or relative perspective of the proletariat as the revolutionary agent that must assert its "will." Rather, I take Lukács to be following Lenin and Luxemburg (and Marx) quite differently than Macnair seems to think, in that the workers' movement for socialism is the necessary mediation for grasping the problem of capital in its "totality," that the workers must not remake the world in their image, but rather lead society more generally beyond capital. Hence, as Macnair characterizes the approach of the Kautskyan "center" of the Second International, the socialist workers' movement must be a leading, practical force in democratic struggles beyond the workers' own (sectional) interests in the transformation of society as a whole.

I disagree that Lenin made a virtue of necessity in the Russian Revolution after October 1917 and adopted a voluntarist (and substitutionalist) conception of the working class and the political party of communism. Rather, Lenin consistently criticized and politically fought against those tendencies of Bolshevism and in the early Third International. I do not think that Lenin's newly found "Hegelianism" after 1914 was the means by which he achieved (mistaken) rapprochement with the "Left."

The key is Luxemburg. I do not think she was a semi-syndicalist spontaneist/voluntarist, or that she neglected issues of political mediation: she

---

5 "The politics of Critical Theory" *Platypus Review* 37 (July 2011).

was not an "ultra-Left." I take her pamphlet, *The Mass Strike, The Political Party, and the Trade Unions* (1906), to have an entirely different political purpose and conclusion. It was not an argument in favor of the mass strike as a tactic, let alone strategy, but rather an analysis of the significance of the mass strike in the 1905 Russian Revolution as a historical phenomenon, inextricably bound up in the development of capital at a global scale, and how this tasked and challenged the social democratic workers' movement (the Second International and the SPD in particular) to reformulate its approach and transform itself under such changed historical conditions, specifically with regard to the relation of the party to the unions.

Luxemburg's perspective was neither anarcho-syndicalist/ spontaneist nor vanguardist, but rather dialectical. The mass strike was not a timeless principle. For Luxemburg, 1905 showed that the world had moved into an era of revolutionary struggle that demanded changes in the workers' movement for socialism. A contradiction had developed between the social democratic party and (its own associated) labor unions, or "social democracy" had become a self-contradictory phenomenon in need of transformation.

Furthermore, I take Lenin's critiques of Kautsky for being "non-dialectical" to be very specific. This is not a critique of Kautsky "philosophically" (although it does speak to his bad practices as a theorist), but *politically*. It is about Kautsky's non-dialectical approach to politics: that is, the relation of theory and practice, or of social being and consciousness, in and through the concrete mediations of the historically constituted workers' movement. Kautsky failed in this. Lenin agreed with Luxemburg in her *Junius Pamphlet* (1915) that the problem was Kautsky thinking that the SPD's Marxism (that is, what became Kautsky's USPD) could "hide like a rabbit" during World War I and resume the struggle for socialism afterward. Or, as Lenin put it in his *Imperialism: The Highest Stage of Capitalism* (1916) and *Socialism and War* (1915), contra Kautsky's theory of "ultra-imperialism," the world war must be seen as a necessary and not accidental outcome of the historical development of capitalism, and so a crisis that was an opportunity for revolutionary transformation, and not merely, as Kautsky thought, a derailment into barbarism to be resisted. This was the essential basis for agreement between Luxemburg and Lenin 1914–19.

I do not think the separation of the pre-World War I Lenin from Luxemburg is warranted, especially considering their close collaboration, both in the politics of the Russian movement and in the Second International more generally, throughout the period 1905–12 and again 1914–19. Throughout their careers, Lenin and Luxemburg (and Trotsky) were exemplars of the Second International left, or "radicals" in the movement. They all more or less mistook Kautsky to be one of their own before August 1914. Also, Kautsky himself changed, at various points and times — which is not to say that Lenin, Luxemburg and Trotsky never changed.

But the question is the nature and character of such change, and how these figures allow us to grasp the history of Marxism. It is not about learning from their trials and errors, I think, but rather from the example of their "consciousness," not merely theoretically, but practically. Moreover, the history of Marxism must be approached as part and parcel, and the highest expression, of the history of post-1848 capital.

## Hegelianism

Lukács's "Hegelian" point was that "subjective" struggles for transformation take place in and through "necessary forms of appearance" that misrecognize their "objective" social realities, not in terms of imperfect approximations or more or less true generalized abstractions, but specifically as a function of the "alienated" and "reified" social and political dynamics of capital. Capital is "objective" in a specific way, and so poses historically specific problems for subjectivity.

The reason for Marxists distinguishing their approach from Hegel is precisely historical: that a change in society took place between Hegel's and Marx's time that causes Hegelian categories, as those of an earlier, pre-Industrial Revolution era of bourgeois society, to become inverted in truth, or reversed in intention. Marx's idea was that the "contradiction" of bourgeois society had changed. Thus the dialectical "law of motion" was specific to the problem of capital and not a transhistorical principle of (social) action and thought. Marx's society was not Hegel's. The meaning of Hegel had changed, just as the meaning of the categories of bourgeois society had changed. Labor-time as value had become not productive (if not unproblematically) — as in Hegel's and Adam Smith's time, the era of "manufacture" — but destructive of society; as a form of social mediation, wage-labor had become self-contradictory and self-undermining in the Industrial Revolution, hence the "crisis of capital."

One fundamental disagreement I have with Macnair's approach, in which I think I follow Lenin, Luxemburg, Lukács and Marx, is with the idea that the potential transformation of capitalist society involves the confrontation of two antithetical social principles, of the workers (collectivism) vs. the capitalists (individual private property). Capital, as Marx understood it, is not based on the mode of existence of the capitalists, falsely generalized to society as a whole, but rather that of the workers. This is not a top-down, but a bottom-up, view — shared by Smith, for example. As Lukács put it, the fate of the worker becomes that of "society as a whole."[6] The contradiction of capital is the contradiction of the workers' — not the capitalists' — existence in society. For Marx, capital is a social mode of production and not merely a relation of production. As a mode of production, capital has become increasingly self-contradictory. As a function of capital's historical development, through the Industrial Revolution, in which the workers' own increasing demands for bourgeois rights, to realize the value of their labor, and not merely capitalist competition, played a key, indispensable role, bourgeois society became self-contradictory and self-undermining. That is, the workers centrally or at base constituted the self-destructive, social-historical dynamic of capital through their laboring and political activity. This development culminated in the crisis of world war and revolution 1914–19.

As Lenin put it in *The State and Revolution*, the social relations of bourgeois society — namely, the mutual exchange of labor as the form of social solidarity in capital — could only be transformed gradually and thus "wither away," and not be abolished and replaced at a stroke.[7] The proletarian socialist revolution was supposed to open the door to this transformation. The potential for emancipated humanity expressed in

---

6   "The phenomenon of reification," in *History and Class Consciousness* (Cambridge, MA: MIT Press, 1971), 91.

7   See chapter 5, "The economic basis of the withering away of the state," part 3, "The first phase of communist society."

communism that Marx recognized in the modern history of capital is not assimilable without remainder to pre- or non-Marxian socialism.

As Marx put it, "Communism is the necessary form and the dynamic principle of the immediate future, but communism as such is not the goal of human development, the form of human society."[8] This was because, according to Marx, "Communism is a dogmatic abstraction and . . . only a particular manifestation of the humanistic principle and is infected by its opposite, private property."[9] Marx was not the pre-eminent communist of his time, but rather its critic, seeking to push it further. Marxism was the attempted Hegelian self-consciousness of proletarian socialism as the subject-object of capital.

As Lukács's contemporary, Karl Korsch, pointed out in "Marxism and Philosophy" (1923), by the late 19th century historians such as Dilthey had observed that "ideas contained in a philosophy can live on not only in philosophies, but equally well in positive sciences and social practice, and that this process precisely began on a large scale with Hegel's philosophy."[10] For Korsch, this meant that "philosophical" problems in the Hegelian sense were not matters of theory, but practice. From a Marxian perspective, however, it is precisely the problem of capitalist society that is posed at the level of practice.

Korsch went on to argue that "what appears as the purely 'ideal' development of philosophy in the 19th century can in fact only be fully and essentially grasped by relating it to the concrete historical development of bourgeois society as a whole."[11] Korsch's great insight, shared by Lukács, took this perspective from Luxemburg and Lenin, who grasped how the history of the socialist workers' movement and Marxism was a key part — indeed the crucial aspect — of this development, in the first two decades of the 20th century.

---

8   *Economic and Philosophic Manuscripts* (1844), manuscript 3, section 2, "Private property and communism."

9   Letter to Arnold Ruge, "Ruthless criticism" (September 1843).

10  In *Marxism and Philosophy*, trans. Fred Halliday (New York: Monthly Review Press, 2008), 39.

11  Ibid., 40.

The problem we have faced since then is that the defeat of the workers' movement for socialism has not meant the stabilization, but rather the degeneration, disintegration and decomposition, of bourgeois society — without the concomitant increase, but rather the regression, of possibilities for moving beyond it. This shows that the crisis of Marxism was a crisis of bourgeois society, or the highest and most acute aspect of the crisis of capital: bourgeois society has suffered since then from the failure of Marxism.

## Crisis of Marxism

The "crisis of Marxism," in which Lenin, Luxemburg and Trotsky took part (especially in 1914–19, but also in the period leading up to this, most significantly from 1905 on), and Lukács tried to address "theoretically" in *History and Class Consciousness* and related writings of the early 1920s, was (the highest practical expression of) the crisis of bourgeois society.

This crisis demanded a Marxist critique of Marxism, or a "dialectical" approach to Marxism itself: that is, a recognition of Marxism, politically, as being a self-contradictory and so potentially self-undermining historical phenomenon (a phenomenon of history — hence the title of Lukács's book, *History and Class Consciousness*), itself subject to necessary "reification" and "misrecognition" that could only be worked through "immanently." This meant regaining the "Hegelian" dimension, or the "self-consciousness" of Marxism. This is because Marxism, as an expression of the workers' "class-consciousness," was — and remains — entirely "bourgeois," if *in extremis*. While self-contradictory in its development, the socialist workers' movement, including its Marxist self-consciousness, pointed beyond itself, "dialectically" — as consciousness of the bourgeois epoch as a whole does.

I follow Adorno's characterization of the problem of workers' consciousness and the necessary role of intellectuals, which he took from Lenin, in his letter to Walter Benjamin of March 18 1936: "The proletariat . . . is itself a product of bourgeois society . . . the actual consciousness of actual workers . . . [has] absolutely no advantage over the bourgeois except . . . interest in the revolution, but otherwise bear[s] all the marks of mutilation of the typical bourgeois character. This prescribes our function for us clearly enough — which I certainly do not mean in the sense of an activist conception of 'intellectuals.' . . . It is not bourgeois idealism if, in full knowledge and without mental prohibitions, we maintain our solidarity with the proletariat instead of making of our own necessity a virtue of the proletariat, as we are always tempted to do — the proletariat which itself experiences the same necessity and needs us for knowledge as much as we need the proletariat to make the revolution."[12]

The problem we face today, I think, is the opacity of the present, due to our lack of a comparably acute, self-contradictory and dialectical expression of the crisis of capital that Marxism's historical self-consciousness, in theory and practice, once provided.

Originally published in *Weekly Worker* 878 (August 10, 2011)

---

12 "Correspondence with Benjamin," *New Left Review* (September – October 1973), 66–67.

# Why still read Lukács?

## The place of "philosophical" questions in Marxism

### The role of "critical theory"

Why read Georg Lukács today?[1] Especially when his most famous work, *History and Class Consciousness*, is so clearly an expression of its specific historical moment, the aborted world revolution of 1917–19 in which he participated, attempting to follow Vladimir Lenin and Rosa Luxemburg. Are there "philosophical" lessons to be learned or principles to be gleaned from Lukács's work, or is there, rather, the danger, as the Communist Party of Great Britain's Mike Macnair has put it, of "theoretical overkill," stymieing of political possibilities, closing up the struggle for socialism in tiny authoritarian and politically sterile sects founded on "theoretical agreement?"

Mike Macnair's article "Lukács: The philosophy trap"[2] argues about the issue of the relation between theory and practice in the history of ostensible "Leninism," taking issue in particular with Lukács's books *History and Class Consciousness* (1923) and *Lenin* (1924), as well as with Karl Korsch's 1923 essay "Marxism and philosophy." The issue is what kind of theoretical generalization of consciousness could be derived from the experience of Bolshevism from 1903–21. I agree with Macnair that "philosophical" agreement is not the proper basis for political agreement, but this is not the same as saying that political agreement has no theoretical implications. I've discussed this previously in "The philosophy

---

1  See M. A. Torres, "Politics as a Form of Knowledge: A Brief Introduction to Georg Lukács," *Platypus Review* 1 (November 2007).

2  *Weekly Worker* 987 (November 21, 2013).

of history"[3] and "Defending Marxist Hegelianism against a Marxist critique,"[4] as well as in "Gillian Rose's 'Hegelian' critique of Marxism."[5] The issue is whether theoretical "positions" have necessary political implications. I think it is a truism to say that there is no sure theoretical basis for effective political practice. But Macnair seems to be saying nothing more than this. In subordinating theory to practice, Macnair loses sight of the potential critical role theory can play in political practice, specifically the task of consciousness of history in the struggle for transforming society in an emancipatory direction.

A certain relation of theory to practice is a matter specific to the modern era, and moreover a problem specific to the era of capitalism, that is, after the Industrial Revolution, the emergence of the modern proletarianized working class and its struggle for socialism, and the crisis of bourgeois social relations and thus of consciousness of society involved in this process.

Critical theory recognizes that the role of theory in the attempt to transform society is not to justify or legitimate or provide normative sanction, not to rationalize what is happening anyway, but rather to *critique*, to explore conditions of possibility for change. The role of such critical theory is not to describe how things are, but rather how they might become, how things could and should be, but are not, yet.

The political distinction, then, would be not over the description of reality but rather the question of what can and should be changed, and over the direction of that change. Hence, critical theory as such goes beyond the distinction of analysis from description. The issue is not theoretical analysis proper to practical matters, but, beyond that, the issue of transforming practices, with active agency and subjective recognition, as opposed to merely experiencing change as something that has already happened. Capitalism itself is a transformative practice, but that transformation has eluded consciousness, specifically regarding the ways change has happened and political judgments about this. This is the specific role of theory, and hence the place of theoretical issues or "philosophical" concerns in Marxism.

---

3   *Weekly Worker* 869 (June 9, 2011).
4   *Weekly Worker* 878 (August 11, 2011).
5   *Platypus Review* 21 (March 2010), in this volume.

Marxist critical theory cannot be compared to other forms of theory, because they are not concerned with changing the world and the politics of our changing practices. Lukács distinguished Marxism from "contemplative" or "reified" consciousness, to which bourgeois society had otherwise succumbed in capitalism. If ostensibly "Marxist" tendencies such as those of the followers of Tony Cliff have botched "theory," which undoubtedly they have, it is because they have conflated or rendered indistinct the role of critical theory as opposed to the political exigencies of propaganda: for organizations dedicated to propaganda, there must be agreement as to such propaganda; the question is the role of theory in such propaganda activity. If theory is debased to justifying propaganda, then its critical role is evacuated, and indeed it can mask opportunism. But then it ceases to be proper theory, not becoming simply "wrong" or falsified but rather *ideological*, which is a different matter. This is what happened, according to Lukács and Korsch, in the 2nd/Socialist International, resulting in the "vulgarization" of Marxism, or the confusion of the formulations of political propaganda instead of properly Marxist critical theorization.

### "Proletarian socialism"

The "proletariat" was Marx's neologism for the condition of the post-Industrial Revolution working class, which was analogous metaphorically to the Ancient Roman Republic's class of "proletarians": the modern industrial working class was composed of "citizens without property." In modern, bourgeois society, for instance in the view of John Locke, property in objects is derived from labor, which is the first property. Hence, to be a laborer without property is a self-contradiction in a very specific sense, in that the "expropriation" of labor in capitalism happens as a function of society. A modern "free wage-laborer" is supposed to be a contractual agent with full rights of ownership and disposal over her own labor in its exchange, its buying and selling as property, as a commodity. This is the most elementary form of right in bourgeois society, from which other claims, for instance, individual right to one's own person and equality before the law, flow. If, according to Marx and Engels, the condition of the modern, post-Industrial Revolution working class or "proletariat" expressed a self-contradiction of bourgeois social relations, this was because this set of social relations, or "bourgeois right," was in need of transformation: the Industrial Revolution indicated a potential condition beyond bourgeois society. If the workers were expropriated, according to Marx and Engels, this was because of a problem of the value of labor at a greater societal level, not at the level of the individual capitalist firm, not reducible to the contractual relation of the employee to her employer, which remained "fair exchange." The wage contract was still bourgeois, but the value of the labor exchanged was undermined in the greater (global) society, which was no longer simply bourgeois but rather industrial, that is, "capital"-ist.

The struggle for socialism by the proletariat was the attempt to reappropriate the social property of labor that had been transformed and "expropriated" or "alienated" in the Industrial Revolution. Marx and Engels thought this could be achieved only beyond capitalism, for instance in the value of accumulated past labor in science and technology, what Marx called the "general (social) intellect." An objective condition was expressed subjectively, but that objective condition of society was itself self-contradictory and so expressed in a self-contradictory form of political subjectivity, "proletarian socialism." For Marx and Engels, the greatest exemplar of this self-contradictory form of politics aiming to transform society was Chartism in Britain, a movement of the high moment of the Industrial Revolution and its crisis in the 1830s–40s, whose most pointed political expression was, indicatively, universal suffrage. The crisis of the bust period of the "Hungry '40s" indicated the maturation of bourgeois society, in crisis, as the preceding boom era of the 1830s already had raised expectations of socialism, politically as well as technically and culturally, for instance in the "Utopian Socialism" of Fourier, Saint-Simon, Owen et al., as well as in the "Young Hegelian" movement taking place around the world in the 1830s, on whose scene the younger Marx and Engels arrived belatedly, during its crisis and dissolution in the 1840s.

One must distinguish between the relation of theory and practice in the revolutionary bourgeois era and in the post-Industrial Revolution era of the crisis of bourgeois society in capitalism and the proletariat's struggle for socialism. If in the bourgeois era there was a productive tension, a reflective, speculative or "philosophical" relation, for instance for Kant and Hegel, between theory and practice, in the era of the crisis of bourgeois society there is rather a "negative" or "critical" relation. Hence, the need for Marxism.

As the Frankfurt School Marxist Critical Theorist Theodor Adorno put it, the separation of theory and practice was *emancipatory*: it expressed the freedom to think at variance with prevailing social practices unknown in the Ancient or Medieval world of traditional civilization. The freedom to relate and articulate theory and practice was a hallmark of the revolutionary emergence of bourgeois society: the combined revolution in society of politics, economics, culture (religion), technique and philosophy — the latter under the rubric "Enlightenment." By contrast, Romantic socialism of the early 19th century sought to re-unify theory and practice, to make them one thing as they had been under religious cosmology as a total way of life. If, according to Adorno, Marxism, as opposed to Romantic socialism, did not aspire to a "unity of theory and practice" in terms of their identity, but rather of their articulated separation in the transformation of society — transformation of both consciousness and social being — then what Adorno recognized was that, as he put it, the relation of theory and practice is not established once-and-for-all but rather "fluctuates historically." Marxism, through different phases of its history, itself expressed this fluctuation. But the fluctuation was an expression of crisis in Marxism, and ultimately of failure: Adorno called it a "negative dialectic." It expressed and was tasked by the failure of the revolution. But this failure was not merely the failure of the industrial working class's struggle for socialism in the early 20th century, but rather that failure was the failure of the emancipation of the bourgeois revolution: this failure consumed history, undermining the past achievements of freedom — as Adorno's colleague Walter Benjamin put it, "Even the dead are not safe." Historical Marxism is not a safe legacy but suffers the vicissitudes of the present. If we still are reading Lukács, we need to recognize the danger to which his thought, as part of Marxism's history, is subject in the present. One way of protecting historical Marxism's legacy would be through recognizing its *inapplicability* in the present, distancing it from immediate enlistment in present concerns, which would concede too much already, undermining — liquidating without redeeming — consciousness once already achieved.

## The division in Marxism

The title of Lukács's book *History and Class Consciousness* should be properly understood directly as indicating that Lukács's studies, the various essays collected in the book, were about class consciousness as consciousness of history. This goes back to the early Marx and Engels, who understood the emergence of the modern proletariat and its political struggles for socialism after the Industrial Revolution in a "Hegelian" manner, that is, as phenomena or "forms of appearance" of society and history specific to the 19th century. Moreover, Marx and Engels, in their point of departure for "Marxism" as opposed to other varieties of Hegelianism and socialism, looked forward to the dialectical "*Aufhebung*" of this new modern proletariat: its simultaneous self-fulfillment and completion, self-negation, and self-transcendence in socialism, which would be (also) that of capitalism. In other words, Marx and Engels regarded the proletariat in the struggle for socialism as the central, key phenomenon of capitalism, but the symptomatic expression of its crisis, self-contradiction and need for self-overcoming. This is because capitalism was regarded by Marx and Engels as a form of society, specifically the form of bourgeois society's crisis and self-contradiction. As Hegelians, Marx and Engels regarded contradiction as the appearance of the necessity and possibility for change. So, the question becomes, what is the meaning of the self-contradiction of bourgeois society, the self-contradiction of bourgeois social relations, expressed by the post-Industrial Revolution working class and its forms of political struggle?

Marx and Engels regarded the politics of proletarian socialism as a form of bourgeois politics in crisis and self-contradiction. This is what it meant for Marx and Engels to say that the objective existence of the proletariat and its subjective struggle for socialism were phenomena of the self-contradiction of bourgeois society and its potential *Aufhebung*.

The struggle for socialism was self-contradictory. This is what Lukács ruminated on in *History and Class Consciousness*. But this was not original to Lukács or achieved by Lukács's reading of Marx and Engels, but rather mediated through the politics of Lenin and Rosa Luxemburg: Lenin and Luxemburg provided access, for Lukács as well as others in the nascent 3rd or Communist International, to the "original Marxism" of Marx and Engels. For Marx and Engels recognized that socialism was inevitably ideological: a self-contradictory form of politics and consciousness. The question was how to advance the contradiction.

As a participant in the project of the Communist International, for Lukács in his books *History and Class Consciousness* and *Lenin* (as well as for Karl Korsch in "Marxism and philosophy" and other writings circa 1923), the intervening Marxism of the 2nd or Socialist International had become an obstacle to Marx and Engels's Marxism and thus to proletarian socialist revolution in the early 20th century, an obstacle that the political struggles of Lenin, Luxemburg and other radicals in the 2nd International sought to overcome. This obstacle of 2nd International Marxism had theoretical as well as practical-political aspects: It was expressed both at the level of theoretical consciousness as well as at the level of political organization.

2nd International Marxism had *become* an obstacle. According to Luxemburg, in *Reform or Revolution?* (1900) and in Lenin's *What is to be Done?* (1902) (the latter of which was an attempted application of the terms of the Revisionist Dispute in the 2nd International to conditions in the Russian movement), the development of proletarian socialism in the 2nd International had produced its own obstacle, so to speak, in becoming self-divided between "orthodox Marxists" who retained fidelity to the revolutionary politics of proletarian socialism in terms of the Revolutions of 1848 and the Paris Commune of 1871, and "Revisionists" who thought that political practice and theoretical consciousness of Marxism demanded transformation under the altered historical social conditions that had been achieved by the workers' struggle for socialism, which proceeded in an "evolutionary" way. Eduard Bernstein gave the clearest expression of this "Revisionist" view, which was influenced by the apparent success of British Fabianism that led to the contemporary formation of the Labour Party, and found its greatest political support among the working class's trade union leaders in the 2nd International, especially in Germany. In Bernstein's view, capitalism was evolving into socialism through the political gains of the workers.

## Marxism of the Third International

Lenin, Luxemburg, and Lukács and Korsch among others following them, thought that the self-contradictory nature and character — origin and expression — of proletarian socialism meant that the latter's development proceeded in a self-contradictory way, which meant that the movement of historical "progress" was self-contradictory. Luxemburg summarized this view in *Reform or Revolution?*, where she pointed out that the growth in organization and consciousness of the proletariat was itself part of — a new phenomenon of — the self-contradiction of capitalism, and so expressed itself in its own self-contradictory way. This was how Luxemburg grasped the Revisionist Dispute in the Marxism of the 2nd International itself. This self-contradiction was theoretical as well as practical: for Luxemburg and for Lenin the "theoretical struggle" was an expression of practical self-contradiction. Leon Trotsky expressed this "orthodox Marxist" view shared by Lenin and Luxemburg in his 1906 pamphlet *Results and Prospects*, on the 1905 Revolution in Russia, by pointing out that the various "pre-requisites of socialism" were self-contradictory, that they "retarded" rather than promoted each other. This view was due to the understanding that proletarian socialism was bound up in the crisis of capitalism which was disintegrative: the struggle for socialism was caught up in the disintegration of bourgeois society in capitalism. For Luxemburg, Lenin and Trotsky, contra Bernstein, the crisis of capitalism was deepening.

One of the clearest expressions of this disintegrative process of self-contradiction in Luxemburg, Lenin and Trotsky's time was the relation of capitalism as a global system to the political divisions between national states in the era of "monopoly capital" and "imperialism" that led to the World War, but was already apprehended in the Revisionist Dispute at the turn of the 20th century as expressing the need for socialism — the need for proletarian political revolution. Lenin and Luxemburg's academic doctoral dissertations of the 1890s, on the development of capitalism in Russia and Poland, respectively, addressed this phenomenon of "combined and uneven" development in the epoch of capitalist crisis, disintegration and "decay," as expressing the need for world revolution. Moreover, Lenin in *What is to be Done?* expressed the perspective that the Revisionist Dispute in Marxism was itself an expression of the crisis of capitalism manifesting within the socialist workers' movement, a prelude to revolution.

While it is conventional to oppose Luxemburg and Lenin's "revolutionary socialism" to Bernstein et al.'s "evolutionism," and hence to oppose Luxemburg and Lenin's "dialectical" Marxism to the Revisionist "mechanical" one, what is lost in this view is the role of historical dynamics of consciousness in Lenin and Luxemburg's (and Trotsky's) view: This is the phenomenon of historical "regression" as opposed to "progress," which the "evolutionary socialism" of Bernstein et al. assumed and later Stalinism also assumed. The most important distinction of Luxemburg and Lenin's (as well as Trotsky's) "orthodox" perspective — in Lukács's (and Korsch's) view, what made their Marxism "dialectical" and "Hegelian" — was its recognition of historical "regression": its recognition of bourgeois society as disintegrative and self-destructive in its crisis of capitalism. But this process of disintegration was recognized as affecting the proletariat and its politics as well. Benjamin and Adorno's theory of regression began here.

### Historical regression

The question is how to properly recognize, in political practice as well as theory, the ways in which the struggle for proletarian socialism — socialism achieved by way of the political action of wage-laborers in the post-Industrial Revolution era as such — is caught up and participates in the process of capitalist disintegration: the expression of proletarian socialism as a phenomenon of *history*, specifically as a phenomenon of crisis and regression.

This history has multiple registers: there is the principal register of the post-Industrial Revolution crisis of bourgeois society in capitalism, its crisis and departure from preceding bourgeois social relations (those of the prior, pre-industrial eras of "cooperation" and "manufacture" of the 16th, 17th and 18th centuries, in Marx's terms); but there is also the register of the dynamics and periods within capitalism itself. Capitalism was for Marx and Engels already the regression of bourgeois society. This is where Lukács's (and Korsch's) perspective, derived from Luxemburg and Lenin's (and Trotsky's) views from 1900-19, what they considered an era of "revolution," might become problematic for us, today: the history of the post-1923 world has not been, as 1848–1914 was in the 2nd International "orthodox" or "radical" Marxist (as opposed to Revisionist) view, a process of increasing crisis and development of revolutionary political necessities, but rather a process of continued social disintegration of capitalism without, however, this being expressed in and through the struggle for proletarian socialism.

It is important to note that Lukács (and Korsch) abandoned rather rapidly their 1923 perspectives, adjusting to developing circumstances of a non-revolutionary era.

Here is where the problematic relation of Tony Cliff's political project to Lukács (and Korsch), and hence to Lenin, Luxemburg and Trotsky, may be located: in Cliff's perspective on his (post-1945) time being a "non-revolutionary" one, demanding a project of "propaganda" that is related to but differs significantly from the moment of Lenin et al. For the Cliffites and their organizations, "political practice" is one of propaganda in a non-revolutionary period, in which political action is less of a directly practical but rather of an exemplary-propagandistic significance. This has been muddled by their strategy of "movement-building."

This was not the case for Luxemburg, Lenin and Trotsky, whose political practice was directly about the struggle for power, and in whose practical project Lukács's (and Korsch's) "theoretical" work sought to participate, offering attempts at clarification of self-understanding to revolutionaries "on the march." Cliff and his followers, at least at their most self-conscious, have known that they were doing something essentially different from Lenin et al.: they were not organizing a revolutionary political party seeking a bid for power as part of an upsurge of working class struggle in the context of a global movement (the 2nd International), as had been the case for Lenin at the time of *What is to be Done?* (1902), or Luxemburg's *Mass Strike* pamphlet and Trotsky in the Russian Revolution of 1905. Yet the Cliffites have used the ideas of Lenin and Luxemburg and their followers, such as Lukács and Korsch as well as Trotsky, to justify their practices. This presents certain problems. Yes, Lenin et al. have become ideological in the hands of the Cliffites, among others — "Leninism" for the Stalinists most prominently. So the question turns to the status of Lenin's ideas in themselves and in their own moment.[6]

Mike Macnair points out that Lukács's (and Korsch's) works circa 1923 emphasized attack and so sought to provide a "theory of the offensive," as opposed to Lenin's arguments about the necessities of "retreat" in 1920 (as against and in critique of "Left-Wing" Communism) and what Macnair has elsewhere described as the need for "Kautskyan patience" in politically building for proletarian socialism (as in the era of the 2nd International 1889–1914), and so this limits the perspective of Lukács (and Korsch), after Lenin and Luxemburg (and Trotsky), to a period of "civil war" (circa 1905, and 1914/17–19/20/21). In this, Macnair is concerned, rightly, with "theory" becoming a blinder to proper political practice: "theoretical overkill" is a matter of over-"philosophizing" politics. But there is a difference between active campaigning in the struggle for power, whether in attack or (temporary) retreat, and propagandizing, to which Marxism (at best) has been relegated ever since the early 20th century.

However, in raising, by contrast, the need for a conscious openness to "empirical reality" of political experience, Macnair succumbs to a linear-progressive view of history as well as of political practice, turning this into a matter of "lessons learned": it becomes a quantitative rather than qualitative matter. Moreover, it becomes a matter of theory in a conventional rather than the Marxist "critical" sense, in which the description of reality and its analysis approach more and more adequate approximations.

Lenin, Luxemburg and Trotsky, and so Lukács (and Korsch), as "orthodox" as opposed to "revisionist" Marxists, conceived of the development of consciousness, both theoretically and practically-organizationally, rather differently, in that a necessary "transformation of Marxism," which took place in the "peculiar guise" of a "return to the original Marxism of Marx and Engels" (Korsch), could be an asset in the present. But that "present" was the "crisis of Marxism" 1914–19, which is not, today, our moment — as even Cliff and his followers, with their notion of "propaganda" in a

---

6    See my "The relevance of Lenin today," *Platypus Review* 48 ( July – August 2012), in this volume.

non-revolutionary era, have recognized (as did Lukács and Korsch, in subsequently abandoning their circa-1923 perspectives).

So what is the status of such ideas in a non-revolutionary era?

### Korsch and the problem of "philosophy"

Karl Korsch, Lukács's contemporary in the 3rd International, whose work Macnair deliberately and explicitly puts aside, offered a pithy formulation in his 1923 essay on "Marxism and philosophy," that, "a problem which supersedes present relations may have been formulated in an anterior epoch." That is, we may live under the shadow of a problem that goes beyond us.

This is a non-linear, non-progressive and recursive view of history, which Korsch gleaned from Luxemburg and Lenin's contributions to the Revisionist Dispute in the 2nd International (e.g., *Reform or Revolution?*, *What is to be Done?*, etc.; and Trotsky's *Results and Prospects*). It has its origins in Marx and Engels's view of capitalism as a regressive, disintegrative process. This view has two registers: the self-contradiction and crisis of bourgeois social relations in the transition to capital-ism after the Industrial Revolution; and the disintegrative and self-destructive process of the reproduction of capitalism itself, which takes place within and as a function of the reproduction of bourgeois social relations, through successive crises.

Marx and Engels recognized that the crisis of capitalism was motivated by the reproduction of bourgeois social relations under conditions of the disintegration of the value of labor in the Industrial Revolution, producing the need for socialism. The industrial-era working class's struggle for the social value of its labor was at once regressive, as if bourgeois social relations of the value of labor had not been undermined by the Industrial Revolution, and pointed beyond capitalism, in that the realization of the demands for the proper social value of labor would actually mean overcoming labor as value in society, transforming work from "life's prime need" to "life's prime want": work would be done not out of the social compulsion to labor in the valorization process of capital, but rather out of intrinsic desire and interest; and society would provide for "each according to his need" from "each according to his ability." As Adorno, a later follower of Lukács and Korsch's works circa 1923 that had converted him to Marxism, put it, getting beyond capitalism would mean overcoming the "law of labor."[7]

Korsch's argument in his 1923 essay "Marxism and philosophy" was focused on a very specific problem, the status of philosophy in Marxism, in the direct sense of Marx and Engels being followers of Hegel, and Hegel representing a certain "end" to philosophy, in which the world became philosophical and philosophy became worldly. Hegel announced that with his work, philosophy was "completed," as a function of recognizing how society had become "philosophical," or mediated through conceptual theory in ways previously not the case. Marx and Engels accepted Hegel's conclusion, in which case the issue was to further the revolution of bourgeois society — the "philosophical" world that demanded worldly "philosophy." The disputes among the Hegelians in the 1830s and 40s were concerned, properly, with precisely the politics of the bourgeois world and its direction for change. The problem, according to Korsch, was that, after the failure of the revolutions of 1848, there was a recrudescence of "philosophy," and that this was something other than what had been practiced either traditionally by the Ancients or in modernity by revolutionary bourgeois thinkers — thinkers of the revolution of the bourgeois era — such as Kant and Hegel (also Rousseau, John Locke, Adam Smith, et al.).

What constitutes "philosophical" questions? Traditionally, philosophy was concerned with three kinds of questions: ontology, what we are; epistemology, how we know; and the good life, how we ought to live. Starting with Kant, such traditional philosophical "first questions" of *prima philosophia* or "first philosophy" were no longer asked, or, if they were asked, they were strictly subordinated or rendered secondary to the question of the relation of theory and practice, or, how we account to ourselves what we are doing. Marxism is not a philosophy in the traditional sense, any more than Kant and Hegel's philosophy was traditional. Lenin, in the Conclusion of *Materialism and Empirio-Criticism* (1908), summed up that the late 19th century Neo-Kantians "started with Kant and, leaving him, proceeded not [forwards] towards [Marxist] materialism, but in the opposite direction,

---

7    Quoted in Detlev Claussen, *Adorno: One Last Genius* (Cambridge, MA: Harvard University Press, 2008), 48.

[backwards] towards Hume and Berkeley." It is not, along the lines of a traditional materialist ontology, that firstly we are material beings; epistemologically, who know the world empirically through our bodily senses; and ethically we must serve the needs of our true, material bodily nature. No. For Kant and his followers, including Hegel and Marx, rather, we consciously reflect upon an on-going process from within its movement: we don't step back from what we are doing and try to establish a "first" basis for asking our questions; those questions arise, rather, from within our on-going practices and their transformations. Empirical facts cannot be considered primary if they are to be changed. Theory may go beyond the facts by influencing their transformation in practice.

Society is the source of our practices and their transformations, and hence of our theoretical consciousness of them. Society, according to Rousseau, is the source of our ability to act contrary to our "first nature," to behave in unnatural ways. This is our freedom. And for Kant and his followers, our highest moral duty in the era of the process of "Enlightenment" was to serve the cause of freedom. This meant serving the revolution of bourgeois emancipation from traditional civilization, changing society. However Kant considered the full achievement of bourgeois society to be the mere "mid-point" of the development of freedom.[8] Hegel and Marxism inherited and assumed this projective perspective on the transitional character of bourgeois society.

Marx and Engels can be considered to have initiated a "Second Enlightenment" in the 19th century the degree to which capitalism presented new problems unknown in the pre-Industrial Revolution bourgeois era, because they had not yet arisen in practice. By contrast, philosophers who continued to ask such traditional questions of ontology, epistemology and ethics were actually addressing the problem of the relation of theory and practice in the capitalist era, whether they recognized this or not. Assuming the traditional basis for philosophical questions in the era of capitalism obscured the real issue and rendered "philosophy" ideological. This is why "philosophy" needed to be abolished. The question was, how?

---

8    Immanuel Kant, "Idea for a universal history from a cosmopolitan point of view" (1784).

The recrudescence of philosophy in the late 19th century was, according to Korsch, a symptom of the failure of socialism in 1848, but as such expressed a genuine need: the necessity of relating theory and practice as a problem of consciousness under conditions of capitalism. In this respect, Marxism was the sustaining of the Kantian-Hegelian "critical philosophy" but under changed conditions from the bourgeois-revolutionary era to that of capitalism. Korsch analogized this to the recrudescence of the state in post-1848 Bonapartism, which contradicted the bourgeois-revolutionary, liberal prognosis of the subordination of the state to civil society and thus the state's "withering away," its functions absorbed into free social relations. This meant recognizing the need to overcome recrudescent philosophy as analogous to the need to overcome the capitalist state, the transformation of its necessity through socialism. "Bonapartism in philosophy" thus expressed a new, late found need in capitalism, to free society. We look to "philosophers" to do our thinking for us the same way we look to authoritarian leaders politically.

As Korsch put it, the only way to "abolish" philosophy would be to "realize" it: socialism would be the attainment of the "philosophical world" promised by bourgeois emancipation but betrayed by capitalism, which renders society — our social practices — opaque. It would be premature to say that under capitalism everyone is already a philosopher. Indeed, the point is that none are. But this is because of the alienation and reification of bourgeois social relations in capitalism, which renders the Kantian-Hegelian "worldly philosophy" of the critical relation of theory and practice an aspiration rather than an actuality. Nonetheless, Marxist critical theory accepted the task of such modern critical philosophy, specifically regarding the ideological problem of theory and practice in the struggle for socialism. This is what it meant to say, as was formulated in the 2nd International, that the workers' movement for socialism was the inheritor of German Idealism: it was the inheritor of the revolutionary process of bourgeois emancipation, which the bourgeoisie, compromised by capitalism, had abandoned. The task remained.

## Transformation of Marxism

Lenin, Luxemburg and Trotsky, "orthodox Marxists" of the 2nd International who radicalized their perspectives in the crisis of the 2nd International and of Marxism in world war and revolution 1914–19, and were followed by Lukács and Korsch, were subjects of a historical moment in which the crisis of bourgeois society in capitalism was expressed by social and political crisis and the movement for "proletarian socialist" revolution, beginning, after the Industrial Revolution, in the 1830s–40s, the attempt to revolutionize society centrally by the wage-laborers as such, a movement dominated from 1889–1914 by the practical politics as well as theoretical consciousness of Marxism.

Why would Lukács and Korsch in the 20th century return to the origins of Marxism in Hegelianism, in what Korsch called the consciousness of the "revolt of the Third Estate," a process of the 17th and 18th centuries (that had already begun earlier)? Precisely because Lukács and Korsch sought to address Marxism's relation to the revolt of the Third Estate's bourgeois glorification of the social relations of labor, and the relation of this to the democratic revolution (see for example the Abbé Sieyès's revolutionary 1789 pamphlet *What is the Third Estate?*): how Marxism recognized that this relation between labor and democracy continued in 19th century socialism, however problematically. In Lukács and Korsch's view, proletarian socialism sustained just this bourgeois revolution, albeit under the changed conditions of the Industrial Revolution and its capitalist aftermath. Mike Macnair acknowledges this in his focus on the English Enlightenment "materialist empiricism" of John Locke in the 17th and 18th centuries and on the British Chartism of the early 19th century, their intrinsic continuity in the democratic revolution, and Marx and Engels's continuity with both. But then Macnair takes Kant and Hegel — and thus Lukács and Korsch following them — to be counter-Enlightenment and anti-democratic thinkers accommodating autocratic political authority, drawing this from Hume's alleged turn away from the radicalism of Locke back to Hobbes's political conservatism, and Kant and Hegel's alleged affirmation of the Prussian state. But this account leaves out the crucially important influence on Kant and German Idealism more generally by

Rousseau, of whom Hegel remarked that "freedom dawned on the world" in his works, and who critiqued and departed from Hobbes's naturalistic society of "war of all against all" and built rather upon Locke's contrary view of society and politics, sustaining and promoting the revolution in bourgeois society as "more than the sum of its parts," revolutionary in its social relations *per se*, seminal for the American and French Revolutions of the later 18th century. Capital, emerging in the 19th century, in the Marxist view, as the continued social compulsion to wage-labor after its crisis of value in the Industrial Revolution, both is and is not the Rousseauian "general will" of capitalist society: it is a self-contradictory "mode of production" and set of social relations, expressed through self-contradictory consciousness, in theory and practice, of its social and political subjects, first and foremost the consciousness of the proletariat. It is self-contradictory both objectively and subjectively, both in theory and in practice.

Marx and Engels's point was to encourage and advance the proletariat's critical recognition of the self-contradictory character of its struggle for socialism, in what Marx called the "logical extreme" of the role of the proletariat in the democratic revolution of the 19th century, which could not, according to Marx, take its "poetry" from the 17th and 18th centuries, as clearly expressed in the failure of the revolutions of 1848, Marx's famous formulation of the need for "revolution in permanence."[9] What this means is that the democratic revolutionary aspirations of the wage-laborers for the "social republic" was the self-contradictory demand for the realization of the social value of labor after this had already taken the form of accumulated capital, what Marx called the "general intellect." It is not the social value of labor, but rather that of this "general intellect" which must be reappropriated, and by the wage-laborers themselves, in their discontents as subjects of democracy. The ongoing democratic revolution renders this both possible and superfluous in that it renders the state both the agency and obstacle to this reappropriation, in post-1848 Bonapartism, which promises everything to everyone — to solve the "social question" of capitalism — but provides nothing, a diversion of the democratic revolution under conditions of self-contradictory bourgeois social relations: the state

---

9  Karl Marx, "Address to the Central Committee of the Communist League" (1850).

promises employment but gives unemployment benefits or subsidizes the lost value of wages; as Adorno put it, the workers get a cut of the profits of capital, to prevent revolution.[10] Or, as Adorno's colleague, the director of the Frankfurt Institute Max Horkheimer put it, the Industrial Revolution and its continued social ramifications made not labor but the workers "superfluous."[11] This created a very dangerous political situation — clearly expressed by the catastrophic events of the 20th century, mediated by mass "democratic" movements.

## Marxism in the 20th century

In the 20th century, under the pressure of mass democracy — itself the result of the class struggle of the workers — the role of the state as self-contradictory and helpless manager of capitalism came to full fruition, but not through the self-conscious activity of the working class's political struggle for socialism, confronting the need to overcome the role of the state, but more obscurely, with perverse results. Lenin's point in *The State and Revolution* (1917) was the need for the revolutionary transformation of society beyond "bourgeois right" that the state symptomatically expressed; but, according to Lenin, this could be accomplished only "on the basis of capitalism itself" (*"Left-Wing" Communism: An Infantile Disorder*, 1920). If the working class among others in bourgeois society has succumbed to what Lukács called the "reification" of bourgeois social relations, then this has been completely naturalized and can no longer be called out and recognized as such. For Lukács, "reification" referred to the hypostatization and conservatization of the workers' own politics in protecting their "class interest," what Lenin called mere "trade union consciousness" (including that of nationalist competition) in capitalism, rather than rising to the need to overcome this in practice, recognizing how the workers' political struggles might point beyond and transcend themselves. This included

---

10 "Late capitalism or industrial society?" (1968), in *Can One Live After Auschwitz?: A Philosophical Reader*, ed. Rolf Tiedemann, trans. Rodney Livingstone and others (Stanford: Stanford University Press, 2009), 125.

11 "The Authoritarian State" (1942) in *The Essential Frankfurt School Reader*, ed. Andrew Arato and Eike Gebhardt (New York: Continuum, 1985), 95.

democracy, which could occult the social process of capitalism as much as reveal it.

One phenomenon of such reification in the 20th century was what Adorno called the "veil of technology," which included the appearance of capital as a thing (as in capital goods, or techniques of organizing production), rather than as Marxism recognized it, a social relation, however self-contradictory.

The anti-Marxist, liberal (yet still quite conservative) Heideggerian political theorist Hannah Arendt (and antagonist of Adorno and other Marxist "Critical Theorists" of the Frankfurt School, who was however married to a former Communist follower of Rosa Luxemburg's Spartacus League of 1919), expressed well how the working class in the 20th century developed after the failure of Marxism:

> The modern age has carried with it a theoretical glorification of labor and has resulted in an actual transformation of the whole of society into a laboring society. The fulfilment of the wish, therefore, like the fulfilment of wishes in fairy tales, comes at a moment when it can only be self-defeating. It is a society of laborers which is about to be liberated from the fetters of labor [by technical automation], and this society does not longer know of those other higher and more meaningful activities for the sake of which this freedom would deserve to be won. Within this society, which is egalitarian because this is labor's way of making men live together, there is no class left, no aristocracy of either a political or spiritual nature from which a restoration of the other capacities of man could start anew. Even presidents, kings, and prime ministers think of their offices in terms of a job necessary for the life of society, and among the intellectuals, only solitary individuals are left who consider what they are doing in terms of work and not in terms of making a living. What we are confronted with is the prospect

of a society of laborers without labor, that is, without the only activity left to them. Surely, nothing could be worse.[12]

This was written contemporaneously with the Keynesian economist Joan Robinson's statement that, "The misery of being exploited by capitalists is nothing compared to the misery of not being exploited at all."[13] (Robinson, who once accused a Marxist that, "I have Marx in my bones and you have him in your mouth."[14]) Compare this to what Heidegger offered in Nazi-era lectures on "Overcoming metaphysics," that, "The still hidden truth of Being is withheld from metaphysical humanity. The laboring animal is left to the giddy whirl of its products so that it may tear itself to pieces and annihilate itself in empty nothingness;"[15] and, in "The End of Philosophy and the Task of Thinking" (1964), the place of Marx in this process: "With the reversal of metaphysics which was already accomplished by Karl Marx, the most extreme possibility of philosophy is attained."[16] But this was Heidegger blaming Marxism and the "metaphysics of labor" championed politically by the bourgeois revolt of the Third Estate and inherited by the workers' movement for socialism, without recognizing as Marx did the self-contradictory character in capitalism; Heidegger, for whom "only a god can still save us" (meaning, only the discovery of a new value to serve),[17] and Arendt following him, demonized technologized society as a dead-end of "Western metaphysics" allegedly going back to the Socratic turn of "science" followed by Plato and Aristotle in Classical Antiquity, rather than recognizing it as a symptom of the need to transform society, capitalism and its need for socialism as a transitional condition of history emerging specifically in the 19th century.

This was the resulting flat "contradiction" that replaced the prior "dialectical" contradiction of "proletarian socialism" recognized by Marxism,

---

12  Hannah Arendt, *The Human Condition [Vita Activa]* (1958).

13  *Economic Philosophy* (Middlesex: Pelican, 1962), 46.

14  See Mike Beggs, "Joan Robinson's 'Open letter from a Keynesian to a Marxist,'" in *Jacobin* (July 2011), which quotes in full Robinson's letter from 1953 to Ronald Meek.

15  In *The End of Philosophy*, ed. and trans. Joan Stambaugh (Chicago: University of Chicago Press, 2003), 87.

16  In *Basic Writings*, ed. David Farrell Krell (New York: HarperCollins, 1993), 433.

17  1966 interview with Heidegger in *Der Spiegel*, published posthumously May 31, 1976.

whose theoretical recovery, in the context of the crisis of Marxism in the movement from the 2nd to 3rd Internationals, had been attempted by Lukács and Korsch. What Arendt called merely the (objective) "human condition," the "vita activa" and its perverse nihilistic destiny in modern society, was, once, the (subjective) "dialectical," self-contradictory "standpoint of the proletariat" in Marxism, as the "class consciousness" of history: the historical need for the proletariat to overcome and abolish itself as a class, including its own standpoint of "consciousness," its regressive bourgeois demand to reappropriate the value of labor in capitalism, which would both realize and negate the "bourgeois right" of the value of labor in society. Socialism was recognized by Marxism as the raising and advancing of the self-contradiction of capitalism to the "next stage," motivated by the necessity and possibility for "communism." What Arendt could only apprehend as a baleful *telos*, the society of labor overcoming itself, Marxism once recognized as the need for revolution, to advance the contradiction in socialism.

When Marxists such as Adorno or Lukács can only sound to us like Arendt (or Heidegger), this is because we no longer live in the revolution. Adorno:

> According to [Marxist] theory, history is the history of class struggles. But the concept of class is bound up with the emergence of the proletariat. . . . If all the oppression that man has ever inflicted upon man culminates in the cold inhumanity of free wage labor, then . . . the archaic silence of pyramids and ruins becomes conscious of itself in materialist thought: it is the echo of factory noise in the landscape of the immutable. . . . This means, however, that dehumanization is also its opposite. In reified human beings reification finds its outer limits. . . . Only when the victims completely assume the features of the ruling civilization will they be capable of wresting them from the dominant power. . . . Even if the dynamic at work was always the same, its end today is not the end.[18]

---

18  "Reflections on Class Theory" (1942) in *Can One Live After Auschwitz?: A Philosophical Reader*, 93–4 and 110.

Lukács:

> [As Hegel said,] directly before the emergence of something qualitatively new, the old state of affairs gathers itself up into its original, purely general, essence, into its simple totality, transcending and absorbing back into itself all those marked differences and peculiarities which it evinced when it was still viable. . . . [I]n the age of the dissolution of capitalism, the fetishistic categories collapse and it becomes necessary to have recourse to the "natural form" underlying them. . . . As the antagonism becomes more acute two possibilities open up for the proletariat. It is given the opportunity to substitute its own positive contents for the emptied and bursting husks. But also it is exposed to the danger that for a time at least it might adapt itself ideologically to conform to these, the emptiest and most decadent forms of bourgeois culture.[19]

## Why still "philosophy?"

The problem today is that we are not faced, as Lukács and Korsch were, with the self-contradiction of the proletariat's struggle for socialism in the political problem of the reified forms of the working class substituting for those of bourgeois society in its decadence. We replay the revolt of the Third Estate and its demands for the social value of labor, but we do not have occasion to recognize what Lukács regarded as the emptiness of bourgeois social relations of labor, its value evacuated by technical but not political transcendence. We have lost sight of the problem of "reification" as Lukács meant it.

As Hegel scholar Robert Pippin has concluded, in a formulation that is eminently agreeable to Korsch's perspective on the continuation of philosophy as a symptom of failed transformation of society, in an essay addressing how, by contrast with the original "Left-Hegelian, Marxist, Frankfurt

---

19  "Reification and the consciousness of the proletariat," in *History and Class Consciousness* (1923), trans. Rodney Livingstone (Cambridge, MA: The MIT Press, 1972), 208.

school tradition," today, "the problem with contemporary critical theory is that it has become insufficiently critical": "Perhaps philosophy exists to remind us we haven't gotten anywhere."[20] The question is the proper role of critical theory and "philosophical" questions in politics. In the absence of Marxism, other thinking is called to address this — for instance, Arendt (or worse: see Carl Schmitt[21]).

Recognizing the potential political abuse of "philosophy" does not mean, however, that we must agree with Heidegger, that, "Philosophy will not be able to bring about a direct change of the present state of the world" (*Der Spiegel* interview). Especially since Marxism is not only (a history of) a form of politics, but also, as the Hegel and Frankfurt School scholar Gillian Rose put it, a "mode of cognition *sui generis*."[22] This is because, as the late 19th century sociologist Emile Durkheim put it, (bourgeois) society is an "object of cognition *sui generis*." Furthermore, capitalism is a problem of social transformation *sui generis* — one with which we still might struggle, at least hopefully! Marxism is hence a mode of politics *sui generis* — one whose historical memory has become very obscure. This is above all a practical problem, but one which registers also "philosophically" in "theory."

The problem of what Rousseau called the "reflective" and Kant and Hegel, after Rousseau, called the "speculative" relation of theory and practice in bourgeois society's crisis in capitalism, recognized once by historical Marxism as the critical self-consciousness of proletarian socialism and its self-contradictions, has not gone away but was only driven underground. The revolution originating in the bourgeois era in the 17th and 18th centuries that gave rise to the modern philosophy of freedom in Rousseauian Enlightenment and German Idealism and that advanced to new problems in the Industrial Revolution and the proletarianization of society, perverting "bourgeois right" into a form of domination rather than emancipation, and expressed through the Bonapartist state's perversion of democracy,

---

20  "*Critical Inquiry* and Critical Theory: A Short History of Non-Being," *Critical Inquiry* 30, no. 2 (Winter 2004), 416–417.

21  See Schmitt's *The Concept of the Political* (1927/32).

22  Review of the English translation of Adorno's *Negative Dialectics* (1973), in *The American Political Science Review* 70, no. 2 (June 1976), 598–599.

which was recognized by Marxism in the 19th century but failed in the 20th century, may still task us.

This is why we might, still, be reading Lukács.

Originally published in *Weekly Worker* 994 (January 23, 2014)
and *Platypus Review* 63 (February 2014)

## Addendum: A century of critical theory: the legacy of Georg Lukács

Almost 10 years ago now already, in late 2013, I wrote the following bulk of my remarks, which is taken from a longer essay, "Why still read Lukács? The place of 'philosophical' questions in Marxism," published in early 2014 in *The Platypus Review* and the Communist Party of Great Britain's *Weekly Worker*. Although my fellow panelist Mike Macnair is familiar with my argument, my other interlocutor here, Andrew Feenberg, perhaps is not. Andrew's early book on Lukács, more recently revised and expanded under the title *The Philosophy of Praxis*, was very formatively educational for me early on — especially on the Rousseauian roots of Marxism and the "red thread" of dialectics from Kant and Hegel to the Frankfurt School.

I will begin with a polemical jab, or perhaps just a jocular nudge, directed at Mike, about his characterization of Kant and Hegel as expressing a philosophical "counterrevolution" against the Enlightenment, and specifically as against Locke and Hume. Regarding Andrew, the dispute between Mike and me over Lukács might seem a debate over Marxism that might not be especially relevant in the present. I hope to explain my perspective on the simultaneous relevance and irrelevance of Lukács today. As I wrote in one of exchanges with Mike and with the CPGB more generally in their *Weekly Worker* publication, "the absence of Marxism is a task of Marxism."

The recovery of Marxism that I think must take place at some point in the future will be over a great chasm of discontinuity and break, of which the present discussion is a symptomatic phenomenon: we are expressions of the very problem that we seek to overcome. I see the gulf between us and Lukács — at least the Lukács of his most significant work from 1923 — as having opened indeed already a century ago, with what has come between since then as muddling the issues and confounding attempts to even address them, presenting a formidable obstacle to making sense of things let alone clearly articulating the problem. Of course, readings of Lukács themselves express the ways we are stuck and prevented from formulating the proper questions to begin with.

The question would be, as I put it 10 years ago, the place of "philosophical questions" in Marxism. Is Marxism a philosophy? Does the struggle for socialism require philosophy, or a specific form of philosophy? This is where the notorious Frankfurt School formulation of "Critical Theory" comes into play, namely, Marxism not as a philosophy but rather a theoretical critique. And a critique not of capitalism merely, but of the struggle for socialism itself, a critical self-consciousness. The issue is what kind?

The aforementioned Frankfurt School considered Marxism to have succumbed in its degeneration to "positivity" and abandoned its negative character — for instance losing the critical recognition of the negative character of the proletarianized working class in capitalism. It had forgotten, as Rosa Luxemburg put it, that the working class had no positive content to oppose to that of capitalism, but stood merely as the "bankruptcy lawyer" to liquidate it — and "liquidate" doesn't mean eliminate but rather translate its value into another form, transforming its value. In this way, the social revolution of the proletariat was unlike that of any other in history. The proletarian struggle for socialism was unprecedented. This included the unprecedented nature of the tasks of its self-consciousness, especially as "critical." What was forgotten was not simply the present's place in the historical process, positively, but what Marx and Engels considered the "prehistorical" character of all history hitherto, how the proletarian struggle for socialism was the final chapter of prehistory and hence negative. Lukács himself called attention to what he called the "positive and negative dialectics" in Hegel, and associated the latter with Marx and the former with bourgeois society. — Not to be undialectical and simply counterpose them, for the bourgeois positive dialectic must also be fulfilled as well as overcome in socialism!

This meant that Marxism as a political movement itself required a Marxist critique; the crisis of Marxism had to be met by more Marxism, not supplementation from without, philosophical or otherwise. In short, the proletarianized working class's struggle for socialism required a critical self-consciousness, and Marxism provided this, without which the workers' economic, political and social struggles would reproduce capitalism and not get beyond it.

Marx had formulated his approach in the critique of the proletarian socialism of his time. Lenin and Luxemburg had critiqued the Marxism of their time. For Lukács, the need for this took place in dramatic form when the majority Marxist party, the SPD, conducted the counterrevolution in Germany in 1918–19, precisely in the name of preserving the workers' interests — namely, their interests in the existing social system of capitalism. Likewise, Stalinist policies in the USSR could be seen as driven by the needs and interests of the workers in the Soviet Union, and elsewhere in a similar reformist and conservative direction. Eventually, Lukács backed off from his own critical perspective when it threatened to estrange him from the dominant Marxism of his time, namely, Stalinism. The Frankfurt School by contrast maintained Marxism, however partially one-sidedly, as Critical Theory. — As Adorno put it, praxis is the "obsession" of theory.

Addendum presented on a panel with Andrew Feenberg and Mike Macnair at the fifteenth annual International Convention of the Platypus Affiliated Society, held at the University of Chicago on April 1, 2023.

# Beyond history?
# Nietzsche, Benjamin, Adorno

History is a way the present *relates* to itself. History *mediates* the present, and anticipates the future. The relation of past and present in history is a *social* relation, a relation of society with itself, as a function of *change*. The proper object of the present is history: the present is historical; it is constituted by history. The present *is* history; history is the *present*. As Hegel put it, the "philosophical" approach to history is concerned with the "eternally present": what in the past was *always* present. This is a function of *modernity*. What is at issue is the form of the present in history, or, the form of history in the present.

Three writings, by Nietzsche, Benjamin and Adorno, respectively, reflect upon the specific form of history in capital, and on the possibility of transcending the historicism that emerged in the 19th century, as it continued to inform the 20th: Nietzsche's 1873 "On the Use and Abuse of History for Life;" Benjamin's 1940 "Theses on the Philosophy of History;" and Adorno's 1942 "Reflections on Class Theory." Nietzsche's essay inspired Benjamin's; Adorno's followed directly upon Benjamin's.

## Nietzsche and the genesis of history

Nietzsche's second "untimely meditation" (or "unfashionable observation"), "On the Use and Abuse of History for Life," critiqued what translator and Nietzsche scholar Peter Preuss called the 19th century "discovery" of history. Nietzsche regarded history specifically as a symptomatic expression of the genuine needs of the time. For Nietzsche, the symptom of history is expression of an illness, but Nietzsche's approach to such illness is as to "pregnancy": not to be cured in the sense that it is eliminated, but rather undergone successfully to bring forth new life.[1]

19th century historicism was, for Nietzsche, the hallmark of a historically peculiar form of life: modern humanity. Modern humanity is historical in a precise sense: "history" is historical. For Nietzsche, the question is what the symptom of history indicates about the need for humanity to overcome itself in present form. Nietzsche's expression for this potential self-overcoming of historical humanity is the "supra-historical." It points beyond history, towards a new form of life that is possible *in* history.

For Nietzsche, there are three forms of the historical: the "monumental;" the "antiquarian;" and the "critical." Nietzsche addressed these different phases of the historical as expressing different "uses" or needs for the historical in the "life" of humanity. In each of them the past figures differently. The forms of the historical are distinguished from the greater three categories with which Nietzsche's essay is concerned: the "unhistorical;" the "historical;" and the "supra-historical." The latter three categories refer, respectively, to the pre-human, the human, and the supra-human. Humanity becomes itself through history; and it potentially overcomes or transforms itself in transcending itself as historical. As Preuss pointed out, history is the record of the "self-production" of humanity. Therefore, the transformation of humanity, the changes in its self-production, changes history, and changes what the past is for humanity. In this respect, it is possible to address Nietzsche's essay as indicating the possibility for going beyond the historical, or overcoming the present relation humanity has to itself, in and through history.

## Benjamin and Adorno on Nietzsche and Marxism

Benjamin, and Adorno following him, appropriated Nietzsche's account of history for their Marxist critical theory of the "philosophy of history," specifying Nietzsche's symptomology of history as symptomatic of *capital*. For Benjamin and Adorno, Nietzsche's account of history was historically

---

1   See *On the Genealogy of Morals: A Polemic* (1887), part II, sections 16–19.

specific to its moment of capital, the late 19th century, with further impli-
cation for the 20th century.

What would it mean to get "beyond history?" First, it is necessary to
identify, as Adorno put it, "what history is": its possibility and necessity.
For Benjamin, history originates in the demand for *redemption*. Follow-
ing Benjamin's "Theses on the Philosophy of History," and responding to
Marx and Engels's *Communist Manifesto*, in "Reflections on Class Theory"
Adorno wrote that,

> According to [Marxian] theory, history is the history of class
> struggles. But the concept of class is bound up with the emer-
> gence of the proletariat. . . . By exposing the historical necessity
> that had brought capitalism into being, political economy
> became the critique of history as a whole. . . . All history is the
> history of class struggles because it was always the same thing,
> namely, prehistory. This gives us a pointer as to how we can rec-
> ognize what history is. From the most recent form of injustice,
> a steady light reflects back on history as a whole. Only in this
> way can theory enable us to use the full weight of history to
> gain an insight into the present without succumbing in resigna-
> tion to the burden of the past.

This relation of pre-history, history, and a potential post-historical condition was, for Adorno, the relation of the present to the "burden of the past":
can it be redeemed?

Adorno addressed a certain problem in Marxism's so-called "dialectical" approach to history, in that it tended to be, paradoxically, one-sided:

> [Marxism has been praised] on account of its dyna-
> mism. . . . Dynamism is merely one side of dialectic: it is the
> side preferred by the belief in practicality. . . . The other, less
> popular aspect of dialectic is its static side. . . . The law that,
> according to the Hegelian dialectic, governs the restlessly
> destructive unfolding of the ever-new consists in the fact that at

every moment the ever-new is also the old lying close at hand. The new does not add itself to the old but is the old in distress.[2]

This was Adorno's interpretation and attempted further elaboration of Benjamin's injunction to read history "against the grain" (Thesis VII). But what did Adorno mean by "the new?"

Potential futures are generated out of the relation of past and present, out of the relation of the present to itself through *history*. The dynamic of history is inherent in the self-contradiction of the present: history is a projection of it. What is the "practicality" of history? The emergence or departure of the new is the self-overcoming of the present, or the self-overcoming of history: its immanent transcendence. Nietzsche's phrase, "self-overcoming" is, literally, the "Selbstaufhebung": self-fulfillment and self-negation. The present provides an opportunity for the self-overcoming of history.

The "new is the old in distress" because it is the present in tension with itself: is the present merely the ever-same? The "static side of the dialectic," in which the "ever-new is the old lying close at hand," means that, as Benjamin put it, "every second is the strait gate through which the Messiah [redemption] might enter" (Addendum B). The "homogeneous" and "empty" time of the ever-same is also, potentially, the "full" time-of-the-now (*Jetztzeit*). History is dialectical, but it is a "negative" dialectic of the present: the present, in its potential for self-overcoming, disintegrates as history disintegrates into the mere facticity of the past. Historicism is a symptom of failed self-overcoming. For Benjamin, the task was to "construct" history, rather than to merely "add" the new to the old (Thesis XVII). This is the contrast Adorno found between the new as "the old lying close at hand" and the "restlessly destructive unfolding of the ever-new" that is "always the same thing, namely, prehistory." The "static side" of the dialectic of history is thus a *resource*. The question is whether it is a resource for the emergence of the new or the perpetuation of the old: either, or both.

---

2   Ibid., 95.

## Nietzsche's "untimeliness"

The discontent of history is the source of Nietzsche's "untimely thought."
What potential *critique* of the present does history offer? Nietzsche
recognized himself as a product of 19th century historicism. Nietzsche
characterized as "antiquarian" the deadly transformation of history into the
mere facticity of the past. As a Classical philologist, Nietzsche was well prepared to address the melancholy of modernity expressed in historicism. As
Benjamin put it, quoting Flaubert, "Few people can guess how despondent
one has to be in order to resuscitate Carthage" (Thesis VII). (The reference to Carthage echoes that with which Nietzsche began his essay, the
*Ceterum censeo* ["I judge otherwise"] of Cato the Elder: "*Carthago delenda
est* [Carthage must be destroyed]." As Nietzsche put it, this was the spirit
with which his "consideration of the worth and the worthlessness of history" began.) In response to such threatening *acedia*, Nietzsche contrasted
his "critical" approach to history.

> Here it becomes clear how badly man needs, often enough, in
> addition to the monumental and antiquarian ways of seeing the
> past, a *third* kind, the *critical*: and this again in the service of life
> as well. He must have the strength, and use it from time to time,
> to shatter and dissolve something to enable him to live: this he
> achieves by dragging it to the bar of judgment, interrogating it
> meticulously and finally condemning it; every past, however, is
> worth condemning.

This approach, Nietzsche pointed out, was counter to the historicist passion of his time, the prevalent "consumptive historical fever." Nevertheless,
Nietzsche found his own philological concerns to motivate a certain dis-
satisfaction with the *ethos* inherent in "the powerful historical tendency of
the times, as it has been, by common knowledge, observed for the past two
generations, particularly among the Germans" since the early 19th century.

> I must be allowed to ascribe this much to myself on account of
> my profession as a classical philologist, for I would not know

what sense classical philology would have in our age unless it is to be effective by its inappropriateness for the times, that is, in opposition to the age, thus working on the age, and, we hope, for the benefit of a coming time.

The consummation and self-destruction of 19th century historicism in Nietzsche presented the demand for the "supra-historical," for getting beyond the historical comportment that had produced Nietzsche, a self-overcoming of history.

### Beyond history?

The question of getting beyond history relates to Nietzsche's characterization of "critical history," that is, the possibility and necessity of "condemning a past" in creating what he called a "new nature." This is the need to *forget*. This is not the forgetting that might be taken to characterize the unhistorical, animal condition (according to Nietzsche, the unhistorical condition is that of the grazing animal, which does not speak because it immediately forgets what it was going to say). "Forgetting," in Nietzsche's sense, is an activity in service of life: it can only be considered, not unhistorical, but post- or supra-historical, that is, a form of historical forgetting that overcomes a form of remembering. There is a human need to forget that is not natural but develops: it is a *new* need.

For Benjamin, the need to "forget" is related to the need to "redeem" history. "Redeemed" history could not only be potentially "cited" in "all its moments," but also, more importantly, *forgotten*. The need to remember is matched by the need to forget. So, the question turns on the necessity for remembering that would need to be overcome in order to make forgetting, in a transcendent sense, possible and desirable.

Benjamin's concept of historical redemption in the "Theses on the Philosophy of History" was informed by the correspondence he conducted with Horkheimer on the *Arcades Project* (for which the "Theses" were drafted as an introduction), specifically concerning redemption. Horkheimer pointed out that any redemption must be qualified: the dead remained dead; their sacrifice could not be redeemed in certain respects.

For Benjamin, this affected the quality of history: it became the record of wasted potential, or "barbarism." This was history's standing reproach to the present.

If, for Nietzsche, "critical history" means standing in judgment over history, by contrast, for Benjamin, the critical value of history was in its judgment over the present: history was an effect of the present's judgment of *itself*. What does the present need to remember; what to forget? What does it need to *judge*? If Nietzsche called for the historian to be "man enough" to judge the past, for Benjamin, the required "strength" was to receive history's judgment and not be devastated by it: the memory of "enslaved ancestors" (Thesis XII). For the nature and character of both the ancestry and the enslavement were precisely the matters to be judged, remembered and forgotten. From what are we descended, and from what must we free ourselves? How do we judge this?

## Capital as form of history to be redeemed

Adorno identifies "how we can recognize what history is" by the "steady light" reflecting "from the most recent form of injustice." The *theory* that is thus enabled, without succumbing to the past, must be able to distinguish the potential for the present to depart from the "ever-same." For Benjamin, this "Messianic" potential for redemption available in every present moment is the product of two opposed vectors: regression and stasis. The "static side" of the historical dialectic that Adorno identified was, for Benjamin, the potential "exploding" of the "continuum of history" (Thesis XVI), a "standstill" (Thesis XVI), or "activating the emergency brake on the locomotive of history" (Paralipomena Thesis XVIIa). The motivation for this was the "regression of society" (Thesis XI). Otherwise, one might "succumb," "in resignation to the burden of the past."

Capital presents an apparently unredeemable history, at least in any traditional (theological) sense of redemption. Benjamin was no melancholic but rather sought to diagnose and potentially overcome the melancholy of modernity. But this could only be achieved immanently, from within modernity's "dialectic" of history. This dialectic had, for Adorno, two sides: dynamic and static. The dialectic of history in capital is one of constantly generated but wasted new potentials. This is its "injustice," what gives modernity its peculiar, specific melancholy, affecting its demand for redemption. While all of human history may have been characterized by the Messianic demand for redemption, modern history's demand for redemption is specific and peculiar. Modern history liquidates all prior history, however rendering it, according to Benjamin, more as "rubble" (Thesis IX) than as resource.

Modern history ruins prior forms of redemption, in favor of what is, for Benjamin, a specious form of remembering: history as the accumulation of mere facts. What would be its "opposite?" The traditional Messianic eschatological "end of time" is matched by the modern "monstrous abbreviation" that summarizes the entire history of humanity (Thesis XVIII) in capital: an appropriation of all of history that threatens to become its barbarization. For Benjamin, this must be countered by a constructed "constellation," in which the demand for the redemption of history transforms the time of the present into one of potential *secular* redemption: not the *negation* of time as in the coming of the Messiah, but the redemption *of* time, *in* time (Addendum A). This would amount to the effective transformation of history, a "fulfillment" of the "here-and-now" appearing as a "charged past" that has the ability to "leap into the open sky of history" (Thesis XIV) as opposed to subordination to a "chain of events" (Thesis IX) or "causal nexus" (Addendum A). Neither celestial redemption outside of time nor secular time without redemption, Benjamin's philosophy of history seeks the relation of modern temporality to the transformed demand for redemption.

The question is how to overcome the ideological abuse of history to which it is subject in modernity. This abuse is due to the form of temporality in capital. For Benjamin, this concerns the "citability" of the moments of the past, which modern society makes possible — and necessary. This is no mere addition to knowledge of the past, a quantitative increase, but rather the fundamental qualitative transformation of what counts as historical knowledge, the self-knowledge of humanity as a function of time. Is the self-production and self-transformation of humanity a function of *time*? In capital, this is the case, but in a certain sense, producing what Benjamin called a "causal chain" of events "anterior" to the present. However, such spatialization of time, once, historically, did not, and so, potentially, would no longer, pertain in a "supra-historical" condition for humanity, as prognosed by Nietzsche.

## The temporality of capital

From the transformation *of* time *in* time, it becomes possible to turn the "abbreviation" of time in capital into the potential supersession of the form of change as a function *of* time. From Nietzsche's "critical" approach to history, as an active appropriation of the present, Benjamin turned to the reception of history as critical to the present: the present as *crisis* of history. Where, for Nietzsche, the culmination of history was the crisis of the historical, and the possibility for a supra-historical form of humanity, for Benjamin, the culmination of the peculiar historical comportment of modern humanity is the crisis of history, the crisis of humanity. All of history becomes citable, but as *amalgamation*. Where, for Nietzsche, a future changed condition "must come" if humanity is to *survive*, for Benjamin, if history is to be redeemed, humanity must be *transformed*. (Benjamin: "Humanity is preparing to outlive culture, if need be;" this is Nietzsche's "strange goal.")

As Adorno concluded his "Reflections on Class Theory," "This means, however, that dehumanization is also its opposite. . . . Even if the dynamic at work was always the same, its end today is not the end." The transformation of humanity envisioned by Benjamin and Adorno, appropriating Nietzsche's discontent in history, was one that would transcend all historical culture "hitherto." Benjamin and Adorno matched Nietzsche's "rumination" with Marx and Engels's *Manifesto*. The self-overcoming of the entire history of civilization and of its "process of transmission" (which cannot be avoided but only "reversed," pointing not to the future but the past) would be "against the grain" of the historical progress that can only be regarded as "regression": the inversion of the meaning of history; the end of history as the end of pre-history in the present, or, the potential redemption of the history of civilization that capital makes possible of itself.

The dialectic of memory and forgetting involves changes in both the forms of remembering and the process of forgetting. A form of remembrance is a way of forgetting. It serves a certain way of life. To remember is to forget in a certain way; to forget is to overcome a certain need to remember, and to overcome the past in a certain way. If the present is an effect of history, then it is in the way the past *causes* the present.

Why is the past, in modernity (according to Benjamin, following Nietzsche), "citable" in all of its moments? Because all of history is (potentially) *negated* by capital — just as it is (potentially) *fulfilled* by it. The question is the possibility and necessity of the appropriation of all of history in capital. The mode of appropriation of the past in capital, its "process of transmission," is the society prevailing throughout "all of history": "barbarism." This means that all moments of the past potentially become culpable in capital, by becoming the endless resource of the present: history. Capital is the literal "Aufhebung" of history. But can capital become the *Selbst*-aufhebung of history? Or does modern history exhibit, rather, a dynamic that is *alien* to all of history, as it was practiced hitherto (prior to the challenge of modernity)? Is capital the potential for redemption in history, or its ultimate denial, its final liquidation? The fundamental ambivalence of history in capital is the key to what it *is*: an injustice to be made good. This is what capital has promised humanity at the end of history. Can it be fulfilled? Will it?[3]

---

3   This link between redemption and forgetting has its utopic as well as dystopic valences. As Kafka wrote in conclusion of his last published story, "Josephine the Singer, or the Mouse Folk" (in *The Complete Stories*, trans. Willa and Edwin Muir [New York: Schocken, 1995], 360–376), in a decidedly non-human, zoomorphic parable:

> Josephine's road, however, must go downhill. The time will soon come when her last notes sound and die into silence. She is a small episode in the eternal history of our people, and the people will get over the loss of her. Not that it will be easy for us; how can our gatherings take place in utter silence? Still, were they not silent even when Josephine was present? Was her actual piping notably louder and more alive than the memory of it will be? Was it even in her lifetime more than a simple memory? Was it not rather because Josephine's singing was already past losing in this way that our people in their wisdom prized it so highly?
>
> So perhaps we shall not miss so very much after all, while Josephine, redeemed from the earthly sorrows which to her thinking lay in wait for all chosen spirits, will happily lose herself in the numberless throng of the heroes of our people, and soon, since we are no historians, will rise to the heights of redemption and be forgotten like all her brothers. (376)

Originally presented on a panel with Fabian Arzuaga, Bo-Mi Choi and
G. S. Sahota at the Critical Historical Studies conference, Chicago Center for
Contemporary Theory (3CT), University of Chicago, December 3, 2011.

## Bibliography

Adorno, Theodor W., "Reflections on Class Theory," translated by Rodney
Livingstone, *Can One Live after Auschwitz? A Philosophical Reader*, ed.
Rolf Tiedemann (Stanford, CA: Stanford University Press, 2003),
93–110.

Benjamin, Walter, "Theses on the Philosophy of History," translated by
Harry Zohn, *Illuminations*, ed. Hannah Arendt (New York: Schocken,
1968), 255–266; "On the Concept of History," translated by Dennis
Redmond (2005). Available online; "Paralipomena to 'On the Con-
cept of History,'" *Selected Writings*, vol. 4 *1938–40* (Cambridge, MA:
Harvard, 2003), 401–11.

Nietzsche, Friedrich, "On the Use and Abuse of History for Life," trans.
Ian Johnston (2010), available online; *On the Advantage and Dis-
advantage of History for Life*, trans. Peter Preuss (Indianapolis, IN:
Hackett, 1980).

# The concept of Left and Right

Leszek Kolakowski's "The concept of the Left" was published in English translation in 1968.[1] Actually, the essay dates from the late fifties, and it was a response to the crackdown that came with the Khrushchev revelations. Most famously, there was an uprising in Hungary in 1956 after Khrushchev's revelations about Stalin, but in fact there were attempts at liberalization in other parts of Eastern Europe, including Poland. Kolakowski participated in that, but also suffered the consequences of the reaction against it, and that's what prompted him to write the essay. Much later, Kolakowski became a very virulent anti-Marxist. But in the late fifties, he's still writing within the tradition of Marxism and drawing from the history of its controversies, specifically the revisionist dispute and the split with the Second International into the Third International.

Kolakowski wrote that the Left needs to be defined at the level of ideas rather than at the level of sociological groups. In other words, Left and right don't correspond to "workers" and "capitalists." Rather, the Left is defined by its vision of the future, its utopianism, whereas the right is defined by the absence of that, by opportunism. Very succinctly, Kolakowski said, "The right doesn't need ideas, it only needs tactics." So what is the status of the ideas that would define the Left?

He says that the Left is characterized by an obscure and mysterious consciousness of history. The Left is concerned with the opening and furthering of possibilities, whereas the right is about the foreclosure of those possibilities. The consciousness of those possibilities would be the ideology of the Left. Kolakowski's use of the term "utopia," when he says the Left is

---

1   In *The New Left Reader*, ed. Carl Oglesby (New York: Grove Press, 1969).

344 · Critical theory: Philosophy

defined by utopia, is a rather peculiar and eccentric use of the term. It's not a definite image of the future; it's rather a sense of possibility — a consciousness of change. This might involve certain images of the future, but it's not defined, for Kolakowski, by those images of the future. Left and right are relative; there's a spectrum that goes from a sense of possibility for change and ranges off to the right with a foreclosure of those possibilities, which is what justifies opportunism and politics of pure tactics.

Another useful category that Kolakowski introduced is "crime." He says politics cannot be fully extricated from crime, but the Left should be willing to call crime "crime," whereas the right needs to pretend that crimes are exigent necessities. In other words, the Left is concerned with distinguishing between true necessities and failures to meet those necessities, which is what political crime amounts to. So Kolakowski says that the Left cannot avoid committing crimes, but it can avoid failure to recognize them as crimes. In this respect, crimes would be compromises that foreclose possibilities — political failure is a crime. This is important, again, because the context in which he was writing was Stalinism, and Khrushchev's revelation of Stalin's crimes. In other words, Khrushchev's concern was, "Okay, Stalin is dead and there's been a struggle for power in his wake. How are we going to make sense of the past twenty or thirty years of history? What were the crimes that were committed?" The crimes that were committed in this respect were crimes against the revolution — crimes against freedom, crimes against the possibility of opening further possibilities for change. In this respect, the Left is concerned with freedom, and the right is concerned with the disenchantment of freedom — the foreclosing of possibilities for freedom. Whereas the Left must believe in freedom, the right does not. Hannah Arendt in the 1960s in *On Revolution* points out how remarkable it was that the language of freedom had dropped out of the Left already at that point.

Today, one of the reasons why Platypus says, "The Left is dead! Long live the Left!" is that the concept of freedom, and therefore the concept of the Left itself, has given way rather to concerns with social justice. Social justice can't be about freedom because justice is about restoring the status quo ante, not advancing further possibilities. While we might say there can be no freedom without justice, we can say that there can be justice without freedom. When the avowed Left concerns itself not with freedom but with justice, it ceases to be a Left. That's because pursuing a politics of justice would stand on different justifications than pursuing a politics of freedom — in the name of justice, crimes against freedom can be committed.

Presented on April 5th, 2014 at the sixth annual Platypus International Convention at the School of the Art Institute of Chicago on a panel discussion with Samir Gandesha (Simon Fraser University) and Nikos Malliaris (Lieux Communs).

Originally published in *Platypus Review* 68 (July – August 2014)

# The Left is a concept — but social revolution is not[1]

Leszek Kolakowski's "The Concept of the Left" (1958) is useful for addressing what it means to say that there is a Left and a Right in Marxism. It is derived from the Revisionist Dispute regarding Orthodox Marxism and the question of reform vs. revolution in the 2nd Socialist International. The actual occasion for Kołakowski's article was Soviet Premier and Communist Party head Nikita Khrushchev's denunciation of Stalin for "crimes against Leninism" and against socialism. What did this mean?

It goes back to the accusation against the Socialist Party-associated labor unions and the Marxist theorist Eduard Bernstein and his Revisionist associates in the 2nd International, who advocated reform struggles within liberal democratic capitalism at the expense of socialist revolution, that they were "opportunists." This is what characterized them as the Right. Kołakowski describes this as adaptation to and expression of the "inertia of the status quo" that characterizes the Right as conservative.

By contrast, Orthodox and "revolutionary" Marxism upheld what Kołakowski called the Left as "utopia." Kołakowski wrote that what characterized the Left was an "idea" and moreover its "negation" of the status quo, not programmatically as in a blueprint for a better society, but rather as a "mysterious and obscure" expression of historical potential and possibility that is not yet realized.

This goes back to the bourgeois revolutionary philosophy of Rousseau, Kant, Hegel and others which contrasted what "is" with what "ought" to be, the process of becoming within a state of being that expressed what could and should be but "is not" yet. Marxism descended from this revolutionary

---

1    A response to "Benedict Cryptofash." See "The Left is not a concept," *Platypus Review* 142 (December 2021 – January 2022).

philosophy of the era of bourgeois emancipation and enlightenment from traditional civilization.

So what is the difference that makes this such a contentious issue? Capitalism has its origins in the bourgeois revolution, but for Marxism expresses a potential beyond it: socialism/communism — "communism" as an Ancient religious ideal of collective equality; "socialism" as a modern political ideology stemming from the potential inherent in capitalism but not possible previously and not yet existing in historical reality.

The problem is not that the Marxist Left — the revolutionary political ideology and "[Hegelian] scientific theory" of historical Marxists such as Karl Kautsky, Rosa Luxemburg, Vladimir Lenin and Leon Trotsky, among others — is descended from bourgeois revolutionary philosophy, but rather that since the failure of Marxism historically to achieve socialist revolution in the early 20th century, capitalism itself has tried to adapt to the threat of proletarian discontent and disorder through "progressive liberal" democratic capitalist welfare-state measures and the national organization of capital accumulation.

Stalinism was an adaptation to this failure of world socialist revolution and assimilation instead to "progressive capitalism," thus making Stalinism the modern expression of the Right wing of Marxism, expressing the inertia of history and society and becoming the ideology of the liquidation of the proletarian struggle for socialism. Trotsky called Stalinism the "antithesis of Bolshevism" — of Marxism.

The Left is dead today because it is the Right — not because it is the Left. The Left as a historical idea of Marxism motivating the proletarian struggle for the socialist transformation of capitalism has become instead a late bourgeois ideology of the "progressive" reform of capitalism. This already happened nearly 100 years ago and is still in effect very strongly today. Marxism is thus entombed in history.

The Left–Right distinction is not social but political and ideological in nature. Its meaning for Marxism comes from a division and split in the political party for socialism — the split of the 3rd Communist from 2nd Socialist International in the Russian Revolution and its world-historic aftermath: the old Socialists were the Right and the new Communists were the Left. From a Marxist perspective, the established Socialist Parties existing today are still the Right, despite being called the "Left." Trotsky and his comrades called themselves the Left Opposition to Stalinism in the Communist International. They made a claim to uphold the true spirit of Marxism and proletarian socialist revolution that still haunts us today.

Lenin (in)famously observed that socialist ideology must come from outside the social and economic and political struggles of the working class within capitalism. What was this "outside"? It wasn't sociological — from bourgeois intellectuals — but rather historical: it comes from the past accumulation of experience of the bourgeois democratic revolution and its self-contradiction and defeat in capitalism. Lenin called socialists "Jacobins indissolubly connected to the workers movement." This is the idea.

The workers movement comes from bourgeois discontents in capitalism: capitalism's contradiction and betrayal of "equality of inalienable rights to life, liberty and the pursuit of happiness" (Jefferson — who importantly led the Left wing of the American Revolution). Only historical experience and its critical lessons can teach the proletarianized working class in capitalism that the goal of its struggle is beyond bourgeois emancipation and freedom, within which their struggles are otherwise inevitably circumscribed, reproducing capitalism.

Only a Marxist socialist Left could possibly lift the horizon of such struggle beyond capitalism. But only the working class can actually achieve the real goals of this struggle in social revolution.

Originally published in *Platypus Review* 143 (February 2022)

# Consciousness is essential —
# why the death of the Left is consequential[1]

Benedict Cryptofash criticizes me for using the "Left" as a concept for its alleged idealism and metaphysical essentialism. But by identifying the "Left" with a group of people, e.g. members of *Jacobin*/DSA et al., Cryptofash reifies the phenomenon of the Left, and in the worst possible way, by personalizing it. But even in colloquial discourse it is well understood that Left and Right represent principles not people. This is why someone who was a Leftist can become a Rightist: he can change his mind.

The Left is not a thing but rather expresses a process; moreover the Left refers to the tendency or force of a historical process. Aaron Benanav criticized Platypus for its preoccupation with the Left rather than with class — similar to the criticism of Platypus by my old ex-comrades of the Spartacist League[2] — and referred as Cryptofash does to the Left as the Left-wing of capitalism, as if this disqualified the concept.[3] But Marxism always considered itself to be the consciousness of the historical tendency of capitalism that pointed beyond it and that was necessary in order to actually get beyond it. For instance, Lenin considered the Marxist approach to socialism to be overcoming capitalism on the basis of capitalism itself. But that tendency was self-contradictory in that it pointed both further beyond capitalism but also back to the reconstitution of its historical roots

---

1   A rejoinder to Benedict Cryptofash, "The Left is not the Right," *Anti-Leftist Marx* (substack: March 10, 2022)

2   See "Platypus Group: Pseudo-Marxist, Pro-Imperialist, Academic Claptrap," *Workers Vanguard* 908 (February 15, 2008), where they wrote that "For Platypus, the fundamental social divide is not the class struggle of proletariat vs. bourgeoisie, but an amorphous and classless contest of 'Left' vs. 'Right.'"

3   See Benanav's remarks on the panel discussion "Program and utopia," *Platypus Review* 58 (July 2015)

in bourgeois society — the society of labor. The modern labor movement of the proletarianized working class was itself the core engine of capitalist development, driving the industrial development of production, which contradicted and undermined and destroyed its bourgeois social relations, producing crisis. The problem with the present Left — and for the past hundred years — is that it no longer expresses the emerging and developing consciousness of the subject of a historical tendency — proletarian socialism — but rather the memory of something that proceeds today seemingly objectively — without a corresponding political movement aiming to go beyond it. In the absence of such a subjective consciousness of history as a phenomenon in practice, capitalism itself appears to regress.[4] This regression is something that can be observed in both long-term and short-term political processes.

In my previous article in this thread, I tried to explain very briefly the mind of original historical Marxism as a political movement.[5] I will now try to illustrate the point with the example of the leader of *Jacobin*/DSA, Bhaskar Sunkara, who recently took over the historically progressive liberal *Nation* magazine. Sunkara has apparently changed since he published an article in *The Nation*, "Reclaiming Socialism" (2015), in which, under the influence of my teachings in Platypus, he cited Kołakowski's "Concept of the Left" to justify his political vision.[6] Back then, Sunkara's influences were Lenin and Kautsky (from "when Kautsky was still a Marxist," as Lenin put it[7]). But this is no longer the case.

More recently, Sunkara claimed that he was less a follower of Kautsky than of Ralph Miliband. This is in keeping with the 2017 statement written by Vivek Chibber to distinguish Jacobin/DSA's perspective from that of the Marxism of Kautsky and Lenin, "Our Road to Power" — by contrast with Kautsky's 1909 *The Road to Power*, which Lenin followed in the

---

4   See "The Decline of the Left in the 20th Century: Toward a theory of historical regression," in this volume and in *Platypus Review* 17 (November 2009).

5   "The Left is a concept — but social revolution is not: A response to 'Benedict Cryptofash,'" *Platypus Review* 143 (February 2022), in this volume.

6   *The Nation*, 150th Anniversary Issue (April 6, 2015), March 23, 2015.

7   "I. In What Sense We Can Speak of the International Significance of the Russian Revolution," in *"Left-Wing" Communism: An Infantile Disorder* (1920).

Revolution of 1917.[8] I addressed this on the 150th anniversary of Lenin's birth, to which Sunkara and Leo Panitch replied, defending Miliband's "Marxist" *bona fides* against my characterization of him as a "liberal" — a proponent of a liberal democratic road to socialism, very much like the reformist Revisionism of Eduard Bernstein et al. from more than fifty years earlier.[9] Miliband's idea, with which Sunkara, Chibber and Panitch agreed, was that the capitalist state could not be overthrown and replaced by the working class's own organizations in the dictatorship of the proletariat, but had to be worked through existing liberal democratic electoral means to a potential transformation of society — the endless dream of reformist social democracy (through the Democratic Party of all vehicles!) that has ensnared the Millennial Left like the generations before them. Most recently, Sunkara said that socialism was probably ultimately impossible in the U.S., but at least some "social democracy" was possible, by which he meant public sector and welfare state expansion.[10] This was an abandonment of Marxist ideas, or at least of their current relevance politically.

Perhaps Sunkara thinks he has remained consistent, but there seems to be some change of mind. Perhaps not in principle — perhaps he still finds socialism desirable but not possible, and ultimately not necessary to meet the needs of the present — but certainly in terms of practical politics and what he takes to be the "art of the possible," which is the essence of politics. In so doing, he has abandoned the Left's role in pushing — and transcending — the envelope of possibility and realizing hitherto unrealized potentials, not even necessarily in changing society but merely in renewing the Left and socialism or Marxism as a political tendency. Sunkara has abandoned the task of building a socialist party. Instead, Sunkara et al. among the Millennial Left have fallen back upon the dead traditions of

8   *Jacobin* (December 5, 2017).

9   See my "Lenin today," *Platypus Review* 126 (May 2020), in this volume.

10   In the Bard College Hannah Arendt Center for Politics and Humanities talk of March 2, 2021, "Tough Talks: Bhaskar Sunkara," Sunkara said that, "Perhaps we will fall short of our loftier ambitions [of socialism], but we will still manage to win a more just United States that will at least have Medicare for All, and a living wage for all, and the chance for decent work for all," available online. See also "The Promise (and Limits) of Social Democracy," *The Jacobin Show* (June 6, 2021) and "Biden Offers Fiscal Liberalism, not Social Democracy," *The Jacobin Show* (June 7, 2021).

the past post-Marxist "Left" — accepting and reinforcing the liquidation of proletarian socialism over the course of the past century, since Lenin's time. This is why and how it takes the form of calls for a "new New Deal" etc.[11]

This downward trajectory in perspectives is a significant degeneration of consciousness on the part of a key leader of the Millennial Left. Five years ago I called it the death of the Millennial Left, in its liquidation into the Democratic Party.[12] It has only grown worse since then. I take Crypto-fash's objection to "Leftism" to be a symptomatic phenomenon of the same degeneration, but one which throws the baby out with the bathwater, in rejecting *Jacobin*/DSA's road back to the Democrats. Cryptofash derogates consciousness by calling it "idealistic" and "metaphysical," an "abstract" and so supposedly unreal "essence." But then one must ask what the purpose of Cryptofash's own writings is. What is the point of his arguments if all that matters is "material reality"? Indeed, in prioritizing empirical reality over consciousness, Cryptofash follows the present dead "Left's" lead into accommodating the power of the status quo, abandoning the conscious-ness of how it could and should be changed — first of all, how the present "Left" must be fundamentally changed. Cryptofash's "anti-Leftist Marx-ism" merely strikes a pose against the "Left."

Marx followed Kant and Hegel's — modern German Idealism's — and bourgeois thought's more general sense of the task of "consciousness" as the necessity of freedom: the struggle for freedom is motivated by conscious-ness of necessity. And the highest necessity is not base "material" need — the animal survival of the workers — but rather *freedom*: the necessity of changing the world, specifically of overcoming capitalism. It was a matter of Rousseau's "general will" of society as more than the sum of its parts in the wills of its members, Kant's "transcendental subject" of freedom, and Hegel's "objective mind" (*Geist*, Spirit) as it develops in history. Marxism's consciousness of "communism" was more specifically — and empirically — that of a political outlook and strategy for pursuing it and the reasons for this historically. Marx did not invent communism, which predated

11  See my "The end of the Gilded Age: Discontents of the Second Industrial Revolution today," *Platypus Review* 102 (December 2017 – January 2018), in this volume.
12  See my "The Millennial Left is dead," *Platypus Review* 100 (October 2017), in *Death of the Millennial Left: Interventions 2006–2022*.

him, but *critiqued* it. Marx's was moreover a "historical" critique of existing society in the contradictions of capitalism to be overcome, a "historical consciousness" or "consciousness of history" and its tasks: why socialism or communism arose as an ideology in the very specific phase of history in the Industrial Revolution. Marx thought that the world had only to recognize what it was struggling for in order to realize it.[13] Marx found the existing communist consciousness of his time to be lacking: its call to abolish private property resulted in a reification of labor rather than its overcoming, especially since capitalism itself already abolished private property.[14] But he thought that proletarian socialism as a movement was capable of learning the bitter lessons of its struggles — why it remained trapped in its opposition to and within capitalism. This learning process was the subjective factor of history. But what can be learned can also be unlearned.

Cryptofash exhibits a striking "historical" liquidation of the historical, reducing things like the splits of Marxism in revolution and civil war as mere "context," which ends up affirming whatever happened. — I am reminded of my late professor Moishe Postone saying that capitalism will be overcome when it is good and ready, despite what the Left wants or thinks. The Marxist critique of history is lacking. The fact is that the workers' movement for socialism has up to now failed, and this has affected history. The issue is the objective vs. subjective character of the proletarianized working class in capitalism. — In his last interview before he died, Postone claimed that we were presently witnessing the historical liquidation of the working class.[15] But for that to actually happen would require a subjective political act, leading to actually overcoming capitalism, since capitalism can objectively by (Marx's) definition not do without workers. As long as there are desperately poor people willing or able to have their labor exploited, capitalism will continue — until the workers themselves put a stop to it. There

---

13  See Marx's September 1843 letter to Arnold Ruge, "For the ruthless criticism of everything existing," in *The Marx-Engels Reader*, 2nd edition, ed. Robert C. Tucker (New York: W. W. Norton & Co., 1978), 12–15.

14  Marx and Engels, "II. Proletarians and Communists," in *Manifesto of the Communist Party* (1848).

15  "Marx in the Age of Trump," at the Vienna Humanities Festival: Hope and Despair, on September 17, 2017. This is available online.

is a necessity of politically achieving the dictatorship of the proletariat.[16] Communism as the "real movement of history" according to Marx is not merely an objective but a subjective issue: "theory gripping the masses" as a "material force"[17] also means the masses grasping theory — or at least a political ideology. That's the role of the Left.

Antonio Negri had an idea that we were already living in communism but just didn't realize it.[18] But the point of the Left is to realize it — not in the sense of just an idea or change of "consciousness" in the colloquial sense, but a critical theory helping make it happen in reality, in practice. The working class won't be able to do so without a Left, without a theory of what they are trying to do in practice. Cryptofash's desire to proceed separately from and in opposition to the Left, and without the necessity of Left theory and ideas, expects communism to happen on its own — with people as not the subjects but the objects of history. But people have perspectives and ideas, and those ideas and perspectives matter. We cannot afford to abdicate on helping to provide them. They are affected by the history of the Left and the historical self-liquidation of Marxism, which is not merely past but a continuing obstacle to the future.[19] The Left's corpse is not something we can ignore.[20] We must remember history.

Originally published in *Platypus Review* 145 (April 2022)

---

16  See my "The dictatorship of the proletariat and the death of the Left," *Platypus Review* 141 (November 2021), in this volume.

17  Marx, "Contribution to a Critique of Hegel's Philosophy of Right" (1843).

18  See Michael Hardt and Negri's books *Empire* (2000), *Multitude* (2004) and *Commonwealth* (2009), where this is elaborated.

19  See my "Remember the future! A rejoinder to Peter Hudis on 'Capital in history,'" *Platypus Review* 8 (November 2008), in this volume.

20  See my "Vicissitudes of historical consciousness and possibilities for emancipatory politics today: 'The Left is dead! — Long live the Left!," *Platypus Review* 1 (November 2007), in *Death of the Millennial Left: Interventions 2006–2022.*

# Revolutionary politics and thought

The last 20th century was characterized as one of wars and revolutions. I would like to re-characterize it slightly, to a century of war and revolution, singular. The 20th century was the century of the crisis of capitalism, and that crisis was expressed through war and revolution. Hannah Arendt's 1962 book *On Revolution* begins its discussion of politics with an introduction on "War and Revolution," offering that these were the two paramount political issues of the day, after all ideological justifications handed down from the 19th century, such as nationalism, capitalism and socialism or communism, had faded.

Arendt began her discussion, properly, with Lenin: Lenin, who called for turning the "world war" among national states into a global "civil war" between the workers and the capitalists — it almost happened. Lenin represented to Arendt the opposition of revolution to war. It is said that a Nazi diplomat once quipped that the only beneficiary of WWII would be Trotsky. For most of the 20th century, this is what was assumed, that war was the failure of politics, and that the political failure of the ruling class in war would lead to social revolution. This was once a reasonable assumption that we cannot however share today, for the political issues of the revolution, while not going away, have been driven underground, no longer manifesting as politics. Arendt's fears have been confirmed: It was her rather hopeful and optimistic prognosis that modern history was the history of revolution, and war merely the revolution's epiphenomenon. Today that is hard for us to perceive.

Arendt predicted that due to "mutual assured nuclear destruction" in the Cold War, the 20th century would cease to be characterized as a century of war but would remain a century of revolution. But the opposite has taken place after the end of the Cold War. It is not that war has been eclipsed by revolution — as Lenin would have hoped — but rather the opposite, that war has eclipsed revolution. Arendt dismissed De Maistre's statement that, "Counterrevolution is not the revolution in reverse but the opposite of revolution."[1] But De Maistre was correct and Arendt mistaken: the 20th century became a century of war not revolution because it was a century of counterrevolution.

To recognize, with von Clausewitz, that "war is politics by other means," does not mean the reverse, that "politics is war by other means." In other words, while the early 19th century liberal Benjamin Constant pointed out that moderns achieve by social commerce and peaceful politics what was once achieved by the Ancients through war, this does not mean that politics is reducible to *war*.[2] If war is politics by other means, then we must add that war is not the best and might indeed be the worst means for achieving political ends. Revolution might be the alternative to war, but that does not mean that war is an acceptable alternative to revolution. It is important as well to note that Arendt recognized that while wars were a timeless, perennial feature of civilization, revolution was quintessentially modern. So, what we might say is that it appears that the 20th century became in retrospect a century of wars rather than revolutions the degree to which revolutionary modernity was rolled back successfully by the counterrevolution.

Arendt discusses "freedom" in an ancient rather than specifically modern sense à la Benjamin Constant, when she points out that for the Ancients wars were fought not for freedom but for gain; and that for moderns revolution is inseparable from freedom: that a particular danger lies in the concept of wars for freedom, precisely because it conflates war and revolution, at the expense of proper political considerations, drowning the separate issues of each in the phenomenon of violence, to which she thought neither revolution nor war could be reduced. However, it would appear that today not only war and revolution are reduced to violence, but also politics and society. Politics seems reduced to "war by other means,"

---

1    *On Revolution* (London: Penguin, 1990), 18.
2    "The Liberty of the Ancients Compared with That of the Moderns" (1819), in *Constant, Political Writings*, ed. Biancamaria Fontana (Cambridge: Cambridge University Press, 1988), 309–328.

indeed to violence by other means. That politics and social power have been reduced to violence is the surest sign of the "success," so to speak, of the counterrevolution. This is what it means for the Left to say that, but for the Right, the revolution would be peaceful, without violence — political force is not violence.

Arendt, like von Clausewitz, sought to preserve the political content of war. But Benjamin Constant, like other liberals, considered war to be, not merely the failure of politics, but a crime. Unlike for the Ancients who celebrated war, indeed as among the highest of values, after every modern war people search for who was criminally culpable for the regrettable catastrophe. Carl Schmitt thought that this pointed to the dehumanization inherent in liberalism, its attempt to suppress the war of politics through its criminalization of war, reducing to his mind society to mere "commerce and entertainment."[3] It should not be for the Left to define politics, like Schmitt, in terms of war. Rather, the issue is the pursuit of freedom without war. If the liberal ideal of bourgeois society as the replacement of war by commerce — by not only peaceful competition but indeed cooperative competition for the benefit of all — has failed, then we must interrogate the nature of that failure and not naturalize it. The liberal ideal may also remain that of socialism.

This raises the issue of war in our particular moment, today, the time of an apparently quickly fading neoconservatism and a continuing if chastened neoliberalism. What are these ideologies with respect to revolution? We might say that there is an antinomy of neoconservatism versus neoliberalism, that neoliberalism prefers to seek to achieve through the market what neoconservatism is content to seek through war, and that this antinomy points to the form of the revolution in our time, that is, *capitalism*, and its political antinomies. For capitalism is the revolution, however it is also the counterrevolution. Both the neoliberals and neoconservatives seek to further the revolution — capitalism — but do so through what Marxists must consider the counterrevolution.

Modern politics, in this sense, can be considered the war, so to speak, within the revolution: the political counterrevolution within the

---

3   *The Concept of the Political* (1927/32).

revolutionizing of society in capitalism, and the yet still ongoing irrepressible revolution of capitalism within the politics of the counterrevolution. Modern politics is concerned with the values of the massive changes occurring within capitalism — the values and direction of the revolution. Once we recognize that modern history does not consist of occasional revolutions but rather of *the* revolution, one single process and trajectory of revolution, which has been more or less poorly manifested, recognized and fought-out, we can better situate the stakes of politics.

The counterrevolution, as the war within the revolution, is the reaction against the failure of the revolution: the degeneration of the revolution into war expressed through the counterrevolution. So what *is* the revolution? The modern era is one of revolution, that is, the overthrow of traditional civilization. The past few hundred years have been characterized by the most far-reaching and deepest ever transformation of the world. More has changed and has changed more rapidly than at any other moment of history. The predominant way in which this change has taken place is through avowed bourgeois social relations, which are essentially the relations of the exchange of labor as a commodity, what Adorno called the "law of labor." This has been recognized clearly by bourgeois protagonists as well as by their adversaries. Both revolutionaries and reactionaries have characterized this process in bourgeois terms, the terms of the modern city.

The American revolutionary Thomas Jefferson offered a clear characterization of the stakes of this revolution of which he was an important advocate and political agent. Jefferson, in his letter of January 3, 1793 to U.S. Ambassador to France William Short about the Jacobins, wrote:

> The tone of your letters had for some time given me pain, on
> account of the extreme warmth with which they censured the
> proceedings of the Jacobins of France. . . . In the struggle which
> was necessary, many guilty persons fell without the forms of
> trial, and with them some innocent. These I deplore as much
> as any body, and shall deplore some of them to the day of
> my death. But I deplore them as I should have done had they
> fallen in battle. It was necessary to use the arm of the people, a
> machine not quite so blind as balls and bombs, but blind to a

certain degree. A few of their cordial friends met at their hands, the fate of enemies. But time and truth will rescue and embalm their memories, while their posterity will be enjoying that very liberty for which they would never have hesitated to offer up their lives. The liberty of the whole earth was depending on the issue of the contest, and was ever such a prize won with so little innocent blood? My own affections have been deeply wounded by some of the martyrs to this cause, but rather than it should have failed, I would have seen half the earth desolated. Were there but an Adam and an Eve left in every country, and left free, it would be better than as it now is.[4]

In 1793, the Jacobins had restarted the calendar, retrospectively beginning with year one of the Republic in 1792. The French Revolution also introduced the metric system of measurements, which has since become the universal standard. A new epoch was to have dawned. That the revolution has since then come to seem not the overthrow but the rather continuation of traditional civilization is only an effect of the need and failure to advance the revolution.

Politics since then has been concerned with the direction of this revolution. Only very isolated extreme figures and only for relatively brief historical intervals have rejected the politics of the bourgeois revolution. For instance, several years ago, in an open letter to President George W. Bush, President of the Islamic Republic in Iran, Mahmoud Ahmadinejad, wrote that the project of liberal democratic capitalism had clearly failed and that therefore it was time to return to the values of traditional civilization in religion, to Islam and Christianity, respectively.[5]

Since the 1970s, there have been two extremely active movements more or less proximate to the centers of political power at a global scale that have sought to further the bourgeois revolution. They have not been of the Left. Neoconservatism and neoliberalism have taken up the mantle abandoned by the Left in promoting the revolution of bourgeois society, promising the

---

4  Available online in the U.S. Government Archives.
5  Available online by the Carnegie Endowment for International Peace (May 9, 2006).

world freedom. In many ways the neoliberals have done so more radically than the neoconservatives. Still, even the neocons must be reckoned as bourgeois revolutionaries — which their traditionalist paleoconservative rivals, let alone the religious fundamentalists, have clearly recognized. The strange bedfellows of Christian conservatives and neoconservatives have fought the properly political battle of what Lenin called the "who-whom" question: Have the Christians used the neocons, or the neocons used the Christians? I think it is clear that the neocons, though now ideologically discredited on certain policy questions (after the Iraq war in particular), won that battle: they used the Christians to attain political power. But the neoliberals have, despite recent global economic crisis of the past several years, really triumphed. Neoliberalism is the "new normal" throughout the world; Margaret Thatcher was right, "There is no alternative." Furthermore, it is under neoliberal leadership that the world is currently being revolutionized. We might say that the neoliberals have fought in the vanguard, and the neoconservatives in the rearguard, of the continuing bourgeois revolution over the course of the past generation, the last 40 years.

Where does this leave the avowed "Left," today? There has been a great deal of confusion in the past generation in particular, but also more broadly since the early 20th century, about the direction and stakes of the revolution from the point of view of the "Left." Arendt, for instance, pointed out how it was remarkable that freedom had dropped out of the vocabulary of revolutionaries. What would have been obvious to Marx and Engels, or to Lenin or Trotsky as Marxists, that the struggle for socialism was to further and complete, and ultimately transcend the bourgeois revolution in freedom, has become an obscure issue today.

Marx and Engels's *Communist Manifesto* parsed out the issue of socialism in the 19th century in terms of conservative-reactionary versus progressive-emancipatory varieties, deeming only "proletarian socialism" a reliable agent of overcoming the problem of capitalism in the emancipatory direction of freedom. Other varieties were deemed "petit-bourgeois," that is, reproductive of the problem of capitalism and obscuring its essential contradictions. The original socialist critique of capitalism was that the capitalists were unreliable revolutionaries, too opportunistically conservative to confidently promote the revolution of which they had been however the beneficiaries historically. Rather, that task of fulfilling the revolution in modern society had fallen to the working class.

In the 20th century, this became muddled, in that "new revolutionary subjects" were sought to promote the revolution after the apparent failure of the working class in the advanced capitalist countries to further the revolutionary advance to socialism. But today these purported new social-revolutionary classes and social groups have also clearly failed. Neither peasants nor anti-colonialists nor oppressed ethno-cultural minorities nor women nor sexual deviants have furthered the advance of socialism. If anything, such politics have only confounded the issue even more. We are left with the problem of the results of incomplete revolution — capitalism — but without any apparent revolutionary subjects to address and overcome this problem. The best on offer seems an indeterminate "democracy," but that has a storied and problematic history as well, going back to the Jacobins themselves if not earlier. Moreover, since the mid-19th century, the democratic revolution has been an engine for the reproduction of capitalism.

What the revolution has given us since Marx's time is not socialism but more extensive and deeper capitalism. Moreover, Marx's recognition of the revolutionary character of capitalism has been lost. The reproduction of capitalism has taken largely conservative-reactionary forms. This is because the issue of capitalism itself has become obscured. This has had a profound effect on politics itself. The ostensible "Left" has allowed itself to become defensive, and to thus imagine that the principal task has been, rather, the "resistance" to capitalism. A one-sided and confused "anti-capitalism" has replaced the struggle for socialism. Worse, the "Left" has internalized not only cynicism about the bourgeois revolution, but even the conservative-reactionary rejection of the revolution itself. Marx has gone from being a revolutionary to becoming a "master of suspicion," and has been profoundly misread as skeptical or even cynical regarding modern, bourgeois society and its revolutionary potential. The "Left" has thus become a new Right. It has not only compromised itself but actively contributes to the confounding and obscuring of the revolution that still tasks the world.

This means that only opportunists — the Right — have allowed themselves to be politically active, but have been compromised in their activity precisely by such opportunism. Neoliberalism and neoconservativism are clear examples of this, but so is political religious fundamentalism. But before them so was Stalinism. As Trotsky put it, Stalinism was the "great organizer of defeat," meaning the political "leadership" of the organized accommodation of defeat. As such, Stalinism was also, ideologically, the apologetics for defeat. This was done through calling defeat victory, or, the affirming of the course of the revolution through opportunistic grief. Thus, the 20th century was called "progress" when there was none. No wonder that postmodernism's opposition to Marxism — really to Stalinism — was first and foremost an opposition to ideas of historical progress and of history — that is, universal history itself.

What characterizes the last two hundred years is the relative lack of consciousness, and unfortunately increasingly so, of the on-going bourgeois revolution. To date, Marxism has offered not merely the best but really the only way out of this deficiency of consciousness. Specifically, Marxism offered the diagnosis of the necessary if symptomatic character of that lack of consciousness. The bourgeois revolution without consciousness is what Marx called "capitalism;" it was the rendering of the revolution "objective" — an object of mere contemplation, an unfolding catastrophe rather than a process of freedom — abdicating the task of consciousness, which alone could offer the possibility of the continuation of the revolution as a matter of freedom.

If we experience the return, the repetition of the bourgeois revolution, then this is as the reproduction of capitalism. But the repetition is an opportunity for advancing the revolution, if however its self-contradiction, the war of the counterrevolution within the failure of the revolution, still dominates us. The task of revolutionary thinking, therefore, would be the recognition of the repetition and of the contradiction.

Presented on April 5th, 2014 at the sixth annual Platypus International Convention at the School of the Art Institute of Chicago on a panel discussion with Samir Gandesha (Simon Fraser University), Nikos Malliaris (Lieux Communs), Dimitrios Roussopoulos (Transnational Institute of Social Ecology) and Joseph Schwartz (Temple University).

Originally published in *Platypus Review* 69 (September 2014)

# When was the crisis of capitalism?

## Moishe Postone and the legacy of the 1960s New Left

Lenin stated, infamously perhaps, that Marxists aimed to overcome capitalism "on the basis of capitalism itself." This was in the context of horrors of not only industrial exploitation but also and especially of war: WWI. Lenin was not, as he might be mistaken to be, merely advocating so-called "war communism" or statist capitalism.[1] No. Lenin recognized state capitalism as the advancing of the contradiction of capitalism. By contrast, after Lenin, there was state capitalism, but no active political consciousness of its contradiction. This affected the Left as it developed — degenerated — subsequently.[2]

The question is, when was the definitive crisis of capitalism, after which it could be plausibly asserted that the world suffered from the overripeness for change? Was it in 1968, as the New Left supposed? Or was it much earlier, in WWI, as Marxists such as Lenin thought?

Moishe Postone is arguably the — by far — most important interpreter of Marx to come out of the generation of the 1960s–70s "New Left." Contributing to that generation's "return to Marx," motivated by the widespread discontents and political crisis of the 1960s, and finding increased purchase in the economic crisis and downturn of the '70s, Postone's work on Marx

---

1    Lenin wrote that,

> The bourgeoisie makes it its business to promote trusts, drive women and children into the factories, subject them to corruption and suffering, condemn them to extreme poverty. We do not 'demand' such development, we do not 'support' it. We fight it. But *how* do we fight? We explain that trusts and the employment of women in industry are progressive. We do not want a return to the handicraft system, pre-monopoly capitalism, domestic drudgery for women. Forward through the trusts, etc., and beyond them to socialism! (*The Military Programme of the Proletarian Revolution*, 1916/17).

2    See my "1873–1973: The century of Marxism," *Platypus Review* 47 (June 2012), in this volume.

participated in the shaping of the self-understanding of the transition from what has been called the "Keynesian-Fordist" synthesis of predominant modes of capitalism in the mid-20th century to its neoliberal form starting in the 1970s. If Postone, as well as others of the New Left generation, found neoliberalism to be the travesty of the emancipatory aspirations of the 1960s, where does this leave his work today? For Postone's work was very much of its moment, the 1960s–70s. It recalls an earlier era.

A full generation has passed since Postone's initial works,[3] and 20 years since publication of his book *Time, Labor and Social Domination* (1993): younger readers of Marx who encounter Postone's interpretation are likely to have been born after Postone's formulations were written and published. The recent economic crisis, the still on-going "Great Recession," has prompted a renewed "return to Marx" moment that has reached back to the prior generation's return to Marx in the 1960s–70s. The most perspicacious of young would-be *Marxisants* have discovered Postone's work, and have begun to try to make sense of the present in Postone's terms.

Such belated recognition of Postone's work is well and long-deserved and can only be welcomed by anyone interested in Marx's distinctive and indeed *sui generis* approach to the problem of capitalism.

Postone's specific contribution was to direct attention to Marx's critique of the relation between abstract labor and abstract time in the self-contradiction of value in capital. This allowed Postone to recognize how Marx grasped the accumulation of history in capital, the antagonism between "dead labor" and "living labor" in the ongoing reproduction of capital and of the social relations of the exchange of labor in the commodity form of value.

Much of the basis for resistance to Postone's critical insights into Marx's approach to capitalism, largely of a political character, has since fallen away. This centered on the question of "proletarian-transcending" vs. "proletarian-constituting" politics and the problem of the "ontology of labor." At the same time, however, the political assumption for Postone's work — the possibility of transcending the politics of labor — has become eroded and undermined along with the basis for resistance to it: Postone's

---

3    See Moishe Postone, "Necessity, Labor, and Time: A Reinterpretation of the Marxian Critique of Capitalism," *Social Research* 45, no. 4 (Winter 1978).

object of critique in recovering Marx in the 1960s–70s has largely if not entirely disappeared. Most importantly, the political prognosis that motivated Postone was falsified by subsequent history: Postone's work was not able to help clarify the New Left moment to itself because the New Left failed in its aspirations. It did not help to transcend capitalism.

## Liberal and statist periods of capitalism — individualist and collectivist discontents

The failure of the New Left is a deeply obscure problem because its success wears the mask of failure and its failure wears the mask of success: the New Left failed precisely where it thought it succeeded; and succeeded precisely where it thought it failed. But neither its failure nor its success had anything to do with being part of the history of the Left but rather with its furnishing the ideological consciousness for a renewed Right.

For instance, where the New Left thought it transformed with greater freedom a diversely heterogeneous multiplicity of socio-cultural practices, relations and identities, for instance, of "race, gender and sexuality," as against what it supposed was a stultifying, oppressive and even genocidal homogenizing social conformism rooted in industrial-capitalist labor, in fact it smoothed the way towards even more widespread and deeper social participation in the capitalist labor process on a global scale that has not made corporations and governments more responsible to their constituencies but rather more intractably elusive as targets of political action.

Few on the avowed "Left" today would claim that there has been greater progress against capitalism let alone towards socialism since the 1960s: whatever the "balance sheet" of "gains and losses" in the past generation, the scale tilts ineluctably in the direction of loss. Still, the idea that "we know better now," as an accomplishment of and development beyond the New Left, is unfortunately prevalent.

But every generation thinks it improves upon previous ones. It is this assumption of progress that is perhaps the most pernicious of ideological phenomena of consciousness.

The metaphysics of consciousness — the fact that consciousness transcends its concrete empirical moment in time and space — means that history does not constitute merely a factual record of events, but rather that purported historical "causality" is grasped only according to changes in "theoretical" perspectives on our on-going practices and their reproduction in society. History is not merely a set of accumulated effects but a development of consciousness — or at least should be, according to Hegel.[4] The question is whether and how the development of social practices has facilitated or rather hindered and retarded — perhaps even blocked — the further development of consciousness.

So, what kind of consciousness is provided by Moishe Postone's work, and how has this been grasped by Postone's followers? What does this tell us about the history from the formative moment of Postone's consciousness to the present?

## The 1960s New Left moment

It is necessary to characterize the moment of the 1960s New Left. What kind of an opportunity was that moment?

The 1960s saw the deepening crisis of the Keynesian-Fordist liberal social-democratic "welfare state." In the United States, which set the pattern for the rest of the world, the New Deal political coalition of the leading Democratic Party became unraveled. First, the Civil Rights Movement undermined the Democrats in the South, the so-called "Dixiecrats." Then, the U.S. military involvement in Vietnam undermined the administration of President Lyndon Baines Johnson. The Civil Rights Movement offered to go "part of the way with LBJ" in the election of 1964, in hopes of trading a quieting of protest against the U.S. anti-Communist war in Southeast Asia for LBJ's support for Civil Rights legislation. Johnson's reelection raised the prospects of a crisis in the Democratic Party, which was seen as an opportunity for its transformation. Bayard Rustin wrote that it was necessary to move the Civil Rights Movement "From Protest to Politics" in order to remake the Democrats into a party of blacks and labor, building upon the labor unions' support for both the Civil Rights Movement and the new Students for a Democratic Society that emerged from the Civil Rights and

---

4    Hegel, *Reason In History: A General Introduction to the Philosophy of History.*

student Free Speech Movements of the late 1950s – early '60s. This didn't happen, but rather the Republicans' "Southern Strategy" first floated in the 1964 election but fully realized in 1968 moved the southern Democratic voters to the Republicans' camp. The tide change in U.S. politics is illustrated by the contrast between the 1952 and 1968 Presidential elections: Where the Democrats lost to Dwight Eisenhower in 1952, Adlai Stevenson winning only states in the Deep South; in 1968 the South provided the base for Republican Richard Nixon's victory. What Rustin's plan would have meant was a rejuvenation of the New Deal Coalition under changed conditions. It failed. The Democrats, who had been the majority party since 1932, went on the defensive, however holding onto Congressional majorities all the way up to the 1994 "Republican Revolution" led by Newt Gingrich. Since the 1930s, the Republicans were the party of opposition, which is still the case today in 2014. The Democrats have remained most often the majority party in Congress. The Republicans have never enjoyed the sustained occupation of the Presidency and majority in Congress that the Democrats have enjoyed more or less consistently since the 1930s. This character of ruling-class politics in the U.S. has meant certain conditions for any purported "Left."

In the 1960s, being on the "Left" politically meant opposing an overwhelming Democratic majority government, and moreover one which claimed to be in the interest of working-class and minority people. The 1930s New Deal Coalition saw an uneasy alliance of white working class people including in the South with ethnic minority constituencies in the Northern cities, cities which exploded in the 1960s. For instance, it was only in the 1930s that blacks began voting in large numbers for Democrats, having supported Republicans since the Civil War and Reconstruction. Blacks were integrated into the Democrats' New Deal Coalition as yet another Northern urban ethnic constituency vote: Adam Clayton Powell personified this politics. There was the Great Migration of blacks out of the South to the North from the period of WWI through WWII and the unionization of blacks through the Congress of Industrial Unions (CIO) in the 1930s Great Depression-era radicalization as well as in the war industries of the 1940s.

By the mid-1960s, LBJ, who was far more supportive of Civil Rights demands than JFK had been, while dramatically escalating the war in Vietnam, was opposed by the emergent New Left as a "fascist" — a representative of the authoritarian state that seemed to stand in the way of social change rather than as its instrument. The Civil Rights Movement's pressure on the Democratic Party (seen in the Mississippi Freedom Democrats' protest at the 1964 national convention) was met by the military risk to the state in the Cold War running hot in Southeast Asia.

A note on the Vietnam War: The U.S. proceeded through the Korean War and into the Vietnam War with the attempt to sustain and mobilize the United Nations of WWII, turning from opposition to fascism to opposing Communist "totalitarianism": the U.S. prosecuted both the Korean War and increasingly in the 1960s the Vietnam War as extensions of strategies pursued in WWII and its immediate aftermath. The Greek Civil War set the pattern for counter-insurgency in the post-WWII world. Already in Korea the U.S. and its allies pursued counterinsurgency and not only a conventional military war. In Vietnam, counterinsurgency gave way to conventional warfare with the bombing campaigns initiated by LBJ and pursued further by Nixon succeeding him. The form of warfare pursued placed certain pressures on the Keynesian-Fordist social-democratic "welfare state" administered by the U.S. Democratic Party's New Deal Coalition. Those pressures were political and socio-cultural as well as economic: such pressures were political-economic and social-political in character, setting the stage for the New Left.

The U.S. New Deal Coalition's alliance of labor with the "welfare state" set the pattern throughout the world in the Cold War era, both in advanced capitalist countries and in newly independent post-colonial states. Its unraveling also set the historical political pattern, for student and worker discontent, in the 1960s. Moreover, discontent with the conservatism of the Soviet-bloc by the end of the 1950s meant an identification of the New Deal Coalition and the social-democratic "welfare state" with Stalinism in "state capitalism" and "state socialism," both regarded as politically compromised obstacles to new upsurges "from below" in the 1960s. Political problems of both capitalism and socialism were thus identified with the state.

The political defections identified with the crisis of the Democrats' New Deal Coalition involved not only the disaffection of blacks and other workers, especially among younger people, but also intellectuals of the establishment. There was a crisis in the ideological edifice of the post-WWII state. For instance, "neo-conservatism" was a phenomenon of the loss of confidence in the Democrats' successful prosecution of the Cold War, both at home and abroad. Many former supporters of and even ideologues for the Democrats provided the brain-trust for the Republicans taking political advantage of this crisis. For instance, there was former Frankfurt School assistant Daniel Bell, who first supported and then opposed the Democrats on grounds of non-ideological technocracy.

Thus discontents with the post-WWII state were far-ranging and even endemic by the 1960s, reaching both down among those marginalized at the bottom of society and up into top echelons of governmental power.

In France, May 1968 was a deep crisis of the post-WWII Gaullist state. It began as a student protest against gender segregation of student dormitories — against the educational — institutional repression of sex — and grew into a student and working class mass mobilization against the state. It was rightly regarded as a potential revolutionary situation. But it failed politically. Many on the French New Left became a New Right.

Moishe Postone characterized this as a crisis of "new social movements" expressing discontents with "state capitalism" as a historical formation. That formation could trace it roots, prior to the 1940s and WWII and the Great Depression of the '30s, back to WWI and perhaps even further, back to the late 19th century transformations that took place after the economic crisis of 1873, such as the post-Civil War and Reconstruction "imperial Presidency" in the U.S., Bismarckian policies in Germany, state-sponsored capitalist development in Meiji Restoration Japan, among other phenomena.

## 1968 and 1917

Postone attributes "state capitalism" to the crisis of WWI and the Russian Revolution of 1917 and characterizes Lenin and Trotsky's Bolsheviks as unwitting instruments of state capitalism. In this view, in certain respects common with and descending from the Frankfurt School of the 1930s, Lassallean social democracy, fascism, Lenin's Bolshevism as well as ostensible "Leninism" (meaning Stalinism), Keynesianism (FDR New Deal-ism), all participated in the turn from 19th century liberal laissez-faire capitalism to 20th century state capitalism, which went into crisis by the time of the 1960s New Left.

The crisis of modernist state capitalism led, however, not to socialism in Marx's sense but rather to the neoliberal "postmodernist" turn of capitalism in the 1970s-80s, leading to the present. Postone's idea was that the 20th century was a "post-bourgeois" form of capitalism. But for the Frankfurt School, it was a form of bourgeois society *in extremis*: as Adorno put it, "the new is the old in distress."[5]

There is an important equivocation with respect to the Russian Revolution in Postone's view. Postone condemns the USSR et al.'s "state capitalism," as not merely inadequate but also misleading regarding potential possibilities for socialism. But such state capitalism was (and remains) a form of political mediation of the working class to the means of production. Postone, despite his critique of and political opposition to Soviet Communism, addresses the USSR as a progressive development, in ways that Adorno, for instance (or Trotsky in his critique of Stalinism), did not. Rather, the USSR et al. (as well as fascism) could be regarded as a decadent, barbaric form of bourgeois society, rather than as Postone attempted to address it, as "post-bourgeois." On the other hand, Postone is (retrospectively) opposed to Lenin and Trotsky's Bolsheviks in the October Revolution, whereas Adorno and other members of the Frankfurt School were supportive. Postone treats such support as a combination of theoretical blindness and historical limitation — unripeness of the means as well as the relations of production for socialism. The character of that "progress" — really, regression — of capitalism in the 20th century would be in terms of advancing the contradiction of the commodity form of labor, and how to make sense of and work through that contradiction politically.

The proletariat would need to be constituted politically, subjectively, and not merely "objectively" (economically). The commodity form of the value of labor needs to be constituted through political action, but such action, today, like at any moment since the Industrial Revolution, would manifest the *self-contradiction* of the commodity form.

The question is, what constitutes a "social relation"? It must be addressed not as a static fact but a developing social activity in history.

---

5    Theodor W. Adorno "Reflections on Class Theory," *Can One Live after Auschwitz?*, ed. Rolf Tiedemann (University of California Press, 2003), 95.

Postone addresses it economically but not politically. In this he follows Marx's *Capital*, which however was left incomplete and hence not mediated "all the way up" to the level of politics — as if Marx never wrote anything else that indicated his politics. Yes, the question is, as Postone puts it, not the existence of a capitalist (that is, private-property-in-the-means-of-production owning) class, but rather the existence of a proletariat, in the sense of a class of people who relate to the means of production through their social activity of wage-labor. That class still exists, "objectively" economically, but the question is, how is it mediated, today, politically?

## Do we still live in capitalism?

James Heartfield has pointed out that the present-day "Left" considers such Marxist categories as "class" to be "objective." This has effaced the purchase of politics regarding capitalism. If the working class has ceased to constitute itself as a class "for itself," subjectively, then this has affected politics more generally.[6] Moreover, it means that the working class is not even constituted as a class "in itself," objectively. For Marx, there was a subject-object dialectic at work — in which subjectivity was objectively determined, and objectivity was subjectively determined, in practice — in the working class's struggle for socialism.

Marx pointed out that after the Industrial Revolution, the working class can only constitute its labor-power as a commodity collectively. Marx also pointed out that the capitalist class is constituted as such, as capitalist, only in opposition to the working class's collective demands for the value of its labor. This was because, as Postone points out, for Marx, the dynamics of the value of the time of labor has become that of society as a whole. For Marx, the collective bargaining for the value of labor-power measured in time does not take place at the level of trade unions in individual firms or even in industrial unions across entire fields of production, but rather at the societal level in the form of the workers' political struggle for socialism. Without that struggle for socialism, the working class is not constituted as such, and so neither is the capitalist class. Rather, as Adorno observed in

---

6    "The left is over? I hate to say I told you so," *Sp!ked* (May 9, 2014).

the mid-20th century, society had devolved into a war of "rackets" and had thus ceased to be "society" in the bourgeois sense at all. Politics for Marx was the "class struggle" — the struggle for socialism. Without that, politics itself, as Marx understood it, ceases.

In this sense, we must confront the question of whether we still live in capitalism as Marxists historically understood it. An admirer of Postone, Jamie Merchant of the *Permanent Crisis* blog, spoke in dialogue with Elmar Flatschart of *EXIT!* and Alan Milchman of *Internationalist Perspective* at a Platypus panel discussion on *Wertkritik*. They stated the following in response to the question that I posed to them:

> *Neoliberalism might well have obscured the experience of the Fordist era, rendering it more esoteric, but didn't Fordism, and the nationalism from which it is inseparable, in its own way occlude even deeper issues of capitalism? Elmar [Flatschart], you warn against "privileging" the workers as a revolutionary subject, but you seem to conflate earlier Marxism, in which the proletariat's role is characterized negatively, with 20th century Stalinism and Social Democracy. What other subject would manifest the self-overcoming of capitalism "on the basis of capitalism itself," as Lenin put it in "Left-Wing" Communism: An Infantile Disorder (1920)?*

**EF:** Marx had a negative notion of class, insofar as he saw it as immanent to capitalism and this is evident in the logical approach of *Capital*. But then again you already have with Marx, and more so with Engels, this political privileging of class as an emancipatory actor. There were no other questions of oppression, and hence no other emancipatory subjectivities. There is no one subject anymore, and this is what we can learn from the New Left and the postmodern turn.

**JM:** Yes, Fordism definitely occluded capital in many ways, especially, in the Cold War context, in terms of the role of the nation-state. But my point was that it was a form of society in which the social whole did appear, and so the idea of society had more currency. There was this concern during the Fordist period of the individual being absorbed into the social whole and losing individualism. But this was just the inversion of the cultural logic of neoliberalism. The point is that different periods of accumulation provide different versions of society and apprehension of the "social"; the social form appears in differently mediated ways. Different regimes of accumulation can lead to different perceptions of what society is, which could open up avenues for new forms of politics.[7]

These responses seem rather optimistic, especially regarding the legacy of the 1960s–70s New Left moment, let alone that of 1980s–90s postmodernism. Postone avers that whereas traditional Marxism affirmed and indeed aspired to the social totality of capitalism, true socialism would abolish it. But the question is its transformation — its "sublation" (*Aufhebung*). If Marxism ever recognized capitalism as a "totality," it was *critically*, as a totality of *crisis*, a *total* crisis of society, which the struggle for socialism would *advance*, and not immediately overcome. But the crisis has been occulted, appearing only in disparate phenomena whose interrelatedness remains obscure.

Postone offered the clearest consciousness of the discontents of the 1960s understood as the first opportunity to transcend capitalism, by transcending proletarian-constituting forms of politics. But this was not transcended but rather liquidated without redemption. To transcend proletarian politics, it would be necessary first to constitute it.

We continue to pay the price for past failures of Marxism, which have become naturalized and hypostatized: reified. In this sense, we must still redeem Lenin. We still need to overcome capitalism on the basis of capitalism itself.

Originally published in *Platypus Review* 70 (October 2014)

---

7   "Marx and 'Wertkritik,'" *Platypus Review* 56 (May 2013).

# The self-overcoming of labor

## Beyond capitalism

Like all great thinkers, Marx ends up being saddled with responsibility for the very category that he is taking under critical consideration. So he is mistaken to be an *advocate*, whereas in fact he is a *critic*, regarding the so-called "labor theory of value." Marx doesn't have a labor theory of value, but he's rather a critic of it — and not merely a critic, rather, he is mounting a *critique* of it, i.e. how labor as value might point beyond itself. An analogy would be Friedrich Nietzsche. If you ask most people about Nietzsche as a philosopher, they would say he's a nihilist — whereas actually what he was doing was not advocating nihilism, but trying to diagnose nihilism as a symptom, specifically one that needed a self-overcoming, a *Selbstauf-hebung*, a self-fulfillment in self-negation. I think that turn of phrase from Nietzsche, which both is and is not in the tradition of German Idealism that Marx is in, is helpful for thinking about Marx's approach to labor as value: He looks forward to the self-overcoming of labor as value. So, with respect to this, we're talking about not a positive theory of labor as value, but a critical theory of labor as value, and specifically labor, as value, is in crisis in capitalism, for Marx. In other words, there's a crisis of labor as value in capitalism, which Marx regards as a symptom of a possible and necessary change. So let me say something about labor, and then I'll say something about value. I know we're going to have a presentation on Hannah Arendt's *The Human Condition* (or *Vita Activa*, as it was titled in German) and a distinction that Arendt makes is helpful in this regard. She distinguishes between: (1) *activity*; (2) *work*, which is transformative activity, as not all activity is transformative, but work is transformative activity, not only of the object that's being worked on, but indeed transformative of the subject; and then there's (3) *labor*, which is work, its transformative activity, in society. In other words, it's the value of work. Not all work is labor, just as not all activity is work.

A famous formulation of Marx's with respect to this is "the emancipation of labor," what he's inheriting from the greater socialist and communist tradition, the idea that the emancipation of society demands the emancipation of labor. But in fact, for Marx, this is a fulfillment of what is already the *desideratum* of bourgeois society — i.e. bourgeois society is itself understood as the emancipation of labor, the emancipation of the transformative activity of work, and its valuation in society. Just to point out the history for this: John Locke, the theorist of the Glorious Revolution in England, really the consolidation of the bourgeois revolution in England in the late 17th century, had formulated that the right to property was grounded in labor; in other words, that the actual right to property was not a right of might, but a right of labor: it's something that needs to be recognized in society. And in the Great French Revolution of 1789, the most prevalent revolutionary pamphlet was the Abbé Sieyès's *What is the Third Estate?*, in which he talked about the estates in the Estates-General that were being called in the crisis of the Ancien Régime. The First Estate, what does it do? It prays, because it is the Church. The Second Estate, the aristocracy, what does it do? It fights. The Third Estate, however, the commoners (which is at least 95 percent of the population), what do they do? They *work*. He said that under the old regime, the Third Estate was nothing, but now it shall be everything. In other words, the value of work, which was negligible in terms of the organization of society in Medievalism, in Christianity, the activity of the commoners counted for nothing, but now it will count for everything, it will be the principle of society. So indeed, the bourgeois revolution was announced in terms of the rights of labor and the social recognition of work.

Now I want to turn to Marx's passage from the *Grundrisse*, just to put this issue of bourgeois society and labor on the table:

Thus the ancient conception, in which man always appears (in however narrowly national, religious, or political a definition) as the aim of production, seems very much more exalted than the modern world, in which production is the aim of man and wealth the aim of production.[1]

What he's doing here is engaging in a reversal of means and ends. He thought that in the ancient conception — meaning everything that came before the modern — a definite form of humanity, or definite forms of humanity in the caste system, was the aim of the activity of society. In other words, everything was geared towards producing a definite way of life. Whereas now, production is not a means towards a definite end, but rather production has become an end in itself, the very aim is production itself. He says:

> In fact, however, when the narrow bourgeois form has been peeled away, what is wealth, if not the universality of needs, capacities, enjoyments, productive powers etc., of individuals, produced in universal exchange?[2]

I want to highlight there that production and exchange are inextricable for Marx, in other words, production is in this sense a *social* form, and exchange is the form of this social production.

> What, if not the full development of human control over the forces of nature — those of his own nature as well as those of so-called "nature"? What, if not the absolute elaboration of his creative dispositions, without any preconditions other than antecedent historical evolution which make the totality of this evolution — i.e., the evolution of all human powers as such, unmeasured by any previously established yardstick — an end in itself? What is this, if not a situation where man does not reproduce in any determined form, but produces his totality? Where he does not seek to remain something formed by the past, but is in the absolute movement of becoming? In

---

1  "Pre-capitalist economic formations," *Grundrisse* (1857-58).
2  Ibid.

> bourgeois political economy — and in the epoch of production to which it corresponds — this complete elaboration of what lies within man, appears as the total alienation, and the destruction of all fixed, one-sided purposes as the sacrifice of the end in itself to a wholly external compulsion. Hence in one way the childlike world of the ancients appears to be superior; and this is so, insofar as we seek for closed shape, form and established limitation. The ancients provide a narrow satisfaction, whereas the modern world leaves us unsatisfied, or, where it appears to be satisfied with itself, is vulgar and mean.[3]

I want to unpack that a little bit, in order to get at what I'm trying to address, namely production for the sake of production. This is the bourgeois epoch's conception — not only theoretically, but in practice — of *freedom*. Freedom is production for the sake of production, in this open-ended manner, the "absolute movement of becoming." But what we have, according to Marx, in the era of capitalism, is that this production for the sake of production has seemed to appear "satisfied with itself," and thus has become "vulgar and mean."

The distinction that I'd like to make is between the idea of society as a society of production for production's sake, and what we have in capitalism, which is not production for the sake of production, but rather production for the sake of *value*. This brings us back to the issue of labor as value — does Marx have a labor theory of value, or rather does he have a critique of labor as value? In other words, has a society that is pursuing production for the sake of production actually outgrown labor as value? In a way, the bourgeois conception is this kind of Promethean notion of human labor as productive. So I wanted to invoke there the classic definition that Marx has of capitalism, namely that the capitalist mode of production is a contradiction — as a mode of production it's a contradiction in itself — between "bourgeois social relations" on the one hand, and, on the other hand, the "industrial forces of production." The industrial forces of production are outstripping and pointing beyond the bourgeois social relations. These

---

3   Ibid.

bourgeois social relations have usually been understood as private property and the market: private property in the means of production, and the market form of the exchange of goods and the realization of value in capital. What I'd like to offer is that in fact the bourgeois social relations are not essentially private property in the means of production by the capitalists, but the value of labor, in other words, wage-labor as a social relation. That's what's holding back the industrial forces of production, for Marx. Again, this is the distinction between production for the sake of production, in which case, for instance for someone like Adam Smith, labor as value is a means to the end — if you want to maximize production for the sake of production, you can use labor as value to mediate a society effectively to emancipate production. What Smith could not have foreseen, but which is Marx's concern, is what happens with the Industrial Revolution, when labor as value ceases to be an adequate means for emancipating production, and thus ceases to be adequate to the task of freeing production in the unlimited way he calls for here.

In that respect, the issue is how labor as value has itself generated and continues to generate these industrial forces of production, in other words, continues to generate a crisis, a situation pointing beyond itself, how labor in its own activity in society points beyond itself, and points beyond the bourgeois conception of humanity as *homo faber* and *homo economicus*. The bourgeois conception is that there has been this long history of human development from the Paleolithic hunter-gatherers, up through settled, subsistence agriculture, and now into bourgeois production, in which humans are the producing animal — they make things, *homo faber* — and they produce with increasing efficiency — *homo economicus*. The history of humanity as the history of *homo faber* and *homo economicus* is of course not actually true of past forms of humanity, but is the way that bourgeois society appropriates all of human history to itself, so, e.g. it appears that the so-called "hunter-gatherers" had a "division of labor." Did they have a division of labor? No, they actually just had a gendered way of relating to the totemic species, in which the men hunted and the women gathered. It's not a division of labor, a mode of production. Did peasants, in the long history of traditional civilization practicing subsistence agriculture, constitute a mode of production? Can we say that agriculture was their mode of "absolute movement of becoming"? Not really. But from the bourgeois standpoint this looks as if this is the case, it looks as if what humans have always been doing is perfecting production, perfecting their production with respect to nature, and with respect to themselves. That has not always been the case, it has rather been the case specifically in the emancipation of society in the bourgeois era, and it will not always be the case. So, for Marx, the crisis of capitalism is actually marking, as he puts it, the potential end of "pre-history," and the beginning of "true" human history. What that would mean is that in fact we would cast the history of the human species that is projected back from bourgeois society as the history of production, as the history in a sense of human labor, into pre-history, if socialism and communism were attained. In other words, we would transcend this conception of human nature that is specific to the bourgeois epoch.

Marx thinks this has happened precisely through the demand, in the industrial era, of workers for the value of their labor. What came up earlier was the distinction between "formal" and "real subsumption," and the related but not identical distinction between "relative" and "absolute surplus value." Of course, these are not discrete periods in time, but are both constitutive, and reproduce a contradiction in capitalism, meaning that we always have an interaction of formal and real subsumption, we always have an interaction of absolute and relative surplus value. We always have the paradox of overwork and unemployment, we always have sweatshops and robots, and in a sense, we've always had that since the very beginning of the Industrial Revolution. Now Marx thought that this has come about precisely because of the political crisis caused by the Industrial Revolution, and by the workers' own class struggle against the capitalists in the Industrial Revolution, for example, with the Chartists in England, or the rising of the weavers in Lyon in France — this period of the early 19th century, at the close of the first phase of the Industrial Revolution. In fact, things like wage levels, subsistence levels, norms for all kinds of aspects of social reproduction, the reproduction of the workforce in society, according to Marx in "The Working Day" chapter of *Das Kapital*, are extremely variable, they're the product of political struggle, of cultural-social norms, legal reforms, etc. For instance, it became "un-Christian" to exploit people, so it was Christian pastors in England who led the fight to get the workers to have at least one day off, Sunday, because it's un-Christian to work them on the Sabbath. And it became un-Christian to work women and children in the factory era. These are all not part of the strictly *economic* logic of labor as value, but are actually extrinsic to it — they are external constraints imposed for political, cultural, social reasons, and it's this that in fact motivates and impels the introduction of machines into the factory process.

I can come around to my end-point, then, quickly. I want to conclude on a paradoxical formulation that Marx has, with respect to a world beyond labor. He says that work will go from "life's prime need," to becoming "life's prime want." We will no longer work because we need to, out of the false necessity of the social valorization-process of capital — in other words, capital itself has to justify itself with respect to labor as value. We will no longer work because we *need* to; in that respect, we will overcome the *social* necessity for work. We will work because we *want* to. In other words, the degree to which humans engage in transformative activity, activity that transforms nature and transforms ourselves, it is because we want to, not because we need to. Therefore, we will have transcended the value of work in society, as we now experience it: we will transcend labor as value. So we will not necessarily transcend *work*, but we will transcend *labor*, labor as a *social* principle, beyond capitalism.

Presented at the symposium on *Architecture as a Political Practice* at Archeworks, Chicago, October 29, 2016.

Originally published in *After the Revolution III Labor* (2017), 807–17

# Ends of philosophy

## Misery

Marxism considered philosophy as "bourgeois ideology." This meant, first and foremost, radical bourgeois philosophy, the modern philosophy of bourgeois emancipation, the thought of the revolt of the Third Estate. But pre-bourgeois philosophy, traditional philosophy, was also addressed as bourgeois ideology, as ideology. But ideology is a modern phenomenon. There's little point in calling either Aristotle or Augustine "ideology." It is when philosophy is invoked in bourgeois society that it becomes ideological. (Religion, too!)

So what is meant by philosophy as "ideology"?

This goes to the issue of Marxist "ideology-critique." What did Marxism mean by ideology as "false consciousness"? "False" in what way? For if bourgeois ideology were considered the ideology of the sociological group of the bourgeoisie — capitalists — then there would be nothing "false" about it: it would be the consciousness adequate to the social being of the ruling class; it would be the true consciousness of the bourgeoisie. So it must be false not for the bourgeoisie but rather for others — for the "proletariat." This kind of "class analysis" of ideology would be concerned that the workers not fall for the ideology of the ruling class. It would be a warning against the workers adopting the idealism of the bourgeoisie that would blind them to their real social condition in capitalism. The idea here is that somehow the workers would remain ignorant of their exploitation by the capitalists if they remained mired in bourgeois ideology.

Of course Marxism was originally no such "material analysis" — debunking — of wrong thinking. No.

Rather, the original Marxist ideology-critique — Marx and Engels's ideology-critique of bourgeois society — was the immanent dialectical critique of the way society in capitalism necessarily appears to its members, bourgeois and proletarian — capitalists and workers — alike. It was the critique of the true consciousness of the workers as well as of the capitalists.

Now, that formulation just lost me 99% of ostensible "Marxists" as well as all of the rest of the "Left," whether socialist or liberal, who do indeed think that the poor benighted workers and other subaltern need us intellectuals to tell them what their true social interests are.

This is not what Marxism — Marx and Engels — originally thought, however.

Marxism began with the critique of socialism, specifically with the critique of the most prominent socialist thinker of Marx and Engels's formative moment in the 1840s, Pierre-Joseph Proudhon. Proudhon — who coined the term "anarchism" — claimed that he respected only three authorities, intellectually, Adam Smith, Hegel and the Bible![1]

Marxism is usually thought of as the synthesis of German Idealist philosophy, British political-economy, and French socialist politics. But what Marxism actually was was the immanent dialectical critique of these three phenomena, which Marx and Engels considered three different forms of appearance of the same thing: the most advanced bourgeois ideology of their time, of the early–mid 19th century. They were all true expressions of their historical moment, of the Industrial Revolution. But as such, they were also all false.

Proudhon wrote of the "philosophy of misery," attacking the heirs of Adam Smith in Utilitarianism — James Mill and Jeremy Bentham — and other contemporary British political economists such as Malthus and David Ricardo and their French counterparts. Marx wrote his first major work on political economy and the class struggle in industrial capitalism as a critique of Proudhon, cleverly inverting its title, *The Misery of Philosophy*.

I was deeply impressed by this work — and especially by its title — when I first read it as an aspiring young "Marxist" in college. It signified to me a basic truth, which is that the problem of capitalism and its potential

---

1    Cited by J.A. Langlois in his preface to *P.J. Proudhon: His Life and Works* (1875).

overcoming in socialism was not a matter of "philosophy," not a problem of thinking. Reading further, in Marx's 1844 *Economic and Philosophic Manuscripts*, I read and deeply internalized Marx's injunction that "communism is a dogmatic abstraction" which was "one-sided," expressing the same thing as its opposite, private property, and, like bourgeois society itself, was internally divided, for instance, between collectivism and individualism, and so could not be considered a vision of an emancipated future society, but only a negation of the present. I had read in Marx and Engels's *Communist Manifesto* their critique of "reactionary socialism," and their observation that everything of which communism stood accused was actually the "specter" of what capitalism itself was already doing — "abolishing private property," among other things.

This all told me that, for Marx and Engels at least, the problem of bourgeois ideology was not a matter that could be addressed let alone rectified by proper methodology — by a kind of right-thinking opposed to it.

In short, I recognized early on that Marxism was not some better philosophy.

Marxism was not a philosophical critique of philosophy, but rather something else entirely. For instance, Marx and Engels's critique of the Young Hegelians was not as philosophers, but in their philosophical claims for politics. This was also true of Lenin's critique of the Machians among the Bolsheviks (in *Materialism and Empirio-Criticism*, 1908). The critique was of the *relation* between philosophy and politics. It was thus also not a political critique of philosophy.

### Ends

I have titled my talk here, "Ends of philosophy," after the title for the week in our Platypus primary Marxist reading group syllabus when we read Karl Korsch's 1923 essay on "Marxism and philosophy," the recommended background reading for today's discussion. In the syllabus week title as well as here, I intend to play on the multiple meanings of the word "ends." What are the ends of philosophy, according to Marxism, in terms of its telos, its goals, its purposes, and its satisfaction; what would it take to attain and thus overcome the aspirations of philosophy?

Specifically, what would it take to satisfy bourgeois — that is to say, modern — philosophy? What would make philosophy superfluous?

This is posed in the same way that Marxism sought to make labor as social value superfluous. How does labor seek to abolish itself in capitalism? The same could be said of philosophy.

What would it take to bring philosophy to an end — to its own end? Not by denying the need for philosophy, but by satisfying it.

But there have been other moments, before (and after) Marxism, which sought to overcome philosophy through its satisfaction, through satisfying the need for philosophy.

The need for — the necessity of — philosophy in the modern world is different from its need previously — fundamentally different. The need to account for freedom in bourgeois emancipation was new and different; this did not motivate and inform traditional philosophy. But it fundamentally tasked modern philosophy — at least the philosophy that mattered most to Marxism, the Enlightenment and German Idealism at its culmination. But the need for philosophy in capitalism is also different from its need in the bourgeois revolution.

Please allow me to address several different historical moments of the end of philosophy. I use this concept of moments of the "end of philosophy" instead of alternative approaches, such as varieties of "anti-philosophy," because I think that trying to address Marxism as an anti-philosophy is misleading. It is also misleading in addressing other such supposed "anti-philosophies," such as those of Kierkegaard, Nietzsche, Existentialism, Heidegger, etc., as well as other traditions entirely, such as the Enlightenment *philosophes* contra "philosophy," or Empiricism and Analytic Philosophy contra "metaphysics." (For instance, Heidegger sought the potential end to "thousands of years of Western metaphysics," going all the way back to Plato.) Yet all these various phenomena express to my mind a common issue, namely the problem of "philosophy" *per se* in the modern era, both in the era of bourgeois emancipation and subsequently in capitalism.

What is "philosophy," such that it can experience an end? It is not merely its etymological meaning, the love of knowledge, or wisdom, or the love of thinking. Philosophers are not merely smart or sage — not merely sophists, clever thinkers: philosophy cannot be considered merely the mastery of logic or of semantics. If that were true, then most lawyers would be better philosophers than most avowed "philosophers."

The end of philosophy cannot be considered an end to sophistry, finally putting the clever fellows down. It cannot be considered an analogue to Shakespeare's "First, we kill all the lawyers." It is not meant to be the triumph of Philistinism. Although you might think so from a lot of "Marxist" deprecation of philosophy, especially as "bourgeois ideology." Such "Marxists" want to put a stop to all mystification by putting a stop to the mystifiers of bourgeois society, the lackeys — the paid liars — of the capitalist bourgeoisie. They want to stop the "philosophers" from pulling the wool down over the eyes of the exploited and oppressed. This is not my meaning. — This was not even Socrates's (Plato's) meaning in taking down the Sophists.

## Authoritarianism

Philosophy cannot be considered, either negatively or positively, as the arrogation of all thinking: it is not some Queen of the Sciences that is to make proper sense of and superintend any and all human thought in every domain. It is not the King of Reason; not the thought-police. Marxism did not seek to replace philosophy in such a role. No. Yet this seems to be precisely what everyone wants from philosophy — or from anti-philosophy. They want their thinking dictated to them.

Korsch addresses this as "Bonapartism in philosophy": we seem to want to be told how and what to think by philosophers — or by anti-philosophers. It is an authoritarian impulse. But one that is an authentic expression of our time: capitalism brings forth its own Philosopher Kings.

This is not at all what the immediate predecessors for Marxist thought in philosophy, Kant and Hegel, considered as their task: Kant, in "beginning" philosophy (anew), and Hegel in "completing" this, did not seek to replace the thinking of others. No. Precisely the opposite: they sought to free philosophy, to make it "worldly." They thought that they could do so precisely because they found that the world had already become "philosophical."

After them, they thought there would no longer be a need to further develop Philosophy as such, but only the need for philosophical reflection in the various different diverse domains of human activity. Our modern academic institutions reflect this: one receives the PhD, Doctor of Philosophy, in Chemistry, meaning one is qualified to "doctor," to minister and correct, to treat the methods and attendant thinking — the "philosophy" — of the science of chemistry, without however necessarily becoming an expert specialist "philosopher of science," or studying the specialized discipline Philosophy of Science *per se*. According to Lukács, such specialized knowledge as found in academia as well as in the various technical vocations — such as law, journalism, art, etc. — exhibited "reification" in capitalism, a disintegrated particularization of atomized consciousness, in which losing the forest for the trees was the very predicate of experience and knowledge. But this was the opposite of what Kant and Hegel had expected. They expected not disintegration but the organic, living and changing *relations* of diverse multiplicity.

Marx found a very different world from Kant and Hegel's, after the Industrial Revolution. It was not a philosophical world in capitalism — not an "enlightened" realm of "sober senses," to which bourgeois philosophy had aspired, but something much darker. It was a "phantasmagoria" of "commodity fetishism," full of beguiling "metaphysical subtleties," for which one needed to refer to the "mist-enveloped regions of religion" for proper models. In capitalism, bourgeois society was sunk in a kind of animism: a world of objects exhibiting "theological niceties."

There was a need for a new Enlightenment, a Second Enlightenment specific to the needs of the 19th century, that is, specific to the new needs of industrial capitalism, for which the prior thinking of bourgeois emancipation, even at its best, for instance by Rousseau, Adam Smith, Kant and Hegel, was not equipped to adequately address. It needed a new recognition of the relation between social being and consciousness.

But for Marx and Engels, this new task of enlightenment was something that could not be accomplished philosophically — could not be brought to fruition in thinking — but only in actual political struggle and the transformation of society.

## History

This was because, unlike the emancipation of bourgeois society, which took several centuries and came to consciousness of itself as such only late, no longer cloaking itself in the religious garb of Christianity — the Protestant Reformation as some return to true Christianity of the original Apostles, freed from the corruptions of the Church — and arrived at self-consciousness only at the end of its process of transformation, in the 18th century. As Hegel put it, "The Owl of Minerva [that is, knowledge] flies at dusk": proper consciousness comes only "post-festum," after the fact of change.

But Marx and Engels found the task of socialism in capitalism to be motivated by a new need. The proletarianization of the bourgeois social relations of labor — the society of cooperative production in crisis with the Industrial Revolution — required a new consciousness of contradiction, a "dialectical" and "historical" "materialism," to properly recognize its tasks. As Marx put it, the social revolution of the 19th century — in contradistinction to the bourgeois revolution — could not take its poetry from the past, but needed to take its poetry from the future. This was quite a paradoxical formulation, especially since Marx and Engels explicitly abjured "utopian socialism," finding it a realm of images of capitalism, and not of a world beyond it.

This was because they found the workers' struggles against the capitalists to be motivated by bourgeois consciousness, the consciousness of the bourgeois revolution. Socialism was born in the Jacobinism of the French Revolution, for instance, in the former Jacobin Babeuf's Conspiracy of Equals, still motivated by the aspirations of "liberty, equality and fraternity." Proudhon, for example, was motivated in his anarchist socialism, avowedly, by Adam Smith and Hegel (and the Bible) — animated, unabashedly, by bourgeois political economy and philosophy.

Marx and Engels didn't think that this was wrong, but only inadequate. They didn't offer an alternative to Proudhon — to Smith and Hegel (or the Bible!) — but only a critique of how bourgeois thought mystified the crisis and task of capitalism. The world necessarily appeared in bourgeois terms — there were no other terms. There was no other form of consciousness. There was no other philosophy. Nor was there a need for a new philosophy.

Bourgeois philosophy, for Marx and Engels, had successfully summed up and appropriated all prior philosophical enlightenment. They agreed with Kant and Hegel. Bourgeois social thought had successfully summed up and completed all prior thinking about society. Marx and Engels neither disputed nor sought to replace it. They were concerned only with its self-contradiction in capitalism. Not its hypocrisy, but its authentic antinomies, which both drove it on and left it stuck. The bourgeois "end of history" turned out to be the opposite of what it intended: not a final stage of freedom, but rather a final stage of unfreedom; the crossroads of "socialism or barbarism."

## Impossibility

This affected the status of philosophy. Bourgeois philosophy no longer described freedom but rather unfreedom. Or, more dialectically, it described both: the reproduction of unfreedom in the struggle for freedom. As a result, the task of freedom was no longer expressed by the need for all human activity to achieve an adequate — Hegelian — philosophically reflective self-consciousness, but rather to realize in practice and thus recognize in consciousness the limits of such self-consciousness, of such philosophical reflection. There was a crisis in radical bourgeois philosophy. The crisis and decay of Hegelianism was an authentic historical phenomenon, not a mistake.

Like liberal democracy, philosophy in capitalism was no longer itself, and was no longer tasked with becoming itself, attaining its aspirations, but rather was tasked with overcoming itself, superseding its achievements. The achievements of bourgeois emancipation seemed ruined in the 19th century.

Indeed, capitalism already accomplished such self-overcoming of bourgeois society, but perversely, negating itself without satisfying itself. In so doing, it constantly re-posed the task of achieving itself, as an impossible necessity. Bourgeois philosophy became the opposite of what it was, utopian. Not worldly philosophy, but an ideal, a mere notion, mocked by the real, ugly and anything-but-philosophical world.

Because of this — precisely because of this — bourgeois philosophy did not end but constantly reinvented itself, however on an increasingly impoverished basis. It radically revolutionized itself, but also, in so doing, radically undermined itself.

Philosophy remained necessary but proved impossible. It disintegrated, into epistemology, ontology and ethics. They went their separate ways. But they also drove themselves into blind alleys — dead-ends. This actually indicates the task of philosophy to overcome itself, however in perverted form.

## Metaphysics

So, what is philosophy? One straightforward way of answering this is, simply, metaphysics. Kant, following Rousseau, had overcome the division and opposition between Rationalism and Empiricism by finding a new foundation for metaphysics. This was the Kantian "Copernican Turn" and "revolution" in philosophy. But it was not simply a new metaphysics, but rather a new account of metaphysics — of philosophy — itself. Moreover, it was revolutionary in an additional sense: it was not only a revolution, but also accounted for itself as revolutionary. This is because it was a metaphysics of change, and not merely change but radical qualitative transformation: it was a revolutionary account of the fundamental transformability of the substance of philosophy itself. In short, it was a philosophy of freedom. It was the self-reflection of practical freedom in society — that society made human life's transcendence of nature possible, at all, but in so doing created new problems to be worked through and overcome.

It is precisely this metaphysics of freedom, however, that has gone into crisis and disintegrated in capitalism. This has been the expression of the crisis and disintegration — the decay — of bourgeois society.

The goal of philosophy in overcoming itself is to free thinking from an overarching and underlying metaphysics at all. Kant and Hegel thought that they had done so already, but capitalism — in its crisis of the metaphysics of bourgeois society — revealed that there was indeed an underlying and overarching metaphysics still to be overcome, that of social practice — society — itself. The self-production and self-overcoming of the subject in its socially and practically objective activity — labor — needed to be overcome.

The end of philosophy — the end of a singular metaphysics, or of metaphysics *per se* — aims at the freeing of both action and thinking from any unitary framework. It is the freeing of an ever-expanding and limitless — without end — diverse multiplicity of new and different forms of acting, being and knowing.

Postmodernism was, as Moishe Postone put it, "premature post-capitalism." It aimed at the freeing of the "small-s subjects from the big-S Subject." It also aimed at freedom from capital-H History. It meant overcoming Hegel's philosophy of history.

We already live in such freedom in bourgeois society, however perverted by capitalism. Diverse activities already inhabit different realms of being and call forth different kinds of ethical judgments. Doctors and lawyers practice activities that define being — define the "rights of life and liberty and the pursuit of happiness" — in different ways, and are hence ethically bound in different ways. Doctors discipline themselves ethically differently from scientists. Among scientists, Biology has a different epistemology from Physics: there are different methods because there are different objects. There is no "philosophy" in the sense of a metaphysical logic that encompasses them all. Lawyers, for example, practice differential ethics: prosecutors and defense attorneys in criminal law are bound by different rules of behavior; the practice of civil law is ethically distinct from criminal law; the rules of evidence are different. We do not seek to bind society to one form of knowledge, one code of conduct, or one way of life. There is no "philosophy" that could or should encompass them all. It would be arrogant to claim that there is one singular logic that can be mastered by anyone for governing everything.

Bourgeois society has already established well the reasonable limits to philosophy and its competence.

In Ancient civilization there were differentiated realms of being, knowing and acting. There was a caste system, in which there were different laws for peasants; for merchants; for artisans (and for different kinds of artisans, for different arts and different sciences); and for the nobility; and for the clergy. But they were unified in a Divine Order of the Great Chain of Being.

There was heterogeneity, but all with a single origin in God: all of God's creatures in all of God's Creation. That mystery was to remain unknown to Man — known only to God. There was a reason for everything, but only God could know it. There was not philosophy but theology, and theology was not to arrogate to itself the place of the Mind of God, but only ponder Man's place in and relationship to it. Theology established the limits to man's knowledge of God: we knew only what God had revealed to us, through his Covenant. We all heard the Word of God; but God told His different creatures different things. In overcoming theology, philosophy did not seek to replace it. It sought to explore the mind of man, not to relate to and limit itself with respect to the Mind of God. It was not concerned with Divine or Natural limits, but with freedom.

There is no possible one single or once-and-for-all account of freedom, for then freedom would not be free. There is no possible account of "being" free, but only of *becoming* free. And there is only one such account, that of bourgeois emancipation from traditional civilization. It was to set free all the diverse and multiple activities of mankind, in relation to other humans, to Nature, and to ourselves.

### Overcoming

Marx was both a Hegelian and departed from Hegel, with a historical and not a philosophical difference. As Marx put it, for Hegel himself the Hegelian system was not ready-made and finished as it was for those who came after. As Marx observed, Hegelianism went into crisis for real historical reasons, not due to misunderstanding by his followers; but rather the crisis came from Hegelian philosophy's actual contact with the world, and that world had become as internally contradictory in capitalism as Hegelianism became in contact with it. The Hegelian dialectic is both appropriate and inappropriate to the problem of capitalism. The crisis and disintegration of Hegelianism was a crisis of metaphysics — of philosophy — at a higher and deeper and not a lower or more superficial level from Hegelianism. Hegelianism was falsified not in itself but by history. But Hegelianism was also borne out by history as the last word in philosophy — in metaphysics. Marxism cannot be purged of its Hegelianism without becoming incoherent; Marxism remains Hegelian, albeit with what Lukács called an "additional twist" in the "pure historicization of the dialectic."[2]

If society in capitalism remains bourgeois in its ideals, with the goal of providing opportunities for social labor, materially, it has become its opposite: as capitalist, it prioritizes not labor but capital, and at the expense of labor. This means society is tasked with the material challenge of overcoming its ideals. But, as Marx recognized, this can only be done on the basis of this society's own ideals, in and through their self-contradiction. In philosophy, this means the task expressed by the self-contradiction of Hegelianism.

Capitalism is the model of the Marxist-Hegelian procedure of immanent dialectical critique: this is how capitalism itself moves, how it reproduces itself through self-contradiction. Capitalism is its own practical critique, reproducing itself by constantly overcoming itself. As Marx put it, the only limit to capital is capital itself; but capital is the transgression of any and all limits. It is the way capitalism overcomes itself, its dynamic process of change, which is its unfreedom, its self-limitation. The Marxian horizon of freedom beyond capitalism is freedom beyond the Hegelian dialectic, beyond the bourgeois dialectic of transformation — beyond labor as a process of self-overcoming through production.

There thus remains a unitary metaphysics binding all social practices, dominating, constraining and distorting their further development in freedom under capitalism: the bourgeois right of labor. The form of total freedom in bourgeois emancipation — self-production in society — has become in capitalism the form of total unfreedom. The social condition for labor has become that of the self-destruction of labor in capital. The goal of labor in capital is to abolish itself; but it can do so only by realizing itself — as self-contradiction. Hegel's "negative labor of the concept" must be completed; short of that, it dominates us.

Overcoming this will mean overcoming metaphysics — overcoming philosophy. At least overcoming philosophy in any way known — or knowable — hitherto.

---

2  *History and Class Consciousness: Studies in Marxist Dialectics*, trans. Rodney Livingstone (Cambridge, MA: MIT Press, 1971), xlvii.

## Introductory remarks on the topic of "Marxism and philosophy"

Earlier this summer, I visited Athens and made a pilgrimage to Aristotle's Lyceum. I was struck by the idea that perhaps what I am doing in Platypus is essentially the same as what Socrates, Plato and Aristotle were doing back in Ancient Greece. Spencer Leonard and I were recently discussing the recurrent trope of Aristotle and Marx, apropos of today's discussion of Marxism and philosophy, and he recalled his feeling nauseous when reading Castoriadis's famous essay on Aristotle and Marx, published in the same issue of the journal *Social Research* alongside Moishe Postone's seminal essay, "Necessity, Labor and Time."[3] Spencer said he had felt sick at the thought that nothing had changed since Aristotle's time.

I recalled how Frantz Fanon wrote, in *Black Skin, White Masks*, that he would be happy to learn that an African philosopher had corresponded with Plato, but this wouldn't make a difference for 8 year-olds in Haiti and the Dominican Republic forced to cut sugar cane for a living.[4] This compares well to the former Black Panther Assata Shakur, who, writing from her exile in Cuba on Black Lives Matter, referred to black Americans as "Africans lost in America." But are blacks any less lost in Africa today? Am I an Italian or Irish lost in America, too? I often feel that way, that my peasant ancestors were dragged into bourgeois society to ill effect, to my present misery. What would it mean not to be lost? Was I returning home, in a sense, when, as an intellectual, I returned to Aristotle's school in Athens? Was I any less lost in Athens?

Adorno wrote, in his inaugural lecture on "The idea of natural history," that "I submit myself, so to speak, to the materialist dialectic."[5] What he meant of course was that he could only speak misleadingly of submitting himself to the materialist dialectic, as if he would not already be dominated by it, whether he was conscious of his submission or not. This reminds us of Trotsky's statement to his recalcitrant followers who rejected Hegelianism

---

3   Vol. 45, no. 4 (Winter 1978).
4   Trans. Charles Lam Markmann (New York: Grover Press, 1967), 230.
5   Trans. Robert Hullot-Kentor, *Telos* 57 (1985), 124. Originally published in 1932.

that, "You may not be interested in the dialectic, but the dialectic is interested in you."

Why should we be interested in "philosophy," then? Adorno did not mean that he was submitting himself to Marxism as the "materialist dialectic" in the sense of submitting to Marx's thought. No. He meant, as we must mean in Platypus, that he accepted the challenge of Marx's thought as thinking which registered a greater reality, as a challenge and call to task for Adorno's own thinking.

Foucault wrote about his chagrin that just when one thinks one has overcome Hegel, Hegel is still there smiling back at you. This rather paranoid claim by Foucault as a mental phenomenon has a real meaning, however, which is that Hegel still speaks in some unavoidable way to our real condition. What is meant by "Hegel" here, of course, is the entirety of the alleged "Master Narrative" of the Western philosophical tradition culminating in bourgeois modernity.

Engaging philosophy then, is not being told how to think, but allowing one's thinking to be challenged and tasked in a specific way. It is a microcosm of how society challenges and tasks our thinking, whether we are inclined to it or not.

Historical philosophers are not some "dead white males" the authority of whose thinking threatens to dominate our own; we do not, or at least ought not, to read philosophy in order to be told how to think. No. The philosophy that comes down to us from history is not the dead weight of the past, but it is part of that past. And the past is not dead or even really past, since past actions still act upon us in the present, whether we like it or not. Marx reminds us that, "Man makes history, but not according to conditions of his own choosing."

We cannot avoid the past, but we are concerned with the symptomatic attempts to free ourselves from the past by trying to avoid it. Especially on the "Left," and especially by ostensible "Marxists."

As Korsch reminds us, among other ways, this can take the form of trying to avoid the "philosophical" aspects of Marxism.

We might recall that Korsch's essay on "Marxism and philosophy," the background reading for today, was the very first text we read in the Platypus reading group. This was before it was called Platypus, of course, but it was still our first collective discussion of a reading as a group. Our reading was predicated on opening up, not philosophy, but rather the political foundations for Adorno's thinking. It was meant to help lead my academic students of Adorno, not from Marxism to philosophy, but rather from philosophy to Marxism.

This is the intention of today's event as well: we come full circle. Perhaps indeed nothing has changed.

Presented at an internal discussion by members of Platypus on "Marxism and philosophy" held on August 11, 2018.

Originally published in *Platypus Review* 108 (July – August 2018)

# On philosophy and Marxism[1]

Karl Korsch concluded his 1923 essay on "Marxism and philosophy" with the declaration that,

Philosophy cannot be abolished without being realized.[2]

Jensen Suther and Teo Velissaris try to explain what Korsch (and Marx before him, and Adorno after) meant by this, but end up avoiding it, and rather restore not only bourgeois philosophy from its fatal crisis, self-contradiction and regression in capitalism and need to overcome it, but restoring traditional philosophy, *prima philosophia*, pre-critical philosophy — before Kant and Hegel. Despite trying to engage this problem, they merely stave it off, and do indeed turn Kant and Hegel into traditional philosophers. They follow many since the 20th century who have mistakenly tried to secure and justify Marxism philosophically. But Marxism is justified, if at all, only politically.

Velissaris and Suther restore metaphysics — albeit that of bourgeois-revolutionary society — and forget that already Kant and Hegel were post-metaphysical thinkers. Marx was post-philosophical.

In my writings on philosophy and Marxism, I have been aware that one is brought — necessarily and not mistakenly — to the very limits of comprehension — and of comprehensibility. Many of Marxism's formulations — for instance on philosophy — are beguilingly opaque. As Lukács wrote in the original 1923 Preface to *History and Class Consciousness*,

---

1   Response to Jensen Suther and Teo Velissaris: "Karl Korsch 1923: The problem of Marxism and philosophy" *Platypus Review* 131 (November 2020).

2   In *Marxism and Philosophy* (New York: Monthly Review Press, 1970 and 2008).

When the professional demolishers of Marx criticise his "lack of conceptual rigour" and his use of "image" rather than "definitions," etc., they cut as sorry a figure as did Schopenhauer when he tried to expose Hegel's "logical howlers" in his Hegel critique. All that is proved is their total inability to grasp even the ABC of the dialectical method. The logical conclusion for the dialectician to draw from this failure is not that he is faced with a conflict between different scientific methods, but that he is in the presence of a *social phenomenon* and that by conceiving it as a socio-historical phenomenon he can at once refute it and transcend it dialectically.[3]

The philosophy of revolution — as Korsch put it — that links Kant, Hegel and Marx is appropriate insofar as we still live in capitalism. But it is the revolution of bourgeois society that is in crisis in capitalism, and so is its philosophy: Korsch's 1923 essay, after all, sought to address the manifest crisis of Marxism itself that had occurred in the revolution; this was the problem of "Marxism and philosophy."

Velissaris and Suther forget the clear statement with which Adorno began his *Negative Dialectics* (1966), that,

Philosophy, which once seemed obsolete, lives on because the moment to realize it was missed.[4]

They forget that the goal of socialism is to overcome the — real — metaphysics of capitalism. The metaphysics of social labor in bourgeois society has become reified and hypostatized in capitalism. Marxism, in its failure in the 20th century, succumbed to adaptation to capitalism, including philosophically — for instance in becoming the official philosophy of "dialectical materialism" in the purportedly "revolutionary" state. The later Korsch renounced his own 1923 work in recoiling from Stalinism

---

3   *History and Class Consciousness: Studies in Marxist Dialectics* (1922), trans. Rodney Livingstone (Cambridge: MIT Press, 1973), xlvii.

4   *Negative Dialectics*, (1966), trans. E.B. Ashton (New York: Continuum, 2007), 3.

and what he called "Marxist metaphysics," blaming Lenin and even Marx for supposed "philosophical errors" of "idealism," and forgetting that the struggle for socialism remained based in capitalism, and so a self-consciously *"critical* (post-)metaphysics" was still required. What is required is not philosophy but what the Frankfurt School called "critical theory."

But ostensible "Marxism" after 1923 did indeed become mystified and mystifying — precisely as "philosophy." Velissaris and Suther's discussion of "achieving full freedom" from "class society," for instance, evinces such mystification: for Marx, bourgeois philosophy is not a "class philosophy" in a sociological sense, but rather expresses a historical horizon of politics in capitalism, which reproduces itself through democracy, including through democratic revolution. This is the true meaning of the problem of the "state," which socialism sought to overcome and abolish as surely as "philosophy."

Both desiderata of Marxism, to abolish philosophy and the state, seem utopian in the pejorative sense of threatening to do more harm than good: wishing to abolish the state and philosophy now seems to want to go back to a pre-philosophical or even pre-social condition. The emancipatory horizon of socialism in Marxism has been lost. Suther and Velissaris express this loss of the original Marxist vision.

As I have written elsewhere, for instance in "Capital in history" (2008), "The Marxist hypothesis" (2010)[5] etc., the principal danger facing the struggle for socialism — revealed clearly in the failure of the Revolutions of 1848 — is its collapse and liquidation into bourgeois-revolutionary democratic (for instance petit bourgeois radical) forms of politics, which reproduce capitalism. This can be seen in the failure to observe, acknowledge, recognize and pursue the difference of Marx and Marxism from Kant and Hegel, who were historically bourgeois-revolutionary thinkers but not socialists. Marxism does take up (*Aufheben*) the bourgeois-revolutionary tradition — including German Idealism philosophically — but seeks to go beyond it. This is because the crisis of bourgeois society in capitalism already goes beyond it.

---

5 "Capital in History: The need for a Marxian philosophy of the history of the Left" and "The Marxist hypothesis: A response to Alain Badiou's 'communist hypothesis,'" both in this volume.

The struggle for socialism is the next necessary step and not the last word in history: there will be no "full freedom" in some absolute sense, but what is foreseeable, however dimly, is only overcoming the unfreedom of capitalism. — Beyond that, who knows?

As I wrote in my "Ends of philosophy" (2018) that Velissaris and Suther reference in their article,

> Kant, in "beginning" philosophy (anew), and Hegel in "completing" this, did not seek to replace the thinking of others. No. Precisely the opposite: they sought to free philosophy, to make it "worldly." They thought that they could do so precisely because they found that the world had already become "philosophical."
>
> After them, they thought there would no longer be a need to further develop Philosophy as such, but only the need for philosophical reflection in the various different diverse domains of human activity. Our modern academic institutions reflect this: one receives the PhD, Doctor of Philosophy, in Chemistry, meaning one is qualified to "doctor," to minister and correct, to treat the methods and attendant thinking — the "philosophy" — of the science of chemistry, without however necessarily becoming an expert specialist "philosopher of science," or studying the specialized discipline Philosophy of Science *per se*. According to Lukács [in "Reification and the consciousness of the proletariat" from *History and Class Consciousness*], such specialized knowledge as found in academia as well as in the various technical vocations — such as law, journalism, art, etc. — exhibited "reification" in capitalism, a disintegrated particularization of atomized consciousness, in which losing the forest for the trees was the very predicate of experience and knowledge. But this was the opposite of what Kant and Hegel had expected. They expected not disintegration but the organic, living and changing *relations* of diverse multiplicity.
>
> Marx found a very different world from Kant and Hegel's, after the Industrial Revolution. It was not a philosophical world in capitalism — not an "enlightened" realm of "sober senses," to

which bourgeois philosophy had aspired, but something much darker. It was a "phantasmagoria" of "commodity fetishism," full of beguiling "metaphysical subtleties," for which one needed to refer to the "mist-enveloped regions of religion" for proper models. In capitalism, bourgeois society was sunk in a kind of animism: a world of objects exhibiting "theological niceties."

There was a need for a new Enlightenment, a Second Enlightenment specific to the needs of the 19th century, that is, specific to the new needs of industrial capitalism, for which the prior thinking of bourgeois emancipation, even at its best, for instance by Rousseau, Adam Smith, Kant and Hegel, was not equipped to adequately address. It needed a new recognition of the relation between social being and consciousness.

But for Marx and Engels, this new task of enlightenment was something that could not be accomplished philosophically — could not be brought to fruition in thinking — but only in actual political struggle and the transformation of society.[6]

In order to clarify this issue, I will let Hegel scholar Robert Pippin speak through what he has written, in a brief but core reading on Platypus's syllabus from the very beginning of our project, "Critical Inquiry and Critical Theory: A Short History of Non-Being" (2004):

The basic claim is that "First Philosophy," the foundation of all premodern university learning and all science, was not in fact any longer regarded as first. A critical account of the possibility of such, or any other claim to know, was first necessary. . . .

The most important result of the all-destroying Kant was the destruction of metaphysics as traditionally understood (*a priori* knowledge of substance). Philosophy, nonempirical claims to know, could not be understood as about the world or things in themselves but rather had to be reconceived as concerned with our mode of knowledge of objects. . . .

6   "Ends of philosophy," *Platypus Review* 108 (July – August 2018), in this volume.

But the most important result for later critical theory concerned the status of necessity in philosophy or Kant's attempt to argue that some philosophical account of the once-and-for-all necessary conditions of knowledge was possible. To make a very long story very short, after Kant, while the critical attack on the very possibility of first philosophy survived, this faith in a formal philosophy, capable of delivering an epistemological form of necessary truth, did not. Retaining the notion of a subjective contribution to, legislation of, the possibility of representational content, or all aspects of human experience "fraught with oughts," but without the necessity or fixity, meant that it wasn't long before the most important aspect of the Kantian aftermath was apparent: Hegel's famous claim in the preface to the *Philosophy of Right* that "philosophy . . . is its own time apprehended in thoughts" or that every philosopher is essentially a "child of his time." . . .

I should say that I still believe that the Hegelian response to this situation (postmetaphysical philosophy, radical historicity, modernist dissatisfactions) is the most promising. It is tagged by such phrases as the causality of fate, internal critique, and determinate negation. . . .

I would say that the level of discussion and awareness of this issue, in its historical dimensions (with respect both to the history of critical theory and the history of modernization) has regressed. . . . [T]here is also a historical cost for the neglect or underattention or lack of resolution of this core critical problem: repetition. . . . [T]he dim understanding we have of the post-Kantian situation with respect to, let's say, "the necessary conditions for the possibility of what isn't." But, however sketchy, that is what I wanted to suggest. I'm not sure it will get us anywhere. Philosophy rarely does. Perhaps it exists to remind us that we haven't gotten anywhere.[7]

---

7   *Critical Inquiry* 30, no. 2 (Winter 2004).

Unfortunately, Velissaris and Suther forget such realization, which Platypus as well as Pippin received from the Frankfurt School and Marxism — as well as from Kant and Hegel themselves. Kant and Hegel demanded to go beyond Kant and Hegel. So did Marx demand to go beyond Marx. The question is fulfilling them as a condition for getting beyond them. Politically, this means the necessity of the democratic revolution leading to socialism.

As I wrote in my "Ends of philosophy,"

> Capitalism is the model of the Marxist-Hegelian procedure of immanent dialectical critique: this is how capitalism itself moves, how it reproduces itself through self-contradiction. Capitalism is its own practical critique, reproducing itself by constantly overcoming itself. As Marx put it, the only limit to capital is capital itself; but capital is the transgression of any and all limits. It is the way capitalism overcomes itself, its dynamic process of change, which is its unfreedom, its self-limitation. The Marxian horizon of freedom beyond capitalism is freedom beyond the Hegelian dialectic, beyond the bourgeois dialectic of transformation — beyond labor as a process of self-overcoming through production.
>
> There thus remains a unitary metaphysics binding all social practices, dominating, constraining and distorting their further development in freedom under capitalism: the bourgeois right of labor. The form of total freedom in bourgeois emancipation — self-production in society — has become in capitalism the form of total unfreedom. The social condition for labor has become that of the self-destruction of labor in capital. The goal of labor in capital is to abolish itself; but it can do so only by realizing itself — as self-contradiction. Hegel's "negative labor of the concept" must be completed; short of that, it dominates us.
>
> Overcoming this will mean overcoming metaphysics — overcoming philosophy. At least overcoming philosophy in any way known — or knowable — hitherto.[8]

---

8    "Ends of philosophy," *Platypus Review* 108 (July – August 2018), in this volume.

Suther and Velissaris forget the fundamental point of Korsch's essay on which they have written their article, the historically new and unprecedented need to "realize philosophy by abolishing it" in socialism.

Originally published in *Platypus Review* 131 (November 2020)

# The negative dialectic of Marxism

I will present on the reason why Marxism was and must be "dialectical" — to demystify this word and specify it and its necessity for Marxism. What is the necessity of the dialectic for Marxism? It is of an essentially negative character. — For instance, all degeneration of Marxism can be called "undialectical," the abandonment of this essentially negative and dialectical character. The Frankfurt School thinker Theodor Adorno titled his last completed book *Negative Dialectic,* and he thus sought to recapture this original sense of Marxism, which had been progressively abandoned in Adorno's lifetime in the 20th century. Moreover, as Adorno emphasized, the task is to "think dialectically and undialectically at the same time,"[1] because getting beyond capitalism would mean getting beyond the dialectic, or as Adorno wrote, "no longer a totality nor a contradiction."[2]

Looking back upon the history of Marxism, there are three different moments for considering this problem: Marx's own formative moment of Marxism; the height of Marxism as a political force in the world, in the time of Lenin; and the degeneration of Marxism into what Adorno called "dogmatization and thought-taboos." — Our own moment today is the product of a century of such degeneration.

By contrast, for Marx in his own time, the necessity of the dialectic was to be found in the self-contradictory character of not only capitalism but of the struggle to overcome it in socialism. Marxism has its origins in the

---

1  *Minima Moralia: Reflections on a Damaged Life,* trans. E.F.N. Jephcott (New York: Verso, 2005), 152.

2  *Negative Dialectics,* trans. E.B. Ashton (New York: Continuum, 1973), 11: "Regarding the concrete utopian possibility, dialectics is the ontology of the wrong state of things. The right state of things would be free of it: neither a system nor a contradiction."

dialectical critique of capitalism which also includes — at its core — the dialectical critique of socialism. It is significant that Marx and Engels began with the dialectical critique of the socialists and communists of their time, of the Young Hegelians and others such as Proudhon.

In the subsequent height of Marxism as a political force, during Lenin's time, the proletarian socialist movement and its organized parties became self-contradictory — subject to a dialectic — for instance, as Rosa Luxemburg critiqued of reformist Revisionism in Marxism, there was a contradiction between the movement and its goal, or between means and ends, which also involved a contradiction between practice and theory, etc. Lenin went so far as to say that this contradiction — division and split — within the workers' movement for socialism was what made political and social revolution possible and necessary. How was this so?

First, it is necessary to address how Marx and Marxism understood capitalism as a problem to be overcome. What kind of society is capitalism, from a Marxist perspective?

Marx defined capitalism as a mode of production as the contradiction of "bourgeois social relations" and "industrial forces of production."[3] This is the essential character of the dialectic for Marxism, from which several other contradictions can be derived, for instance, the contradiction between the bourgeois "ideological superstructure" of "false consciousness" and the "socioeconomic base." There, Marx defined the contradiction as temporal and historical in nature: the ideological superstructure "changes more slowly" than the socioeconomic base.

"Bourgeois consciousness" is of a historical and not class character in a sociological sense of a particular group of people. Bourgeois means "urban" in the original French, and workers as well as capitalists are bourgeois in the sense of not members of the traditional rural classes — castes — of preceding agricultural civilization (peasants, manorial lords, parsons of the parish church, guild craftsmen of the village and traveling merchant traders serving the lord, et al). The new situation of society in the bourgeois epoch brought with it new forms of self-understanding that are well-established

---

3    Preface to *Contribution to a Critique of Political Economy* (1859), in *The Marx-Engels Reader*, ed. Robert C. Tucker, 2nd ed. (New York: Norton, 1978), 4–5.

and continue in capitalism, especially the autonomous individual as social subject of production and exchange.

Another way of describing capitalism is the contradiction between social being and consciousness. For Marxism, this contradiction of capitalism began with the Industrial Revolution. The consciousness of participation in society in practice and theory is bourgeois while its actual social being has become industrial. The most important bourgeois ideology for Marxism is the consciousness of the workers as subjects of bourgeois society. The proletariat is a peculiar term referring to how the working class retained its formal rights as bourgeois citizens while substantially becoming expropriated of its property in its labor as a commodity, harking back to the Ancient Roman class of *proletarii* citizens without property.

The Marxist critique of bourgeois consciousness as ideology is in its self-contradictory character. Hence, what distinguishes the Marxist dialectic is its critical character — from which it is distinguished for example from the Hegelian dialectic, which as a description of bourgeois emancipation of free labor from slavery and caste constraint — the bourgeois revolution — became an affirmative dialectic unable to address the problem of capitalism after the Industrial Revolution. So the critical theory of Marxist politics — to invert the title of this panel discussion — is essentially its negative character: the self-negation of bourgeois society in the Industrial Revolution, in which, for example bourgeois right became self-contradictory, self-undermining and self-destructive in capitalism.

It is important that most avowed "Marxists" today adopt Marxism in a false way as a positive theory, a theory of what capitalism is, for example, rather than as Marx and original Marxism approached capitalism, which was as a contradiction and crisis of society, a contradiction of its self-understanding and self-consciousness. I mentioned for instance social being and consciousness: for Marxism, social being does not define consciousness — in theory and practice — but rather consciousness, or bourgeois ideology as "false consciousness" is contradicted by the social being of industrial production in capitalism.

The temporal and historical character of this is crucially important — and usually neglected. From a Marxist perspective, bourgeois society was not capitalist — not self-contradictory — from the beginning (in the Renaissance and subsequent 16th, 17th and 18th centuries) but rather became so only in the 19th century, after the Industrial Revolution — in Marx's own time. This means an essentially negative approach to history in capitalism. History in capitalism for Marxism does not unfold positively — as with Hegel, as the development of consciousness of freedom — but rather negatively, a broadening and deepening crisis of society, borne of the essential contradiction of industrial forces of production against bourgeois social relations.

Capitalism is not a form of society for Marxism but rather a self-contradiction and crisis of society — of bourgeois society specifically. The history of capitalism was for Marxism that of the unfolding task of socialism. But for the last 100 years, the task of socialism was abandoned in favor of the mere denunciation of capitalism, which was thus accepted as a positive fact rather than regarded properly as a negative task, something to be overcome. Involved in this was a collapse of the original distinction Marxism made between bourgeois society and capitalism — an elision of the contradiction between industrial forces and bourgeois social relations of production.

The bourgeois social relations for Marxism are those of labor — cooperative social production. As Marx early on described about "alienation" — that is, the self-estrangement of social relations — in capitalism, social relations are not only between people in society, but also between humanity and nature, and our relations with ourselves. — Marx added to this three-fold character of bourgeois social relations a fourth dimension of alienation in capitalism, namely the estrangement of labor from capital as its product. So, for Marxism, social relations in capitalism are phenomena of contradiction and crisis, and no longer (primarily) the constitutive dimensions of society, as they had been in bourgeois consciousness, for instance for Locke, Rousseau, Adam Smith, Kant, Hegel and others. For Marxism, capitalism is not really a mode of production, but the self-contradiction of the bourgeois mode of production, that is, of the cooperative social production through the social relations of labor as a commodity.

Marx defined bourgeois society as commodity-producing society: a society of commodities that produce other commodities. Labor — and later in manufacture and industry, labor-power and labor-time — as a commodity produces other commodities. But in the Industrial Revolution, labor (including labor-power and labor-time) as a commodity becomes divided against itself: it produces two opposed commodities: use-values whose consumption reproduces labor in society; and capital as the objectification — and alienation or self-estrangement — of the social value of labor, which ends up contradicting and undermining the basis for the reproduction of labor in society — the social relations of cooperative production. Capital investment becomes divided between human labor and scientific technique in production. Marx called science and technology the "general social intellect," which mediated social production in a fundamentally different way from that of individual human labor.

Social cooperation in capitalism was mediated by capital (hence, "capitalism") — and for Marxism as a form of Hegelianism, what "mediates" is also what embodies contradiction: what mediates also contradicts. So capital contradicts social cooperation; but also social cooperation — the bourgeois social relations of labor as a commodity — contradicts capital, hence, the class struggle of the workers as subjects of social cooperation versus the capitalists as stewards of the social value of accumulated labor in capital. Labor and capital confront each other as aspects of social self-contradiction — capital is the self-contradiction of labor, and labor is the self-contradiction of capital in industrial production.

The workers' demand for the value of their labor in capitalism is historically regressive in that it seeks to restore the value of labor as a commodity that industrial production has contradicted and undermined. However, although the workers demand the reconstitution of the social value of labor as a commodity, and thus the reconstitution of bourgeois society, this is also the inevitable form in which the demand for socialism will be manifested: socialism will inevitably be posed as the restoration of society in bourgeois terms, that is, in terms of the social relations of labor.

This means that the workers' struggle for socialism is inherently self-contradictory: it is divided and indeed torn between the contradictory impulses to restore and reconstitute labor as well as to transcend labor as a social relation and value.

In the crisis of Marxism itself that came at the end of the First World War as the cataclysmic culmination of the Second Industrial Revolution, there was a division between the old Socialist and new Communist Parties over the issue of whether and how to save society from the devastation of war and political and social collapse and to revolutionize it beyond capitalism. There was an actual civil war within Marxism in the revolution that unfolded 1917–19. One side defended the working class as it existed in capitalism, while the other sought to overcome it. Socialism itself became divided between the interests of the workers. The anti-communists considered revolution to be a threat above all to the working class itself.

The socialist political party that had been built up to overcome capitalism became its last bulwark of defense. The power to overthrow and smash the capitalist state proved to be the power to save it. And both sides claimed not only to represent the true interests of the working class but the ultimate goal of socialism itself. Both had right on their side — at least apparently.

This was the most powerful demonstration of the dialectic ever in world history. And that is entirely appropriate since the Marxist dialectic was designed to address precisely this problem, as it had first manifested in the workers movement for socialism in the 1840s and the Revolutions of 1848, repeating itself on a higher level and in more drastic and dramatic — and violent — form in the Revolutions of 1917–19, and the division of Marxism between the parties of the old Socialist Second and new Communist Third Internationals.

But this political conflict within the Marxist-led workers movement was not a *de novo* phenomenon but had long historical roots, which pointed to the development of contradictions within Marxism itself. This demanded a dialectical critique — a Marxist critique — of Marxism itself. Just as Marx had engaged in the dialectical critique of the socialism and communism of his time, so Lenin, Rosa Luxemburg and other radical revolutionaries in the Second International engaged in the dialectical critique of their own Marxist socialist movement. — Later, Trotsky engaged in the dialectical critique of Stalinism. In subsequent history, successive generations' rediscovery of Marxism was the rediscovery of the dialectic, which however proved ephemeral and elusive, and fragile as a red thread that has been lost — broken — many times.

This tradition of negative dialectical critique was carried on by the Frankfurt School, under the rubric of "Critical Theory" — as I already mentioned, including Adorno's magnum opus *Negative Dialectic,* but also Horkheimer and Adorno's *Dialectic of Enlightenment,* etc.

But the dialectic fell out of style in the 20th century, with Marxism itself rendered undialectical and discontents of the failure of Marxism blaming the dialectic for the impasse of Marxism. Undialectical "Marxists" made explicit return to pre-critical — indeed pre-Socratic — philosophy such as Althusser and his followers. Postmodernists such as Foucault rejected the "grand narrative" of history as the struggle for freedom. Unable to grasp the nature and character of the dialectic at a standstill in capitalism as the crossroads of socialism or barbarism, the domination of the contradiction of capital was blamed on the dialectic — and often on Marxism — itself. And yet the ironies of the Hegelian cunning ruse of reason were hard to shake off entirely, leaving the lingering question of meaning at the supposed "end of history."

This is the most difficult aspect of Marxism but also the most essential; it is the most esoteric but also the substantial core of Marxism: it is the most enchanting but also most frustrating quality of Marxism. It will inevitably return, as Marxism continues to haunt the world of capitalism and its manifest contradictions: but can it be sustained? Will the capitalist world be brought back to the point of its dialectical contradiction that points beyond itself? If so, then the necessity of the Marxist negative dialectic will be felt again and anew.

Presented on a panel discussion with Dennis Graemer (Association for the Design of History), Doug Lain (Zer0 Books) and Douglas Kellner (UCLA) at the thirteenth annual Platypus Affiliated Society International Convention on Saturday, April 3, 2021.

# The party

# Review of Andrew Feenberg, *The Philosophy of Praxis: Marx, Lukács and the Frankfurt School*

The mastery of nature (so the imperialists teach) is the purpose of all technology. But who would trust a cane wielder who proclaimed the mastery of children by adults to be the purpose of education? Is not education, above all, the indispensable ordering of the relationship between generations and therefore mastery (if we are to use this term) of that relationship and not of children? And likewise technology is the mastery of not nature but of the relation between nature and man.

> – Walter Benjamin,
> "To the planetarium," *One-Way Street* (1928)

Andrew Feenberg's new book *The Philosophy of Praxis*[1] is a substantial revision of a much earlier work, *Lukács, Marx and the Sources of Critical Theory* (1981)[2]. If one were to sum up Feenberg's main point it would be to recover Marxist Critical Theory's ability to recognize technology as a social relation, and to thus grasp the crisis of capitalism expressed through the crisis of technology. Feenberg arrives at this recognition of Marxism through an investigation of critical theory as the self-reflection of social and political practice, "praxis," with its roots in the origins of social theory in Rousseau and the German Idealism of Kant and Hegel that had followed upon Rousseau's breakthrough. The sources of Critical Theory are thus critical theory's origins in the critique of society. Society, indeed, is a modern invention, in that only modern society recognizes social relations as such, as part of the emancipation of those social relations. The new,

---

1   New York: Verso, 2014.
2   Oxford: Oxford University Press.

modern concept of freedom beginning with Rousseau — Hegel had written that "the principle of freedom dawned on the world in Rousseau, and
gave infinite strength to man, who thus apprehended himself as infinite"
(*Lectures on the History of Philosophy*) — originated in the revolution of
bourgeois society: a new consciousness of social relations came with the
experience of their radical transformation. As Adorno, one of the subjects
of Feenberg's book, put it pithily, "Society is a concept of the Third Estate."[3]

Technology as a social phenomenon, specifically as a phenomenon
of social relations, or, technology as a social relation, is Feenberg's way
into political questions of capitalism. His new title for the revised book
takes its name from Gramsci's term for and description of Marxism (in
*The Prison Notebooks*), the "philosophy of praxis," which Gramsci took
over from Croce's Neo-Hegelian concept of self-reflective practice. The
question for politics, then, is the degree of social reflexivity in the recognition of technology. In this, Feenberg follows from Marcuse's writings from
the 1960s, which were concerned with the post-WWII world's exhibiting
what Horkheimer and Adorno had earlier called the "veil of technology,"
or, "technology as ideology." There was a deliberate attempt to overcome
the prevailing Heideggerian critique of technology, in which humans
became victims of the tools they had fashioned. As Heidegger succinctly
phrased it in a barb directed against Marxism, "The laboring animal is
left to the giddy whirl of its products so that it may tear itself to pieces
and annihilate itself in empty nothingness."[4] Feenberg asks, what would
it mean to overcome this reification of technology? And, what would it
mean to overcome the political pessimism that the problem of technology
seems to pose in capitalism?

The "philosophy of praxis," then, is Feenberg's attempt to recognize
technology as self-alienated social practice, or to use Lukács's term, "reified"
action that engenders political irresponsibility, the false naturalization or
hypostatization of activity that could be changed. Feenberg traces this problem back to the origins of social theory in Rousseau's critique of civilization,
the inherently ambivalent character of social "progress" in history. Feenberg

3 "Society" in *Salmagundi*, no. 10/11 (Fall 1969 – Winter 1970).
4 "Overcoming Metaphysics" (1936–46), in *The End of Philosophy*, ed. and trans. Joan
  Stambaugh (University of Chicago Press, 2003), 87.

locates in Rousseau what he calls the origins of the "deontological" approach to society: a new conception of freedom which is not merely a "right" but is indeed a "duty." What Feenberg calls the "deontological grounds for revolution" in Marx, then, is the Rousseauian tradition that Marx inherited from Kant and Hegel, if however in a "metacritical approach."

Why "metacritical?" Because in the Rousseauian tradition followed by Kant and Hegel, there remains the possibility of a theoretical affirmation and justification of society as being free already, where it would need to *become* free through radical transformation. Hence the peculiarity of "critical theory" in Marx. According to Feenberg, it was necessary for Marx to transcend the post-Rousseauian "utilitarian" framework of maximizing happiness through addressing "true needs." For Feenberg, Marx overcomes the "split between reason and need," or between freedom and necessity, precisely because freedom is understood by Marx as the transformation of necessity. Marx thus followed upon the most radical implications of Rousseauian recognition of "second nature."

This bears on the centrality of the problem of "technology" in capitalist utilitarianism, which is subject to a precipitous lowering or narrowing of horizons through concern with needs that are falsely naturalized: what is "second nature," a social product, is mistaken for "first nature," or what Marx considered a "false necessity." Such critique of ideology is how Marx overcame the potential conservative implications of how Kant and Hegel regarded "necessary forms of appearance" of social reality. Social practices such as those reified in "technology" seem responsive to necessities that can actually be transformed.

For Feenberg, there is a recurrent problem of neglect but also a red thread of rediscovery of this problem from Marx up to the present, with Lukács and the Frankfurt School providing key moments for recovery along the way.

This is a problem specific to capitalism precisely because of the centrality of labor. Marxism's point of departure was to regard capital not as a "thing" in terms of the means of production or as "technology" but rather as a social relation, specifically as a social relation of the commodity form of labor. Marx regarded capital as labor's own product in order to demystify the capitalist estrangement of social relations in technologized production.

What Marx called the "capitalist mode of production" was a "contradiction" between the "bourgeois social relations" of production in labor and their unrealized potential beyond themselves, or "industrial forces" that had yet to be mastered socially — that is, *politically*.

The danger lay in accepting false limits to politics seemingly imposed by technology which poses "nature" as static where it is actually the existing social relations that are recalcitrant obstacles to be overcome.

However, capitalism is not only a problem of false static appearance, but also a "reified" or self-alienated dynamic, in which concrete practices or "technologies" change, but without adequate social-political awareness and agency. This is why the dynamics of technical change and its invidious social effects appear *deus ex machina* (literally a theodicy for Heidegger; *techne* as a god), and why it makes sense at all to characterize the problem in Marx's terms as *capital*-ism. It is not a problem of "capitalist-ism," that is, a problem of society subject to the greed and narrow interests of the capitalists, but rather a deeper and more endemic problem of overall participation in social practice.

This brings us back to the original Rousseauian problem of society and political sovereignty: the unlimited, free development both collectively and individually that Rousseau apotheosized in the "general will." What does it mean, following Marx, that the "general will" appears in the form of "capital," and, in the 20th century, in the even more alienated form as the imperative of "technology?" It means that the problem of capitalism deepened, and social freedom became even more obscure.

Feenberg provides an important Appendix to his book that addresses the history of Marxism as a phenomenon of this problem. There, Feenberg discusses the issue of Lukács's "self-identical subject object" of the proletariat in the form of the Communist Party. For Feenberg, Lukács followed both Luxemburg and Lenin's approaches to the problem of political party and social change. In Feenberg's formulation, for Lukács, following Lenin and Luxemburg, the political party for proletarian socialism, or the Communist Party, was not only or even especially the "subject" but was at least as if not more importantly the "object" of the working class's political action in trying to overcome capitalism.

In this sense, the problem of "reification" was not merely an economic or even "political-economic" problem (in the sense of the workers versus the capitalists), but was indeed first and foremost for Lukács a problem of *politics*. The party was objectified political practice. The question was its critical recognition as such. What had motivated Lukács's recovery of Marx's original point of departure, what Feenberg calls the "deontological grounds for revolution," was precisely the phenomenon of how Marxism itself had become reified and thus went into political crisis by the time of WWI and the revolution — the civil war in Marxism — that had followed in Russia, Germany, Hungary, Italy, etc. It was Lukács's attempt to explain the underlying problem of that crisis in which Luxemburg and Lenin had been the protagonists that led to his rediscovery of Marx, specifically in the form of the "subjective," "conscious" or "Hegelian" dimension of Marxism that had fallen out as Marxism had degenerated or become "vulgarized" as a form of objectivistic economic determinism. The crisis of Marxism had led Lukács following Lenin and Luxemburg to a rediscovery of the potential for freedom concealed in capitalism.

The subsequent reification of Marxist politics in Stalinism presented a new problem that the Frankfurt School following Lukács had tried to address. This was paralleled by others, according to Feenberg, such as Merleau-Ponty and Lucien Goldmann. There were problems and some stumbles along the way, however, as Feenberg addresses in discussing the recently translated and published (2011) conversation in 1956 between Horkheimer and Adorno regarding the crisis of official Communism in Khrushchev's (partial and abortive) attempt at de-Stalinization[5], which Feenberg finds them to have failed to adequately pursue, an opening only taken up by the 1960s New Left, encouraged not by Adorno and Horkheimer but rather by Marcuse.[6]

Thus the New Left was another such moment of recovery for Feenberg, motivating an attempted further development of Marxist Critical Theory under changed historical conditions of society and politics. Feenberg's

---

5   "Towards a New Manifesto," trans. Rodney Livingstone, *New Left Review* 65 (September – October 2010).

6   *Philosophy of Praxis*, 167–171.

book, both in its original and its newly revised form, is an ongoing testament to that moment and its continued tasks up to the present.

Originally published in *Marx & Philosophy Review of Books* (February 14, 2015)

# 1873–1973: The century of Marxism

## The death of Marxism and the emergence of neo-liberalism and neo-anarchism

In the tradition we established just two years ago, there is a Platypus President's report, speaking to the historical moment. At our convention last year, I presented on the "anti-fa" vs. "anti-imp" Left, as a division in the history of the Left that bears upon the present.[1] In the year prior to that, in my first report, I presented on the 1970s as a decade in the history of the Left that continues to inform the present, but in ways that are usually not acknowledged.

This year, I am presenting on "1873 to 1973: The century of Marxism." The reason that I, in consultation with my comrades and colleagues, chose this topic, is to attempt to grasp the crisis of 2007–08 as closing the period of neoliberalism that began with the crisis of 1973. One thing to consider, therefore, is the parallel but also lack or disparity between the period from 1873 to, say, 1912 vs. the period from 1973 to today. I think this bears upon how we might consider our present historical moment. So the provocative formulation I have is to call the period from 1873 to 1973 the "century of Marxism," locating Marxism itself historically in this period.

### Historical periodization

I will begin with some historical dates, the birth and death years of various figures in the history of Marxism that are of prime importance for Platypus. The "century of Marxism" is, principally, after Marx's time, and ends, roughly, around the time of Adorno's death.

---

1   See Chris Cutrone, "The 'anti-fascist' vs. 'anti-imperialist' Left: Some genealogies and prospects," in *Death of the Millennial Left: Interventions 2006–2022*.

1818–1883 Karl Marx
1820–1895 Friedrich Engels
1870–1924 Vladimir Ilyich Lenin
1871–1919 Rosa Luxemburg
1879–1940 Leon Trotsky
1885–1971 Georg Lukács
1889–1914 Second International
1892–1940 Walter Benjamin
1895–1973 Max Horkheimer
1903–1969 Theodor W. Adorno

If, according to Jim Creegan, in his article on #Occupy, "Hot autumn in New York,"[2] the events of 2011 were similar to but different in certain key respects from those of 1968 and 1999, this is due to 1968, as a crisis year of the New Left, and 1999, the year of the Battle of Seattle, taking place during periods of economic boom, whereas 2011 took place during the economic crisis that began in 2007–08. However, in terms of similarities and differences, what this comparison neglects is the crisis of 1973, the crisis of Keynesianism and Fordism that occurred in the aftermath of the New Left explosion of 1968. One can say, perhaps, that 1968 took place during an economic boom, but the 1970s phase of the New Left took place during a period of economic crisis, after 1973. Why Creegan, among others, may choose to forget this is that it raises the question of Marxism in the 1970s, the last time that there was a potential renascence of the Left during an economic crisis on the order of magnitude we're facing today. The 1970s were a period whose failure conditions any attempts at Marxism in the present.

The last apparent renascence of Marxism, in the 1970s "Marxist-Leninist" turn of the New Left, may indeed be considered, rather, Marxism's long-delayed *death*. In other words, Marxism didn't come back to life in the '70s so much as it finally died then. This is quite different from considering the collapse of the Soviet Bloc beginning in 1989 to be the crisis and death of Marxism. For it was in the 1970s that the crisis of Keynesian Fordism led to the neoliberal era, symbolized by the election of Thatcher and Reagan by

---

2   *Weekly Worker* 886 (October 20, 2011).

the end of the decade. Neoliberalism has this crucial history in the 1970s, two decades before the 1990s, despite the preponderant consciousness today of later anti-globalization protests.

If the recent crisis is to be considered a crisis of neoliberalism, then it recalls the birth of the neoliberal era in the failure of the New Left, specifically the failure of New Left Marxism in the 1970s. The Marxist-Leninist turn of the New Left is coincidental historically with neoliberalism, so neoliberalism can be considered a historical phenomenon of the failure of the New Left. It was this failure that led to "postmodernist" anti-Marxism, specifically the death of the Left in its "post-political" phase of the 1980s–90s that we describe in Platypus's official Statement of Purpose.

### The century of Marxism: 19th and 20th centuries

The question before us, then, is the century of Marxism, considered as the emergence, crisis, death, and memory of Marxism. That question can be historically periodized as 1873–1973.

Marx's thought predates this period, and is properly considered a phenomenon circa and in the aftermath of the Revolutions of 1848.[3] If Marx's own thought was born in the crisis of the 1840s (the "hungry '40s"), then Marx-*ism* (as distinct from Marx's own thought and practice), as a form of politics *sui generis*, a Marxist politics *per se*, dates from the collapse of the First International (International Workingmen's Association) and the formation of the German Social Democratic Workers' Party (SPD) in the 1870s. As such, Marxism is contemporaneous with the first Great Depression that began with the crisis of 1873. Marxism, as a form of politics distinct from other forms of socialism, dates from this period. Prior to this, there was no question of "Marxism" but, rather, Marx and Engels and their close colleagues participated in the broader socialist movement.

1873 is commonly regarded as the end of the mid-19th century "liberal" era (which saw a certain heyday in the 1860s, also when Leftist politics emerged from post-1848 reaction). In Marxist historiography, the

---

3   See Cutrone, "The Marxist hypothesis: A response to Alain Badiou's 'communist hypothesis,'" *Platypus Review* 29 (November 2010), in this volume.

period after 1873 dates the emergence of the "monopoly" era of capitalism, the era of modern "imperialism." By contrast, the 1860s is the decade, for instance, marked by the U.S. Civil War, which conditioned the formation of the First International.[4] However, that period ended by the 1870s.

Significantly, 1873 was a blow to, and not a boon for, the First International. If we take the First International as paradigmatic of 19th century socialism, the crisis of 1873 did not boost 19th century socialism as much as it was coincidental historically with the crisis of 19th century socialism, namely, the collapse of the First International. The 1870s signaled a shift. This shift, towards what became "Marxism," therefore, was bound up with other changes.[5] These changes can be summed up in the historical shift from the liberal era to the state-centric era of capitalism.

## "State capitalism" and Marxism

"State capitalism" is a tricky category, with a variety of different meanings. For instance, Friedrich Pollock, a member of the Frankfurt School, wrote an influential essay on "state capitalism," published in the early 1940s, which referred to changes in the inter-war years of the early 20th century.[6] But, in another sense, "state capitalism" can be dated in two very different ways: from 1873 or 1914, either Bismarck or WWI. The fact that state capitalism can be characterized as having such very different start dates is significant: it places, specifically, the period between these two dates under certain questions. This period, 1873–1914, is coterminous with another historiographic period, the time between the Franco-Prussian War and WWI (in France, this is the period of the Third Republic, after the collapse of the Louis Bonaparte's Second Empire and the suppression of the Paris Commune), which developed towards a certain flowering of global capitalism in the Belle Époque. This is also the period of Marxism. Thus, it is significant that Marxism, in its "classical" era, can be considered a phenomenon of the

---

4    See Karl Korsch, "The Marxism of the First International" (1924).

5    See Cutrone, "Lenin's liberalism," *Platypus Review* 36 (June 2011), in this volume. See also Cutrone, "1917," *Platypus Review* 17 (November 2009), in this volume.

6    "State Capitalism: Its Possibilities and Limitations," in *The Essential Frankfurt School Reader*, ed. Andrew Arato and Eike Gebhardt (New York: Continuum, 1990), 71–94.

turn to state capitalism. Marxists of this period called this era "imperialism," or the "highest stage of capitalism," the eve of socialist revolution. In other words, the period of the emergence of Marxism as a politics *sui generis* was also understood by Marxists of the time as sharing the historical moment of capitalism's highest possible stage. "State capitalism," in this view, was not the overcoming but rather the exacerbation of the contradictions of capitalism. Marxism was thus bound up with heightening contradiction.

The late-19th to early-20th century period of "imperialism" resulted in the First World War, which was, of course, the crisis of Marxism: the collapse of the Second International. The question is how Marxism was bound up with the imperialist phase of capitalism, and how the crisis of Marxism in WWI was connected to the other results of this period of history. In other words, how did the crisis of Marxism itself share in the historical moment of the emergence and crisis of state capitalism, understood by Marxists at the time as "imperialism"?

For the Marxists of this time, WWI was the crisis of capitalism in its period of "revolution," which was signaled, in an inaugural sense, by the Russian Revolution of 1905. Marxists such as Lenin, Luxemburg, and Trotsky regarded this period as one confronted by the choice of "socialism or barbarism," or, more specifically, the "civil war" of the workers against the capitalists or a "world war" between imperialist states. This was the prognosis.

### The 20th century (1): The death of Marxism

Both predictions, of civil war and world war, in fact, came spectacularly true. Up to that time, Marxists understood this as either one alternative or the other. As it turned out, it was both. There was a world war and a civil war in 1914–19, in which the Second International collapsed and Marxism was divided. Marxism was divided specifically on the questions of both the imperialist world war and the class-struggle civil war that followed. So the crisis of Marxism was not only over the world war but was also over the civil war.

Marxism, specifically as a form of politics *sui generis* (distinguished from the greater 19th century history of socialism, from the Utopians to Proudhon, Blanqui, Lassalle, Bakunin, et al.) that had developed in the preceding period, from 1875–1914, did not survive its crisis in WWI and the revolutions that followed. Rather, Marxism died then.

The failure of Marxism can be seen most clearly in the birth of a new right-wing form of politics, fascism, in this period, issuing directly out of the crisis of Marxism in WWI (see, for instance, Benito Mussolini, who before the war was a leading member of the Marxist Left of the Italian Socialist Party). Fascism, 20th century social-democratic reformism, 20th century forms of nationalism (i.e., "anti-colonialism"), and Stalinism were the predominant (but not exclusive) results of the failed crisis of Marxism 1914–19.

So, how are we to regard the history of Marxism post-1919? Precisely as its post-history, its *memory*.

## The 20th century (2): The memory of Marxism

The memory of Marxism was carried, for the purposes of our project in Platypus, principally by two figures: Trotsky and Adorno. Trotsky, as the major surviving figure of Second International radicalism (Luxemburg died in 1919, and Lenin in 1924); and Adorno, as the "Critical Theorist" who tried to sustain the insights of Lukács and Korsch in the aftermath of 1917–19 (also through the attempt to sustain Benjamin's work, which was itself inspired by Lukács and Korsch's work of the early 1920s). Trotsky and Adorno represented the disintegration of theory and practice that had characterized the crisis and failure of Marxism as a *relation* of theory and practice, as a form of thinking and political action *sui generis*, as it had developed up to 1914. In other words, Marxism developed from the 1870s, it ran into a crisis by 1914, and then it became divided in its theory and practice, especially around the revolutions of 1917–19. These two figures, Trotsky and Adorno, exemplify the effects of this history. But what they actually exemplify, to be more precise, is not the separation of theory (Adorno) from practice (Trotsky), but, rather, *both* Adorno and Trotsky are symptoms of the disintegration of Marxism as a relation of theory and practice that developed in the preceding period. The theory and practice problem exists on both sides of Trotskyism and the Frankfurt School.

The memory of Marxism haunted the 20th century, especially regarding the grotesque farce of Marxism in Stalinism. If there was a tragedy of

Marxism in 1914–19, then this was followed by the farce of Stalinism. Both Trotsky and Adorno exemplify the possibilities for anti-Stalinist Marxism.

What died in the 1970s (let alone in 1989!) was not Marxism but rather the memory of Marxism, which had been only tenuously sustained. Between 1919 and 1973, we had the memory of Marxism, which faded out: this memory did not really survive Adorno's death. This is not to say that Adorno was the personal embodiment of the memory of the Marxism, but that it didn't really survive the time of Adorno's death. The reason that the passing of the memory of Marxism might date, coincidentally, with the death of Adorno (who was more a thinker and not a very overtly political actor), is that "Trotskyism" as a form of Marxist politics did not really survive Trotsky's death in 1940.

What is of interest, then, is how the last great renaissance of interest in Marxism, in the 1970s, actually marked the "death" of its effective memory. The apparent recovery of Marxism in the '70s was actually the effective obscuring of its memory.

What we have been living through more recently, say, since the 2000s, is the exhaustion and falling away of the *means for obscuring* the memory of Marxism that emerged and developed in the 1970s–80s–90s, which were a process of forgetting Marxism. The 1990s were an especially interesting period in this history, as there were already some intimations of the exhaustion of the postmodernism of the previous 1970s–80s. In this sense, 1989 can be considered a certain end to the "long 1960s" that had extended into the '70s and '80s (or, '89 can be considered as an "inverted '68").

The period from 1914 to 1973 (or, perhaps, 1989) was the essential, "short" 20th century.[7]

### Platypus: Marxism in the 21st century?

Now, what does this say about Platypus in this regard? There are two different generations of Platypus, broadly speaking: the generation of the 1990s and that of the 2000s. These two generations express (the tensions within)

---

7   Cf., Eric Hobsbawm, *The Age of Extremes: The Short Twentieth Century 1914–1991* (New York: Vintage, 1994).

the possible recovery of the memory of Marxism against its passing means of effacement. Thus, two different founding moments of Platypus's own historical consciousness — 1999, Seattle, and 2007, the exhaustion of the anti-war movement — are interrelated and interact specifically as different modulations of the exhaustion of processes for obscuring the memory of Marxism. Platypus, therefore, has two histories: a pre-history, 1999–2007; and an actual history, 2007–11/12.

If we compare our historical period with one a hundred years ago, the specificity of our project can be thrown into stark relief.

Whereas Marxism up to 1914 responded to and participated in the culmination of the imperialist phase of post-1873 capitalism, Platypus circa 2012 faces the very different challenges of the crisis of the neoliberal phase of post-1973 capitalism. In other words, our project in Platypus is a product of the end of the post-1973 neoliberal era. In this respect, the era of Marxism 1873–1914 could not contrast more starkly with our time, 1968/73–2011. Where one, 1873–1914, was a mounting crisis and a deeply ambivalent process of historical progression *and* regression, the other, our period, is one of spiraling decomposition.

This is how Platypus must relate to the history of Marxism: through the profound contrasts of post-1873 vs. post-1973 history.

## Unprecedented historical moment

The reason that our project in Platypus is unprecedented is precisely because our historical moment is unprecedented: without the post-1848 and post-1873 projects of Marxism, and without the memory of Marxism 1914/19–73. Our period is a "post-Marxist" time in a totally unparalleled way. We are entering into a time not only very much unlike post-1873 or post-1914, but also significantly unlike the decades post-1973 (1970s–80s) and post-1989 (1990s–2000s).

This is why our project is so specifically one of the 21st century, of its first, and, now, its second decade. We need to attend closely to the various ways in which our project is so conditioned. The specificity of our time is our *task*.

Reference to the history of Marxism, as the ghost that might still haunt us, helps specify the peculiarities of our time, in which a fundamental transformation of Marxism is necessary for it to continue at all — for Marxism to be reborn, or, more precisely, to be reincarnated, in the traditional sense of spirit forgetting its past life. Such forgetting today, however, is a pathological repression. We must make Marxism remembered, if however, and necessarily, obscurely.

### Unredeemable legacy of the 20th century

The 20th century, the period of the emergence, crisis, death, and memory of Marxism, cannot really be redeemed. In other words, the language of redemption you find in the Second International, with figures such as Rosa Luxemburg, or even with figures such as Benjamin or Adorno (who followed Luxemburg), their notion of redemption doesn't apply for us in the 21st century. The reason that the 20th century cannot be redeemed is that, unlike the 19th century, we can say that the 20th century was one of *unnecessary* suffering. This is because the failure of Marxism was unnecessary — which is why it cannot be properly forgotten.

Rather, all of (prior) human history is now filtered through the 20th century — not through capital (as in the 19th century, for Marx), but rather through the failure of Marxism. The postmodernist attempt to overturn "grand narratives" of history was first and foremost the attempt to overcome Marxism as the grandest of all narratives of history. But postmodernism was not successful in this.

Whereas, for Marx, capital was the crossroads of human history as it had culminated in the 19th century, the 20th century was characterized by the crossroads of Marxism. This affects what came after. All ideology today is anti-Marxism, thus always returning to the question of Marxism. This is why Platypus is not about Marxism as an answer to the crisis of history, but rather as a question. That means that Platypus as a project is peculiar and unlike any other Marxist project historically, and the reason that we are unlike any other Marxist project today is that we emerged when we did. Our historical moment is unlike any other period. We cannot pose Marxism as an answer but only as a question.

Now, our claim is not that Marxism is *a* question, but is, rather, the more emphatic one, that Marxism is *the* question.

Because of the nature of the last year, 2011–12, this narrative requires a postscript, on anarchism.

## Neo-anarchism and neo-liberalism

I just narrated 1873–1973 with respect to Marxism. Now, I'd like to narrate 1873–1973 in terms of anarchism.

Post-1873, anarchism was a waning ideology in the wilderness, excluded from the Second International, and thus cast into the shadows.

Post-1973, by contrast, it has become impossible to avoid anarchism. There is a way in which everything has become a kind of anarchism. Everything becomes filtered through an ethos of anarchism. Such (pseudo-) "anarchism" is more ideologically prevalent today than ever before.

It is significant that anarchism was excluded from the Second International. For the Second International, it didn't seem that this was to any political detriment.

Starting in 1905, however, with the Russian Revolution, there began to be a changed relationship between anarchism and Marxism. After the 1870s, Marxism felt entirely justified in regarding anarchism as an antiquated and obsolete ideology. After 1905, however, this is no longer really the case. There are splits in both Marxism and anarchism that point to a changed relationship between Marxism and anarchism. Starting with 1905, anarchists become Marxists and, also, Marxists become (somehow) more anarchist. For instance, it was important for Rosa Luxemburg to argue, with respect to her pamphlet on 1905, *The Mass Strike, the Trade Unions and the Political Party* (1906), that she was *not* offering an anarchist argument or apologia for anarchism.

And, later, again, with the Russian Revolution in 1917, significantly, anarchists became Marxists.

From 1920/24–73, however, dissident Marxism becomes ("neo"-) anarchism, as seen in "council-communism," Korsch's later (post-1924) trajectory, figures such as Castoriadis, Murray Bookchin, the Situationist International, etc.

In 1969, Adorno wrote, in his last essay, "Resignation," that "the return of anarchism is that of a ghost," that (historical) Marxism's critique of anarchism remained valid (see there Adorno's paraphrasing of Lenin's 1920 pamphlet *"Left-Wing" Communism: An Infantile Disorder*).[8] Marxism's failure to transcend anarchism post-1919 means that the recrudescence of anarchism becomes an important symptom of the failure of Marxism. But this return of anarchism is not true but rather "pseudo."

More broadly speaking, socialism's failure to transcend liberalism in the 20th century means that liberalism becomes an important symptom of the failure of socialism, i.e., neo-liberalism. There are thus significant parallels between neo-liberalism and what we might call neo-anarchism after the failure of Marxism in the world revolution 1917–19.

Why characterize (pseudo-")anarchism(") as "dishonest liberalism," or, as "hysterical" liberalism?[9] What might we mean by that? This is because anarchism is the only serious non-Marxian approach to socialism — other versions of socialism, for instance 20th century Social Democracy, are more clearly apparently relapses into (decadent, "ideological" forms of) liberalism. (Hence, Luxemburg's characterization, in *Reform or Revolution?*, 1900/08, of Eduard Bernstein's "reformism" as "liberalism.")

The failure of Marxist socialism thus has two essential results: neo-anarchism and neo-liberalism. They are distinguished not in principle, as their proponents might imagine, but only on a spectrum of opportunism. Hence, the indicative, symptomatic ideology of "libertarian socialism" in our post-1973 era. Libertarianism is merely an ideologically cruder version of anarchism, or, (neo- or pseudo-)anarchism post-1973 is merely an ideologically overwrought libertarianism. Anarchists are libertarians who take themselves too seriously; and libertarians are anarchists who are content to remain muddled in their thinking.

Following the Marxism of Lenin and Trotsky (and Luxemburg), Stalinism, as a form of "state socialism" is not to be defined properly as "authoritarian" but rather as *opportunist*. It was not simply a "wrong way,"

---

8   In *Critical Models: Interventions and Catchwords*, trans. Henry W. Pickford (New York: Columbia University Press, 1998), 292.

9   See "The Occupy Movement, a Renascent Left, and Marxism Today: An interview with Slavoj Žižek," in *Platypus Review* 42 (December 2011 – January 2012).

but an opportunistic adaptation to defeat (or failure), what Trotsky called the "great organizer of defeat." Hence, neo-anarchism is to be defined as dishonest opportunism, or as "(reactionary-)utopian ideology."

The primary character of such ideology is the obscuring of history – the effacing of post-1848 political authoritarianism ("Bonapartism") as a historical symptom that cannot be avoided but must be worked through. Anarchism is indicted by its anti-Marxism. This is what it means to say that (neo-)anarchism lacks historical consciousness or theory, replacing this with anthropology or psychology.

### Q & A

*In speaking about the "unnecessary suffering" of the 20th century, what did you mean?*

It is significant that it is only in the late 19th century that one finds, for instance, a *genocidal* policy towards indigenous peoples (e.g., Native Americans). But, also, there is a new kind of racism, whether Dreyfus Affair anti-Semitism, or the new post-(collapse of) Reconstruction anti-black racism in the U.S. These came to characterize the 20th century. I would assert that such pathologies were not historically necessary but avoidable.

*What about Bonapartism, as a post-1848 vs. post-1873 phenomenon?*

This is related to the difference between Marx and Marxism, which is potentially obscure. Is there a difference in Bonapartism post-1848 and post-1873? Perhaps. This is the importance of "state capitalism." What is the difference between the 1848 Revolutions and the (1870–71) Paris Commune? What is the difference between the First and Second Internationals? Marx and Engels did not seek to make "Marxism," whatever that would be, hegemonic in the First International. But it seems to become necessarily hegemonic in the Second International. This expresses a historical shift.

*I have two questions about the historical periodization: perhaps two blind spots. What about the period between the death of Trotsky in 1940 and the emergence of the New Left in the 1960s? This would appear to be an important bridge period. Also, aren't you collapsing the post-1973 and post-1989 periods? What about the 1980s, before the collapse of Stalinism, but after the efflorescence of the 1970s? One sees this, for example, in the degeneration of the Spartacist League, among other Marxist organizations, after the 1970s.*

The 1980s were importantly characterized by the disintegration of the Left into academicism and activism. Hence, there were two phases of what I'm calling the obscuring of the memory of Marxism, in which this occurred differently: the 1970s and the 1980s.

In terms of the mid-20th century period, one could say this was the heyday of Stalinism, as well as of ersatz or quasi-Stalinism, that is, Third World nationalism and Maoism, Castroism/Guevarism, etc. The Cold War films of the period showed the "blob" of the "Red Menace" growing. But this was not, I would contend, the growth of Marxism.

The memory of Marxism was sustained by the farce of Marxism in Stalinism.

*But wasn't Adorno's own work a response to this mid-20th century moment?*

I would say that neither the Frankfurt School nor Trotskyism experienced any real development in the mid-20th century, after 1940. At best, they held their ground. At worst, they retreated.

*What about the 1860s? What about Bonapartism as an epochal development? What about Marx's own growth and maturity as a political thinker? In 1873, from my understanding of European history, the kind of state interventionism one sees then is a political choice, not (merely) an economic one. When was the crisis of Marxism? How does this relate to the crisis of neoliberalism in the present? Why do you place such emphasis on Trotsky and Trotskyism? I know you were once around the Spartacist League. But wasn't Trotskyism a farce as much as Stalinism? Didn't Trotsky underestimate the profound, paralyzing influence of Stalinism? Wasn't Stalinism a profounder problem than Trotsky thought?*

*Isn't there a problem with the "red thread" argument, linking Marx, through Lenin, Trotsky, etc.?*

I must say that I don't think Trotsky's Fourth International project was particularly viable. But I also don't think the Third, Communist International project was viable. Now, of course, Lenin and Trotsky had to hope against hope with the Third International.

But this is not to fault Trotsky (or Lenin!). When Trotsky was launching the Fourth International — people had spoken of the October Revolution as one characterized by "youth;" the soldiers were teenagers — there was still a living memory of the Revolution in the 1930s. Those who were once 20 were then 40, and thus still capable of making revolution. There is also the problem of what I would call Trotsky's self-vulgarization, his propaganda orientation. Moreover, there was a problem in Trotsky trying to split the Third International, and basing his politics on the early Third International. But we must bear in mind that after 1933 Trotsky also oriented towards the remnants of Second International Social Democracy (as expressed in the so-called "French turn"), and refused to characterize Stalinism as somehow more Left than Social Democracy. I think that Trotsky's "crisis of leadership" estimation of political possibilities meant something more supple than what his followers offered later. I think he recognized the profundity of the problem and its historical roots.

Let me be clear: The failure of Marxism was profound. Hence, there is no Marxism to return to. There is no answer, only a question. The question is the failure of Marxism.

The reason I am putting such emphasis on post-1873 history is to raise the issue of Marxism *per se*. Not the question of the workers' movement or of socialism, but of Marxism. This is not posed later, in 1938 (the founding of the Fourth International) or 1933 (the failure of Third International to stop Nazism), or 1923 (the definitive end of the post-WWI revolutionary wave) or 1919 (the crushing of the German Revolution) or 1917 (the October Revolution as revolutionary split in Marxism) or 1914 (the collapse of the Second International in WWI). The question of Marxism is posed already at the outset in the 1870s. Why was the SPD necessary? Why does the SPD take the form it does? Why did Marxists join a Lassallean party?

So, there is the issue of the SPD, founded in 1875, being what Moishe Postone, for one, has called a "Lassallean party with Marxist verbiage." Wasn't it always a Lassallean party with "Marxist" window-dressing? My question is, is there such a thing as a "Marxist party?" Or, is there, rather, a socialist party with Marxists participating in it? Marxism was the "historical consciousness" of the socialist workers' movement. There's a famous photograph of Rosa Luxemburg, flanked on stage by portraits of Lassalle and Marx. Now, what did that mean? Certainly, Luxemburg was aware of Marx's critique of and political opposition to Lassalle. So, what did it mean for an avowed "Marxist" such as Luxemburg to participate in a socialist workers' movement and political party with a strong tradition of Lassalleanism?

But the history of Marxism was always characterized by the critique of socialism, starting with Marx in the 1840s, but carried forward, for instance, in Lenin's critique of Narodnism, "Legal Marxism," and "Economism." Or, more generally, in the Marxist critique of anarchism, whether of Proudhon or Bakunin, et al. There is also the "Revisionist Dispute" within Marxism itself in the 1890s. What would it mean, then, to speak of Marxism as a form of politics *per se*?

Just as Marxism as a philosophy or theory is peculiar, as a political practice it is also quite peculiar. If, for Marxists, the socialist workers' movement always shades off into liberalism and anarchism, is always overlaid with anarchist and liberal ideology, then Marxism is always in a constant struggle against these. But this is not a struggle merely of opposition but of critical *recognition*.

About the "maturity" of Marxism, there is a question. I don't think of the "mature Marx" as the writer of *Capital*, but also and perhaps more importantly as a political figure. In the critique of Korsch's "Marxism and Philosophy" (1923) by Kautsky that we published,[10] Kautsky accuses Korsch, along with Lenin and the Bolsheviks (including Trotsky), for being enamored of "primitive Marxism," i.e., that of Marx and Engels in the 1840s, and ignoring subsequent development.[11] Both Korsch and Kautsky have some points to score in that debate. What's the difference,

---

10 See Karl Kautsky, "A Destroyer of Vulgar Marxism," in *Platypus Review* 43 (February 2012).

11 Ibid.

for example, between Marx in the *Manifesto* and in the "Programme of the Parti Ouvrier" (1880)?[12] These differences are potentially vital. But can they be considered simply as *development*?

There is, for instance, the issue that Marx himself was accused (in the 1860s) of being right-wing or opportunistic, in his endorsement of unions and workers' consumer cooperatives, etc. Lukács is good at pointing this out (in "Reification and the Consciousness of the Proletariat," in *History and Class Consciousness*, 1923), that is, the symptomatic character of Lassalle's criticism of Marx for supposedly being "economistic" and neglecting politics. But Lassalle criticized the "economic" struggles of the workers more generally, going so far as to call this the mere struggle of economic "objects" as objects (of capitalism). But Lukács's point was that Marx recognized a dialectic of economics and politics, or, of the workers as both "objects" and "subjects" of capitalism. Marx didn't take unions or cooperatives as good in themselves, but rather as historical (and symptomatic) forms that the workers' movement was taking, to be pushed through. They are the forms through which the possibility for socialism can be grasped. They can't be accepted in their own terms, but they're also not to be criticized, let alone rejected as such.

That's why I emphasize this period of the collapse of the First International and the birth of the SPD in the 1870s, to bring out the issue of Marxism as such.

*What about the crisis of liberalism? When does the crisis of liberalism become the necessity for Marxism? When was this shift?*

For Marx, certainly liberalism was "dead" as an *emancipatory* politics already in 1848. It was liberals, after all, who put down the workers in June 1848. Liberalism dies several deaths. The death of liberalism in 1848 is different from that in the 1870s (for example, with the failure of Reconstruction in the U.S.).

This raises the question of historical "progress." The necessity for socialism grows between 1848 and 1873. Engels, for example, in his 1895

---

12 Jules Guesde and Karl Marx, "The Programme of the Parti Ouvrier."

Introduction to Marx's *The Class Struggles in France*,[13] discusses the still not exhausted potential for capitalist development after 1848. But this wasn't for Engels merely "economic" but *political*. Capitalism continues to grow, economically, in a sense. The question was whether such growth was a political advance. The evidence of "progress," for Engels, was the growth of the socialist workers' movement. What Marx and Engels had "underestimated" was the potential for capitalism to contribute to the growth of the workers' movement for socialism. But that is precisely what we have *not* seen since 1973! Perhaps not since 1919.

*What about Marx's (infamous) Preface to the Contribution to the Critique of Political Economy (1859), about "productive forces" and "relations of production?" To call the 20th century one huge ball of unnecessary suffering seems to belie Marx's sense of contradiction. This is part of the continuing strange character of "what it means to live." Chris, I've heard you address, for instance, financial techniques as forces of production, still contributing to the development of social possibilities. The 20th century as unnecessary suffering fails to get at that aspect of history. Capitalism hasn't shut down yet. On the other hand, Marx and Engels, in the Manifesto, project the rest of the 19th century as unnecessary. So, the 20th century could be seen still as necessary, while the 19th century could also be seen as unnecessary.*

The reason I put it this way, highly tendentiously, is to focus the question of Marxism. In other words, will Marxism play a role in emancipation? If it does, then the 20th century was unnecessary. If it does not, then perhaps the 20th century was necessary, in getting beyond, and transcending, Marxism. If the history of actual Marxism as politics plays no role, then the New Left was right, revolution in 1917 had been premature. If this history still has a role to play, however, then perhaps 1917 was not so premature, and what came later was not so necessary.

We must ask, in what ways might the history of Marxism play a role? As practical politics? As theory? How? As a relation of theory and practice,

---

13  See Friedrich Engels, "Introduction to Karl Marx's *The Class Struggles in France 1848 to 1850*" (1895).

as Adorno puts it in "Marginalia to Theory and Praxis" (1969)?[14] In what way was and is Marxism necessary?

Why should a project such as ours, beginning in the 21st century, be "Marxist?" Why shouldn't we be "post-Marxist?" Why can't we say, simply, that the history of Marxism has some contributions to make, but look at all these other things, anarchism, etc.?

*How is it that Stalinism, Maoism, etc., weren't Marxism? Is it because they abandoned an emancipatory vision? Is it because they became one-sided in their opposition to capitalism, and denied its contributing to emancipatory possibilities? So that, today, it doesn't seem that capitalism holds such possibilities. What would it take to make that possibility active again? It would seem that the only way to do that would be to work through the history of the 20th century.*

I'm not exactly saying that (about Stalinism and Maoism, etc.). To get back to the issue of Trotskyism, yes, Trotskyism was farcical in a sense. It was not the Marxism practiced by Lenin, Luxemburg, and Trotsky himself in an earlier period. It was not the relation between theory and practice that Marxism once was. This is what makes the history of Trotskyism, including Trotsky's own in the 1920s and '30s, farcical, in a sense.

Why isn't Trotsky a tragic figure, why is he farcical? Well, because the real tragic figures of Marxism, to my mind, are Lenin and Luxemburg. Lenin, to me, was a tragic figure. Also, Marx and Engels themselves. Marxism was the tragedy.

*The ambiguity of the 20th century raises the issue of ideology. Could Marxism again become a guiding ideology?*

There is the difference of the dialectic of history, as expressed by Marxism in the late 19th and early 20th centuries, and the exhaustion of history in our present period. That's what Fukuyama meant by the "end of history." While untrue in a certain sense, it is symptomatically expressive in another sense.

---

14  In *Critical Models: Interventions and Catchwords*, trans. Henry Pickford (New York: Columbia University Press, 2005).

What is the possibility of the recovery of the memory of Marxism? I think that the casualty of the death of Marxism was the workers' movement itself, despite the 1930s, let alone the '60s and '70s. The "class struggle," as previously found in history, ended. Not labor militancy, but class struggle. The failure of Marxism is the failure of the socialist workers' movement. Stalinism was not only the farce of Marxism but also of the socialist workers' movement. This is related to social democracy and even fascism. When Friedrich Hayek, in *The Road to Serfdom* (1944), said that the roots of fascism are to be found in pre-WWI social democracy, even a benign case like Austrian Social Democracy, he had a point. Horrific if true, still, there is the problem of the *plausibility* of Hayek's account, which was influential. Hayek, after all, is a key progenitor of neo-liberalism, that is, 20th century liberalism.

The 20th century was the rehash of 19th century ideology. There's nothing new. Hayek, for instance, doesn't come up with anything new, but rather goes back to liberalism, to ideology before socialism. The recrudescence of old ideologies is indicative. The 19th century, by contrast, was very new at the level of ideology.

*What about fascism? What about fundamentalism? Aren't they new in the 20th century?*

Well, fundamentalism might be new, but I am emphasizing the Left. Fundamentalism is obviously conservative, and reaches back well before the 19th century. Fascism has roots in the 19th century, specifically in history after the 1870s. But, on the Left, liberalism and anarchism, as forms of anti-Marxism, still claim to be emancipatory, not conservative ideologies. They, like Marxism, originate in the 19th century. They are still with us today. The question is whether and how Marxism still is.

Presented at the Platypus Affiliated Society's fourth annual International Convention, held at the School of the Art Institute of Chicago March 30–April 1, 2012.

Originally published in *Platypus Review* 47 (June 2012)

# Internationalism fails

The "anti-imperialist Left" considers itself opposed to all U.S. government action as "imperialist" on principle. But, as Trotsky wrote to his followers in 1938, "Learn to think!" while one may oppose the government politically, to oppose the government putting out a fire, especially when there is no alternative agency for doing so, is nonsense. But the "Left" today is not the inheritor of Trotsky, but rather of what he pitilessly assailed, the policy of the Stalinist "Popular Front Against War and Fascism" of the 1930s, for which the shibboleth was, "Which side are you on?"

The idea is that the defeat of imperialist policy creates possibility for an alternative, and therefore one must always be against imperialism to be on the side of an alternative to it. Historically, Marxists have understood such a strategy in terms of either "revolutionary defeatism" or "revolutionary defencism." Simply put, the defeat of an imperialist power is seen as providing the possibility for a political alternative to the government of the imperialist country; whereas the defense of a country against imperialist attack is seen as providing the possibility for a political alternative in the subaltern country. Importantly, these are not pacifist positions against war, but rather political military strategies in time of war, moreover with the aim of *revolution*.

Historically, there are two examples of success of these strategies of revolutionary defeatism and revolutionary defencism: the role of the Bolsheviks in the Russian Revolution is regarded as a success of revolutionary defeatism, in which the defeat of the Tsarist Russian Empire undermined the government and gave rise to political and social revolution; and Mao's Communists in the Chinese Revolution, in which the defense of China against Japanese imperialist attack undermined the nationalist Kuomintang and allowed for Communist-led revolution. The point of revolutionary defencism was to be better defenders of the country than the nationalists could be, in that the nationalists, in upholding the nation-state as such, must necessarily compromise with global capitalism — "imperialism" — in ways the Communists, as anti-capitalist, would not. This did not mean to be better nationalists than the nationalists. Socialism, let alone Marxism, was not meant to be a political ideology of "national liberation," but rather of global political and social transformation, which was meant to better — and indeed truly, because more fundamentally able to — meet the needs of liberation from national oppression under capitalism.

Today, such specificities and true horizons of politics of social emancipation are lost in the "anti-imperialism" of the pseudo-"Left." Today's "Left" has more in common with the Indian National Army (INA), which sought help from the Japanese against the British during WWII. But this was not the Communist but rather the fascist version of "anti-imperialism." It should not be the Left's. (Indeed, Hitler hosted INA leader Subhas Chandra Bose in Berlin as a fellow "anti-imperialist.") As the Burmese nationalist Aung San, father of democratic activist Aung San Suu Kyi, put it, "The British sucked our blood, but the Japanese ground our bones."[1] Mao and his Chinese Communist Party celebrated their WWII allies U.S. atomic bombing of Hiroshima and Nagasaki. The German and Japanese national-fascist oppositions to the U.K. and U.S.-led global capitalist "imperialist" order were no good. Neither are today's oppositions.

The question today is whether supposed "revolutionary" defeatism in the U.S. and "revolutionary" defencism in the targets of its military interventions, for example, will actually lead to socialist revolution or any kind of beneficial outcome in either the U.S. or those countries it attacks.

The Left must ask: What might be the actual political effects of a defeat for the U.S.?

It is a mistake perpetuated by the 1960s-era New Left, with its experience of the Vietnam anti-war movement, that somehow imperialist counterinsurgency must necessarily fail. Indeed, historically, counterinsurgencies

---

1    Quoted in Field Marshal Sir William Slim, *Defeat into Victory*, 2nd edition (London: Cassell & Co., 1956).

have been far more successful than unsuccessful. The Indian Mutiny of 1857 was quelled; so were the Taiping and Boxer Rebellions of 1850–64 and 1899–1901. The Boers were subdued in 1880–81 and 1899–1902. The U.K. maintained control of Iraq in the 1930s-40s; they waged a successful counter-insurgency against Communists in Malaysia after WWII. The U.S. was successful in rolling back peasant *jacquerie* in South Korea in 1950–53. The Greek Civil War 1946–49 resulted in defeat for the Communist insurgents.

Furthermore, the question of political-military strategy regarding "imperialism" is not exhausted or even well informed by ostensible Left-Right distinctions. The U.S. supported the Maoist Communists in Cambodia, the Khmer Rouge, both in and out of power; the U.S. opposed the regime installed by Vietnamese Communist intervention in Cambodia in 1979 by supporting the Khmer Rouge — well after the revelation of the "killing fields" — just as they opposed the USSR-supported regime in Afghanistan with the Mujahideen Islamists. Maoists supported both out of "anti-imperialism," which found the People's Republic of China on the same side as the U.S. against "Soviet imperialism" (also in various wars in Africa). Most of the "Left" supported Solidarity in Poland as well. In these instances "anti-imperialism" worked: "Soviet imperialism" was defeated, and there was a "revolution" in the USSR and its Eastern European "sphere of influence."

Should we expect something similar today regarding the U.S.-led world order? Will defeat for the U.S. in one of its military campaigns result in its collapse? Hardly.

For it would appear that the only instances in which "anti-imperialism" has ever been successful — including in the Russian and Chinese Revolutions — were when there was military support from a more powerful imperialist power: Germany against Russia in WWI; and the U.S. against Japan in WWII.

The mistake of "anti-imperialism" today is in its naturalization of all national states as existing political actors and as domains of potential political action. We are today well past the political compromises of Stalin's strategy of "socialism in one country."

However, the deeper history of Marxism, before Stalinism, may yet be instructive in certain ways. Rosa Luxemburg and Karl Liebknecht's

Spartacus League in WWI Germany was "revolutionary defeatist" regarding the German war policy. They did not regard the greater imperialist powers of the time and their alliance, the U.K., the U.S., France and Russia, as the greater enemies of potential progressive-emancipatory political and social change, but rather "the main enemy is at home" meant the German government. This did not mean that they "sided" with the other imperialist powers, as their political opponents — and ultimate executioners — on the German Right insisted. Neither did Lenin and Trotsky's Bolsheviks side with Germany as the Russian nationalists and their Entente international allies averred. The Provisional Government, overthrown by the Bolshevik-led soviets, fled in a U.K. diplomatic car, but that didn't change the fact that for Lenin and Trotsky the Russian nationalists were the "main enemy." Luxemburg feared the political consequences of Lenin and Trotsky's potential "embrace" of German imperialism in the Treaty of Brest-Litovsk — what caused the Bolsheviks' Russian "socialist" opponents to unleash a terrorist campaign against them, bombing Bolshevik Party headquarters and attempting to assassinate Lenin and the German ambassador — but Luxemburg nonetheless endorsed the Bolsheviks in the October Revolution and their soviet government and joined the Third International they led.

The "Left" today is hardly up for the challenge posed by such political necessities, let alone the task of social revolution. "Anti-imperialism" today is not revolutionary but rather counter-revolutionary in that it is a species of the most powerful actually constituted counterrevolutionary political force, nationalism.

"Internationalism" is no longer what it was for Lenin, Luxemburg and Trotsky in the 2nd, 3rd and 4th Internationals, but is rather inter-*nationalism*, that is, conjunctural alliances between nationalisms, and not revolutionary *anti*-nationalism as it was historically for socialism and Marxism.

Defeatism and defencism today have no progressive-emancipatory political and social content either, for they are not "revolutionary" in any sense beyond, perhaps, the conventional and superficial one of "regime change." Today's "Left" agrees with the imperialists in their horizon of politics: the existing international system of national states. The "Left" today may be divided among and within the nation-states, between those who "side with" this or that government policy, but they are all on the same side of accommodating global capitalism — imperialism.

There is no real anti-imperialism, but only various forms of compromise with imperialism, which is regarded pejoratively to denounce merely this or that governmental policy, but is accepted at a deeper level as an unshakeable reality. However, historical Marxists once knew that it will not be possible to move beyond it on this basis.[2]

Originally published in *Platypus Review* 60 (October 2013)

---

2   See the Platypus Affiliated Society public fora on: "Imperialism: What is it, and why should we be against it?," in January 2007, an edited transcript of which was published in *Platypus Review* 25 (July 2010). Also see "What is imperialism? (What now?)," held in April 2013, in *Platypus Review* 59 (September 2013).

# 1914 in the history of Marxism

One hundred years later, what does the crisis and split in Marxism, and the political collapse of the major parties of the 2nd International in 1914, mean for us today?

The Spartacists, for example, are constantly in search of the "August 4" moment, the moment of betrayal of the proletariat's struggle for socialism by various tendencies in the history of Marxism. The Spartacists went so far as to confess their own "August 4th" when they failed to call for the immediate withdrawal of U.S. troops from Haiti in the aftermath of the earthquake there.

So, what happened, from a Marxist perspective, on August 4, 1914, when the Social Democratic Party of Germany (SPD) members of the Reichstag voted to finance the Prussian Empire's war budget?

Two things: the parliamentary representatives of the SPD went against past resolutions to vote down the war effort of the German government; and the disorganization of the SPD leadership, what has been called the effective but illegitimate takeover of the party by the parliamentary delegation. No legitimate political authority of the party sanctioned this action. In all respects of principle and practice, the SPD was destroyed as a political organization as it had existed up to that point.

August 4, 1914, has been called — by the Spartacists — the first great internal counterrevolution in the history of Marxism. This is entirely true.

But it was a counterrevolution conducted not merely by the leadership of the SPD, however they may have abetted it, but rather by the Reich's government against the SPD membership.

What was the specific character of this counterrevolution, and how was it made possible?

There was a famous pair of sayings by the SPD's chairman, Bebel: "Not one man or one penny for this rotten system!" and "If it's against Russia, I myself will pick up a gun!"

The German High Command, in preparation for war, took aim precisely at the contradiction between these two statements by Bebel.

The German High Command wielded the specter of counterrevolution through occupation by Tsarist Russian troops against the SPD in order to prompt their preemptive counterrevolution, which they saw as an act of self-preservation, as the lesser evil. Furthermore, they thought that getting behind the war would allow them to (somehow) control it, to make the government dependent on them and so wrest political concessions from it, perhaps even undermining it, in political favor of the proletariat.

This was not an unreasonable judgment. The question is whether their compromise was too much, whether the act of ostensible self-preservation was in fact actually an act of self-destruction.

The SPD leadership did not want the war. They thought, however, that they couldn't prevent it: unleashing a class-struggle civil war to stop the international war was not feasible in terms of success, but would only result in the crushing of the SPD's organization, which was at least preserved if subordinated to the government through the war.

So the issue is what was preserved through the compromise, the surrender to the blackmail of the war?

The German government, which the original Spartacus League of Rosa Luxemburg and Karl Liebknecht considered responsible for the war, adopted a strategy of a two-front war — against both the Russians and the British and the French — despite the evident military risks of doing so. They did so in order to ensure the adherence of the Social Democrats to the war effort, out of defense against the Russians. The threat of Russian invasion and occupation, and destruction of the social-democratic workers' movement, was enough to preempt such active counterrevolution with the passive counterrevolution of the social-democratic cooperation with the war effort.

In all politics there is, as Lenin put it, a "who-whom?" question: who is the agent and who is the object. The most catastrophic political mistakes the Left has made historically are in terms of this who-whom problem: for instance, the Iranian Left tried to use the Ayatollah Khomeini's Islamists, but it was Khomeini who instead used the Left.

The German Social Democrats, by contrast, did not seek so much to undermine the German government through cooperation, but rather merely to survive the war.

Still, when the German war effort collapsed in 1918, the Social Democrats were, as a result of their collaboration, in the position to have the mantle of government fall to them, in what they considered to be a democratic — and not socialist — revolution.

The apparent separation of the democratic from the socialist revolution in 1918 is what retrospectively condemns the SPD's collaboration with the German government's war effort. What confirms the political character of the vote for war credits of August 4, 1914, was the counterrevolutionary role played by the SPD in 1918–19. If the SPD had fought for socialism in 1918, then its choice to avoid confrontation and repression in 1914 would have been justified. It was not only the horror of the war that indicted the SPD's compromise in 1914, but the division around the struggle for socialist revolution later at the conclusion of the war that confirmed Luxemburg, Liebknecht, and Lenin's perspective.

However, there was the perspective of Kautsky, who was consistent in considering the war an utter calamity and not any kind of occasion for struggling for socialism, either in 1914 or in 1917, and 1918–19.

Kautsky condemned the Bolsheviks' overthrow of the Russian Provisional Government in 1917, which stood with the Entente against the Germans. Lenin and Trotsky's Bolsheviks were regarded by Russian nationalists as German agents for promoting an armistice, to pull Russia out of the war. But Lenin wanted to pull Russia out of the international war in order for it to participate in the civil war between the global classes of workers and capitalists.

Thus Kautsky and Lenin could accuse one another of complicity in the war: Kautsky for voting for war credits to defend the SPD in the present, and thus the possibility of the struggle for socialism in the future; and Lenin for trying to use the war as an occasion for socialist revolution. Each could accuse the other of opportunism in the historical moment and of undermining — betraying — the true struggle for socialism.

Luxemburg agreed with Lenin that, in itself, and apart from the immediate application of the goal in the struggle for socialism, the SPD was nothing or indeed worse than nothing, part of sustaining capitalism.

For Luxemburg and Lenin, the SPD was duty-bound to launch a civil war against the German government rather than allow it to launch an international war. This is precisely the repression of the SPD Kautsky and other leaders of the SPD feared, why they thought it was impossible to stage a political confrontation with the government in 1914. Its failure to do so rendered it, in Luxemburg's terms, a "stinking corpse;" that is, dead for long enough that it was putrefying already in 1914. August 4 revealed the SPD as already dead: its past failures accumulated in it. This was not a matter of mere tactics, a military appraisal of the SPD's chances against the government's forces in 1914, but rather a matter of principle — preserving the honor of Marxism and of the workers' movement for socialism more generally.

Recently, the anarchist Wayne Price spoke on a Platypus panel about the dual failure of Marxism in the 2nd and 3rd Internationals, that Marxism revealed its authoritarian statism at two clear moments, when Marxists of the 2nd International supported the war in 1914, and when Lenin suppressed other socialists in the Russian Revolution and Stalin did so in the Spanish Civil War.[1]

The role of Marxist parties in these instances was to serve the counter-revolution rather than the revolution.

The question, then, would be not what Kautsky and Lenin had in common, but how they differed. And they differed most clearly around the issue of the war in 1914, from which their later difference over the revolution in both Russia and Germany in 1917–18 was derived.

The question is the workers' movement for socialism. Kautsky considered it an end in itself, thus retroactively agreeing with Bernstein's Revisionist-reformist view of the "movement is everything, the goal nothing." Preserving the movement meant betraying its goals, whereas Luxemburg and Lenin were willing to sacrifice the movement for the goal of socialism. That is the only reason they opposed the war by opposing the

---

1   See Wayne Price's remarks for the Platypus panel discussion "Radical Ideologies Today: Marxism and Anarchism," at the University of Illinois at Chicago (UIC), March 19, 2014. Sound recording available online.

war policies of the various antagonistic governments, to precipitate a global civil war of workers against capitalists. They thus did not reject the war on pacifist grounds, as Kautsky might have done, compromising with it on defensive grounds, but rather identified the war as the necessary expression of, and occasion for, the need for the struggle for socialism.

As it turns out, perhaps the preemptive counterrevolution by the German government through the war must be deemed in retrospect to have been successful. Certainly the struggle for socialism let alone Marxism in the advanced capitalist countries never did recover from it.

Luxemburg, Lenin, and Trotsky tried to make the First World War really into what Woodrow Wilson merely promised, a "war to end all wars." Wilson thought it was to defeat remnant feudalism; Marxists understood rather that it was to overcome capitalism.

As such, Luxemburg, Lenin, and Trotsky launched a civil war: first and foremost a civil war within Marxism itself, between those who accepted the task and those who rejected and thus betrayed the duties of that civil war. That they failed in this is not proof against the task of socialism. Wilson regarded and fought against the Marxists as extremists — extremism bred of political repression in undemocratic states. But of course the conservative and opportunist character of Wilson's politics was different from that of the SPD's capitulation to the war. Or was it? Wilson didn't think that Prussian militarism or Tsarism indicted bourgeois society but were backward violations of its norms. The SPD similarly addressed the war as an abnormality. Luxemburg, Lenin, and Trotsky addressed the war as the norm: the endemic crisis of capitalism raised to a fever pitch. But the SPD and Wilson considered them to be opening the world to greater war and horror, to the greater barbarization of bourgeois society. If Wilson was no socialist, he still considered himself a defender against the threats of both Prussian militarism and Bolshevism of the norms of liberal democratic bourgeois society, which socialists considered the base-line minimum of the standards for a better society. The question and the political dispute was over how to best protect, defend, and promote the principles of that better society, to which all political actors might claim adherence, and what compromises can be justifiable in that pursuit. It is thus not a matter of pure principles but of means to their end, the true dispute of politics.

Nineteen fourteen was not proof of the Marxist analysis of "imperialism" or the demonstration of the horrors of capitalism, or any other such thing: It was the division of Marxism in war and revolution at the *Götterdämmerung* of bourgeois society that haunts the struggle for socialism to this day, the task and duty of civil war from which the "Left" today shrinks, thus becoming a "stinking corpse," now as before.

The war and the revolution are all around us, all the time. As Lenin put it, it is not as conveniently posed as the capitalists lining up on one side and the workers on the other, which would make the task very simple. No: 1914 is still with us to the extent that the workers are on both sides, and both sides could plausibly claim to be on the true side of the struggle for socialism, or at least for a better society, which is what "socialism" after all means.

Nineteen fourteen was the division in the workers' movement for socialism, which was the precondition for the politics of revolution. The fact that we no longer have that politics can be traced back to the problem and task that 1914 revealed.

## Q & A

*The idea that we've inherited from 1914 — Lenin as revolutionary defeatist, and defeatism as Marxist orthodoxy — really represents an innovation. It was not the norm even of Marxists who opposed the war at the time, e.g. the Zimmerwald center. Marx and Engels did not take a revolutionary defeatist stance in the wars of German unification or Franco-Prussian war, but instead tactically adopted different positions in different wars. The idea of a principled revolutionary defeatism came from Lenin's consciousness that bourgeois society had changed in the decades since then. To him, 1914 represented simultaneously the overripeness and rottenness of both bourgeois society and the SPD. This is expressed in the theory of imperialism, which is taken to be a new stage of bourgeois society. The problem with the "Leninist" view is that after the long period from 1914–1933, the principle of revolutionary defeatism becomes detached from concrete politics and is upheld simply as a principle. This is especially pronounced after WWII. When this principle is detached from the concrete possibility of a global class civil war, everything is changed.*

CC: I want to touch on something I glossed over in my comments in light of this. On the one hand, Luxemburg and Lenin were on the same side in the war; but on the other, they were on opposite sides. They were both revolutionary defeatists in certain respects. But one of Luxemburg's first critiques of the Bolsheviks in power is of their armistice with Germany. Luxemburg thought that by doing this Lenin would be embracing German militarism. We forget this in light of other criticisms, but it was a live issue at the time. The way these disputes — imperialism, revolutionary defeatism, etc. — are remembered by the Left now is in terms of principles, but in a particular way. Rather, we should raise the issue of the need to split the worker's movement post-1914. Lenin's "principled" assessment of WWI was bound up with this need at his historical moment. It's a principled stance with respect to a certain historical situation, but not principled in the manner of pacifism. It is actually in a way a kind of pro-war sentiment.

*When you said, "1914 is still with us," could you relate this to the anti–Iraq war protests? Was there still some kind of consciousness on the Left of the way the problems of 1914 are still with us? If not, what factors stand in the way of raising these problems to consciousness on the Left?*

CC: A government going to war takes a huge political risk, even in the case of the U.S. invading a far weaker country. The government could delegitimate itself, and thus release all sorts of problems. But the anti-war protests before the war gave the Left the false impression that there was a kind of mass sentiment, waiting to take advantage if the governments took a misstep in the war. But the anti-war protests didn't have the content the Left wanted to attribute to it. Both these protests and the Left were bound up in a conservative opposition to war, a kind of fear. But in 1914 the situation is quite different — there is the presence of the Second International. I brought up Lenin's critique of Luxemburg's *Junius Pamphlet*, where he's basically saying, "OK, comrade, just hold on, these governments are undermining themselves and revolution can still happen." Of course this isn't just based upon the war, but of his perception of the strength of the Second International and the SPD. Now where Luxemburg may have been right against Lenin was in thinking that the SPD was a paper tiger. But Lenin had the cooler head with respect to the historical moment.

The main organizers in the 2003 anti-war movement were the International Socialist Organization, Revolutionary Communist Party (RCP), and the Workers World Party and its various offshoots like the Party for Socialism and Liberation. So the RCP would show up with their sound system and their rabble-rousers, and they would deliver speeches that sounded like they were out of a monster truck rally — except with Leftist language as their content. They thought the war just showed how fascistic the world really is. They were stuck in this 1930s frame of fascism versus communism: if you aren't a communist, you're a fascist, and if you don't think you're living under fascism, the war shows that you really are. This is far degraded, neither Luxemburg nor Lenin.

Let's say the U.S. government had been completely delegitimated in the course of the Iraq war, and hundreds of thousands of soldiers were left in Iraq. Do we really think socialism would have been the result of that? Obviously not. What would have happened was a military takeover of the U.S. government, and it would have been popular. People would think only the military could save the troops in Iraq; if the executive and congress can't do it, the military will. There would have been a military coup, a state of emergency; there would not have been socialist revolution — that's for sure.

*I want to bring anarchists into the discussion. In 1914, many anarchists opposed the Bolsheviks and supported the war. But nowadays we see anarchists taking up the defeatist position in an even more consistent manner than Leninists. So it seems there is an opposite course over time.*

CC: The anarchists who supported the war in 1914 capitulated in the same manner as Marxists in the Second International. So it is interesting that the Third International emerges not only from a split within the Second International, but also among anarchists. However, today's anarchists and Marxists aren't in a position of political responsibility, so theirs are a pseudo-anarchism and pseudo-Marxism. These people aren't going to capitulate to anything, because they don't have the political responsibility that would force them into a choice. Anarchists in 1914 were actually faced with a political choice.

Richard Rubin: *I would like to raise the issue of nationalism. We have until now talked about the stances of the so-called leadership of the worker's movement — but WWI showed how deeply rooted nationalist sentiments were in the masses. Before 1914 the view was that workers internationally had a common interest that would lead them to fight together against their exploiters. But this illusion was destroyed by WWI. As anti-nationalists we need to keep this in mind, as it seems there is the mistaken impression that nationalism can be dispensed with easily. People think that common interests are enough to overcome nationalist ideology. Marxists — Lenin included — thought that it would not be a problem, and so the USSR gave land to various ethnicities. But we could actually say that the nation was the necessary ground for the growth of the workers' movement, and nationalism was deeply rooted in it.*

CC: I take exception to this, very strongly. First of all, the question of the workers "supporting the war" is tricky. That young, 18–20-year-old people could be recruited to be very nationalistic troops is very different from saying that 30–40-year-old workers organized in the SPD supported the war. There was a cosmopolitan — not merely international — culture among workers before WWI that was actively destroyed during the war. The German government estimated that the SPD was anti-war, but could be maneuvered into supporting one. They thought that as the SPD grew, and as Germany generally became more liberal and democratic, any hope of reordering Europe by military means would be progressively undermined. So the German government blackmailed them with the threat of Russian invasion. So it's not as if the war occurred independently, and the SPD underestimated the workers' support for it. These are much more closely bound up phenomena, where the thinking was of the SPD as a piece on the playing field militarily. None of the workers wanted the war.

Richard Rubin: *The earlier points about Lenin and Luxemburg are important here. I do believe it is correct to say that Lenin had a "cooler head" than Luxemburg with respect to their historical conjuncture. The problem is that regression in a way makes it appear that Luxemburg was right. I think that Lenin's response to nations, nationalism, and self-determination was basically a continuation of a bourgeois-democratic project. But having experienced the 20th century, there is a way that Luxemburg's anti-nationalism seems more accurate. But I think one has to separate oneself from the sense that we know what happened; there can be a kind of historical optical illusion. This issue came up in current debates about Ukraine. Putin said that the Bolsheviks irrationally gave away historically Russian territory to the Ukrainians. But this was a perfectly reasonable belief: Ukrainians, as a separate people, should have the right to self-determination within the overarching bounds of a soviet socialist federation. You can say at this point in history that it was a naïve belief; but it only became a naïve belief. It was at the time a very sane, rational belief that was an extension through Marxism of basic liberal ideas.*

Presented at the Platypus Affiliated Society's sixth annual International Convention, held at the School of the Art Institute of Chicago April 4–6, 2014.

Originally published in *Platypus Review* 66 (May 2014)

# Israel-Palestine and the "Left"

*Legalities.* — What the Nazis did to the Jews was unspeakable: language has no word for it, since even mass murder would have sounded, in face of its planned, systematic totality, like something from the good old days of the serial killer. And yet a term needed to be found if the victims — in any case too many for their names to be recalled — were to be spared the curse of having no thoughts turned unto them. So in English the concept of genocide was coined. But by being codified, as set down in the International Declaration of Human Rights, the unspeakable was made, for the sake of protest, commensurable. By its elevation to a concept, its possibility is virtually recognized: an institution to be forbidden, rejected, discussed. One day negotiations may take place in the forum of the United Nations on whether some new atrocity comes under the heading of genocide, whether nations have a right to intervene that they do not want to exercise in any case, and whether in view of the unforeseen difficulty of applying it in practice the whole concept of genocide should be removed from the statutes. Soon afterwards there are inside-page headlines in journalese: East Turkestan genocide programme nears completion.[1]

This bitter aphorism was written by Adorno, as part of his book *Minima Moralia*, at the end of World War II, and at the same time he and Frankfurt School Director Max Horkheimer were writing their *Dialectic of*

---

1    Theodor W. Adorno, orphaned from *Minima Moralia* (1944–47), published as "Messages in a Bottle," trans. Edmund Jephcott, *New Left Review* I/200 (July – August 1993).

*Enlightenment* by the poolside in Santa Monica, in which they (outrageously) wrote that perhaps the Hegelian *Weltgeist* — World-Spirit — of freedom dictated the destruction of small nations — in this case, that of the Jews — and that Marxists must accept and go along with this irresistible trend.* For after all socialists were powerless to prevent it, but must still struggle to achieve socialism in its wake. "Never again!" after the Holocaust meant: *always* again. Makes you think.

There have been many instances in the meantime. For example, at around the same time as the Israeli War of Independence, there was the post-colonial Partition of India, which involved millions of victims in the creation of a Muslim state in Pakistan — repeated again when Bangladesh separated from the latter in the 1970s. And there is still Kashmir.

Is Alan Dershowitz to be proven right, that no one cares unless it is Jews who are doing it? (Or is it because they are "white"? But Jews are no more — or less — white than their fellow Semites, the Arabs, and anyway the majority of Israel's Jewish population is Mizrahi and Sephardic not Ashkenazi.) Or are the Islamists right that it matters because it's about al-Aqsa? Or are the millenarian Christians right about Armageddon and the beginning and end of the world? Or Hasidim who judge Zionism a blasphemy? Or is this the "Left's" Rapture, in which God's Elect ascend to Salvation and the rest are Left Behind? At least Hamas has "martyrdom" as consolation for the occupants of the former Roman province of Palestine.

## Lenin and Trotsky

Speaking of the United Nations, this later fulfillment of Woodrow Wilson's League of Nations was embraced by Stalin, whereas the League was rejected by Lenin. This is a good way of illustrating the difference between Leninism and Stalinism: Stalinism is based on acceptance of the racist nationalist Wilson's vision instead of world proletarian socialist revolution and global dictatorship of the proletariat pursued by original historical Marxism.

This was the basis of Adorno's critique of "international law" under capitalism and its inherently ambiguous and hypocritical concepts such as "genocide." The United Nations definition of "genocide" includes that of so-called "cultural genocide." — What did Lenin say about that?

> The Socialists of *oppressed* nations must, in their turn, unfailingly fight for the complete (including organizational) unity of the *workers* of the oppressed and oppressing nationalities. The idea of the juridical separation of one nation from another (so-called "cultural-national autonomy" advocated by Bauer and Renner) is reactionary.[2]

Later on, Trotsky wrote that proletarian socialists must "Learn to Think":

> Ultra-left scholastics think not in concrete terms but in empty abstractions. They have transformed the idea of defeatism into such a vacuum. They can see vividly neither the process of war nor the process of revolution. They seek a hermetically sealed formula which excludes fresh air. But a formula of this kind can offer no orientation for the proletarian vanguard.[3]

Trotsky goes on to point out that "revolutionary defeatism" can only be *revolutionary* if it leads to proletarian socialist revolution. And that is not the case today. Today it can only be defeatism in a non-revolutionary way, playing into capitalist politics not building a socialist movement. It is bourgeois defeatism. The bourgeoisie can benefit — indeed profit — from the defeat of their opponents. Not so the workers. At least not as proletarian socialists, who are not the beneficiaries of capitalist competition, of which war is just a usual event. Capitalists always make a killing off war — no matter who wins or loses, the capitalists as such always profit. Capital always finds an opportunity.

It is a Stalinist contrivance to justify their opportunism that somehow divisions in the ruling class benefit the working class, regardless of the actual state of the latter's struggle and movement.

---

2   *Socialism and War* (1915).
3   *The New International* IV, no. 7 (July 1938), 206–07.

## Demands

There is simply no proletarian socialist movement today. There is only petit bourgeois radicalism, more or less. This is what Lenin called "liberalism with bombs" and "reformism with guns" — at best. At worst, it is not even liberalism or reformism, but is just reactionary capitalist pseudo-politics. Actually, it is only ever more or less *crime*.

So let's examine the current demands of the Palestinian solidarity movement in the U.S.: "Ceasefire now!" and "Defund Israel!"

The latter of course is a repetition of the Black Lives Matter demand, to "defund" the police. It is a variety of impossibilism and hence of BLM's avowed nihilism. But not in the case of U.S. aid to Israel, military and otherwise, which could happen: Republican Presidential candidate Vivek Ramaswamy as well as Right-wing commentator Tucker Carlson have called for sun-setting U.S. aid to Israel, to cut the strings in the relationship and make it more an alliance — marriage of convenience? — than a dependency.

What "Defund Israel!" also is connected to is BDS — what I like to call BDSM, namely, Bondage, Domination, Sadism, Masochism — oh, excuse me! Boycott, Divest, Sanction. (The latter is really a matter of the former, but anyway:) The latter is an attempted repetition of the Anti-Apartheid Movement of South Africa in the 1970s–80s. The "Left" likes to think that it brought down Apartheid, but, no, that was the result of the end of the Cold War and the resolution of proxy conflicts between the U.S. and USSR. Israel-Palestine was supposed to be another, hence the Intifada and Oslo Accords peace process. It failed.

So this leaves history seemingly unfinished — no, not really. "Resistance" to "Apartheid" or "settler-colonialism" in Israel is not some unfinished business of the last century — although it might appear so.

What both "Ceasefire now!" and "Defund Israel!" have in common, whatever their merits and defects, is that they are demands on the capitalist state, and moreover on its political parties — specifically, demanding these things of one Party in particular, the Democrats.

But the Biden Administration has indeed called for a ceasefire: it wants different tactics and even strategy of Israel. Most importantly, it wants Israel to give "land for peace," end the settlements in the West Bank, and, most pertinently, not to devastate Gaza or displace the Palestinians there. Or so at least they say.

Why not believe them?

## Genocide

And this brings us back to the charge of "genocide." There's no *mens rea*, and hence no consciousness of guilt with which to convict the Israelis. "Slow-motion genocide" is no genocide at all — unless history itself is the story of endless "genocides." The UN's International Court of Justice will take many years to come to a decision about the current Israeli war against Hamas.

Why not call it "ethnic cleansing," for example — a horrible enough crime? It is not at all clear even that this is the current Israeli intent in Gaza.

So what is going on here, between Israel and Palestine? Why was a two-state solution not achieved in the aftermath of the Cold War in the 1990s? It's actually very simple:

The Palestinian "political leadership" has refused to officially accept the existence of Israel as a state.

After many wars, uprisings, terrorism, etc., the Palestinians lost and the Israelis won.

The stronger were victorious and the weaker were defeated. Case closed. History's pronouncement is undeniable — and irreversible.

The Israelis expected a peace treaty of surrender by the Palestinians, which the Palestinians have refused. So Israel has continued its war against an enemy that has refused to surrender.

But the Palestinians have been defeated. This is not going to change. Ever.

Indeed, the recent Hamas attack was an act of desperation in a condition of defeat. This doesn't justify or condone it — indeed it convicts it of futility and wanton, pointless destructiveness. Hamas has admitted as much, as they say they expected an Israeli overreaction and the destruction of Gaza and the Palestinians there, which they thought at best would create a wider regional war and at worst would make the Palestinian question impossible to ignore by the international community. Hamas spent everything it had in one final bid for political relevance. So it's all in the end a public-relations stunt. How grotesque!

Is there any doubt that Israel would live at peace with the Palestinians if given the chance? But the "Left" don't want peace here.

Should "Marxists" or "socialists" accept the verdict of war — accept the victory of one side over another? Not necessarily. But the point would not be to rearrange capitalist settlements — which are indeed merely deck-chairs on the Titanic — but to struggle to overcome them entirely in socialist revolution.

### Gangster rap

How to do so? Well, for one thing, we can aspire to not miseducate Palestinian, Arab or Muslim-Americans or any others in the U.S. and beyond: Rashida Tlaib is a travesty and tragedy of today's pseudo-"Leftism," specifically in its spurious "Palestinian solidarity." Progress means: Congress now has its very own Palestinian mascot. But no less tragic is the rest of the Squad of Democrat "socialists" in the U.S. Congress. — So is Bernie Sanders. Their miseducation and now willing complicity in the crimes of capitalist politics runs deeply historically. It has unfolded over many generations. It should not continue. The dead-end closing in Gaza bears a lesson.

Hamas is a capitalist group. What does this mean? It accepts capitalism and is not in any way a challenge to it. It is a particularly Right-wing form of capitalism. It is a criminal gang. They are indeed terrorists. Terrorism is by its very nature capitalist and not socialist politics. Capitalist crime. — Crime is capitalist, not socialist. It is the capitalism of the weak, not socialism. And the weak shall not inherit the Earth. They never have. They have perished irremediably — dust.

Hamas are the Kapos in the concentration camp, recruited from ordinary criminals to rule over the rest, and hoping to slip away and survive through the mayhem. They were literally chosen by Israel to rule the Gaza Strip. The game of "military transactions" (Hegel) played between Israel and Hamas, no matter how violent and gruesome, is merely negotiating the terms of capitalism, through extremely sensationalist marketing propaganda — in images as well as deeds. And the bargaining-chips that are played consist of ordinary people's lives — as victims and not agents, objects and not subjects of bloody capitalist politics. As the workers always are.

Historically, Marxists always rejected terrorism as a tactic and as a strategy. Why? Because it did not advance the working class's own necessary self-organization and action to achieve socialism, and indeed set it back, working against it, including but not only by provoking state repression. And what Marxism meant by the "terrorism" that they opposed was not at all what Hamas committed on October 7, which was targeted mass murder of civilians, but rather military actions against the capitalist state and its repressive apparatus — "legitimate" warfare. By contrast, Hamas has aimed and aims to divide the civilian population along religious or ethnic lines. This means dividing the working class. They wagered — and lost — the lives of Palestinians in ways capitalist politicians always do. Hamas's leadership are literally billionaires whose individual personal wealth rivals that of Donald Trump. But what have they built? Their wealth is skimmed off the misery of others — as with all gangsters. They will retire comfortably, while their fighters are slaughtered. Hamas is a criminal enterprise, both literally and figuratively — at least from a Marxist perspective.

Today's "Left" are a parody side-show of capitalist gangsterism, cheerleading the slaughter. They are the psychotics viewing events from the windows of the insane-asylum, expressing and enacting what British Leftist psychoanalyst Juliet Mitchell called the "normative psychosis of the capitalist social-political world"[4] — no less and perhaps a great deal more so than what the Symbionese Liberation Army's audiotaped communiqués called the "fascist insects" in what the "Left" has called the "Zionist entity." Or are we to be agents rather of *Aeon Flux*'s Monica contra Bregna? But Trevor Goodchild always wins, however resurrecting Aeon in the next episode after death each time. Can we wake from this nightmare film-loop of history? We've seen this movie already — billed as the Next Big Thing and quickly forgotten in the clickbait revenue stream of the latest Breaking News in capitalist exploitation. Gaza will be rebuilt by the workers of the world, Palestinian and otherwise.

---

4    E. Efe Çakmak and Bülent Somay, "There is never a psychopathology without the social context: An interview with Juliet Mitchell," *Eurozine* (April 12, 2006).

## Lenin again

This brings us back to Lenin's rejection of "national" capitalist states and of Woodrow Wilson's League of Nations after World War I. — By contrast with Stalin's acceptance and even embrace of the United Nations after WWII, which was the institutionalization of the victorious Allies for managing world politics set up by the U.S.: the terms of the USSR et al.'s participation in global capitalist politics. The world political order is the capitalist system of nation-states preferred by the U.S.

Lenin called the League of Nations set up by Woodrow Wilson after WWI a "den of thieves and their victims;" how much more so is the UN today: the complaint-office of the U.S.-led global order.

Unlike spurious fake "Marxists'" attempts to treat nations — let alone capitalist nation-states — as coherent fundamental units of political economy, Marx and subsequent Marxists recognized that political economy and its social relations — society — are not national but international and indeed global and cosmopolitan in nature and character. Nationalism — the reification of "national" identities — has always been and will always be retrograde. Even Hamas are not nationalists.

The PFLP, Popular Front for the Liberation of Palestine, an ostensibly "Marxist" socialist or communist force in Palestine, treats what they call the "national liberation struggle" over and prior to the struggle for socialism. As such, they support Hamas as the supposed "vanguard" of the national struggle of the Palestinians. The PFLP see themselves as the "Left" of the "national" or "democratic" struggle and movement — and Hamas as the Right wing. What does this mean? It means that, after the purported successful "national liberation struggle," then the political differences between Hamas and themselves will become manifest. But before that, the PFLP says that they don't want "ideological" differences to stand in the way of "political unity" with Hamas. They want a "cross-class popular alliance," very explicitly. It is vintage 1930s Stalinist Popular Frontism. It failed to stop "fascism and war" ever since then, and continues to do so now.

As counter-intuitive as it might sound, this is very much like how the supposed "Palestinian solidarity" movement in the U.S. conceives of itself:

in "political unity" with "progressive liberal d/Democratic capitalist" politicians despite any and all "ideological differences."

But are these merely "ideological" differences? From a socialist let alone Marxist perspective, they must rather be recognized as political differences: socialists have an entirely different aim and goal from Hamas, in any number of respects.

But this is where the present "Left" is fundamentally confused and mistaken: socialism is not a matter of "progressive" capitalism or "progressive" reforms of capitalism. Nor is it about separate "stages" of struggle, which since the 1930s has never gotten beyond, nor ever even fulfilled this first "popular democratic national" stage. It has been a dead-end — always.

What is required in Palestine or Israel is the working-class political unity of Jewish and Arab and Muslim and Christian and other (for instance, "foreign/guest") workers in the struggle for socialism. This is entirely contrary to either Arab nationalism — such as that of the PFLP — or Islamism — as with Hamas. It is also contrary to Zionism. It is against the nation-state — the nationalist basis for politics.

### Aftermath

In the Middle East specifically we see the aftermath of the collapse of the Ottoman Empire over a hundred years ago, after WWI, and the failure to create out of this any viable national states. There are rather many different ethnic and religious and linguistic and other cultural groups in the region — as indeed there are in every part of the world. There has been the necessary and not accidental oppression of minorities throughout the world in the attempt to enforce nationalist politics. "Decolonization" has necessarily and not accidentally meant this for the last century: forced population transfers, genocides, and continued oppression and exploitation. Socialists should not accept this let alone apologize for it — and certainly not regard it as somehow "progress." Which side should socialists have taken in the Biafra War? With Boko Haram today? The civil wars in Congo have not been merely about exotic metals.

But pluralistic liberal democracy has also failed in capitalism in places like the U.S. — not as spectacularly as in the Middle East and elsewhere, but still a failure. Division of the working class according to various sectarian and communitarian lines has prevailed. Where does this division originate? In capitalism itself, which both brings people together through trade and commerce and cooperation in labor, locally and globally, and divides them in competition in a situation of industrial production in which there are periodic crises of economic value of social activity and unemployment, commonly seen as due to technological innovation and necessity. There will be no possible restoration of petit-bourgeois democratic localism, "national" or otherwise.

So long as capitalism persists and is not overcome in socialism, globally, there will be social and geographical divisions that invite political divisions to which the working class and other people will become inevitably subject. There will be war, inter-national state and/or civil, "legitimate" or otherwise. Always capitalist war.

But original historical Marxism said, "No war but class war!" — refusing the terms of capitalist warfare. — I know that this is regarded as "ultra-Leftism" and "Marxist purism" and "dogmatism," but still. I prefer to maintain my self-respect as a dogmatic Marxist than pose in the mirror as a wannabe gangsta, mouthing the words to someone else's rap. "Intifada until victory!" will be a very long time. Forever. Never.

But we can still refuse to endorse and support the capitalist politics that actively seeks to exploit and enforce such divisions and warfare: Hamas and other dominant Palestinian political forces as well as Zionism are clear examples of such destructive politics, whose devastating and anti-social results we are seeing now as well as for the past century.

Do you get it yet, children?

Originally published in *Platypus Review* 163 (February 2024)

---

\*    Actually, it was in Horkheimer's 1940 essay on "The authoritarian state" *Telos* 15 (Spring 1973), 20:

> It would be sentimental to remain opposed to state capitalism merely because of those who have been slain. One could say that the Jews were for the most part capitalists, and that the small nations have no justification for their existence. State

capitalism is said to be the only thing possible today. As long as the proletariat does not make its own revolution, there remains no choice for it and its theoreticians but to follow the *Weltgeist* on the path it has chosen. Such opinions, and there are plenty of them, are neither the most stupid nor the most dishonest. This much is true, that with the return to the old free enterprise system, the entire horror would start again from the beginning under new management.

Note that this is not voiced as Horkheimer's own opinion but rather that of others, with whom nonetheless he cannot disagree — an important distinction, however. I still think that the spirit of this passage is found in *Dialectic of Enlightenment*, especially in the "Elements of Anti-Semitism" chapter, but I could not hunt down a corresponding passage there.

# What is political party for Marxism? Democratic revolution and the contradiction of capital[1]

Mike Macnair's *Revolutionary Strategy* is a wide-ranging, comprehensive and very thorough treatment of the problem of revolutionary politics and the struggle for socialism. His focus is the question of political party and it is perhaps the most substantial attempt recently to address this problem.

Macnair's initial motivation was engagement with the debates in and around the French Fourth International Trotskyist Ligue Communiste Révolutionnaire prior to its forming the Nouveau Parti Anti-capitaliste electoral party in 2009. The other major context for the discussion was the Iraq anti-war movement and the U.K. Respect electoral party, which was formed around this in 2004, with the Socialist Workers Party driving the process. This raised issues not only of political party, democracy and the state, but also united fronts among socially and politically heterogeneous groups and the issue of imperialism. One key contribution by Macnair to the latter discussion is to raise and call attention to the difference between Bukharin's and Lenin's writings on imperialism, in which the former attributed the failure of (metropolitan) workers' organization around imperialism to a specifically *political* compromise with the (national) state, whereas Lenin had, in his famous 1916 pamphlet, characterized this in terms of compromised "economic" interest. So with imperialism the question is the political party and the state.

Macnair observes that there are at least two principal phases of the party question: from the 16th, 17th and 18th centuries; and beginning in the middle of the 19th century. He relates these phases to the development of the problem of the state. He offers that constitutional government

---

1    On Mike Macnair's *Revolutionary Strategy: Marxism and the Challenge of Left Unity* (London: November Publications, 2010).

involves the development of the "party state" and that revolutionary politics takes its leave of such a "party state" (which includes multiple parties all supporting the constitutional regime). Furthermore, Macnair locates this problem properly as one of the nation-state within the greater economic and political system of capitalism. By conflating the issue of government with "rule of law," however, Macnair mistakes the contradiction of the modern state and its politics in capitalism.

Elsewhere, Macnair has criticized sectarian "Marxism" for "theoretical overkill" in a "philosophy trap." But he might thus mistake effect for cause: "philosophical" questions might be the expression of a trap in which one is nonetheless caught; and Marxist "theory" might go beyond today's practical political concerns. Philosophy may not be the trap in which we are caught but rather an expression of our attempts — merely — to think our way out of it. The mismatch of Marxism today at the level of "theoretical" or "philosophical" issues might point to a *historical* disparity or inadequacy: we may have fallen below past thresholds and horizons of Marxism. The issue of political party may be one that we would need to re-attain rather than immediately confront in the present. Hence, "strategy" in terms of Marxism may not be the political issue now that it once was. This means that where past Marxists might appear to be in error it may actually be *our* fault, or, a fault in the present situation. How can the history of Marxism help us address this?

### New politics

The key to this issue can be found in Macnair's own distinction of the new phenomenon of party politics in the late 19th century, after the revolutions of 1848 and in the era of what Marx called "Bonapartism," the pattern set by Louis Bonaparte, who became Napoleon III in the French Second Empire, with its emulation by Bismarck in the Prussian Empire, as well as Disraeli's Tories in the U.K., among other examples. While Macnair finds some precedent for this in the 18th century U.K. and its political crises as well as in the course of the Great French Revolution 1789-1815 especially regarding Napoleon Bonaparte, the difference of the late 19th century party-politics from prior historical precedent is important to specify. For Macnair it is the world system of capitalism and its undermining of democracy.

It is important to recall Marx's formulation, in the *Eighteenth Brumaire of Louis Bonaparte*, that (neo-)Bonapartism was the historical condition in which the bourgeoisie could "no longer" and the proletariat "not yet" rule politically the modern society of capitalism. Bonapartism was the symptom of this crisis of capitalism and hence of the need for socialism revealed by the unprecedented failure of revolution in 1848 — by contrast with 1830 as well as 1789 and 1776 and the Dutch Revolt and English Civil War of the 17th century. The bourgeoisie's "ruling" character was not a legal-constitutional system of government descended from the 17th century political and social revolutions in Holland and England so much as it was a form of civil society, a revolutionary system of bourgeois social relations that was supposed to subordinate the state. What requires explanation is the 19th century slipping of the state from adequate social control, and its "rising above" the contending political groups and social classes, as a power in itself. Even if Bonapartism in Marx's late 19th century sense was the expression of a potential inherent in the forms of bourgeois politics emerging much earlier, there is still the question of why it was not realized so until after 1848. There is also the matter of why Marx characterized Louis Napoleon as a "lesser" and "farcical" phenomenon of post-1848 history by contrast with Napoleon Bonaparte's "tragedy" in the Great Revolution. It was not the mere fact of repetition, but *why* and *how* history "repeated itself," and repeated with a *difference*.

This was according to Marx the essential condition for politics after 1848, the condition for political parties in capitalism. That condition was not only or primarily a matter of politics due to constitutional legal forms of bourgeois property and its social relations, but rather was for Marx the expression of the crisis of those forms as a function of the Industrial Revolution. There was for Marx an important contradiction between the democratic revolution and the proletarianization of society in capitalism.

Macnair addresses this by specifying the "proletariat" as all those in society "dependent on the total wage fund" — as opposed to those (presumably) dependent upon "capital." This is clearly not a matter of economics, because distinguishing between those depending on wages as

opposed to capital is a political matter of differentiation: all the intermediate strata depending on both the wage fund and capital would need to
be compelled to take sides in any political dispute between the preroga-
tives of wages versus capital. Macnair addresses this through the struggle
for democracy. But this does not pursue the contradiction far enough.
For the wage fund according to Marx is a form of capital: it is "variable" as
opposed to "constant capital." So the proletarianization of society according to Marx is not addressed adequately as a matter of the condition of
labor, but rather the social dependence on and domination by capital. And
capital for Marx is not synonymous with the private property in the means
of production belonging to the capitalists, but rather the relation of wages,
or the resources for the reproduction of labor-power (including the "means
of consumption"), to society as a whole. This is what makes it a *political*
matter — a matter of politics in *society* — rather than merely the struggle
of one group against another.

Macnair characterizes the theory of Marxism specifically as one that
recognizes the necessity of those dependent upon the wage fund *per se* to
overcome capitalism; he characterizes the struggle for this as the struggle
for democracy, with the adequate horizon of this as "communism" at a
global scale, as opposed to "socialism" which may be confined to the internal politics of individual nation-states. Macnair points out that the working
class is necessarily in the "vanguard" of such struggle for adequate social
democratization insofar as it comes up against the condition of capitalism
*negatively*, as a *problem* to be overcome. The working class is thus defined
"negatively" with respect to the social conditions to be overcome rather
than "positively" according to its activity, its concrete labor in society. The
goal is to change the conditions for political participation as well as economic activity in society.

## Class and history

Conventionally, Marxists have distinguished among political parties on
their "class basis," regarding various parties as "representing" different class
groups: "bourgeois," "petit bourgeois" and "proletarian." This is complicated by classic characterizations such as that by Lenin of the U.K. Labour

Party as a "bourgeois workers' party." Furthermore, there has been the bedeviling question of what is included in the "petite bourgeoisie." But Marxists (such as Lenin) did not define politics "sociologically" but rather *historically*: as representing not the interests of members of various groups but rather different "ideological" horizons of politics and for the transformation of society. So, for instance, what made the Socialist Revolutionaries in the Russian Revolution of 1917 "represent" the peasants was not so much their positions on agrarian matters as the "petit bourgeois" horizon of politics they shared with the peasants as petty proprietors. SRs were not necessarily themselves petty proprietors — they were like Lenin "petit bourgeois intellectuals" — but rather had in common with the peasants a form of *discontent* with capitalism, but one "ideologically" hemmed in by what Marxism regarded a limited horizon.

In Marx's (in)famous phrase from *The Eighteenth Brumaire of Louis Bonaparte*, the peasants as a group, as a "petit bourgeois" "sack of potatoes" of smallholders, could not "represent themselves" but must rather "be represented" — as they were, according to Marx, by Louis Bonaparte's Second Empire's succeeding the counterrevolutionary Party of Order in 1848. Marx called attention to the issue of *how* representation functioned in the politics of capitalism. Likewise, "bourgeois" parties were not so much pro-capitalist as much as they sought to manage the problems of capitalism from a certain historical perspective: that of "capital." This was the horizon of their politics; whereas "petit bourgeois" parties were concerned with the perspective of smaller property holdings; and "workers parties" that of wage-labor. To be a "bourgeois workers' party" such as Labour in the U.K. meant to represent the horizon of wage-labor in terms compatible with (especially but not exclusively U.K. "national") capital. This was the character of ideology and political action — "consciousness" — which was not reducible to, let alone determined by, economic interest of a particular concrete social group.

So, various political parties as well as different political forms represented different *historical* horizons for discontents within capitalism. For Marxists, only "proletarian socialist" politics could represent adequately the *problem* — the crisis and contradiction — of capitalism. Others ideologically obscured it. A "bourgeois workers' party" would be a phenomenon of "Bonapartism" insofar as "nature abhors a vacuum" and it filled the space evacuated by the failure of bourgeois politics while also falling short of the true historical horizon of the political tasks of proletarian socialism. It was a phenomenon of the contradiction of *capitalism* in a particular way — as were *all* political parties from a Marxist perspective.

There are great merits and significant clarity to Macnair's approach to the problem of politics in capitalism and what it would require to transcend this.

The issue, though, is his taking as a norm the parliamentary system of government in the European mode and thus neglecting the U.S. Constitutional system. For at issue is the potential disparity and antagonism between legislative and executive authority, or between the law and its enforcement. The American system of "checks and balances" was meant to uphold liberal democracy and prevent the tyranny of either the executive or the legislative (or the judicial) aspects of government. There is an important domain of political struggle already, between executive and legislative authority, and this would affect any struggle to transform politics. The question is the source of this antagonism. It is not merely formal. If the "separation of powers" in the U.S. Constitutional system has served undemocratic ends, it is not essentially because it was *intended* to do so. The problem of adequate and proper democratic authority in society is not reducible to the issue of purported "mob rule." Any form of government could be perverted to serve capitalism. So the issue is indeed one of *politics* as such, the social content of or what informs any form of political authority.

### "Party of the new type"?

Macnair notes potential deficits and inadequacies in the Third Communist International's endorsement of "soviet" or "workers' council" government, with its attempt to overcome the difference between legislative and executive authority, which seems to reproduce the problem Macnair finds in parliamentary government. For him, executive authority eludes responsibility in the same way that capitalist private property eludes the law constitutionally. This is the source of Macnair's conflation of liberalism and Bonapartism, as if the problem of capitalism merely played out in terms of liberalism rather than contradicting it. Liberal democracy should not be conceived as the constitutional limit on democracy demanded by capitalist private property. The "democratic republic" Macnair calls for by contrast should not be conceived as the opposite of liberal democracy. For capitalism does not only contradict the democratic republic but also liberal democracy, leading to Bonapartism, or, *illiberal* democracy.

Dick Howard, in *The Specter of Democracy*[2] has usefully investigated Marx's original formulations on the problem of politics and capitalism, tracing these back to the origins of modern democracy in the American and French Revolutions of the 18th century, specifying the problem in common between (American) "republican democracy" and (French) "democratic republicanism." Howard finds in both antinomical forms of modern democracy the danger of "anti-politics," or of society eluding adequate political expression and direction, to which either democratic authority or liberalism can lead. Howard looks to Marx as a specifically political thinker on this problem to suggest the direction that struggle against it must take. Socialism for Marx in Howard's view would fulfill the potential that has been otherwise limited by both republican democracy and democratic republicanism — or by both liberalism and socialism.

Macnair equates communism with democratic republicanism and thus treats it as a goal to be achieved and a norm to be realized. Moreover, he thinks that this goal can only be achieved by the practice of democratic republicanism in the present: the political party for communism must exemplify democratic republicanism in practice, as an alternative to the politics of the "party-state" in capitalism.

Marx, by contrast, addressed communism as merely the "next step" and a "one-sided negation" of capitalism rather than as the end goal of emancipation: it is not the opposite of capitalism in the sense of an undialectical antithesis but rather an expression of it. Indeed, for Marx, communism would be the completion and fulfillment of capitalism, and not in terms of one or some aspects over others but rather in and through its central self-contradiction, which is political as well as economic, or, "political-economic."

---

2   New York: Columbia University Press, 2002.

What this requires is recognizing the non-identity of various aspects of capitalism as bound up in and part and parcel of the process of capitalism's potential transformation into communism. For example, the non-identity of law (as legislated), its (judicial) interpretation, and (executive) enforcement, or, the non-identity of civil society and the state, as expressed by the specific phenomenon of modern political parties. States are compulsory; political parties are voluntary, civil society formations. And governments are not identical with legislatures. Politics as conditioned by capitalism could provide the *means* but cannot already embody the *ends* of transforming capitalism through communism. If communism is to be pursued, as Macnair argues, by the means of democratic republicanism, then we must recognize what has become of the democratic revolution in capitalism. It has not been merely corrupted and degraded but rather rendered self-contradictory, which is a different matter. The concrete manifestations of democracy in capitalism are not only opportunist compromises but also struggles to assert *politics*.

## Symptomatic socialism

The history of the movement for socialism or communism generally and of Marxism in particular demonstrates the problem of capitalism through symptomatic phenomena of attempts to overcome it. This is not a history of trials and errors but rather of discontents and exemplary forms of politics, borne of the crisis of capitalism as it has been experienced through various phases, none of which have been superseded entirely.

Lenin and Trotsky were careful to avoid, as Trotsky put it, in *The Lesson of October* (1924), the "fetishizing" of the soviet or workers' council form of politics and (revolutionary) government. Rather, Marxists addressed this as an emergent phenomenon of a specific phase of history, one which they sought to advance through the proletarian socialist revolution. But, according to Lenin, in *"Left-Wing" Communism: An Infantile Disorder*, the soviet form did not mean that preceding historical forms of politics, for instance parliaments and trade unions, had been superseded in terms of being left behind. Indeed, it was precisely the failure of the world proletarian socialist — communist — revolution of 1917–19 that necessitated a "retreat" and reconsideration of perspectives and political prognoses. Certain forms and arenas of political struggle had come and gone. But, according to Lenin and Trotsky, the political *party* for communism remained indispensable. What did they mean by this?

Lenin and Trotsky meant something other than what Rosa Luxemburg's biographer J.P. Nettl called the "inheritor party" or "state within the state" exemplified by the Social Democratic Party of Germany (SPD) as the flagship party of the Second International. The social-democratic party was not intended by Luxemburg, Lenin or Trotsky to be the democratic republican alternative to capitalism. They did not aim to replace one constitutional party-state with another. Or at least they did not intend so beyond the "dictatorship of the proletariat," which was meant to rapidly transition out of capitalism to socialism. Beyond that, a qualitative development was envisioned, beyond "bourgeois right" and its forms of social relations — and of politics. "Communism" remained the essential horizon of potential transformation.

One key distinction that Macnair elides in his account is the development of bourgeois social relations within pre-bourgeois civilization that will not be replicated by the struggle for socialism: socialism does not develop within capitalism so much as the proletariat represents the potential negation of bourgeois social relations that has developed within capitalism. The proletariat is a phenomenon of crisis in the existing society, not the exemplar of the new society. Socialism is not meant to be a proletarian society but rather its overcoming. Capitalism is already a proletarianized society. Hence, Bonapartism as the manifestation of the need for the proletariat to rule politically that has been abandoned by the bourgeoisie. Bonapartism is not a form of politics but rather an indication of the *failure of politics*. Marxism investigates that failure and its historical significance. The dictatorship of the proletariat will be the "highest" and most acute form of Bonapartism, but one that intends to immediately begin to overcome itself, or "wither away."

The proletariat aims to abolish itself as a class not simply by abolishing the capitalist class as its complementary opposite expression of the self-contradiction and crisis of capitalism. This is why Marx recognized the persistence of "bourgeois right" in any "dictatorship of the proletariat" and down into the transition to socialism in its "first stage." Bourgeois right would overcome itself through its crisis and self-contradiction, which the dictatorship of the proletariat would "advance" and not immediately transcend. The dictatorship of the proletariat or "(social-)democratic republic" would be the form in which the struggle to overcome capitalism would first be able to take place politically.

Macnair confuses the proletariat's struggle for self-abolition in socialism with the bourgeois — that is, modern urban plebeian — struggle for the democratic republic. He ignores the self-contradiction of this struggle in capitalism: that capitalism has reproduced itself in and through crisis, and indeed through revolution, through a process of "creative destruction" (Schumpeter) in which the bourgeois revolution has re-posed itself, but resulting in the re-proletarianization of society, the reconstitution of wage labor under changed concrete conditions. This has taken place not only or perhaps even primarily through economic or political-economic crises and struggles, but through specifically *political* crises and struggles, through the recurrence of the democratic revolution. The proletariat cannot either make society in the image of itself or abolish itself immediately. It can only seek to lead the democratic revolution — hopefully — beyond itself.

## Liberalism and socialism

The problem with liberal democracy is that it proceeds as if the democratic revolution has been achieved already, and ignores that capitalism has undermined it. Capitalism makes the democratic revolution both necessary and impossible, in that the democratic revolution constitutes bourgeois social relations — the relations of the exchange of labor — but capitalism undermines those social relations. The democratic revolution reproduces not "capitalism" as some stable system (which, by Marx's definition, it cannot be) but rather the *crisis* of bourgeois society in capitalism, in a *political*, and hence in a potentially *conscious* way. The democratic revolution reconstitutes the crisis of capitalism in a manifestly political way, and this is why it can possibly point beyond it, if it is recognized as such: if the struggle for democracy is recognized properly as a manifestation of the crisis of capitalism and hence the need to go beyond bourgeois social relations, to go beyond democracy. Bourgeois forms of politics will be overcome through advancing them to their limits — in crisis.

The crisis of capitalism means that the forms of bourgeois politics are differentiated: they express the crisis and disintegration of bourgeois social relations. They also manifest the accumulation of past attempts at mediating bourgeois social relations in and through the crisis of capitalism. This is why the formal problems of politics will not go away, even if they are transformed. The issue is one of recognizing this historical accumulation of political problems in capitalism, and of grasping adequately how these forms are symptomatic of the development — or lack thereof — of the politics of the struggle for socialism in and through these forms. For example, Occupy, which took place after the writing of Macnair's book, clearly is not an advance in politically effective form. But it is symptomatic of our present historical moment, and so must be grappled with as such. It must be grasped as an endemic phenomenon, a "necessary form of appearance" of the problem of capitalism in the present, and not treated merely as an accidental and hence avoidable error.

Macnair's preferred target of critical investigation is the "mass strike" and related "workers' council" or "soviet" form. But this did not exist in isolation: its limits were not its own but rather also an expression of the limits of labor unions and parliamentary government as well as of political parties in the early 20th century. For Macnair the early Third or Communist International become a blind alley, proven by its failure. But its problems cannot be thus settled and resolved so summarily or as easily as that.

If Occupy has failed it has done so without manifesting the political problem of capitalism as acutely as the soviet or workers' council form of revolutionary politics did circa 1917, precisely because Occupy did not manifest, as the soviets did, a crisis of parliamentary democracy, labor union organization and political party formation, as the workers' council form did in the Russian Revolutions of 1905 and 1917 and the German Revolution of 1918-19 and the Hungarian Revolution of 1919 as well as the crisis in Italy beginning in 1919, and elsewhere in that historical moment and subsequently (e.g., in the British General Strike of 1926 and the Chinese Revolution of 1927). Indeed, Occupy might be regarded as an attempt to *avoid* certain problems, through what post-New Leftists such as

Alain Badiou have affirmed as "politics at a distance from the state," that nonetheless imposed themselves, and with a vengeance — see Egypt as the highest expression of the "Arab Spring." Occupy evinced a mixture of liberal and anarchist discontents — a mixture of labor union and "direct democracy" popular-assembly politics. The problem of 20th century Third (and Fourth) International politics, regarding contemporaneous and inherited forms of the mass strike (and its councils), labor unions and political parties, expressed the interrelated problems accumulated from different prior historical moments of the preceding 19th century (in 1830, 1848, and 1871, etc.), all of which needed to be worked through and within, together, along with the fundamental bourgeois political form of (the struggle for) the democratic republic — which Kant among others (liberals) already recognized in the 18th century as an issue of a necessary "world state" (or at least a world "system of states") — not achievable within national confines.

### Redeeming history

Political forms are sustained practices; they are embodied history. Because none of the forms emerging in the capitalist era — since the early to mid-19th century — has existed without the others, they must all be considered together, as mediating (the crisis of) capitalism at various levels, rather than in opposition to one another. Furthermore, these forms do not merely instantiate the bourgeois society that must be overcome — in a reified view — but rather mediate its crisis in capitalism, and inevitably so.

History cannot be regarded as a catalogue of errors to be avoided, but must be regarded, however critically, as a resource informing the present, whether or not adequately consciously. If past historical problems repeat themselves, they do not do so literally but with a difference. The question is the significance of that difference. It cannot be regarded as itself progressive. Indeed the difference often expresses the degradation of a problem. One cannot avoid either the repetition or the difference in capitalist history. An adequate "proletarian socialist" party would immediately push beyond prior historical limits. That is how it could both manifest and advance the contradiction in capitalism.

History, according to Adorno (following Benjamin), is the "demand for redemption." This is because history is not an accumulation of facts but rather a form of past action continuing in the present. Historical action was transformative and is again to be transformed in the present: we transform past action through continuing to act on it in the present. No past action continues untransformed. The question is the (re-)direction and continuing transformation of that action. Thinking is a way, too, of transforming past action.

Political party is not a dead form, but rather lives in ways dependent at least in part on how we think of it. The need for political party for the Left today is a demand to redeem past action in the present. We can do so more or less well, and not only as a function of quantity but also of quality. Can we receive the task of past politics revealed by Marxism as it is ramified down to the present? Can the Left sustain its action in time; can it be a form of *politics*?

Marxism never offered a wholly new or distinct form of political action, but only sought to affect — consciously — forms of politics already underway. Examples of this include: Chartism; labor unions (whether according to trade or industry); Lassalle's political party of the "permanent campaign of the working class;" the Paris Commune; the "mass" or "general strike;" and "workers' councils." But not only these: also, the parliament or congress, as well as the sovereign executive with prerogative. These are all descended to us as forms not merely of political action and political struggle over that action, but also and especially of *revolution*, revolutionary change in society in the modern, bourgeois epoch.

One thing is certain regarding the history of the 19th and 20th centuries as legacy, now in the 21st century: since the politics of the state has not gone away, neither has the question of political party. We must accept forms of revolutionary politics as they have come down to us historically. But that does not mean inheriting the forms of state and party as given but rather transforming them — in revolution. Capitalism is a social crisis that calls forth political action. The only questions are how and why — with what consciousness and with what goal?

If social and political crisis — revolution — has up to now given us only more capitalism, then we need to accept that — and think of how communism could be the result of revolutionary politics in capitalism. Again, as Marx and the best Marxism once did: we need to accept the task of *redeeming* history.

The difference Macnair observes, between the political party formations of the early original bourgeois era of the 17th and 18th centuries and in the crisis of capitalism manifesting circa 1848 (including prior Chartism in Britain), is key to the fundamental political question of Marxism as well as of proletarian socialism more broadly (for instance in anarcho-syndicalism) — as symptoms of *history*. There is not a static problem but rather a dynamic of the historical process that is moreover regressive in its repetition in difference. Marxism once sought to be conscious of the difference, and so should we.

Originally published in *Weekly Worker* 1030 (October 16, 2014)
and in *Platypus Review* 71 (November 2014)

## Postcript on party politics

The Frankfurt School of the 1930s recognized that the two historic constituencies of revolutionary politics, the masses and the party, had failed: the masses had led to fascism; and the party had led to Stalinism.

Trotsky had remarked, in his *History of the Russian Revolution* (1930), on the "interference of the masses in historical events": "Whether this is good or bad we leave to the judgment of moralists."

> The most indubitable feature of a revolution is the direct interference of the masses in historical events. In ordinary times the state, be it monarchical or democratic, elevates itself above the nation, and history is made by specialists in that line of business — kings, ministers, bureaucrats, parliamentarians, journalists. But at those crucial moments when the old order becomes no longer endurable to the masses, they break over the barriers excluding them from the political arena, sweep aside their traditional representatives, and create by their own interference the initial groundwork for a new régime. Whether

this is good or bad we leave to the judgment of moralists. We ourselves will take the facts as they are given by the objective course of development. The history of a revolution is for us first of all a history of the forcible entrance of the masses into the realm of rulership over their own destiny.[3]

But, as Lenin had written in *What is to be Done?* (1902), this was not a spontaneous development, but rather such apparent "spontaneity" could be explained by the prior history of the workers' movement for socialism.[4] The Russian Revolution had broken out on International Women's Day, a working class holiday invented by Marxists in the socialist parties of the Second International.

Trotsky wrote, in "Stalinism and Bolshevism" (1937), that Bolshevism was "only a political tendency closely fused with the working class but not identical with it" and had "never identified itself with either the October Revolution or the Soviet state that issued from it."

Bolshevism considered itself as one of the factors of history, its "Conscious" factor — a very important but not decisive one. We never sinned on historical subjectivism. We saw the decisive factor — on the existing basis of productive forces — in the class struggle, not only on a national scale but on an international scale.[5]

So, what was political party for Marxists such as Trotsky, Lenin and Luxemburg? It was one part of a differentiated whole of society and its political struggles, a political form that allowed for conscious participation in all the variety of arenas for politics that had developed in capitalism: parliaments, labor unions, mass strikes and their councils, and popular assemblies including workers' councils for revolutionary governance. However, as a political form — as Andrew Feenberg has pointed out, in *The Philosophy of Praxis* (2014), about Lukács's account of the articulation of theory

---

3  Trotsky, *History of the Russian Revolution* (1930).
4  Lenin, *What is to be Done?* (1902).
5  Trotsky, "Stalinism or Bolshevism" (1937).

and practice in Bolshevism in *History and Class Consciousness* (1923) and related writings — the party was not only or even especially a subject, but also, and perhaps most importantly, an object of political action.[6] It fell to Trotsky, in the aftermath of the failure of Bolshevism, to attempt to sustain this Marxist concept of political form, against Stalinism's liquidation of politics in the USSR and in the international Communist movement.

In this, Trotsky followed Lenin and Luxemburg as well as Marx and Engels. Trotsky followed Marx in regarding both Stalinism and fascism — as well as FDR New Deal-ism — as forms of the Bonapartist state. The death of the Left as a political force is signaled by its shying away from and anathematizing the political party for social transformation — revolution — not only in anarchism and "Left communist" notions of politics without parties, but most of all in the long and pervasive, if largely unrecognized, Stalinist inheritance that justifies the party only by identifying it with the people, which puts an end to politics, including political consciousness. What Dick Howard, following Marx, warns of the "anti-political" crisis of politics in capitalism expressed by Bonapartism, is this unmediated identification of politics with society, whether through the subordination of society or the liquidation of the party in the state, all in the name of quieting the inherent instability of politics, which society in its crisis of capitalism cannot afford.

For, as Marx recognized in the aftermath of failed revolution in 1848, Bonapartism was not only undemocratic liberalism, unbridled capitalism without political accountability to society, but was also the state run amok, dominating society, and with a great deal of popular support — for instance by what Marx called the "lumpenproletariat," an example of the reduction of society to a politically undifferentiated mass, the very opposite of what Marx considered the necessary "class consciousness" of the proletariat. This is why Trotsky rightly regarded Stalinism as the "antithesis" of Bolshevism.

Stalinism's suppression of politics in the Marxist sense was not only undemocratic but also popular, both in the USSR and internationally. It was borne of the same social and thus political crisis in capitalism. Stalinism

---

6    Andrew Feenberg, *The Philosophy of Praxis: Marx, Lukács and the Frankfurt School*, rev. edition (London: Verso, 2014).

was not the cause but was an effect of the failure of politics in capitalism. We still need to try to overcome this problem of capitalism by constituting it through the inherently dangerous game of party politics.

Originally published in abridged form as a letter in
*Weekly Worker* 1035 (November 20, 2014) and in
*Platypus Review* 72 (December 2014 – January 2015)

# Proletarian dictatorship and state capitalism

Tamás Krausz's recent book *Reconstructing Lenin* (2015)[1] notes the foundational opposition by Lenin to "petty bourgeois democracy" — Lenin's hostility towards the Mensheviks was in their opportunistic adaptation to petty bourgeois democracy, their liquidation of Marxism.

The real objects of Lenin's political opposition in proletarian socialism were the Narodniks and their descendants, the Socialist Revolutionaries, who were the majority of socialists in Russia in 1917. The SRs included many avowed "Marxists" and indeed supported the "vanguard" role of the working class in democratic revolution. The split among the SRs over World War I is what made the October revolution in 1917 possible — the alliance of the Bolsheviks with the Left SRs.

Conversely, the collapse of that alliance in 1918, due to the Bolsheviks' policy of pursuing a peace treaty with Germany at Brest-Litovsk, led to the Russian civil war. The SRs, calling for a "third Russian revolution," remained the most determined enemies of the Bolsheviks, all the way up through the Kronstadt mutiny of 1921, calling for "soviets without political parties": ie, without the Bolsheviks. The Bolsheviks considered them "petty bourgeois democrats" and thus "counterrevolutionaries." As Engels had already foretold, opposition to proletarian socialism was posed as "pure democracy." It was "democracy" versus the "dictatorship of the proletariat."

Hal Draper's four-volume *Marx's theory of revolution* (1977-90) similarly finds Marx's essential lesson of 1848 in the need to oppose proletarian socialism to petty bourgeois democracy. In the democratic revolution "in permanence" the proletariat was to lead the petty bourgeoisie.

---

1    *Reconstructing Lenin: An Intellectual Biography*, trans. Balint Bethlenfalvy (New York: Monthly Review Press, 2015).

What has happened since Marx and Lenin's time, however, has been the opposite: the liquidation of proletarian socialism in petty bourgeois democracy, and the workers' acceptance of the political lead of the latter — what Trotsky in the 1930s called the "crisis of revolutionary leadership," the result of the self-liquidation of Marxism by Stalinism in the popular front. Today, the left is characterized by the utter absence of proletarian socialism and the complete domination of politics by what Marxism termed petty bourgeois democracy.

This did not, however, prevent Marx — and Lenin, following him — from endorsing the "bourgeois democratic revolution," which remained necessary not only in apparently holdover feudal-aristocratic states, such as Germany in 1848 or Russia in 1905 and 1917, but also in the US Civil War of 1861-65 and the Paris Commune of 1871. This is because capitalism in the 19th century was a crisis undermining the bourgeois revolution begun in the 16th-17th centuries (in the Dutch Revolt and English Civil War).

The question is, what is the relation between the task of the still ongoing bourgeois democratic revolution, the contradiction of capital and the struggle for socialism? How has Marxism regarded the problem of "political action" in modern society?

### Program

Mike Macnair's four-part series on the "maximum program" of communism — "Thinking the alternative"[2] — argues for the need "to proletarianize the whole of global society." Macnair means this more in the political than economic sense. So what is the proletariat as a *political* phenomenon, according to Marxism? Georg Lukács, following Marx, however, would have regarded the goal of the complete "proletarianization of society" precisely as the "reification" of labor: i.e., a one-sided opposition and hypostatization that Macnair articulates as the proletariat's "denial of property claims" of any kind. But this leaves aside precisely the issue of "capital" in Marx's sense: the self-contradictory social relation of the workers collectively to the

---

2   *Weekly Worker* (April 9, 16 and 30 and May 14, 2015).

means of production, which for Marxism is not reducible to the individual capitalists' property.

"Capital," in Marx's sense, and the petty proprietorship of shopkeepers, for example, let alone the personal skills of workers (either "manual" or "intellectual"), are very different phenomena. Macnair addresses this issue in the final, fourth part of his series, "Socialism will not require industrialization"[3], which clarifies matters as regards his view of *wage-labor*, but not with respect to *capital* specifically as the self-contradiction of wage-labor in society. Moreover, there is the issue of how capital has indeed already "proletarianized the whole of global society," not only economically, but also politically. This cuts to the heart of what Marx termed "Bonapartism."

Macnair's "maximum program," if even realizable at all, would only reproduce capitalism in Marx's sense. Whereas, for Marx, the proletariat would begin to abolish itself — i.e., abolish the social principle of labor — immediately upon the workers taking political power in their struggle for socialism. If not, then petty bourgeois democracy will lead the lumpen-proletariat against the workers in Bonapartist politics, typically through nationalism — a pattern seen unrelentingly from 1848, all the way through the 20th century, up to the present. It has taken the various forms of fascism, populism, ethno-cultural (including religious) communalism (e.g., fundamentalism), and Stalinist "communism" itself. How have the workers fared in this? They have been progressively politically pulverized and liquidated, up to today.

Marxism's political allegiance to the working class was strategic, not principled. What Marxism expressed was the socialist intelligentsia's recognition of the "necessity of the dictatorship of the proletariat" as a *means* to achieve socialism, not as an abstract utopia, but rather, as Lenin put it, "on the basis of capitalism itself," and thus the necessary "next stage" of history.

This is because capitalism produces not only proletarianized workers, but also their opposite: a reserve army of lumpenized unemployed to be used against them — not merely economically, but also politically — as fodder for petty bourgeois demagogy and objects of capitalist technocratic manipulation, but also as enraged masses of capitalism's discontented. If

---

3  *Weekly Worker* (May 14, 2015)

the working class in revolution would open its ranks to all and thus abolish the lumpenproletariat as well as the petty bourgeoisie through universalizing labor, then this would be a civil war measure under socialist leadership, to immediately attack and dismantle the valorization process of capital, as well as to mobilize the masses against competing petty bourgeois democratic leadership: it will not be as a new, ostensibly emancipatory principle of society. It would be rather what Lukács dialectically considered the "completion of reification" that would also lead potentially to its "negation." It would be to raise to the level of conscious politics what has already happened in the domination of society by capital — its "proletarianization" — not to ideologically mystify it, as Macnair does in subsuming it under the democratic revolution, regarded as "bourgeois" or otherwise.

But this can only ever happen at a global and not local scale, for it must involve a predominant part of the world working class asserting practical governing authority to be effective. This would be what Marxism once called the "proletarian socialist revolution." But it would also be, according to Marx and Lenin, the potential completion of the bourgeois democratic revolution, going beyond it. This ambivalent — "dialectical" — conception of the proletarian socialist revolution as the last phase of the bourgeois democratic revolution that points beyond it has bedeviled "Marxists" from the beginning, however much Marx was clear about it. Lenin's and Trotsky's practical political success in October 1917 was in pursuing the necessity Marx had recognized. However, consciousness of that original Marxist intention has been lost.

## Democracy

This must be ideologically plausible as "socialism," not only to the workers, but to the others they must lead politically in this struggle. That means that socialism must be as compelling ideologically as the working class is politically organized for the dictatorship of the proletariat — what Marx called "winning the battle of democracy." Note well that this was for Marx the battle *of* democracy, which he took to be already established, and not the battle "for" democracy as some yet unattained ideal. For Marx democracy was *constitutive* of the modern state in bourgeois society and capitalism:

hence his statement that the "secret of every constitution is democracy" — a notion Marx had in common with bourgeois revolutionary thought going back to Machiavelli, but especially with respect to Locke and Rousseau. "Socialism," as the phenomenon of a new need in capitalism, must win the battle of the democratic revolution. The political party for socialism would be the means by which this would take place.

The issue is whether we are closer to or rather further away from the prospect of socialism today, by contrast with a hundred years ago. If socialism seems more remote, then how do we account for this, if — as Macnair, for instance, asserts — we have already achieved socially what Marx demanded in the *Critique of the Gotha Program*? The return to predominance of what Marx considered Bonapartism through petty bourgeois democracy after the liquidation of proletarian socialism in the early 20th century would seem to raise questions about the "progress" of capitalism and of the very social conditions for politics. Have they advanced? It could be equally plausible that conditions have *regressed*, not only politically, but socially, objectively as well as subjectively, and that there has been a greater *divergence* of their interrelation by comparison to past historical moments, especially the revolutionary crisis of 1914–19.

The question, then, would be if the *necessity* of Marx's "dictatorship of the proletariat" has been overcome or rather *deepened*. Redefining the dictatorship of the proletariat, as Macnair, along with many others, has tried to do, will not suffice to address adequately the issues raised by consideration of historical Marxism, specifically how Marxists once regarded the workers' movement for socialism itself, as well as capitalism, as self-contradictory. And, most pointedly, how Marxism considered capitalism and socialism to be "dialectically" intertwined, inextricably — how they are really two sides of the same historical phenomenon — rather than seeing them as standing in undialectical antithesis.

The task posed by capitalism has been for proletarian socialism to lead petty bourgeois democracy, not adapt to it. The classic question of politics raised by Lenin — "Who-whom?" (that is, who is the subject and who is the object of political action) — remains: the history of the past century demonstrates that, where ostensible Marxists leading proletarian socialist parties have tried to use the petty bourgeois democrats, really the latter have used — and then ruthlessly disposed of — them.

So let us return to Marx's formulation of the problem and retrace its history — for instance, through the example of the revolutionary history of the US.

## Dictatorship

In a letter of March 5 1852, Marx wrote to Joseph Weydemeyer that his only original contribution had been recognizing the necessity of the "dictatorship of the proletariat." Bourgeois thought, Marx wrote, had already recognized the existence and the struggle of classes: indeed, the existence and struggle of classes — the struggle of the workers against the capitalists — had been recognized by bourgeois thought in terms of liberalism. Recognition of the class struggle was an achievement of liberal thought and politics. Marx thought that socialists had fallen below the threshold of liberalism in avoiding both the necessity of the separation of classes in capitalism and the necessity of the class struggle resulting from that division of society. Socialists blamed the capitalists rather than recognizing that they were not the *cause*, but the *effect*, of the self-contradiction of society in capitalism.[4] So Marx went beyond both contemporary liberal and socialist thought in his recognition of the historical necessity of the dictatorship of the proletariat revealed by capitalism.

Marx wrote this letter in the wake of the *coup d'état* by Louis Bonaparte and his establishment of the Second Empire. It was the culmination of Marx's writings on the 1848 revolution and its aftermath. Weydemeyer was Marx's editor and publisher for his book on *The Eighteenth Brumaire of Louis Bonaparte*.

Later, in his writings on the Paris Commune in *The Civil War in France*, Marx summarized the history of Louis Bonaparte's Second Empire in terms of its being the dialectical inverse of the Commune, and wrote that the Commune demonstrated the "dictatorship of the proletariat" in action. How so?

---

4   See my "Class-consciousness (from a Marxist perspective) today," *Platypus Review* 51 (November 2012), in this volume.

Marx's perspective on post-1848 Bonapartism was a dialectical conception with respect to the necessity of the dictatorship of the proletariat that Bonapartism expressed. This was why it was so important for Marx to characterize Louis Bonaparte's success as both "petty bourgeois" and "lumpenproletarian," as a phenomenon of the reconstitution of capitalism after its crisis of the 1840s. Bonaparte's success was actually the failure of politics; and politics for Marx was a matter of the necessity of the class struggle of the workers against the capitalists. Bonapartism was for Marx a "dictatorship of the bourgeoisie" — not in the sense of the rule of the capitalists, but rather in terms of the political necessity of the state continuing to organize capitalism on a bourgeois basis and the imperative for doing so after the capitalists had lost the ability to lead through civil society. After all, as Marx put it in *The Eighteenth Brumaire*, in Bonaparte's coup, "bourgeois fanatics for order [were] shot down on their balconies in the name of . . . order." It was a "dictatorship of the bourgeoisie" in the sense that it did for them what they could not.

The crisis of bourgeois society in capitalism ran deep. Marx wrote:

> Every demand of the simplest bourgeois financial reform, of the most ordinary liberalism, of the most formal republicanism, of the most insipid democracy, is simultaneously castigated as an "attempt on society" and stigmatized as "socialism."[5]

It was in this sense that the Bonapartist police state emerging from this crisis was a travesty of bourgeois society: why Louis Bonaparte was for Marx a "farcical" figure, as opposed to his uncle Napoleon Bonaparte's "tragedy" in the course of the Great Revolution. Where Napoleon tried to uphold such bourgeois values, however dictatorially, Louis Bonaparte and others who took their cue from him after 1848 abjured them all. 1848 was a parody of the bourgeois revolution and indeed undid it. The "tragedy" of 1848 was not of bourgeois society, but of proletarian socialism: Marx described the perplexity of contemporaries, such as Victor Hugo, who considered Bonapartism a monstrous historical accident and, by contrast, Pierre-Joseph

---

5   *Eighteenth Brumaire.*

Proudhon, who apologized for it as some expression of historical necessity, even going so far as to flirt with Louis Bonaparte as a potential champion of the working class against the capitalists — a dynamic repeated by Ferdinand Lassalle in Germany with respect to Bismarck, earning Marx's excoriation. Marx offered a *dialectical* conception of Bonapartism.

## State capitalism

Frankfurt Institute for Social Research director Max Horkheimer's essay on "The Authoritarian State" was inspired by Walter Benjamin's "Theses on the Philosophy of History," which were his draft aphorisms in historiographic introduction to the unwritten *Arcades Project*, concerned with how the history of the 19th century prefigured the 20th: specifically, how the aftermath of 1848 was repeating itself in the 1920s–30s, the aftermath of failed revolution from 1917–19; how 20th century fascism was a repeat and continuation of 19th century Bonapartism. So was Stalinism.

Horkheimer wrote that the authoritarian state could not be disowned by the workers' movement or indeed separated from the democratic revolution more broadly. It could not be dissociated from Marx's dictatorship of the proletariat, but could only be understood properly dialectically with respect to it. The authoritarian state was descended from the deep history of the bourgeois revolution, but realized only after 1848: only in the crisis of bourgeois society in capitalism, which made the history of the bourgeois revolution appear in retrospect rather as the history of the authoritarian state. What had happened in the meantime?

In the 20th century, the problem of the Bonapartist or authoritarian state needed to be addressed with further specificity regarding the phenomenon of "state capitalism." What Marx recognized in the "necessity of the dictatorship of the proletariat" was the same as that of state capitalism in Bonapartism. Hence, the history of Marxism after Marx is inseparable from the history of state capitalism, in which the issue of the dictatorship of the proletariat was inextricably bound up. Marx's legacy to subsequent Marxism in his critique of the Gotha Programme (1875) was largely ignored.

The question is how the Lassallean Social Democratic Workers' Party that Marx's followers joined in Bismarckian Germany was a state capitalist party, and whether and how Marx's followers recognized that problem: would the workers' party for socialism lead, despite Marxist leadership, to state capitalism rather than to socialism? Was the political party for socialism just a form of Bonapartism?

This is the problem that has beset the Left ever since the crisis of proletarian socialism over a hundred years ago, in World War I and its aftermath. Indeed, Marxism has seemed to be haunted by this historical verdict against it, as state capitalism, and so disqualified forever as a politics for emancipation.

Marxism fell apart into mutual recriminations regarding its historical failure. Anarchists and council communists blamed "Leninism"; and "Leninists" returned the favor, blaming lack of adequate political organization and leadership for the grief of all spontaneous risings. Meanwhile, liberals and social democrats quietly accepted state capitalism as a fact, an unfortunate and regrettable necessity, to be dispensed with whenever possible. But all these responses were in fact forms of political irresponsibility, because they were all avoidance of a critical fact. Marx's prognosis of the "dictatorship of the proletariat" still provoked pangs of conscience and troubling thoughts. What *had* Marx meant by it?

We should be clear: state capitalism in the underdeveloped world was always a peripheral phenomenon; state capitalism in the core, developed, capitalist countries posed the contradiction of capitalism more acutely, and in a politically sharpened manner. What was the *political* purpose of state capitalism in post-proletarian society? Rather than in "backward" Russia or China and other countries undergoing a process of industrializing-proletarianizing. Socialism was not meant to be a modernizing capitalization project. And yet this is what it has been. How did socialism *point beyond* capitalism?

## Neoliberalism

Organized capitalism relying on the state is a fact. The only question is the *politics* of it. Lenin, for one, was critically aware of state capitalism, even if he can be accused of having allegedly contributed to it. The question is not whether and how state capitalism contradicts socialism, but how to grasp that contradiction *dialectically*. A Marxist approach would try to grasp state capitalism, as its Bonapartist state, as a form of *suspended revolution*; indeed, as a form of suspended "class struggle." The struggle for socialism — or its absence — affects the character of capitalism. Certainly, it affects the *politics* of it.

A note on neoliberalism. As with anything, the "neo" is crucially important. It is not the liberalism of the 18th or even the 19th century. It is a form of state capitalism, not an alternative to it. Only, it is a form of politically *irresponsible* state capitalism. That is why it recalls the Gilded Age of the late 19th and early 20th centuries, the era of "imperialism," of the imperial — Bonapartist — state. However, at that time, there was a growing and developing proletarian movement for socialism, or "revolutionary social democracy," led by Marxists, in nearly all the major capitalist countries. Or so, at least, it seemed.

Historically, Marxism was bound up with the history of state capitalism, specifically as a phenomenon of politics after the crisis of 1873. For this reason, the history of capitalism is impacted by the absence of Marxism 100 years later, today, after the crisis of 1973.[6] After 1873, in the era of the second industrial revolution, there was what Marxists once called the "monopoly capitalism" of global cartels and financialization, organized by a world system of states, which Marxists regarded as the "highest (possible) stage of capitalism." It was understood as necessarily bringing forth the workers' movement for socialism, which seemed borne out in practice: the history from the 1870s to the first decades of the 20th century demonstrated a growth of proletarian socialism alongside growing state capitalism.

Rosa Luxemburg pointed out — against social democratic reformists, who affirmed this workers' movement as already in the process of achieving socialism within capitalism — that "the proletariat ... can only create political power and then transform [*aufheben*] capitalist property."[7] That *Aufhebung* — the "dictatorship of the proletariat" — would be the *beginning*, not the "end," of the emancipatory transformation of society. As Michael Harrington noted, drawing upon Luxemburg and Marx, "political

---

6    See my "1873–1973, the century of Marxism: the death of Marxism and the emergence of neoliberalism and neo-anarchism," *Platypus Review* 47 (June 2012), in this volume.

7    "Speech to the Hanover Congress" (October 11, 1899).

power is the unique essence of the socialist transformation."[8] It is this political power that the "Left" has avoided since the 1960s.

## History

In the US, the liberal democratic ideal of Jeffersonian democracy, the idyll of the American Revolution, was shattered by the crack of the slave whip — and by the blast of the rifle shot to stop it. Jefferson had tried to call for abolition of slavery in his 1776 Declaration of Independence, accusing British policy of encouraging slavery in the colonies, but the Continental Congress deleted the passage. Jefferson fought against slavery his entire political life. Towards the end of that life, in a letter of August 7 1825, Jefferson wrote to the abolitionist, women's rights activist and utopian socialist, Frances Wright, supporting her founding the Nashoba Commune in Tennessee for the emancipation of slaves through labor:

> I do not permit myself to take part in any new enterprises, even for bettering the condition of man, not even in the great one which is the subject of your letter [the abolition of slavery], and which has been thro' life that of my greatest anxieties. The march of events has not been such as to render its completion practicable within the limits of time allotted to me; and I leave its accomplishment as the work of another generation. and I am cheered when I see that on which it is devolved, taking it up with so much good will, and such mind engaged in its encouragement. The abolition of the evil is not impossible: it ought never therefore to be despaired of. Every plan should be adopted, every experiment tried, which may do something towards the ultimate object. That which you propose is well worthy of trial. It has succeeded with certain portions of our white brethren, under the care of a [Christian communist

---

8    Michael Harrington, "Marxism and democracy," *Praxis International*, no. 1 (April 1981).

George] Rapp and an [utopian socialist Robert] Owen; and
why may it not succeed with the man of colour?[9]

Jefferson's election to president in 1800, through which he established the
political supremacy of his new Democratic-Republican Party, was called
a "revolution," and indeed it was. Jefferson defeated the previously dominant Federalists. What we now call the Democratic Party, beginning under
Andrew Jackson, was a split and something quite different from Jefferson.
The Republican Party, whose first elected president in 1860 was Abraham Lincoln, was a revolutionary party, and in fact sought to continue the
betrayed revolution of Jefferson's Democratic-Republicans. The Republicans came out of the destruction of the Whig party, which produced a
revolutionary political crisis leading to the Civil War. They were the party
of the last great political revolution in American politics, the Civil War and
Reconstruction under Ulysses S ("Unconditional Surrender") Grant that
followed. Its failure demonstrated, as the revolutions of 1848 had done in
Europe, the limits of political and social revolution in capitalism: it showed
the need for socialism.[10]

The last major crisis of US politics was in the 1960s "New Left" challenge to the ruling Democratic Party's New Deal coalition that had been the
political response to the 1930s great depression.[11] In the 1930s Franklin D
Roosevelt had disciplined the capitalists in order to save capitalism, subordinating the working class to his efforts. He thus remade the Democratic
Party. Trotsky, for one, considered FDR New Dealism, along with fascism
and Stalinism, despite great differences, a form of "Bonapartism."[12] The crisis

---

9   The letter can be found in the National Archives online.

10  Lincoln's Gettysburg address declared the goal of the Union in the US Civil War to be
    a "new birth of freedom." But its declaration that it was fought so that "government of
    the people, by the people, for the people shall not perish from the Earth" expressed the
    sobering consciousness that, by contrast with the European states after the failures of
    the revolutions of 1848, the US was the last remaining major democratic-republican
    state in the world.

11  See my "When was the crisis of capitalism? Moishe Postone and the legacy of the 1960s
    New Left" *Platypus Review* 70 (October 2014), in this volume.

12  See Leon Trotsky, *The Death Agony of Capitalism and the Tasks of the Fourth Internation-
    al* aka *Transitional Programme for Socialist Revolution* (1938).

of the 1960s was essentially the crisis of the Democratic Party, challenged by both the Civil Rights Movement and the Vietnam war. The Republicans, first led by Richard Nixon in 1968 then by Ronald Reagan in 1980, were the beneficiaries of that crisis. Both the 1930s and 1960s–70s, however, fell below the standard of Radical Republicanism in the 1860s–70s, which was the most democratic period in US history. It is something less than ironic that the Democrats, considered the "Left" of the American political party system, have been the most acutely counterrevolutionary of Bonapartist parties. This despite Democratic Party presidential candidate John F Kennedy's declaration on October 12 1960 that the strife of the 20th century — expressed by the cold war struggles of communism and decolonization — was an extension of the American Revolution to which the US needed to remain true.[13]

The history of the state in the modern era is inextricable from the politics of revolution.[14] The crisis of the state is always a crisis of political parties; crises of political parties are always crises of the state. The crisis of the state and its politics is a phenomenon of the crisis of capitalism.

The question of Left and Right is a matter of the degree of facilitation in addressing practically and with consciousness the problem of capitalism, and the problem of capitalism is inextricable from the state.

## Regression

Politics today tends to be reduced to issues of policy, of *what* to do, neglecting the question of *who* is to do it. But this is depoliticizing. Politics is properly about the matter of mobilizing and organizing people to take

---

13  Kennedy was speaking at the Hotel Theresa in New York:

> I am delighted to come and visit. Behind the fact of Castro coming to this hotel, Khrushchev coming to Castro, there is another great traveler in the world, and that is the travel of a world revolution, a world in turmoil. I am delighted to come to Harlem and I think the whole world should come here and the whole world should recognize that we all live right next to each other, whether here in Harlem or on the other side of the globe. We should be glad they came to the United States. We should not fear the 20th century, for this worldwide revolution which we see all around us is part of the original American Revolution.

14  See "Revolutionary politics and thought," *Platypus Review* 69 (September 2014), in this volume.

action: their very empowerment is at least as important as what they do with it. Marxism never identified itself directly with either the working class or its political action, including workers' revolution and any potential revolutionary state issuing from this.[15] But Marxism advocated the political power of the working class, recognizing why the workers must rule society in its crisis of capitalism. Marxism assumed the upward movement of this trend from the 1860s into the early 20th century. But, in the absence of this, other forces take its place, with more or less disastrous results. After 1919 matters have substantially regressed.

Marxism recognized the non-identity of socialism and the working class. "Revolutionary social democracy" of the late 19th century, in its original formulation by Bebel and Kautsky, followed by Lenin and Luxemburg, was the union of the socialist ideological movement of the revolutionary bourgeois intelligentsia with the workers in their class struggle against the capitalists.[16] For Marxism "politics" is the class struggle. For Marx, the capitalists are only constituted as a class through opposing the working class's struggle for socialism (see Marx's 1847 *The Poverty of Philosophy*). Otherwise, as Horkheimer recognized, there is no capitalist class as such, but competing rackets. Adam Smith, for instance, had recognized the need for the workers to collectively organize in pursuit of their interests; Smith favored high wages and low profits to make capitalism work. Marx's critique of political economy was in recognition of the limits of bourgeois political economy, including and especially that of the working class itself. Marx was no advocate of proletarian political economy, but its critic.

The antagonism of workers against the capitalists is not itself the contradiction of capital. However, it expresses it.[17] The goal of socialism is the abolition of political economy, not in terms of the overthrowing of the capitalists by the workers, but the overcoming of and going beyond

---

15  See Leon Trotsky, "Stalinism and Bolshevism" (1937).

16  See V.I. Lenin *What is to Be Done? Burning Questions of our Movement* (1902), and *One Step Forward, Two Steps Back: The Crisis in our Party* (1904), where, respectively, Lenin argues for the non-identity of socialist and trade union consciousness, and defines revolutionary social democracy as Jacobinism tied to the workers' movement.

17  See my "Democratic revolution and the contradiction of capital," *Weekly Worker* (October 16, 2014), in this volume; and my follow-up letters in debate with Macnair (November 20, 2014, January 8, January 22, and April 16, 2015).

the principle of labor as value that capital makes possible.[18] The question is how the potential for socialism can transcend the politics of capitalism — can emerge out from the class struggle of the workers against the capitalists — that otherwise reconstitutes it.

### Rejecting

A political party is necessary to preserve the horizon of proletarian socialism in capitalism over time. Otherwise, the workers will have only consciousness of their interests that reproduces capitalism, however self-contradictorily. A political party is necessary for class struggle to take place at all. According to Marx, the democratic republic is the condition under which the class struggle in capitalism will be fought out to completion; and the only possibility for the democratic republic in capitalism is the dictatorship of the proletariat, or a revolutionary workers' state.

Such a revolutionary politics would be concerned not with the *whether*, but only the *how*, of socialism. It will be marked by great social strife and political struggle, with competing socialist parties. Its purpose will be to make manifestly *political* the civil war of capitalism that occurs nonetheless anyway. We are very far from such a politics today.

The notion of politics apart from the state, and of politics apart from parties is a bourgeois fantasy — precisely a *bourgeois* fantasy of liberal democracy that capitalism has thrown into crisis and rendered obsolete and so impossible. Capitalism presents a new political necessity, as Marx and his best followers once recognized. Anarchism is truly "liberalism in hysterics" in denying the necessity of politics, in denying the need for political party. Neo-anarchism today is the natural corollary to neoliberalism.

In the absence of a true Left, politics and the state — capitalism — will be led by others. In the absence of meeting the political necessity of the dictatorship of the proletariat, we will have more or less, hard or soft, and more or less *irresponsible* capitalist state dictatorship. We will have political irresponsibility.

---

18  See my "Why still read Lukács? The place of 'philosophical questions' in Marxism" *Platypus Review* 63 (February 2014), in this volume.

To abandon the task of political party is to abandon the state, and to abandon the state is to abandon the revolution. It is to abandon the political necessity of socialism, whose task capitalism presents. It is to abandon politics altogether, and leave the field to pseudo-politics, to political irresponsibility. The "Left" has done this for more than a generation, at least since the 1960s. What would it mean to do otherwise?

Presented on a panel at the closing plenary of the seventh annual Platypus Affiliated Society International Convention in Chicago with Mike Macnair of the Communist Party of Great Britain (CPGB), Adolph Reed, Jr. (University of Pennsylvania), and Tom Riley of the Internationalist Bolshevik Tendency (IBT), April 11, 2015.

Originally published in *Weekly Worker* 1064 ( June 25, 2015) and in *Platypus Review* 78 ( July – August 2015)

# Back to Herbert Spencer!
# Industrial vs. militant society

Herbert Spencer's grave faces Marx's at Highgate Cemetery in London. At his memorial, Spencer was honored for his anti-imperialism by Indian national liberation advocate and anti-colonialist Shyamji Krishnavarma, who funded a lectureship at Oxford in Spencer's name.

What would the 19th century liberal, Utilitarian and Social Darwinist, Herbert Spencer (1820–1903), who was perhaps the most prominent, widely read and popular philosopher in the world during his lifetime — that is, in Marx's lifetime — have to say to Marxists or more generally to the left, when such liberalism earned not only Marx's own scorn but also Nietzsche's criticism? Nietzsche referred to Spencer and his broad appeal as the modern enigma of "the English psychologists." Nietzsche critiqued what he took to be Spencer's assumption of a historically linear-evolutionary development and improvement of human morality leading to a 19th century epitome; where Nietzsche found the successive "transvaluations of values" through profound reversals of "self-overcoming."[1] Nietzsche regarded modern liberal morality not as a perfection but rather as a challenge and task to achieve an "over-man," that, failing, threatened to result in a nihilistic dead-end of "the last man" instead. Marx regarded Spencerian liberalism as an example of the decrepitude of bourgeois-revolutionary thought in decadence. Marx's son-in-law, the French socialist Paul Lafargue, wrote, just after Marx's death, against Spencer's "bourgeois pessimism," to which he offered a Marxist optimism.[2] Such Marxism fulfilled Nietzsche's "pessimism of the strong." By the late 19th century, Marxists could be confident about transcending bourgeois society. Not so today.

---

1   *On the Genealogy of Morals: A Polemic* (1887).
2   "A Few Words with Mr. Herbert Spencer" (1884).

Spencer's distinction of "militant" vs. "industrial" society[3] — that is to say, the distinction of *traditional civilization* vs *bourgeois society* — is still, unfortunately, quite pertinent today, and illuminates a key current blindspot on the ostensible "Left," especially regarding the phenomenon of war. Spencer followed the earlier classical liberal Benjamin Constant's observation[4] that moderns get through commerce what the ancients got through war; and that for moderns war is always regrettable and indeed largely unjustifiably criminal, whereas for ancients war was virtuous — among the very highest virtues. Do we moderns sacrifice ourselves for the preservation and glory of our specific "culture," as "militants" do, or rather dedicate ourselves to social activity that facilitates *universal freedom* — a value unknown to the ancients? Does the future belong to the constant warfare of particular cultural differences, or to human society? Marx thought the latter.

The question is whether we think that we will *fight* or, rather, *exchange* and *produce* our way to freedom. Is freedom to be achieved through "militant" or rather "industrial" society? Marx assumed the latter.

When we seek to extol our political leaders today, we do not depict them driving a tank but waking at 5 o'clock and staying up past midnight to do society's business. We do not speak of their scars earned in combat but their gray hairs accumulated in office. Not enjoying the spoils of war on a dais but getting in their daily morning jog to remain fit for work. We judge them not as cunning warriors but as diligent workers — and responsible negotiators. In our society, it is not the matter of a battle to win but a job to do. Carl Schmitt thought that this has led to our dehumanization. But few would agree.

What would have appeared commonplace to Spencer's contemporary critics, such as Nietzsche and Marx, must strike us today, rather, as profoundly insightful and indeed critical of our society. This is due to the historical regression of politics and society since Marx's time, and, moreover, to the liquidation of Marxism. What Marx would have regarded as fatally one-sided and undialectical in Spencer, would today seem adequate to the prevailing condition, in the absence of the Marxist-Hegelian dialectic. The Marxist critique of liberalism has been rendered moot, not in the

---

3   *The Principles of Sociology*, vol. 2, (1879/98).

4   In "The liberty of the Ancients as compared with that of the Moderns" (1816).

sense of liberalism's actual social supersession but by historical regression. Society has fallen below the historical threshold of not only socialism but of classical liberalism — of bourgeois emancipation itself. Not only have we fallen below the criteria of Kant and Hegel that surpassed 18th century Empiricism, we have fallen below its 19th century successor, Positivism, as well. The question is the status today of liberalism as *ideology*. It is utopian. As Adorno put it, it is both promise and sham.

Militant and industrial tendencies confront each other today not as different societies, but as opposed aspects of the same society, however contradictorily and antagonistically, in capitalism. Similarly, the phases of "religious," "metaphysical" and "positive" forms do not succeed one another sequentially in a linear development but rather interact in a dynamic of social history. What Spencer regarded as regressive "metaphysics" remains valid in capitalism, as "ideology" calling for dialectical critique. We cannot now claim to address problems in the clear air of Enlightenment.

If Adorno, for instance, critiqued sociological "positivism," this was not as a Romantic anti-positivist such as Max Weber, but rather as a critique of positive sociology as *ideology* in capitalism. For Adorno, positivism and Heideggerian ontology, as well as Weberian "cultural sociology," opposed each other in an antinomy of capitalism that would be overcome not in one principle triumphing over another, but rather in the antinomy itself being succeeded dialectically in freedom. Weber denied freedom; whereas Spencer assumed it. Both avoided the specific problem of capitalism. To take a condition of unfreedom for freedom is the most salient phenomenon of ideology. This is what falsified positivism as liberal Enlightenment, its false sense of freedom as already achieved that still actually tasked society. Freedom is not to be taken as an achieved state but a goal of struggle.

An emancipated society would be "positivist" — Enlightened and liberal — in ways that under capitalism can only be ideologically false and misleading. Positivism should therefore be understood as a desirable goal *beyond* rather than a possibility *under* capitalism. The problem with Herbert Spencer is that he took capitalism — grasped partially and inadequately as bourgeois emancipation — to be a condition of freedom that would need yet to be really achieved. If "metaphysics," contra positivism, remains valid in capitalism, then this is as a condition to be overcome. Capitalist metaphysics is a real symptom of unfreedom. Positivism treats this as merely an issue of mistaken thinking, or to be worked out through "scientific" methodology, whereas it is actually a problem of society requiring political struggle. The antinomy of positivism vs metaphysics is not partisan but *social*. As Adorno observed, the same individual could and would be scientifically Positivist and philosophically ontological-Existentialist.

Spencer's opposition to "socialism" in the 19th century was in its undeniable retrograde illiberal aspect, what Marx called "reactionary socialism."[5] But Marx offered a perspective on potentially transcending socialism's one-sidedness in capitalism. Spencer was entirely unaware of this Marxian dialectic. Marx agreed with Spencer on the conservative-reactionary and regressive character of socialism. Marx offered a dialectic of socialism and liberalism presented by their symptomatic and diagnostic antinomy in capitalism that pointed beyond itself. 18th century liberalism's insufficiency to the 19th century problem of capitalism necessitated socialist opposition; but liberalism still offered a critique of socialism that would need to be fulfilled to be transcended, and not dismissed let alone defeated as such.

Only in overcoming capitalism through socialism could, as Marx put it, humanity face its condition "with sober senses."[6] This side of emancipation from capital, humanity remains trapped in a "phantasmagoria" of bourgeois social relations become self-contradictory and self-destructive in capital. This phantasmagoria was both collective and individual — socialist and liberal — in character. Spencer naturalized this antinomy. His libertarian anti-statism and its broad, popular political appeal down through the 20th century was the necessary result of the continuation of capitalism and its discontents.

Spencer regarded the problem as a historical holdover of traditional civilization to be left behind rather than as the new condition of bourgeois society in capitalist crisis that Marx recognized needed to be, but could not be, overcome in Spencer's liberal terms. Marx agreed with Spencer on the goal, but differed, crucially, over the nature of the obstacle and, hence, how to get there from here. Not only Spencer's later followers (more egregiously

---

5   *Communist Manifesto* (1848).
6   Ibid.

than Spencer himself), but Marx's own, have falsified this task. It has been neglected and abandoned. We cannot assume as Marx did that we are already past Spencer's classical liberalism, but are driven back to it, ineluctably, whether we realize it or not. Only by returning to the assumptions of classical liberalism can we understand Marx's critique of it. The glare of Marx's tomb at Highgate stares down upon a very determinate object. If one disappears, they both do.

Originally published in *Weekly Worker* 1088 (January 7, 2016) and in *Platypus Review* 82 (December 2015 – January 2016)

# Horkheimer in 1943 on party and class

## Without a socialist party, there is no class struggle, only rackets

Horkheimer's remarkable essay "On the sociology of class relations" (1943)[1] is continuous with Adorno's contemporaneous "Reflections on class theory" (1942) as well as his own "The Authoritarian State" (1940/42), which similarly mark the transformation of Marx and Engels's famous injunction in the *Communist Manifesto* that "history is the history of class struggles."[2] All of these writings were inspired by Walter Benjamin's "On the concept of history" (AKA "Theses on the philosophy of history," 1940), which registered history's fundamental crisis. Instead, for Horkheimer and Adorno in the 1940s, history has become the history of "rackets."[3] As Horkheimer concludes his draft, parenthetically citing Marx

---

1   Unpublished manuscript available online in Goethe University Frankfurt Max Horkheimer archives. See the symposium "Max Horkheimer and the Sociology of Class Relations" on Horkheimer's essay with Todd Cronan, James Schmidt, John Lysaker, Nicholas Brown and David Jenemann published in *nonsite.org* (January 11, 2016), from which this essay is taken.

2   In *Can One Live After Auschwitz?: A Philosophical Reader*, ed. Rolf Tiedemann, trans. Rodney Livingstone and others (Stanford: Stanford University Press, 2009) and in *The Essential Frankfurt School Reader*, ed. Andrew Arato and Eike Gebhardt (New York: Continuum, 1985, respectively).

3   Horkheimer specified the concept of "rackets" in "On the sociology of class relations" as follows:

> The concept of the racket referring to the big and to the small units struggling for as great a share as possible of the surplus value designates all such groups from the highest capitalistic bodies down to the little pressure groups working within or without the pale of the law among the most miserable strata of the population. It has arisen as a theoretical concept when, by the increasing absoluteness of the profit system the disproportion between the functions of the ruling class in production and the advantages which they draw from it became even more manifest

on Hegelian methodology, "the anatomy of man is key to that of the ape": the past is explicable from the present, in the form of clique power-politics. But this change is for Horkheimer a devolution — regression. It stemmed from the failure of proletarian socialist revolutionary politics after 1917–19. Without Marxism, there was no class struggle.[4]

The significance of this change is the relation of the individual to the collective in capitalism. This affects the character of consciousness, and thus the role of theory: the critical theory of the capitalist totality — Marxism — is fundamentally altered. Specifically, the role of working-class political parties in developing this consciousness is evacuated. At stake is what Horkheimer later (in his 1956 conversation with Adorno translated as *Towards a New Manifesto* (2011)) called, simply, the "memory of socialism." It disappears. This was Horkheimer's primary concern, why he points

---

than at the time of . . . [Marx's] *Capital*.

4   A half-century earlier, Rosa Luxemburg had expressed this succinctly in her October 3, 1898 speech to the Stuttgart Congress of the Social-Democratic Party of Germany (SPD), that, "It is the final goal alone which constitutes the spirit and the content of our socialist struggle, which turns it into a class struggle":

Think about it: what really constitutes the socialist character of our whole movement? The really practical struggle falls into three tags: the trade-union struggle, the struggle for social reforms, and the struggle to democratize the capitalist state. Are these three forms of our struggle really socialism? Not at all. Take the trade-union movement first! Look at England: not only is it not socialist there, but it is in some respects an obstacle to socialism. Social reform is also emphasized by Academic Socialists, National Socialists, and similar types. And democratization is specifically bourgeois. The bourgeoisie had already inscribed democracy on its banner before we did. . . .

Then what is it in our day-to-day struggles that makes us a socialist party? It can only be the relation between these three practical struggles and our final goals. It is the final goal alone which constitutes the spirit and the content of our socialist struggle, which turns it into a class struggle. And by final goal we must not mean, as [Wolfgang] Heine has said, this or that image of the future state, but the prerequisite for any future society, namely the conquest of political power. . . . This conception of our task is closely related to our conception of capitalist society; it is the solid ground which underlies our view that capitalist society is caught in insoluble contradictions which will ultimately necessitate an explosion, a collapse, at which point we will play the role of the banker-lawyer who liquidates a bankrupt company. (In *Selected Political Writings of Rosa Luxemburg*, ed. Dick Howard [New York: Monthly Review Press, 1971], 38–9.)

out that the socialist party was not focused on fighting against exploitation, and was indeed indifferent to it. This is because exploitation does not distinguish capitalism from other epochs of history; only the potential possibility for socialism does. That is why, without socialist politics, the pre-capitalist past reasserts itself, in the form of rackets.

At the conclusion of "The Authoritarian State," Horkheimer wrote that, "with the return to the old free enterprise system, the entire horror would start again from the beginning under new management." Regarding the specific topic stated in the title of this essay in particular, we should note Horkheimer's unequivocal observation in "The Authoritarian State" that,

> Sociological and psychological concepts are too superficial to express what has happened to revolutionaries in the last few decades: their will toward freedom has been damaged, without which neither understanding nor solidarity nor a correct relation between leader and group is conceivable.[5]

If there was a "sociology of class relations" to be had, then it would be, as usual for the Frankfurt School, a "negative" and not positive phenomenon. The issue was how to grasp the significance of the original proletarian socialist revolutionary "will toward freedom" degenerating into a matter of mere "sociology" at all. We need to pay attention to the problem indicated by the "On . . . " in the title of Horkheimer's essay. "Class" in Marx's sense was not amenable to sociology; but "rackets" are. Sociology is about groups; but the proletariat for Marx was not a sociological group but rather a negative condition of society. The proletariat in capitalism was for Marx a negative phenomenon indicating the need for socialism. The political task of meeting that necessity was what Marx called "proletarian socialism."

Horkheimer was in keeping with Marx on this score. As the former SYRIZA Greek Finance Minister Yanis Varoufakis pointed out in a recent (October 23, 2015) interview, Marx was not concerned with "equality" or "justice," but "liberty" — freedom.[6] Moreover, as Varoufakis correctly

---

5   In *The Essential Frankfurt School Reader*, ed. Andrew Arato and Eike Gebhardt (New York: Continuum, 1985), 117.

6   Novara Media, "Yanis Varoufakis on Europe, UKIP and Post-Capitalism." Available on

observes, for Marx, capitalism is a condition of unfreedom for the *capitalists* and not only for the workers.[7]

As Marx wrote, at least as early as *The Poverty of Philosophy* (1847), the capitalist class is constituted as such, as a class, only in response to the demands of the workers. It treats the demands of the workers as impossible under capitalism, as a more or less criminal violation of society. It is only in meeting the political challenge of a unified capitalist class that the working class constitutes itself as a class "in itself," not only subjectively but also objectively. For Marx, the historical turning point in this development was Chartism in England, which inaugurates the "class struggle" of the working class *per se*.

Only in fulfilling the task of proletarian socialism, transcending not only the workers' (competing, racket) economic interests in capitalism but also democracy in bourgeois society, that is, coming up against the limits of liberalism, does the proletariat become a class "for itself" — on the way to "abolishing itself" in overcoming the negative condition of society in capitalism: its politics is not about one group replacing another. But Chartism in the U.K., like the revolutions of 1848–49 on the Continent, failed. For

---

YouTube (October 23, 2015).

7   See also Horkheimer's "The little man and the philosophy of freedom," in *Dawn and Decline, Notes 1926–31 and 1950–69*, trans. Michael Shaw (New York: Seabury, 1978), 50–52. There, Horkheimer wrote that,

> [A]lthough [the capitalists] did not themselves create the world, one cannot but suspect that they would have made it exactly as it is. . . . But for the little man who is turned down when he asks for a job because objective conditions make it impossible . . . [n]ot only his own lack of freedom but that of others as well spells his doom. His interest lies in the Marxist clarification of the concept of freedom.

Horkheimer paraphrased Marx and Engels's *The Holy Family* (1845), where they wrote that,

> The property-owning class and the class of the proletariat represent the same human self-alienation. But the former feels at home in this self-alienation and feels itself confirmed by it; it recognizes alienation as its own instrument and in it possesses the semblance of a human existence. The latter feels itself destroyed by this alienation and sees in it its own impotence and the reality of an inhuman existence.

(Quoted in Georg Lukács, "Reification and the consciousness of the proletariat," part III, "The standpoint of the proletariat," *History and Class Consciousness: Studies in Marxist Dialectics*, trans. Rodney Livingstone [Cambridge, MA: MIT, 1971], 149.)

Marx, this is the need for "revolution in permanence" (1850) indicated by the failure of the democratic revolution and of the "social republic" in 1848. This is why Adorno (1965) characterized the *critical* concept of "society" itself, negatively, as originating "around 1848."[8] The Chartists' last act was to translate Marx and Engels's *Manifesto*.[9]

So what, for Marx, was missing in 1848? This is key to what is missing for Horkheimer a hundred years later: an adequate political party for proletarian socialism; the means for making capitalism a *political* issue.

The role of the political party, specifically as non-identical with the workers' consciousness, both individually and collectively, was to actually preserve the individuality of the workers — as well as of intellectuals! — that is otherwise liquidated in the corporate collectives of capitalist firms, labor unions and nation-states. These rackets have replaced the world party of proletarian socialist revolution, which was itself a dialectical expression of the totality of market relations and of the otherwise chaotic disorder of the concrete conditions of the workers. For Horkheimer, workers related to the political party individually, and only as such constituted themselves as part of a class — in revolutionary political struggle to overcome capitalism through socialism. It was not that Lenin's party *caused* the liquidation of the individual, but the later travesty of "Leninism" in Stalinism was the *effect* of a broader and deeper socially regressive history of capitalism — what Marx called "Bonapartism" in the 19th century — that the 20th century authoritarian state and its concomitant "sociological" problem of political "atomization" expressed.

Liquidating the political party paves the way for conformism: individuality in society instead becomes individualism, whether of persons or corporate bodies. As Margaret Thatcher succinctly put it, "There is no such thing as society." Not only as wish but in fact. By contrast, the party was the negative political discipline adequate to the societal crisis of liberal capitalism in self-contradiction. But for Horkheimer, now, instead positivity rules, in a direct authoritarian manner that capitalism eludes. Avoidance of the party means avoiding capitalism — which suits the power of the rackets as such.

---

8   "Society" in *Salmagundi*, no. 10/11 (Fall 1969–Winter 1970).
9   See David Black, "The elusive threads of historical progress: The early Chartists and the young Marx and Engels," in *Platypus Review* 42 (December 2011 – January 2012).

The problem of society's domination by anonymous social forces was revealed by the struggle against exploitation, which demonstrated the limits of the power of the capitalists and hence the problem of and need to transform "society" as such. The "social question" dawned in the political crisis of 1848: the limits of the democratic republic. This becomes replaced by overt power relations that are mystified, by appearing to know no limits. For Horkheimer, following Lenin,[10] the party's struggle for socialism picked up where the struggle against exploitation reached its limits; without the party there is no struggle for socialism: no pointing beyond but only accommodating capitalism as nature — or at least as a condition seemingly permanent to society.

This is why Horkheimer likens the ideology of organized "racket" capitalism in the 20th century to traditional civilization, by contrast with the liberal capitalism of the 19th century mediated by markets. Indeed, the problem with the rackets is that they falsify precisely the universalism of ideology, which in liberalism could be turned into a negative critique, an

---

10  See Lenin's *What is to be Done?* (1902), where Lenin distinguished "socialist" from "trade union consciousness":

> We have said that *there could not have been* Social-Democratic consciousness among the workers. It would have to be brought to them from without. The history of all countries shows that the working class, exclusively by its own effort, is able to develop only trade union consciousness, i.e., the conviction that it is necessary to combine in unions, fight the employers, and strive to compel the government to pass necessary labor legislation, etc. The theory of socialism, however, grew out of the philosophic, historical, and economic theories elaborated by educated representatives of the propertied classes, by intellectuals.

> Furthermore, in a January 20, 1943 letter debating Henryk Grossmann on Marxist dialectics, Horkheimer wrote that, "It is no coincidence that Lenin the materialist thinker who took these questions [in Hegel] more seriously than anyone else placed all those footnotes next to the [*Science of*] *Logic* rather than next to the *Philosophy of History*. It was he who wanted to make the study of Hegel's *Logic* obligatory and who, even if it lacked the finesse of the specialist, sought out the consequences of Positivism, in its Machian form, with the most determined single-mindedness [in *Materialism and Empirio-Criticism*, 1908]. It was still in this Lenin sense that Lukács was attacked for his inclination to apply the dialectic not to the whole of reality but confine it to the subjective side of things." Translation by Frederik van Gelder and original letter in German both available online under "Max Horkheimer's critique of Marxist Positivism in Henryk Grossmann."

index of falsity. Universality is no longer claimed, so the universal condition of domination by capital is rendered occult and illegible. As Adorno put it, "The whole is the false." Only by confronting the negative totality of capitalism politically was class struggle possible. The power-struggles of rackets do not point beyond themselves. There is no history.

Originally published in *nonsite.org* 18 ( January 11, 2016)
and *Platypus Review* 82 (December 2015 – January 2016)

# Rosa Luxemburg and the party

In one of her earliest interventions in the Social-Democratic Party of Germany (SPD), participating in the notorious theoretical "Revisionist Dispute," in which Eduard Bernstein infamously stated that "the movement is everything, the goal nothing," the 27 year-old Rosa Luxemburg (1871–1919) clearly enunciated her Marxism: "It is the final goal alone which constitutes the spirit and the content of our socialist struggle, which turns it into a class struggle."[1]

## Critique of socialism

What did it mean to say that socialist politics was necessary to have "class struggle" at all? This goes to the heart of Luxemburg's own Marxism, and to her most enduring contribution to its history: her Marxist approach to the political party for socialism — a *dialectical* understanding of class and party, in which Marxism itself was grasped in a critical-dialectical way. When Luxemburg accused Bernstein of being "undialectical," this is what she meant: That the working class's struggle for socialism was itself self-contradictory and its political party was the means through which this contradiction was expressed. There was a dialectic of means and ends, or of "movement" and "goal," in which the dialectic of theory and practice took part: Marxism demanded its own critique. Luxemburg took the controversy of the Revisionist Dispute as an occasion for this critique.

In this, Luxemburg followed the young Karl Marx's (1818–83) own formative dialectical critiques of socialism when he was in his 20s, from

---

1   *Selected Political Writings of Rosa Luxemburg*, ed. Dick Howard (New York: Monthly Review Press, 1971), 38–39.

the September 1843 letter to Arnold Ruge calling for the "ruthless critique of everything existing," to the critique of Pierre-Joseph Proudhon in the 1844 *Economic and Philosophic Manuscripts* and *The Poverty of Philosophy* (1847), as well as in *The German Ideology* and its famous *Theses on Feuerbach* (1845). Marx had written of the socialist movement that:

> The internal difficulties seem to be almost greater than the external obstacles. . . .
>
> [W]e must try to help the dogmatists to clarify their propositions for themselves. Thus, communism, in particular, is a dogmatic abstraction; in which connection, however, I am not thinking of some imaginary and possible communism, but actually existing communism as taught by Cabet, Dézamy, Weitling, etc. This communism is itself only a special expression of the humanistic principle, an expression which is still infected by its antithesis — the private system. Hence the abolition of private property and communism are by no means identical, and it is not accidental but inevitable that communism has seen other socialist doctrines — such as those of Fourier, Proudhon, etc. — arising to confront it because it is itself only a special, one-sided realization of the socialist principle. . . .
>
> Hence, nothing prevents us from making criticism of politics, participation in politics, and therefore *real* struggles, the starting point of our criticism, and from identifying our criticism with them. . . . We do not say to the world: Cease your struggles, they are foolish; we will give you the true slogan of struggle. We merely show the world what it is really fighting for. . . .
>
> The reform of consciousness consists *only* in making the world aware of its own consciousness, in awakening it out of its dream about itself, in *explaining* to it the meaning of its own actions.

Such formulations recurred in Marx's *Theses on Feuerbach* a couple of years later:

But that the secular basis detaches itself from itself and establishes itself as an independent realm in the clouds can only be explained by the cleavages and self-contradictions within this secular basis. The latter must, therefore, in itself be both understood in its contradiction and revolutionized in practice.

For Marx, this meant that socialism was the expression of the contradiction of capitalism and as such was itself bound up in that contradiction. A proper dialectical relation of socialism with capitalism required a recognition of the dialectic within socialism itself. Marx followed Hegel in regarding contradiction as manifestation of the need for change. The "proletariat" — the working class after the Industrial Revolution — contradicted bourgeois society, not from outside but from within. As such, the contradiction of capitalism centered on the proletariat itself. This is because for Marx "capitalism" is nothing in itself, but only the crisis of bourgeois society in industrial production and hence its only meaning is the expression of the *need for socialism*. The very existence of the proletariat — a working class expropriated from its bourgeois property-rights in labor as a commodity — demanded socialism.

### Lassallean party

But had the social-democratic workers' party been from its outset a force for counterrevolution — for preserving capitalism — rather than for revolutionary transformation and the achievement of socialism? Its roots in Ferdinand Lassalle's formulation of its purpose as the "permanent political campaign of the working class" evinced a potential contradiction between its Lassalleanism and Marxism. Marxists had not invented the social-democratic workers' party, but rather joined it as an emergent phenomenon of the late 19th century. The social-democratic workers' party in Germany, what became the SPD, had, through its fusion of 1875 at Gotha, attained Marxist or "revolutionary" leadership. But this had elicited Marx's famous *Critique of the Gotha Programme*, to which Marx's own followers, Wilhelm Liebknecht and August Bebel, could only shrug their shoulders at the difficulty of pleasing the "old men in London" (that is, Marx and Engels).

The development of the SPD towards its conscious direction beyond mere Lassalleanism was more clearly enunciated in the SPD's Erfurt Programme of 1891. Nonetheless the ghost of Lassalle seemed to haunt subsequent developments and was still present, according to Engels's critique of it, in the "Marxist" Erfurt Programme itself. (Indeed, one of Rosa Luxemburg's earliest achievements in her participation in the life of the SPD was to unearth and discover the significance of Engels's critique of Bebel, Kautsky, and Bernstein's Erfurt Programme.)

Luxemburg, in her critique of the SPD through regarding the party as a manifestation of contradiction, followed Marx and Engels, whose recognition was the means to advance it beyond itself. Lassalle had made the mistake of opposing the political against and derogating the economic action of the workers, rejecting labor unions, which he called merely the "vain efforts of *things* to behave *like human beings*."[2] Lassalle thus ontologized the political struggle. For Lassalle, the workers taking political power would be tantamount to the achievement of socialism; whereas for Marx this would be merely a transitional revolutionary "dictatorship of the proletariat" that would lead to socialism. Engels called it the transition from the "governing of men" to the "administration of things"[3] — an eminently *dialectical* formulation, since humans are both subjects *and* objects of society.

Lassalle's political ontology of socialism was complementary to the one-sided "vulgar Marxist" misapprehensions of the Revisionists who prioritized and indeed ontologized the economic over the political, reducing the social to the economic, and relating the social to the political "mechanically" and "undialectically" — neglecting the *contradiction* between them in an "economic determinism" that subordinated politics. Where Lassalle subordinated economics to politics in a "state socialism," Marx regarded this rather as a state *capitalism*. Indeed, despite or rather *due* to this antinomy, the Lassalleans and the economistic reformists actually converged in their political perspectives — giving rise later to 20th century welfare-state capitalism through the governance of social-democratic parties.

---

2  Quoted in Georg Lukács, "The Standpoint of the Proletariat," Part III of "Reification and the Consciousness of the Proletariat" in *History and Class Consciousness: Studies in Marxist Dialectics* (1923), trans. Rodney Livingstone (Cambridge, MA: MIT Press, 1971), 195.

3  *Anti-Dühring: Herr Eugen Dühring's Revolution in Science* (1877).

Rather than taking one side over the other, Luxemburg, as a Marxist, approached this problem as a real contradiction: an antinomy and dialectic of capitalism itself that manifested in the workers' own discontents and struggles within it, both economically and politically. For instance, Luxemburg followed Marx in recognizing that the Lassallean goal of the workers achieving a "free state" in political revolution was a self-contradiction: An unfree society gave rise to an unfree state; and it was society that needed to be emancipated from capitalism. But this was a contradiction that could be *posed* only by the workers' revolutionary political action and seizing of state power — if only to "wither" it away in the transformation of society beyond capitalism. In this way the Lassallean party was not a mistake but rather a necessary stage manifesting in the history of the workers' movement. So it needed to be properly recognized — "dialectically" — in order to avoid its one-sided pitfalls in the opposition of Revisionist, reformist economic evolutionism versus the Lassallean political revolutionism. Kautsky followed Marx in a critical endorsement of Lassalleanism in regarding the dictatorship of the proletariat as the seizing of state power by the workers' party for socialism. Hence, Luxemburg expressed her sincere "gratitude" that the Revisionists had occasioned this critical self-recognition, by posing the question and problem of "movement" and "goal."

### Antinomy of reformism

Luxemburg made her great entrance onto the political stage of her time with the pamphlet *Social Reform or Revolution?* (1900). In it, Luxemburg laid out how the original contradiction of capitalism, between its chaotic social relations and its socialization of production had been further developed, exacerbated, and deepened by the development of a new contradiction, namely the growth of the workers' movement in political organization and consciousness: Its movement for socialism was a self-contradictory expression of the contradiction of capitalism. This contrasted with Bernstein's view that the growth and development of the workers' movement was the overcoming of the contradiction of capitalism and the gradual "evolution" of socialism. For Bernstein, the movement for socialism was the achievement of socialism, whereas the goal of socialism was a dispensable figment, a useful enabling fiction.

For Luxemburg, however, the contradiction of the industrial forces of production against their bourgeois social relations in capitalism was recapitulated in the contradiction between the means and ends of the workers' movement for socialism. Socialism was not built up within capitalism; but only the contradiction of capital deepened through workers' struggle against exploitation. How so? Their demand for a share of the value of production was a *bourgeois* demand: the demand for the value of their labor as a commodity. However, what was achieved by increases in wages, recognition of collective bargaining rights, legal protections of workers in capitalist labor contracts and the acceptance of responsibility of the state for the conditions of labor, including the acceptance of the right to political association and democratic political participation in the state, was not the *overcoming* of the problem of capital — that is, the overcoming of the great divergence and social contradiction between the value of capital and wages in industrial production — but rather its exacerbation and deepening through its broadening onto society as a whole. What the workers received in reforms of capitalism was not the value of their labor-power as a commodity, which was relatively minimized by developments of industrial technique, but rather a cut of the profits of capital, whether directly through collective bargaining with the employers or indirectly through state distribution of social welfare benefits from the tax on capital. What Bernstein described optimistically as the socialization of production through such reforms was actually, according to Luxemburg, the "socialization" of the *crisis* of capitalist production.

The workers' party for socialism, through its growth and development on a mass scale, thus increasingly took political responsibility for capitalism. Hence, a new contradiction developed that was focused on the party itself. Was its purpose to manage capitalism, or rather, as Luxemburg put it in her 1898 Stuttgart speech, to "play the role of the banker-lawyer who liquidates a bankrupt company"? Luxemburg posed the political task of the socialist party in *Reform or Revolution?* succinctly: "It is an illusion, then, to think that the proletariat can create economic power within capitalist society. It can only create political power and then transform [*aufheben*] capitalist property." The proletarian socialist party was the means for creating that political power. This differed from the development of bourgeois social relations in feudalism that led to revolution:

> What does it mean that the earlier classes, particularly the third estate, conquered economic power before political power? Nothing more than the historical fact that all previous class struggles must be derived from the economic fact that the rising class has at the same time created a new form of property upon which it will base its class domination.

However, according to Luxemburg, "The assertion that the proletariat, in contrast to all previous class struggles, pursues its battles, not in order to establish class domination, but to abolish all class domination is not a mere phrase." This is because the proletariat does not develop a new form of "property" within capitalism, but rather struggles economically, socially and politically, on the basis of "bourgeois property" — on the basis of the bourgeois social relations of *labor*, or of labor as a commodity. What the working class's struggle within capitalism achieves is consciousness of the need to overcome labor as a commodity, or, to transform capital from bourgeois property into social property that is no longer mediated by the exchange of labor. This is what it meant for Marx that the proletariat struggles not to "realize" but to *abolish* itself, or, how the proletariat goes from being a class "in itself" to becoming a class "for itself" (*The Poverty of Philosophy*, 1847) in its struggle for socialism.

For Luxemburg, the achievement of reforms within capitalism accomplish nothing but the greater practical and theoretical realization, or "consciousness," of the need to abolish labor as a commodity, since the latter has been outstripped by industrial production. The further economic, social, and political reforms only dramatically increase this disparity and contradiction between the economic value of labor as a commodity and the social value of capital that must be appropriated by society as a whole.

In other words, the workers' movement for socialism and its institution as a political party is necessary to make the otherwise chaotic, unconscious, "objective" phenomenon of the economic contradiction and crisis of wage-labor and capital into a conscious, "subjective" phenomenon of *politics*. As Luxemburg wrote later, in *The Crisis of German Social Democracy* (AKA the "Junius Pamphlet," 1915):

> Socialism is the first popular movement in world history that has set itself the goal of bringing human consciousness, and thereby free will, into play in the social actions of mankind. For this reason, Friedrich Engels designated the final victory of the socialist proletariat a leap of humanity from the animal world into the realm of freedom. This leap' is also an iron law of history bound to the thousands of seeds of a prior torment-filled and all-too-slow development. But this can never be realized until the development of complex material conditions strikes the incendiary spark of conscious will in the great masses. The victory of socialism will not descend from heaven. It can only be won by a long chain of violent tests of strength between the old and the new powers. The international proletariat under the leadership of the Social Democrats will thereby learn to try to take its history into its own hands; instead of remaining a will-less football, it will take the tiller of social life and become the pilot to the goal of its own history.

Why "violent tests of strength"? Was this mere "revolutionary" passion, as Bernstein averred? No: As Marx had observed in *Das Kapital*, in the struggle over the "working day," or over the social and legal conventions for the condition of labor-time, workers and capitalists confronted each other, both with "bourgeois right" on their side. But, "Where right meets right, force will decide." Such contests of force did not *decide* the issue of right in capitalism, but only channeled it in a *political* direction. Both capital and wage-labor retained their social rights, but the political arena in which their claims were decided shifted from civil society to the state, posing a crisis — the need for "revolution."

## 1848: state and revolution

For Luxemburg, the modern state was itself merely the "product of the last revolution," namely the political institutionalization of the condition of class struggle up to that point. The "last revolution" was that of 1848, in which the "social question" was posed as a crisis of the democratic republic. As such, the state remained both the subject and the object of revolutionary politics. Marx had conflicted with the anarchists in the First International over the issue of the need for "political" as well as "social action" in the working class's struggle for socialism. The Revisionists such as Bernstein had, to Luxemburg's mind, reverted to the pre-Marxian socialism of anarchism in abandoning the struggle for political power in favor of merely social action. In this, Luxemburg characterized Bernstein as having regressed (like the anarchists) to mere "liberalism." What Bernstein like the anarchists denied was what Marx had discovered in the experience of the revolutions of 1848, namely, the necessity of the "dictatorship of the proletariat," and hence the necessary political separation of the workers' "social democracy" from the mere "democracy" of the bourgeois revolution, including the necessary separation from the "petit bourgeois democrats" who earned Marx's most scathing scorn.

While liberals denied the need for such "social democracy" and found political democracy to be sufficient, anarchists separated the social from the political, treating the latter as a fetishized realm of collusion in the bourgeois state and hence capitalism. Anarchists from the first, Proudhon, had avoided the issue of political revolution and the need to take state power; whereas Marxists had recognized that the crisis of capitalism inevitably resulted in political crisis and struggle over the state: If the working class failed to do so, others would step in their place. For Marx, the need for workers' political revolution to achieve socialism was expressed by the phenomenon of Louis Bonaparte's election in 1848 and coup d'état in 1851, which expressed the inability of the "bourgeoisie to rule" any longer through civil society, while the proletariat was as yet politically undeveloped and thus "not ready to rule" the state. But for Marx the necessity of the "dictatorship of the proletariat" was that the "workers must rule" politically in order to overcome capitalism economically and socially.

Marx characterized Louis Bonaparte's politics as both "petit bourgeois" and "lumpenproletarian," finding support among the broad masses of capitalism's discontented. But according to Marx their discontents could only reproduce capitalism since they could only at best join the working class or remain dependent on the realization of the value of its labor as a commodity. Hence, there was no possible withdrawal from the crisis of bourgeois politics and the democratic state, as by libertarians and anarchists, but the need to develop political power to overcome capitalism. For the capitalist wage-labor system with its far-reaching effects throughout society to be abolished required the political action of the wage laborers. That the "workers must rule" meant that they needed to provide political leadership to the exploited and oppressed masses. If the organized working class did not, others would provide that leadership, as Bonaparte had done in 1848 and 1851. The means for this was the political party for socialism. As Luxemburg put it in her 1898 Stuttgart speech:

> [B]y final goal we must not mean . . . this or that image of the future state, but the prerequisite for any future society, namely the conquest of political power. This conception of our task is closely related to our conception of capitalist society; it is the solid ground which underlies our view that capitalist society is caught in insoluble contradictions which will ultimately necessitate an explosion, a collapse, at which point we will play the role of the banker-lawyer who liquidates a bankrupt company.

The socialist political party was for Luxemburg the means for this necessary achievement of political power. But the party was not *itself* the solution, but rather the necessary manifestation and concretization of the *problem* of political power in capitalism and indeed the problem of "society" itself.

### 1905: party and class

Luxemburg took the occasion of the 1905 Revolution in Russia to critique the relation of labor unions and the Social-Democratic Party of Germany (SPD) in her pamphlet on *The Mass Strike, the Political Party and the Trade*

*Unions* (1906). This was a continuation of Luxemburg's criticism of the reformist Revisionist view of the relation of the economic and political struggles of the working class for socialism, which had found its strongest support among the labor union leadership. In bringing to bear the Russian experience in Germany, Luxemburg reversed the usual assumed hierarchy of German experience over Russian "backwardness." She also reversed the developmental order of economic and political struggles, the mistaken assumption that the economic must precede the political. The "mass" or political strike had been associated with social- and political-historical primitiveness, with pre-industrial struggles and pre-Marxian socialism, specifically anarchism and anarcho-syndicalism (especially in the Latin countries), which had prioritized economic and social action over political action. Luxemburg sought to grasp the changed historical significance of the political strike; that it had become, rather, a symptom of advanced, industrial capitalism. In the 1905 Russian Revolution, the workers had taken political action before economic action, and the labor unions had originated out of that political action, rather than the reverse.

The western Russian Empire was rapidly industrialized and showed great social unrest in the 1890s–1900s. It exhibited the most up-to-date techniques and organization in industrial production: The newest and largest factories in the world at this time were located in Russia. Luxemburg was active in the Russian Social-Democratic Labor Party (RSDLP) in the Russian part of Poland, through her own organization, the Social-Democratic Party of the Kingdom of Poland and Lithuania (SDKPiL). The 1905 Russian Revolution was precipitated by a *political* and not "economic" crisis: the shaking of the Tsarist state in its losing war with Japan 1904–05. This was not merely a liberal-democratic discontent with the arbitrary rule of the Russian absolutism. For Luxemburg, the Russo-Japanese War was a symptom of capitalism, and so was the resulting crisis of Tsarism in Russia triggered by this war. The political strike was, as she put it, a revolt of "bourgeois Russia," that is, of the modern industrial capitalists and workers, against Tsarism. What had started out in the united action of the capitalists and workers striking economically against the Tsarist state for liberal-democratic political reasons, unfolded into a class struggle by the workers against the capitalists. This was due to the necessity of reorganizing social provisions during the strike, in which mass-action strike committees took over the functions of the usual operations of capitalism and indeed of the Tsarist state itself. This had necessitated the formation of workers' own collective-action organizations. Luxemburg showed how the economic organization of the workers had developed out of the political action against Tsarism, and that the basis of this was in the necessities of advanced industrial production. In this way, the workers' actions had developed, beyond the liberal-democratic or "bourgeois" discontents and demands, into the tasks of "proletarian socialism." Political necessity had led to economic necessity (rather than the reverse, economic necessity leading to political necessity).

For Luxemburg, this meant that the usual assumption in Germany that the political party, the SPD, was "based" on the labor unions, was a profound mistake. The economic and social-cooperative actions of the unions were "based," for Luxemburg, on the political task of socialism and its political party. This meant prioritizing the political action of the socialist party as the real basis or substance of the economic and other social action of the working class. It was the political goal of the dictatorship of the proletariat through socialist revolution that gave actual substance to the workers' economic struggles, which were, for Luxemburg, merely the necessary preparatory "school of revolution."

Luxemburg wrote her pamphlet while summering at a retreat with Lenin and other Bolsheviks in Finland. It was informed by her daily conversations with Lenin over many weeks. Lenin had previously written, in *What is to be Done?* (1902) (a pamphlet commissioned and agreed-upon by the Marxist faction of the RSDLP as a whole, those who later divided into Bolsheviks and Mensheviks), that economism and workerism in Russia had found support in Bernsteinian Revisionism in the SPD and the greater Second International, trying to subordinate the political struggle to economic struggle and thus to separate them. In so doing, they like the Revisionists had identified capitalist development with socialism rather than properly recognizing them as in growing contradiction. Lenin had, like Luxemburg, regarded such workerism and economism as "reformist" in the sense of separating the workers' struggles for reform from the goal of socialism that needed to inform such struggles. Luxemburg as well as Lenin called this "liquidationism," or the dissolving of the goal into the movement, liquidating the need for the political party for socialism. In *What is to be Done?* Lenin had argued for the formation of a political party for the workers' struggle for socialism in Russia. He took as polemical opponents those who, like the Revisionists in Germany, had deprioritized the necessity of the political party, thus deprioritizing the *politics* of the struggle for socialism, limiting it to economic action.[4] The political party had thus redeemed itself in the 1905 Revolution in Russia, showing its necessary role for the workers' political, social, and economic action, confirming Lenin and Luxemburg's prior arguments against economism.

Luxemburg regarded the lessons of the 1905 Revolution in Russia to be a challenge to and hence a "crisis" — a potential critical turning point — of the SPD in Germany. Continuing her prosecution of the Revisionist Dispute, Luxemburg argued for the concrete necessity of the political leadership of the party over the unions that had been demonstrated by the 1905 Revolution in Russia. By contrast, the tension and indeed contradiction between the goal of socialism and the preservation of the institutions of the workers' movement — specifically of the labor unions' self-interest — which might be threatened by the conservative reaction of the state against the political action of the socialist party, showed a conflict between movement and goal. The Revisionists thought that a mass political strike would merely provoke the Right into a coup d'état.

### Demand for redemption

Walter Benjamin, in his draft theses "On the Concept of History" (AKA "Theses on the Philosophy of History," 1940), cited Luxemburg in particular when describing history itself as the "demand for redemption." Not only did Luxemburg raise this demand with her famous invocation of Marx and Engels on the crossroads in capitalism of "socialism or barbarism," but as a historical figure she herself calls out for such redemption.

The conflict in and about the party on which Luxemburg had focused was horribly revealed later by the outbreak of war in 1914, when a terrible

---

4    See also my "Lenin's Liberalism," *Platypus Review* 36 (June 2011), in this volume.

choice seemed posed, between the political necessity to overthrow the *Kaiserreich* state to prevent or stop the war, and the need to preserve the workers' economic and social organizations in the unions and the party. The war had been the *Kaiserreich's* preemptive coup d'état against the SPD. The party capitulated to this in that it facilitated and justified the unions' assertion of their self-preservation at the cost of cooperation with the state's war. This self-preservation — what Luxemburg excoriated as trying to "hide like a rabbit under a bush" temporarily during the war — may have been justified if these same organizations had served later to facilitate the political struggle for socialism after the Prussian Empire had been shaken by its loss in the war. But the SPD's constraining of the workers' struggles to preserve the state, limiting the German Revolution 1918–19 to a "democratic" one against the threat of "Bolshevism," meant the party's suppression of its own membership. Past developments had prepared this. The Revisionists' prioritization of the movement and its organizations over the goal of socialism had been confirmed for what Luxemburg and Lenin had always warned against: the adaptation and liquidation of the working class's struggles into, not a potential springboard for socialism, but rather a bulwark of capitalism; the transformation of the party from a revolutionary into a counterrevolutionary force. As Luxemburg had so eloquently put it in WWI, the SPD had become a "stinking corpse" — something which had through the stench of decomposition revealed itself to have been dead for a long time already — dead for the purposes of socialism. The party had killed itself through the Devil's bargain of sacrificing its true political purpose for mere self-preservation.

In so doing, supposedly acting in the interests of the workers, the workers' true interests — in socialism — were betrayed. As Luxemburg put it in the *Junius Pamphlet*, the failure of the SPD at the critical moment of 1914 had placed the entire history of the preceding "40 years" of the struggles by the workers — since the founding of the SPD in 1875 — "in doubt." Would this history be liquidated without redemption? This underscored Luxemburg's warning, decades earlier, against dissolving the goal into the movement that would betray not only the goal but the movement itself. Reformist revisionism devoured itself. The only point of the party was its goal of revolution; without it, it was "nothing" — indeed worse than nothing: It became a festering obstacle. The party was for Luxemburg not only or primarily the "subject" but was also and especially the *object* of revolutionary struggle by the working class to achieve socialism. This is why the revolution that the party had facilitated was for Luxemburg merely the beginning and not the end of the struggle to achieve socialism. The political problem of capitalism was manifest in how the party pointed beyond itself in the revolution. But without the party, that problem could never even manifest let alone point beyond itself.

During the German Revolution — provoked by the collapse of the *Kaiserreich* at the end of WWI — Luxemburg split and founded the new Communist Party of Germany (KPD), joining Lenin in forming the "Third" or Communist International, in 1919: to make clear the political tasks that had been manifested and advanced but ultimately abdicated and failed by the social-democratic parties of the Second International in war and revolution. Just as Luxemburg and Lenin had always maintained that the political party for socialism was necessary to advance the contradiction and crisis of capitalism as it had developed from Marx's time to their own, so it became necessary in crisis to split that party and found a new one. Turning the international war of capitalism into a socialist revolution meant manifesting a civil war within the workers' movement and indeed within Marxism itself. Whereas her former comrades in the SPD recoiled from her apparent revolutionary fanaticism, and "saved" themselves and their party by betraying its goal (but ultimately faded from historical significance), Luxemburg, as a loyal party-member, sacrificed herself for the goal of socialism, redeeming her Marxism and making it profoundly necessary, thus tasking our remembrance and recovery of it today.

Originally published in *Weekly Worker* 1115 (July 14, 2016)
and in *Platypus Review* 86 (May 2016)

# What was social democracy?

Communism is an ancient concept of the community sharing everything in common. It has its roots in religious communes. Socialism by contrast is a modern concept that focuses on the issue of "society," which is itself a bourgeois concept. Marx sought to relate the two concepts of communism and socialism to capitalism.

Social democracy is a concept that emerged around the 1848 revolutions, which posed what was at the time called the "social question": namely the crisis of society evident in the phenomenon of the modern industrial working class's conditions. Social democracy aimed for the democratic republic with adequate social content.

Marxism has in various periods of its history used all three concepts — communism, socialism and social democracy — not exactly interchangeably, but rather to refer to and emphasize different aspects of the same political struggle. For instance, Marx and Engels distinguished what they called "proletarian socialism" from other varieties of socialism, such as Christian socialism and utopian socialism. What distinguished proletarian socialism was twofold: the specific problem of modern industrial capitalism to be overcome; and the industrial working class as a potential political agent of change.

Moreover, there were differences in the immediate political focus, depending on the phase of the struggle. "Social democracy" was understood as a means for achieving socialism; and socialism was understood as the first stage of overcoming capitalism on the way to achieving communism. Small propaganda groups such as the original Communist League of Marx and Engels, for which they wrote the *Communist Manifesto*, used the term "communism" to emphasize their ultimate goal. Later, the name "Socialist Workers Party" was used by the followers of Marx and Engels in Germany to more precisely focus their political project specifically as the working class struggling to achieve socialism.

So where did the term "social democracy" originate, and how was it used by Marxists — by Marx and Engels themselves as well as their immediate disciples?

The concept of the "social republic" originates in the revolution of 1848 in France — specifically with the socialist, Louis Blanc, who coined the expression, "From each according to his ability, to each according to his need," to describe the goals of the society to be governed by the democratic republic. Marx considered this to be the form of state in which the class struggle between the workers and capitalists would be fought out to a conclusion.

The essential lesson Marx and Engels learned from their experience of the revolutions of 1848 in France and Germany, as well as more broadly in Austria and Italy, was what Marx, in his 1852 letter to his colleague and publisher, Joseph Weydemeyer, called his only "original discovery": namely the "necessity of the dictatorship of the proletariat;" or, as he had put it in his summing-up report on the revolutions of 1848 in his address to the central committee of the Communist League in 1850, the need for "the revolution in permanence," which he thought could only be achieved by the working class taking independent political action in the leadership of the democratic revolution.

This was a revision of Marx and Engels's position in the earlier *Communist Manifesto* on the eve of 1848, which was to identify the working class's struggle for communism with the democratic revolution. They claimed that "communists do not form a party of their own, but work within the already existing [small-d!] democratic party." Now, after the experience of the failure of the revolutions of 1848, Marx asserted the opposite: the necessary separation of the working class from other democratic political currents.

### Petty bourgeois

What had happened to effect this profound change in political perspective by Marx and Engels?

Marx had come to characterize the failure of the revolutions of 1848 in terms of the treacherous and conservative-reactionary role of what he called the "petty bourgeois democrats," whom he found to be constitutionally incapable of learning from their political failures and the social reasons for this.

The historical horizon for the petty bourgeois democratic discontents in the social crisis of capitalism was too low to allow the contradiction of capital to come within political range of mere democracy, no matter how radically popular in character. The problem of capitalism was too intractable to the ideology of petty bourgeois democracy. The problem of capitalism exceeded the horizon of the French revolutionary tradition, even in its most radical exponents, such as Gracchus Babeuf's Jacobin "conspiracy of equals." Such democracy could only try to put back together, in essentially liberal-democratic terms, what had been broken apart and irreparably disintegrated in industrial capitalism.

This was not merely a matter of limitation in so-called "class interest or position," but rather the way the problem of capitalism presented itself. It looked like irresponsible government, political hierarchy and economic corruption, rather than what Marx thought it was: the necessary crisis of society and politics in capitalism, the necessary and not accidental divergence of the interests of capital and wage-labor, in which society was caught. Capital outstripped the capacity for wage-labor to appropriate its social value. This was not merely a problem of economics, but politically went to the heart of the modern democratic republic itself.

The petty bourgeois attempt to control and make socially responsible the capitalists, and to temper the demands of the workers in achieving democratic political unity, was hopeless and doomed to fail. But it still appealed nonetheless. And its appeal was not limited to the socioeconomic middle classes, but also, and perhaps especially, to the working class, as well as to "enlightened, progressive" capitalists.

The egalitarian sense of justice and fraternal solidarity of the working class was rooted in the bourgeois social relations of labor, the exchange of labor as a commodity. But industrial capital went beyond the social mediation of labor and the bourgeois common sense of cooperation. Furthermore, the problem of capital was not reducible to the issue of exploitation, against which the bourgeois spirit rebelled. It also went beyond the social discipline of labor — the sense of duty to work.

For instance, the ideal of worker-owned and -operated production is a petty bourgeois democratic fantasy. It neglects the fact that, as Marx observed, the conditions for industrial production are not essentially the workers' own labor, but rather more socially general: production has become the actual property of society. The only question is how this is realized. It can be mediated through the market, as well as through the state — the legal terms in which both exchange and production are adjudicated (that is, what counts as individual and collective property): issues of eminent domain, community costs and benefits, etc. Moreover, this is global in character. I expect the foreign government of which I am *not* a citizen to nonetheless respect my property rights. Bourgeois society already has a global citizenry, but it is through the civil rights of commerce, not the political rights of government. However, capitalism presents a problem, and a crisis, of such global liberal democracy.

Industrial capital's value in production cannot be socially appropriated through the market, and indeed cannot at all any longer be appropriated through the exchange-value of labor. The demand for universal-suffrage democracy arose in the industrial era out of the alternative of social appropriation through the political action of the citizenry via the state. But Marx regarded this state action no less than the market as a hopeless attempt to master the social dynamics of capital.

At best, the desired petty bourgeois political unity of society could be achieved on a temporary national basis, as was effected by the cunning of Louis Bonaparte, as the first elected president of Second Republic France in 1848, promising to bring the country together against and above the competing interests of its various social classes and political factions. Later, in 1851 Bonaparte overthrew the republic and established the Second Empire, avowedly to preserve universal (male) suffrage democracy and thus to safeguard "the revolution." He received overwhelming majority assent to his *coup d'état* in the plebiscite referenda he held both at the time of his coup and 10 years later to extend the mandate of the empire.

Marx and Engels recognized that to succeed in the task of overcoming capitalism in the struggle for proletarian socialism it was necessary for the working class to politically lead the petty bourgeoisie in the democratic revolution. This was the basis of their appropriation of the term "social democracy" to describe their politics in the wake of 1848: the task of achieving what had failed in mere democracy.

The mass political parties of the Second, Socialist International described themselves variously as "socialist" and "social democratic." "International social democracy" was the term used to encompass the common politics and shared goal of these parties.

They understood themselves as parties of not merely an international, but indeed a cosmopolitan politics. The Second International regarded itself as the beginnings of world government. This is because they regarded capitalism as already exhibiting a form of world government in democracy; what Kant had described in the 18th century, around the time of the American and French revolutions, as the political task of humanity to achieve a "world state or system of states" in a "league of nations" — the term later adopted for the political system of Pax Americana that US president Woodrow Wilson tried to achieve in the aftermath of World War I. As the liberal chronicler of Napoleon, Benjamin Constant, had observed 100 years before Wilson, in the wake of the French Revolution and its ramifications throughout Europe, the differences between nations were "more apparent than real" in the global society of commerce that had emerged in the modern era. But capitalism had wrecked the aspirations of Kant and Constant for global bourgeois society.

The International offered the alternative, "Workers of the world, unite!", to the international strife of capitalist crisis that led to the modern horrors of late colonialism in the 19th century and finally world war in the 20th.

### Redefinition

The political controversy that attended the first attempt at world proletarian socialist revolution in the aftermath of World War I divided the workers' movement for socialism into reformist social democracy and revolutionary communism and a new Third International. It made social democracy an enemy.

This changed the meaning of "social democracy" into a gradual evolution of capitalism into socialism, as opposed to the revolutionary political struggle for communism. But what was of greater significance than the "revolution" sacrificed in this redefinition was the cosmopolitanism of the socialist workers who had up until then assumed that they had no particular country to which they owed allegiance.

The unfolding traumas of fascism and World War II redefined social democracy yet again, lowering it still further to mean the mere welfare state, modeled after the dominant US's New Deal and the "four freedoms" the anti-fascist Allies adopted as their avowed principles in the war. It made the working class into a partner in production, and thus avoided what Marx considered the inevitable contradiction and crisis of production in capitalism. It turned socialism into a mere matter of distribution.

For the last generation, since the 1960s, this has been further degraded to a defensive posture in the face of neoliberalism, which, since the global crisis and downturn of the 1970s, has reasserted the rights of capital.

The "specter of communism" that Marx and Engels had thought haunted Europe in the post-industrial revolution crisis of capitalism in the 1840s continues to haunt the entire world today, after several repetitions of the cycle of bourgeois society come to grief — not as a desired dream misconstrued as a feared nightmare, but rather as the evil spirit that does not fail to drive politics, no matter how democratic, into the abyss. And, as in Marx's time, the alternating "ethical indignation" and "enraptured proclamations of the democrats" continue to "rebound" in "all the reactionary attempts to hold back" the ceaseless crisis of capitalism, in which "all that is solid melts into air."

We still need social democracy, but not as those who preceded Marxism thought — to mitigate capitalism, as was attempted again, after the failure of Marxism to achieve global proletarian socialism in the 20th century — but rather to make the necessity for communism that Marx recognized over 150 years ago a practical political reality. We need to make good on the "revolution in permanence" of capitalism that constantly shakes the bourgeois idyll, and finally leverage the crisis of its self-destruction beyond itself.

Presented on a panel with Bernard Sampson (Communist Party USA), Karl Belin (Pittsburgh Socialist Organizing Committee) and Jack Ross (author of *The Socialist Party of America: A Complete History*) at the eighth annual Platypus Affiliated Society International Convention April 1, 2016 in Chicago.

Originally published in *Weekly Worker* 1114 (July 7, 2016) and in *Platypus Review* 87 (July – August 2016)

# 1917–2017

The Frankfurt School approached the problem of the political failure of socialism in terms of the revolutionary subject, namely, the masses in the democratic revolution and the political party for socialism. However, in the failure of socialism, the masses had led to fascism and the party had led to Stalinism. What was liquidated between them was Marxism, or proletarian socialism; what was liquidated was the working class politically constituted as such, or, the class struggle of the working class — which for Marxists required the goal of socialism. The revolutionary political goal of socialism was required for the class struggle or even the working class per se to exist at all. For Marxism, the proletariat was a Hegelian concept: It aimed at fulfillment through self-abolition. Without the struggle for socialism, capitalism led the masses to fascism and led the political party to Stalinism. The failure of socialism thus conditioned the 20th century.

The legacy of the Russian Revolution of 1917 is a decidedly mixed one. This variable character of 1917's legacy can be divided between its actors — the masses and the party — and between the dates, February and October 1917.

The February 1917 revolution is usually regarded as the democratic revolution and the spontaneous action of the masses. By contrast, the October Revolution is usually regarded as the socialist revolution and the action of the party. But this distorts the history — the events as well as the actors involved. What drops out is the specific role of the working class, as distinct from the masses or the party. The soviets or workers' and soldiers' councils were the agencies of the masses in revolution. The party was the agency of the working class struggling for socialism. The party was meant to be the political agency facilitating the broader working class's and the masses' social revolution — the transformation of society — overcoming capitalism. This eliding of the distinction of the masses, the working class and the political party goes so far as to call the October Revolution the "Bolshevik Revolution" — an anti-Communist slander that Stalinism was complicit in perpetuating. The Bolsheviks participated in but were not responsible for the revolution.

As Trotsky observed on the 20th anniversary of the 1917 Revolution in his 1937 article on "Stalinism and Bolshevism"[1] — where he asserted that Stalinism was the "antithesis" of Bolshevism — the Bolsheviks did not identify themselves directly with either the masses, the working class, the revolution, or the ostensibly "revolutionary" state issuing from the revolution. As Trotsky wrote in his 1930 book, *History of the Russian Revolution*, the entrance of the masses onto the stage of history was something Marxism had to reckon with, for good or for ill. How had Marxists done so?

Marx had observed in the failure of the revolutions of 1848 that the result was "Bonapartism," namely, the rule of the state claiming to act on behalf of society as a whole and especially for the masses. Louis Bonaparte, who we must remember was himself a Saint-Simonian Utopian Socialist, claimed to be acting on behalf of the oppressed masses, the workers and peasants, against the capitalists and their corrupt — including avowedly "liberal" — politicians. Louis Bonaparte benefited from the resentment of the masses towards the liberals who had put down so bloodily the rising of the workers of Paris in June 1848. He exploited the masses' discontent.

One key reason why, for Trotsky, Stalinism was the antithesis of Bolshevism — that is to say, the antithesis of Marxism — was that Stalinism, unlike Bolshevism, identified itself with the state, with the working class, and indeed with the masses. But this was for Trotsky the liquidation of Marxism. It was the concession of Stalinism to Bonapartism. Trotsky considered Stalin to be a Bonapartist, not out of personal failing, but out of historical conditions of necessity, due to the failure of world socialist revolution. Stalinism, as a ruling ideology of the USSR as a "revolutionary state," exhibited the contradictions issuing out of the failure of the revolution.

---

1 *Socialist Appeal* I, no. 7 ( September 25, 1937).

In Marxist terms, socialism would no longer require either a socialist party or a socialist state. By identifying the results of the revolution — the one-party state dictatorship — as "socialism," Stalinism liquidated the actual task of socialism and thus betrayed it. Claiming to govern "democratic republics" or "people's republics," Stalinism confessed its failure to struggle for socialism. Stalinism was an attempted holding action, but as such undermined itself as any kind of socialist politics. Indeed, the degree to which Stalinism did not identify itself with the society it sought to rule, this was in the form of its perpetual civil-war footing, in which the party was at war with society's spontaneous tendency towards capitalism, and indeed the party was constantly at war with its own members as potential if not actual traitors to the avowed socialist mission. As such, Stalinism confessed not merely to the on-going continuation of the "revolution" short of its success, but indeed its — socialism's — infinite deferral. Stalinism was what became of Marxism as it was swallowed up by the historical inertia of on-going capitalism.

So we must disentangle the revolution from its results. Does 1917 have a legacy other than its results? Did it express an unfulfilled potential, beyond its failure?

The usual treatment of 1917 distorts the history. First of all, we would need to account for what Lenin called the "spontaneity of spontaneity," that is, the prior conditions for the masses' apparently spontaneous action. In the February Revolution, one obvious point is that it manifested on the official political socialist party holiday of International Working Women's Day, which was a relatively recent invention by Marxists in the Socialist or Second International. So, the longstanding existence of a workers' movement for socialism and of the international political party of that struggle for socialism was a prior condition of the apparently spontaneous outbreak of revolution in 1917. This much was obvious. What was significant, of course, was how in 1917 the masses seized the socialist holiday for revolution to topple the Tsar.

The October Revolution was not merely the planned coup d'état by the Bolshevik Party — not alone, but in alliance, however, we must always remember, with the Left Socialist Revolutionaries or SRs. This is best illustrated by what took place between February and October, namely the July

Days of 1917, in which the masses spontaneously attempted to overthrow the Provisional Government. The Bolsheviks considered that action premature, both in terms of lack of preparation and, more importantly, in terms of the Provisional Government not yet having completely exhausted itself politically. But the Bolsheviks stood in solidarity with the masses in July, while warning them of the problems and dangers of their action. The July uprising was put down by the Provisional Government, and indeed the Bolsheviks were suppressed, with many of their leading members arrested. Lenin went into hiding — and wrote his pamphlet *The State and Revolution* in his time underground. The Bolsheviks actually played a conservative role in the July Days of 1917, in the sense of seeking to conserve the forces of the working class and broader masses from the dangers of the Provisional Government's repression of their premature — but legitimate — rising.

The October Revolution was prepared by the Bolsheviks — in league with the Left SRs — after the attempted coup against the Provisional Government by General Kornilov, which the masses had successfully resisted. Kornilov had planned his coup in response to the July uprising by the masses, which to him showed the weakness and dangers of the Provisional Government. As Lenin had put it at the time, explaining the Bolsheviks' participation in the defense of the Provisional Government against Kornilov, it was a matter of "supporting in the way a rope supports a hanged man." Once the Provisional Government had revealed that its crucial base of support was the masses that it was otherwise suppressing, this indicated that the time for overthrowing the Provisional Government had come.

But the October Revolution was not a socialist revolution, because the February Revolution had not been a democratic revolution. The old Tsarist state remained in place, with only a regime change, the removal of the Tsar and his ministers and their replacement with liberals and moderate "socialists," namely the Right Socialist Revolutionaries, of whom Kerensky, who rose to the head of the Provisional Government, was a member. To put it in Lenin's terms, the February Revolution was only a regime change — the Provisional Government was merely a "government" in the narrow sense of the word — and had not smashed the state: the "special bodies of armed men" remained in place.

The October Revolution was the beginning of the process of smashing the state — replacing the previously established (Tsarist, capitalist) "special bodies of armed men" with the organized workers, soldiers, and peasants through the "soviet" councils as executive bodies of the revolution, to constitute a new revolutionary, radical-democratic state, the dictatorship of the proletariat.

From Lenin and the Bolsheviks' perspective, the October Revolution was merely the beginning of the democratic revolution. Looking back several years later, Lenin judged the results of the revolution in such terms, acknowledging the lack of socialism and recognizing the progress of the revolution — or lack thereof — in democratic terms. Lenin understood that an avowedly "revolutionary" regime does not an actual revolution make. The events of 1917 exhibited this on a mass scale.

Most of the Bolsheviks' political opponents claimed to be "revolutionary" and indeed many of them professed to be "socialist" and even "Marxist," for instance the Mensheviks and the Socialist Revolutionaries.

The Bolsheviks' former allies and junior partners in the October 1917 Revolution, the Left Socialist Revolutionaries, broke with the Bolsheviks in 1918 over the terms of the peace the Bolsheviks had negotiated with Germany. They called for overthrowing the Bolsheviks in a "third revolution": for soviets, or workers', soldiers', and peasants' councils, "without parties," that is, without the Bolsheviks. As Engels had correctly observed, opposition to the dictatorship of the proletariat was mounted on the basis of so-called "pure democracy." But, to Lenin and the Bolsheviks, their opponents did not in fact represent a "democratic" opposition, but rather the threatened liquidation of the revolutionary democratic state and its replacement by a White dictatorship. This could come about "democratically" in the sense of Bonapartism. The opponents of the Bolsheviks thus represented not merely the undoing of the struggle for socialism, but of the democratic revolution itself. What had failed in 1848 and threatened to do so again in 1917 was democracy.

Marx had commented that his only original contribution was discovering the necessity of the dictatorship of the proletariat. The dictatorship of the proletariat was meant by Marxists to meet the necessity in capitalism that Bonapartism otherwise expressed. It was meant to turn the political crisis of capitalism indicated by Bonapartism into the struggle for socialism.

The issue of the dictatorship of the proletariat, that is, the political rule of the working class in the struggle to overcome capitalism and achieve socialism, is a vexed one, on many levels. Not only does the dictatorship of the proletariat not mean a "dictatorship" in the conventional sense of an undemocratic state, but, for Marxism, the dictatorship of the proletariat, as the social as well as political rule of the working class in struggling for socialism and overcoming capitalism, could be achieved only at a global scale, that is, as a function of working-class rule in at least several advanced capitalist countries, but with a preponderant political force affecting the entire world. This was what was meant by "world socialist revolution." Nothing near this was achieved by the Russian Revolution of 1917. But the Bolsheviks and their international comrades, such as Rosa Luxemburg in Germany, thought that it was practically possible.

The Bolsheviks had predicated their leading the October Revolution in Russia on the expectation of an imminent European workers' revolution for socialism. For instance, the strike wave in Germany of 1916 that had split the Social-Democratic Party there, as well as the waves of mutinies among soldiers of various countries at the front in the World War, had indicated the impending character of revolution throughout Europe, and indeed throughout the world, for instance in the vast colonial empires held by the European powers.

This had not happened — but it looked like a real, tangible possibility at the time. It was the program that had organized millions of workers for several decades prior to 1917.

So what had the October Revolution accomplished, if not "socialism" or even the "dictatorship of the proletariat"? What do we make of the collapse of the 1917 revolution into Stalinism?

As Leo Panitch remarked at a public forum panel discussion that Platypus held in Halifax on "What is Political Party for the Left?" in January 2015, the period from the 1870s to the 1920s saw the first as well as the as-yet only time in history in which the subaltern class organized itself into a political force.[2] This was the period of the growth of the mass social-ist parties, around the world, of the Second International. The highest and perhaps the only result of this self-organization of the international working class as a political force was the October Revolution in Russia of 1917. The working class, or at least the political party it had constituted, took power, if however under very disadvantageous circumstances and with decidedly mixed results. The working class ultimately failed to retain power, and the party they had organized for this revolution transformed itself into the institutionalized force of that failure. This was also true of the role played by the Social-Democratic Party in Germany in suppressing the revolution there in 1918–19.

But the Bolsheviks had taken power, and they had done so after having organized for several decades with the self-conscious goal of socialism, and with a high degree of awareness, through Marxism, of what struggling towards that goal meant as a function of capitalism. This was no utopian project.

The October 1917 Revolution has not been repeated, but the Feb-ruary 1917 Revolution and the July Days of 1917 have been repeated, several times, in the century since then.

In this sense, from a Marxist perspective what has been repeated — and continued — was not really 1917 but rather 1848, the democratic revolu-tion under conditions of capitalism that has led to its failure. For Marx, the Paris Commune of 1871 had been the repetition of 1848 that had however pointed beyond it. The Paris Commune indicated both democracy and the dictatorship of the proletariat, or, as Marx had put it, the possibility for the "revolution in permanence." 1871 re-attained 1848 and indicated possibil-ities beyond it.

In this sense, 1917 has a similar legacy to 1871, but with the further paradox — actually, the contradiction — that the political agency, the political party or parties, that had been missing, from a Marxist perspec-tive, leading to the failure of the Paris Commune, which in the meantime had been built by the working class in the decades that followed, had, after 1917, transformed itself into an institutionalization of the failure of the

2   *Platypus Review* 74 (March 2015).

struggle for socialism, in the failure of the world revolution. That institutionalization of failure in Stalinism was itself a process — taking place in the 1920s and continuing up to today — that moreover was expressed through an obscure transformation of "Marxism" itself: avowed "Marxists" (ab)used and distorted "Marxism" to justify this institutionalization of failure. It is only in this self-contradictory sense that Marxism led to Stalinism — through its own failure. But only Marxism could overcome this failure and self-distortion of Marxism. Why? Because Marxism is itself an ideological expression of capitalism, and capitalism must be overcome on its own basis. The only basis for socialism is capitalism. Marxism, as distinct from other forms of socialism, is the recognition of this dialectic of capitalism and the potential for socialism. Capitalism is nothing other than the failure of the socialist revolution.

So the legacy of 1917, as uniquely distinct from other revolutions in the era of capitalism, beginning at least as early as in 1848 and continuing henceforth up to today, is actually the legacy of Marxism. Marxism had its origins in taking stock of the failed revolutions of 1848. 1917 was the only political success of Marxism in the classical sense of the Marxism of Marx and Engels themselves, and their best followers in the Socialist or Second International such as Lenin, Rosa Luxemburg and Trotsky, but it was a very limited and qualified "success" — from Lenin and his comrades' own perspective. And that limited success was distorted to cover over and obscure its failure, and so ended up obscuring its success as well. The indelible linking of Marxism with 1917 exhibits the paradox that its failure was the same as in 1848, but 1917 and so Marxism are important only insofar as they might point beyond that failure. Otherwise, Marxism is insignificant, and we may as well be liberals, anarchists, Utopian Socialists, or any other species of democratic revolutionaries. Which is what everyone today is — at best — anyway.

1917 needs to be remembered not as a model to be followed but in terms of an unfulfilled task that was revealed in historical struggle, a potential that was expressed, however briefly and provisionally, but was ultimately betrayed. Its legacy has disappeared with the disappearance of the struggle for socialism. Its problems and its limitations as well as its positive lessons await a resumed struggle for socialism to be able to properly judge. Otherwise they remain abstract and cryptic, lifeless and dogmatic and a matter of thought-taboos and empty ritual — including both ritual worship and ritual condemnation.

In 1918, Rosa Luxemburg remarked that 70 years of the workers' struggle for socialism had achieved only the return to the moment of 1848, with the task of making it right and so redeeming that history. In *Results and Prospects*, on the 1905 Revolution in Russia, Trotsky had observed that it was only because of Marxism that the 19th century had not passed in vain.

Marx's concept of Bonapartism resonates today because it depicts politics and society absent the working-class struggle for socialism. The masses remain, but the working class and its political party for socialism are missing. The "specter" not of proletarian socialism but of the petite bourgeoisie's and lumpenproletariat's Bonapartism is what haunts the world today, a century after the failure of 1917 — just as it did after the failure of 1848.

Today, in 2017, on its hundredth anniversary, we must recognize, rather, just how and why we are so very far from being able to judge properly the legacy of 1917: It no longer belongs to us. We must work our way back towards and reattain the moment of 1917. That task is 1917's legacy for us.

Presented on April 8, 2017, at the closing plenary of ninth annual International Convention of the Platypus Affiliated Society on a panel discussion with Bryan Palmer, professor at Trent University and author of numerous histories of the Left, and Leo Panitch, professor at York University, author, and co-editor of the *Socialist Register*.

Originally published in *Platypus Review* 99 (September 2017)

# The end of the Gilded Age

## Discontents of the Second Industrial Revolution today

The account of history is the theory of the present: How did we get here; and what tasks remain from the past — that however appear to be "new" today? As Adorno put it, "the new is the old in distress."[1] This is true of capitalism and its crisis now.

The present crisis is a crisis of the world system of capitalism that emerged in the 20th century, a crisis of the capitalist world created by the Second Industrial Revolution at the end of the 19th century — in fits and starts (such as the two World Wars and the Cold War) but nonetheless consistently and inexorably. That system has been led by the countries newly industrialized at the end of the 19th century, the U.S., Germany and Japan. All three have come to be in crisis in the early 21st century — the crisis of the EU can be regarded as a crisis of the management of "German" capital.

David Harvey, in his book *The Condition of Postmodernity* (1990)[2], written and published in the heyday of neoliberalism, regarded the history of capitalism as a succession of "regimes of accumulation" — concrete forms for socially and politically mediating the need to accumulate capital in its valorization process. But since, according to Marxism, capitalism is itself a form of social contradiction and thus a crisis and decay of society and politics, each successive form of capitalism takes up and perpetuates the crisis of the preceding form, however in an altered way.[3] Capitalism really

---

1   "Reflections on Class Theory" (1942), in *Can One Live after Auschwitz: A Philosophical Reader*, ed. Rolf Tiedemann (Stanford: Stanford University Press, 2003), 93–110.

2   *The Condition of Postmodernity: An Enquiry into the Origins of Cultural Change* (New Jersey: Wiley-Blackwell, 1990).

3   See my "Symptomology: Historical Transformations in Social-Political Context," *Platypus Review* 12 (May 2009), in *The Death of the Millennial Left: Interventions 2006–2022*.

is a matter of "kicking the can down the road," apparently indefinitely. But the banging can eventually returns, and we must ultimately pay the added costs of its deferral.

The characterization by critical contemporaries of the late-19th – early-20th century era as the "Gilded Age"[4] expressed its quality as what Kant warned about a century earlier, in his 1784 essay on the "Idea for a Universal History from a Cosmopolitan Point of View," namely, "the danger that the vitality of mankind may go to sleep": "Everything good that is not based on a morally good disposition, however, is nothing but pretense and glittering misery."[5] Gilded Age capitalism was such "glittering misery." This quality of capitalism continues today, especially in the last generation of neoliberalism whose spell was broken in the recent crisis. Joseph Schumpeter tried to put a happy face on capitalism by calling it "creative destruction," but Marxism recognized to the contrary that it is actually destructive creation.[6] And its destructiveness is not only immediate but has long-term consequences. The destruction of capitalism is cumulative: it makes claims on future generations that cannot be settled cheaply.[7]

### Industrial production and Robber Barons

It was during the period of the late 19th century Gilded Age that capitalists appeared not as entrepreneurs of production but as "Robber Barons" — an aristocracy of looting. Marx had already mordantly observed that in industrial production, with its high capital requirements, it was not the case that being a

---

4   The term originated from Mark Twain's 1873 novel, co-written by Charles Dudley Warner, *The Gilded Age: A Tale of Today*, which expressed disappointments with the post-Civil War boom era in the U.S. It was adopted in the 1920s and retrospectively applied to the entire preceding era, especially the 1870s–1890s.

5   Immanuel Kant, "Idea for a Universal History from a Cosmopolitan Point of View" (1784).

6   Marx and Engels had observed in their *Manifesto of the Communist Party* (1848) that the crisis of capitalism would end "either in a revolutionary reconstitution of society at large, or in the common ruin of the contending classes."

7   See Walter Benjamin, "On the concept of history" (1940), AKA "Theses on the philosophy of history," in *Illuminations*, trans. Harry Zohn (New York: Schocken Books, 1969), 253–64.

captain of industry made you money, but rather that having money made you a captain of industry. In industrial capitalism, it was not, as Adam Smith had thought, production developed by reinvestment of relatively low profits in the long run, with high wages facilitating increased consumption — wealth — in a virtuous cycle, but rather, as Marginal Utility Theory, developed precisely in this late 19th century era, regarded more cynically, that use-values of commodities decrease over time, so investors in their production better get in early and take their profits out while the going is still good and before it becomes a matter of diminishing returns — the miserable reasoning of what Smith regarded as "mercantile interest," the profiteering of "buying cheap and selling dear," that he thought actually constrains and undermines the productivity of wealth in society, and so needed to be overcome as an impediment to growth. Marx pursued rather the self-contradiction in what became of Smith's labor theory of value in industrial capitalism.

The accelerated technical production of the Industrial Revolution increased along with it the accumulation and concentration of capital, which Marx thought produced a crisis of value in industrial capitalism, in that such production was still socially mediated by the value of wage-labor, however anachronistically. Wage labor was inadequate for the social appropriation of industrial production. This was the self-contradiction of the capitalist mode of production in political-economic terms, according to Marx: the "bourgeois social relations" were contradicted by the "industrial forces of production;" industrial technique served to increase capital but this outstripped the actual social productivity of human labor, eliminating workers from production so that, as Max Horkheimer wryly observed, "machines have made not work but the workers superfluous."[8] Adam Smith's "proprietors of stock" were only a slight variation on the prior traveling merchants collecting the products of cottage industry, now gathering the previously disparate producers in factories; they were not capitalists in the Marxist sense of "owners of the means of production": the role of the proprietors in Smith's view of production was minimal by comparison to the laborers who were actually making things with increased efficiency. Where Smith would have expected higher productivity to result in the

8  "The Authoritarian State" (1942), *Telos* 15, no. 2 (Spring 1973), 3.

increased value of time in work through cooperation that would not only increase the purchasing power of labor but also decrease labor-time and increase leisure-time, what happened for labor instead, at a societal level, was the pernicious combination of over-work and unemployment, not attributable merely to temporary labor-market corrections. Human labor was progressively eliminated from production in absolute and not only relative terms: increased production was no longer based primarily on human labor-power inputs in efficient cooperation (as in Adam Smith's example of the pin-factory), but rather on the development of science and technology, or what Marx called the "general social intellect," objectified in machine production.[9]

The "combined and uneven [i.e. self-contradictory] development" of capitalism is exhibited by the paradoxical phenomena of simultaneously coexisting "robots and sweatshops." Industrial development and the accumulation of capital undermine the entire bourgeois social ethos of rewarding productivity through work, the exchange of labor as a commodity. Contrary to Smith's expectation, Marx observed how in capitalism labor sinks from the most precious to "the most wretched of commodities."[10] The workers are expropriated of the value of their labor at a societal level, and not merely through being super-exploited by their employers. There is a glaring problem in the development of wealth in society based on the value of labor. The ramifications of this are found in capitalism's social effects.

This is what makes capitalists appear ambiguously as performing a social duty as investors but also as criminals ripping off society — what Smith had warned about, the constant danger of their "conspiracy against the public." Bernard Mandeville's 1714 book *Fable of the Bees*, a parable of "private vices, public benefits," seemed mocked by what was actually happening in the Gilded Age. Were the capitalists really, as today's parlance goes, "job creators?" Yes and no: as often as not. When President Theodore Roosevelt went after J.P. Morgan for violation of anti-trust laws, and Morgan, a Republican supporter, complained, asking what he could do to avoid prosecution by the government, Roosevelt replied with a variation

---

9   *Grundrisse* (1858) in Robert C. Tucker, ed., *Marx-Engels Reader*, 2nd edition (New York: Norton, 1978), 285.

10  *Economic and Philosophic Manuscripts of 1844*, "Estranged Labour."

of Robespierre's injunction that if someone feels implicated by the gaze of judgment it is because he is guilty. Who wouldn't side with Roosevelt's sentiment against the Robber Baron? But Roosevelt was motivated not by altruism but what he regarded as necessary policy, to make capitalists responsible investors: Build the railroads, just don't rip us off. Marx thought that socialism would allow industrial production to go beyond capital and overcome the need for and value of labor in a socially beneficial and not destructive way. This was a problem of society, not reducible to the criminality of the individual capitalists. Even Roosevelt recognized the need for a change in policy beyond the mere curbing of excesses. For Marxism, the accumulation of capital in industrial production was a crisis for bourgeois society, but also an opportunity for changing it. Indeed, realizing the social potential of capitalism was a necessity — a task: it was "inevitable." The only question was the depth and breadth of the needed change in society.

## Discontents old and new

In the 20th century, the discontents of Gilded Age capitalism of the Second Industrial Revolution led to what Harvey (after Antonio Gramsci) called "Fordism," a new "regime of accumulation" or concrete form for the valorization process of capital. It was a new and different form of production and consumption, a new economics and new politics, a new culture: a new way of life. The 20th century and its continuing legacy today express unresolved problems inherited from Gilded Age capitalism that Fordist capital was not able to overcome. We suffer today from discontents with the results not, for instance, of the 16th–18th century African slave trade or the 15th century Reconquista and New World discovery, but rather from, for example, the failure of Reconstruction in the U.S.,[11] and the late, 2nd-wave colonialism from the era of what Marxists called "imperialism" at the end of the 19th century — hence the problem of so-called "neo-colonialism." We live in the world created by the early 20th century's attempts to solve those problems.

---

11  For instance, W.E.B. Du Bois, in his high-Jim-Crow-era book, *Black Reconstruction in America* (1935), recognized it was the capitalist crisis of the 1870s after the Panic of 1873 that had spelled the doom of Reconstruction.

Eric Hobsbawm wrote of the "long 19th" and "short 20th" centuries.[12] He regarded 1789–1914 as one cycle, and 1914–1991 as another. But perhaps we should consider the short 19th century, the core of which runs from the 1820s–70s (from the aftermath of the French Revolution until the U.S. Civil War, the Meiji Restoration and Franco-Prussian War), and the long 20th century which began, perhaps as early as the 1870s but certainly by the 1890s, and continued until the recent crisis of the 2000s–10s.[13] The high 19th century of liberalism contrasts with the 20th century of state capitalism.

In the 1990s, it seemed as if, after the "long detour" of fascism and "Communism" (Stalinism) in the 20th century,[14] a responsibly reformed "progressive" capitalism of the Second Industrial Revolution would finally have its unobstructed day in the sun: the U.S., Germany and Japan could inherit a progressively productive world at peace. The mirage of the purported Third Industrial Revolution of the post-WWII mid–late 20th century was revealed to be merely the full flowering of the turn-of-the-20th century electromagnetic revolution that had succeeded the original Industrial Revolution's thermodynamics: cybernetics turned out to be the latest expression of liberal democracy; however Steampunk fantasies haunted historical memory in the 1990s. But already in the 1970s, *Star Wars*, *Alien* and *Blade Runner* showed us the "used future" of decrepit Fordist capital. Neoliberalism naturalized this.

## Retrospective history

The retrospective view from the present allows for regarding the 20th century as the outcome of the Gilded Age — of the Second Industrial Revolution. But the 20th century was conditioned by the mounting discontents

---

12  See Hobsbawm's books *The Age of Revolution: 1789–1848* (1962), *The Age of Capital: 1848–1875* (1975), *The Age of Empire: 1875–1914* (1987), and *The Age of Extremes: The Short Twentieth Century, 1914–1991* (1994).

13  Another way of considering this history is to regard the history of Marxism relative to the phenomenon of the emergence of so-called "state capitalism." See my "1873–1973: The century of Marxism: The death of Marxism and the emergence of neo-liberalism and neo-anarchism," *Platypus Review* 47 (June 2012), in this volume.

14  See James Weinstein, *The Long Detour: The History and Future of the American Left* (2003). Excerpts in *The Nation* (July 7, 2003) and *In These Times* (May 28, 2003).

of the Gilded Age and its crisis in the early 20th century — most apocalyptically in the First World War and its aftermath. We still live in the after-effects of the crisis that conditioned the 20th century. The inability to overcome the discontents of capital from a century ago still swamps us today.

In the late 19th century U.S., the Second Industrial Revolution was governed largely by the Republican Party, which was the combined party of progressive liberalism and big capital. The Democratic Party in this period, by contrast, was the party of the middle class and conservatism. So, for instance, Populism as a 1890s Depression phenomenon fed into the Democratic Party, with William Jennings Bryan the Democrats' (unsuccessful) candidate for President in 1896 and (again in) 1900. But Progressivism emerged as a reform effort from within the Republican Party against manifest problems of liberal capitalism in the 1890s–1900s — most dramatically under President Theodore Roosevelt.

In Europe, discontents with the Gilded Age / Second Industrial Revolution manifested in the Socialist Parties of the Second International. Liberal capitalism was opposed by a mass industrial workers' politics — most significantly in the major party of the Second International, the SPD (Social-Democratic Party of Germany). In the U.K., discontents with liberalism led to the formation of the Labour Party. These parties had origins in the 1870s but experienced phenomenal growth especially in the aftermath of the crisis of the 1890s. Countries drawn into the Second Industrial Revolution more broadly but on a subordinate subsidiary basis included the Russian Empire and Italy, which also experienced mass radicalization in the form of new Social-Democratic and Socialist Parties.

However these new socialist parties also experienced a crisis of their growth in the 1890s — a crisis of their political purpose: Were they, as they claimed, parties of political revolution, or rather of social reform? Eduard Bernstein was the most perspicacious of the commentators on the developments of this period in the 1890s. He regarded the growth of the U.K. workers movement that led to the formation of the Labour Party as evidence that a revolutionary socialist political party may not be necessary for the transformation of capitalism into socialism: socialism may socially evolve within capitalism rather than requiring its political overthrow. The eventual election of majority socialist or labor parties may be sufficient to crown the development of the social movement of the working class through its civil society organizations such as labor unions and other social collectives (such as women's organizations, etc.).

The 20th century belied this socialist optimism of the late 19th century that Marxism had in common with liberalism. Just as Progressivism expressed manifest problems of liberal capitalism, so the new distinctly "revolutionary" current in socialism beginning circa 1900 represented by Rosa Luxemburg, Lenin and Trotsky as well as by Debs (who was converted to Marxism in the late 1890s) expressed discontent with socialist reformism. Luxemburg for instance called Bernstein simply a "liberal." What this meant was that Bernstein regarded liberal democracy as politically adequate for the activity of the working class in its struggle for socialism. Bernstein thought that the capitalist interest could be subordinated to a political majority. What Bernstein didn't reckon with was how the working class would become politically split in the crisis of capitalism.[15] In the First World War and the Revolutions in Russia, Germany, Italy and Hungary that broke out in its aftermath 1917–19, the former socialist parties of the Second International divided between reformist Social Democrats and revolutionary Communists. In 1919, responding to criticisms of the course of the Russian Revolution, Debs declared that, "From the crown of my head to the soles of my feet I am Bolshevik, and proud of it."[16]

This is related to how Progressivism emerged contemporaneously from the crisis of liberalism. It was acrimonious as well, with incumbent President Taft condemning his challenger, his former friend and colleague Theodore Roosevelt, the Progressive Party candidate for President in 1912, as "the most dangerous man in America." It led, via the actual beneficiary of the split among the Republicans, Woodrow Wilson's more socially conservative (for example, avowedly racist) Democratic Party Progressivism, to (Theodore Roosevelt's nephew-in-law) Franklin Delano Roosevelt's New Deal.[17]

---

15  See my "Rosa Luxemburg and the Party," *Platypus Review* 86 (May 2016), in this volume.

16  "The Day of the People" (February 1919), written about the assassinations of Karl Liebknecht and Rosa Luxemburg during the Spartacist Uprising of the German Revolution.

17  See Ken Burns's recent documentary series, *The Roosevelts: An Intimate History* (2014), which traces this lineage of Progressivism from TR to FDR, including that of TR's niece, FDR's wife Eleanor Roosevelt.

## "Progressive" capitalism

The question is the alternative to capitalist progressivism offered by Marxist socialism. In the U.S. Eugene Debs's Socialist Party of America sought to intervene with working-class socialism across the division of Republican Party big-capitalist liberalism versus Democratic Party middle-class conservatism. "Industrial democracy" was the term of this socialist opposition under Marxist leadership.

As a Marxist, Debs like Rosa Luxemburg understood that this pressed a contradiction.[18] Marxism was not an authoritarian collectivist opposition to liberalism, but sought to combine and transcend middle class conservative-reactionary discontents over the destructive effects of capitalism with the revolutionary social potential of the dynamism of big capital. Debs articulated this in his 1900 election manifesto, first delivered as a speech in Chicago, on "Competition versus cooperation":[19]

> The Republican platform is a self-congratulation of the dominant capitalist class. "Prosperity galore, give us four years more." The Democratic platform is the wail and cry of the perishing middle class; calamity without end. The Social Democratic platform is an indictment of the capitalist system; it is the call to class consciousness and political action of the exploited working class; and it is a ringing declaration in favor of collective ownership of all the means of production and distribution, as the clarion voice of economic freedom.

Progressivism sought to similarly transcend the liberal capitalist vs. conservative populist divide emerging from industrialization, which is why liberals could observe in 1912 that Theodore Roosevelt's Progressive Party was seeking to usurp the mantles of both William Jennings Bryan's Populist Democrats and Debs's Socialists. Democrat Woodrow Wilson's election as President was the result of the split among the Republicans between

---

18  See Rosa Luxemburg, *Social Reform or Revolution?* (1900/08).

19  Eugene Debs, "Competition versus cooperation."

Progressives and old-style liberals. This set the stage for the triumph of New Deal progressivism under FDR — however 20 years later, after the crisis of the Great Depression.

But FDR's New Dealism, specifically as a Democratic Party phenomenon, combined but did not transcend the split of progressive capitalism with middle-class conservatism. The working class was thus bound in the Democratic Party to both big capital and the middle class. The working-class struggle for socialism found earlier in the old Socialist Party of America was squeezed out between these two aspects of the progressive New Deal Democrats. Socialism in the U.S. never recovered from this suppression. The New Deal Coalition Democrats became the ruling party in the U.S. in the high 20th century.

The Democrats have tried ever since FDR to retain a progressive capitalist alliance of liberal capital with middle-class conservatism. But what happened in the political crisis of the New Deal Coalition in the 1960s (signaled by the Civil Rights Movement as well as the U.S.'s losing war in Vietnam), combined with the crisis of capitalism in the 1970s, was that the form of middle-class conservatism changed — and was captured by the Republicans instead. This was not only expressed in the Southern Strategy that captured the Dixiecrat middle class (racial) conservatives, but also the appeal to "law and order" that captured the Northern urban and suburban working class ethnics who had previously supported the New Deal Democrats.

Subsequently, this has taken the otherwise longstanding form of the old split within liberalism that Progressivism represented: progressive liberalism versus conservative liberalism. The conservative liberals have promised the middle class that it will benefit from big capital; whereas the progressive liberals have actively sought policies that will ensure this. But neither the promise nor the policies have been able to prevent the social destruction and hence the conservative reaction of the middle class. Both the Republicans and Democrats have exploited middle-class discontents without satisfying them.

The working class has been the passive object of this process, oscillating between big-capitalist liberalism and middle-class conservatism, however in the obscure form of oscillating between greater or lesser support for progressive liberalism — greater or lesser support for the Democrats.

Politically, this means the subordination of the working class to the middle class. But which middle class?

The 20th century saw the rise of the "new middle class" of corporate capitalist managers, as opposed to the old middle class of small proprietors as well as of artisanal workers. The old middle class were the petite bourgeoisie, which were always distinct from the new industrial working class ever since the 19th century. So the question in the 20th century became the relation between the proletarianized working class of wage-earners and the capitalist managerial middle class. Could the middle class be captured by progressive liberalism? Or would the perennial crisis of capitalism lead instead to populist conservatism? How could populism, whether middle or working class, be neutralized as a disruptive threat to the negotiations of big-capitalist politics?

From the era of the late-19th century Second International, Debs serves as an example of how a populist could become a socialist — and not a progressive liberal. By contrast, Eduard Bernstein shows how a Marxist could become a progressive liberal, via the liquidation of proletarian socialism by neglect of the appeal of middle-class conservatism to which the working class could succumb in its trade unionism.

### Proletarian socialism vs. middle-class revolt

The working class is susceptible to middle-class conservatism insofar as it remains attached to a prior form of capitalism — the accumulated ensemble of previous concrete forms of wage labor — that undergoes crisis and is destroyed. Progressivism depends conversely upon the amenability and "liberalism" of the middle class to go along with changes in capitalism led by big capital. Big capital benefits from all changes anyway — capitalists can shift their investments or retire into philanthropy and entire countries can adopt what Lenin called "coupon-clipping"[20] — so the real issue is the struggle to come out on top or simply not to sink entirely but keep one's head above water in the next wave of capitalism. Conservatives are always there to try to take advantage of those swamped and potentially left behind,

---

20  See Lenin's pamphlet on *Imperialism, the Highest Stage of Capitalism* (1916).

with demagogic appeals to the status quo that people forget was itself once something new.

The question is, who are the progressives and who are the conservatives, politically? Perhaps the progressives are the more cunning conservatives — or the conservatives are the more cunning progressives. In the last generation of neoliberalism the Republicans could plausibly claim to be the "true revolutionaries" in advancing capitalism, and thus addressed and exploited the manifest liabilities of the Democrats' conservatism. The game is to capture middle-class discontents in "progressive" capitalist "reforms" (e.g. "welfare reform," "trade reform" etc.). The Republicans did so through the "Reagan Revolution," just as the Democrats had done in the 1930s FDR New Deal Coalition through which they had replaced the Republicans as the dominant majority party since the Civil War. Every "old conservative" was once a "new revolutionary" in capitalism.

Proletarian socialism — Marxism — by contrast sought to subordinate the middle class to the working class in reappropriating capital, which it proposed could only happen through the "dictatorship of the proletariat." The political party for proletarian socialism thus sought to lead the broader "masses" in "social democracy" in order to achieve socialism.

This would be especially true of the new managerial middle class which could simply take direction from the working class where they formerly did so from the capitalists — including from the capitalist state and its state capitalist managerial policies. Thus the capitalists could be retired into philanthropy. This was the vision of the Second International (1889–1914) and of mid-20th century Social Democratic politics. Especially since it was understood by Marxism, for instance by Lenin's conception of contemporary "imperialism" or monopoly capitalism, that not only the new middle class as corporate employees but also the working class itself subsisted not on the value of their own laboring activity but rather on a cut of the profits of capital, which was granted to them for political reasons, through a myriad of government subsidies, to prevent revolution — not merely to soften the blows of the business cycle of boom and bust.

Theodore Roosevelt called this the need for a "Square Deal" — indicatively not a "fair" deal, not merely enforcing liberal capitalism, but the government actively ameliorating its defects — and understood it explicitly as required to stave off socialism. But Roosevelt had, not Marx's vague "specter of communism," but Debs's actual mass Socialist Party of America staring him down to draw this political conclusion: it was a rear-guard action, but with a visionary long view. Progressivism was meant to institute political reforms required to be up-to-date with capitalist development: it was a matter not so much of advancing history as catching up with it; in this sense it still accorded with classical liberalism that the state should follow society and not try to determine it. But since Roosevelt's time, new problems arising from reforms attempted in the 20th century have clouded the issue; however, the essential political predicament of liberal democracy in the industrial era remains.

The problem and task of "progressive capitalism" is the attempt to maintain capitalism through its manifest social and political crisis. The alignment of the working class with the middle class in common capitalist interest with big capital is always temporary and inevitably fraught. There is always a struggle for supremacy in the fractious, politically negotiated social alliance of capital, which will eventually burst forth from the inexorable obsolescence of any and all concrete forms of capitalism in society.

The question the capitalists periodically face is: Can the conservative-reactionary middle class be made to go in peace (e.g. overdose on opioids — before that, on whiskey: it is important to note that the Progressives advocated Prohibition), or will it freak out and disrupt society and politics in uncontrollable ways? Trotsky called fascism the "petite bourgeoisie run amok."[21] But every old middle class was once a new middle class — just as every old form of wage-labor was once a new form of capitalism: the working class's discontents are subsumed under middle-class conservatism; the potential for socialism in capitalism thus disappears. The contradiction of capital that Marxism once recognized is submerged.

The "progressive capitalist" political forms that emerged as an alternative to Marxist socialism after the crisis of the Gilded Age and were carried through the 20th century have exhausted themselves in two waves of crisis: the crisis of the 1960s–70s that led to neoliberalism; and the present

---

21   Trotsky's writings on fascism were collected in *Fascism: What It Is, and How to Fight It* (Pioneer Publishers, U.S., 1944).

crisis of neoliberalism itself in the 2000s–10s.[22] The attempted return to
the Gilded Age since the 1980s–90s has clearly failed — which is why this
deeper history leading to the present reasserts itself today. It is undigested.

Glenn Beck was not wrong to panic at the sight of Trump and take his
ascendancy as the occasion to condemn the Progressivism of Theodore
Roosevelt and Woodrow Wilson from a century ago.[23] Beck counterposed
the "America of the Founding Fathers Washington and Jefferson" to that
of the "Progressivism of Theodore Roosevelt and Woodrow Wilson," calling the 2016 election the final defeat of the former by the latter. Neglected
by Beck in his division of American history is Abraham Lincoln and the
Civil War as a second founding moment of the U.S. But the evident desire
for return to the apparently more innocent time of the Second Industrial
Revolution and its liberal optimism neglects its real discontents and actual
crisis in the Gilded Age, which once were expressed by Marxist socialism
in the era of the Marxist-led parties of the Second International, including
the Socialist Party of America of Eugene Debs, but were captured instead
by "progressive" state capitalism in the 20th century that Beck and other
conservative liberals constantly bemoan — regretting its political necessity.

Today, the question is the future of that 20th century state capitalism
that, no matter how rickety, still dominates the world. Its prospects look
grim — China notwithstanding.

But actually it is no more grim than the 20th century itself — or the
late 19th century Gilded Age of Second Industrial Revolution capitalism
that gave birth to the 20th century.

Now as before, the Republicans and Democrats compete over the
political capture of middle-class conservative reaction by big capital in

---

22  See my "Symptomology," op. cit.

23  See for instance, Glenn Beck, "Why Teddy Roosevelt is America's New Founding Father" *Glenn* (May 11, 2016). Beck says that,

So the country is going to vote – the parameters are the Roosevelts. Those are the
bookends. Theodore Roosevelt, the beginning of progressivism, to FDR, heavy
statism. That's where we'll vote. And we've just voted two people in the FDR category. Hillary Clinton is FDR. Trump could be Woodrow Wilson, where he silenc-
es people and throws them into jail if you have a differing opinion. He could be
Woodrow Wilson. But she's probably FDR.

service of a capitalist "progress" that is none. What disappears is the possibility once recognized by Marxism of the working class, through proletarian socialism, superseding both "progressive" capital and middle-class reaction. Without it, capitalism is permanent, the middle class under threat periodically runs amok, old tenements are torn down, slums cleared, and new dormitories for the working class are hastily constructed, and in the end the best we can hope for is another Industrial Revolution — with all the destruction that it will inevitably bring.

Originally published in *Platypus Review* 102 (December 2017 – January 2018)

# Gilded Age socialism

## Historically past?

The great question regarding Marxism today is whether it is still current or rather belongs to the past: was Marxism in its highest moment confined to its contemporary period of the 2nd Industrial Revolution? — to the industrialization of the United States after the Civil War, which took place contemporaneously with that of the other countries where the 2nd Industrial Revolution was centered, Germany, Japan, Italy and Russia, where Marxism also, as in the U.S., had its greatest influence over the socialist movement.

By "Marxism" I mean, of course, not the theory of Karl Marx, but rather proletarian socialist politics in the historically Marxist mould, which combines social and political action, economic and political struggle, as opposed to other forms of socialism.

The question before us today (on this panel) is that of the historical Socialist Party of America, member of the 2nd or Socialist International, and led by Marxists such as Eugene Debs, its most prominent public political figure. Was the SPA a phenomenon specific to the era of the rapid industrialization of the U.S., the Gilded Age between the Civil War and World War I? For the SPA did not really survive the war and its aftermath, split as it was into the new Communist Party of the Third or Communist International, and repressed by the government both during the war and afterwards, in the notorious Palmer Raids.

I am going to deliberately place certain blinders on my consideration, namely confining my history to specifically American socialism. In so doing, I am going to have to ignore some glaring omissions — for instance leaving aside the Russian Revolution and the subsequent history of Soviet Communism and Stalinism. That being said:

The long legacy of the SPA is found today in such phenomena as First Amendment freedom of speech and association disputes contra public safety, as in the expression that "one cannot yell 'Fire!' in a crowded theater," which dates back to the suppression of the SPA, as Debs's vocal opposition to the war was the supposed threat to public safety not protected by the First Amendment, according to the Supreme Court. The SPA's members had previously established the ACLU American Civil Liberties Union — as well as having established the NAACP National Association for the Advancement of Colored People.

The issue, then, is the relationship between the Socialist Party and Progressivism, for the latter eclipsed socialism in the United States, starting with Woodrow Wilson's election in 1912 and culminating in FDR's election in 1932 and New Deal reforms implemented in the 1930s that flipped the U.S. capitalist political party system, and replaced the prior ruling Republican Party since the Civil War with the Democrats as the progressive liberal party. — This latter change was so profound that it has been regarded as a Third American Revolution — after the original and the Civil War.

It is significant that the SPA peaked in 1912 — when it so happens that the SPD in Germany also peaked — and Progressivism replaced it since then, namely, replacing the struggle for socialism with the reform of capitalism.

As I have written in "The end of Millennial Marxism," historically, workers have engaged in new organizing efforts with each successive wave of capitalist development, motivated by transformed conditions created by new industries.

Socialist Party leader Eugene Debs, for instance, had his formative experience in the 1894 Pullman Strike, which took place in the era of the rapid expansion of American railroads. We might observe that the wave of worker militancy and socialist organizing that made Marxism into a mass political movement took place around the world in the wake of the 1893 Panic. This led to the growth and development of the SPD in Germany and led to the birth of the Labour Party in the U.K. and the SPA in the United States. It also created the conditions for the formation of the Russian Social Democratic Labor Party of Lenin.

In capitalism, great economic depressions — nowadays called "recessions" — have not brought an end to capitalism but rather to its reinvigoration. Capitalism reproduces itself through crises and resulting regeneration. Capitalism is reconstituted through its self-destruction. Working class movements are part of this process. The question, then, is how this could lead to socialism instead of rebooting capitalism.

What is peculiar is how, although capitalism has experienced countless business cycles of boom and bust in the last 200 years, only one era saw the emergence and blooming of Marxism as a mass movement in the advanced capitalist countries, namely, the historical period in question, that of the 2nd Industrial Revolution Gilded Age, or roughly the 50 years between 1870 and 1920, scarcely two generations in time.

These two generations, those of August Bebel, Wilhelm Liebknecht, Karl Kautsky, Eduard Bernstein, Georgi Plekhanov, and Eugene Debs, on the one hand, and Vladimir Lenin, Rosa Luxemburg and Leon Trotsky, on the other, brought the Marxist movement into existence and experienced its historical crisis and downfall.

What we are concerned with here is the potential reproduction of such an achievement for our time — or at least at some point in the foreseeable future. Is there a future for Marxism?

So the question hinges on conditions for social mobilization and political radicalization: how to build a revolutionary movement? Unfortunately, many misconceptions abound regarding what that even means: what a revolutionary movement fundamentally is. These misconceptions have their basis in distortions of memory, how this history is misremembered, subject to a selective reduction in hindsight.

There are two questions: How did workers become radicalized? And, how did intellectuals become revolutionaries? For normally workers, like everyone else, are not especially radical under capitalism, and intellectuals serve not to change but rather to preserve the status quo. In both cases, we are concerned with workers and intellectuals becoming socialists: workers might be mobilized in capitalist politics; and intellectuals might contribute to change, but within the overall maintenance of capitalism.

Capitalist politics plays a role in the periodic crises and waves of destruction and reproduction in capitalism. Is there a specifically socialist as opposed to capitalist way that workers and intellectuals might take part in these cycles of history?

In certain respects, the period 1870–1920 was the first and remains the only time that the subaltern have constituted a mass social and political movement, and not been merely the followers of those already dominant in society. Certainly, it was the period of its greatest extent in the advanced capitalist countries. What made this period so unique? Was it contingent and unrepeatable, or was there something of this time that continues in its essence today?

I've already mentioned the succession of progressive liberal capitalist politics over socialism at the end of this historical era. How did Progressivism succeed over socialism? Was socialism a variety of progressivism, but just an inferior or antiquated one?

I would offer that we still live with the consequences of the failure of Marxism, and with the continuing effects of how that failure was institutionalized in progressive capitalist policy and politics.

Progressivism has provided a successful way of managing capitalism as a substitute for socialism — although lately it seems to have itself reached certain limits. Insofar as it has succeeded, economically, politically and socially, progressivism has made the struggle for socialism redundant or unnecessary, and considering the great effort required for the latter, undesirable, if not impossible. We have experienced now two waves of progressivism: those of the early and late 20th centuries, or, in terms more familiar to Platypus, of the 1930s Old Left and the 1960s New Left. In both cases, the struggle for socialism was replaced by capitalist reforms. Today, we are facing the limits of the progressive capitalist reforms instituted in the wake of the New Left, namely neoliberalism. We are also apparently facing the limits of the progressive capitalist reforms that were instituted in the era of the Old Left, in response to the Great Depression, the welfare state.

Intellectuals in our time — the Millennial Left — have harked back, first to the Old Left reforms and more recently to the New Left reforms, hoping to rejuvenate them. What has been forgotten by the Millennials is how those historical reforms were expressions of crises that were supposed to lead not to reconstituting capitalism but to socialism — at least in the minds of the original Old and New Leftists of the 20th century. In this way, socialism has been confused and mistaken for the reform of capitalism.

In this way, the dialectical relationship between capitalism and socialism has been misapprehended.

An example to help illustrate how this has functioned can be found in the history of the labor movement that is related but not identical with and at some distance from the history of socialist politics.

The American Federation of Labor or AFL was led by Samuel Gompers, who was a socialist educated in his perspective by Marxists. Eugene Debs had a famous conflict and contest with Gompers over the direction and character of the labor movement, with Gompers representing older craft-based trade unionism and Debs representing a newer perspective of industrial unionism. Eventually this led Debs with other socialists to found the IWW, the Industrial Workers of the World. Related to this was Gompers's preference for supporting Progressivism in the Democratic Party instead of Debs's Socialist Party. Later, after Debs and Gompers's time, industrial unionism was accomplished by the Congress of Industrial Organizations or CIO, with leading participation by socialists of a variety of ideological tendencies, including the Communist Party, which filled the new needs of labor organizing neglected by the old AFL. Eventually the AFL and CIO merged, and they are now a key constituency of the Democratic Party.

But the older craft trade unionism was radical for its time — it was led by socialists and even Marxists. As was industrial unionism. But both became not movements leading beyond capitalism but rather institutions within and part of capitalism.

There was an upsurge of labor militancy and organizing in the 1960s and 1970s, but it did not transform the existing labor unions nor produce a new form of unionization as might have been required by the new form of capitalism that emerged at that time, what we now call neoliberalism, namely, the more service-based and decentralized forms of work, at least as compared to the older.

What prevented the last major wave of new capitalism from producing new forms of labor organizing as well as new forms of socialist politics?

One could say that the surviving legacy organizations and political parties stood in the way of meeting the challenge and achieving this.

What is remarkable about our time, then, is the test to which the existing political parties and civil social organizations are being subject in the latest crisis of capitalism. Unlike the 1960s and '70s, the existing formations seem unable to meet the new needs, in however minimal ways.

This is what makes the Millennial capitulation to the Democratic Party so painful to witness: it was so unnecessary. But there was evidently a significant lack of imagination — filled, however spuriously, by the haunting ghosts of past Leftism. There was a sense of an old need being presented anew, but it was ill-defined. The lack of clarity was precisely over the meaning of socialism and Marxism for which the Millennials reached back: they became subject and beholden to the confusion and mistakes of their ancestors.

Perhaps it is inevitable that the past should be recalled and rehearsed. But the question is, which past, and how? It is specifically tragic that the past that was remembered was not the Socialist Party of Eugene Debs and the 2nd International but rather the Great Depression-era Communist Party of Stalin and the Comintern and the New Left of the 1960s and '70s. The Millennials could only imagine emancipation as expansion of the welfare state and of identity politics. They could only imagine more Democratic Party policies.

There are failures and there are failures: not all are equal in significance or poignancy in their tragedy. The 1930s and '60s were much lesser failures than that of original historical Marxism. And worse still, the 1930s and '60s are misremembered not as failures but as successes, not as tragedies but as heroism — forgetting that what makes heroes heroic is their tragedy.

The question is what results from the tragedy: what is the lesson to be learned in the cosmic story that is told? The story at this point is the history of capitalism. What is the lesson to be learned from the history of socialism? What was the purpose of that struggle? Was it to reform capitalism or to get beyond it? That is the question we are faced with today.

It is clear in hindsight that, unlike the original era of Marxism at the turn of the 20th century, both the 1930s and 1960s lacked dedication and belief in overcoming capitalism, at least not directly. Now that we are reaching the exhaustion of the capitalist reforms born from those times, we might be haunted rather from that earlier time which was so much more hopeful and organized, but which bequeathed us no significant reforms of capitalism — nothing to be confused with and mistaken for socialism. The old socialism accomplished nothing, not even to change capitalism. It is this that might be its redeeming virtue.

Presented on a panel with Spencer Leonard, Pamela Nogales and Edward Remus at the fifteenth annual International Convention of the Platypus Affiliated Society, held at the University of Chicago on March 30, 2023.

# 1918–2018

## The century of counterrevolution

Recently, I came across a 1938 article by the "Left communist" Paul Mattick, Sr., titled "Karl Kautsky: From Marx to Hitler." In it, Mattick asserted that the reformist social democracy that Kautsky ended up embracing was the harbinger of fascism — of Nazism.[1] There is a certain affinity to Friedrich Hayek's book on *The Road to Serfdom* (1944), in which a similar argument is made about the affinity of socialism and fascism. If Marxism (e.g. Kautsky) led to Hitler, as Hayek and Mattick aver, then this is because the counterrevolution was in the revolutionary tradition. The question we face today is whether and how the revolutionary tradition is still within the counterrevolution. For that is what we live under: it is the condition of any potential future for the revolutionary tradition whose memory we seek to preserve.

2018 marks two anniversaries: the 100th anniversary of the failed German Revolution of 1918; and the 50th anniversary of the climax of the New Left in 1968.

Moishe Postone died this year, and his death marks the 50th anniversary of 1968 in a certain way.

A strange fact of history is that both Thomas Jefferson and his fellow Founding Father but bitter political opponent, whose Presidency Jefferson unseated in his Democratic-Republican Revolution of 1800, John Adams, died on the precise 50th anniversary of the Declaration of Independence to the day, on July 4, 1826. John Adams's dying words were "Jefferson still lives." He was mistaken: Jefferson had died several hours earlier. But he was correct in another, more important sense: Jefferson had lived just long enough to see the survival of the American Revolution for its first half-century.

---

1    In *Anti-Bolshevik Communism* (London: Merlin Press, 1978).

Perhaps Moishe Postone lived just long enough to see the survival of the New Left 50 years later. If that is true, however, then he lived just long enough to see the survival of not the revolution but the counterrevolution.

As I presented all the way back at our very first annual Platypus convention in 2009, in my contribution to *The Platypus Synthesis*, on "History, theory," the Spartacists and Postone differ on the character of historical regression: Postone taking it to be the downward trend since the missed opportunity of the New Left in the 1960s; while the Spartacists account for regression since the high-point of the revolutionary crisis after WWI in which the October Revolution took place in 1917. But perhaps we can take the occasion this year to date more precisely the regression affecting both the Spartacists and Postone, the failure of the German Revolution of 1918, whose centennial we mark this year.

The question of historical regression raises its potential opposite, that is, history as Hegel took it to be, the progress in (the consciousness of) freedom. What we face in 2018 is that the last 50 years and the last 100 years have not seen a progress in freedom, but perhaps a regression in our consciousness of its tasks, specifically regarding the problem of capitalism. Where the Spartacists and Postone have stood still, waiting for history to resume, either from 1918 or from 1968, we must reckon with not history at a standstill but rather as it has regressed.

In this we are helped less by Hegel or Marx than by Friedrich Nietzsche, whose essay on "The Use and Abuse of History for Life" (1874/76) I cited prominently in my *Platypus Synthesis* contribution. There, I quoted Nietzsche that,

> A person must have the power and from time to time use it to break a past and to dissolve it, in order to be able to live.... People or ages serving life in this way, by judging and destroying a past, are always dangerous and in danger.... It is an attempt to give oneself, as it were, a past after the fact, out of which we may be descended in opposition to the one from which we are descended ...

Here it is not righteousness which sits in the judgment seat or, even less, mercy which announces judgment, but life alone, that dark, driving, insatiable self-desiring force . . .

[But there is a danger in the] attempt to give oneself, as it were, a past after the fact, out of which we may be descended in opposition to the one from which we are descended. It is always a dangerous attempt, because it is so difficult to find a borderline to the denial of the past and because the second nature usually is weaker than the first.[2]

So the question we have always faced in Platypus is the borderline between freeing ourselves from the past or rather participating in its liquidation. Are we gaining or losing history as a resource? In losing its liability we might sacrifice history as an asset. We must refashion history for use in our present need, but we might end up — like everyone else — abusing it: it might end up oppressing rather than freeing us.

Indiana Jones, who as we know was a Professor of Archaeology, in the 1989 film *The Last Crusade*, said that "Archaeology is about the search for fact, not the search for truth — for the search for truth, see Philosophy!" If Steven Spielberg and George Lucas can get it, then certainly we should!

In our approach to history, then, we are engaged not with its "facts" but with the *truth* of history. We are not archeologists: we are not antiquarians or historians — at least not affirmatively: we are not historicists. The events and figures of the past are not dead facts awaiting discovery but are living actions — past actions that continue to act upon the present, which we must relate to. We must take up the past actions that continue to affect us, and participate in the on-going transformation of that action. How we do so is extremely consequential: it affects not merely us, today, but will affect the future. History lives or dies — is vital or deadly — depending on our actions.

We are here to consider how the actions of not only 50 years ago in 1968 but 100 years ago in 1918 affect us today. But to understand this, we must consider the past actions that people 100 years ago in turn were

---

2    "The Platypus Synthesis: History, theory," in this volume.

affected by. We must consider the deeper history that they inherited and sought to act upon.

Last year we marked the 100th anniversary of the Russian Revolution of 1917. In the closing plenary panel discussion at our international convention in which I participated, alongside Bryan Palmer and Leo Panitch, I raised the possibility that, after a century, we had the opportunity of approaching this history differently. There, I said that,

> The paradox of 1917 is that failure and success are mixed together in its legacy. Therefore, the fact that 1917 is becoming more obscure is an opportunity as well as a liability. We are tasked not only with understanding the opportunity, but also with trying to make the liability into an asset. The various ways in which 1917 is falsely claimed, in a positive sense — we can call that Stalinism, we can call it all sorts of things — has dissipated. We have to try to make use of that. What has faded is not the revolution, perhaps, but the counter-revolution. In other words, while not entirely gone, the stigmatization of 1917 throughout the 20th century and the horror at the outcome of revolution [i.e., Stalinist repression] — these are fading. In *that* way we might be able to disentangle the success and the failure differently than it has been attempted in the past.[3]

This year we must reckon with the changing fortunes over the last century, not of the revolution, but rather of the counterrevolution. If not the revolution but the counterrevolution has disappeared, perhaps this is because it has become invisible — naturalized. It is so much the fundamental condition of our time that we don't even notice it. But that does not mean that it doesn't continue to act upon us. It might be so powerful as to not even provoke resistance, like atmospheric pressure or gravity. The effort it takes to read history against the grain — Benjamin said it must be done with the leverage of a "barge-pole"[4] — is in denaturalizing this history of the

---

3   "1917–2017," *Platypus Review* 99 (September 2017), in this volume.

4   Walter Benjamin, "Paralipomena to 'On the Concept of History'" (1940), *Selected Writings*, vol. 4 *1938–40*, Howard Eiland and Michael William Jennings, eds. (Cambridge:

counterrevolution, to make it visible or noticeable at all. Can we feel it? This has changed over the course of the past century. In the first half-century, from 1918 to 1968, the naturalization of the counterrevolution took certain forms; in the last half-century, since 1968, it has taken other forms. We can say indeed that the action of the counterrevolution provoked more resistance in its first 50 years, from 1918–68, than it has in its second 50 years, from 1968 to the present. That would mean that 1968 marked the decisive victory of the counterrevolution — to the degree that this was not entirely settled already in 1918.

As Richard Rubin pointed out at my presentation at this year's 4th Platypus European Conference in London, on "The Death of the Millennial Left," there has been nothing new produced, really, in the last 50 years. I agreed, and said that whatever had been new and different in the preceding 50 years, from 1918 to 1968 — Heidegger's philosophy, for example — was produced by the counterrevolution's active burial of Marxism. Max Weber had remarked to Georg Lukács in 1918 that what the Bolsheviks had done in Russia in the October Revolution and its aftermath would mitigate against socialism for at least 100 years. He seems to have been proven right. But since 1968, such active efforts against the memory of Marxism have been less necessary. So we have had, not so much anti-Marxism, as the naturalization of it. Ever since 1968, everyone is already a "Marxist" — as Foucault himself said — precisely because everyone is already an anti-Marxist. This is how things appear especially this year, in 2018. And necessarily so.

The failure of the 1918 German Revolution was not only that, but was the failure of Marxism as a world-historical movement. As Rosa Luxemburg posed the matter, the failure of revolution in Germany was the failure of revolution in Russia. 1918 and 1917 are inextricably linked. But the failure of 1918 has been hidden behind the apparent of success of 1917. The failure of 1917 wears the deceptive mask of success because of the forgetting of the failure of 1918.

Marxism failed. This is why it continues to fail today. Marxism has forgotten its own failure. Because Marxism sought to take up the prior — bourgeois — revolutionary tradition, its failure affected the revolutionary

---

Harvard University Press, 2003), 407.

tradition as a whole. The victory of the counterrevolution in 1918 was the victory of counterrevolution for all time.

What do we mean by the "counterrevolution"?

Stalin declared the policy — the strategy — of "socialism in one country" in 1924. What did it mean? What was it predicated upon? The events in Germany in 1923 seemed to have brought a definitive end to the post-WWI revolutionary crisis there. Stalin concluded therefore that Russia would not be saved by revolution in Germany — and even less likely by revolution elsewhere — but needed in the meantime to pursue socialism independently of prospects for world revolution. Stalin cited precedent from Lenin for this approach, and he attracted a great deal of support from the Communist Party for this policy.

Robert Borba, a supporter of the Maoist Revolutionary Communist Party (RCP), USA, speaking at our 4th European Conference in London earlier this year, addressed the Trotskyist critique of Stalinism in response to Hillel Ticktin on the panel discussion of "50 Years of 1968," as follows:

> Hillel [Ticktin] defined Stalinism as socialism in one country, which supposedly cannot exist. It is not viable. We should think seriously about what that means. Imagine you are Lenin in 1918. You have led a revolution. You are counting on the German revolutionaries to come to your aid, as you envision this whole process of revolution throughout Europe. But it does not happen. Now what do you do? Say, "This cannot exist, it is not viable," and give up? Lenin and the Bolshevik Party did not give up. The proletariat had taken power in one country. The imperialists were invading. They did the best they could for the world revolution. They retained a base from which to spread revolution. To give that up would harm the interests of oppressed humanity.[5]

This blackmail of the necessity to "defend the gains of the revolution" is crucial to understanding how the counterrevolution triumphed within the revolution — how Bolshevism led to Stalinism.

---

5   "50 years of 1968," *Platypus Review* 105 (April 2018).

Even supposed "Trotskyists" however ended up succumbing to the exigencies of supposedly "defending the gains" — Trotsky himself said that an inability to defend the gains of the revolution would mean an inability to advance it: Trotsky was still addressing Stalinism as a retreat. His followers today are even more willing than Trotsky himself to defend any and all purported "gains" — but at the expense of possibilities for any advance. What was perhaps a temporary necessity for Trotsky has become permanent for the supposed "Left."

So-called "Marxism" today is in fact an agency of the counterrevolution — has become part of the counterrevolution's on-going action — which is why it is not surprising that the "Left" today even champions the counterrevolution — by denouncing the revolutionary tradition. But this didn't happen just recently, but has been going on increasingly over the course of the past century. First, in small ways; but then finally comprehensively. Equivocations became judgments against the revolutionary tradition. It began in marked ways at least as early as the late 1960s. For instance, in 1967 Susan Sontag wrote, in the formerly Communist- and then Trotskyist-affiliated journal *Partisan Review*, that,

> If America *is* the culmination of Western white civilization, as everyone from the Left to the Right declares, then there must be something terribly wrong with Western white civilization. This is a painful truth; few of us want to go that far. . . . The truth is that Mozart, Pascal, Boolean algebra, Shakespeare, parliamentary government, baroque churches, Newton, the emancipation of women, Kant, Marx, Balanchine ballets, *et al*, don't redeem what this particular civilization has wrought upon the world. The white race *is* the cancer of human history; it is the white race and it alone — its ideologies and inventions — which eradicates autonomous civilizations wherever it spreads, which has upset the ecological balance of the planet, which now threatens the very existence of life itself.[6]

---

6 "What's happening to America?" *Partisan Review* 34, no. 1 (1967), 57–58.

Sound familiar? It is a voice very much for our time! Here, Sontag explicitly rejects the revolution — "parliamentary government," the "emancipation of women," and "Marx" included — because of its "eradication of autonomous civilizations wherever it spreads," and as "what this particular civilization has wrought upon the world." Let's accept this characterization of "Western white civilization" by Sontag, but try to grasp it through the *revolution*. For this is what revolution does, eradicate the prior form of civilization. What is America the "culmination" of, exactly? Let's look to its Founding Father, Thomas Jefferson, and think about the American Revolutionary leader alongside the protagonist of the 1918 German Revolution, Rosa Luxemburg.

I will start with the concluding scene of the 1995 film *Jefferson in Paris*. Here, Jefferson negotiates a contractual agreement with his slave James Hemings for the freedom of himself and Sally Hemings and her children — Jefferson's own offspring. It is observed by his white daughter. This scene encapsulates the revolution: the transition from slavery to social contract.

In the 1986 film *Rosa Luxemburg*, Sonja Liebknecht says to Luxemburg in prison that, "Sometimes I think that the war will go on forever" — as it has indeed gone on forever, since we are still fighting over the political geography and territorial results of WWI, for instance in the Middle East — and, responding to Luxemburg's optimism, about the mole burrowing through a seemingly solid reality that will soon be past and forgotten, "But it could be us who will soon disappear without a trace." In the penultimate scene of the film, Karl Liebknecht reads the last lines of his final article, "Despite Everything," and Luxemburg reads her last written words, "I was, I am, I shall be!" — referring however to "the revolution," not Marxism![7]

Luxemburg's "I was, I am, I shall be!" and Liebknecht's "Despite everything!" — are they still true? Is the revolution still on-going, despite everything? If not Luxemburg's, then at least Jefferson's revolution?

But aren't Thomas Jefferson and Rosa Luxemburg on "opposing sides" of the "class divide" — wasn't Luxemburg's Spartakusbund ["Spartacus

---

7   Karl Liebknecht, "Despite everything" (1919), in John Riddel, ed., *The Communist International in Lenin's Time: The German Revolution and the Debate on Soviet Power: Documents 1918–19: Preparing for the Founding Conference* (New York: Pathfinder, 1986), 269–271; Rosa Luxemburg, "Order prevails in Berlin" (1919).

League"] on the side of the slaves (named after a Roman slave who revolted); whereas, by contrast, Jefferson was on the side of the slave-owners? No!

To quote Robert Frost, from his 1915 poem "The Black Cottage,"

> . . . the principle
> That all men are created free and equal . . .
> That's a hard mystery of Jefferson's.
> What did he mean? Of course the easy way
> Is to decide it simply isn't true.
> It may not be. I heard a fellow say so.
> But never mind, the Welshman [Jefferson] got it planted
> Where it will trouble us a thousand years.
> Each age will have to reconsider it.[8]

How will we reconsider it for our age? Apparently, we won't: Jefferson's statues will be torn down instead. We will take the "easy way" and "decide" that Jefferson's revolutionary character "simply isn't true." This has long since been decided against Luxemburg's Marxism, too — indeed, as a precondition for the judgment against Jefferson. As Max Horkheimer said, "As long as it is not victorious, the revolution is no good."[9] The failure of revolution in 1918 was its failure for all time. We are told nowadays that the American Revolution never happened: it was at most a "slaveholder's revolt." But it certainly did not mark a change in "Western white civilization." Neither, of course, did Marxism. Susan Sontag tells us so!

Platypus began in 2006 and was founded as an organization in 2007, but we began our conventions in 2009. In 2018, our 10th convention requires a look back and a look ahead; last year marked centenary of 1917; this year marks 1918, hence, this specific occasion for reflecting on history from Platypus's point of view. What did we already know in 2006–08 that finds purchase especially now, in 2018? *The persistence of the counter-revolution.* Hence, our special emphasis on the failure of the 1918 German Revolution as opposed to the "success" of the 1917 Russian Revolution,

---

8    Robert Frost, "The Black Cottage," in *North of Boston*.
9    Horkheimer, "A discussion about revolution," in *Dawn & Decline: Notes 1926–31 and 1950–69* (New York: Seabury, 1978), 39.

which has been the case throughout the history of our primary Marxist reading group pedagogy. But we should reflect upon it again today.

I would like to refer to some of my convention speeches for Platypus:

In my 2012 convention President's report, "1873–1973: The century of Marxism," I asserted that the first 50 years saw growth and development of Marxism, as opposed to the second 50 years, which saw the steady destruction of the memory of Marxism.[10]

So today, in regarding 1918–2018 as the century of counterrevolution, I ask that its first 50 years, prior to 1968, be considered as the active counterrevolution of anti-Marxism, as opposed to the second 50 years, after 1968, as the naturalization of the counterrevolution, such that active anti-Marxism is no longer necessary.

But I would like to also recall my contribution to a prior convention plenary panel discussion in 2014, on "Revolutionary politics and thought,"[11] where I asserted that capitalism is both the revolution and the counterrevolution. To illustrate this, I quoted a JFK speech from 1960:

We should not fear the 20th century, for this worldwide revolution which we see all around us is part of the original American Revolution.

Kennedy was speaking at the Hotel Theresa in New York:

I am delighted to come and visit. Behind the fact of [Fidel] Castro coming to this hotel, [Nikita] Khrushchev coming to Castro, there is another great traveler in the world, and that is the travel of a world revolution, a world in turmoil. I am delighted to come to Harlem and I think the whole world should come here and the whole world should recognize that we all live right next to each other, whether here in Harlem or on the other side of the globe. We should be glad they came to

---

10  See my "1873–1973: The century of Marxism," *Platypus Review* 47 (June 2012), in this volume.

11  "Revolutionary politics and thought," *Platypus Review* 69 (September 2014), in this volume.

the United States. We should not fear the 20th century, for this worldwide revolution which we see all around us is part of the original American Revolution.[12]

With Kennedy, the counterrevolution, in order to be successful, still needed to claim to be the revolution: the counterrevolution still struggled with the revolution. By the end of the 1960s — at the other end of the New Left — however, this was no longer the case.

We can observe today that what was lacking both in 1918 and in 1968 was a political force adequate to the task of the struggle for socialism. The problem of political party links both dates. 1968 failed to overcome the mid-20th century liquidation of Marxism in Stalinism and related phenomena, in the same way that 1918 had failed to overcome the capitulation of the SPD and greater Second International in WWI, and thus failed to overcome the crisis of Marxism.

For this reason, we can say, today, 50 years after 1968, that the past 100 years, since 1918, have been the century of counterrevolution.

Presented as the President's report at the closing plenary of the tenth annual International Convention of the Platypus Affiliated Society in Chicago on April 7, 2018.

Originally published in *Platypus Review* 106 (May 2018)

---

12  The speech is available online at *The American Presidency Project*.

# Redeeming the 20th century

## Statism and anarchy today

A senior teaching colleague of mine at the University of Chicago revised the college core syllabus, which he said needed to be "brought into the 21st century." What he really meant by this was brought into the 20th century — specifically, the late 20th century. But the 20th century was determined by the 19th century. There was very little that was new, and most of it was bad. I spoke at previous conventions about 1873–1973, 1917–2017 and 1918–2018.[1] In those discussions, I divided the 100-year cycles into their first and second halves of 50 years. What was new was Marxism and anti-Marxism. As Marxism died and its memory faded in the second half of the last century, there was absolutely nothing new. My colleague invoked ideas that had their genesis in the early 20th century as anti-Marxism: for example, Foucault – Heidegger – Nietzsche.

The Stalinist historian Eric Hobsbawm defined the "short 20th century" as the period 1914–91, from WWI to the fall of the Soviet Union. But perhaps the 20th century could be defined not by the catastrophe of world war in 1914 but the failure of the world socialist revolution in 1919, which was already prefigured by the capitulation of Marxism in 1914 — and the war certainly contributed to not only the crisis and the revolutionary opportunity but also the counterrevolutionary reality, in whose brutality the war continued.[2] 2019 marks the centenary of 1919, which was not the failure of the revolution, as we marked last year in 2018 as a function of both 1918 and 1968, but the triumph of the counterrevolution.

---

1   "1873–1973: The century of Marxism: The death of Marxism and the emergence of neo-liberalism and neo-anarchism"; "1917–2017"; "1918–2018: The century of counterrevolution," all in this volume.

2   "1914 in the history of Marxism," *Platypus Review* 66 (May 2014), in this volume.

## 100 years

This year we observe the 100th anniversary of the defeat of the German Revolution in 1919 and the 30th anniversary of the collapse of Stalinism in 1989. It is unclear to me which of these takes priority in my talk now. I therefore want to build upon the last two years of anniversaries I have observed in my remarks at the annual Platypus conventions, namely, the centenaries of 1917 and 1918, and 50 years of 1968.

In my remarks last year on 1918–2018 as the "century of counter-revolution," I thematized the issue of the presence of the revolution in the counterrevolution as the converse and complement to the issue of 1917 as the presence of the counterrevolution in the revolution. Usually, the 20th century is treated by the "Left" as one of accomplishment. The supposed advances and gains of the 20th century take two forms: the so-called "actually existing socialism" of the East in the Stalinist-ruled states of the USSR, Eastern Europe, China, North Korea, Vietnam and Cuba; and the social-democratic welfare state in the West. Today, in 2019, we are faced with what has been evident for the past few years: the reemergence of the legacies of neo-Stalinism and neo-social democracy, both of which are called "socialism." In the Democratic Socialists of America and in the Momentum movement of the U.K. Labour Party, we see both tendencies present. In the abiding "continuing struggles" of "anti-imperialism" and "anti-fascism" — including "anti-sexism" and "anti-racism" — we find the united front of neo-social democracy and neo-Stalinism: street-fighting as well as imposed government and para-state civil society — corporate and academic — "hate speech" code restrictions.

This is because, as Trotsky and the Frankfurt School observed already back in the 1930s, the liquidation of historical Marxism after the failure of the world proletarian socialist revolution of 1917–19 was present in both Social Democracy and Stalinism. They are the twin headstones at the grave of Marxism. In the 1930s, Trotsky treated both equally as varieties of reformist opportunism, whose residual differences were actively liquidated at the time in the Popular Front Against War and Fascism. Trotsky anticipated by one year the official announcement of the Popular Front in 1935 with his "French Turn," having his followers join the official social-democratic parties world-wide in 1934. The fact that these parties had betrayed Marxism both in WWI and in the revolutions that followed, that Social Democracy was on the side of active counter-revolution as opposed to Stalinism's apparent continuity with the revolution, did not matter one bit to Trotsky: Stalinism was just as proven in his mind to be counterrevolutionary; and social-democratic parties were just as potentially transformable into revolutionary socialist parties as the ostensibly "revolutionary" Communist Parties could have been.

The first assumption I must ask you to entertain is that both Social Democracy and Stalinism were forms of avoidance of the struggle for socialism in the 20th century, and that everything accomplished under their auspices was actually stepping back and away from and not towards socialism. As such, both Stalinism and Social Democracy represented obstacles to socialism. — Here, the anarchists and "Left communist" Marxists would apparently agree. But historically, this was the perspective shared by the Frankfurt School and Trotsky, both of which must be distinguished from and recognized properly in their opposition to such "Left communism" and anarchism, for both Trotsky and the Frankfurt School represented the memory of original historical Marxism, and of its last protagonists, Lenin and Luxemburg, among others.

The forms of the liquidation of Marxism in the post-failed revolutionary aftermath of the 1920s–30s are various, but have continued to endure ever since then: they express the same problems we see on the "Left" today, in both its neo-Stalinist and neo-social democratic guises. — These problems are also present in anarchism and so-called "Left communism." As such, they express not only problems of the "Left" but the political antinomies of capitalism itself. In this sense, they were not new problems of the 20th century, but old problems that Marxism had already addressed and at least theoretically "overcome" in the 19th century — at least, Marxism had appeared to have overcome these problems. This is the reason for Platypus's emphasis on pre-WWI Marxist history, to find the sources for 20th century problems that were originally obvious to Marxists historically but in the meantime have become obscure, elusive and intractable today. While it would seem that history proved in fact that the old problems had not actually been overcome by Marxism, such a perspective would assume that we somehow "know better" today, that the 20th century had provided lessons that have been learned — even if some anarchists had already warned of them in the 19th century. So it is incumbent upon me in my defense of and advocacy for Marxism to prove otherwise.

## Redemption

The question of the potential "redemption" of the 20th century hinges on the question of historical "progress." If progress has been made since 1919, then no redemption of the 20th century is really necessary: we can simply build upon past practices in the present and proceed accordingly. So the issue of redemption is actually based on the reverse evaluation, that the 20th century did not progress beyond the original issues of historical Marxism, and indeed regressed below it. This was the assumption of both Trotsky and the Frankfurt School by the 1930s. They regarded the problems of Stalinism and Social Democracy as repetitions of past problems that Marxism had already consciously processed in its history before WWI.

The "Left" has tried to preserve itself through appropriating past history in a certain way. The paradox — actually a contradiction — is as follows: On the one hand, the "Left" treats itself as independent of the dominant society in capitalism, thus treating the society it seeks to change as outside of itself (perhaps treating the presence of capitalist society within itself as an outside contagion to be fought against and expelled); on the other hand, the "Left" claims the supposed "progress" of society in the 20th century as its own, as the result of its own doing.

But this is the way capitalist society always grasps itself: as an autonomous subject trying to take hold of an extrinsic object. Originally, by contradistinction, Marxism characterized itself — "communism" or "proletarian socialism" — as the "actual self-consciousness of the real movement of history." Both Stalinism and Social Democracy (reformist Revisionism) followed original Marxism in this, by identifying themselves with the real movement of history.

The problem is that history and its movement in capitalism is self-contradictory, and is thus non-identical with itself. So, in identifying oneself with history, one inevitably falls into a partial, one-sided antinomical perspective that privileges some aspects of historical movement over others. The "Left" thus leaves itself at the mercy of capitalism and is merely tossed about by the *Sturm und Drang* of its contradictions and historical changes. When one looks soberly and honestly at the actual history of the action and thought of the "Left" — Stalinism and Social Democracy, as well as anarchism and "Left communism," and liberalism, too — in the 20th century, one finds it always on all sides of all issues. The "Left," in one form or another, has variously justified and supported in certain moments of history even imperialism and fascism. It has been pro-imperialist and anti-imperialist, pro-fascist and anti-fascist — revolutionary and counter-revolutionary. The actual history in its violent vicissitudes is hence forgotten — repressed. The way this is done is to resolve history by ironing it out, and rest content that, through it all, "progress" has been made in the end. — That is, until the next historical shift of capitalism unsettles history once again, throwing progress into doubt.

## Antinomies

I have raised one set of antinomies already, namely, anti-imperialism and anti-fascism (the subject of a prior convention talk of mine in 2011[3]). There are others. For instance, parliamentarism-electoralism as opposed to extra-parliamentary activity, or the battle of the "ballots" vs. that on the "streets." There is also "anti-exploitation" vs. "anti-oppression," or socio-economic "class" vs. "race, gender and sexuality." In the time of the historical origins of Marxism, there was also "social" vs. "political action" — the debate which broke up the First International Workingmen's Association, in the original split in socialism between anarchism and Marxism. There is also the antinomy of political and economic struggles. What one will find today is that all tendencies on the "Left" are actually riven by such divisions, still. For instance, all these oppositions are present in the DSA and in Labour's Momentum movement.

---

3   "The 'anti-fascist' vs. 'anti-imperialist' Left," in *Death of the Millennial Left: Interventions 2006–2022.*

This shows that the 20th century is still with us — as is indeed the 19th century. That is actually cause for hope. The fact that such antinomies still beset the "Left" shows that the problem of capitalism as Marxism originally understood it has not been overcome — if only we can continue to recall it.

These antinomies must be regarded properly as forms for the social and political movement of capitalism itself. Capitalism is internally divided and destroys itself periodically, only to reconstitute itself again, through its characteristic social and political struggles, whether between "classes" or "nations," etc. So the first task of redeeming the 20th century would be to recognize properly that the only "progress" made was progress in *capitalism* — namely, actually the *regression* from socialism, at least as far as the political struggle for socialism as Marxism originally understood it is concerned.

Hypothetically, the perpetuation of capitalism also means sustaining the possibility for socialism. The only question is how this potential possibility is manifest and grasped in practice and theory. There, we can observe an obvious regression in political potential for socialism from the early 20th century to today. — Unless we assume that the election and policies of "socialist" Democrats and Labourites and/or demands of those engaged in street fighting or guerilla warfare immediately promise the achievement of socialist revolution, which I think we have reason to doubt: the mid-20th century is not about to be repeated.

Indeed, the implementation of what would now be considered "socialist" policies by either elected officials or leaders of political revolutions in the 20th century can be considered today as part of the history of *capitalism* — the history for whatever potential for socialism exists concretely in the world today, which is after all how Marxism originally addressed capitalism to begin with: capitalism is the possibility and necessity for socialism.

### Oscillation — vicissitude

Towards the end of his life, my old professor Moishe Postone raised the specter of history oscillating between liberal and authoritarian state-centric forms of capital — this was always Postone's great apprehension and suspicion of Platypus with our positive appraisal of Lenin and Trotsky — so that the state-mediated capitalism succeeding the original liberal forms of capitalism in the early 20th century reverted by the end of the 20th century to neoliberalism, but might be followed by another phase of statist capital as a result of the crisis of neoliberalism in the 21st century. I addressed this phenomenon of reaction against the failure of Marxism in my Platypus convention President's report in 2012, in the wake of the demise of Occupy Wall Street, on "1873–1973: The century of Marxism: The death of Marxism and the emergence of neo-liberalism and neo-anarchism."[4]

What is striking now is how, at the terminus of the Millennial Left, anarchism has been nearly completely suppressed in favor of statist forms of "socialism," in both neo-social democracy and neo-Stalinism. This is very different from where the Millennial Left originally started out, in the new Students for a Democratic Society (established in the same year, 2006, as Platypus), steeped as it was in neo-anarchism, especially as inherited from the 1990s anti-globalization and avowedly "post-" if not simply "anti-political Left" of Generation X. Despite the anti-imperialism of the anti-war movement at that time, which prioritized defense of Third World regimes against the U.S., this neo-anarchism persisted through #Occupy. It can be seen in the more general anti-austerity movement in response to the post-2008 global economic crisis. But as the Great Recession wore on, eventually there was a turn to state-oriented and capitalist electoral politics, for instance with SYRIZA in Greece, but also Podemos in Spain — despite the latter's avowedly "anti-political" stance, which, unlike SYRIZA, failed to take power and faded, Podemos having lost out to the traditional Socialists.

The turn towards the Labour Party in the U.K. through Momentum under Jeremy Corbyn's leadership, and towards the Democrats in the U.S., first via Bernie Sanders's campaign for the Democratic Party nomination for President, and then through its ostensibly "socialist" progressive liberal fringe, the Democratic Socialists of America, after the Brexit vote and Trump's election, shows the utter collapse — indeed, I called it the "death" — of the Millennial "Left."[5] "Marxism" was originally disputed by the Millennial Left in opposition to both Social Democracy and Stalinism, but now has been completely assimilated to these two latter legacies. Whatever

---

4    In this volume.

5    See "The Millennial Left is dead," in *Death of the Millennial Left: Interventions 2006–2022.*

potential possibility and hope for opportunity of historical change that had come with the Millennial Left was expressed by its rejection of the traditional identification of Marxism with statism. Now this has disappeared. This repeated the failure of the 1960s New Left to overcome the problems of its elders in Stalinism and Social Democracy and subsequent assimilation to their legacy.

As I wrote in "The Sandernistas," about the Millennial Left's enthusiasm for Bernie, what "socialism" means is merely return to the New Deal and Great Society government programs of the Democratic Party in the 20th century.[6] Similarly, the Corbynistas want to return to the old Labour policies before neoliberalism. Where has the original "anarchist" spirit of the Millennials gone? — This is as striking as the disappearance of ostensible "libertarian" discontents from the Republican Party under Trump, however they are still expressed positively in moves to criminal justice reform as well as "free speech" efforts against Political Correctness that Trump has initiated. Trump remains the central phenomenon of our time, however shadowed by militant neo-social democracy and neo-Stalinism in response to him. The crisis of neoliberalism will deepen before it abates. In any case, the center of action remains the state. What the "Left" wants above all is to unelect Trump and reverse the Brexit vote, to which everything else is subordinated. The calls for increased welfare provisions, nationalization of industry and other capitalist state reforms are just enabling fictions.

### Statism and anarchy today

Significantly, I myself would characterize the task of socialism today as essentially "anarchist" in nature, but not as "post-political" as with post-New Left neo-anarchism, but rather *pre*-political, namely, the necessity to organize the potential for civil-social action independent of the state and capitalist politics, as a precondition for any kind of political formation, let alone socialist party-building. This must be distinguished sharply from "movement-" or "base-building," however, in that they are, by contrast,

---

6   "The Sandernistas: The final triumph of the 1980s," in *Death of the Millennial Left: Interventions 2006–2022.*

dependent on their converse and complementary phenomenon, electoralism: the "movement" is always understood as a pressure-tactic on elected officials, whether in government or legislative-parliamentary opposition. The ostensible "base-building" is according to the model of "community organizing" and NGO activism, that is, as civil society constituencies for electoral parties, especially in the neoliberal mode of privatized outsourcing of political action. In this way, I would distinguish the actual present historical necessity from the past neoliberal model, which expressed not a return to but actually the thinning-out of civil society and capitulation to statism, however post-Fordist in character. The "Left" today is stuck in the characteristic post-New Left neoliberal modality of social-movement activism, which is actually just a training ground for NGO lobbyism and its group identity-politics and professional-managerial cultural racketeering. Any pre-socialist organizing today would need to cut sharply across the established divisions in the capitalist-state management of civil society. The crisis of neoliberalism provides an opportunity for this — which the Millennial Left in its death is precisely avoiding.

The new phase of capitalism now emerging from the crisis of its past neoliberal forms since the 1970s will offer possibilities for such organizing, as existing civil society is destroyed and reconstructed according to the new needs of capital. This is an opportunity to return to the original Marxist vision of socialism as immanent to and building upon the foundations of capitalism. The statist turn of the Millennial Left fails at this in its clinging to the established prior forms of neoliberal capitalism embodied by the existing Democrat and Labour Parties, which will be as slow to change now as they were in the face of the neoliberal shift beginning in the 1970s — they didn't complete their turn for another 20 years, in the 1990s. The Millennials joining them now will be their unopposed official leadership in 20 years' time, just as Hillary and Bill Clinton came to power in 1992, 20 years after their youthful participation in the (losing) 1972 McGovern Democrat campaign for President. The Millennials will learn through their defeats now how to adapt to capitalist politics in the long run, as usual, through a backward and shamefaced movement — by contrast, the avowed Right will be more straightforward, unabashed, and hence successful. This will give the Millennials' electoralism and statist orientation an apparently more "principled and responsible" character, by contrast to the more blatant opportunism of the Right in pushing through whatever capitalism requires. But "resistance" or not, the overall drift is the same.

## History

By contrast to Postone, I regard neoliberalism as a form of statism and not anti-statism, with anarchism and libertarianism always marginalized fringe ideological phenomena, and so post-neoliberalism will not require any profound changes in capitalist politics at the level of the state, which however requires periodic fine-tuning. The mid-late 20th century New Left, with its characteristic confusions about the capitalist state, mistaking it as a compromise formation with socialism (in this way recapitulating the old opportunist reformist Revisionism), was always deeply ambivalent in its neo-anarchist social-movementism, by the 1980s resigning itself to and even celebrating its powerlessness as some principled virtue — the "Left" itself came to be actually identified with such powerlessness, mocking the original 1960s New Left vision of "be realistic, demand the impossible." That is not going to change in the least with the present electoral turn of the Millennial Left. The resulting statist managerial professionals emerging from the Millennial generation will always be regarded as bastard children and not recognized as the Left's own — just as the 1980s yuppies and the 1990s Clintons were never recognized as the offspring of the New Left that they were. But the continuing "Left" on the marginal fringe won't matter at all, other than as the usual paragon of hypocritical denial for which the New Left has served as eminent historical example. See the "long march through the institutions" through which New Left Maoists gave us academic "Left" blather, charter schools and Obama's Presidency. Before them, the Old Left Stalinists had always been what they ended up being, bureaucrats of corporate management and the capitalist state — many more of them lived out illustrious post-WWII careers than were purged by McCarthyism, in which they had not been "coopted" or "sold out" but rather fulfilled their original 1930s youthful Great Depression vision for reformed capitalism.

As Lenin observed and Adorno repeated 50 years later, the apparent rebirth of anarchism in the wasteland of the defeat of Marxism was only a symptom of historical failure and never more than a return of a "ghost" (or, as Lenin put it, a "phantasm").[7] But the ghost was not actually of anarchism itself but rather of what Marxism originally had been, the effective union of social and political action. That the historical mission accepted by Marxism became divided between the reduction of politics to statism and the reduction of social freedom to capitalist anarchy is the symptom that must be worked through towards any possibility for socialism.

Historically, Marxism already traversed this path, in the 1860s–70s, in the prelude to the mass socialist parties of the late 19th – early 20th centuries. Marxism emerged ascendant and anarchism diminished in the 1880s–90s, and the Second Industrial Revolution expanded the ranks of the proletariat and of socialist politics internationally through the Second or Socialist International, as the geopolitical order of capitalism found new players in the rise of Germany, Japan and the United States, and the older 19th century British and French socialist traditions were taken up and subsumed by Marxism. At the same time, Bonapartist states in the industrializing countries led capitalism into a new and even greater era. The freewheeling Gilded Age saw the most massive quantitative transformations in the history of civilization. The Second Industrial Revolution of the late 19th century resulted in mass socialist parties unprecedented in world history, and within a generation they were prepared to take power.[8] This produced what Luxemburg and Lenin regarded as the welcome "crisis of Marxism" itself, which they took as opportunity to clarify the tasks of socialism. We are nowhere near such a condition today. Indeed, the question of the meaning of socialism is being suppressed through its advocacy: precisely when everyone is claiming to be "socialist," its memory is being buried. Socialism currently is being not constituted, but liquidated. The last time this happened was in the mid-20th century, when Stalinism and

---

7 See V.I. Lenin, *"Left-Wing" Communism: An Infantile Disorder* (1920), trans. Julius Katzer (Moscow: Progress Publishers, 1964) chap. 4, "The Struggle Against Which Enemies Within the Working-Class Movement Helped Bolshevism Develop, Gain Strength, and Become Steeled"; and Theodor W. Adorno, "Resignation" (1969), in *Critical Models: Interventions and Catchwords*, trans. Henry W. Pickford (New York: Columbia University Press, 1998), 292.

8 See "The end of the Gilded Age: Discontents of the Second Industrial Revolution today," *Platypus Review* 102 (December 2017 – January 2018), in this volume.

Social Democracy liquidated Marxism and adapted to continuing capitalism. It is happening yet again.

Redeeming the 20th century, then, means recognizing its repetition today. The reigning statism of the Millennial Left arriving at adulthood, whether neo-social-democratic or neo-Stalinist, is the death-mask imposed upon it by its 20th century forebears, smothering it from birth — especially the 1960s New Left, internalizing, through "anti"-authoritarian rebellion, the mocking face of state "socialism." Any haunting reminders of anarchism that may trouble its conscience moving forward will be a mere spectral apparition and no living spirit of socialism. That spirit can only find life in a rebirth of Marxism, which for now exists outside and against the stream of the present, and, like Benjamin's Angel of History, sees not a chain of events, carrying us helplessly from one "damned thing" to another, but only one single mounting catastrophe.[9] As for Benjamin, the only hope is not in the flow of time, but in the monstrous abbreviation and compression of history that can blast the continuity of the present.

Presented at the closing plenary of the eleventh annual Platypus Affiliated Society International Convention, April 6, 2019, at the School of the Art Institute of Chicago.

Originally published in *Platypus Review* 116 (May 2019)

---

9   Walter Benjamin, "On the concept of history" (1940), AKA "Theses on the philosophy of history," in *Illuminations*, trans. Harry Zohn (New York: Schocken Books, 1969), 253–64.

# Kautsky in the 21st century

For me, the question of the legacy of Karl Kautsky's Marxism is not as *a* Marxist, but rather as *the* Marxist. He was the theorist, not of capitalism or socialism, but of the working class's struggle for socialism, the social and political movement and most of all the political party that issued from this movement and struggle. Kautsky articulated the historical and strategic perspective and the self-understanding of the proletarian socialist party. He helped formulate the political program of Marxism — the Erfurt Programme in which the German Social-Democratic Party became officially Marxist — and explained it with particular genius. He was not a theorist of German socialism but rather of the world-historic social and political task of socialism, for the entire Socialist International.

He was rightly if ironically called the "Pope of Marxism," and this meant as a world political movement, indeed of the world party for socialism, in every country. For instance his writings converted the American socialist Eugene Debs to Marxism. Lenin, Rosa Luxemburg, Trotsky and countless others learned Marxism from Kautsky. Kautsky provided the theoretical self-understanding and strategic vision for all Marxists and for the broader socialist movement led by Marxism throughout the world, precisely when Marxism was a mass form of social struggle and politics, and precisely when this was so in the core metropolitan advanced capitalist countries.

In this respect Kautsky was one of the greatest political leaders of all time, in all of world history. However, he was the leader of a movement that failed, for Marxism failed.

This makes Kautsky a peculiar historical figure, and makes his thought — as we inherit from his writings — a specific kind of object and legacy. Kautsky explains something to us that no longer exists, namely the mass socialist political party and the class struggle for socialism of the working class, aiming for the world dictatorship of the proletariat taking over and transforming global capitalism.

Kautsky's Marxism summarized and appropriated the entire history and experience of the socialist workers' movement up to that point, namely, the radical tradition of the bourgeois revolution, the industrial social visions of the Utopian Socialists, the unfinished tasks of the failed revolutions of 1848, the civil collective and social cooperative movements of labor organizers and anarchists, and the party as what Ferdinand Lassalle called the "permanent political campaign of the working class" aiming to win the "battle of democracy."

But the history of socialism had exhibited antagonisms and conflicts between its various aspects and protagonists. The disputes within socialism were considered by Marxism such as Kautsky's as not mere differences and disagreements, but rather expressed the self-contradictory character of the struggle for socialism and its tasks. The question was how the working class must work through such self-contradiction.

One catch-phrase from 19th century history preceding Kautsky was "social and political action." Kautsky understood the proletarianized working class's struggle for socialism to require both kinds of activity, and moreover sought to combine them in the political party for socialism and its associated civil-social movement organizations. This is what Kautsky and the greater Second International Marxism meant by "social democracy," a legacy of the unfulfilled tasks of 1848, to achieve the "social republic." Marxists understood this to require the independent political and social action of the working class leading the broader discontented, exploited and oppressed masses under capitalism.

Otherwise, the task of socialism in capitalism was liable to fall out into an antinomy of having to choose between social movement activism and political activity. It was Kautsky's Marxism's ability to comprehend and transcend this antinomy and achieve the combined tasks of both.

This is what the subsequent socialist movement since Kautsky's time — since the failure of Second International Marxism — has foundered upon, starting at least as early as the 1930s Old Left of Stalinism and reformist Social Democracy, and especially since the 1960s New Left and its eschewing of the tasks of building the political party for socialism.

The historical wound of this history we face is that the Kautskyan political party both made the revolution and prosecuted the counterrevolution. Both Social Democracy and "Marxist-Leninism" — Stalinism — are descended from Kauskyan socialism — from this history of Marxism.

But rather than engaging and trying to work through the problematic legacy of Kautsky's Marxism, socialists and the greater Left — and indeed democracy — has drawn back and retreated from it — avoided it.

The reason the question of Kautsky's legacy specifically as well as that of Marxism more generally returns periodically is that it represents the unfinished work and task of history that must still be worked through.

In one way or another, we must engage the tasks — and contradiction — of social and political action in capitalism that points beyond it to socialism. So long as this task remains we will be haunted by Kautsky's Marxism.

Presented on a Platypus panel discussion with Adam J. Sacks (professor of history at the University of Hong Kong and contributor to *Jacobin*), Ben Lewis (member of the Communist Party of Great Britain), Jason Wright (member of the Bolshevik Tendency), September 5, 2020.

Originally published in *Platypus Review* 136 (May 2021)

# The fate of the American Revolution

In this lecture series,[1] we are talking about the way that the American Constitutional republic and democracy have been reconstituted several times in the course of its history. We are talking about the emergence of the problem of capitalism, the problem of politics, and the relationship between state and society in that process.

My first lecture was on the Jeffersonian revolution. That phrase elides a difference between Thomas Jefferson's participation in the 1776 American Revolution and his electoral revolution of 1800. You could say that the first political party in the United States is Jefferson's Democratic Republicans running for office in 1800, and that he understood this as a renewal of the original revolutionary party — small "p" party instead of capital "P" Party — in the original 1776 Revolution, namely, the Committees of Correspondence.

However, Pam Nogales's lecture on Jacksonian democracy, really traces the emergence of the first modern political party, not only in American history, but perhaps in world history: the Democratic Party of Andrew Jackson. The Civil War and Reconstruction are incomprehensible without thinking about the new Republican Party that emerges in the 1850s and wins the election of 1860, precipitating the Civil War and precipitating a revolution.

The lecture that I gave last in the series was on the Gilded Age and the emergence of socialism as a mass political force in the United States, which, however, was unable to realize such a revolutionary transformation of American politics and society. My point there — as in Reid Kotlas'

---

1    The following excerpted remarks were presented on a panel culminating a lecture series hosted by the Platypus Affiliated Society in the summer of 2020 and titled "The Legacy of the American Revolution" with lectures given by Platypus members James Vaughn, Chris Cutrone, Pamela Nogales, Spencer Leonard and Reid Kotlas.

lecture — was that socialism succumbed to progressivism, to progressive liberal capitalism. That is behind both the failed election of 1912 — the campaign of Theodore Roosevelt as a Progressive — and the ultimate success of FDR and the Democratic Party. There was a new configuration of American politics with FDR through the New Deal coalition when he was elected in 1932. In many respects we still live in that system. That was not fundamentally modified or overthrown by the Reagan revolution of 1980, but only modified.

We are thinking about politics and the relationship between politics and society, and how much more problematic the relationship between politics and society becomes as a function of capitalism. The narrative we've been telling is of what might be perceived as a divergence between society and politics, as a function of capitalism and the transformations of the American political party system over the course of the history of the United States. We are perhaps living through yet another transformation of the political party system in the United States, or at least a crisis of that political party system, signaled by not only Donald Trump, but Bernie Sanders.

The ghost of American socialism stalks this crisis, precisely in the way that Bernie Sanders invoked — also through his own personal political history as a New Left activist — the older history of American socialism and the Socialist Party of America of Eugene Debs, even while he mounted an attempt to repair the New Deal coalition Democratic Party politics in the United States, first in 2016 and again in the primaries of 2020. He sought not to win the nomination or the office of the presidency, but rather to try to rally what remains of the New Deal coalition and progressive liberalism in the Democratic Party. That he had to do that under the moniker of socialism is significant, even if it is misleading and false in fundamental ways. It is, nonetheless, significant that the industrialization of the United States in the Gilded Age did not lead to socialist revolution in the United States, and yet we are haunted by the possibility that it could and should have. Reid's lecture was all about the folding of American socialism and the Communist Party that emerged out of the crisis in American socialism into progressive liberal capitalism in the 1930s Great Depression era, as a function of the FDR New Deal settlement of American politics and society. That is the red thread traced through the series.

As I said in my lecture on the Gilded Age, this is not a Marxist approach to American history necessarily. The narrative that I just laid out does not depend on Marxism. It would be widely acknowledged by liberals and conservatives that there was a crisis in American politics with the emergence of industrial capitalism in the United States, and that there was a fundamental shift in the relationship between politics and society that has put a question mark over the Constitutional republican order of American politics, ever since the Progressive Era and, especially, FDR.

We still live with that question. What kind of democracy, democratic republic and Constitutional order is the United States? It doesn't take much of a crisis, but just a weakness of the major capitalist political parties, to throw the whole system into question, not only on the avowed Left, but across the political spectrum, across all varieties of political thinkers in the United States and around the world. In other words, over the past four years, and again with this election, people around the world are wondering about the United States' Constitutional order and its political system. That is the occasion for our lectures. Marxism would have to make sense within that broader world historic narrative of the American Revolution and the Constitutional republic that it gave birth to. Again, it's not an accident that rage was directed towards the statues of American Revolutionaries in this year. As I've written in my essay "Republicans and riots," it's a deeply ambivalent rage.[2] It's not a simple rejection but it's anger at the failure of the revolution that we've been facing this year.

## Q & A

**Richard Rubin:** Since I wrote in *The Platypus Synthesis* about the "Four types of ambiguity," which Pam mentioned, there's been a general political degeneration.[3] I was already speaking nostalgically when I spoke about liberals and Spartacists in 2009, and since then there's been a deterioration in

---

2    "Republicans and riots: The Left in death, 1992 and 2020," *Platypus Review* 130 (July – August 2020), in *Death of the Millennial Left: Interventions 2006–2022*.

3    "The Platypus Synthesis: Four types of ambiguity," (panel discussion, Platypus Affiliated Society International Convention, Chicago, June 2009), transcript available online at *Platypus1917*.

both. I agree with Pam's meta-question about how that affects Platypus. I think that the general Right-wing trend has subtle effects not only on liberals and the Spartacists, but also on Platypus.

The general emphasis in Platypus is on the general continuity and unity of the bourgeois revolution. But there are individual bourgeois revolutions. I wonder to what extent you see differences, as well as continuity, specific to the American Revolution, both from those that preceded it — like the Anglo and Dutch revolutions — and also perhaps the French Revolution succeeding it.

Two of the dates that were set up in this whole series were the opposition between 1619 and 1776. If we move to a period that follows the period that was covered in this lecture series, namely, the Cold War — Chris' quote from John F. Kennedy[4] brought this up, as well as comments by Reid — couldn't you say that after 1945 the two dominant states in the world were states that were born in revolution, the Soviet Union and the United States, in whatever deformed ways they represented those revolutions? Is there not a way that after 1945 the fundamental opposition in world politics begins to seem an opposition between 1776 and 1917? What is the relationship between those two dates?

**CC:** I think that it came up in one of the preceding lectures that in the 19th century the United States and Russia were seen, however differently, as resources, wellsprings for the counter-revolution. Russia as a political force of reaction in Europe, and the United States was a kind of pressure release valve for the European proletariat to emigrate to. Hegel, in his introduction to the Philosophy of History, observed that Russia and America were not in his consideration because they were the lands of the future. He left very unspecified what that meant, but we might assume that he meant they are the lands of the future of freedom since that was the subject of his lectures on the introduction to the philosophy of history. Certainly, the counter-position of 1776 and 1917 featured for the New Left, both the early New Left and figures who come out of the Trotskyist tradition,

---

4    "The American Revolution and the Left," *Platypus Review* 124 (March 2020), in *Death of the Millennial Left: Interventions 2006–2022*.

such as Raya Dunayevskaya, who wrote a book on "the spirit of 1776," precisely as a Hegelian Marxist or Marxist-Humanist. This contention has been occasionally explicitly referenced, for instance in the John F. Kennedy quote from 1960 that I gave in my *American Revolution and the Left* public form panel discussion opening remarks.

But after the Cold War we don't really have the juxtaposition of 1917 and 1776 any longer. Rather, we're left with what Christopher Hitchens called, from the early days of Platypus, the "last surviving revolution" — the American Revolution — to which he dedicated himself in his émigré status, as a New Leftist who became an American citizen and champion of American democracy, American liberalism and the American Revolution.

I hope that we are not living in a completely different era now than when Richard Rubin, Ian Morrison and I spoke in 2009 on the Platypus Synthesis.[5] That was right after the election of Barack Obama. I hope that we don't think that politics has qualitatively degenerated only with the election of Donald Trump. I hope that we don't concede to that canard, because I think that that would be a serious mistake.

At the same time, I do want to say something rather outlandish and provocative myself. The 2020 election promises to be quite tumultuous, and after 2016 we already had the specter of what James brought up: secession. People have said that now is the time, perhaps, for progressive liberal America to secede from conservative liberal America. Insofar as the results of the 2020 election might occur under some cloud of doubt, the specter of civil war is raised. I want to recall from comments from our panel back on the American Revolution in New York, that the US accomplishes through elections what in other countries requires civil wars, and in that respect every election is a little civil war, however peacefully conducted. We are looking at that in a particularly extreme form in 2020, precisely because, in many respects, the Democratic Party has never quite accepted the election results of 2016 and it would be an irony of history if the Democrats did lead a new secessionist movement that precipitated another civil war after 2020.

---

5   op. cit.

*It's somewhat old fashioned to ask, but I'm wondering how people respond to the issue that Socialism has always been historically weak in the US, and is this related to the American Revolution? It does appear that greater democracy in the US has made it such that parties like the SPD were not the right model. What is at issue? Is American civil society different? Is it constitutional? Or, is it simply a deficiency in organizing?*

*In our summer reading group in Platypus on Kautsky's Marxism, I was very surprised to see Kautsky say that the Second International had thought at its inception that America would have one of the fasted growing parties, and this was halted by the Haymarket affair in 1886, when suddenly public opinion side-lined the socialists. I was also struck by Spencer and Pam pointing out that a lot of these revolutionaries and socialists came to America in the 1850s, and the First International does seem to play some sort of role in the American Revolution. Could you clarify the relationship of the First and Second International to the American Revolution and within America?*

**CC:** There is an important parallel between our two different summer activities: our summer reading group on Kautsky's Marxism and on Second International Marxism more broadly, and this lecture series on the legacy of the American Revolution. They complement each other in a particular way. When Kautsky said that the expectation of the growth of American socialism taking off more rapidly was contradicted or checked by the reaction against the Haymarket uprising, that's perhaps true in the 1880s but by the end of the 1890s and the early 1900s that had been reversed. The Socialist Party of America did grow very rapidly. It was belated in comparison to the SPD but their rapid growths are contemporaneous, in the late 1890s and early 1900s.

Regarding the comparative weakness of American socialism, for instance as addressed by someone like Werner Sombart, the SPD has a much more proportionally significant place in German society and politics than the Socialist Party of America does in that era. But I wouldn't draw too sharp a distinction between the two because in the United States the Socialist Party of American was not merely a sect, it was not marginal the way we might imagine. I think that historical imagination is affected by later Stalinism. Stalinism starts the history of Marxism in 1917 and therefore the only significant socialist party in American history becomes the CPUSA, specifically the CPUSA of the 30s and 40s, before McCarthyism.

This willful neglect and forgetting of the Socialist Party of America before the First World War is tendentious and distorting in a particular way, and suppresses history in a particular way. This false memory hides the question of socialism behind the question of progressive liberalism and progressive capitalism. Of course, the Stalinists also claim that the New Deal is somehow a response to the pressure of American socialists or American communists, which is simply not true. It's far less true in 1932 and 1933 when FDR took office and implemented the New Deal, than it was in 1912 when Theodore Roosevelt ran as a Progressive. Theodore Roosevelt running as a Progressive was less of a response to the growth of the Socialist Party of America than it was a response to the growth of capitalism itself and the political crisis it brought about. The Left likes to claim that progressive liberal reforms are a response to the pressure of socialists or communists but that's really a rationalization for their own social movement activist pressure tactics on elected officials which is essentially the model adopted by the Left ever since the 1930s Stalinist era continuing through the New Left and up to today.

The history of American socialism goes all the way back to the early 19th century and does have a vital role in American civil life and maybe an indirect role in American political life, all the way up through WWI, in a way that it doesn't really subsequently. If we are going to say that the American Revolution is the one that endures in the 19th century — it's not about enduring today but enduring in the 19th century — not only liberal democracy as a political form, but bourgeois civil society is particularly vibrant in the United States in the 19th century, all the way up through the Gilded Age. Obviously, there is a certain brutality to the second industrial revolution in the United States but this doesn't contradict the fact that the United States remains bourgeois society throughout that period. That is why the question of progressivism, of a kind of progressive statism, is dated to either Woodrow Wilson or FDR. In other words, it is a fairly late development and the vibrancy of American socialism coincides precisely in the historical era of the 19th and early 20th century in which you could say that civil society had the advantage over the state and its politics; and, loses that purchase in civil society precisely with the rise of a kind of statist, progressive liberal capitalism, first with Woodrow Wilson through WWI and then finally with FDR and the New Deal.

*Chris said that you can say that the first party was Jefferson's Democratic Republican Party. Aren't the British Whigs the first real party, and Britain in the 18th century the first one-party state?*

**CC:** Jefferson had to win the election of 1800 against a growing consensus among the ruling class, in terms of the John Adams administration and Alexander Hamilton and what becomes of Federalism, so he has to mount a political campaign in the election of 1800 that perhaps he didn't anticipate ever having to do when the Constitution was ratified in 1787 and 1788 and under the Washington administration.

This raises the question of what that [new Democratic-Republican] political party is. It is the dominant party until its crisis, which Pam addressed, with its splitting and the rise of the new Jacksonian Democratic Party. That's why I distinguish between the first political party, because the Federalists didn't have to be a political party and there really is no place for political parties in the American Constitution in its original conception. It isn't set up to be a two-party system; it's set up to be a no-party system. And yet it becomes a party system, first with this push to renew and properly interpret the Constitution through the Jeffersonian revolution of 1800, but then in a totally different way with the rise of Andrew Jackson's Democratic Party.

It's interesting that the party in the US that opposes the Andrew Jackson Democrats call themselves the Whigs, and are precisely harking back to a kind of non-party democracy — namely, that of the 18th century in the United Kingdom. It would be a little bit anachronistic to call 18th century Britain a one-party state, in the sense of what we take that to mean. I think that it would be more accurate to say that it's really a no-party state, in the sense of modern political parties.

*Was not the main difference between the Democratic Party coalition in FDR's day and today the trading away of the southern racist vote who filled their shoes?*

**CC:** This is why I emphasized in my talk the fact that it's utterly forgotten that the Republicans were the black party. That's really the trade that occurs as a function of the Civil Rights movement. The Dixiecrats are abandoned in favor of the black vote. The Dixiecrats go from the Democrats to the Republicans and blacks go from the Republican to the Democratic Party. I would say that the difference between the Democratic Party of FDR's day and today is that it has a black constituency that it didn't have when FDR was elected, quite obviously.

But there was a black Republican patronage system, a very strong patronage system. They were given all sorts of jobs and offices in the federal bureaucracy throughout the US. When Woodrow Wilson is elected in 1912, there's a kind of purge of the federal government of blacks and part of that is seen in the segregation of Washington D.C. which up to that point had not been segregated. People forget that Martin Luther King's father famously said he'd never vote for a Democrat.

*Why doesn't Platypus start talking to the Right, since the Republican Party is ideologically bankrupt, and since the New Left is atrocious and undermining the country?*

**CC:** We always recognized that someone like Christopher Hitchens was Right-wing. But we also recognized — and this is really the stakes of my Gilded Age article and the whole question of progressive liberalism versus conservative liberalism and where socialism fits into that — that since FDR, in fact, certainly since the New Left, the degree to which the Left abandons the struggle for freedom then that's expressed by the Right. That's why there's the whole question of the New Right — neoliberalism and neoconservatism — both of which have roots before they emerge in the 1970s as a strong political force and feed into the Reagan revolution.

I always like to point out that, in a very literal sense, the neoliberals and neoconservatives are defectors from the Democratic Party. In other words, the Reagan revolution is really about dissent and defection from the ruling New Deal liberal progressive Democratic Party. There's an anecdote about the famous Mont Pelerin society where Ludwig von Mises, a classical liberal libertarian type, shows up and screams, "You're all socialists!" to people like Hayek and Milton Friedman, the ordo-liberals who became the neoliberals, because they had already accepted the prominent role of the state in society. They had already given in to progressive liberal capitalism. Even though they were dissenters from it in certain respects, they'd already conceded to it too much and therefore were already "socialists."

This problem is really a long-standing one. And I think it's the one on which the Millennial Left was defeated. How is socialism fundamentally different from progressive liberal capitalism?

*To the extent that we recognize that Marxism should be judged by the standards of 1776, rather than that 1776 should be judged by the standards of Marxism, are we not relinquishing Marxism as the determinant of our philosophical, historical, and political perspectives?*

**CC:** Well, 1776 can't survive unaltered in capitalism. The question is, what does Marxism mean to bourgeois freedom? Is it the negation of bourgeois freedom? Or is it rather the fulfillment of bourgeois freedom? Well, really that's the question of capitalism. Reid pointed out the fact that when, during the Cold War, the United States became the upholder of capitalism, the question of bourgeois freedom was submerged in a particular way. I would modify something about that, which is to say that in the Cold War, the East bloc called the West bloc "the fascist bloc." And the West called the Eastern bloc "red fascism." They both upheld the revolution but accused the other of betraying the revolution. That second part is really important.

Marxism remains important insofar as capitalism is a specific problem. If, however, capitalism is not a specific problem, in other words, if the problem of today's society is not capitalism but white supremacy, for example, then neither 1776 nor Marxism are relevant. Our point is that Marxism is only relevant if we're living in bourgeois society in crisis in capitalism and not living in white supremacy. If we're living in white supremacy, then of course Marxism is irrelevant because the bourgeois revolution is irrelevant.

**Richard Rubin:** If one accepts the diagnosis that everything is Right-wing because the Left is dead, is Platypus in some sense already Right-wing like everything else?

**CC:** I would say, also, about the colloquial sense of Right-wing, there was the avowed conservatism of the Socialist Party of America and its 1904 platform, meaning that it sought to conserve the values of the American Revolution. When Platypus first started, at the School of the Art Institute of Chicago and the University of Chicago simultaneously, the students at SAIC who were involved in starting Platypus were told by one of my colleagues, one of the faculty members there, "Oh, Platypus is trying to take us back 50 years?" So, conservative in that sense. My response to that was: "A hell of a lot longer than that! I want to take us back 100 years."

In this respect, built into our project is an emphasis on the question of history and how the past critiques the present, how the past surpasses the present, and consciousness of that. I think in the colloquial sense we're already seen as conservative, or as reactionary. I'm often called a reactionary and what's meant by that is that I want to take the Left back to some older style, more precisely, before the new social movements. Whether it's 50 years or 100 years, the accusation is that you want to undo the New Left. Yes! So, is that Right-wing? What would be Right-wing about that? Especially if the Socialist Party of America was trying to reclaim 1776 in 1904, does that mean they want to turn back the 19th century? Well, of course, in some ways they do: they want to overcome the effects of capitalism. And we want to overcome the effects of the 20th century, absolutely. But, as Reid just pointed out, because we're not a political project, we never aimed to do it ourselves, but rather to perform a necessary function in facilitating the possibility of that happening.

Adorno called this the dialectic of progressive and conservative viewpoints. Also, we should just admit that Adorno's usually seen as Right-wing, or at least conservative. But he's seen as Right-wing in the sense of a kind of cultural mandarin, someone stuck in the 19th century — very anachronistically because of course he's a 20th-century person. Also, interestingly, Lenin is often characterized as some kind of hold-over from the 19th century as well, as a conservative-bourgeois type of person in his sensibility.

It's all very loaded and, again, the legacy of the New Left is actually quite deep, in the sense that the Left is seen as necessarily counter-cultural, and if you're not counter-cultural, then you're Right-wing and you're conservative in the pejorative sense. That is the legacy of the New Left's own antinomianism, its own counter-culture but also more politically it's the way that the Cultural Revolution — the Maoist Cultural Revolution — was taken up as a model, very broadly.

Even when Richard has invoked the *Nation* magazine as the Right-wing of the Left and the Spartacist League as the Left-wing of the Left, the *Nation* magazine was no longer what it used to be. Adolph Reed, my old mentor, used to write for the *Nation*, but then he had a falling out with Katrina vanden Heuvel and the editorial mandate of the *Nation* magazine became more inimical to an Adolph Reed perspective. He saw that as a caving in to the racial politics of the Democratic Party which it, of course, was. When we see Keeanga-Yamahtta Taylor writing for the *New Yorker* and we see Bhaskar Sunkara writing regular op-eds in the *New York Times*, I think that it's nothing new. I think rather that something has been revealed, that already was the case when Platypus started out. Of course, when we said the Left was dead, when we started out in 2006-2007, we were saying liberalism, social democrats, Marxists, Trotskyists, Maoists, anarchists, were all dead in this respect. The reason that we wanted to include the broad Left was to include all of the symptoms of the death of the Left and our consideration of the historical legacy of the failure of Marxism and the disintegration — liquidation — of socialism. It is very unfortunate if we allow the suspicion that the very topic of the American Revolution is somehow Right-wing.

Originally published in *Platypus Review* 130 (October 2020)

# Socialism and capitalism

# The 3 Rs: Reform, revolution, and "resistance"

## The problematic forms of "anticapitalism" today

When we in Platypus conceived the topic of this forum on "Resistance" and the Left, we had in mind the title of a pamphlet written over a hundred years ago by the brilliant Marxist radical Rosa Luxemburg, titled *Reform or Revolution?*, which sought to argue for the necessity of *revolutionary* politics on the Left, not against *reforms*, but against a reform-*ist* perspective that was developing on the Marxist Left at the time, in which it was regarded that only reforms were possible — and hence that political and social revolution was not only unlikely and unnecessary, but undesirable as well.

We in Platypus seek to respond, in the present, to the development of the perspective on the Left that assumes that only "resistance" is possible. We find this to be a symptom of the degradation and degeneration of the Left over at least the past generation — over the last 40 years, since the 1960s "New" Left — and, indeed, for much longer than that. We find the current self-understanding of the Left as "resistance" to express despair not only at prospects for revolutionary transformation, but also for substantial institutional reforms.

We in Platypus seek to develop critical consciousness of the history of the Left, which we think is necessary for the possibility of emancipatory politics today and in the future. We understand the last, 20th Century, as one of the history of the defeat and decline — and ultimate disappearance — of the Left, as the 19th Century was of the Left's emergence and rise. We consider how we might suffer from a more obtuse grasp, a less acute consciousness, of socially emancipatory politics than those on the Left that came before us were able to achieve, how the Left has degenerated in both practice and theory.

In Rosa Luxemburg's phrase, the world in the crisis of the early 20th Century faced the choice of "socialism or barbarism."[1] But socialism was not achieved, and so perhaps the present is the descendant and inheritor of barbarism — including on the "Left."

So we seek to re-open the question and problem of anti-capitalist politics at the most fundamental levels, asking what it means to struggle against and seek to move beyond capitalism, and what makes this possible — and desirable. — This is what the name and the works of Marx signify to us.

Marx did not *invent* anti-capitalist politics or socialism, but rather sought to understand the significance of Left politics in light of history. Marx saw himself, and we regard him principally in his capacity of offering a critique of the Left, understanding its assumptions and aspirations in light of the historical development of possibilities, and thus seeking to push these further, through seeking to understand how the Left pointed beyond itself.

For instance, we follow Marx as a critic of the Left to the extent that we find that the conception of emancipation remains inadequate if understood as deriving primarily from struggles against exploitation and oppression. Rather, following Marx and his liberal predecessors, we seek to specify the freedom-problem expressed in the history of capitalist society, to clarify how capitalism is bound up with changes in the character of free humanity.

We find the true significance and meaning of anti-capitalist politics in its expression of how capital itself is the product of and continually creates possibilities for its own self-transformation and self-overcoming. Modern categories for emancipatory social struggles should be understood as part and parcel of capital and how it might point to its own transformation and self-abolition.

We find evidence of failure to grasp capital in this double-sided sense to the extent that the very conception of emancipation — as the freedom-in-becoming of the *new*, rather than the freeing of the prior-existent — to be virtually tabooed on the Left today. The Left today almost never

---

1   *The Crisis in German Social Democracy* (AKA *The Junius Pamphlet*), (1915).

speaks of freedom or emancipation, but only of "resistance" to the dynamics of change associated with capital and its transformations. The spirit of Marx's observation that in bourgeois society, under capital, "all that is solid melts into air," has been displaced by his other famous observation from the *Communist Manifesto* that "history is the history of class struggle" — but even this has been debased to the sense of the perennial suffering of the oppressed, taking the subaltern in its alterity, and not, as Marx meant in his notion of the proletariat, in the figuration of the new — and the new not as an end, but as an opening onto yet further possibilities.

A crucial distinction Marx found it important to make over a hundred and fifty years ago was between a progressive-emancipatory and reactionary-conservative critique and opposition to capital. Marx spoke of "reactionary" socialism, and categorized socialists of his day such as Proudhon, the coiner of the term "anarchism," among conservative and not progressive responses and oppositions to capital. Marx resisted the one-sided, Romantic critique of capital prevalent in his time, and understood socialism as being made possible by capital itself, as becoming possible only through capitalism.

But, with the reconsideration of Marx and Marxian critical theory must come reconsideration of the meaning of the history of subsequent Marxism. But this means treating the tradition of the revolutionary Marxist Left of the turn of the 19th and 20th and of the early 20th century, especially of its best and most effective exponents, Lenin, Luxemburg, and Trotsky, not in terms of what this Left actually accomplished, which from the standpoint of emancipation was minimal and quickly stifled and undone, but rather what the historical revolutionary Marxist Left strived for but failed to achieve.

Platypus seeks to reconsider the legacy of Marxist politics in order to understand our present as being conditioned — and haunted — by its failure, so that we can marshal its suppressed and buried history, its unfulfilled emancipatory potential, to the service of the critique of and the attempt to overcome the most fundamental assumptions of the present, including and especially those on the "Left."

Presented on a Platypus panel with Michael Albert (*Z Magazine*, author of *Parecon: Life After Capitalism*), Stephen Duncombe (Gallatin School of New York University, editor of *Cultural Resistance Reader*), Brian Holmes (Continental Drift and Université Tangente) and Marisa Holmes (new Students for a Democratic Society), November 6, 2007.

Originally published in *Platypus Review* 4 (April – May 2008)

# The future of socialism

## What kind of illness is capitalism?

The liquidation of [Marxist] theory by dogmatization and thought taboos contributed to the bad practice.... The interrelation of both moments [of theory and practice] is not settled once and for all but fluctuates historically.... Those who chide theory [for being] anachronistic obey the *topos* of dismissing, as obsolete, what remains painful [because it was] thwarted.... The fact that history has rolled over certain positions will be respected as a verdict on their truth-content only by those who agree with [Friedrich] Schiller that "world history is the world tribunal." What has been cast aside but not absorbed theoretically will often yield its truth-content only later. It festers as a sore on the prevailing health; this will lead back to it in changed situations.

– Adorno, *Negative Dialectics* (1966)[1]

The future of socialism is the future of capitalism — the future of capitalism is the future of socialism.

Socialism is an illness of capitalism. Socialism is the prognosis of capitalism. In this respect, it is a certain diagnosis of capitalism. It is a symptom of capitalism. It is capitalism's pathology. It recurs, returning and repeating. So long as there is capitalism there will be demands for socialism. But capitalism has changed throughout its history, and thus become conditioned by the demands for socialism. Their histories are inextricably connected and intertwined. This is still true today.

---

1    Trans. E. B. Ashton (London: Seabury Press, 1973), 143–44.

Society under capitalism in its concrete form will be conditioned by the need to realize capital. This means that society will be conditioned by the contradiction of capital. The future of socialism will be conditioned by that contradiction. This is an illness of self-contradiction of society in capitalism.

## Illness

What kind of illness is capitalism?

Friedrich Nietzsche described the modern affliction of nihilism in capitalism — he didn't use the term "capitalism" but described it — as an "illness, but the way pregnancy is an illness."[2]

Socialism is the pathology of capitalism — in terms of Marx and Engels's *Manifesto*, "communism" is the "specter" — and capitalism is the pathology of socialism, always threatening its return. The question is the prognosis of socialism — the prognosis of capitalism.

Capitalism is an illness — a pathology — of *potential*. We suffer from the unrealized potential of capital.

Capitalism is an imbalance of production and appropriation. It is a problem of how society produces, and how society appropriates its own production. As such it is a problem of metabolism. This is often referred to, for instance by Keynesians, as a problem of overproduction — a problem of underconsumption. But it is more self-contradictory than that. It is more than a temporary market imbalance awaiting correction, either by the state or by the market itself. Turning over the issues of production and consumption, we find that capitalism is also a problem of an overconsumption of resources — Marx called it the wearing-out of both the worker and nature — and an underconsumption of value, for instance in an overabundance of money without outlet as capital investment. It is also, however, an underproduction of resources — a wastage of nature and labor — and an overproduction of value. It is, as Marx called it, a problem of surplus-value — of its production and consumption.

The pathology of capitalism is a metabolic disorder. As capitalism is usually addressed by contemporary commentators, it is not however a

---

2　See *On the Genealogy of Morals: A Polemic* (1887), part II, sections 16–19.

disorder of scarcity or of (over-)abundance, nor of hierarchy or of equality — for instance, a problem of leveling-down. But, rather, as a problem of what Marx called the "social metabolism," it exhibits all of these symptoms, alternately and, indeed, simultaneously.

In the way that Nietzsche regarded capitalist modernity as an illness, but an illness the way pregnancy is an illness, it is not to be cured in the sense of something to be eliminated, but successfully gone through, to bring forth new life.

Is it a chronic or an acute condition? Capitalism is not well analogized to cancer because that would imply that it is a *terminal* condition. No. Rather than socialism waiting for capitalism to die, however, the question is whether socialism is merely a fever-dream of capitalism: one which chronically recurs, occasionally, but ultimately passes in time. Capitalism is not a terminal condition but rather is itself a form of life. A pathological form of life, to be sure, but, as Nietzsche — and Christianity itself — observed, life itself is a form of suffering. But what if capitalism is not merely a form of life — hence a form of suffering — but also a potential form of *new* life beyond itself? What if the recurrent symptom of socialism — the crisis of capitalism — is a pregnancy that we have failed to bring to term and has instead miscarried or been aborted? The goal, then, would be, not to eliminate the pregnancy of socialism in capitalism, not to try to cure the periodic crises of capitalism, but for capitalism to successfully give birth to socialism.

This would mean encouraging the health of capitalism in a certain sense. Perhaps humanity has proven too ill when undergoing capitalism to successfully give birth to socialism; but the pregnancy has been mistaken for an illness to be cured, rather than what it actually was, a symptom of potential new life in the process of emerging.

Past Marxists used the metaphor of "revolution as the midwife of history," and they used this very precisely. Socialist revolution would make socialism possible, but would not bring forth socialism ready-made. An infant — moreover one that is not yet born — is not a mature form of life.

These are the stakes of properly recognizing capitalism for what it is — the potential for socialism. If we mistake capitalism for an illness to be eliminated, then we undergo its pathology periodically, but fail to bring forth the new life that capitalism is constantly generating from within itself. The point then would be, not to avoid capitalism, not to avoid the pregnancy of socialism, but to allow capitalism to give birth to socialism. Bourgeois ideology denies that there is a new form of life beyond itself — that there is socialism beyond capitalism — and so seeks to terminate the pregnancy, to cure the ailment of capitalism, to eliminate the potential that is mistaken for a disease, whether that's understood as the infection by a foreign body, or a metabolic imbalance to be restored. But capitalism is not a malignant tumor but an embryo. The recurrent miscarriage of socialism, however, makes capitalism appear as a tumor — more or less benign, so long as it passes — or is extracted or otherwise extirpated.

As a cancer, capitalism appears as various kinds of cancer cells running rampant at the expense of the social body: whether of underclass criminals, voracious middle classes, plutocratic capitalists, or wild "populist" (or even "fascist") masses, all of whom must be tamped down if not eliminated entirely in order to restore the balanced health of the system. But capitalism does not want to be healthy in the sense of return to homeostasis, but wants to overcome itself — wants to give birth to socialism. Will we allow it?

For this would mean supporting the pregnancy — seeing the symptoms through to their completion, and not trying to stop or cut them short.

### Diagnosis

What is the prognosis of socialism?

Socialism is continuous with the "rights of human beings and citizens," according to the principles of "liberty, equality and fraternity," that "all men are created equal," with "inalienable rights" of "life, liberty and the pursuit of happiness." Socialism seeks to realize the bourgeois principle of the "free association of producers," in which each is provided "according to his need" while contributing "according to his ability." The question is how capitalism both makes this both possible and impossible, and what it would take to overcome its impossibility while realizing its possibility.

Moishe Postone, in his 2006 essay on "Theorizing the Contemporary World: Brenner, Arrighi, Harvey"[3] — a companion-piece to his

---

3  In *Political Economy of the Present and Possible Global Future(s)*, ed. Rob Albritton, Bob

other well-known essay from 2006, "History and Helplessness"[4] — grasped this contradiction of our time as that between islands of incipient post-proletarian life surrounded by seas of superfluous humanity — postmodernist post-humanism and religious fundamentalist defense of human dignity, in a world simultaneously of both post-proletarian cities of abundance and sub-proletarian slums of scarcity.

Peter Frase, in an early foundational article for the Democratic Socialists of America's *Jacobin* magazine in 2011, wrote of the "Four Possible Futures" — this was later expanded into the 2016 book subtitled "Life after Capitalism"[5] — on the supposed "inevitable end" of capitalism in four potential outcomes: either in the "communism of abundance and egalitarianism;" the "rentism of hierarchy and abundance;" the "socialism of egalitarianism and scarcity;" or the "exterminism of hierarchy and scarcity." The future was supposed to lie between two axes of contradiction: egalitarianism vs. hierarchy; and scarcity vs. abundance.

Unlike Postone — who, like Slavoj Žižek around the same moment, grasped the simultaneous existence of postmodernism and fundamentalism as two sides of the same coin of late capitalism — Frase neglects the dialectical proposition that all four of his "possible futures" will come true — indeed, that all four are already the case in capitalism. They are not merely in the process of coming true, but have been the actual condition of capitalism throughout its history, ever since its inception in the Industrial Revolution. There has been the coexistence of hierarchy and egalitarianism and of scarcity and abundance, and each has been the precondition for its — dialectical — opposite.

One could say that this has been the case since the early emergence of bourgeois society itself — that capitalist contradiction was always the case — or, indeed, since the beginning of civilization itself. One could say that this has been the condition of "class society as a whole," the condition of the existence of a "social surplus" throughout history.

---

Jessop, and Richard Westra (London: Anthem Press, 2010).

4  "History and Helplessness: Mass Mobilization and Contemporary Forms of Anticapitalism," *Public Culture* 18, no. 1 (2006), 93–110.

5  The article is from December 13, 2011. *Four Futures: Life After Capitalism* (London: Verso, 2016).

This is the perspective of Alain Badiou's "communist hypothesis," for example. Badiou has mobilized a rather literal reading of Marx and Engels's *Communist Manifesto*, and a straightforward, if rather naïve, interpretation of communism or socialism from Babeuf's "conspiracy of equals" onwards — indeed perhaps all the way back from Jesus and His Apostles onwards. "Communism" — in Peter Frase's terms, "egalitarian abundance" — is the "land of milk and honey," where the "last shall be first, and the first shall be last."

Capitalism, understood undialectically, then, is, by contrast, the exterminism of rentism, the inhumanity of exploitation, in which scarcity and hierarchy rule through elite appropriation of the surplus. But this has been true since the dawn of civilization, since the beginning — in terms of Engels's clever footnote to the *Manifesto*'s assertion that "history is the history of class struggle" — of "recorded history."

So what is different with capitalism? What has changed is the form of the social surplus: "capital." To say, as Marxists did, that, as the possibility for socialism, capitalism is the potential "end of prehistory" is to say that all of history is the history of capital: the history of civilization has been the development of the social surplus, until it has finally taken the form of capital.

Ancient civilizations were based on a specific kind of social surplus, however. The surplus of grain beyond subsistence produced by peasant agriculture allowed for activity other than farming. Peasants could tighten their belts to feed the priests rather than lose the Word of God, and so that some knights could protect them from the heathen. But for us to return to the religious basis of civilization would also mean embracing values quite foreign to the bourgeois *ethos* of work, such as that "the sick are blessed," with the divine truth of the vanity of life, whereas we rightly consider sickness to be a curse — at the very least the curse of unemployability in society.

So what is the social surplus of capital? According to Marx, capital is the surplus of labor. It is also, however, the source of possibilities for employment in production: the source of social investment. Does this make it the source of hierarchy or of equality, of scarcity or of abundance, of post-humanism or of ontological — fundamental — humanity? It is the source of all these different apparently opposed values. It is their common condition. It is society itself, albeit in "alienated" form. As such, it is also the source of society's possible change.

Socialism aims at the realization of the potential of society. But it will be achieved — or not — on the basis of capitalism, under conditions of capital. The social surplus of capital is the source of potential societal change, of new forms of production — manifold new forms of human activity, in relation to others, to Nature, and to ourselves. Changes in capital are changes in our social relations. Capital is a social relation.

Capital is the source of endless new forms of social scarcity and new forms of social abundance — of new forms of social expropriation and of social production — as well as of new forms of social hierarchy and of new forms of social equality. Capital is the source of all such changes in society over the course of the last two centuries, since the Industrial Revolution.

Hillary Clinton, in an interview during her failed campaign for President of the U.S., said that what keeps her "awake at night" is the problem of figuring out policy that will encourage the investment of capital to produce jobs. Indeed, this is precisely what motivated Trump's — successful — campaign for President as well. Interestingly, it is unclear whether this is what properly motivated Bernie Sanders as an alternative to Clinton, or if this now motivates Jeremy Corbyn as the head of the U.K. Labour Party. In the case of Corbyn and Sanders, it seems that they have been motivated less by the problem of capital and labor than by a more nebulous concern for "social justice" — regardless of the latter's real possibilities in capitalism. In the U.K., for example, Theresa May's "Red Toryism" — by prioritizing the circumstance of the "British worker," like Trump's stated priority for the "American worker" — is actually more realistic, even if it presently has a rather limited organized political base. Corbyn, as a veteran New Leftist "social justice warrior," is actually closer to the criteria of neoliberal politics than May, whose shifting Conservative Party is not (yet) able to support her agenda. By contrast, it is a solidly neoliberal Blairite Labour Party that Corbyn leads. But Brexit, and the crisis of the EU that it expressed, is changing the landscape. May is still, however, leading the way. As is, of course, Trump.

In this sense, the issue of socialism was closer to the actual concerns of Clinton and Trump than to Sanders. Sanders offered to his followers the

Obama Presidency that never was, of a "new New Deal" that is never going to be. By contrast, both Clinton and Trump were prepared to move on from the 2008 economic crisis: How to make good of the crisis of neoliberalism, now a decade old? For every crisis is an opportunity for capitalism. This is what must be the concern of *politics*.

This is the ageless question of capitalism: How is society going to make use of its crisis of overproduction, its surplus in capital — its surplus of labor? How are the social possibilities of capital going to be realized? What is the actual potential for society in capitalism?

Of course, the narrow horizons of the perspectives of both Clinton and Trump and of May for realizing the potentials of capitalism are less appealing than the apparent idealism of Corbyn and Sanders. But, realistically, it must be admitted that the best possible outcome — with the least disruption and danger — for U.S. and thus global capitalism at present would have been realized by a Clinton Presidency. If Trump's election appears to be a scary nightmare, a cruise into the unknown with a more or less lunatic at the helm, then, by contrast, a Sanders Presidency was merely a pipe-dream, a safe armchair exercise in idealism. Today, the stock market gambles that, whatever Trump's gaffes, the Republican Party remains in charge. The captain, however wild-eyed, cannot actually make the ship perform other than its abilities. The question is whether one trusts a CEO trying to build the company by changing it, or one trusts the shareholders who don't want to risk its profitability. Trump is not a safe bet. But he does express the irrepressible impulse to change. The only question is how.

### Prognosis

So the question of the future of socialism is one of potential changes in capitalism. The question is how capitalism has already been changing — and will continue to change.

What seems clear is that capitalism, at least as it has been going on for the past generation of neoliberalism, will not continue exactly the same as it has thus far. There has been a crisis and there will be a change. Brexit and the fall of David Cameron as well as Trump's victory and Hillary's defeat — the successful challenge by Sanders and the rise of Corbyn alongside

May's Premiership — cannot all be chalked up to the mere accidental mistakes of history.

In the face of historical change, continuity must be reckoned with — precisely as the basis for this change. How is neoliberal capitalism changing out of its crisis?

Neoliberalism is old and so is at least in need of renewal. The blush has gone off the rose. Its heroic days are long behind us. Obama rallied it to a certain extent, but Hillary was unable to do so again. The Republicans might be stuck in vintage 1980s Reaganism, but Trump is dragging them out of it. In the face of Trump, the question has been posed: But aren't we all good neoliberals? Not only Nancy Pelosi has said that, all respect to Bernie, we need not try to become socialists but remain capitalists. The mainstream Republican contender Marco Rubio said the same about Trump, while Ted Cruz retired to fight another day, against what he indicatively called Trump's "socialism." But the Tea Party is over. Now, the specter of "fascism" in the crisis of neoliberalism — which, we must remember, regards any and all possible alternatives to itself as more or less fascist — is actually the specter of *socialism*.

But what does the actual hope for socialism look like today? Does it inevitably appear as nationalism, only with a difference of style? Must the cosmopolitanism of capitalism take either the form of unmediated globalization (which has never in fact existed) or rather inter-nationalism, relations between nations? These apparent alternatives in themselves show the waning of neoliberal optimism — the decline of Clinton's "global village." We are now living — by contrast with the first Clinton era of the 1990s — in the era of neoliberal *pessimism*, in which all optimism seems reckless and frightening by comparison: Hillary's retort that "America is great already!" raised against Trump's "Make America Great Again!" Trump was critical of, and quite pessimistic about, existing conditions, but optimistic against Hillary's political pessimism — to which Hillary and Obama could only say that things aren't so bad as to justify (either Sanders or) Trump.

Were the Millennials by contrast too optimistic to accept Hillary's sober pragmatism — or were they so pessimistic as to eschew all caution of *Realpolitik* and embrace Sanders and Corbyn? Have they clung, after the election of Trump, now, to the shreds of lip-service to their concerns, as the best that they could hope for? Does Sanders — like Corbyn in the U.K. — merely say, better than Hillary or Obama, what they want to hear? By comparison, Hillary and Trump have been a salutary dose of reality — which is bitterly resented. Obama was the "change we can believe in" — meaning: very little if any. Clinton as the continuation of Obama was the sobriety of low-growth "realism." Now Trump is the reality of change — whether we like it or not. But it is in the name of the optimism for growth: "Jobs, jobs, jobs."

The problem of capitalism — the problem that motivates the demand for socialism — is that of managing and realizing the possibilities of a global workforce. This is in fact the reality of all politics, everywhere. All countries depend on international and, indeed, global trade, including the circulation of workers and their wages. Even the "Hermit Kingdom" of North Korea depends not only on goods in trade but on remittances from its workers abroad. This issue of the global workforce is the source of the problem of migration — the migration of workers. For instance, wars are waged with the problem of refugees foremost in mind. Political crisis seeks alleviation in either benign ways such as the "brain drain" of the emigrating middle-class, or malignantly in ethnic cleansing — in either case the exodus of restive surplus populations that cannot be integrated. International aid as well as military intervention is calculated in effects on migration: how to prevent a refugee crisis? The U.S. has paid countries like Egypt and Pakistan to subsidize their unemployed through bloated militaries. What is to be done with all those seeking work? Where will they find a job? It is a global problem.

Capital is the social form of this surplus of labor — the social surplus of production. Capital is the way society tries to manage and realize the potential of that surplus. But the source of that surplus is no longer so much human activity — labor — as it is science and technology. The problem is that, politically, we have no way of marshaling this surplus other than through possibilities for labor — for instance, through managing nation-states as labor markets. The question is realizing the potential possibilities of the social surplus beyond the reproduction of an increasingly redundant laboring workforce. Will they be starved or exterminated? Or will they be freed?

The only alternatives capitalism offers is in freedom *to* work — not the worst form of freedom the world has ever known, but its possibilities in capitalism are increasingly narrow. The question is the freedom *from* work. How will this be realized? There has been mounting evidence of this problem ever since the Industrial Revolution: unemployment. Social Darwinism was not a program but a rationalization for the crisis of capitalism. It remains so today. Will humanity free itself from the confines of capital — the limits of labor?

### Future

Were *Jacobin*'s Peter Frase's four possible alternative futures merely alternatives in rhetoric? Nearly no one claims to favor exterminism, scarcity, or inequality. The real future of capitalism does not actually belong to such expressions of pessimism. Fortunately, it will be appreciably better than our worst fears — even if, unfortunately, it will be much worse than our best desires. Capitalism for better or worse does indeed have a future, even if it will be different from what we are now used to. It will also be different from our dreams and nightmares.

*Jacobin*'s Frase seems to assume that not what he calls "communism" but "socialism" — the combination of egalitarianism and scarcity — is both more possible and more desirable: for Frase, abundance carries the danger, rather, of continued capitalist "rentism" and hierarchy. For Frase, among others, the future of social conflict seems to be posed over the terms of scarcity: equality vs. "extermination;" for instance, egalitarianism vs. racism.

Both Moishe Postone's and Peter Frase's antinomies — of postmodernism and fundamentalism, and of scarcity and egalitarianism (the latter combination as Frase's formula for "socialism") — are expressions of pessimism. They form the contemporary face of diminished hopes. But capitalism will not tarry over them. It will move on: it is already moving on.

What is the future of abundance, however with hierarchy — that of continued capitalism, that is, of "capital rents" — in society, and how does this potential task any future for socialism? Where will the demand for socialism be raised? And how is it to be realized?

We should not assume that capitalist production, however contradictory, is at an end. No. We are not at an end to forms of scarcity under conditions of abundance, or at an end to hierarchies conditioned by social equality.

Citizen Trump shows us this basic fact of life under continued capitalism.

As Walter Benjamin observed in conversation with Bertolt Brecht during the blackest hour of fascism at the midnight of the last century, we must begin not with the "good old days" — which were in fact never so good — but with the "bad new ones." We must take the bad with the good; we must take the good with the bad.

We must try to make good on the reality of capitalism. As Benjamin put it, we must try to redeem its otherwise horrific sacrifices, which indeed are continuous with those of all of civilization. History — the demand for socialism — tasks us with its redemption.

The future of capitalism is the future of socialism — the future of socialism is the future of capitalism.

### Addendum

Perhaps capitalism is the illness of bourgeois society, and socialism is the potential new form of life beyond the pregnancy of capitalism. Bourgeois society does not always appear as capitalism, but does so only in crisis. We oscillate in our politics not between capitalism and socialism but between bourgeois ideology and anti-capitalism — nowadays usually of the cultural ethno-religious fundamentalist communitarian and identitarian type: forms of anti-bourgeois ideology. But socialism was never, for Marxism at least, simply anti-capitalism: it was never anti-bourgeois. It was the promise for freedom *beyond* that of bourgeois society. The crisis of capitalism was regarded by Marxism as the tasking of bourgeois society beyond itself by socialism. It was why Lenin called himself a Jacobin; and why Eugene Debs called the 4th of July a socialist holiday. Socialism was to be the realization of the potential of bourgeois society, which is otherwise constrained and distorted in capitalism. So long as we live in bourgeois society there will be the promise — and task — of socialism.

Presented at the fourth Platypus European Conference closing plenary panel discussion, "What is the Future of Socialism?" with Boris Kagarlitsky (Institute of Globalization and Social Movements), Alex Demirovic (Rosa Luxemburg Foundation), Mark Osborne (Alliance for Workers' Liberty, Momentum) and Hillel Ticktin (*Critique* journal), at Goldsmiths University in London on February 17, 2018.

Originally published in *Platypus Review* 105 (April 2018)

# What is capitalism?

## Robots and sweatshops

Starting with the Industrial Revolution, there have been two contrary tendencies in the development of social production: increased automation lowering socially necessary labor-time; and the desperation of people rendered superfluous as workers.

For Marxism, this presented a social and political task for the working class to demand higher wages for fewer hours.

An alternative to this would be for workers to try to fight against technology — the Luddites.

Conversely, the capitalists could invest in machines instead of labor.

Thus was born the antagonism between wage-labor and capital.

The outcome of the class struggle between the workers and capitalists was to be the realization of the potential for both increased production and the reduction of human toil: socialism.

However, since machine production created a permanent class of unemployed people, there would always be a demand for work that could be exploited by the capitalists to pay lower wages.

Paying lower wages decreases the market for produced goods, which means a drive for higher profitability, leading to further pursuit of cost-efficiency in production as well as depression of wages.

That leads to both robots and sweatshops.

Disparities and imbalances between capitalist profits and workers' wages lead to periodic crises in which there is money that cannot find profitable investment and workers who cannot find employment.

638 · Socialism and capitalism

But eventually balance is restored through the cheapening of money-capital — and the cheapening of labor.

New forms of work are developed to serve new technologies of production. — Until the next crisis begins the cycle all over again.

This meant that the working class as a whole — both employed and unemployed — needed to be organized as a social and political force to ensure increased social wealth and to prevent exploitation.

Since this is a matter of the organization of society as a whole — including internationally, and indeed globally, in the cosmopolitan exchange of wage-labor and capital — it requires the political act of taking state power: world socialist revolution.

### Jobs and free stuff

The current political polarization in the U.S. is not Democrat vs. Republican or the minorities of race, gender and sexuality against straight white men: It is between the politics of free stuff vs. the politics of jobs — demands for more free stuff vs. demands for more jobs.[1]

"Democratic socialist" candidate for Democratic Party nomination for President Bernie Sanders has responded to charges that he is actually a communist with the assertion that the U.S. is already socialist, but it is a socialism for billionaires. The kernel of truth in this is that there is already government subsidy and other kinds of support for capital. The question is, why is this so? Corruption? Or rather is it actually in the interest of society? Of course it is the latter — the general interest of capitalist society, which both Parties serve (as best they can).

Karl Marx observed that the productive activities of general social cooperation are a "free gift to capital." What did he mean? The social process of production is not at all reducible to the paid wage-labor of capitalist employees, but includes the activity of everyone in society. As Frankfurt School Director Max Horkheimer wrote, in "The little man and

---

1   See my "Why not Trump again?" in *Death of the Millennial Left: Interventions 2006–2022*; and "The end of the Gilded Age: Discontents of the Second Industrial Revolution today" and "The future of socialism: What kind of illness is capitalism?" both in this volume.

the philosophy of freedom," "All those who work and even those who don't, have a share in the creation of contemporary reality."[2]

Whether in terms of Andrew Yang's proposed "freedom dividend" of free money for all in a UBI or free public education and health care for all, the question is not who's going to pay for it, but rather how can capital make use of it. These are not anti-capitalist demands but demands for the better functioning of capital. The question is, what are we going to do in our society with all the fruits of our production — with all our free stuff? How can we make it benefit everyone? Is it just a matter of better shaving off more crumbs?

Yang proposes that the invaluable but currently unpaid labor of mothers, inventors and artists should be supported by society. Marx called this the communism of the principle of "from each according to ability, to each according to need" in a society in which the "freedom of each is the precondition for the freedom of all." We already live in capitalism according to this principle, but capital fails to fulfill it.

The Democrats propose to make capital fulfill its social responsibility; the Republicans think it already does so as best as possible, and any attempts at government intervention to make it do better, no matter how well intentioned the reforms, will actually be counterproductive. The result will be stagnation and lack of growth, undermining society along with capital. Without people working there can be no greater social benefits of production; without jobs there can be no free stuff.

This is the essential difference in U.S. politics or really in capitalist politics everywhere: progressive capitalism vs. conservative capitalism. Not spendthrift vs. frugality or kindheartedness vs. cynicism or liberality vs mean-spiritedness, nor is it optimism vs. pessimism or idealism vs. realism. It is a division of labor in debate over advocating how to keep people working and how to distribute freely the products of their labor. It is not a difference in principle or one of honesty vs. deception: both sides are sincere — and both sides are self-deceiving.

---

2   Horkheimer, *Dawn & Decline: Notes 1926–31 and 1950–69* (New York: Seabury, 1978), 51.

Marx observed that the free gift to capital is the "general social intellect." But that general social intellect has become the "automatic subject" of capital. How do we make it serve us, instead of us serving it? All politicians in capitalism want the same thing. The problem is that capitalist politics is not as intelligent as the society it represents. This is the true meaning of socialist politics — to realize the general social intellect — which today unfortunately is inevitably just a form of capitalist politics, whether by Sanders, Yang or Trump. They all want to better serve us — which means better serving capital.

## Capital and Labor

According to Marx, capitalism is the contradiction of bourgeois social relations and industrial forces of production. The effect of this self-contradiction of bourgeois society in industrial production is the division of capital and labor. It is from this division that the opposed classes of capitalists and workers derive. The class struggle between workers and capitalists is a phenomenon — the phenomenal expression — of the self-contradiction of capitalism. It expresses labor's contradiction with itself — which is also capital's contradiction with itself. When referring to "capital and labor" there are actually just two forms of capital — Marx called these "variable and constant" as well as "fixed and circulating" capital — and both refer to labor — Marx called capital "alienated labor." Labor and capital are two aspects of the same thing in capitalism. The bourgeois social relations of production are the social relations of labor.

The usual oppositions posed by the labor movement and by socialism, such as profit vs. human needs (and the needs of the natural world beyond humanity), are expressions of this self-contradiction of society in capitalism, the needs of capital as opposed to the needs of labor. The contradiction of capital is not external but internal.

Marx described capitalism as "false necessity." What he meant by this was not simply wrong necessity, but rather self-contradictory necessity. For the needs of capital and the needs of labor are the same. In becoming opposed in capitalism, there is the conflict of labor with itself as well as of capital with itself.

In capitalist politics, there is another phenomenon — expression — of capital's self-contradiction, namely, the disputes among capitalist politicians over government policy, which can also express conflicting interests of different capitalists, including different sectors of industry, between different capitalist nation-states, etc. Workers employed in different occupations as well as in industries can thus have different and conflicting interests, competing over the priorities of social investment in capital. The opposed aspects of capital — and of labor — are inseparable. Labor cannot be extricated from capital any more than capital can be from labor.

The goal of socialism is to realize capital as well as labor — to negate labor as well as capital. It is to realize as well as negate — overcome — capitalist necessity. What would such *Aufhebung* [sublation] mean?

Discontents in capitalism take various different and even opposed forms. The history of socialism itself as well as the history of capitalism expresses self-contradictory desires and goals. At different moments in the history of capitalism, the goals of socialism have taken various different and indeed opposed forms. For instance, socialism has variously regarded its goals as realizing the potential of capitalist production as opposed to abolishing capitalist production: achieving hyper-industrialism versus returning to subsistence primitivism[3] have both found home at one time or place or another in the struggle for socialism. Socialism could be defined as both and neither of the opposed alternatives that capitalism generates as its own positive goals and its own self-negations. All the various opposed demands arising from the discontents in capitalism will be both fulfilled and negated — overcome — in socialism.

Capital seeks to abolish labor and labor seeks to abolish capital — but more importantly in capitalism capital seeks to abolish itself and labor seeks to abolish itself. By making labor more productive it becomes less necessary; by producing excess capital it becomes more superfluous — less a real measure of social value. Labor seeks to abolish itself in capitalism, and thus to abolish capital, tasking socialism.

---

3   See the articles in the *Platypus Review* issue 125 (April 2020) published to commemorate the 50th anniversary of the first observation of Earth Day, April 22 (the same date as Lenin's birthday), in 1970 (thus on the 100th anniversary of Lenin's birth in 1870).

Only by encompassing the wide variety of discontents within the working class and across the history of its developments in capitalism could the political movement for socialist revolution to overcome capitalism become adequate to its task and mission, by becoming conscious of it. Since capital is the product of labor and labor the product of capital, this would mean encompassing the divisions among the capitalists as well as within capitalism itself as a total movement of society. The achievement of socialist revolution would be when the working class can take responsibility politically for capitalism as a whole. In so doing, the working class would confront the choices posed by the contradictions of capitalism that are otherwise expressed by the conflicts between the different capitalists and thus among workers of the world. All the conflicts exhibited in the world must be grasped as expressions and various forms of the self-contradiction of capitalism. Such conflicts are necessary — to be overcome.

The false necessity of capitalism as self-contradictory but opposed real needs can only be truly engaged and overcome from the standpoint of universal world history.[4] This can only take place from within the social antagonisms of capitalism, and not from partial, single-sided aspects of its contradictory totality.

The "workers of the world must unite" because the world is united in its self-contradiction and crisis in capitalism. The laborers must themselves take up and overcome the social relations of labor in crisis in capitalism by assuming the socialist political responsibility for capital that is eluded by capitalist politics.

Otherwise, the social conflicts in capitalism — between and among its capitalists and workers — will reproduce its contradictions forever.

---

4   See my "Capital in history: The need for a Marxian philosophy of history of the Left," in this volume.

Presented on a panel discussion with Dick Howard (Distinguished Professor Emeritus at Stony Brook University), Chris Nineham (founding member and vice chair of the Stop the War Coalition), Shane Mage (former senior editor of Economics and Social Science for *Collier's Encyclopedia*), Leo Panitch (Distinguished Research Professor of political science at York University), May 23, 2020.

Originally published in *Platypus Review* 129 (September 2020)

# Socialism in the 21st century

## The 21st century

Last year at the Platypus international convention closing plenary discussion, I spoke on the issue and problem of "Redeeming the 20th century."[1] There I commented on the phenomenon of the neo-social democratic and neo-Stalinist turn of the Millennial Left in the Bernie Sanders campaign[2] of 2016 and the Jeremy Corbyn-aligned Momentum caucus of the UK Labour Party. I titled my talk "Statism and anarchy today" and addressed the phenomenon of socialism and Marxism being mistakenly identified with statism and freedom being mistakenly identified with the anarchy of capitalism. — I have been thinking a lot lately about Karl Popper's liberal "open society" of freedom and unavoidable risk contra socialism's false and self-defeating promise of security.

In previous convention talks over the last few years, I have sought to address the problems we inherit from the past 100 years, which I called the "century of counterrevolution,"[3] following the failure of socialism after the 1917 Russian Revolution.[4]

I intended today to elaborate on the difference recognized by original historical Marxism between progressive capitalism and socialism,[5] and to

---

1   "Redeeming the 20th century: Statism and anarchy today," *Platypus Review* 116 (May 2019), in this volume.

2   "The Sandernistas: The final triumph of the 1980s," in *Death of the Millennial Left: Interventions 2006–2022*.

3   "1918–2018: The century of counterrevolution," *Platypus Review* 106 (May 2018), in this volume.

4   "1917–2017," *Platypus Review* 99 (September 2017), in this volume.

5   "The end of the Gilded Age: Discontents of the Second Industrial Revolution today,"

review the history from the late 19th century origins of Progressivism up to today. I was going to take the occasion of the impending defeat of Bernie Sanders's primary campaign this year for nomination as Democratic Party candidate for President.

But the coronavirus crisis has intervened, rekindling hopes in far-reaching government reforms of capitalism, for instance seeming to pose the need for Medicare for All public insurance for health care as well as student loan debt forgiveness and even a Universal Basic Income (UBI)[6] to deal with the pandemic. Trump[7] and the Republicans he leads and not only the Democrats have been alleged to have embraced "socialism" in the crisis.

In the aftermath of the 2016 election and sudden explosion of growth of the Democratic Socialists of America (DSA) in response to Trump,[8] I declared the Millennial Left "dead."[9] At the time, it was commented that my declaration was "sublimated spleen" — repressed melancholy at the losses of the Millennial Left. Now, regarding the growing wave of disease about to engulf us and desperate attempts to stem the menacing tide of misery from economic and other social devastation and dislocation, I am struck by how the Millennial generation has had to endure the worst catastrophes to have occurred during my lifetime, the War on Terror, the Great Recession, and now perhaps the worst plague in more than a century — the gravest scourge since the 1918 Spanish Flu. This does not change the verdict of history,[10] which, as the young Nietzsche recognized, is not merciful let alone sympathetic in its judgments, but is rather relentlessly ruthlessly "critical." As Marx observed, in his historical moment, and at his similarly relatively young age of 25 years, it is necessary to be "ruthless" in the "critique of everything existing." And as Engels observed, quoting

---

*Platypus Review* 102 (December 2017 – January 2018), in this volume.

6    "Jobs and free stuff," *Platypus Review* 129 (September 2020), in this volume.

7    "Why not Trump again?," *Platypus Review* 123 (February 2020), in *Death of the Millennial Left: Interventions 2006–2022.*

8    "Why not Trump?," *Platypus Review* 89 (September 2016), in *Death of the Millennial Left: Interventions 2006–2022.*

9    "The Millennial Left is dead," *Platypus Review* 100 (October 2017), in *Death of the Millennial Left: Interventions 2006–2022.*

10   "Capital in history: The need for a Marxian philosophy of history of the Left," *Platypus Review* 7 (October 2008), in this volume.

Goethe's Mephistopheles, "everything that exists deserves to perish." — Is this the perishing we deserve?

## Back to basics

In the interest I serve that Marxism not perish entirely, I want to get back to basics and define the task of socialism properly. This means defining the problem of capitalism properly.

First, it is important to address what capitalism is not. It is not greed or profiteering, nor is it exploitation — all recognized sins and crimes in this society. Capitalism is not a social system or moral order or set of values — it is a crisis of the social system, moral order and set of values. The society we live in is bourgeois society.[11] We live in bourgeois values and morality. Capitalism is the contradiction of that society and its values. And contradiction does not mean hypocrisy.

Rosa Luxemburg called capitalism "the wage system," and her book masterpiece was on *The Accumulation of Capital*. This suggests the problem of capitalism that Marxism thought tasked socialism, namely, the crisis of capital accumulation that undermined and destroyed the social value of wage labor.[12]

Georg Lukács observed the phenomenon of "reification" in capitalism, and described this, among other things, as a reversal of cause and effect.

We commonly identify capitalism with class inequality and hierarchy[13] and its resulting relationships of exploitation, but we are given to think that this is the cause of the problem of capitalism, rather than, as Marxism properly recognized, the effect of capitalism.

---

11  "Class consciousness (from a Marxist perspective) today," *Platypus Review* 51 (November 2012), in this volume.

12  "The future of socialism: What kind of illness is capitalism?" *Platypus Review* 105 (April 2018), in this volume.

13  "Class consciousness," op cit.

648 · Socialism and capitalism

## Marxist recognition of capitalism

For Marxism, after the Industrial Revolution,[14] capitalism exhibits a crisis of the value of labor in social production. But the value of labor, specifically of labor-time, is still the measure and still mediates the value of social production in capitalism. In short, and without explaining how this works in Marx's view, it is the self-contradiction of the value of labor-time that produces as a result the conflict between the value and social right of capital with the social right and value of wage-labor. In capitalism there is a conflict of social rights between labor and capital; but Marxism understood this as a conflict of labor with itself, since capital was nothing but alienated labor. Reification in Lukács's sense meant a reversal of cause and effect such that capital appeared as a thing separate from labor; but as Nikolai Bukharin put it, in *The ABC of Communism*, capital is not a thing but a social relation. Specifically, it is the self-contradictory social relation of labor with the means of production, or, the contradiction of two aspects of value in social production, capital and labor, namely, between past accumulated dead labor and present living labor.

The self-undermining and self-destructive character of the disparity between the diminishing value of human labor-time in industrial social production and capital as the "general social intellect" of technique and organization in production and the reproduction of society — what my old professor Moishe Postone described after Marx as the "shearing effect" and resulting antagonism between labor and the needs of its reproduction and its results and effects in society — has as its expression the phenomena of inflation, the necessity of interest in credit, and finance as the necessary form of speculation — namely, the claim of the past and present on the future — in investment in production.

The result of massive and constantly increasing productivity in industry is the cheapening of labor and thus the cheapening of value. But this cheapening threatens the value of investment and its speculation, hence the crisis of social value in capital. Attempts to preserve value in capital result in accumulation and concentration, producing a separate capitalist class of

---

14 "Robots and sweatshops," *Platypus Review* 129 (September 2020), in this volume.

investors, who, in Marx's words, are not rich because they are captains of industry, but rather become captains of industry merely because they are rich: they are capitalists in the sense of not merely owners of capital, but rather are the agents and servants of capital. Capital does not follow the dictates of the capitalists; but the capitalists follow the dictates of capital.

Capital is not profiteering, because profiteering is compelled by constantly diminishing value in capital, to preserve the value of investment. All production in capitalism is in this sense profit-driven, but not because profit is the goal or the ends of production, but rather because profit is the means by which capital preserves its value. Workers have an interest in the profitability of the capital that employs them, to preserve social investment in their work.

Marxism thus considered capitalism to be a general social compulsion to produce and preserve value in the form of capital to which all — everyone — in society are subject. In this sense, everyone in capitalism is a capital-ist, namely a follower of capital.

And capital does not mean money; rather, as we already call it, "human capital," labor itself is a form of capital, and is of course the most important form of capital: Marx called it "variable" as well as "circulating capital."

Crises of value in capital characteristically result — as in the recent Great Recession — in the twin phenomena of superfluous labor and superfluous money: money that cannot find investment as capital; and labor that cannot find employment in social production. This results in the destruction of existing concrete forms of production — the destruction of the concrete manifestations of capital — which means the depreciation of money and the unemployment, starving and perishing of the workers, the idling of machines and factories, the bankruptcy and dissolution of firms, etc.

All of this is to help explain what Marxism originally meant by capitalism being not a social system, but rather a contradiction of the bourgeois social relations by the industrial forces of production. Bourgeois social relations, for instance private property, meant the social relations of labor — for as we know from the bourgeois revolutionary thinker John Locke, the social rights of property are based in the social rights of labor — namely, the self-ownership of the workers to freely dispose of their labor as a commodity, for instance in the employment contract. For Marxism, industrial production represented the self-contradiction of the social relations of labor.

As Marx and Engels put it in the *Communist Manifesto*, it was capitalism itself which abolished — undermined and destroyed — private property, not only in the form of capital but also and most importantly in the form of labor: industrial production abolished the value of labor as a commodity. Nonetheless, this constant self-destruction of value was the occasion for its reconstitution and reproduction in different concrete forms after each crisis in value. In short, so long as there were starving workers desperate for employment, the social value of labor would be reconstituted — however, it was subject to self-destruction, restarting the cycle of capital accumulation again.

## The true task of socialism

Socialism arose, from the perspective of Marxism, from this constant self-contradiction, crisis, destruction, and demand for the reconstitution of the social value of labor. As such, socialism was an expression of capitalism, namely, an expression of the contradiction of bourgeois social relations and industrial forces of production. As the advocacy of the social value of labor, socialism was an expression of the demands of the reconstitution of the bourgeois social rights of labor, namely, its social value.

As all serious thinkers of capitalism have recognized, capital is meant to be a means to the ends of social production, namely, of serving and sustaining a society of labor. That capital has reversed this and become an end in itself and social labor a mere means to capital, this is the perversion that is denounced as capitalism, or the subordination and domination of society to the dictates of capital, to the compulsion to produce, reproduce and preserve the value of labor after it has been diminished, undermined and destroyed by industrial production.

In this sense, the task of socialism that Marxism recognized in industrial capitalism already nearly two centuries ago remains today.

However, the clarity that Marxism achieved about the true nature and hence purpose or end of this true task of socialism, to overcome the social relations of labor, has been obscured and lost. Instead, we have at present calls for socialism, as were posed already before Marx and Marxism, by pre-Marxian socialism, more naïvely and less critically consciously, based on preserving the value of labor. Even calls for UBI, for instance in the recent Presidential campaign of Andrew Yang, are based on the social value of labor that fails to find monetary compensation on the market.

Supposed "socialism" today means the state and hence political management of capitalism — the administrative maintenance of the working class when capital fails to do so. But this means trying to preserve capitalism against its own self-contradiction and crisis in social production.

Finally, a note on another way that capitalism is characteristically misrecognized, namely as competition and resulting individualism, including the competition of social groups in capitalism as "individuals," for example, nations and other concrete collectives (hence nationalism and other forms of competitive communitarianism): it is the self-contradiction and crisis of value in labor that drives workers against each other competitively in zero-sum games for survival — rather than, as the original consciousness of bourgeois society recognized, a function of the development of cooperation, to lose one's job in an obsolescent industry that loses to competition just means switching to a new and different form of employment. This development of social cooperation in production still occurs in capitalism, of course, but it is the tendency of diminishing and self-undermining value of labor in capitalism that renders such development fragmentary and unfulfilled, unnecessarily destructive and wasteful. So individualism and competitiveness are, again, not the cause but rather the effect of the problem of capitalism.

Presented on a panel with Jamal Abed-Rabbo (Democratic Socialists of America), Patrick Quinn (Solidarity, Democratic Socialists of America) and Earl Silbar at the closing plenary discussion of the twelfth Platypus Affiliated Society International Convention, April 4, 2020.

Originally published in *Platypus Review* 126 (May 2020)

# We are all Friedmanites now!

Milton Friedman famously declared, on the threshold of the neoliberal revolution he helped usher in, "We are all Keynesians now!" Also around this time, Michel Foucault said that "We are all Marxists now." The point was to thus thrust aside, by treating as safely past, something longstanding as a banality that could be ignored — as Marx said the Young Hegelians had done to Hegel. Friedman, like Hegel, might be wrongly overlooked by subsequent generations as a "dead dog."

Jennifer Burns, in her monumental biography, *Milton Friedman: The Last Conservative* (2023)[1], wants to do the opposite: make us recognize the enduring power of Friedman's ideas in our current post-neoliberal moment, even and precisely when we might think we are past them. Burns quotes Joe Biden from his 2020 campaign for President that, "Milton Friedman isn't running the show anymore!" But the question then would be, "Who is?" Burns's point is not that Friedman still is, but that perhaps he should be. But it is not the Friedman most people know. If we are haunted by Friedman, it is not his fault but ours. So the challenge is to read Friedman against the grain of his own and subsequent history, in terms of unfulfilled potential.[2]

For it is not only the case that Friedman's profound legacy will remain with us concretely in the ongoing practices we inevitably inherit from neoliberalism in multiple and manifold domains, but also in our thinking; and not merely as undigested, unreflected and unconscious repetition, but at the level of the truth of his vision. We might remain with Friedman because he was right. And not simply in terms of what he grasped about capitalism, but

---

1   New York: Farrar, Straus and Giroux.
2   See my "Friedrich Hayek and the legacy of Milton Friedman," in *The Death of the Millennial Left* (Sublation, 2023).

as he tasks us to change it. So it is not a matter of how he was wrong or right in this or that issue. Friedman's thought might see beyond his time — and ours.

This is what Friedman himself meant about Keynes. Part of the problem is that we treat Friedman as an intellectual figure opposed to Keynes rather than growing out of him. We are misled to do so by considering matters merely in terms of policies and polarized differences. As his biographer writes, "his work lies at the intersection of fundamental problems that will never be solved and ongoing tensions that will never be eased."[3] Neither Keynes nor Friedman had their desired programs fulfilled. They were taken up only partially in policy, and so, in important respects, not at all. This is what makes them pertinent to us, still: to not forget what they wanted, and recall their incomplete projects. Friedman declaring himself a Keynesian meant that he wanted to fulfill Keynes better than he had been able to achieve himself. In becoming common sense, Keynes was betrayed. The same has now happened to Friedman. The attempt to discard Friedman, as Burns writes, "betrays an anxiety" that implicitly acknowledges "how fundamental Friedman's style of economic analysis and his skepticism about government regulation have become to liberals as well as conservatives."[4]

The same had happened earlier with Keynes and his cohort of reformers of mid-20th century capitalism. Their ideas were not enacted so much as used to authorize the designs of others. In Keynes's case, this involved ignoring his decided internationalism, indeed cosmopolitanism, in favor of nationalist economic projects. Because Friedman is associated with neoliberal globalization leading to socioeconomic disparities and hierarchies within rather than between countries, we might forget, as Burns is anxious to remind us, Friedman's egalitarian concerns. But not directed against the rich — whose wealth he considered incidental — but rather in favor of the poor, whose condition is the true index of the wealth and health of society. This is why for Friedman the latter were to be the true beneficiaries of his policies apparently favoring the former, the infamous "rising tide that raises all boats" we are tempted to mock — at our peril. There is still a crisis of capitalism.

---

3    Ibid., 481.
4    Ibid., 475.

How this apparently "reversed" Keynes has become obscure to us today: Keynes recognized that the only meaningful variable in the economy was the money in the hands of the working class as consumers; the amount of money as capital in the hands of the rich investors was by comparison secondary and of little effect. (Keynes's observation was confirmed in the recent Great Recession investment drought, in which the capitalists were for a significant time sitting on their money and failing to invest their capital.) This was the difference between so-called "supply-side" economics ostensibly advocated by Friedmanite neoliberalism versus the "demand-side" approach attributed to Keynes. But, looked at more closely, the supposed "social welfare" aspect of Keynesianism vs. the more limited and technical "monetarist" (money-supply) concern of Friedmanism disappears: both are varieties of monetary policy; both are based on desire for freeing up money-capital to grease the stuck wheels of the economy. Keynes and Friedman agreed on the basic nature of the problem, and they even agreed fundamentally on the solution.

But circumstances change, and so do the implications at the level of policy implementation. Just as Burns observes that Friedman's solutions remain operant in today's proposed post-neoliberal policies, it was true back in his day that the neoliberal revolution was a continuation in its essentials of Keynesian economics. Burns is not unsympathetic to Friedman, even while her biography of him reads as a forensic case against him as much as a tragicomedy of Friedmanism's follies. In her account, Friedman appears most clueless precisely when he's seemingly in the driver's seat. Her narrative of Pinochet's Chile — Friedman's most notorious affair — depicts a dictator interested neither in Friedman's goals nor his philosophy, and former students calling upon the master to endorse them in doing what they wanted to do anyway. As Burns writes, "How important was Friedman's visit to shaping economic policy in Chile? As it turns out, the decision to shift away from gradualism had already been taken by the time he arrived. . . . To brace the government for what was to come, the Chicago Boys had flown in a ringer."[5] Their honoring him hardly affirmed his thought, but served only to make him culpable — not that Friedman was guileless.

---

5   Ibid., 368.

The epigraph with which Burns begins her book is telling in this respect: that Friedman's "ideas were lying around" when the policy-crisis came in the 1970s, but their "impossibility" becoming "inevitability" was more in serving as an opportunist rationalization rather than a genuine historical triumph. If Friedman was guilty of anything, it was not for his ideas but in allowing them to be misused.

What about MMT (Modern Monetary Theory), then — is this the "idea lying around" in the current crisis and transition to a form of capitalism after neoliberalism? Is it Keynesian? Is it Friedmanite? Paradoxically, although it is called "modern," its foundational roots in economic thinking are actually more than a century old, predating both mid-20th century Keynesianism and subsequent Friedmanite neoliberalism. Like both of them, however, MMT is "heterodox" — a departure from reigning orthodoxy — and yet is still recognizable according to existing thinking. Like prior orthodoxies that started out as heresies, it might be taken up only in a partial and not total way.

For Friedman never did cease playing the part of a "pixie or pest" to which he had been consigned before his long belated official recognition. To the end, in life he remained a gadfly with a twinkle in his eye rather than a revered authority. In this respect he was very much like another seeming titanic figure of the New Right, William F. Buckley, Jr., founder of *National Review*. Their faces might have been plastered all across the public square, their voices ringing in everyone's ears — both, notably, through the medium of the television screen — but this cannot be equated with the real power of their ideas: was anyone actually listening to them, or hearing only what they wanted them to say? Bestowing laurels is the surest way to silence the critic, since the public can consider their case to have been won — and thus closed.

One way of understanding how and why Friedman's desired program was implemented only in part — or by half — is to find the tension, perhaps even contradiction, between "free markets" and "upward redistribution" of income. In neoliberal capitalism, we might have gotten only the latter and not the former — and under the former's mere banner.

So the question is, why was there a need to redistribute income upwards in the crisis of the 1970s, after the preceding period's by comparison greater economic "egalitarianism"? Especially considering that Friedman's own aims were to raise the wealth of society as a whole — primarily that of the working class — which he thought was hampered precisely by the mistaken established "Keynesian" policies.

Burns notes that the specter of unemployment had already reared its head in the 1960s, with the later founder of the DSA Democratic Socialists of America, Michael Harrington's book, *The Other America*, published in the early 1960s, around the time of the greatest tax breaks — enacted by JFK — before those of Ronald Reagan in the 1980s. The issue was how the desired economic growth — Keynesian "growth liberalism" — failed to materialize in the 1960s, shifting the issues to other domains. By the end of the '60s, the crisis leading to neoliberalism started to manifest.

Burns points to the scourge of "automation," whose effects of "deindustrialization" were most glaringly seen after the 1970s, having already emerged much earlier, in the aftermath of WWII. This is where Friedman was already on the case at the time in the 1940s–50s, his investigations auguring the policy needs that would not be fully felt until the late 1960s. Burns touches on the ways the 1930s New Deal had neglected and bypassed a great deal of African-American poverty, which became salient in the climax of the Civil Rights era and Great Society expansions of the New Deal, and recognizes that this was Friedman's concern as well — paving the way to post-Civil Rights policies in the era of neoliberalism such as "charter-school" voucher program public education reform, against the government-monopoly teachers-union "closed shop" education rackets that Friedman thought kept the teachers' wages down as well as doing a disservice to their "consumers," the families whose children were being educated there.

This is where Friedman's post-Keynesian character enters the picture, in the form of a UBI Universal Basic Income "negative income tax," which, again, was only partially implemented later, as the "Earned Income Tax Credit" innovation of the Reagan era. But the UBI, then as now, was directed at the problem of automation as well as redistribution, and potential stagnation due to Keynesian "under-consumption." The problem, in Burns's account, was regarding the lack of desired spending in the economy: was it by consumers or rather by "business" — producers? Of course it is both, as workers are producers as well as consumers, albeit as employees of strapped-for-capital firms faced with the prospect of layoffs or potential expansion: how can government policies help or hinder employers to hire more workers? It is not simply a matter of providing a freer and hence more open market — as Friedman himself well knew.

Burns retails the story of Jack Kemp's rise in Congress during the 1970s, and then serving a pivotal role in Reagan's tax cuts of the 1980s, as representing a constituency hard-hit by unemployment, and how his policies of refunding of homeowner property taxes as well as business-owner expenses sought to apply Friedmanite remedies to get capital flowing again. The issue is the ambiguous socioeconomic "middle class" — those who are neither rich nor poor. What are the political limitations inherent in such a conception of the core of society, in which the role of producer and consumer is mixed? The problem of maintaining asset value, whether business or private (e.g. homes) was made shockingly apparent by the rampant inflation in which Friedman's "monetarist" ideas found a hearing in the 1970s.

This problem of depreciation via economic crisis back in the 1970s seems to foreshadow the more recent housing bubble in the 2008 financial crash leading to the Great Recession. But the return of 1970s–80s era inflation is now coming after, rather than before, the initial shock, depending on how and when one sees it. If Friedman's prescription, otherwise dismissed by contemporaries as "voodoo economics," appeared to have shrewdly corrected for the stubborn and beguiling "stagflation" of the late 1970s — economic stagnation combined with inflation — back then, today the opposite problem presents itself: Friedmanite economics producing inflation and menacing us chimerically with an as-yet unseen stagnation. Whereas then Friedman's approach was dangerous as untried innovation, today it has become threatening as doxa. The deeper question is, when were the seeds planted for the manifest economic crisis? For Friedman it was in the post-WWII era, long predating the currency of his ideas in the 1970s. Similarly, today the problem appears to have been sown back in the 1980s–90s heyday of neoliberalism itself. For the depreciation of capital, both business and consumer assets, if merely in earning potential — including in children depending on inheriting their parents' home value — is what is expressed in the monetary inflation.

Then, as now, the problem of implementing policy is marshaling enough of an electorate to support it. Of course demagogy is inevitably involved in democracy — voters don't really understand what they are voting for. But the question is, do politicians truly know the policies they are advocating?

Burns's story of the origins and paradoxical "triumph" of Milton Friedman's thought provides a great deal to consider regarding capitalism and its past and current travails. What we have in Burns's biography is the narrative of the journey of a thought from a preceding era succeeding in a later time. This is appropriate insofar as a subsequent crisis of capitalism is prepared by the character of the previous boom period. What was propitious in one time proves pernicious in another.

But we must be careful in attributing the nature of the disease that emerges only later. While Friedman detected problems with the "Keynesian" policies of his own time, really, these were made apparent by the actual shape of their success, through which could be recognized the disfiguration of the original intention.

In this respect, Friedman could build upon as well as "correct" what was essentially a Keynesian framework that had established the criteria with which to judge its own deficiencies: the task was to hold Keynesianism to its own standards. Burns finds in Friedman's own thinking and intentions the criteria for how we must evaluate and judge its apparent failures today.

Just as Keynes's own "monetarism" laid the groundwork for Friedman's neoliberal reforms, so must now Friedman's vision itself provide the lens through which new solutions can be found within today's configuration of capitalism produced by neoliberalism. Burns warns that in our rush to re-bury Friedman after planting a wooden stake in his dreaded vampire's heart, we risk entombing along with his troubled memory the resources that could unseal the problem we face in his wake. The blame for our current woes seems a bit too obvious in the Friedmanite legacy we seek to leave behind. But it might lie elsewhere from the place in the rearview mirror we think we have put it to rest. Our lingering fear after moving on from past mistakes is that we are destined to unknowingly make them again.

It is important to note that Friedman intended his proposed reforms to be implemented on the basis of prosperity in the 1950s–60s, not downturn and austerity, but were taken up in a period of crisis in the 1970s that he didn't anticipate. Friedman wanted to not merely defend capitalism but realize its unfulfilled potentials.

This is why Milton Friedman's memory haunts us, and why his character as ideological apologist for capitalism threatens to come at the expense of recognizing his true value as capitalism's reformer. For, as Burns shows, Friedman did not place faith in capitalism to solve its own problems, but actively championed bringing about its potential that would otherwise lie dormant and unrealized. Friedman did not, as his critics tell it, call us to bow down at the altar of capitalism, but rather to take it in hand and make it work better.

As Burns reminds us, Friedman was no mere "economist" running rampant ideologically outside his own narrow province of actual expertise, but his vocation and discipline was actually "political economy," whose concerns are much broader and deeper, and speak to the improvement of society as a whole, in which economics, culture and politics coincide and participate together. Moreover, Burns notes that Friedman's primary concern was "freedom." What did this mean?

Friedman's contemporary Daniel Bell called himself a "conservative in culture, liberal in politics and socialist in economics" to describe his own brand of "neoconservatism," in which the aim was to preserve the best qualities and potentials of society. Ludwig von Mises denounced Friedman and other fellow members of the Mont Pelerin Society as "socialists." What this meant was their accepting the state as the indispensable agent of economic equality. This is where monetary policy is located, whether Keynesian or Friedmanite — whether old-style "progressive" liberal or later "neoliberal." Bell's post-Marxist "socialist economics" was more vaguely elaborated, but still concerned the contradiction Friedman had faced of automation in a society of consumption based on the wage-earnings of work, what Bell called the opposed criteria of "socialization" and "efficiency" in the economy, which he found to be at odds in the inexorable logic of technological advancement, and to which he found the (modern, bourgeois) "culture" he wanted to "conserve" fall victim, in a nihilistic, "trivialized" culture of "multiples for the *culturati*," "hedonism for the middle classes" and "pornotopia for the masses."[6] Bell found that in the post-WWII world "heterodoxy" and even "antinomianism" has become "conformist" — think *Rebel Without a Cause* (1955) — at the expense of any "moral" criteria of "orthodoxy" with which to even be able to judge society's "adequacy." A full historical period later, today, after neoliberalism, we face this specter even more starkly, in the form of social disintegration alongside perfected automated efficiency. As in Bell and Friedman's time, the "ends" of society have been sacrificed to the "means" of capitalism.

Burns recalls that the true concern of "political economy" is not only not economic efficiency but also not the mere maintenance of society, but rather its "freedom." The problem with "economic stagnation" is that it delivers society into a dead end from which the resources of escape are bereft: a lack of freedom.

It should be remembered that Margaret Thatcher's infamous statement that "there is no such thing as society" was not a denial of society per se, but an attack on the dishonest political rhetoric of "socialism" or "social democracy" by her opponents in both the Conservative and Labour Parties that she thought provided cover for and justified the actual violation in practice of society, the "individuals and families" she sought to champion.

As a true egalitarian, Milton Friedman attributed the necessary freedom to change things not in government or corporate enterprise but among the working people. Friedman's animus towards the established labor unions, for example, was not in their collective bargaining rights for workers but their betrayal of the latter in collusion with a state-corporate system that constrained — political as well as economic and broader social — choices, at all levels of society. Friedan assailed the "crony capitalism" that resulted from the post-New Deal economic and political order to which the working class had been increasingly subordinated after WWII. The problem today is that the "crony capitalism" remains, while the collective agencies of the working class have declined. But what are those agencies? And are they not still beholden to and collusive with the political-crony state-managed capitalism Friedman sought society's freedom from? Have they done or been able to do anything at all in the last 50 years — really, in

---

6    1978 Foreword to *The Cultural Contradictions of Capitalism* (1976).

the last century — to stop or even slow the increasing vulnerability and descent of the working class and of the greater society along with it? We may not be happy with Friedman's proposed solutions or their results, but we can at least agree on the problem: the mismanagement of society by an elite to which we are subject and to whose rule we fall casualty.

The problem is how we see capitalism: is it something over which we can exert control for our benefit; or is it something "objective" to whose reality we must inevitably submit? Burns points out that Friedman despised treating economics as some kind of "hard science" of unchangeable "mathematical" laws, which he considered an abominable intellectual and moral abdication. But the problem remains.

Though we might now see Friedman as an actor on behalf of the elite political management that managed to continue through his policies, we must recognize how his ideas were not only appropriated but hijacked and held hostage to their self-interest — at the expense of the true character of Friedman's own concerns.

Burns's book is subtitled "the last conservative." But Friedman considered himself to be a true "progressive" advocating needed change against an ailing status-quo. Indeed he might have been the "last rebel" — to paraphrase Newt Gingrich's proclamation in the 1994 Congressional election "Republican Revolution" majority he led, the "true revolutionary." Friedman sought to intervene in the impasse of the 1970s, but ended up as a neutered and banalized ornament gracing a status quo which preserved itself by prostituting his ideas and "revolutionizing" the political and social order only superficially. What Friedman sought to conserve was society and its economic, political and social resources for the prosperity of the working masses of the people, to which he found the capitalism of his time to be invidious. Friedman was the "last conservative" in Burns's telling insofar as he represented the fading memory of that which the neoliberal reforms of capitalism conducted under the auspices of his ideas accelerated the destruction: the very society of his working-class childhood and its opportunities in the earlier 20th century that Friedman had sought to conserve and whose potential he wanted to realize. The tragedy of Milton Friedman was how he failed through "success."

The lesson is that intellectuals' ideas become captive and hostage to fortune in the course of historical events, serving to justify things they were originally formulated to critique and oppose. But their neglected sides might come to the fore later and redeem them in time.

The Epilogue to Burns's book is titled "Helicopter Drop" and discusses recent economic interventions that seemed to have followed Friedman's prescription. The phrase is Friedman's own, advocating direct cash infusions such as was done with the COVID relief payments, but refers mordantly if never explicitly to the atrocity perpetrated by the Pinochet regime of dropping dissident political prisoners from helicopters to their deaths. The point could not be more clear: such "helicopter drops" saved the economy but also brought about the inflation that threatens to undo it. As Hegel said, the very virtue through which a community thrived historically — in this case that of neoliberal capitalism of the last era — becomes the "poison draught" that brings about its downfall, which, not able to be fully realized by its originators, in an apparent reversal is then taken up by its successors. In this instance, it is Friedman's "conservatism" that, as Burns puts it, "paradoxically," is providing rather an opportunity today for the "progressive" reconsideration of his legacy and the substance of his thinking and even of his advocated policies, which, again, were hardly implemented by his supposed followers in neoliberalism but might prove more fruitful and in different ways now. This speaks not only to Friedman's social and political goals but even to his economic theory — where the danger is precisely that the latter seems discredited, but it might be to the ultimate detriment of the former for us to reflexively and unthinkingly accept this apparent verdict of history. In Burns's view, Friedman might be key to achieving future equality where in his own time he contributed to producing deeper inequities — and even iniquities.

How capitalism has undone society since neoliberalism can be understood well from Friedman's own theoretical point of view and out of his own concerns. For what Friedman wanted to "conserve" was our freedom to "choose" — and beyond the limited, self-serving and false alternative policies on offer in the existing political order of capitalism, as much now as back then.

Hopefully not in the mere inertia of lack of imagination, but in his neglected, buried and unfulfilled potential: Just as neoliberalism was still Keynesian, post-neoliberalism will still be Friedmanite.

Originally published in *Platypus Review* 165 (April 2024)

# Epilegomena

# The dictatorship of the proletariat and the death of the Left

## Marxism and the necessity of the dictatorship of the proletariat

The dictatorship of the proletariat is the most controversial proposition by Marxism — and is indeed how Marxism distinguishes itself politically, ideologically and theoretically, and intellectually as well as practically and organizationally. The death of the Left is a measure of its abandonment of this prognosis, intellectual project and political program of Marxism that culminated in the dictatorship of the proletariat.

What did Marx and Marxism mean by the "dictatorship of the proletariat"? Very simply, the political rule by the working class. The form of such rule was meant to be "dictatorial" in the sense of revolutionary, politically and socially transformative, overruling social and political norms of constitutional government. It was meant to be a "state of emergency" and hence a dictatorship in the sense of the Ancient Roman Republic, an active political intervention into society of limited duration.

What was meant by a dictatorship of the "proletariat," specifically? It meant the political rule of the workers, but not in the restricted sense of those employed in wage labor, but in a more expansive sense that would include both the unemployed or only potentially employed, and those not employed in wage labor strictly speaking, for instance "middle class" salaried professionals, including the middle-management "white collar" workers of corporate capitalism. But the center of political power was to be the wage-laboring working class.

The dictatorship of the proletariat was a world-historical and hence geopolitical proposition. It was meant to be a global rule of the working class, with revolution encompassing the preponderance of the capitalist world, which means where capital itself is concentrated: not where money is concentrated, but rather labor, where the production and reproduction of capital is concentrated.

Positively, this meant the production of value in global capitalism, which is not identical to the production of material wealth in terms of articles of consumption as subsistence goods, but rather where capital as the means of production is produced. This meant the core capitalist countries.

This meant the countries where capital as the expression of the "general social intellect" is concentrated. The dictatorship of the proletariat must be in the position to at least begin to appropriate the means of production on a global scale. Capital as "dead labor" — historically accumulated labor in the current existing means of production — must be appropriated by the "living labor" of the present working class.

Strategically, this meant a complex and potentially politically quite complicated intervention in the existing capitalist production process, or the current conditions for the production of material wealth (including intellectual wealth), in an ongoing way.

Negatively, it meant that the global working class must be in a position to overcome the reproduction of wage labor as the source of valuation for material wealth. The working class must be in a position to outlaw unemployment and prevent the exploitation of the labor of desperate poor people, in favor of gearing global production towards the production of wealth for human needs and overcoming the social compulsion to labor as part of the valorization process of capital, breaking its cycle of reproduction. What Marx called the "necessity" of the dictatorship of the proletariat was the necessity of breaking the cycle of capitalist reproduction, necessarily on a world-historical and hence global scale.

Until this happens, capitalism will continue. — So long as wage labor exists, capital and its contradiction will persist.

So what is capitalism — what is it that needs to be overcome?

Capitalism is the constraint and distortion and deformation of society by the imperative to produce and reproduce the value of capital.

Capital is past labor — the potential for producing wealth or material (including intellectual) goods in society — but in the form of the contradiction Marxism found between the potential of industrial production and the social value of living human labor and the social and political rights deriving from that value. Capitalism, or the capitalist mode of production that produces and reproduces capital, is the contradiction between the bourgeois social relations of labor and the industrial forces of production that are constrained — dominated — by those relations.

It is not the case, as is commonly mistakenly assumed by supposed "Marxists," that bourgeois social relations means the individual private property in the means of production by members of the capitalist class, and that industrial forces of production means the collective social productive capacity of the working class. No.

The basis of the social rights of property in bourgeois society is the labor of the producers. This is the right of bourgeois social relations. The issue is how this social right is contradicted by the necessities and possibilities of industrial production.

As I have pointed out elsewhere (in my "What is capitalism?" and "Socialism in the 21st century"[1]), there are two different and increasingly divergent commodities produced by industry: goods for the subsistence of the working class; and surplus value as the fund for investment in production, which can take the form of either paying workers' wages and/or for technology. It is the apparent conflict of technology vs. human labor that characterizes capitalism on a societal scale.

The industrial forces of production are the productive capacities of society as a whole, what Marx called the "general social intellect," whose potential for the production of social wealth has outstripped the social and political rights of appropriation through living human labor by the working class.

The capitalist class represents not the exploitation of the workers but the social value of accumulated labor in capital, the surplus value produced by labor that becomes the precondition for further future production. When the capitalists fail to support the social value of capital as the basis for production, they cease to be capitalists, cease to be stewards of capital, and become mere moneybags. As Marx put it, a miser is an irrational capitalist whereas a capitalist is a rational miser. The miserliness or "misery"

---

1  Chris Cutrone, Dick Howard, Shane Mage, Chris Nineham, Leo Panitch, "What is capitalism and why should we be against it?" *Platypus Review* 129 (September 2020), and "Socialism in the 21st century," *Platypus Review* 126 (May 2020), in this volume.

of capitalism that Marx had in mind was not the economic efficiency of social investment in production but the impoverished basis for measuring and valuing the social potential of production according to the surplus value that can be produced by human labor and its wages. The wager of labor in capitalism is that current present production will provide the basis of future production — that human activity and life will thus support itself in an ongoing way through capitalism.

The contradiction Marxism found in capitalism was that what began as a means to an end of social production and wealth, capital, became an end in itself, and what was an end in itself, human life and activity, becomes a mere means to the ends of capital.

The proletariat was Marx's term for describing and critiquing the existence of the working class in industrial conditions in which there was an increasing divergence and disparity between the value of capital and the value of wages in social production. Marxism called this the expropriation of the working class by capital, in which the workers became less and less able to appropriate the total social product and — most importantly — its potential for future production through its wages as a means of consumption. This was how the working class became "propertyless," increasingly socially divested of the property of its labor.

The "virtuous cycle" of bourgeois society became the circuit of capital in production and consumption, as bourgeois social relations and right increasingly undermined and destroyed themselves. There were thus value-crises in capital, which were crises of society as a whole. The result of these crises was the destruction of the value of both wages and capital. Capital became less profitable, the wage-earning potential of labor decreased, money went without opportunities for productive investment, and workers went unemployed. This was especially true at a generational level in which the reproduction of capital did away with jobs and the continued reproduction of workers created masses of unemployed and unemployable people.

Industrial production made human labor increasingly superfluous to the production of wealth, and thus the social value of human activity and life became not realized through productive activity but negated by it. Marxism thought that this meant the possibility and necessity of overcoming the valuing of human activity and life through labor as a measure of social wealth. This was the motivation for the proletarianized working class's struggle for socialism.

In today's terms of measuring social wealth through GDP (Gross Domestic Product) and Per Capita Productivity and Purchasing Power Parity, there is a contradiction between these indices of economic activity and actual individual and collective life and wellbeing in society. The United States has remained the highest GDP and PPP country in the world, with the highest productivity of labor. And yet there are increasing numbers of unemployed and unemployable people, and what labor employment exists and increases consists of new forms of work that are — temporarily — not yet replaceable by technology, for instance the "service sector."

This is the immiseration of society in capitalism that Marx observed and which has continued up to today.

In socialism, the industrial superfluousness of workers was to be replaced by the superfluousness of work. As Marx envisioned it, work was to go from "life's prime need" to "life's prime want" — people would work because they wanted to, not because they needed to do so, either individually or collectively. The possibilities of science and technology as a higher form of social cooperation than the division of labor would allow "from each according to his ability and to each according to his need."

The increased specialized division of labor in bourgeois social cooperation continues, but with an increasing and intensifying gulf opening between the new forms of social interdependence thus created and the forms of socially valuing and supporting the laboring activity and human lives thus employed.

Bourgeois demands for recognition of equal social and political rights to participation in and contribution to as well as share in consumption and production and reproduction of present and future wealth come up against the limits of the bourgeois form of such rights — the value of laboring activity — and the value of capital as measure of social production and consumption: the limits of capitalism as a self-contradiction of bourgeois society in industrial production.

The politically strategic vision of Marxism was that, to break the repetitive cycle of capitalist crisis and destruction, the wage-laborers would need to abolish wage labor — the laborers would need to abolish labor. It was not enough that the capitalists destroyed capitalism — that capitalism destroyed capital. The very basis for the reproduction of capital — labor — must be overcome. What society already was doing in capitalism in an unconscious and self-alienated way must be overcome in a disalienated and self-conscious way. But first it would need to be done consciously: the working class must politically and socially take over and appropriate capitalism before it can be overcome.

Thus was the Marxist vision of the dictatorship of the proletariat.

## The death of the Left

Today, the ostensible "Left" — the avowed "socialists" — have abandoned the goal of the dictatorship of the proletariat, either in words or in fact, the latter by reinterpreting the dictatorship of the proletariat to mean the governing of capitalism by sociologically working-class political parties in a welfare-state or so-called "social democracy."

For instance, the DSA (Democratic Socialists of America) *Jacobin* magazine publisher Bhaskar Sunkara has recently offered that perhaps achieving socialism in the United States is impossible, but what is possible is "social democracy," by which he meant a better social welfare state.

But even to the extent that Sunkara and his *Jacobin* comrades still claim to be not social democrats but rather (small-d) democratic socialists and aspire for something greater than welfare-state capitalism, they still base their vision on an earlier 20th-century liquidation of Marxism and its goal of the dictatorship of the proletariat. For instance, Ralph Miliband is a major influence for *Jacobin*. This is true for *Jacobin*-associated *Catalyst* journal editor Vivek Chibber's essay "Our Road to Power," which contrasted the current DSA's political program to the older Marxism of Kautsky, Luxemburg and Lenin.[2]

Miliband's idea was that in the 20th century the state had become much more important as an actor in capitalism, and that the working class was less socially and politically excluded than it had been in the time of classical Marxism, with the result being that the working class neither could nor

2   *Jacobin* (December 5, 2017).

should renounce participation politically in the capitalist state, for instance through working-class parties elected to government. The working class is supposedly no longer barred from political power in capitalism.

This is of course far less plausible today, after a generation — 40–50 years of neoliberalism — now, than when Miliband originally formulated his perspective, in the decades after WWII.

But even conceding Miliband's — and the current DSA's — point, the issue is the identification of workers' or labor parties with socialist politics, or governing the capitalist state with the dictatorship of the proletariat.

The issue is the Marxist vision of the dictatorship of the proletariat as a transition to, and not identical with, socialism. It is not merely a matter of political exclusion producing a need for revolution. At issue is the possibility of gradually evolving socialism out of capitalism through increasing state control over and welfare provisions in capitalism.

Historically, this has produced not the working class transforming capitalism into socialism, but rather the transformation of nominally "socialist" parties into political parties of governing capitalism, turning the working class's social and political organizations into appendages of the capitalist state.

Because there has not been by any means the uninterrupted governance of capitalism by working-class and ostensibly "socialist" parties, this hypothetical reforming of capitalism into socialism appears to not have been definitively disproven, and remains a tantalizing prospect.

Whereas "socialist" or "communist" parties were meant to be more than merely social democratic, what has happened rather is the lowering of socialist and even communist politics to social democracy or welfare-statist capitalism. This has been called the "betrayal" of socialism by these parties, and has produced new movements for socialism, for instance by the 1960s–70s New Left and even more recently, during the crisis of the Great Recession, in the however brief upsurges, at least electorally, of new "Left" movements and parties claiming to be socialist, against the existing social-democratic and socialist parties, such as SYRIZA in Greece and Podemos in Spain. Furthermore, there were the phenomena of Jeremy Corbyn's "socialist" leadership of the Labour Party and the Bernie Sanders Campaign for President in the Democratic Party in the U.S. All of these held out the promise of "democratic socialism," at least eventually, even if it was posed merely as reversing the erosion of the welfare state in the past generation of neoliberal capitalism.

There is also of course the 20th-century counterexample of the "undemocratic socialism" in the Soviet Union and associated countries. Even though the recent cycle of "socialism" by the Millennial Left in its social-democratic aspirations was accompanied, as its shadow, by a neo-Stalinism of "tankie" Marxist-Leninists, the "democratic socialism" of the new social democrats is not really pitched against the threat of Stalinist authoritarian socialism of communism, but the latter does remain an obstacle to a true understanding of the original Marxist vision of the dictatorship of the proletariat.

Moreover, Stalinism is seen as an authoritarian welfare state to which is opposed a more "democratic" one. What this ignores is that Stalinism was (and remains) democratic — perhaps as democratic as or even more so than capitalist democracy — (see for instance Cuba), but is not as liberal as the (ostensible) liberal democracy of capitalism.

Perhaps the most pernicious legacy of Stalinism is its equation of liberalism and capitalism, as if civil and social liberty and freedom is essentially the individual "liberty" of social irresponsibility (whether by individual people or by capitalist firms as corporate individuals) and the "freedom" to exploit and oppress others.

What this ignores is that capitalism itself — the domination of society by the imperatives of producing and reproducing capital — undermines the freedom and liberty of bourgeois civil society, not only for the working class but for others as well, including the capitalists.

The social democrats complain that the social-democratic welfare state is still constrained by the dictates of capital, threatened by "capital flight," etc., but by this they mean the nefarious actions of the capitalist class, ignoring the issue of capitalism itself in the Marxist sense. Earlier historical Marxists were much clearer about the true nature and character of the problem, which is precisely why they advocated the dictatorship of the proletariat as the beginning and not the end of political and social revolution, opening the door to and beginning the process of overcoming capitalism, and not yet beyond capitalism, let alone the achievement of socialism, itself.

The recent historical cycle of the Millennial Left failed to grasp either in theory or practice the true nature and character of the problem they faced in capitalism. They failed to become truly Marxist.

Marx argued that, short of the dictatorship of the proletariat, the state remained the "dictatorship of the bourgeoisie," by which he meant the dictatorship of capital, or the state ruling in the interests of capital as a whole. This includes the workers who live and benefit by capital as it presently exists.

In the 20th century, the socialist and communist Left historically liquidated the Marxist vision of the necessity and possibility of the dictatorship of the proletariat not least by neglecting and abandoning the actual reasons for it.

The propaganda of working-class struggle politics by historical Marxism was mistaken in subsequent generations for theoretical substance, confusing cause and effect in capitalism. The class division and conflict between workers and capitalists was mistaken as the cause and not recognized properly as the effect of capitalism and its contradiction. The self-contradiction of social value in production between wages and capital was mistaken for a conflict of interests between workers and capitalists, with the latter regarded merely as exploitative profiteers and not as Marx saw them as "character-masks" of the greater social imperatives of capital. The workers were meant to replace the capitalist ruling class not to do away with exploitation but to make politically explicit and thus "conscious" the contradiction of capital.

Instead, socialism and communism reverted to their pre-Marxian meaning of mere social and political egalitarianism, a complaint against political and social hierarchy and the inequality in distribution and consumption between the working class and the capitalists.

The dictatorship of the proletariat was the intermediate and not ultimate political and social goal of socialist politics in capitalism, as originally understood by Marxism. While the motivations of the working-class struggle for socialism included the egalitarianism of labor — the bourgeois principles of "equal rights for all" to "life, liberty and the pursuit of happiness" in the freedom of "liberty, equality and fraternity" in a "free association of producers"

— Marxism also assumed civil and political liberty, a liberal society and political order of voluntary participation and association.

It is precisely because bourgeois society in capitalism still exhibits such liberty and embodies such an egalitarian spirit of participation that there are discontents in such terms within it and indeed that there is any social and political movement at all against its failures.

The Left has fallen apart into either accommodating capitalist politics through welfare statism or accommodating society's disintegration in capitalism through antinomian opposition of anti-bourgeois nihilism and anti-social attitudes — including the tribalism of communitarian social-group identity politics. In either case, it has abandoned the task of socialism and the political goal of the next historically necessary step of the dictatorship of the proletariat, to begin to move society beyond capitalism.

This is why and how the Left died historically — why it remains dead today.

Presented as a teach-in at the Platypus Midwest Regional Conference on September 25, 2021 at Northwestern University, Evanston, Illinois.

Originally published in *Platypus Review* 141 (November 2021)

# The end of Millennial Marxism

Marxism has been falsified and disproved definitively in both theory and practice in every conceivable way. And yet Marxism still seems to speak, and always newly. Karl Marx asserted that capitalism wouldn't be overcome until the dictatorship of the proletariat was globally achieved. This was based on his conclusion that the inherent contradiction of bourgeois society during the Industrial Revolution posed an insoluble problem. He believed that the proletarianized working class, those at the bottom who embody and suffer the most from this contradiction, would inevitably try for political power in a democratic revolution.

As early as the 1830s, workers suffering displacement by technology revolted. By the 1840s, this working-class discontent had taken political form, as Chartists in England called for universal suffrage. Marx and his comrade Friedrich Engels expected proletarian uprisings to happen during the Revolutions of 1848. They wrote the celebrated *Manifesto of the Communist Party* in anticipation of this outcome.

But it didn't happen. The main lesson that Marx and Engels took away from this failure was that without prior organization as a social and political force, the working class would never be able to cast off its fetters. They agreed with German Chancellor Otto von Bismarck, who famously said of the failed 1848 Revolutions that it was "not by speeches and majority resolutions that the great questions of the time are decided . . . but by iron and blood." They considered the only alternative to the dictatorship of the proletariat to be the dictatorship of the bourgeoisie, and a more or less Bonapartist dictatorship. Not merely strong-man rule — for example, Louis Bonaparte as Napoleon III — but a strong state became necessary.

The capitalist state has been henceforth required to manage capitalism through recurrent crises.

For Marxism, the classic crisis of capitalism was an excess of money without opportunities for profitable investment and a "reserve army" of surplus workers without jobs: both labor and capital were devalued in inflation and unemployment, respectively. Social production became ever more expensive under capitalism and stagnated. This wasn't a problem society could spontaneously solve on its own, for it went beyond mere market corrections. An "imperial" state rose above all rival social and political groups and established its permanent role, for instance the emergence of modern police and bureaucracies (including social-service agencies, which are merely unarmed police forces), necessary to preserve society. Yet this state only fed into and exacerbated social disintegration. Modern political parties arose to seize the state for competing interests — more or less vainly.

The state itself persisted, metastasizing at society's expense. As Marx described it, this was a situation in which the bourgeoisie could no longer rule through civil society and subordinate the state, as in the original bourgeois-revolutionary, liberal-democratic vision, but the proletariat couldn't yet take power in socialist revolution. The bourgeois-cosmopolitan "brotherhood of nations" was contravened as the imperialist capitalist state extended into empire, seeking control not only at home, but abroad, through international "police actions." A prevailing "state of emergency" came into effect.

Capitalism has remained stuck since the mid-19th century. It is noteworthy that, as Lenin underscored in *The State and Revolution* (1917), the Marxist vision for the "dictatorship of the proletariat" was meant to be not only transitional and temporary, but the most minimal possible state, reduced severely from its capitalist excrescence, thereby restoring the civil-social freedom of liberal democracy and immediately "withering away" as capitalism was overcome by the proletariat.

Capitalism will never be able to avoid civil-social and political strife. It will never be able to avoid wars, *coups d'état*, and revolutions. Indeed, it already has exhibited such phenomena in all countries at one time or another in the last two centuries. It will continue to do so. The only question is whether social progress — the progress of society — could possibly result from such concentrated violence, destruction, and sacrifice. It has not done so yet. Political power has been periodically overthrown and rearranged, but the domination of society by the imperatives of capitalism has remained unshaken. Marx wrote that the secret of every state is democracy. But democracy isn't the opposite of dictatorship, but its constitution. Democracy has remained the basis for the dictatorship of capital. But capitalism is a constant crisis of the state.

Even if all the capitalists got together and decided to implement socialism, it wouldn't be possible for them to do so. If all the managers, including the politicians, got together and decided to implement socialism, it wouldn't be possible for them to do so. So long as there are desperately poor people willing to be exploited to survive, capitalism will continue. As long understood by Marx and subsequent Marxist thinkers, the logic of capitalism invariably concludes with the proletariat abolishing itself by its own agency.

But why? Why, according to Marxism, is it necessary for the working class in particular to overcome capitalism? Why did Marx call for the dictatorship specifically of the proletariat? The Marxist vision is that bourgeois society is the product of the everyday activity of people laboring and exchanging the products of that labor — it is the society that arises from modern commodity production. Capitalism is essentially the crisis of the commodity relations of that bourgeois society as the result of the Industrial Revolution: the laboring bourgeois Third Estate became divided between workers and capitalists, each upholding one antagonistic side of production, labor and capital. Marxism is the theory that the demands of the working class for its fair share drives society into a choice between funding laborers' wages and subsistence, versus funding advancements in production through science and technology. Insofar as it is more immediately profitable, capitalists both individually and as a class will always favor technology over human labor, increasingly leaving the working class vulnerable to unemployment. Or, conversely, labor will be exploited at the expense of technical progress. In fact, both occur, however contradictorily, in capitalism. Despite the best intentions of society to employ technology for human benefit, the reverse takes place.

The demands of the working class thus led to a contradictory result of eliminating jobs while requiring that society continue to provide employment. This has driven several waves of industrial transformation since Marx's time, in which not only technology but also forms of work have changed. In each case, however, the crisis of the social value of human labor in production has caught up with capitalism and produced a bust after every boom. As Marx put it, capitalism has developed in "fits and starts." Every affluent generation's offspring, whose biological reproduction was encouraged by a relatively high standard of living, reaches adulthood only to find that there aren't enough jobs. Only the working class as subjects, and not merely objects, of this process could possibly put an end to this evil cycle of destructive creation. The question is how this recurrent generational dynamic has repeatedly raised the specter of socialism — or "communism" — for two centuries.

Marxism has necessarily appeared differently in different moments of history. We can discern several such moments between Marx's formative time of the 1840s and our present moment: the later period of Marx's life, specifically the aftermath of the 1848 Revolutions, and leading to the formation and dissolution of the First International Workingmen's Association in the 1860s and '70s; the time of the Second International leading to World War I and the Marxist-led revolutions that followed, from the 1890s to the 1910s; the time of the Old Left and the Third and Fourth Internationals of Stalinism and Trotskyism in the 1930s and '40s, leading to World War II and the subsequent revolutions of the mid-20th century; the post-Stalinist New Left of the 1960s–70s; and the Millennial Left of the early 21st century, leading to the present.

In each moment, the prevailing form of capitalism shaped how Marxism appeared and appealed to a new generation seeking societal change. There were also intervals of history between these key moments, such as in the 1950s and in '80s and '90s, when Marxism disintegrated into various post-Marxist ideologies (we might be entering such a period of interregnum now, as the Millennial moment has subsided).

So now might be a good moment for reflection on the substance of Marxism, what is fundamentally essential to Marxism, and what has proven continuous despite all this intervening history of change.

Differences within Marxism originated over strategic and political disagreements. Factions sought to justify themselves "theoretically" by looking at changing historical situations in which the struggle for socialism has taken place. Unfortunately, these have been misremembered and perpetuated falsely as differences in principle, in which tactics have been mistakenly evaluated in moral and ethical terms. Perhaps this has been inevitable, since "Marxists" have found themselves on "both sides of the barricade" — on opposite sides of ostensible revolution and counter-revolution for more than 100 years. Worse still, these differences have not been clarified but only further muddled through constant historical revisionism, as succeeding generations have sought to explain this history to themselves anew, often in contrary and indeed directly opposed ways. As a result, the basic "philosophy" of Marxism — especially its philosophy of history itself — has been buried, several times over. What has been lost sight of is the "end" of Marxism, the goal to which it leads.

We might be living in a nightmare of Marx's — a reality too terrible for him to have consciously contemplated. Marxism in its original historical moment never reckoned that we would accept the hellish unfreedom of capitalism, as we appear to have done for the last 100 years.

What was Marxism, then, and what is its potential continued relevance today? The question is especially pressing, since Marxism, despite some spectacular historical events associated with it, seems to have consistently failed to produce the desired social emancipation from capitalism that Marx originally prognosed. Why do people periodically return to reconsiderations of Marxism, reaching back across so much history?

First, we must review the Millennial Left's return to Marxism, which took several forms through the various phases of the Millennials' career through recent history. The distinctly Millennial Left arose after 9/11, protesting against the War on Terror. This was originally an "anti-imperialist Left," seeking to oppose and potentially change the American empire. Marxism at this time was seen as explaining the causes of war in the nature of the international system of American-led capitalism, why and how US imperial policy sought to uphold the global political and economic order against discontents, oppositions, and resistance and rebellions within it. Specifically, neoconservative foreign policy was regarded as the political form of US global hegemony. But liberal human-rights interventionism was also part of this international politics. (The subsequent election of Barack Obama, which to many on the Left seemed to signal the end of empire, was anything but.)

This moment of origin for the Millennial Left was soon followed by the 2008 financial crash leading to the Great Recession. Marxism was looked to for an explanation of the causes of the crisis. An early expression of renascent "socialism" was also found during this moment. The Obama presidency promised a (Green) New Deal, health care for all, and perhaps even a jobs program — none of which came to pass. This crisis of capitalism led to anti-austerity protests, including the Arab Spring toppling of regimes and outbreaks of civil war in the Middle East and North Africa, and Occupy Wall Street in the United States, as the costs of the collapse were felt across the world.

Frustration with the Obama presidency and with the apparent limitations of the greater progressive liberal and social democratic politics of the metropolitan capitalist world led to the Bernie Sanders and Jeremy Corbyn campaigns and emergence and growth of the Democratic Socialists of America and the Momentum movement inside the UK Labour party. Elsewhere, the rise of Syriza in Greece and Podemos in Spain expressed the crisis of the traditional center-Left political parties.

Since 2015, there has clearly been a crisis of neoliberalism: the fraying and breakdown of the combination of economic conservatism and social liberalism that had dominated mainstream capitalist politics since the 1970s.

A key phenomenon of this crisis was the 2016 Trump campaign and election that wrangled the Republican Party and occurred alongside the Sanders and Corbyn bids for leadership of their respective parties, as well as the Brexit referendum vote. That last, Brexit, was a response to the crisis of the reigning neoliberal politics of the European Union that had been made manifest in the sovereign debt crisis of Greece and other states in

Southern Europe afflicted by the Great Recession. Discontent with and opposition to the regime of trade and other international exchange (such as immigration) that favored the ruling interests of global capital could be found across the entire political spectrum. A populist right and a socioeconomic Left both seemed on the rise.

But the apparent success of right-wing opposition to neoliberalism pushed the Millennial Left in an anti-racist, "anti-fascist" direction, centered around Black Lives Matter protests. The Millennial Left was drawn back into the Democratic Party's ethnic-constituency racket, group-identity politics, and electioneering. With this emergence of social identity movements about race and gender, #MeToo and BLM, Marxism appeared yet again as an explanation for racism and sexism under capitalism, eclipsing concerns over socio-economic crises. The Millennial Left is not, as it likes to imagine, the present embodiment of Marxism — "intersecting" the concerns of class-based and international imperialist exploitation, as well as race, sex, and gender oppression. Instead, it has replayed the liquidation of historical Marxism that occurred through the various phases of the last century, reanimating the corpse of every hoary myth and nightmarish self-delusion.

Sanders and Corbyn themselves seemed to stylistically embody this combination, though they were both vintage 1960s activists of the New Left, and had successful political careers at the dawn of the neoliberal era. Their advanced age and cantankerous oratory seemed to make them blasts from the 1930s past. As such, they served as effective if unlikely standard-bearers for the Millennial Left, symbolizing and expressing its complaints and aspirations better than anyone else. They were "anti-imperialist" and upheld the New Left social movements against racism and sexism, all the while expressing socio-economic grievances. Indeed, they ticked all the boxes for the Millennial Left. But their combination of such divergent concerns could not hold, falling apart into the perennial "race vs. class" debates from the 20th-century Left.

This represented less a set of problems inherited from historical Marxism than a present crisis of progressive neoliberalism in the Democratic and Labour parties. The battle wasn't over socialism or Marxism, but progressive liberal capitalism — a battle for Millennial leadership of capitalist politics.

But one significant problem the Millennials came up against was that of motivation. Were they acting out of optimism or pessimism? Was a better world possible or not? BLM's avowed "Afro-pessimism" and "black nihilism," for example, pointed to the disproportionate loss of black middle-class assets in the 2008 financial crisis, resulting in demands for "equity" — vocabulary taken from terms for mortgages and shareholder assets. There has been an attempt to shore up and restore the Democratic Party's electoral coalition of organized labor with social-identity interest groups. But the Democrats' New Deal coalition has been in disrepair for quite some time, salvaged however briefly by the Clinton and Obama presidencies. After Trump, the Biden-Harris administration is a "dead-man-walking" warning to the Millennial Left of the tenuous viability of Democratic Party politics. The Millennial Left's response: the DSA's *Jacobin* magazine's test-marketing opinion research for turning out the youth vote. (It won't work.)

The crisis of the 1930s–40s Old Left was one of pessimism; capitalism in a downturn of the Great Crash of 1929 and subsequent Depression, and the rise of fascism and renewed world war. Whereas, by contrast, the crisis of the 1960s was one of optimism; the "revolt against affluence," discontented with the apparent success of capitalism in the postwar boom under the New Deal Democrats. The 1960s New Left wanted to go beyond capitalism and its evident limitations, not merely fight against it. The subsequent 1970s stagflation economic crisis caught them unprepared and brought about another round of pessimism. This was answered not by the Left, but by Reagan's "morning again in America" turn toward neoliberal capitalism in the 1980s, completed by the "man from Hope," Bill Clinton, ushering in the 1990s boom. "Hope and change" was Obama's neoliberal coda in the new millennium.

Until the emergence of the Millennial Left, Marxism seemed permanently sidelined, its irrelevance dramatically confirmed by the belated collapse of the Soviet Union and Communist regimes in Eastern Europe. But history, and hence Marxism, has returned in the new century.

The Marxism of the Second or Socialist International at the turn of the last century was motivated by the optimism of the Second Industrial Revolution, which came to a dramatic end with the Great War. But

Marxist figures of those revolutions that resulted from the crisis of World War I, figures such as Lenin in Russia and Rosa Luxemburg in Germany, were animated by the same optimism, recovering from the failure of the Second International, in launching their new Third or Communist International in 1919. The subsequent 20th century was a paradoxical product of failed world socialist revolution (despite its grotesque Stalinist caricature expanding after World War II into the voids vacated by global capital in the zones devastated by fascism). As with the Gilded Age a century earlier, the turn of the 21st century seemed to bring new problems, and perhaps with them opportunities for change, and yet it still stubbornly recalled the past. Whence this lack of imagination?

The Millennial Left originated in a combination of the optimism of the 1990s of their early childhood — the last boom period of global capitalism — and the shocks and pessimism of the War on Terror and the Great Recession. The progressivism of Millennial Leftists still expresses that enduring optimism, even if tempered by a catastrophic cast of mind regarding phenomena such as climate change. In many respects, their pessimism is that of diminished career prospects — hence their anxiety around the obvious meaning of their middle-class, professional-managerial sociological composition.

Generally, Marxism seems to fare better during optimistic periods — when capitalism appears as an obstacle to its own potential, rather than a mere baleful malady besetting society. The socialist movement of the working class was facilitated by upsurges of capitalist development, led by workers in new industries. This was true of the high period of historical Marxism in the advanced capitalist world, during the period before World War I which gave rise to Eugene Debs's Socialist Party of America as part of the greater Second or Socialist International of August Bebel, Karl Kautsky, and Rosa Luxemburg's SPD, as well as Lenin's Bolsheviks. But the socialist Left has been on the defensive and in retreat since at least the 1960s (if not the '30s). There hasn't been a significant movement for proletarian socialism in many generations.

The "post-political Marxism" of my own formative years in the 1980s had more in common with the later period of the Boomer experience of the 1970s economic downturn, and recalled the 1930s anti-fascist "resistance"-era Stalinism of defensive retreat in the face of Reaganism and Thatcherism. It was characterized by academic Leftism and social-movement activism. The 1980s Left was nothing if not pessimistic. But the Millennial transition to the reborn Left of today marked a regained optimism. The question is what this optimism has to do with Marxism. What was "Millennial Marxism"? Perhaps it wasn't as optimistic as it appeared.

"Marxism" is commonly used as a shorthand for socialism, so some necessary clarification is in order, to be able to discuss productively the present moment's "socialism" and its relation to the history of Marxism. Marxism has been regarded by the Millennials as the theoretical justification for socialism and for opposition to and criticism of capitalism. The preceding 1990s–2000s World Social Forum Left's slogan of "a better world is possible" was not really a euphemism for socialism, but only for reformed capitalism against what was seen as the abuses and excesses of neoliberalism in the 1990s. But the Millennials' socialism is more earnest, and seems to have been based on more than mere desire.

It is difficult to disentangle the exhaustion and crisis of the neoliberalism of the older generations from the progressivism of the new generation. But if the real possibilities expressed by the latter are actually to be found in their "progressive" political and social agenda, then the question is what, if anything, this has to do with socialism in any even remotely "Marxist" sense. Isn't this just a "progress" in capitalism? Especially since it has resolved to try to reform — restore — the Democratic Party from within its existing electoral coalition? Apart from right-wing hysteria, this isn't "socialism."

To clarify this issue, we must address the perspective of original historical Marxism and its vision of socialism, before showing how it is quite distant from and at odds with the Left's concerns today.

Marxism was born of critique. Critique is not mere criticism, not fault-finding or debunking or falsifying of things, but exploring conditions of possibility for change, and not merely accidental, random or otherwise "objective" change, as in entropic processes, but conditions for the transformation of the world by free, subjective agents. Furthermore, critique is not opposition, not treating phenomena as if from the outside, but finding potential from within something of which we are inextricably parts and participants. The aim of critique is to recognize the possibilities for being subjects rather than objects of change: not change as something that happens to us, but change for which we can claim responsibility as the product of our own action.

Marxism was born of the critique of an existing socialist and communist movement that arose in the 19th century. Marxism sought to clarify the aims of a movement already underway. Socialism pointed beyond capitalism from within capitalism. As such, socialism was a capitalist phenomenon. It aimed to realize the potentialities of capitalism that capitalism itself held back. Conversely, liberals have regarded socialism as the abandoning of the free potential of capitalism in favor of the retrograde restoration of a more traditional community. Marxism was always aware of this downside of "reactionary or conservative socialism." Marx and Engels themselves, for example, esteemed the ambitious visions of the utopian socialists, born of the optimism of the Industrial Revolution, but they considered that capitalism itself actually outstripped and went beyond the utopians. There was a self-contradictory character in socialism; it both pointed back as well as ahead. This duality followed from capitalism itself, which constantly goes beyond while also restoring bourgeois society.

Socialism wasn't possible before capitalism. Nor was it necessary — nor even desirable. Marxism hence held a dialectical relationship between capitalism and socialism. For Marxism, capitalism is nothing but the possibility and necessity of socialism. Capitalism was for Marxism the crisis born of the contradiction of bourgeois social relations by the industrial forces of production that were the product of the historical progress of bourgeois social relations. In this way, Marxism found the industrial forces of production pointing beyond the bourgeois social relations to be the expression of the self-contradiction of those social relations. What were these "bourgeois social relations," according to Marxism? They were the social relations of labor: the exchange of labor as a commodity as the basis for society, emerging in and through and as the product of the dissolution of the preceding caste community of traditional civilization. Bourgeois society was the liberation of production through the emancipation of labor.

The bourgeois revolution regarded itself as the revolt of labor: the revolt of the Third Estate against the illegitimate authority of the religious and noble-aristocratic orders, the First and Second Estates. The Third Estate comprised all those who worked, as opposed to those who prayed and those who fought. Bourgeois right was the right of labor against the right of might, the right of conquest, upon which the preceding social and political order had been based, and which the Church had blessed. This was the rule of society for thousands of years — perhaps of nature for eons. Bourgeois society is one in which there are "no gods and no masters," no traditionally sanctioned patriarchs and no slaves, but only human social rights: it was the rule of freedom over nature. The struggle for socialism or communism proceeds from this already-accomplished bourgeois emancipation. If there was still illegitimate power — not right based on labor and its exchange-relations in freedom—Marxism regarded this not as a holdover from the ancient past, but a new, modern problem due to capitalism. In this respect, Marxism regarded capitalism as the regression of bourgeois society — the regression from bourgeois freedom: "wage-slavery." It was the regression from a history of freedom to prehistory, a reversion to nature.

Marxism regarded the emerging self-contradiction of bourgeois social relations in capitalism to point beyond the emancipation of labor from traditional civilization, which was necessary but insufficient for full freedom. Alongside the subjective phenomenon of the socialist or communist movement for working-class freedom emerging after the Industrial Revolution, there was a new objective phenomenon of a proletarianized working class, workers expropriated of the social property of their labor as self-possessing owners of commodities, their labor-power and its products as contributions to social cooperation, participating as bourgeois citizens in society through their labor. The "proletariat" refers to citizens without property in the ancient Roman Republic: tribal Romans who were entitled to rights as citizens despite not owning property — which meant not possessing the land of Rome's conquests. (Tribal Romans were a ruling class in the sense of an aristocratic warrior caste of conquerors ruling over subjugated peoples and territories.)

But in bourgeois society, property is not a physical possession claimed through conquest, but a social right recognized through the social relations of labor in free association and cooperation. Hence, a proletarianized working class in bourgeois society is a contradiction in terms, an expression of the self-contradiction of society. For Marxism, it is the Industrial Revolution that divides the bourgeois Third Estate of labor and its social relations into antagonistic interests of capitalists and workers: owners of capital as the means of social production and owners of labor-power as a commodity that is increasingly stripped of its concrete material contribution to social cooperation. This division was an expression of the self-contradiction of freedom in social production, the self-production of society and its free self-transformation.

This is why Marxism regards capitalism as a self-contradiction and crisis of production — and not a matter of unequal distribution and inequitable consumption. It is a crisis of society and its freedom. It is a real crisis of the basis or substance of society, in which workers as citizens lose their social rights, not intentionally or deliberately, but as a result of a seemingly "objective" process of the development of social production. It isn't the result of ruthless exploitation or theft — which bourgeois society condemns as not only illegitimate, but criminal — but something that took place "objectively," as a result of the actions of the workers themselves, and was their responsibility. Workers' demands for the social value of their labor as participants in bourgeois cooperation — the cooperation of citizens in bourgeois society — is an engine driving the improvement of production, to realize and maximize the value of labor in the production of wealth, but undermines the social measure of wealth according to the human time of labor, as industrial production — science and technology — outstrips the measure of human labor-time as the basis for the value of wealth in society. The unintended consequence of this is the devaluation of labor even while social wealth increases.

This is a complex phenomenon that is expressed at both a micro and a macro level. It manifests as a phenomenon of the reproduction of the human species in the historical succession of generations, in which a surplus of workers is experienced as overpopulation — the crisis of the overproduction of both material wealth and of the human race itself. But Marxism regarded it not as surplus humanity, but surplus labor and surplus capital, the waste of social production and of human life, pressing for a resolution. It was a contradiction of wealth and value, or of wealth and the means for appropriating that wealth by society in its social relations of labor. The struggle for the appropriation of social wealth and its potentialities beyond itself between capital and labor isn't a struggle for possession between groups, but a self-contradiction of wealth and its social value in capitalism.

Thus, Marxism regarded communism as the "real movement of history" in capitalism — namely, the real potential possibility of industrial production pointing beyond bourgeois society and its relations of labor. But this real movement of history is contradictory. It is not only linear, but also cyclical: It points backwards as well as forwards, as society struggles to restore the social value of labor even while the industrial condition of material production leaves it behind. The result of this contradictory movement of society in history is not only to divide the bourgeois Third Estate between workers and capitalists, but also and more importantly to divide the proletarianized working class between high-wage and low-wage sectors as well as between employed and unemployed, among other distinctions, in a disparity and hierarchy of exploitation and wealth and participation in social production within the working class, which takes place not only within local communities, but between localities in global production; and not only in space, but in time, for instance between generations, in which older workers might benefit from capitalism at the expense of younger workers or younger workers benefit at the expense of older ones.

In short, capitalism creates competition between workers as a new dynamic of historical movement, fundamentally affecting the concrete forms of social production in capitalism, especially as the conditions for production are struggled over, economically, socially, and politically. But this competition not only promotes innovation or improvement of production as in the original bourgeois vision, but actually undermines and destroys the basis of social production. It devalues both labor and capital, throwing human beings and concrete forms of production prematurely on the scrapheap of history before their full potentials are realized.

In Marx's own time, it appeared that the widening contradiction between bourgeois right and industrial production in society led directly to social and political crisis and antagonism — a political struggle — that demanded resolution. As Marx put it, the capitalists and workers both had bourgeois right — the right of the social value of labor in production, whether in the form of wages or capital — on their side and "where right meets right, force will decide," namely politics (not violence!). Hence, capitalism was a condition of "insoluble contradiction"; the "class struggle" was inevitable.

This class struggle, however, was understood originally by Marxism to be not merely the antagonism of different social groups, capitalists and workers, but the struggle for the proletarianized working class to constitute itself as a social and political force and thus as a class: the proletariat vs. the bourgeoisie. But since the working class not only suffers under but benefits from capitalism — depending on wage-labor to survive and, indeed, to thrive — the class contradiction of the proletariat vs. the bourgeoisie is not the same as the antagonism of the capitalists and the workers — which itself is not identical to the contradiction of capital and labor.

The workers' labor is capital — it is, for instance, "circulating capital vs. fixed capital" and "variable vs. constant capital," according to Marx — and so the social antagonism of capital and labor is always also an antagonism within labor as well as an antagonism within capital. It was not enough for Marxism that the social disintegration of production in capitalism manifest as antagonism, for instance the Darwinian struggle for existence among capitalist firms or among many capitals — for example, between "national" capitals — but also such a struggle among workers — including among "national working classes [sic]" or national sectors of the global working class.

What Marxism regarded as necessary was the self-constitution of the working class as a class in-itself objectively, through the constitution of itself as a class for-itself subjectively. For example, Marxism recognized that, for the value of labor as a commodity to be constituted in industrial (as opposed to artisanal) production at all requires collective bargaining. Without collective bargaining, labor is not even a commodity, not even a unit of social exchange, and there is no bourgeois social relation or bourgeois right of labor to be found at all — this is why liberal democratic bourgeois thought found labor union collective-bargaining to be necessary not only to preserve, but to constitute bourgeois social rights in capitalism.

But the workers' struggle to constitute their social right in capitalism was for Marxism the constitution of the contradiction of capitalism: the contradiction of industrial forces by bourgeois social relations. Society itself seemed to face a choice between supporting human labor in the working class and supporting scientific technique and technology in production. It is society as a whole that faces the choice and contradiction of capital vs. labor. This includes the working class in its collective bargaining as a social subject in capitalism — whether this takes place economically through trade-union negotiation in private employment contracts, or as the public subject of citizenry in political democracy adjudicating law and policy.

For Marxism, the limits — the self-contradiction — that the proletarianized working class came up against in capitalism had already been faced in bourgeois society and liberal democracy, in both civil society and political democracy, in the early 19th century, and the struggle for socialism or communism had emerged as a consequence of such limits being reached and contradictions made manifest as an inevitable impasse in history. But this contradiction and limit had manifested and reached an impasse in the socialist or communist movement itself, producing divisions and antagonisms in both theory and practice among the socialists who predated and lived into and as contemporaries of Marx's own time.

Not only that, but the self-contradictory character of socialism had already been recognized in bourgeois economic, social, and political thought and among bourgeois politicians — sometimes more acutely than among the socialists themselves. Not only Marxists and socialists, but bourgeois thinkers and political actors found the real movement of history to lead inevitably to socialism. Conservative bourgeois and reactionary observers in the 19th century bemoaned it, but nonetheless recognized the inexorable tide of history moving against them, toward socialism. So the problem was one to be faced and overcome by the would-be reformers and "revolutionaries" of capitalism themselves, whether from among the workers or the capitalists. For Marxism, the class struggle was one over the direction of society within and beyond capitalism.

The workers' struggle for socialism was motivated by a conservative impulse to restore bourgeois social relations — the value of labor in society promised by the bourgeois revolution — but this pointed beyond capitalism in that industrial production foreclosed any such return to the idyll of a community of cooperative producers. In capitalism, we live in a community not of labor, but of capital, and this must lead us beyond bourgeois society. But capitalism's crises lead us back into bourgeois society — if we fail to constitute the political will of socialism. Because such will is itself self-contradictory — simultaneously Luddite and techno-utopian — it tasks consciousness in specific ways, in both practice and theory, and demands sustained effort over significant historical periods, long enough for the problem to come into view with an adequate horizon of proper perspective.

Marxism began by taking up and critiquing the crisis and confusion of contemporary 19th-century reformers and revolutionaries as a matter of their self-contradictory social and political aspirations and visions — how these were not observations from outside, but perspectives from within capitalism itself, from within its self-contradiction and crisis, pointing not only to potential possibilities beyond itself, but to its seemingly inevitable end.

The purpose of Marxism in its original historical moment was to serve as a critical faculty in the progress of the proletarianized working class's struggle for socialism. It was to arm socialists with an awareness of the reasons for the historical crises besetting their own movement, and precisely in its success and forward motion. But not only that success and forward motion, but the movement itself ended long ago.

Today, by contrast, after the rise and fall of historical Marxism over a century ago, and due to its failure, capitalism no longer appears to have an inevitable end expressed by the possibility and necessity of socialism, but rather "socialism" seems to be a mere desire, a utopian vision divorced from practical reality, whether economic, political, or social. For instance, socialism has become an aspiration that, as the DSA's *Jacobin* magazine founder and editor Bhaskar Sunkara put it recently, is "at its core moral and ethical in nature," but which drives not inevitably towards its revolutionary realization, but rather motivates capitalist reforms to render distribution more "equitable," and this is primarily on a national-state and not international, let alone global, level. This necessarily and not accidentally avoids the contradiction of capital — and guarantees its perpetuation.

The problem of capitalism is today no longer faced, let alone grasped as a self-contradiction of the workers' struggles leading to the necessity of socialism as a historic task, but is just a matter of unbearably excessive social pathologies and suffering demanding capitalist political measures to try to deal with mounting discontents: *Jacobin* and the DSA are formulating solutions for capitalism to continue, albeit under new leadership.

The current crisis of neoliberalism is not a terminal crisis of capitalism — not even one that could be made so politically — but merely an opportunity for the reconstitution of it. And not through the self-constitution of the working class as an economic, social, and political subject of history, but just as an electoral constituency of liberal democracy. And not even a subject of political democracy, but an object of state policy.

*Jacobin* agonizes over its role as would-be professional managers of the working class; really, they aren't even that, but just self-deluded ideologues opining their craft of spin for the latest capitalist messaging. More or less unemployed Millennial and Zoomer workers watch YouTube videos as neurasthenics between anxious applications for their next gigs, seeking to explain the reasons for their endless misery. Hopefully, they will quickly forget them for the niche click-bait ephemera that they are, in favor of more mainstream, and hence more socially rational, pursuits.

This is why the existential crisis of humanity and society shows up today not in the battle of politics and democracy in a proletarianized society and its working class's struggles, but rather in culture and psychology, about which Marxism has nothing to say beyond how these are already expressed by humanistic bourgeois culture in crisis, including its most radical "anthropological" questioning, such as speculations on the "trans-" or "post-human" condition of society in capitalism. It is not raised to the level of collective politics in public life — not even as matters of technocratic management, which is just a reified and ossified mechanized bourgeois humanism in crisis — but devolves upon isolated individuals in their private misery.

Supposed "Marxism" today isn't the critical self-clarification it once was of a historic revolutionary or even reform movement for socialism, but is just an obscure justification for choosing among policies for managing the crisis of capitalism that is no longer regarded as an insoluble contradiction and historical impasse, but has become naturalized as a permanent condition of society and of humanity, purported "human nature" itself — including the degraded condition of what passes for "politics" today as the gang warfare telling you which "side" to be on — among the ruins of bourgeois society in capitalism.

Marxism today has no goal to work toward, but serves only as a reminder that there once was a purpose, a purpose to capitalism, in socialism. Without an existing struggle for socialism, Marxism has no purpose. Without the purpose of socialism, there is no Marxism.

The end of Millennial Marxism has been to realize this — or not.

Parts presented on a panel at the fourteenth annual Platypus International Convention in conversation with Benjamin Studebaker (formerly of the *What's Left?* podcast and author of *The Chronic Crisis of American Democracy: The Way Is Shut*), Donald Parkinson (editor-in-chief of *Cosmonaut* magazine and a member of the Marxist Unity Group organizing committee), and James Heartfield (historian and activist, author of *Britain's Empires* among others), at Northwestern University on April 2, 2022, a transcript of which is available in *Platypus Review* 153 (February 2023).

Originally published in *Compact* (July 1, 2022)

# Dogmatization and thought-taboos on the Left

The title for my opening remarks is "Dogmatization and thought-taboos on the 'Left,'" which is a phrase taken from Theodor Adorno's 1966 book *Negative Dialectics* on what Marxism succumbed to in the 20th century.[1] I want to begin with a quotation from Georg Lukács's essay on "Class Consciousness" from his 1923 book *History and Class Consciousness*. Lukács wrote that,

> Only the consciousness of the proletariat can point to the way that leads out of the impasse of capitalism. As long as this consciousness is lacking, the crisis remains permanent, it goes back to its starting-point, repeats the cycle until after infinite sufferings and terrible detours the school of history completes the education of the proletariat and confers upon it the leadership of mankind. But the proletariat is not given any choice. As Marx says, it must become a class not only "as against capital" but also "for itself;" that is to say, the class struggle must be raised from the level of economic necessity to the level of conscious aim and effective class consciousness. The pacifists and humanitarians of the class struggle whose efforts tend whether they will or no to retard this lengthy, painful and crisis-ridden process would be horrified if they could but see what sufferings they inflict on the proletariat by extending this course of education. But the proletariat cannot abdicate its mission. The only question at issue is how much it has to suffer before it achieves

---

1 Trans. E. B. Ashton (New York: Continuum, 2007), 143.

ideological maturity, before it acquires a true understanding of its class situation and a true class consciousness.[2]

We have a lot more suffering yet to endure, it seems. The true understanding of the working class's situation and of its true class consciousness has yet to be achieved. Marxists do not have it ready-made for them. But they act like they do. This is how and why Marxism has become a parody of itself, a farce of proletarian class consciousness. Marxism has come to serve entirely other ends than those of proletarian socialism: It has become a middle class — bourgeois — ideology of discontents within capitalism, actually of aspirations for more "progressive" capitalism, and not for overcoming it. The bitter lesson of history — attended to by the avowed Right — is that attempts to improve capitalism have made it "progressively" worse. At least worse in the sense of accumulated problems more difficult to overcome. And certainly worse in terms of a more confounding task politically difficult to engage and achieve. In comparison to past times, the working class seems hopelessly lost in the labyrinth of capitalism, confronted immediately by a host of every conceivable problem more directly than by capitalism itself. It is wishful thinking or ugly naïveté to think that as Marxists we can point to all these problems and simply call them "capitalism." In this sense, the problem of capitalism has yet to actually present itself. It must be made to. And that will not happen before the working class is organized as a social and political force to confront it. The issue is what stands in the way of that. The Left today is itself an obstacle to working class struggle. If not the most major obstacle, still a very significant one.

The topic of this panel is "censorship on the Left," but I am going to address that indirectly, by articulating myself the Marxism that is censored on the Left, and not just recently but for a long time already. What is censored is what is tabooed, and what is tabooed is proletarian socialism as Marxism understood it. When Marxism is expressed today it is in self-censored form, as dogmatic. The certitudes of Marxism cover up a crucial uncertainty, namely the content of the task of proletarian socialism.

---

2   Trans. Rodney Livingstone (Cambridge, MA: MIT Press, 1971), 76.

One thing that frustrates students of Marxism is its lack of a blueprint for the liberated society beyond capitalism — what socialism or communism is meant to look like. But while Marxism accepted and promulgated the Hegelian notion of "determinate negation," this did not mean a determination of the socialist society. Rather, capitalism was the determinate negation of bourgeois society in the contradiction of industrial production. The proletarianized working class was the determinate negation of bourgeois social relations as objectified in capitalism, the contradiction of living and dead labor. Etc. What Marxism was certain of was not the content of emancipation — freedom — that will have overcome capitalism, but rather the negative necessity with which the working class must overcome capitalism. Capitalism is the negation of bourgeois society that must itself be negated, and by a negatively determined subject, the proletariat. Marxism was not positive about anything but this. The proletariat was not to posit its own being in the place of bourgeois society, but to abolish itself in overcoming capitalism.

The present condition of the ostensible "Left" is due to its thought-taboos about socialism. Everything flows from fear of and hostility to the working class. There is no trust in empowering the working class, which is seen as racist, sexist, homophobic etc. or otherwise ignorant and backward. Socialist revolution is regarded as impossible, unnecessary, and undesirable by the "Left." The Marxist concept of the dictatorship of the proletariat, apart from any technical details, is something to which the present Left is fundamentally averse. One key reason for this is avoidance of objective criteria for societal transformation beyond capitalism in favor of more subjective concerns, indeed matters of cultural taste. The old Marxist adage that the goal and task is to change conditions not attitudes has been forgotten.

Leftist intellectuals today are unable to subordinate their activity to the requirements of building working class social and political power, but assume rather that the working class ought to submit to the ideology of the Left, a complete reversal of the historical Marxist approach. The Left regards the working class as its instrument for implementing its ideology rather than aspiring to become the working class's political instrument in changing society. It seeks support from the working class for its power, rather than offering its support for working class power.

Looking out onto our audience, I would love to be able to say that you are proletarian socialist revolutionaries, but, no, you are petit bourgeois intellectuals, with all the problems this entails. How do I know this? By everything that you say and do, what you think and how you feel. (I don't mean this pejoratively or to call out or disqualify you, but just to attend to the actual roles you play and functions you perform, which cannot be changed but only potentially turned to a different purpose, to serve proletarian socialist revolution, through discipline to its social and political tasks, rather than to reproduce capitalism.) You find the problem of capitalism — when you are really considering this at all, which is very rare — to be a moral one of unfairness and injustice, of abject suffering and misery. This is not how Marxists once approached things.

Sohrab Ahmari recently published in *Compact Magazine* a report on the *Labor Notes* conference in Chicago, where he observed a cultural divide between unionized workers in attendance and the conference organizers — one might say simply, between the workers and the organized labor bureaucrats. The latter, as dutiful Democrats, engaged in woke culturalism, while the former ignored the discursive and behavioral rules for the conference, for instance neglecting COVID masking and proclamations of gender identity. Why do things like the latter matter, if they do at all? Perhaps they don't. But in trying to model behavior prefiguratively, the Left gives a misleading impression of the kind of society we are living in and the one proletarian socialists aspire for. By following the lead of Democratic Party woke capitalism, the Left proclaims itself to be part of the ruling ideology. It wrongly identifies the interests of the working class and "socialism" itself with the political fortunes of "progressive liberal" capitalism. They channel working-class organizing and any potential struggle into the terms of the capitalist employers and managers, if not their immediate ones then the more general staff of the capitalist state and its crony corporate rackets and their interests. It is a massive concession to workplace discipline imposed by the bosses to protect them from lawsuit litigation. Indeed, this is because organized labor today is mostly in the business of legal disputes over labor contracts and not class struggle at all.

How can I say that? Because I am a Marxist, and hence for me class struggle means the struggle for socialism, and the struggle for socialism means the constituting and growing, building and developing of the social and political organization and power of the proletarianized working class, leading to their taking over the control of society as a whole. Organized labor has nothing to do with that today, but only for managing an increasingly raw deal for the workers to protect the unions' own vested interests. They are not organs of working class power but rather the opposite, for capitalist power over the workers, only negotiating the terms for the latter. This is why they concede all the major points and terms to the capitalists, all the way up to the culture demanded and promulgated by the state and corporations for the everyday practices of capitalism.

To the degree that this culture remains utterly foreign to the working class in its lived reality and consciousness, this is a good thing and a great opportunity for actual socialist organizing. If workers are cynical about the rules and etiquette they are forced to observe on the job, then this means that their hearts and minds are available for entirely other consciousness. For the most part this is taken by religion and other traditional cultural values. The latter are wise enough to concede to this fallen world its sinfulness and to "render unto Caesar" whatever might be demanded, while preserving true spiritual values separately and apart from this.

But the Left makes it seem that practical struggles over matters of life — pursuit of which was never foresworn entirely but accepted by religion, again wisely! — must take place within a framework of social and political power that must be accepted as such, and this massively undercuts and hobbles not merely the attitudes and ideas of the working class but its material concerns as well. It actively lowers the political horizon of what seems possible and necessary, and indeed creates the very space in which socially, culturally and politically reactionary ideology — and the regrettable cynicism — can flourish.

If working class people seem to agree or say what you want to hear, it is because they have learned the wisdom to keep their mouths shut and their true feelings private. They have learned to suffer in silence. Occasionally, they might find some resonance in what you say and find a glimmer of hope of recognition, but it is always qualified with a great deal of reservation, hard-bitten with past discouragement. Workers are seldom in the position to indulge in the enthusiasms of true belief. But the Left are nothing if not true believers — they can afford their illusions, however disposable they prove to be, blown from one passing fad to the next. The working class knows the difference between entertainment and real life. The Left are hucksters — who are themselves the most easily bamboozled. But social-ism will not be a swindle — that is, if it is not merely another capitalist ideology. "Socialism" today is just that, what Marx criticized ruthlessly as a pernicious illusion of capitalism by another name.

This is because the Left, as a petit bourgeois intellectual phenomenon, itself can neither feel nor see, let alone believe in, the necessary task and potential society as a goal beyond capitalism to be engaged and achieved. The Left's vision and imagination are conditioned by the very wrong — opposite — perspective of considering only what can be controlled or managed differently, rather than as a fundamentally different state of being.

Not that working class people can imagine or envision this, either, but at least they know that it is not a matter of managing or controlling, getting others to do what they want or convincing themselves of something to do, since that is not true to their experience, but only of cooperation, motivated by working together. The labor bureaucracy takes advantage of this to the detriment of the workers by posing matters as those of co-management of work by unions in cooperation with employers, labor and capital working together. A fine bourgeois sentiment, but woefully inadequate — need I say so? — to the struggle for proletarian socialism, from a Marxist perspective.

You will always remain mere petit bourgeois democrats — whether lower-case or upper-case Democrats — not socialists, because you will always submit to whatever "progressive" capitalists dangle before you.

What is the true task of socialist intellectuals, then? To grasp the truth of this society that underlies and transcends its immediate realities, but which constrains things in a deformed image of what they could and should become beyond them. The trick is how to distinguish overcoming cap-italism from merely its next phase. Generations of purportedly "socialist" intelligentsia have performed the function of more or less brain-trusting the renovation of capitalism. But this is actually the very least of their crimes.

The principal issues of present society, today, globally and historically — as a matter of world history — how it is that conditions everywhere came to be as they are now, are not racism, sexism, homophobia, etc. (for instance, religious sectarianism and ethno-cultural differences), which are either thousands of years old or, on the contrary, indeed very modern phenomena, but rather are due to capitalism, which is only two hundred years young.

This is not a world of blacks and whites, or Muslims, Jews, Christians, animists, Buddhists, and Hindus etc., or men and women, or queers and straights, or nonbinaries and cisgendered, or Latins, Anglos, Germans, Slavs, Celts, Scandinavians, Nordics, Mediterraneans, Turks, Arabs, Semites, Caucasoids, Negroids, and Mongoloids, Neolithics and Paleolithics, etc., but of workers — and a few capitalists who have thankfully saved the funds necessary for investment in old and new production.

The fact that Leftists today must mis-imagine socialism in progressive liberal terms of pluralist democracy and cultural tolerance and respect — which is actually the more or less official dogma of liberal democratic and international cosmopolitan capitalism, and not only recently, but for the past 200 years — means they are profoundly mistaken from the start, and proceeding in a way utterly foreign and alien(ating) to the working class, both of their own and of any other country in the world. If workers ever listen to them, it is actually as their social and cultural "betters," as their friendly bosses, rather than the strict hard-asses following more directly the imperatives of capital without the polite discursive couching and legalistic disclaimers and expressions of sympathy.

Insofar as young people appear to be more idealistically Leftist, this is only because they haven't yet learned, let alone mastered, the actual rules of the game, and have been misled by their teachers into thinking that something different is possible in capitalism than is actually the case: They call "capitalism" everything that thwarts or disappoints their ingenuously naïve sense — actually lack of sense — of reality.

Not that their fantasies are utterly valueless, but they must be recognized as what they are, capitalist fantasies, to be actually useful in any way. This society does generate felt senses of possibility that are cruelly betrayed constantly by the onrush of history in capitalism. But they are not exact and indeed are necessarily and not accidently indeterminate. We do not — cannot — know what a socialist society beyond capitalism will look like. This is because the future will not in fact be our doing. Nor will it be that of anyone today who is able to deliberately determine it consciously — of whom there is in fact no one now.

This is not so bad as it might sound, since we neither are nor ever will be in a position to create such a world. Only the working class could ever be in that position, precisely because the world as it is now is the result of their action — and inaction — for the last two hundred years. If we hate the world as it now is, it is because it is the world the working class has created — and we hate them for it.

By contrast, if we ever confront actual capitalists about the state of the world, they can legitimately shrug their shoulders, sincerely express their regrets, and point to conditions beyond their control — by which they mean the billions of workers. If we resent them for this, it is because we are under the illusion that, if instead of them we were in charge, things would be so much better. It is not as workers but rival capitalists — as petit as opposed to haut bourgeois — that we challenge their authority (we don't really dispute their power but only envy it).

And that is the point: The world will not be what we as Leftist or socialist intellectuals might imagine or envision or want it today in capitalism, but only what the working class might make it in the future, whether or not they ever overcome capitalism, they will have made the world as they will — and precisely not as we would. Our task is to support and help them in their overcoming of the capitalist limitations to their remaking the world.

The best we can do is to understand the limitations of capitalism. And to do so means overcoming — actually, first recognizing — the dogmatization and thought-taboos of capitalism that we will otherwise enforce, over ourselves and over any (mercifully few) workers within our reach, even and especially when we don't think that we are doing so.

We ourselves, in everything we feel and think, do and say, are the blinders from which we as well as others must be freed. We are the instruments which will be used, more or less, to remake the world, either as capitalist — through the capitalist tools that we are — or otherwise. Can we allow ourselves to be remade — by the working class — to help remake the world other than as we would?

Remarks originally delivered on a panel on "self-censorship" with Norman Finkelstein, Spencer Leonard, Jason Myles and Kuba Wrzesniewski at the *Sublation Media* launch event held in New York City on June 26, 2022.

Published in *Sublation Magazine* (July 1, 2022)

# Postscripta

# Why not Trump, again?

I identify strongly with the wrongly accused. So does America more broadly. And Trump has been wrongly accused. If you are in the right, then there is no need to lie. And they have lied about Trump.

All the criminal charges and civil lawsuits against Trump — literally every single one — are using "novel legal theories" and "unprecedented applications of the law." This is not because he was once President and no President has been tried previously. Anyone sued or prosecuted this way would be in the same untested waters of injustice.

And it is injustice. The idea of liberal democracy is that rights come before the law. Even those proven guilty have rights, and that includes the right not to be prosecuted even if you are indeed guilty of the crime with which you are accused — even if you had criminal intent and deliberately did wrong, prosecuting you can violate your rights. Prosecutorial discretion means that a choice not to do so can serve the ends of justice. That there is a choice and decision involved in prosecution — that it is not automatic — gives it an air of arbitrariness and hence injustice. This is indeed the point of criminal trials: to prove that the state has the right, so to speak, to violate your rights, and an injustice will be allowed by representatives of the people, who are thus shown to be responsible for it: in this case, the rights to life, liberty and the pursuit of happiness will not be respected. It is understood that the law and the state that enforces it are inherent violations of your rights — of everyone's rights.

Critics of Trump's prosecution are correct that it is a Stalinist Beria-style "show me the man and I will find the crime" targeting not of an offense but a person whose guilt is presumed. This is contrary to the presumption of innocence that favors the rights of the accused — including the right not to be investigated, let alone charged, at all. Who will defend such rights? The people. — Certainly not the state.

In the U.S., the trial favors the defendant — not so elsewhere, where it favors the state. When found not guilty before the law, a defendant is not thus found to be innocent — which can never be proved — but merely not culpable in the eyes of the state: the state is prevented from punishing you, but it does not find that you did no wrong. This is why a defendant who is not found guilty in criminal court can still be sued civilly and subject to civil judgment. Courts do not decide morality but only law — legal liability.

A jury votes on whether the state is permitted to violate your rights. That is democracy. This is why a jury can say, regardless of whether the state has proved its case beyond a reasonable doubt or not, that you are not to be held guilty before the law, even if you did indeed do the crime of which you are accused.

We don't like that. But this is what freedom requires. The law is not absolute. Neither do facts amount to judgments. This is why factual innocence is not a legal defense in appeal of a conviction. If the law has been followed, then the facts are immaterial, for the people have decided to hold you accountable anyway.

But you can always be pardoned. The law and the people can convict you, and you can still be relieved of responsibility. The chief executive can decide otherwise. Your rights even as a guilty person can be vindicated ultimately.

In a criminal trial are present the three branches of government in the U.S. Constitutional Republic that we hear so much about — it is a democratic republic, even if not simply a democracy. The executive branch elected to enforce the law is present in the prosecutor. The judicial branch in the judge. And the people are in the jury of your peers. All interpret the law. All decide whether and how the law will be applied, if at all.

In the separation of powers of checks and balances in divided government, the legislature is composed of representatives of the people who make the laws. But since it is representative and not direct democracy, the people are supposed to continually decide on whether the laws actually represent them: this is why they are constantly revised, and why representatives are constantly replaced — or at least hypothetically are supposed to be, though in practice most serve interminably entrenched in office.

But who actually writes the laws in advanced capitalism? Not the legislative representatives themselves or their staff, but corporate lobbyists and government bureaucrats — laws so elaborate and complex that the public cannot understand them, but only those same bureaucrats and corporate agents who game the legal system that they themselves create, in which their own sophistry prevails. But this violates what is supposed to be the spirit of the laws.

The legislative representatives judge the will of the people in writing the law; the executives interpret the law and make decisions about enforcing it or not; and the judicial branch judges whether the execution of the law accords with rights — and indeed whether the laws themselves are right: they both review the law itself as well as its execution. All are elected — all are understood to be political in nature, namely, that they are functions of constituting the *polis* in action.

The law does not have divine but only human status: provisional, fallible, revisable, imperfect — and hence fundamentally unjust. In a criminal trial, justice is not to be achieved but is only at best a by-product of the application of the law. It is the justice in the application of the law that is at issue, not justice for the crime, which is impossible — as God says, "Vengeance is Mine."

In modern, that is to say, bourgeois society, it is understood that the law does not make society but society makes the law. Society does not serve the state, but the state serves society.

The U.S. is not a democracy — not like Ancient Athens, in which the state was society and society was the state — but a constitutional republic. Moreover, the Constitution is interpreted according to the principles of the Declaration of Independence — according to the principles of the American Revolution.[1]

It is not democracy because it is not the rule of the people but rather the rule of law. And the rule of law is not identical with the rule of society.

---

1   See Cutrone, "The American Revolution and the Left" (2020) in *The Death of the Millennial Left* (Sublation, 2023).

There are civil rights, meaning, the rights of civil society against the state — and against the laws the state enforces.

These rights are inalienable. You can never lose your rights but only have them abrogated — violated. And these rights are not only for citizens, but are human rights: they apply to everyone where the U.S. Constitution can hold sway. — The U.S. is not a nation-state, because the principles of the Declaration of Independence and U.S. Constitution are understood to apply everywhere and to everyone — at least where feasible: the scope and reach of the Revolution.

The U.S. Constitutional order and system is revolutionary. It is expansive and ever-deepening. We continue to recognize and explore the full dimensions of rights — of freedom. This is not a local but a world-wide phenomenon. The Revolution has the power to protect all escaped slaves on its free soil — and beyond.

Do we still believe it? People around the world do. Perhaps some haven't heard it yet — that somewhere they have been recognized as free.

Citizen Trump is trying to go back to Washington. Who is trying to stop him? Certainly not the people. Or at least not all of them. Perhaps not even a majority.

Liberal democracy means — unlike Ancient democracy — recognizing and protecting the rights of minorities against the majority — not least why there are civil rights against the law voted by the majority. And this includes a minority of one. A single person with whom no one agrees nonetheless has rights against everyone else. — Do we still believe it?

Capitalism demands that we surrender our rights to the needs not of society but of capital. But we are liable to misrecognize the needs of capital as those of society. And of course they are: the needs of an alienated society. When we think we are serving the needs of society we are inevitably always serving the needs of capital. We surrender our rights to the needs not of society but of capital. Always.

Marx recognized long ago that socialism is capitalism — capitalism is socialism. Socialism is not freedom but its alienated projection: a projection of capitalism. Capitalism is alienated society and socialism is a projection of that alienation. This includes political alienation, which becomes a mystification of the law and state, their reification and hypostatization

— ironically, since the bourgeois revolution had secularized law and the state and removed them from the domain of divine justification and religious authority, bringing them within the realm of consciousness of society in history. That consciousness has withered.

Marx critiqued socialism as an alienated misrecognition of the content of freedom, in which it appears as either anarchy or totalitarian statism: as pure irrationalism or pure rationalism. But as usual for the Marxist dialectic, it is both and neither.

Socialism was meant to work through this crisis of bourgeois emancipation and its political form of liberal democracy in capitalism, not negate it in either libertarianism or totalitarian democracy.

Classical liberal thought is usually associated with the so-called "minimal state," but this is misleading. In the conception of the U.S. Constitutional order envisaged by the Founders — the American Revolutionaries — the tyranny of the state was not merely counterposed to the freedom of society, but the different elements of state power were counterbalanced against each other as opposed tyrannies: the tyranny of law; the tyranny of judicial judgment; and the tyranny of executive action. Each was a dictatorship checking and balancing the others: a legislative dictatorship; judicial dictatorship; and executive dictatorship.

It is the third of these that concerns us here, regarding Trump. Trump stands accused of abusing power and wanting to establish dictatorship. But against this the dictatorial powers of the law and the state enforcement of it are being mobilized against his candidacy for reelection to the Presidency. In so doing, Trump's opponents are threatening the authority and power of the executive embodied in the Presidency as such. The President is an elected monarch — an elected dictator. This is especially so in capitalism which brings out the necessity of dictatorial methods especially prominently, turning it from a rare occasion of emergency into the normal exercise in managing the rolling crises of capital. Marx called this the "Bonapartism" of the capitalist state, as distinct from its earlier, pre-Industrial Revolution bourgeois form. This is seen in the rise of a permanent police force and prisons, both of which are inventions of the industrial era, to control the proletariat. From the subsequent Progressive era, we get a "fourth branch of government," namely the permanent bureaucracy of the administrative state. It is the dictatorship of this Deep State that has conflicted with that of the elected Presidency. This has raised the issue of civilian government per se. Trump represents elected civilian authority over the state where they clash.

Trump claims Presidential immunity from criminal prosecution — the Lockean executive prerogative to break the law in order to preserve it. There is already legislative (parliamentary) and judicial immunity, to prevent abusive exercise of the law by the executive — which in Locke's moment was that of the hereditary monarchy and its appointed Majesty's deputies (including judges). What is usually overlooked is the need to prevent the reverse, the legislative (and judicial) abuse of the executive function of government. There is indeed a Deep State of permanent bureaucratic "special bodies of armed men" in the state of capitalism, which has sought to escape political responsibility to the civilian authority of elected office in the Presidency. Trump was targeted by the Deep State as well as by his political adversaries (Democrats and Republicans) from the beginning of his candidacy.

The Unitary Executive Theory raised in response to the Nixon-era reforms curtailing Presidential authority and power is both legally and politically correct: that without untrammeled executive power, there is tyranny. The bureaucratic administrative changes made after Watergate, establishing independence of federal law enforcement from the Presidency at the dawn of the neoliberal era were long in the making, and blind or indifferent to the fatal compromise of politics involved in it. Nixon was ousted by the CIA and FBI — as they've now tried to do with Trump. It is not surprising that along with Trump and the crisis of the electoral political parties manifesting at the end of neoliberalism, the problematic rationale of these post-Nixon changes is surfacing again now. Nixon said he thought that if the President did it, it wasn't illegal. He might have been right about that. He resigned to avoid impeachment — which is importantly a political and not legal process, conducted by elected politicians not career prosecutors and law enforcement officers. The post-Watergate reforms removed the Deep State in the executive branch of federal government from elected political civilian authority.

Trump maintains that the decision of his case will affect not only his own fate, but that of the U.S. Presidency as such. This is simply true. Should the President become a mere figurehead for the permanent Deep State? Are Presidential initiatives merely suggestions to the bureaucracy? Congress has set up unelected bureaucratic executive agencies whose decisions have the force of law. Is the Presidential election merely a rallying-point for down-ballot candidates to Congress? Is there only to be legislation and lawfare in the courts, and no longer any executive prerogative by electoral mandate? The Presidency is the only office chosen by the entire electorate — however mediated by the federal state system, still, the President is the only nationally elected politician. This is what makes him dangerous.

Trump is wrongly accused not because he didn't do what they say, but because his prosecution is wrongly motivated, and is intended to abrogate liberal democracy in a very pointed way: by violating the personal rights of an individual and denying the collective political rights of democracy.

Marx declared the goal of communism to be a situation where the "freedom of each is the precondition for the freedom of all." This was no utopian goal but an existing value already in bourgeois society, however violated by capitalism, but still to be aspired as a task in getting beyond it. It was a principle to be observed in practice — so that its compromise could be recognized as a problem in the here and now, not to be accepted in its apparent but false necessity in capitalism. Socialism was to realize this.

But the pseudo-"Left" has long fallen into the antinomy of individualism vs. collectivism in capitalist contradiction, and has taken on the latter value as its own — abandoning personal liberty to the avowed Right. However, conservative collectivism also belongs to the Right, demanding the sacrifice of the individual. We should not agree to this demand, and certainly not in the name of "social justice."

The fact that Trump appears politically as both a private person only selfishly motivated and a public menace unleashing the demons of popular fury is indicative of the contradiction that liberal democracy presents in capitalism. He thus perfectly embodies the issue. That he is an unremarkably moderate conservative Centrist in his policies and politics only emphasizes this fact: Citizen Trump is the problem.

The threat of "fascism" — the specter of Ancient democracy and tribal republicanism — has haunted the capitalist world from the inception of its crisis. After long crying wolf at Trump, finally on January 6, 2021, Trump seemed to confirm the worst fears by summoning a mob to riot at the Capitol to delay or prevent certification of his electoral defeat — to "stop the steal." Perhaps, as Nixon said in 1960, "they stole it fair and square," and so there's no point in challenging it. But the man has a right to speak, however demagogically, and the people have a right to protest against their government at its public buildings, whose physical structures and political procedures after all belong to them — and no one but them. They belong to us.

Trump's election was protested by Democrats, so why is protesting Biden's election forbidden?

The Democrats and established Republicans sought to delegitimize Trump's election, and Trump returned the favor. Evidently his most prized classified documents were those that showed his innocence of the Russia collusion hoax manufactured against him by the Democrats and Deep State.

In this sense, we have the historic right and obligation, the duty as a society, to experience politically the phenomenon of Trump, for it shows all the weak and blind spots of liberal democracy in capitalism. As Tocqueville said ironically of American democracy, the public receives the government it deserves: as a society we also get the public we deserve. Trump demands that we confront the problem of politics this society has produced in capitalism. But Trump is — by far — not the worst example of it.

As I wrote more than eight years ago, when Trump first appeared on the political stage, the crisis of neoliberalism has been a crisis of its politics, and this takes the form of a crisis of liberal democracy, specifically of its political parties. All the anxious talk about "populism" betrays this fact.

In Ancient Rome, every election was attended by gang warfare and blood on the streets spilled by the competing factions. Candidates were assassinated, and elections triggered civil wars — as in capitalism. Every election was a political revolution. This is still the case, and it shows. The bug is a feature; the glitch is the algorithm; the noise is the music — of democracy. It is a *Gesamtkunstwerk* — but not necessarily a *Götterdämmerung*. Especially in the U.S., which is a continuation of the original American

Revolution. Vivek Ramaswamy called for reinvigorating the spirit of 1776: he sees that in Trump.

The answer proposed by Trump's traumatized opponents is to suspend rights and avoid election: to cancel liberalism and democracy; to ban the opera and imprison its diva. This is no exaggeration. They have done and will do everything they possibly can to try preventing Trump's election and taking office, in a most remarkable series of events in the history of the U.S. Neither Trump and his supporters nor his opponents are wrong in saying that the fate of American democracy is on the line. The only question is what this says and what it means. Are we afraid to learn? We have yet to figure it out.

Trump and Trumpism are not going away, whatever we might wish. The task of politics remains — even and perhaps especially in the crisis of capitalist politics. It points the way to socialist politics, from the very heart of liberal democracy in crisis. Without a political party for socialism, this is the — very best — politics capitalism has to offer. Are we afraid of it?

So, I repeat the question, for the third time,[2] now: why not Trump — again?

Presented on April 5, 2024, at the opening plenary panel discussion on "Liberal democracy in crisis?" of the Platypus Affiliated Society's sixteenth annual International Convention, with Jordan De Anda (For the People), Howie Hawkins (U.S. Green Party), Ralph Leonard (writer at *Unherd*, *Areo*, et al.) and Matt McManus (author of *The Political Theory of Liberal Socialism*).

Originally published in *Platypus Review* 166 (May 2024)

---

2    See Cutrone, "Why not Trump?" (2016) and "Why not Trump again?" (2020) in *The Death of the Millennial Left*.

# The alternative to genocide

The alternative to extermination is slavery — labor. The only reason for conquerors not to kill the defeated is to put them to work — to make them useful. If they cease to be useful or prove to be more trouble than they are worth, they will be killed. That is the lesson of history.

The Keynesian economist Joan Robinson famously said that, "The misery of being exploited by capitalists is nothing compared to the misery of not being exploited at all."

The terrorism of the Second Intifada 2000–05 brought an end to Palestinian labor in Israel. Not entirely, but substantially: the Palestinians became disposable. That was actually the end. We have been living in its aftermath for the past quarter of a century. It is coming to a conclusion now. Hamas was elected, and that election is coming to fruition.[1]

October 7 was a no-turning-back moment for Israel. Palestinian terrorism is to be utterly crushed in a way that has never been attempted previously. It will succeed. The only alternative to this will in fact be genocide — not rhetorically, but literally. Let us hope it doesn't come to that.

Hamas calls the Palestinians a "nation of martyrs." Palestinian activists loudly proclaim that they will "never surrender." It's easy for them to say. In the meantime, mere survival will demand otherwise. The Palestinians will work. Or they will die. — They will work.

Before October 7, there was a *modus vivendi* in which Israel allowed tens of thousands of Gazans to work in Israel, supporting their families back home: tens of thousands more. After October 7, tens of thousands have been killed, with further tens of thousands grievously wounded: hundreds

---

1    See "Israel-Palestine and the Left," in this volume.

of thousands more are left bereft. Israel is teaching a horrifying lesson, and it is the lesson of the modern world, if not for all of history. It is a lesson not worth the teaching, because it is already known by everyone — at least by every worker: The alternative to labor — slavery — is extermination.

What does Marxism have to say about that? — What doesn't Marxism have to say about it? Nothing and everything. But the point is not Marxism but socialism. And for Marxism that means the working class.

Tens of thousands of Palestinian workers in Israel and abroad: What do they have to do with socialism? They are the only ones in fact to have anything to do with socialism. Not upper- or middle-class or social-climber radicals — not nationalists or Islamists: workers. What they can and should do will decide socialism — or not. Perhaps not today or tomorrow, but the next day.

Palestinian workers should have gone to the Israeli kibbutzim not for hostile reconnaissance but labor solidarity: to work alongside Israelis and others, not target them for killing, as before October 7.

Hamas killed that possibility — the only possibility for socialism: in Palestine and everywhere.

Hamas recruits from the otherwise unemployed and unemployable: angry young (wo/)men. It seeks not workers but soldiers, as with any gangsters. — It does no good to point out that the same is true of the IDF: Israel is a state with compulsory conscription; Palestine is not. That's the point. But Palestinians don't need a state; and Israelis must overcome the need for theirs. This is not what Hamas wants: Hamas wants war. Hamas wants to be the state: and states mean wars. But the war is over — for a long time, now. A Palestinian state is either impossible or undesirable for the workers. But it is what Hamas might be getting them. The Israeli state is the Palestinian state: and the state means violence. Whether by Hamas or the IDF — the official or unofficial state: the state of war.

The Palestinians are a conquered people. Perhaps not for all time, but at least for now. This is not going to change — no amount of protest will change it. This is the reality. The only alternative to extermination is slavery. The only alternative to living with defeat is not living with it: dying from it. But there is an alternative to death: life. Life as a worker — it is actually preferable to death! Every worker knows this.

Pick your battles; and live to fight another day. — But Hamas denied Palestinians this option. Purposefully: if they cannot be lords, then there will be no subjects — only, there are: will they be allowed to live? Or will their defeated lords demand their death to honor them?

The idea of a "noble death" is an aristocratic one — perhaps it is also virtuous for priests. The point is that it is not for the people to die nobly: the people can only die miserably. This is what makes them ignoble and dishonorable: clinging to bare life at all cost, no matter the compromise of virtues. — Good!

What does Marxism have to say about that? It does not promise redemption but only possible change in mode of production: an exchange of miseries. And not out of morality but history: objective necessity. The only good is life itself; and the only change that is possible is in how the good of life is to be achieved.

There is no objective reason for an end to suffering, but only for transforming its necessity. Marxism is resolutely "materialistic," placing "happiness" as the goal in the struggle for freedom — not principle.

Marx wrote his dissertation on Epicurus and Democritus — Marx was a democratic epicurean. This is what is called "socialism." "Communism" seems nobler — which is why Marx criticized it: Marx was not interested in the subjective communism of intellectuals, but the objective communism of workers. Will they have it?

Marx found in communism the scent of religion, and not from the "rose in the cross" but something baser and meaner, in the odor of priests and nuns wafting out of the cloister — the academy.

What are the children doing in their tents but practicing their religion? — It is best kept out of sight.

The alternative to genocide is the working-class struggle for socialism. Short of that, it is the struggle of the workers to survive in capitalism — and perhaps of intellectuals to abandon their illusions, whether in "communism" or whatever else: their sentimental projections onto the workers, who they can only value in their misery and wretchedness of victimhood, the direr the better. But that is their psychology.

Don't listen to the priests or shamans or holy fools, for they are false prophets: The world is not ending.

Nietzsche was right about the priests tricking not only the nobles but the slaves into an evil *ressentiment* for tearing down the good. Thankfully, this was never so successful and was mostly ignored, confined to the middle class of Nietzsche's own bourgeois milieu — that of today's enraged protesters: Nietzsche was right about them. Nietzsche was right.

It is in fact necessary to surrender to your boss. It is not just, but necessary: necessary to live. Workers are not privileged to do otherwise: they are not bosses; nor do they want to be. They just want to live. Shall we let them? Or do we demand their sacrifice to our crazed ideas? Thankfully, they are not listening.

Only the bosses are listening: Be careful not to make the workers' life harder in order to satisfy your own perverse desires and deranged visions. Keep them where they belong: in the monastery or nunnery — get thee there, and stay put in your chosen torture-chamber for the measurement of souls. Or else:

A healthy dose of philistinism would be salutary: The intellectuals need to get a job — make themselves useful in their labor. They can start by stopping their preaching of extermination as the only alternative to slavery: they can stop preaching "genocide," which doesn't help anyone but themselves; it doesn't save anyone but their own "beautiful souls" — which the world can actually do without, thank you.

What the world cannot do without is the people sacrificed to the worshiping of false idols — including those of true religions. Let us not have a democide. Let the people struggle for socialism. Let them work.

There is an alternative to genocide.

Originally published in *Sublation Magazine* (May 17, 2024)

# Why I want Kamala to win

I don't want to be a target.

If Trump wins, "cis-gender straight white males" will be blamed — perhaps also "gay" ones like me. We have had 8 years of attempted reeducation of the population to try to prevent the election of anyone like Trump ever again. Schoolchildren have been told in no uncertain terms that they are guilty for our bad, bad society. Trump paints a target on me.

Evidently, cis-gender (straight) white males are the largest market for masochism. They are gluttons for punishment. Also for sadism. At least in fantasy. But I'm not — not so privileged. It's a turn-off, actually. But, evidently, it turns on so much of politics.

8 years of Trump is enough; 12 might be too much. I have tried to make it into a teachable moment, but if no one has learned by now, they never will. I am not that much of a masochist. There was a viral video early on titled "Stop making me defend Donald Trump." I am frankly sick of still having to do so. Not defending Trump, but defending the truth against Democratic Party — and mainstream established Republican — lies. As I said earlier this year, if you are in the right, you shouldn't have to lie. And they have lied about Trump.

I have tried to take Trump as expressing the historical crisis of neo-liberalism and potential change in capitalism. I have written entire books about it — a learning opportunity. Evidently, it's not over yet.

If Trump wins, we could have 8 more years after him of J.D. Vance. If Kamala wins, we nip all that in the bud. — Don't we? If Trump is stopped, that's the end of Trumpism, isn't it? — But won't Trumpism continue after Trump? Might it be Vance in 4 years for another 8 after all? Who knows? But both are betting on it: one as hope; the other as fear.

One of the candidates is lying more than the other. — They're both lying.

But in one case I might want the lies to be true — not in the other case.

They blame Trump for COVID. But after Kamala said she would not trust the safety and effectiveness of a vaccine developed under Trump, her Administration forced people to take it. Both the epidemic and the suffering caused by the measures supposed to prevent it increased immeasurably under Biden and Kamala. They also censored any dissent from it. They called this "trusting the science" — and denied any evidence to the contrary. Anthony Fauci came out of retirement a last time to preach shots and masks after getting COVID this year — before falling to a mosquito carrying West Nile Virus.

Kamala is going to "build that wall." — Do I want that? No. But it might be an inevitability. After all, it started out as a Democrat promise in the Clinton era, contra Republican neoliberal open borders policy. — As late as 2019, Bernie himself said that open borders is not a "policy of the Left" because it undermines workers and strengthens capitalists. But I hope she's lying about that just to get elected, due to the unpopularity of recent events. — Democratic Party New York City Major Eric Adams was targeted for prosecution after he criticized the Biden Administration's immigration policies. But I don't mind the hundreds of Venezuelans and Haitians sheltered in my neighborhood. They actually make me feel more at home amidst all the rich white people. They are here to join the working class — part of any potential future for socialism in the U.S. Perhaps the Democrats let in enough people already, so that now they want to close the door again.

Kamala is running for President as a prosecutor. Do I support that? No. But there has been a reversal, from the promise of criminal justice reform just a few years ago under Trump — when Kamala encouraged "defund the police" protesters and rioters — to a more law-and-order policing mindset — with Trump cast by her as the very quintessence of criminality. But he markets his mugshot grinningly.

Kamala is going to be "strong" on foreign policy, militarily backing both Ukraine and Israel — even as the current Administration's policies have failed to end both wars — assuming they want to. They've trapped Putin in Ukraine and are trying to bleed him dry. And the U.S. is not going to stand in the way of getting rid of Hamas and Hezbollah, especially since the latter are responsible for hundreds of dead Marines, albeit 40 years ago. Their families remember. Trump is derided as dangerously unpredictable and unreliable to U.S. allies. But is he? Trump might not change anything, or even represent changing anything, but Kamala promises more of the same. Trump vows to stop the wars — both of them — and prevent future ones. "Make America Great Again" means making peace. Is it a lie?

Protesters blame Biden and Harris for not controlling Israel. But maybe it's not about who can control them, but who can be controlled. Netanyahu seems pretty good at playing the U.S. and its politicians. And perhaps Trump is no different. But at least his pride can be hurt, and he will not hide behind apparent institutional and geopolitical insurmountabilities, by which the Democrats unblinkingly and shamelessly justify everything they do — and fail to do. — Is there no alternative — no alternative to "genocide"? But there are genocides, and there are genocides: not all are created equal.

Economically, the Biden Administration has been equally an abject failure, erasing wage gains with inflation. They claim Trump will raise inflation with his tariffs, which is kind of rich coming from them. Trump promises to lower inflation dramatically, specifically by driving down energy costs through supporting fossil fuel production and use. But Kamala says proudly that the U.S. is drilling and pumping oil and gas at levels higher than in Trump's first term. Not that the Democrats want to bring prices down — no, they want to lower consumption, at least by the working class. People will adapt or die.

Kamala claims that Trump will destroy Obamacare and wreck the already strained U.S. healthcare system. But Trump maintained and expanded it and promises to only improve and not eliminate it. It's a cost-benefit analysis for him — as it is for her.

Kamala says Trump is supported by the nefarious Project 2025, while Trump disavows it and says his agenda is different. But Obamacare was based on the same healthcare reform proposal that Project 2025's authors, the Heritage Foundation, had originally drafted.

LGBTQ? But this is a fraught issue, even in the "community." There are many divisions and conflicts, which the Democrats suppress and pretend don't exist, to hold their voting constituency together, and which Trump is happy to leave alone, apart from some "common sense conservatism." He criticized DeSantis for going after Disney on gender. When he was President he even proudly held up a rainbow flag — albeit upside down. But in the meantime that flag has been replaced — by what exactly, no one knows.

Have I left anything out? Oh yeah, "climate change." But no one wants to hear about that. Not when blowing up Nord Stream 2 released more methane into the atmosphere than anything else on record. Not when not only the U.S. but the world depends on American economic recovery.

I grew up in the 1970s and have heard it all before about environmental catastrophe and capitalism. As back then, it is still now an expression of pessimism and nihilism, appropriate to the political times.

(Abortion cannot Constitutionally be legislated at the national level in the U.S.)

I represent the cause of socialism and Marxism. My interest is not in this election or any other in capitalist politics, but in the task of educating young people in the need to change the world.

To do this takes time and energy, and incredible patience and resilience — which can be tested and even broken, not by long hard struggle, but by silliness and stupidity. What Trump has unleashed in response to him has been stupid and silly — and yet it is in deadly earnest. Trump Derangement Syndrome is a reality I can attest to from personal experience.

Trump has made not himself but his opponents farcical. And yet it is all taken very seriously. They are ugly, not amusing. Clowns can be frightening — especially sadistic clowns. But which ones, and how? Insane Clown Posse endorsed Kamala. Of course they did. The clowns I face are the Democrats. The Republicans are a more distant threat, however real. Yet I have to go unnoticed by the Democrat clowns, and avoid attracting their attention while living under their noses. I've lived in Chicago my entire adult life — the town of John Wayne Gacy: unfortunately, it makes all too much sense that he lived here. It is home of International Mr. Leather. Makes sense. Suburban Illinois gave us Speaker of the House Dennis Hastert, the disgraced wrestling coach who helped shepherd the anti-gay Defense of Marriage Act through Congress — signed by Bill Clinton. Sad clowns, all. Sad in their silliness. Silly in their sadness. Kamala and Walz. Trump and Vance. Ren and Stimpy. Itchy and Scratchy. Cats and dogs — eating each other. But I don't want to be a target.

I have always said that Trump's critics have misread him, taking him literally but not seriously enough. Actually, they've just lied about him. What they have taken seriously is not Trump but their own preoccupations — their obsessions — and feelings. I am tired of dealing with hurt Democrats. They have made it impossible to think or even to live properly — to feel anything besides anxiety and depression. They have become the most grim humorless people, holding a grudge and seething with anger and a lust for revenge, all while proclaiming "Joy!" at the prospect. And, unlike Trump and his supporters, they actually have the power to act on it. — I don't want to be a target.

I would like to say that I am bored of it, but really I have gone numb with fear. I am worn out — worn down after more than 8 years. I am not alone. I was never a fan of Naomi Klein's *Shock Doctrine* thesis on "disaster capitalism." But who can deny that the last gasp of neoliberalism has been just that, and for the last 4 years on the greatest scale yet? But we are not supposed to notice. They are doing it while pretending not to. It's the denial that's frightening. Gas-lighting: they are scaring us into submission. And it works. The cowed working class keeps its head down and goes quietly to and from work, thankful for their jobs, just trying to survive it all. Will they register their protest anonymously at the ballot-box? Not nearly enough.

I want Kamala to win so I can get a break from the madness, an end to the intimidation and blackmail, the manipulation and the mind-games. What they promised 4 years ago: getting back to normal — going back to the "new normal." That is the reason — the only reason — anyone will vote for her. Dare I hope for it? But they have lied about everything else, so why should we believe they're not lying about this, too? Will they finally leave us alone? The promise of an end to the drama might be enough to elect Kamala. I want it to be true.

But it is a lie.

Presented on October 30, 2024, for the panel discussion "The Left and the 2024 election" with Eddie Liger Smith (American Communist Party) and Jorge Mujica (Morena), hosted by the Platypus Affiliated Society at the University of Chicago.

·

Originally published in *Sublation Magazine* (November 1, 2024) and in *Platypus Review* 171 (November 2024).

# Why not Greenland?

## The future belongs to America — so should Greenland

Recently, in a scene recalling the X-Files, NASA satellite imagery discovered the ruins of an old U.S. nuclear weapons base, Camp Century, under the permafrost in Greenland, an abandoned relic of the Cold War. Its resurfacing is an apt metaphor for Donald Trump's proposal to expand U.S. territory into the circumpolar North, which seems to have come out of nowhere, but in fact draws upon a long history.

When Nazi Germany conquered Denmark in 1940, Britain and later the United States invaded and occupied Iceland. Four years later, Iceland ended its union with Denmark and became an independent republic. Greenland could certainly have followed. Both islands remain of strategic importance for NATO, which makes Trump's proposal to acquire Greenland for military reasons seem redundant: Doesn't Greenland already occupy a forward position regarding the Arctic and Russian threats? But perhaps Trump aims to abolish NATO — as he has threatened and his critics have accused him of planning to do — after all. Maybe it is not merely a ruse or negotiating position, but a real prospect. Greenland seems to be part of the calculation.

Trump's suggestion has prompted the indigenous people of Greenland to demand their independence. Meanwhile, the King of Denmark has added Greenland and the Faroe Islands to his Royal Coat of Arms, but Danish Prime Minister Mette Frederiksen has sent out mixed signals. Don Jr. is visiting Greenland as I write this.

Trump's calling Canada the "51st State" caused the downfall of its "governor," Prime Minister Justin Trudeau. The president-elect has since declared the benefits of a union with Canada that would erase the "artificial border." But political frontiers represent history and its after-effects. The early Scandinavian — Viking — contact with the New World informs the Danish claim to Greenland. (The Inuit who make up most of the population now actually arrived later.)

The U.S.-Canada border is the frontier of the American Revolution. Benjamin Franklin demanded Canada from the British in the treaty settling the American War of Independence. After the Civil War, the victorious Union offered to take Canada as the compensation the British owed for their support of the Confederacy. Secretary of State William H. Seward had to settle for purchasing Alaska. Canada, then, remains the frontier of the counter-revolution after both American revolutionary wars. It remains the most European part of the Western Hemisphere. This has not been a good thing.

Trump's promise to Make America Great Again begins with making America America again. Making Greenland and Canada American is part of this initiative. Trump declared the Gulf of Mexico to be the Gulf of America. Perhaps saying so blatantly what is nonetheless a fact is in bad taste. Whether literally or figuratively, the gesture is unmistakable. This is not imperialism, but a reminder of the Empire of Liberty that Thomas Jefferson declared the mission of the new United States. It is an evergreen promise. America is revolutionary or it is nothing. The United States of America liberated the world twice — three times with the Cold War. Its mission continues.

(This is no time to abandon the Monroe Doctrine, which was not about U.S. supremacy but protection of American freedom.)

Ever since the Civil War, the United States has demanded unconditional surrender from its enemies. It has treated all its opponents as it did the Confederacy — as echoes of the counterrevolution, the threat of undoing the revolution. The Confederates regarded the values of the revolution — life, liberty, and the pursuit of happiness as the inalienable rights of all equally — as mistaken. So have all of America's opponents. They have been and remain Slave States.

But the revolution cannot be undone. The question is how Greenland or Canada or Panama or Mexico or the rest of the Americas — the rest of America — might still follow and not oppose it.

The real question, though, is how America still follows the revolution. Trump seems to accept its call. The United States does not desire to rule but only to free people and places. How it does so has come now to be in doubt. But there will be no retreat to Little America. The sheer scope of American power won't allow it. Can America find itself again — re-found itself — on these frontiers?

The alliance between Washington and Beijing forged by Nixon and Kissinger ended with the defeat of the Soviet Union. It was supposed to shape the next century, and it has done so. Unfortunately, the original intention of the pact for the two countries — both victors of World War II, but one more damaged by it — to keep each other honest, has failed, as did that of the original Allies, the United States and the Soviet Union.

Vladimir Putin, in interviews he conducted with Oliver Stone before Trump's first term and after the Russian seizure of Crimea, stated that while he accepts American predominance, Washington cannot possibly govern the world. Recalling that throughout U.S. history, Russia has been its ally in all wars except one (namely, the War of 1812 — the Napoleonic Wars), he advised that regional powers such as Russia and China be allowed their own domains. The problem is that their neighbors won't consent, hoping instead for American protection.

Trump is decried by his political opponents in both the Democratic and Republican Parties as an "isolationist" — the old pejorative from the pre-World War II era. But ever since Woodrow Wilson's War to End All Wars, to "make the world safe for democracy," which was forced on America by Europe (that is, by the counterrevolution), American involvement in global affairs has been a given. Theodore Roosevelt had already negotiated the end of the 1905 Russo-Japanese War, and had warned against America coming into conflict with either Japan or Germany, which he saw menacing on the horizon.

Trump has promised to end the current wars in Ukraine and Gaza; to launch no new wars; and invited Chinese President Xi Jinping to his Inauguration, extending the hand of friendship to the only potential rival of American power. Xi politely demurred, not needing the reminder of the vitality of American democracy.

Trump has not ruled out a military solution to either the Greenland or Panama Canal issues that he has identified. He did, however, rule it out for Canada — ironically enough, considering its origins as the redoubt of

America's foes in the Revolutionary War. Is Trump's audacious overture to his second term a prelude to a new geopolitical competition — a new Cold War or even World War III? Or is it rather a preview of a restored American world leadership, as Trump apparently intends?

The key to hard bargaining is willingness to walk away from a deal rather than accept bad terms. Trump is wagering that his negotiating partners are at least as in need of peace as America, and that in the wake of both the Great Recession and the COVID crisis, the world depends on American recovery.

The danger is that the United States might overplay its hand. It might not be a time for brinksmanship or confrontation. It might not be a matter of tests of strength. But it might require a match of wills.

Washington has been bogged down by policy impasses and decided lack of vision in the new millennium. Former Representative Joe Walsh, who briefly opposed Trump for the GOP presidential nomination in 2020, speculated at the 2024 never-Trump Republican counter-convention in Milwaukee that winning the Cold War had doomed America. He might have meant that China was the ultimate beneficiary of the fall of the Soviet Union. But such pessimism is unrealistic. The post-Cold War crisis is indeed being met — however undesirably to Walsh and the GOP old guard — by Trump. Unlike China or Russia, America has greater resources for political change in direction and leadership. There is a refusal to see the obvious regarding Trump: that he represents the "hope and change" that was merely a marketing slogan for Obama before him.

The gravitational attraction of the United States is in its social and not merely its economic power. This extends to its political capacities. There are many sources of power, not just one, and this creates a much more resilient polity than one finds in America's would-be enemies.

Over the course of American history, every 40 or 50 years has seen a crisis that called for renewal. Jefferson's Revolution of 1800, Jackson's 1828 election, the Civil War, the Progressive Era, the New Deal, and the Reagan Revolution all changed the political parties and the nature of their competition, fulfilling Jefferson's estimation that a revolution would be needed every generation or so. We are living through such a shift now.

While there might not exactly be a plan, there is a vision. Trump setting his sights on Greenland might seem to prove his critics right about the danger of his folly. It symbolizes the apparent absurdity of the moment. But it would be wrong to fall back on the lack of imagination that has afflicted U.S. politics for far too long.

The neglected and forgotten Danish colony in the Western Hemisphere captures something of the nature of Trump's character, which is bombastic but not empty. Where others have been complacent to let spaces lie unutilized, he has set to building. Could this be done on the mostly vacant territory of the world's largest island? Where others now see a barren wasteland, Trump finds not only possibilities but necessities — the necessity for American growth and change.

In this and other fields, Trump sees the need for a broader American future. Approaching the quarter-millennium of the American Revolution, perhaps the borders of the Empire of Liberty are set to be revised again.

Originally published in *Compact* (January 9, 2025)

# Appendix

# What is a platypus?

## On surviving the extinction of the Left

A story is told about Karl Marx's collaborator and friend Friedrich Engels, who, in his youth, as a good Hegelian Idealist, sure about the purposeful, rational evolution of nature and of the place of human reason in it, became indignant when reading about a platypus, which he supposed to be a fraud perpetrated by English taxidermists. For Engels, the platypus made no sense in natural history.

Later, Engels saw a living platypus at a British zoo and was chagrined. Like Marx, a good materialist and a thinker receptive to Darwin's theory of evolution, which dethroned a human-centered view of nature, Engels came to respect that "reason" in history, natural or otherwise, must not necessarily accord with present standards of human reason.

This is a parable we find salutary to understanding the condition of the Left today.

In light of the history of the present, we might ask, what right does the Left have to exist?

Every right — as much as the platypus has, however difficult it might be to categorize!

We maintain that past and present history need not indicate the future. Past and present failures and losses on the Left should educate and warn, but not spellbind and enthrall us.

Hence, to free ourselves, we declare that the Left is *dead*. — Or, more precisely, that we are all that is left of it.

This is less a statement of fact than of intent.

— The intent that the Left should live, but the recognition that it can, *only* by overcoming itself. And *we* are that overcoming!

So, then, *what* are we?

We are thinkers on the Left educated and warned by the history of the 20th Century — but not terrorized by it! "Let the dead bury the dead." Our actions might redeem their suffering yet.

We are motivated, after failed and betrayed attempts at emancipation, and in light of their inadequate self-understanding, to re-appropriate this history in service of possibilities for emancipatory struggle in the present — and the future.

Towards such ends, we might begin (perhaps provocatively) with the list of names that indicate the thoughts and problems issuing from events that, reading history against the grain (with Benjamin), still speak to us in the present: Marx, Lenin, Luxemburg, Trotsky, Adorno. — Not much more than what is represented by these figures, but absolutely nothing less.

We will overcome any easy and false recognition of such names, and all received wisdom about the thoughts and actions identified with them, to better possible *critical* recognition and development of *our* purpose.

In the history of the Left, the dates 1848 and 1917, but less 1968, and *not* 1989: the aftermath of ambiguous defeats and victories; but, more, the insights yielded by defeats, and the recognition of a present and a history that need not have been, for a future that need not yet be. The restive spirits of 1848 and 1917, in their unfulfilled possibilities, will continue to speak to an unredeemed future.

The history of modernity is not finished yet, nor will it be, short of redeeming its promise. Therefore, we do not share the (mislaid) feelings of exhaustion with the modern, but we recognize a certain abdication of its emancipatory transformation, which haunts us with its necessity.

We recognize *our* necessity.

We agree with the young Marx in "the ruthless criticism of everything existing." Unlike Hegel in his struggle against Romantic despair after 1789, we recognize the necessity of our present only as "bad." Our present does not deserve affirmation or even respect, for we recognize it only for what came to be when the Left was destroyed and liquidated itself.

And so, with the story of Engels and the platypus, let us begin to address the improbable but not impossible tasks and project of the *next* Left.

(July 2006)

# Index

www.ingramcontent.com/pod-product-compliance
Lightning Source LLC
Chambersburg PA
CBHW032046020426
42335CB00011B/212